II. RESTATEMENT (SECOND) OF TORTS

(Selected Sections & Comments)

■ ■ ■

Table of Sections

Title B. Absolute Privilege Irrespective of Consent

Topic 3. Conditional Privileges
Title A. Occasions Making a Publication Conditionally Privileged
Subtitle III. Abuse of Privilege

Division Six. Injurious Falsehood
Chapter 28. Injurious Falsehood (Including Slander of Title and Trade Libel)
Topic 1. General Principle

Topic 2. Disparagement of Property in or Quality of Land, Chattels and Intangible Things

Topic 3. Rules Applicable to All Publication of Injurious Falsehood

Topic 4. Privileges to Publish Injurious Falsehood

Topic 5. Burden of Proof and Functions of Court and Jury

Division One.   Intentional Harms to Persons, Land, and Chattels
Chapter 1.   Meaning of Terms Used Throughout the Restatement of Torts

§ 8A   Intent

The word "intent" is used throughout the Restatement of this Subject to denote that the actor desires to cause consequences of his act, or that he believes that the consequences are substantially certain to result from it.

Comment:

a.   "Intent," as it is used throughout the Restatement of Torts, has reference to the consequences of an act rather than the act itself. When an actor fires a gun in the midst of the Mojave Desert, he intends to pull the trigger; but when the bullet hits a person who is present in the desert without the actor's knowledge, he does not intend that result. "Intent" is limited, wherever it is used, to the consequences of the act.

b. All consequences which the actor desires to bring about are intended, as the word is used in this Restatement. Intent is not, however, limited to consequences which are desired. If the actor knows that the consequences are certain, or substantially certain, to result from his act, and still goes ahead, he is treated by the law as if he had in fact desired to produce the result. As the probability that the consequences will follow decreases, and becomes less than substantial certainty, the actor's conduct loses the character of intent, and becomes mere recklessness, as defined in § 500. As the probability decreases further, and amounts only to a risk that the result will follow, it becomes ordinary negligence, as defined in § 282. All three have their important place in the law of torts, but the liability attached to them will differ.

Illustrations:

1. A throws a bomb into B's office for the purpose of killing B. A knows that C, B's stenographer, is in the office. A has no desire to injure C, but knows that his act is substantially certain to do so. C is injured by the explosion. A is subject to liability to C for an intentional tort.

2. On a curve in a narrow highway A, without any desire to injure B, or belief that he is substantially certain to do so, recklessly drives his automobile in an attempt to pass B's car. As a result of this recklessness, A crashes into B's car, injuring B. A is subject to liability to B for his reckless conduct, but is not liable to B for any intentional tort.

Division Two.   Negligence
Chapter 12.   General Principles
Topic 5.   Misrepresentations Threatening Physical Harm

§ 311   Negligent Misrepresentation Involving Risk of Physical Harm

(1) One who negligently gives false information to another is subject to liability for physical harm caused by action taken by the other in reasonable reliance upon such information, where such harm results

(a) to the other, or

(b) to such third persons as the actor should expect to be put in peril by the action taken.

(2) Such negligence may consist of failure to exercise reasonable care

(a) in ascertaining the accuracy of the information, or

(b) in the manner in which it is communicated.

Comment:

a. The rule stated in this Section represents a somewhat broader liability than the rules stated as to liability for pecuniary loss resulting from negligent misrepresentation, stated in § 552, to which reference should be made for comparison.

b. The rule stated in this Section finds particular application where it is a part of the actor's business or profession to give information upon which the safety of the recipient or a third person depends. Thus it is as much a part of the professional duty of a physician to give correct information as to the character of the disease from which his patient is suffering, where such knowledge is necessary to the safety of the patient or others, as it is to make a correct diagnosis or to prescribe the appropriate medicine. The rule is not, however, limited to information given in a business or professional capacity, or to those engaged in a business or profession. It extends to any person who, in the course of an activity which is in furtherance of his own interests, undertakes to give information to another, and knows or should realize that the safety of the person of others may depend upon the accuracy of the information.

Illustrations:

1. A train of the A Railroad is approaching a grade crossing. An employee of the Railroad negligently raises the crossing gates, and so informs approaching automobile drivers that no train is coming. B sees the gates raised, drives onto the crossing, and is struck by the train. A Railroad is subject to liability to B.

2. The A Company is conducting blasting operations near a railroad. B, an employee of the railroad, comes to inquire as to the progress of the work. As he arrives a blast is being set off, and he is advised to take cover. Immediately after the blast the foreman of A Company negligently informs B that all danger is over and he can safely come into the open. A delayed explosion occurs, and B is struck and injured by a rock. A Company is subject to liability to B.

3. A has charge of B, a lunatic of violent tendencies. A advertises for a servant, and C applies for the employment. A informs C that B is insane, but negligently gives C the impression that B is not violent or dangerous. C accepts the employment, and is attacked and injured by B. A is subject to liability to C.

c. The rule stated in this Section may also apply where the information given is purely gratuitous, and entirely unrelated to any interest of the actor, or any activity from which he derives any benefit. In this respect the rule stated here differs from that stated in § 552, which is concerned only with pecuniary loss suffered as the result of a negligent misrepresentation. Where only such pecuniary loss is sustained, the gratuitous character of the information prevents any liability for negligence in giving it. Where, as under the rule stated in this Section, the harm which results is bodily harm to the person, or physical harm to the property of the one affected, there may be liability for the negligence even though the information is given gratuitously and the actor derives no benefit from giving it.

The fact that the information is gratuitous may, however, affect the reasonableness of the other's reliance upon it in taking action. There may be no reasonable justification for taking the word of a casual bystander, who does not purport to have any special information or any interest in the matter, as to the safety of a bridge or a scaffold, where the plaintiff would be fully justified in accepting the statement of one who purports to have special knowledge of the matter, or special reliability, even though the plaintiff knows that he is receiving gratuitous advice.

Illustrations:

4. A buys a tombstone from B, a dealer in tombstones. A is in doubt as to how to transport it. C, a casual bystander, volunteers the information that the tombstone weighs only 50 pounds, and that A can easily and safely pick it up and carry it to his car. Relying on C's statement, A attempts to do so. In fact the tombstone weighs 150 pounds, and A suffers a hernia as the result of his efforts. C is not liable to A.

5. The same facts as in Illustration 4, except that the statement is made by B. B is subject to liability to A.

6. A large trailer truck of the A Company is being driven on a winding highway. B is following it in his automobile, and seeking to pass it, but has not done so because his view is obstructed. At a particular point the driver of the truck signals to B to pass it, thereby representing to B that the highway ahead is clear. In reliance upon the signal B attempts to pass the truck, and is injured by a collision with an approaching car. A Company is subject to liability to B.

7. The same facts as in Illustration 6, except that the driver calls verbal assurance to B that he can safely pass. The same result.

Comment on Clause (a) of Subsection (2):

d. *Care in ascertaining facts and forming judgment.* Where the actor furnishes information upon which he knows or should realize that the security of others depends, he is required to exercise the care of a reasonable man under the circumstances to ascertain the facts, and the judgment of a reasonable man in determining whether, in the light of the discovered facts, the information is accurate. His negligence may consist of failure to make proper inspection or inquiry, or of failure after proper inquiry to recognize that the information given is not accurate.

Illustration:

8. The A Boiler Insurance Company undertakes as part of its services to inspect the boiler of B. It issues a certificate that the boiler is in good condition for use. In reliance upon this certificate, B uses the boiler. The boiler bursts, owing to a defect which a reasonably careful inspection would have disclosed. Explosion of the boiler wrecks the adjacent building of C and causes bodily harm to him. The A Company is

subject to liability to C for his bodily harm and the wrecking of his building caused by the explosion of the boiler.

Comment on Clause (b) of Subsection (2):

e.   *Care in use of language.* The negligence for which the actor is liable under the statement in this Subsection consists in the lack of reasonable care to furnish accurate information. It is, therefore, not enough that the actor has correctly ascertained the facts on which his information is to be based and has exercised reasonable competence in judging the effect of such facts. He must also exercise reasonable care to bring to the understanding of the recipient of the information the knowledge which he has so acquired.

Illustration:

9.   The A Boiler Insurance Company undertakes as part of its service to inspect the boiler of B. The A Company makes a careful inspection, and correctly concludes that the boiler is unsafe. Through the negligence of its clerk, it issues a certificate which, while correctly stating all the defects in the boiler, gives the misleading impression that the boiler is nevertheless safe. In reliance on the certificate, B continues to use the boiler, which bursts because of the defects and wrecks the adjacent building of C, causing bodily harm to C. The A Company is subject to liability to C for his bodily harm and the wrecking of his building.

f.   Comments *c* and *d* on § 310 are applicable to this Section.

Division Four.   Misrepresentation
Chapter 22.   Misrepresentation and Nondisclosure
Causing Pecuniary Loss
Topic 1.   Fraudulent Misrepresentation (Deceit)

§ 525   Liability for Fraudulent Misrepresentation

One who fraudulently makes a misrepresentation of fact, opinion, intention or law for the purpose of inducing another to act or to refrain from action in reliance upon it, is subject to liability to the other in deceit for pecuniary loss caused to him by his justifiable reliance upon the misrepresentation.

Comment:

a.   The rules that determine the fraudulent character of a misrepresentation are stated in §§ 526–530. The rules that deal with the requirement that the representation must be made for the purpose of inducing that conduct of the other from which his harm results are stated in §§ 531–536. The rules that determine whether the recipient of the misrepresentation is justified in relying upon it are stated in §§ 537–545. The measure of damages is stated in § 549.

As to the liability for negligent misrepresentation inducing reliance that causes pecuniary loss, see § 552. As to innocent misrepresentation, see § 552C.

b. *Misrepresentation defined.* "Misrepresentation" is used in this Restatement to denote not only words spoken or written but also any other conduct that amounts to an assertion not in accordance with the truth. Thus, words or conduct asserting the existence of a fact constitute a misrepresentation if the fact does not exist.

Illustration:

1. A, a dealer in used automobiles, offers a second-hand car for sale in his showroom. Before doing so he turns the odometer back from 60,000 to 18,000 miles. B, relying on the odometer reading, purchases the car from A. This is a misrepresentation.

c. A representation of the state of mind of the maker or of a third person is a misrepresentation if the state of mind in question is otherwise than as represented. Thus, a statement that a particular person, whether the maker of the statement or a third person, is of a particular opinion or has a particular intention is a misrepresentation if the person in question does not hold the opinion or have the intention asserted.

d. *Representations of fact, opinion and law.* Strictly speaking, "fact" includes not only the existence of a tangible thing or the happening of a particular event or the relationship between particular persons or things, but also the state of mind, such as the entertaining of an intention or the holding of an opinion, of any person, whether the maker of a representation or a third person. Indeed, every assertion of the existence of a thing is a representation of the speaker's state of mind, namely, his belief in its existence. There is sometimes, however, a marked difference between what constitutes justifiable reliance upon statements of the maker's opinion and what constitutes justifiable reliance upon other representations. Therefore, it is convenient to distinguish between misrepresentations of opinion and misrepresentations of all other facts, including intention.

A statement of law may have the effect of a statement of fact or a statement of opinion. It has the effect of a statement of fact if it asserts that a particular statute has been enacted or repealed or that a particular decision has been rendered upon particular facts. It has the effect of a statement of opinion if it expresses only the actor's judgment as to the legal consequence that would be attached to the particular state of facts if the question were litigated. It is therefore convenient to deal separately with misrepresentations of law.

e. *Representation implied from statement of fact.* A misrepresentation of fact may concern either an existing or past fact. A statement about the future may imply a representation concerning an existing or past fact. (See Comment *f*). To be actionable, a misrepresentation of fact must be one of a fact that is of importance in determining the recipient's course of action at the time the representation is made. Thus a statement that a horse has recently and consistently trotted a mile in less than two minutes may justifiably be taken as an implied assertion of the capacity of the horse to repeat the performance at the time the statement is made. So, too, a past fact may be one that makes it obligatory or advisable for the recipient to take a particular course of action, as when A falsely tells B that he has caused the arrest of a criminal for whose arrest B has offered a reward, or when in an insurance policy the insured has falsely stated that his father did not die of tuberculosis. A fraudulent misrepresentation of such a fact may be the basis of liability.

f.   Representation implied from statement promissory in form. Similarly a statement that is in form a prediction or promise as to the future course of events may justifiably be interpreted as a statement that the maker knows of nothing which will make the fulfillment of his prediction or promise impossible or improbable. Thus a statement that a second-hand car will run fifteen miles on a gallon of gasoline is an implied assertion that the condition of the car makes it capable of so doing, and is an actionable misrepresentation if the speaker knows that it has never run more than seven miles per gallon of gasoline.

Illustrations:

2.   A, in order to induce B to buy a heating device, states that it will give a stated amount of heat while consuming only a stated amount of fuel. B is justified in accepting A's statement as an assurance that the heating device is capable of giving the services that A promises.

3.   A, knowing that the X Corporation is hopelessly insolvent, in order to induce B to purchase from him shares of its capital stock assures B that the shares will within five years pay dividends that will amount to the purchase price of the stock. B is justified in accepting these statements as an assurance that A knows of nothing that makes the corporation incapable of making earnings sufficient to pay the dividends.

g.   Representation implied from statement as to past events. On the same basis, a statement that a particular condition has recently existed or that an event has recently occurred or that a particular person has recently by words or acts expressed a particular opinion or intention, may, if reasonable under the circumstances, be understood and accepted as asserting that the situation has not changed since the time when the condition is said to have existed, the event to have occurred or the opinion or intention to have been expressed.

Illustrations:

4.   A, in order to induce B to buy a horse, falsely states that a veterinary surgeon a week before had examined the horse and had pronounced it sound. Unless B knows of something that might have changed the horse's condition in the interim, B is justified in

14

interpreting A's statement as implying that the horse is sound at the time of the sale.

    5.   A tells B that C had the day before offered him $2000 for a particular piece of land. In the absence of anything known to him that might indicate the contrary, B is entitled to assume that C's opinion as to the value of the land is unchanged.

    h.   Misrepresentation causing physical harm. This Section (and this Chapter) covers pecuniary loss resulting from a fraudulent misrepresentation, and not physical harm resulting from the misrepresentation. As to the latter, see § 557A, which also covers the economic loss deriving from the physical harm. This type of economic loss is not intended to be included in the term, pecuniary loss, as used in this Chapter. See also § 310 (liability in negligence for a conscious misrepresentation involving risk of physical harm) and § 311 (negligent misrepresentation involving risk of physical harm).

Title A.   Fraudulent Character of Misrepresentation

§ 526   Conditions Under Which Misrepresentation Is Fraudulent (Scienter)

A misrepresentation is fraudulent if the maker

    (a) knows or believes that the matter is not as he represents it to be,

    (b) does not have the confidence in the accuracy of his representation that he states or implies, or

    (c) knows that he does not have the basis for his representation that he states or implies.

Comment:

    a.   The word "fraudulent" is here used as referring solely to the maker's knowledge of the untrue character of his representation. This element of the defendant's conduct frequently is called "scienter" by the courts. Intent and expectation of influencing the other's conduct by the misrepresentation are dealt with in §§ 531–536 as a separate and distinct element necessary to liability under the rule stated in § 525.

    b.   This Section states merely the rules that determine whether a misrepresentation is fraudulently made. In order that a misrepresentation even though fraudulently made, may be actionable, it is necessary that the other conditions stated in § 525 exist. The rules that deal with the further conditions necessary to liability under § 525, namely, the maker's purpose to induce the recipient to act in reliance upon the misrepresentation and the recipient's justifiable reliance upon the misrepresentation are stated below, the former in §§ 531–536, the latter in §§ 537–545. The rules that deal with causation of the pecuniary loss are stated in §§ 546–548, and in § 549A.

Comment on Clause (a):

c. If the maker of the representation knows the matter to be otherwise than as represented, the fraudulent character of the misrepresentation is clear. However, knowledge of falsity is not essential; it is enough that he believes the representation to be false.

d. The fact that the misrepresentation is one that a man of ordinary care and intelligence in the maker's situation would have recognized as false is not enough to impose liability upon the maker for a fraudulent misrepresentation under the rule stated in this Section, but it is evidence from which his lack of honest belief may be inferred. So, too, it is a matter to be taken into account in determining the credibility of the defendant if he testifies that he believed his representation to be true. For the rules that determine the liability of the maker of a representation that he believes to be true, but which through his negligence is misleading, see § 552. As to strict liability for innocent misrepresentation, see § 552C.

Comment on Clause (b):

e. In order that a misrepresentation may be fraudulent it is not necessary that the maker know the matter is not as represented. Indeed, it is not necessary that he should even believe this to be so. It is enough that being conscious that he has neither knowledge nor belief in the existence of the matter he chooses to assert it as a fact. Indeed, since knowledge implies a firm conviction, a misrepresentation of a fact so made as to assert that the maker knows it, is fraudulent if he is conscious that he has merely a belief in its existence and recognizes that there is a chance, more or less great, that the fact may not be as it is represented. This is often expressed by saying that fraud is proved if it is shown that a false representation has been made without belief in its truth or recklessly, careless of whether it is true or false.

Comment on Clause (c):

f. A representation of fact may be expressly stated to be based upon the maker's personal knowledge of the fact in question or even upon his personal investigation of the matter. So, too, though not expressly so stated, the representation may be made in a form or under such circumstances as to imply that this is the case. A misrepresentation so made is fraudulent even though the maker is honestly convinced of its truth from hearsay or other sources that he believes to be reliable.

Illustration:

1. A states to B that C's financial position justifies B in giving him credit in a particular sales transaction. A knows that B will understand that the statement is based upon A's personal dealings with C. In fact A has had no dealings with C but has heard from what he regards as reliable sources that C's financial position is first rate. C is insolvent and B is unable to collect his debt from him. A is subject to liability to B for the loss that B suffers through relying upon his statement if the

circumstances justify his reliance upon A's supposed personal knowledge.

§ 529   Representation Misleading Because Incomplete

A representation stating the truth so far as it goes but which the maker knows or believes to be materially misleading because of his failure to state additional or qualifying matter is a fraudulent misrepresentation.

Comment:

a. A statement containing a half-truth may be as misleading as a statement wholly false. Thus, a statement that contains only favorable matters and omits all reference to unfavorable matters is as much a false representation as if all the facts stated were untrue. Thus a prospectus that accurately states the assets, bonded indebtedness and net earnings of a manufacturing corporation but omits any reference to its floating debt is a false representation of the financial position of the company. So, too, a statement by a vendor that his title has been upheld by a particular court is a false representation if he fails to disclose his knowledge that an appeal from the decision is pending.

b. Whether or not a partial disclosure of the facts is a fraudulent misrepresentation depends upon whether the person making the statement knows or believes that the undisclosed facts might affect the recipient's conduct in the transaction in hand. It is immaterial that the defendant believes that the undisclosed facts would not affect the value of the bargain which he is offering. The recipient is entitled to know the undisclosed facts in so far as they are material and to form his own opinion of their effect. Thus, in the example last given, the fact that the vendor had good grounds for believing that the appeal would fail does not prevent his statement from being a fraudulent misrepresentation.

c. Except where it is sold "as is," one who offers land or a chattel for sale on inspection by so doing impliedly asserts that he knows of nothing that makes the appearance of the article deceptive and that cannot be discovered by such an inspection as a purchaser at the sale should make. In this case the vendor knows that the buyer will assume that, except for faults discoverable by the inspection, the thing is as it appears to be and is guilty of actionable fraud if he does not disclose a latent defect known to him.

Illustrations:

1. A, selling a tract of land to B, warns B that plans for city development already drawn show two unopened streets which, if opened, may condemn a part of the tract. A knows, but does not tell B, that the plans show a third unopened street which, if opened, will condemn part of the tract and cut it in half. B buys the land, believing that there are only the two streets. A's statement is a fraudulent misrepresentation.

2.   A, selling an apartment house to B, informs B that the apartments in it are all rented to tenants at $200 a month. This is true, but A does not inform B that the rent of $200 has not been approved by the local Rent Control authorities, and without this approval it is not legal. B buys the apartment house, believing that the rent of $200 is legal and he can continue to collect it. A's statement is a fraudulent misrepresentation.

§ 530   Misrepresentation of Intention

(1) A representation of the maker's own intention to do or not to do a particular thing is fraudulent if he does not have that intention.

(2) A representation of the intention of a third person is fraudulent under the conditions stated in § 526.

Comment on Subsection (1):

a.   The state of a man's mind is as much a fact as the state of his digestion. A false representation of the actor's own intention to do or not to do a particular thing is actionable if the statement is reasonably to be interpreted as expressing a firm intention and not merely as one of those "puffing" statements which are so frequent and so little regarded in negotiations for a business transaction as to make it unjustifiable for the recipient to rely upon them. As to the rules that determine whether the recipient may justifiably rely upon the statement of intention as an inducement to enter into the transaction, see § 544.

b.   To be actionable the statement of the maker's own intention must be fraudulent, which is to say that he must in fact not have the intention stated. If he does not have it, he must of course be taken to know that he does not have it. If the statement is honestly made and the intention in fact exists, one who acts in justifiable reliance upon it cannot maintain an action of deceit if the maker for any reason changes his mind and fails or refuses to carry his expressed intention into effect. If the recipient wishes to have legal assurance that the intention honestly entertained will be carried out, he must see that it is expressed in the form of an enforceable contract, and his action must be on the contract.

c.   *Misrepresentation of intention to perform an agreement.* The rule stated in this Section finds common application when the maker misrepresents his intention to perform an agreement made with the recipient. The intention to perform the agreement may be expressed but it is normally merely to be implied from the making of the agreement. Since a promise necessarily carries with it the implied assertion of an intention to perform it follows that a promise made without such an intention is fraudulent and actionable in deceit under the rule stated in § 525. This is true whether or not the promise is enforceable as a contract. If it is enforceable, the person misled by the representation has a cause of action in tort as an alternative at least, and perhaps in some instances in addition to his cause of action on the contract. If the agreement is not enforceable as a contract, as when it is without consideration, the recipient still has, as his only remedy, the action in deceit under the rule stated in § 525. The same is true when the agreement is oral and made unenforceable by the statute of frauds, or when it is unprovable and so unenforceable under the parol evidence rule. The tort action may have other advantages, as when it is subject to a longer statute of limitations. In all of these cases, it is immaterial to the tort liability that the damages recoverable are identical with, or substantially the same as, those which could have been recovered in an action of contract if the promise were enforceable.

   d.   Proof of intention not to perform agreement. The intention that is necessary to make the rule stated in this Section applicable is the intention of the promisor when the agreement was entered into. The intention of the promisor not to perform an enforceable or unenforceable agreement cannot be established solely by proof of its nonperformance, nor does his failure to perform the agreement throw upon him the burden of showing that his nonperformance was due to reasons which operated after the agreement was entered into. The intention may be shown by any other evidence that sufficiently indicates its existence, as, for example, the certainty that he would not be in funds to carry out his promise.

Comment on Subsection (2):

   e.   When the intention misrepresented is that of a third person, it stands on the same footing as any other representation of an existing fact. The maker is subject to liability in an action of deceit only if the misrepresentation is fraudulent, as that term is defined in § 526. If it is honestly made there is no liability in deceit, although there may still be liability in an action for negligence under the rule stated in § 552, or strict liability under the rule stated in § 552C. On the other hand, if the statement is made when the maker knows that he does not have the basis for knowledge or belief concerning the intent of the third person that is professed by his assertion, the statement is fraudulent under the rule stated in § 526.

Title B.   Expectation of Influencing Conduct

§ 531   General Rule

One who makes a fraudulent misrepresentation is subject to liability to the persons or class of persons whom he intends or has reason to expect to act or to refrain from action in reliance upon the misrepresentation, for pecuniary loss suffered by them through their justifiable reliance in the type of transaction in which he intends or has reason to expect their conduct to be influenced.

Caveat:

   The Institute expresses no opinion on whether the liability of the maker of a fraudulent representation may extend beyond the rule stated in this

Section to other persons or other types of transactions, if reliance upon the representation in acting or in refraining from action may reasonably be foreseen.

Comment:

a. This Section deals with the persons to whom the maker of a fraudulent misrepresentation may be liable. The general rule of liability for fraudulent misrepresentation is stated in § 525. As to what constitutes a fraudulent misrepresentation, see § 526. As to the extent of liability for negligent misrepresentation, see § 552.

b. *Unintended and unexpected persons.* The rule stated in this Section governs the liability of the maker of a fraudulent misrepresentation to those plaintiffs whom he intends or has reason to expect to act, or to refrain from action, in reliance upon it. If the maker neither intends nor has reason to expect that the misrepresentation will reach a particular person or class of persons or that they will act or refrain from acting in reliance upon it, the fact that it does reach them and they do so act does not bring him within the rule stated in this Section. In this respect, the rule stated in this Section as to liability for pecuniary loss is somewhat more narrow than that stated in § 310, as to the liability for conscious misrepresentation resulting in physical harm. (See Comment *d* below).

Illustrations:

1. A, an agent of X Company, is seeking to sell stock owned by the company to B. For this purpose he makes fraudulent statements concerning the character of the stock to B, in the presence of C. A does not desire to sell the stock to C, and has no reason to know that C has any interest in it. In reliance upon A's statements, C purchases the stock directly from X Company, and suffers pecuniary loss. A is not liable to C under the rule stated in this Section.

2. A makes fraudulent statements concerning the financial standing of B to C and asks him to repeat them to D for the purpose of inducing D to extend credit to B. A does not intend and has no reason to expect that C will repeat the statements to any one other than D. C repeats them to E, who relies upon the statements and extends credit to B, and as a result suffers pecuniary loss. A is not liable to E under the rule stated in this Section.

3. A, seeking to sell corporate stock to B, C and D, sends them a private prospectus marked "Confidential," in which he makes fraudulent statements concerning the financial condition of the corporation. A does not intend and has no reason to expect that the prospectus will be shown to any one else. B exhibits it to E, who in reliance upon the fraudulent statements comes to A and buys some of the stock from him, without mentioning the fact that he has seen the prospectus. A is not liable to E under the rule stated in this Section.

c.   *Intended results.* A result is intended if the actor either acts with the desire to cause it or acts believing that there is a substantial certainty that the result will follow from his conduct. (See § 8A). Thus one who believes that another is substantially certain to act in a particular manner as a result of a misrepresentation intends that result, although he does not act for the purpose of causing it and does not desire to do so.

d.   *"Reason to expect."* One has reason to expect a result if he has information from which a reasonable man would conclude that the result will follow or would govern his conduct upon the assumption that it will do so. (Compare, in § 12(1), the meaning of "reason to know.")

In order for the maker of a fraudulent misrepresentation to have reason to expect that it will reach third persons and influence their conduct it is not enough that he recognizes, or as a reasonable man should recognize, the risk that it may be communicated to them and they may act upon it. When physical harm results from the misrepresentation, the maker may be liable under the rules stated in §§ 310 and 552A. When only pecuniary loss results, the magnitude of the extent to which misrepresentations may be circulated and the losses that may result from reliance upon them has induced the courts to limit the liability to the narrower rule stated in this Section.

Virtually any misrepresentation is capable of being transmitted or repeated to third persons, and if sufficiently convincing may create an obvious risk that they may act in reliance upon it. (See Illustrations 1 to 3, above). This risk is not enough for the liability covered in this Section. The maker of the misrepresentation must have information that would lead a reasonable man to conclude that there is an especial likelihood that it will reach those persons and will influence their conduct. There must be something in the situation known to the maker that would lead a reasonable man to govern his conduct on the assumption that this will occur. If he has the information, the maker is subject to liability under the rule stated here. For example, one who gives fraudulent information concerning his finances to a commercial credit agency cannot be heard to say that he does not expect that it will be communicated to its subscribers.

e.   *Class of persons.* The maker may have reason to expect that his misrepresentation will reach any of a class of persons, although he does not know the identity of the person whom it will reach or indeed of any individual in the class. Thus the business man who furnishes fraudulent information concerning his credit to the commercial credit agency has reason to expect that it will reach and influence any subscriber of the agency who may be interested in extending credit to him, although he does not know who the subscribers are. The class may include a rather large group, such as potential sellers, buyers, creditors, lenders or investors, or others who may be expected to enter into dealings in reliance upon the misrepresentation.

Illustrations:

4. A, a certified public accountant, fraudulently certifies an erroneous balance sheet for B Company. A is informed that B Company intends to exhibit the balance sheet to one or more of a group of banks or other lenders or investors for the purpose of obtaining a loan. A does not know the identity of any of the persons whom B Company may decide to approach. B Company exhibits the balance sheet to C Company, which, in reliance upon it, makes a loan to B Company, and as a result suffers pecuniary loss. A is subject to liability to C Company.

5. A, an architect, fraudulently furnishes erroneous specifications for a building to B, who is under contract to construct it. A is informed that B intends to obtain bids from subcontractors for work on the building as called for by the specifications, but A does not know the identity of any of the persons who may bid. B publishes an invitation for bids. In response to it C, in reliance upon the specifications, bids for the plumbing work on the building, is awarded the contract and as a result suffers pecuniary loss. A is subject to liability to C.

f. Specific individuals. A fortiori, the maker of the fraudulent misrepresentation is subject to liability to a specific, known and identified person if he knows that the representation is likely to reach that person, and knows of any special reason to expect that he will act or refrain from action in reliance upon it.

Illustration:

6. The same facts as in Illustration 1, except that A knows when he makes the statements that C is interested in buying some of the land, and has been making inquiries about the matter stated. A is subject to liability to C.

g. Type of transaction. The liability under this Section of the maker of a fraudulent misrepresentation is also limited to pecuniary losses suffered in the type of transaction in which he intends or has reason to expect the conduct of others to be influenced. On "intends" and "has reason to expect," see Comments *c* and *d* above.

This does not mean that the transaction into which the plaintiff enters must be identical with that contemplated by the defendant. It may differ in matters of detail or in extent, unless these differences are so great as to amount to a change in the essential character of the transaction. Whether it does so may be to a considerable extent a matter of degree. Thus one who expects a mortgage in the amount of $10,000, secured by particular land, is not relieved from liability when the mortgage is in fact made for $20,000 and secured by the same land; but when the result is a bond issue in the amount of $1,000,000, secured by all of the assets of a corporation, the transaction is of a different type. No definite rules can be stated, and the question in each case is whether the transaction that in fact results is sufficiently similar to that which the defendant has reason to expect to hold him responsible for the loss incurred in it.

Illustration:

7. A, seeking to sell a lot owned by him, publishes in newspapers fraudulent statements concerning the character of all lots in the real estate development in which it is located. B reads these statements, and in reliance upon them purchases another lot in the same development from C. A is not liable to B under the rule stated in this Section.

Comment on Caveat:

h. The area of the law covered by this Section has been undergoing change in the direction of liberalizing the rules as to the expected reliance. This Section is not intended to foreclose or discourage further developments. The Caveat therefore leaves open the question of whether there may be cases in addition to those covered by the rule stated in this Section, in which there is no special reason to expect that a given person or a class of persons will take action or refrain from it in reliance upon the fraudulent representation, but it is foreseeable that they may do so, and the circumstances are such that the maker of the presentation may be held subject to liability. On these cases the Institute takes no position.

Illustrations:

8. A, seeking to sell sheep to B, fraudulently tells C, who is B's agent negotiating the purchase, that the sheep are physically sound, although they are in fact diseased. A does not intend that C shall buy the sheep and has no reason to know that he has any interest in them. C buys the sheep for B, and then, in reliance upon A's statement, himself buys the sheep from B and as a result suffers pecuniary loss. The Institute expresses no opinion as to whether A is subject to liability to C.

9. A, seeking to float an issue of bonds on his land, issues circulars that fraudulently state that the mortgage securing the bonds is a first mortgage and that there is no prior lien. There is in fact a prior vendor's lien on the land. B reads one of the circulars and in reliance upon it comes to A and buys from him a part of the land, without mentioning the circular. As a result B suffers pecuniary loss. The Institute expresses no opinion as to whether A is subject to liability to B.

§ 532 Misrepresentation Incorporated in Document or Other Thing

One who embodies a fraudulent misrepresentation in an article of commerce, a muniment of title, a negotiable instrument or a similar commercial document, is subject to liability for pecuniary loss caused to another who deals with him or with a third person regarding the article or document in justifiable reliance upon the truth of the representation.

Comment:

a. On what constitutes justifiable reliance, see §§ 537 to 545A.

b. The rule stated in this Section is a special application of that stated in § 531. It may be expressed by saying that the maker of a fraudulent misrepresentation incorporated in a document has reason to expect that it will reach and influence any person whom the document reaches.

c. The rule stated in this Section is usually applicable when certificates are issued for shares that the corporation is not authorized to issue, when the names of the makers or endorsers of negotiable instruments are forged or the amounts payable are altered, when false recitals are inserted in deeds or bonds and when merchandise is placed on the market in containers with misleading labels or in a form that misrepresents its basic character. In all these cases the maker has reason to expect that the document or chattel in which the misrepresentation is incorporated will pass into the hands of persons other than the one to whom he immediately delivers it and that the misrepresentation will influence their conduct. He is therefore subject to liability when the third person suffers pecuniary loss through dealing with the document or article.

These misrepresentations differ materially from independent misrepresentations of value or quality or article sold or other misrepresentations of the advantages of a bargain, in that those considered here are incorporated in a document of a character that makes it expected to be transmitted and to be relied on by third persons in commercial dealings with it, on the faith of the honesty of what it conveys. Thus a deed to land or other muniment of title is not merely a means by which the title is transferred to the purchaser, but is also a symbol of the title itself; and a negotiable instrument is not merely a contract to pay, but an embodiment of the contract itself, which passes with the instrument to each successive holder.

The rule stated is therefore limited to those documents or chattels that are in themselves articles of commerce. It does not apply to an ordinary letter misrepresenting the title to land or to a report furnished by an accountant to a corporation concerning its finances, because these documents are not to be expected to have commercial circulation.

Illustrations:

1. A fraudulently draws a negotiable promissory note, which he signs "X Corporation, by A, President." A is not the president of X Corporation and has no authority to sign for it. A borrows money from B, giving him the note, and B negotiates it to C, who purchases it in good faith. A is subject to liability to C for any pecuniary loss sustained through his purchase.

2. A markets sacks of clover seed, which he fraudulently labels "Alfalfa Seed." B, in reliance upon the label, buys a sack of the seed from

a dealer, plants it, and suffers pecuniary loss when the crop turns out to be clover. A is subject to liability to B.

§ 533   Representation Made to a Third Person

The maker of a fraudulent misrepresentation is subject to liability for pecuniary loss to another who acts in justifiable reliance upon it if the misrepresentation, although not made directly to the other, is made to a third person and the maker intends or has reason to expect that its terms will be repeated or its substance communicated to the other, and that it will influence his conduct in the transaction or type of transaction involved.

Caveat:

The Institute expresses no opinion on whether the liability of the maker of a fraudulent representation may extend beyond the rule stated in this Section to other persons or other types of transactions, if reliance upon the representation in acting or refraining from action may reasonably be foreseen.

Comment:

a.   On what constitutes justifiable reliance, see §§ 537 to 545A.

b.   The rule stated in this Section is a special application of that stated in § 531. It is stated in a separate Section in order to make it clear that the rule applies when the misrepresentation is made to a third person. The Comments and Illustrations under § 531 are therefore applicable to this Section, so far as they are pertinent.

c.   *Inducing action between third persons.* The rule stated in this Section is applicable not only when the effect of the misrepresentation is to induce the other to enter into a transaction with the maker, but also when he is induced to enter into a transaction with a third person.

d.   *Reason to expect repetition.* In accordance with Comment *d* under § 531, it is not enough to make the rule stated in this Section applicable that the maker of the misrepresentation does recognize, or should recognize, the possibility that the third person to whom he makes it may repeat it for the purpose of influencing the conduct of another. He must make the misrepresentation with that intent, or must have information that gives him special reason to expect that it will be communicated to others, and will influence their conduct.

If the misrepresentation is made for the purpose of having it communicated, the maker is subject to liability. Thus one who, to aid a friend in selling his land, gives him for transmission to a prospective purchaser a fraudulent misrepresentation as to the quantity or quality of the land, is subject to liability to the purchaser under the rule stated in this Section. On the same basis, an architect who gives a fraudulent certificate as to the amount of work done to a builder for use in obtaining an advance from a bank is subject to liability to the bank. This is also true of one who supplies a fraudulent abstract of title to be transmitted to a prospective purchaser or mortgagor.

The liability, however, extends beyond those whom the maker of the misrepresentation intends to reach or to influence. It includes those whom he has reason to expect it to reach and influence, although he does not make the misrepresentation with that intention or purpose. If he is aware of the intention of the third person to make use of the misrepresentation by communicating it to others, he has a special reason to expect that it will be so communicated and will be relied on. There may be other circumstances that give him reason to expect the repetition, as when, for example, he is informed that the other is interested in the matter misrepresented and proposes to make inquiry of the third person for guidance in his conduct.

e. Maker's interest in the transaction. As stated in Comment *d*, the fact that the maker of the misrepresentation has no interest in the transaction does not take the case out of the rule stated in this Section. However, the fact that the maker has an advantage to gain, even though it is in some other transaction, by furnishing the misrepresentation for repetition to the third person is of great significance in determining whether he has reason to expect that the original recipient should so repeat it. Thus, the customary practice of bankers who purchase bonds of a corporation, to summarize reports made by the corporation to them in the prospectus that they issue to the investing public, will support a finding that the officers of the corporation have reason to expect the substance of their reports to be communicated to the investing public in order to influence the public's purchase of the bonds from the bankers. These considerations apply with added force when the corporation has an indirect interest in the sale of the bonds to the investing public because of the bankers' agreement to take a further issue of bonds when the first issue is distributed to the public.

f. Misrepresentation to credit-rating company. One of the situations to which the rule stated in this Section is frequently applied is where misrepresentations are made to a credit-rating company for the purpose of obtaining a credit rating based on them. In this case the maker is subject to liability to any person who may be expected to and does extend credit to him in reliance upon the erroneous rating so procured. The fact that the rating company does not communicate the figures misstated by the maker of the misrepresentations is immaterial. It is enough that their substance is summarized with reasonable accuracy or that the rating given expresses the effect of the misstatements made. The fact that the misrepresentations are made to a company that purports to give only credit ratings is usually sufficient to justify a finding that their purpose is to obtain credit through the unwarranted ratings and unless the circumstances are sufficient to show some further reason to expect action the maker is subject to liability only to those who extend credit to him in reliance upon the ratings. On the other hand, if the company is one whose ratings purport to show the general financial position of those who make reports to it, the maker of the misrepresentation is subject to liability to anyone who in reliance upon the rating deals with him in any one of the ways in which the maker's financial position is material.

g. *Repetition to unidentified person.* Although the maker of the representation is liable only if it is repeated to a person to whom he intends or has reason to expect to have it repeated, it is not necessary that he have any particular person in mind. It is enough that he intends or has reason to expect to have it repeated to a particular class of persons and that the person relying upon it is one of that class. Thus, if a firm of accountants employed to audit the books of a corporation gives a certificate fraudulently overstating its assets, knowing that the corporation intends to make use of it to obtain a loan, it is immaterial that the identity of the prospective lender is not known to the accountants. Indeed, even though the audit is asked for the purpose of obtaining a particular loan from a particular bank, the circumstances may justify a finding that the maker was aware that the identity of the particular bank was immaterial, and hence that he had reason to expect that the certificate would be used by the corporation to obtain a loan of a similar amount from any bank. In this case it makes little or no difference to the accountants whether the bank which advances the money is one bank or another. The important thing is that they are aware of the intent to obtain a loan from some bank. On the other hand, if the certificate is used by the corporation, not to obtain a loan in the contemplated amount, but obtain unlimited credit, the transaction is of a different type, and there is no liability. (See Comment *f* under § 531).

Comment on Caveat:

h. A developing trend toward extending the scope of liability in this area of the law may eventually extend beyond the rule stated in this Section. The Section is not intended to foreclose or discourage further developments. The Caveat therefore leaves open the issue. For elaboration, see § 531, Comment *h.*

§ 536   Information Required by Statute

If a statute requires information to be furnished, filed, recorded or published for the protection of a particular class of persons, one who makes a fraudulent misrepresentation in so doing is subject to liability to the persons for pecuniary loss suffered through their justifiable reliance upon the misrepresentation in a transaction of the kind in which the statute is intended to protect them.

Comment:

a.   On what constitutes justifiable reliance, see §§ 537 to 545A.

b.   The rule stated in this Section is concerned only with fraudulent misrepresentation. On the liability for negligent misrepresentation under similar circumstances, see § 552(3).

c.   This Section is a special application, and not a limitation, of the rule stated in § 531. The rule may be expressed by saying that when a statute requires information to be furnished, filed, recorded or published for the protection of a particular class of persons in particular kinds of transactions, one who complies with the requirement always has reason to expect that the information will reach the class of persons and influence their conduct. This Section does not limit or restrict liability under the rule stated in § 531, apart from the statute.

d.   In the situation dealt with in this Section the controlling factor is the purpose of the legislature, and not that of the person who furnishes the information. It is therefore immaterial that the information is not furnished voluntarily but under compulsion of the statute. Whether the statute is intended for the protection of a particular class of persons such as investors or those lending money, or whether it is intended to give protection only in a particular type of transaction, or in all transactions in which the information furnished may be material, is a question of statutory construction. No general rules can be stated. Certain situations have, however, arisen with sufficient frequency to make it possible to state the construction that is generally given to certain types of statutes.

e.   A statute that requires corporations to make reports of their financial position that are to be published or open to public inspection is generally regarded as one enacted for the purpose of making the information available to those to whom knowledge of the financial position of the corporation in question is important in determining their course of action in any type of transaction with the corporation in question. Thus a financial statement required to be made by a bank or insurance company is regarded as being made, not only for the information of those who are considering the making of deposits in the bank or taking out insurance, but also for the information of persons considering the purchase of shares or lending money to the bank or insurance company.

f.   A statute that requires information to be given to a state banking department or a state insurance commissioner as a prerequisite to permitting a bank or insurance company to be incorporated or to do business in the state may be regarded as intended only to control the action of the department in permitting the incorporation or granting the permit. A court may so interpret the statute although it is a matter of common knowledge that the favorable action will not be taken unless the report states facts which, if stated directly to the public, would be misrepresentations material in business transactions with the company. In this case, even if a bank can not be incorporated or permitted to do business unless it has a certain amount of cash capital, the risk that some members of the public may rely upon the information in dealings with the company does not impose liability upon the makers of the misrepresentation. The fact that incorporation is granted as a result of the misrepresentation of the cash assets of the bank does not make them liable for losses suffered by persons who, knowing these requirements, make deposits with the bank in reliance upon the incorporation as an assurance that this capital is in existence.

On the other hand, when its terms or language call for the interpretation, the statute may be construed as intended to give protection to those who rely upon the filed information in their dealings.

  g. The rule stated in this Section is not necessary to the liability of one who, having made a misrepresentation in a report that is required by a statute, adopts it as a true statement by showing it to another or by calling his attention to it. In this case it is immaterial that the report is one that the statute requires to be made solely to influence the official action of the governmental officers. Thus, when an insurance company before writing insurance is required by statute to obtain a license that is granted only upon the presentation of a satisfactory report of its financial standing, and an officer of the company, in order to induce another to take out a policy, shows him the report knowing it to contain false statements, the officer is subject to liability to the insured for loss resulting from reliance upon the false statements, although the report was required only for the guidance of the licensing authority.

  h. The rule stated in this Section includes administrative regulations and other governmental orders issued pursuant to a statute.

Title C. Justifiable Reliance

§ 537   General Rule

The recipient of a fraudulent misrepresentation can recover against its maker for pecuniary loss resulting from it if, but only if,

  (a) he relies on the misrepresentation in acting or refraining from action, and

  (b) his reliance is justifiable.

Comment:

  a. The recipient of a fraudulent misrepresentation can recover from the maker for his pecuniary loss only if he in fact relies upon the misrepresentation in acting or in refraining from action, and his reliance is a substantial factor in bringing about the loss. (See § 546 and Comments). If the recipient does not in fact rely on the misrepresentation, the fact that he takes some action that would be consistent with his reliance on it and as a result suffers pecuniary loss, does not impose any liability upon the maker.

  b. The recipient must not only in fact rely upon the misrepresentation, but his reliance must be justifiable. The rules that determine whether he is justified in reliance upon various types of misrepresentations are stated in §§ 538 to 545 and in § 547.

§ 538   Materiality of Misrepresentation

(1) Reliance upon a fraudulent misrepresentation is not justifiable unless the matter misrepresented is material.

(2) The matter is material if

    (a) a reasonable man would attach importance to its existence or nonexistence in determining his choice of action in the transaction in question; or

    (b) the maker of the representation knows or has reason to know that its recipient regards or is likely to regard the matter as important in determining his choice of action, although a reasonable man would not so regard it.

Comment:

a.   The rules stated in this Section are concerned only with whether the recipient's reliance upon the misrepresentation is justifiable. The rules that determine the fraudulent character of the misrepresentation are stated in §§ 526 to 530. The rules which determine the persons to whom the maker of the misrepresentation may be liable are stated in §§ 531 to 536. The general rule requiring that the recipient in fact rely on the misrepresentation and that his reliance be justifiable is stated in § 537.

b.   The rule stated in this Section applies not only to misrepresentations of fact but also to those of opinion, intention and law. When the representation is one of opinion or intention, the question of materiality concerns not only the facts about which the opinion is expressed or the proposed action or inaction to which the intention relates, but also the existence of the opinion or intention itself in the particular individual who asserts it. (See §§ 542, 543, and 544).

c.   The rule stated in this Section differs from the rules that determine the right to rescind a contract induced by fraudulent misrepresentation (see Restatement, Second, Contracts § 306) and to obtain restitution for benefits procured by fraudulent misrepresentation. (See Restatement of Restitution, § 9, Comment *b*). In neither of these cases is it required that the misrepresentation, if fraudulent, be as to a matter that is material, materiality being important in them only when the misrepresentation is negligent and not fraudulent.

Comment on Clause (2), (a):

d.   In determining whether a fact is material it is not necessary that it be one that a reasonable man would regard as affecting the pecuniary advantages of the transaction. There are many more-or-less sentimental considerations that the ordinary man regards as important. Thus it is natural that a person should wish to possess portraits of his ancestors even though they have no value as works of art. A fraudulent misrepresentation that a particular picture is a portrait of the purchaser's great-grandfather is a misrepresentation of a material fact.

e. As in all cases in which the conduct of the reasonable man is the standard, the question of whether a reasonable man would have regarded the fact misrepresented to be important in determining his course of action is a matter for the judgment of the jury subject to the control of the court. The court may withdraw the case from the jury if the fact misrepresented is so obviously unimportant that the jury could not reasonably find that a reasonable man would have been influenced by it. Compare § 285, especially Comments *f* and *g* which state the respective functions of court and jury in negligence cases.

f. Even though the matter misrepresented is one to which a reasonable man would not attach any importance in determining his course of action in the transaction in hand, it is nevertheless material if the maker knows that the recipient, because of his own peculiarities, is likely to attach importance to it. There are many persons whose judgment, even in important transactions, is likely to be determined by considerations that the normal man would regard as altogether trivial or even ridiculous. One who practices upon another's known [idiosyncrasies] cannot complain if he is held liable when he is successful in what he is endeavoring to accomplish.

Illustrations:

1. A, seeking to induce B to buy stock in a corporation, knows that B believes in astrology and governs his conduct according to horoscopes. A fraudulently tells B that the horoscopes of the officers of the corporation all indicate remarkable success for the corporation during the coming year. In reliance upon this statement, B buys the stock from A and as a result suffers pecuniary loss. The misrepresentation is material.

2. A, seeking to induce B to give money to a college about to be founded, fraudulently informs B that it is to be named after X, a deceased friend of B of bad character, whom B has regarded with great affection. A knows that the statement is likely to be regarded by B as an important inducement to make a gift. In reliance upon the statement, B makes the gift. The statement is material.

§ 538A   Opinion

A representation is one of opinion if it expresses only

   (a) the belief of the maker, without certainty, as to the existence of a fact; or

   (b) his judgment as to quality, value, authenticity, or other matters of judgment.

Comment:

a. So far as justifiable reliance by the recipient of the misrepresentation is concerned, a distinction is made in §§ 539, 542 and 543 between representations of fact and those of opinion. As is indicated in those Sections, the recipient may under some circumstances not be justified in relying upon a representation of opinion concerning a fact, although he would be justified in reliance upon a representation of the fact itself.

b. *Fact and opinion.* A representation of fact is a positive assertion that the fact is true. It implies that the maker has definite knowledge or information which justifies the positive assertion. A representation of opinion, on the other hand, is only one of the maker's belief as to the fact. It implies that he does not have definite knowledge, that he is not sufficiently certain of what he says to make the positive statement, or at most, as stated in § 539, that he knows of no facts incompatible with the belief, or that he does know some facts that justify him in forming it. The difference is one between "This is true," and "I think this is true, but I am not sure."

One common form of opinion is a statement of the maker's judgment as to quality, value, authenticity or similar matters as to which opinions may be expected to differ. Thus the statement that an automobile is a good car is a relative matter, depending entirely upon the standard set as to what is a good automobile and what is not, and it is a matter upon which individual judgments may be expected to differ. The maker of a statement of this nature will normally be understood as expressing only his own judgment and not as asserting anything concerning horsepower, riding qualities or any of the dozen other factors that would influence his judgment.

c. *Form of the statement.* The form of the statement is important and may be controlling. "I believe that there are ten acres here," is a different statement, in what it conveys, from "The area of this land is ten acres." The one conveys an expression of some doubt while the other leaves no room for it.

d. The form of the statement is not, however, controlling in all cases. A statement that is in form one of positive assertion of a fact may be made under such circumstances that it must be understood as conveying only an expression of the maker's belief, not free from doubt. This may be true particularly when the recipient knows that the maker has not information concerning the fact asserted and therefore can only be stating his belief. Less frequently a statement made, for the sake of politeness or modesty, in the form of an opinion may reasonably be understood as an assertion of definite knowledge. The question is thus not alone one of the language used but of the sense in which it is reasonably understood.

Illustration:

1. A, seeking to sell land to B, says to B: "There is water under this land, and if you dig a well anywhere on the land you will strike it." B knows that no water survey has been made and that A has no

information concerning the presence or absence of subterranean water. The statement is one of opinion.

e.   Quantity as a fact. A statement of the quantity of either land or chattels is a statement of fact. A purchaser of either is entitled to assume that the vendor knows the acreage of the land or the quantity of a lot of goods that he is selling. This is true although the vendor's statement does not assert or imply that it is based upon a survey of the land or a measurement, weighing or count of the goods.

The words "more or less" accompanying a statement of quantity do not make the statement one of opinion. They merely indicate that there is a certain margin offeror and, although they do not justify the recipient in believing that the statement is intended to express an exact measurement, they justify him in believing that the quantity is substantially as stated.

f.   Quality, when a fact. A representation of quality is usually a representation of opinion, particularly when goods are bought upon inspection. Therefore the recipient's justification for his reliance upon such a representation is determined by the rules stated in §§ 542–543. There are, however, many articles in which the gradations of quality are so marked that they are customarily sold as of a specified grade. A false representation that such an article is of a particular grade is a misrepresentation of fact.

g.   Price, when a material fact. A statement of the price at which goods have been sold or offered for sale is a statement of a fact, which may or may not be material. The price at which goods or securities are sold on a commodity or stock exchange represents a concurrence of the opinion of the interested public as to their value, and therefore justifies the recipient of a statement of market quotations in accepting it as conclusive proof of the value of the article in question. A sale of auction of goods or securities differs in one particular from a sale on an exchange in that there is normally no such attendance of a sufficient number of prospective buyers and sellers as to make the price realized conclusive as to the value of the articles sold. It is, however, evidence of their value; and the recipient of a statement of the price realized at an auction sale may justifiably take it into account in forming his own opinion, although in doing so he should make allowance for the lack of publicity and, in the case of a forced sale, for the exigencies of the vendor. Normally the price realized at a private sale of the article in question or an offer made for it is a fact properly taken into account in determining the value of the article. When, however, the recipient of a representation as to the price realized or offered knows the circumstances of the transaction and the characteristics of the persons engaged therein, the price paid or offered is important primarily as implying the opinion that the parties to the sale or offer had of the value of the article in question. To this extent the question whether the recipient of a misstatement of such a fact is justified in relying upon it as showing the value of the article in question is determined by the rules stated in § 542 if the purchaser or offeror is known to have an interest in the pending transaction antagonistic to that of the recipient and by the rules stated in § 543 when the recipient reasonably believes that the purchaser or offeror is disinterested.

§ 539   Representation of Opinion Implying Justifying Facts

(1) A statement of opinion as to facts not disclosed and not otherwise known to the recipient may, if it is reasonable to do so, be interpreted by him as an implied statement

(a) that the facts known to the maker are not incompatible with his opinion; or

(b) that he knows facts sufficient to justify him in forming it.

(2) In determining whether a statement of opinion may reasonably be so interpreted, the recipient's belief as to whether the maker has an adverse interest is important.

Comment on Subsection (1):

a. Frequently a statement which, though in form an opinion upon facts not disclosed or otherwise known to their recipient, is reasonably understood as implying that there are facts that justify the opinion or at least that there are no facts that are incompatible with it. Thus, when land is bought as an investment, a statement, even by the vendor, that a tenant under a long term lease is a good tenant implies that his conduct has been such that it would not be entirely inappropriate to call him a good tenant. Such a representation is therefore fraudulent if the vendor knows that the tenant has rarely paid his rent except under pressure of legal proceedings, since the vendor is giving a materially false picture of the tenant's conduct. So, too, a statement that a bond is a good investment, even though made by a person attempting to sell it, is a fraudulent misstatement of the actual character of the bond if the vendor knows that the interest on the bond has for years been in default and the corporation that issued it is in the hands of a receiver. Although some allowance must be made for puffing or depreciation by an adverse party, such a statement is so far removed from the truth as to make it a fraudulent misrepresentation of the character of the bond.

Illustration:

1. A, seeking to sell B machinery for the manufacture of ice cream, fraudulently tells B that in his opinion a room in the rear of B's building is suitable for the manufacture. A knows, but B does not, that the room is not at present suitable and can be made so only by changes that would involve prohibitive expense. In reliance on the statement B purchases the machinery. A is subject to liability to B.

b. The statement of opinion may not only imply that the maker knows of no fact incompatible with the opinion, but, when the circumstances justify it, may also reasonably be understood to imply that he does know facts sufficient to justify him in forming the opinion and that the facts known to him do justify him.

This is true particularly when the maker is understood to have special knowledge of facts unknown to the recipient. (See § 542(a)). Thus when an auditor who is known to have examined the books of a corporation states that it is in sound financial condition, he may reasonably be understood to say that his examination has been sufficient to permit him to form an honest opinion and that what he has found justifies his conclusion. The opinion thus becomes in effect a short summary of those facts. When he is reasonably understood as conveying such a statement, he is subject to liability if he has not made the examination, or if he has not found facts that justify the opinion, on the basis of his misrepresentation of the implied facts.

Illustrations:

2.   A, a famous expert on violins, is employed by B, who knows nothing about them, to examine a violin that B is about to purchase. Without looking at the violin or examining its history, A informs B that in his opinion it is a genuine Stradivarius. In reliance on the opinion B buys the violin and suffers pecuniary loss when it turns out to be spurious. A is subject to liability to B.

3.   The same facts as in Illustration 1, except that A examines the violin and its record and is unable to discover anything that throws light on whether it is genuine. The same conclusion.

Comment on Subsection (2):

c.   The habit of vendors to exaggerate the advantages of the bargain that they are offering to make is a well recognized fact. An intending purchaser may not be justified in relying upon his vendor's statement of the value, quality or other advantages of a thing that he is intending to sell as carrying with it any assurance that the thing is such as to justify a reasonable man in praising it so highly. However, a purchaser is justified in assuming that even his vendor's opinion has some basis of fact, and therefore in believing that the vendor knows of nothing which makes his opinion fantastic. On the other hand, a representation that a person who is reasonably believed by the recipient to be disinterested has a particular opinion, may reasonably be understood as impliedly asserting that the opinion expressed is an honest one and that he knows of no facts that make it incorrect. This is true since there is no apparent reason for a disinterested person to exaggerate the facts upon which it may be assumed that his opinion is based and of which the recipient knows nothing.

§ 540   Duty to Investigate

The recipient of a fraudulent misrepresentation of fact is justified in relying upon its truth, although he might have ascertained the falsity of the representation had he made an investigation.

Comment:

a. The rule stated in this Section applies not only when an investigation would involve an expenditure of effort and money out of proportion to the magnitude of the transaction, but also when it could be made without any considerable trouble or expense. Thus it is no defense to one who has made a fraudulent statement about his financial position that his offer to submit his books to examination is rejected. On the other hand, if a mere cursory glance would have disclosed the falsity of the representation, its falsity is regarded as obvious under the rule stated in § 541.

b. The rule stated in this Section is applicable even though the fact that is fraudulently represented is required to be recorded and is in fact recorded. The recording acts are not intended as a protection for fraudulent liars. Their purpose is to afford a protection to persons who buy a recorded title against those who, having obtained a paper title, have failed to record it. The purpose of the statutes is fully accomplished without giving them a collateral effect that protects those who make fraudulent misrepresentations from liability.

Illustration:

1.   A, seeking to sell land to B, tells B that the land is free from all incumbrances. By walking across the street to the office of the register of deeds in the courthouse, B could easily learn that there is a recorded and unsatisfied mortgage on the land. B does not do so and buys the land in reliance upon A's misrepresentation. His reliance is justifiable.

§ 541   Representation Known to Be or Obviously False

The recipient of a fraudulent misrepresentation is not justified in relying upon its truth if he knows that it is false or its falsity is obvious to him.

Comment:

a. Although the recipient of a fraudulent misrepresentation is not barred from recovery because he could have discovered its falsity if he had shown his distrust of the maker's honesty by investigating its truth, he is nonetheless required to use his senses, and cannot recover if he blindly relies upon a misrepresentation the falsity of which would be patent to him if he had utilized his opportunity to make a cursory examination or investigation. Thus, if one induces another to buy a horse by representing it to be sound, the purchaser cannot recover even though the horse has but one eye, if the horse is shown to the purchaser before he buys it and the slightest inspection would have disclosed the defect. On the other hand, the rule stated in this Section applies only when the recipient of the misrepresentation is capable of appreciating its falsity at the time by the use of his senses. Thus a defect that any experienced horseman would at once recognize at first glance may not be patent to a person who has had no experience with horses.

§ 542 Opinion of Adverse Party

The recipient of a fraudulent misrepresentation solely of the maker's opinion is not justified in relying upon it in a transaction with the maker, unless the fact to which the opinion relates is material, and the maker

(a) purports to have special knowledge of the matter that the recipient does not have, or

(b) stands in a fiduciary or other similar relation of trust and confidence to the recipient, or

(c) has successfully endeavored to secure the confidence of the recipient, or

(d) has some other special reason to expect that the recipient will rely on his opinion.

Comment:

a. On when a fact is material, see § 538.

b. The rule stated in this Section applies only when the representation is in itself nothing more than a statement of the maker's opinion. As stated in § 539, a statement of opinion may, when the circumstances justify it, reasonably be interpreted to include an implied assertion of the existence or non-existence of facts. In that case the maker may be subject to liability on the basis of the implied representation of fact. This is frequently the case in the situations covered by Clause (a) of this Section, which is included here in order to complete the Section.

c. The rule stated in this Section applies when the opinion is stated as to facts, all or part of which are not known to the recipient. It applies also when the opinion is an expression of the maker's judgment upon facts known to the recipient.

d. If the subject matter of the transaction is one upon which both parties have an approximately equal competence to form a reliable opinion, each must trust to his own judgment and neither is justified in relying upon the opinion of the other. The law assumes that the ordinary man has a reasonable competence to form his own opinion as to the advisability of entering into those transactions that form part of the ordinary routine of life. The fact that one of the two parties to a bargain is less astute than the other does not justify him in relying upon the judgment of the other. This is true even though the transaction in question is one in which the one party knows that the other is somewhat more conversant with the value and quality of the things about which they are bargaining. Thus the purchaser of an ordinary commodity is not justified in relying upon the vendor's opinion of its quality or worth. For example, one who is purchasing a horse from a dealer is not justified in relying upon the dealer's opinion, although the latter has a greater experience in judging the effect of the factors which determine its value.

e. This is true particularly of loose general statements made by sellers in commending their wares, which are commonly known as "puffing," or "sales talk." It is common knowledge and may always be assumed that any seller will express a favorable opinion concerning what he has to sell; and when he praises it in general terms, without specific content or reference to facts, buyers are expected to and do understand that they are not entitled to rely literally upon the words. "Such statements, like the claims of campaign managers before election, are rather designed to allay the suspicion which would attend their absence than to be understood as having any relation to objective truth." [Learned Hand, C.J., in Vulcan Metals Co. v. Simmons Mfg. Co., (2 Cir.1918) 248 F. 853, 856.]

Thus no action lies against a dealer who describes the automobile he is selling as a "dandy," a "bearcat," a "good little car," and a "sweet job," or as "the pride of our line," or "the best in the American market." On the other hand, a statement that a machine will be satisfactory for the buyer's purposes may, under the circumstances, reasonably be understood to carry the assertion of fact that it has the capacity to do the work known to be required.

Comment on Clause (a):

f. The complexities and specializations of modern commercial and financial life have created many situations in which special experience and training are necessary to the formation of a valuable judgment. In this case if the one party has special experience or training or purports to have them, the other, if without them, is entitled to rely upon the honesty of the former's opinion and to attach to it the importance that is warranted by his superior competence. The ordinary purchaser of jewelry cannot be expected to know the quality or value of the gems shown to him by a jeweler. He must rely and is therefore justified in relying upon the jeweler's statement that a diamond is of the first water; and, after making allowance for the natural tendency of a vendor to praise his wares, he is justified in relying upon the jeweler's statement of the value of the diamond. So, too, one who consults an attorney concerning a question of law, concerning which the layman knows nothing, is justified in relying upon the attorney's opinion. On the same basis, the ordinary purchaser of antiques is entitled to rely upon the statement of a vendor who specializes in such articles that a piece of furniture is an antique and not a modern imitation. Again, a purchaser of a picture may rely upon the dealer's representation that it is painted by a particular artist, since only those who make a study of such matters are able to form a reliable opinion upon them.

Comment on Clause (b):

g. This Clause is substantially identical with Clause (2)(a) of § 551. The Comment on that Clause is equally pertinent here.

Comment on Clause (c):

h. One who has taken steps to induce another to believe that the other can safely trust to his judgment is subject to liability if the confidence so acquired is abused. This is true not only when the maker of the fraudulent misrepresentation of opinion is or professes to be disinterested, as when the transaction is between the recipient and a third person, as to which see § 543, but also when he is known to have an adverse interest in the transaction. The situation to which the rule stated in this Clause is usually applicable occurs when the maker gains the other's confidence by stressing their common membership in a religious denomination, fraternal order or social group or the fact that they were born in the same locality.

Illustration:

1.   A, professing friendship, offers to advise B, an elderly widow inexperienced in business, concerning her investments. He does so for five years, giving her good advice and acquiring her confidence. At the end of this time he advises her to buy from him worthless corporate stock, telling her that in his opinion it is a good investment. B buys the stock and suffers pecuniary loss. A is subject to liability to B.

Comment on Clause (d):

i.   The chief application of this Clause is to cases in which the maker of the representation knows of some special characteristic of the recipient, such as his lack of intelligence, illiteracy or unusual credulity and gullibility, which gives the maker special reason to expect that the opinion will be relied on. One who deliberately practices upon such a special characteristic, and takes advantage of it, cannot be heard to say that the reliance he sought to induce was not justified because his statement was one of opinion and therefore should have been distrusted.

§ 543   Opinion of Apparently Disinterested Person

The recipient of a fraudulent misrepresentation of opinion is justified in relying upon it if the opinion is that of a person whom the recipient reasonably believes to be disinterested and if the fact that such person holds the opinion is material.

Comment:

a.   Opinion of interested and disinterested person distinguished. The rule stated in this Section is applicable to three situations. The first occurs when the person who expresses his opinion has no adversary interest in the transaction. The second occurs when the person who misrepresents his opinion has an interest in the transaction adverse to that of the recipient but purports to be disinterested. The third occurs when a party to the transaction misrepresents that an apparently disinterested person has expressed the opinion or done an act from which the opinion may be implied. In the last two situations the fact that the recipient correctly, or reasonably though

39

erroneously, believes that the person expressing the opinion has no adverse interest is sufficient to justify him in believing that the opinion of the person in question is as it is stated to be. Therefore, it is not necessary, as it is when the opinion is that of a person known to have an adverse interest in the transaction, that the actually or supposedly disinterested person should have any special or superior knowledge of the subject matter or that he should stand in any particular relation to the recipient or should have succeeded in securing the latter's confidence. (Compare § 542). A purchaser who knows all the material facts necessary to an intelligent decision may well be required to be on his guard against attaching too much importance to the laudatory statements of his vendor as to the value or quality of the article which the latter is trying to sell. It is quite a different matter to require him to distrust the opinion of persons whom he believes to be competent and who so far as he knows have no interest in the sale. Thus a purchaser is not entitled to rely implicitly upon a statement of a bond salesman that the bonds are first class. (See § 542). On the other hand, he may regard the opinion of a trust officer of an important trust company as an assurance that the bonds are a reasonably safe investment, unless he knows that for some reason the trust officer or the company has an interest in the sale of the bonds.

b. *Honesty of opinion.* In determining whether the recipient of a representation of opinion is justified in believing that the opinion is as represented the circumstances under which and the manner in which the opinion is expressed are important. The habit of men to give offhand opinions that often do not express their considered judgment is well known. The recipient of an opinion that he knows is so given is not justified in relying upon it. On the other hand, the fact that the statement of opinion is supported by a statement of action taken upon it in a matter in which the interests of the actor are concerned, or that the opinion is implied from conduct that indicates its existence, is sufficient to justify the recipient in believing that the opinion is firmly entertained and well considered.

c. *Materiality.* Even though the recipient of a misrepresentation of the opinion of a person who is or whom he reasonably believes to be disinterested is justified in believing that the person in question actually holds that opinion, the recipient is not justified in acting in reliance upon it unless its existence is material. In conformity with the definition of materiality in § 538, the opinion is material only if reliance upon it is justified because the person in question is one upon whose judgment a reasonable man would place reliance or is justified as between the maker and recipient by the fact that the maker knew that the recipient would be influenced by the opinion of the person in question although reasonable men would distrust his judgment.

The opinion can never be material unless the matter to which it relates is itself material. (See § 538). Thus when a statement of a fact itself would not be material a statement of opinion concerning that fact is no more so.

d. There are many matters upon which every reasonable man relies for guidance. Thus purchasers of land habitually and properly rely upon the opinion of experts in real estate values and buyers of securities rely upon the advice of persons who have made a special study of these matters. So, too, the official position of the persons whose opinion is misrepresented may carry with it a duty to give an honest and well considered opinion.

    e.   Opinions of disinterested persons. Unlike an opinion of one known to have an adverse interest (see § 542) the recipient of a misrepresentation of the opinion of a disinterested person may justifiably rely upon the judgment expressed by it although it is the opinion of a person whose competence to form it is not superior to his own. Indeed, in the absence of reason to know that the judgment of the person in question is bad, he is entitled to rely upon the opinion of any other person, especially if the statement of his opinion is supported by a statement that he has acted on it or his opinion is implied by the fact that he has acted upon it in a matter in which his own interests are concerned. Thus a representation that an unknown purchaser has paid a particular price for a particular thing is material as implying an opinion of its value that an intending purchaser is entitled to take into account in determining whether to buy.

    f.   Opinions of interested persons. The habit of vendors to exaggerate and of purchasers to depreciate the value of the article which they are selling or buying is well known. A purchaser or vendor is, therefore, not justified in attaching any substantial importance to his adversary's opinion as to the value of the article in question. These statements are often mere dealer's talk, or that puffing of value as well as quality that is an accepted part of bargaining transactions.

§ 544   Statement of Intention

The recipient of a fraudulent misrepresentation of intention is justified in relying upon it if the existence of the intention is material and the recipient has reason to believe that it will be carried out.

Comment:

    a.   Existence of intention. The rule stated in this Section applies only when the representation gives its recipient reason to believe that the intention is firmly entertained and, therefore, to expect that it will be carried out. Whether the recipient has reason for this belief depends upon the circumstances under which the statement was made, including the fact that it was made for the purpose of inducing the recipient to act in reliance upon it and the form and manner in which it was expressed.

    b.   Materiality of the intention. Under the rule stated in this Section it is not enough that the maker has given the recipient reason to believe that he will carry out his expressed intention; it is also necessary that the existence of the intention be material, in the sense in which that term is defined in § 538(2). In order for this to be true, it is first necessary that the action or inaction to which the intention relates be itself material to the transaction; and it is also necessary that it be material that the particular individual has the intention. Thus a representation by the directors of a corporation that it is their intention to apply the money realized by the sale of bonds to the enlargement of the business when the purpose that they actually have in mind is the payment of a floating indebtedness is a material misrepresentation. This is true because buyers of bonds properly regard the purpose to which the money is to be put as of the utmost importance in determining the advisability of the investment. So, too, the holder of an option is justified in regarding the constantly reiterated statements of a prospective purchaser that he intends to buy the property covered by the option as soon as minor questions are settled as sufficiently material to justify the holder in refraining from offering the option to other possible purchasers until its near expiration has made it impossible for him to dispose of it.

    c.   Justifiable reliance. In order for reliance upon a statement of intention to be justifiable, the recipient of the statement must be justified in his expectation that the intention will be carried out. If he knows facts that will make it impossible for the maker to do so, he cannot be justified in his reliance.

Illustration:

    1.   A, the owner of a real estate development, seeking to sell a lot in it to B, fraudulently tells B that he intends to construct a golf course in the development. B knows that the terrain is not suitable for a golf course and that there is not enough available land for it, and that it could only be constructed by purchase of a large quantity of additional land beyond A's means. B is not justified in relying on the representation.

§ 545   Misrepresentation of Law

(1) If a misrepresentation as to a matter of law includes, expressly or by implication, a misrepresentation of fact, the recipient is justified in relying upon the misrepresentation of fact to the same extent as though it were any other misrepresentation of fact.

(2) If a misrepresentation as to a matter of law is only one of opinion as to the legal consequences of facts, the recipient is justified in relying upon it to the same extent as though it were a representation of any other opinion.

Comment:

    a.   A statement of law may be a statement of fact or a statement of opinion. (See Comment *d* on § 525). Thus a statement that a particular statute has been enacted or repealed, or that a particular decision has been rendered by a court upon a particular state of facts is a statement of fact. On the other hand, if all the pertinent facts are known and there is no misrepresentation of the existence or nonexistence of a pertinent statute or judicial decision, the statement of the legal consequences of those facts is a statement of opinion as to what a court would determine to be the legal consequences of the facts if the matter were litigated.

Comment on Subsection (1):

b. A statement that a statute has been enacted or repealed or that a particular court has decided thus and so on a particular state of facts is as much a representation of fact as a statement that an automobile has a steering gear of a specified pattern. These are actual happenings and form a part of the data necessary to determine the consequences that the law attaches to another state of facts. The rules that determine the liability for a fraudulent misrepresentation of these matters of law are the same as those determining liability, for the fraudulent misrepresentation of any other fact. (See §§ 538–541).

c. Even though the language of a representation concerns only legal consequences and is in form an expression of opinion, it may, as in the case of any other statement of opinion, carry with it by implication the assertion that the facts known to the maker are not incompatible with his opinion or that he does know facts that justify him in forming it. (See § 539). Thus the statement that the maker has good title to land, although in form one of a legal conclusion, ordinarily will be understood to assert the existence of those conveyances or other events necessary to vest good title in him. So likewise a statement that one mortgage has priority over another may imply an assertion that one was made before the other; and a statement that a corporation has the legal right to do business in a state may carry with it an assurance that it has as a matter of fact taken all of the steps necessary to be duly qualified. When the recipient does not know the facts, he may justifiably rely upon these implied assertions and recover on the basis of a misrepresentation of the implied fact.

Illustrations:

1. A, seeking to induce B to invest in a mining enterprise, fraudulently tells B that certain lands can be obtained from the government by patent free from mineral reservations. Government land is classified as mineral and non-mineral land, and only non-mineral land can be obtained by patent without a mineral reservation. B reasonably understands A to assert that the particular land is classified by the government as non-mineral land. In reliance on the implied assertion he makes the investment and suffers pecuniary loss. A is subject to liability to B.

2. A, seeking to sell frozen fish to B, fraudulently informs B that there is no legal maximum price on frozen fish. B reasonably understands A to assert that government authorities regulating prices have not established any maximum price for the commodity, although they have in fact done so. In reliance on the implied assertion, B buys the fish from A and suffers pecuniary loss. A is subject to liability to B.

Comment:

d. A representation of law that might otherwise imply assertions of fact may be so clearly a statement solely of opinion that it does not carry an implication of fact. Thus one who says, "I think that my title to this land is good, but do not take my word for it; consult your own lawyer," is not reasonably to be understood as asserting any fact at all with respect to the title. A statement limited to the maker's opinion as to the legal consequences of facts that are not asserted and not implied, is to be treated as one solely of opinion. This is true particularly when all of the facts are known to both parties or are assumed by both of them to exist. Such a statement may be relied upon to the same extent and only to the same extent as any other representation of opinion.

Thus, as between bargaining adversaries there can ordinarily be no justifiable reliance upon an opinion, as stated in § 542. The recipient is not justified in accepting the opinion of a known adversary on the law and is expected to draw his own conclusions or to seek his own independent legal advice. On the other hand, if the maker of the representation purports to have special knowledge of the law that the recipient does not have, reliance upon the opinion may be justified. Thus a layman who asks the opinion of a lawyer on a point of law may assume that he has special knowledge of the law, and is entitled to an honest opinion from him. The layman may justifiably rely on the lawyer's opinion even though he knows that the lawyer is representing a client whose interest is adverse to his own. He may, in other words, reasonably assume professional honesty.

The fact that the lawyer is employed by the recipient or that he is merely giving gratuitous advice as a friend may be important in determining whether he professes to be exercising professional competence or has given the matter sufficient attention; but it makes no difference in the recipient's justification in relying on his honesty. (Compare § 552).

It is not necessary, however, that the person making the fraudulent misrepresentation of law be a lawyer. It is enough that he purports to have superior information that will enable him to form an accurate opinion. Thus the ordinary layman dealing with a real estate or insurance agent may be justified in relying upon the agent to know enough about real estate or insurance law to give a reliable opinion on the simpler problems connected with it. On the other hand, if both parties to the transaction are real estate dealers, neither may justifiably assume that the other has so superior a knowledge of the law as to make his opinion a reliable guide.

The rules as to liability for statements of opinion in general are covered in §§ 538A, 539, 542 and 543.

e. *Foreign law.* "Foreign law" is the law of a state or country in which the recipient of the representation does not reside or habitually do business. When there is a representation of foreign law, the recipient usually cannot reasonably be expected to draw his own conclusions or to have ready access to sources of information as to the law in question; and the chief reason for holding that his reliance is unjustified is lacking. He is normally, therefore, justified in relying upon the representation.

Statements of foreign law are customarily treated by the courts as statements of fact, even though the statement may purport to cover only the legal consequences of other facts fully known to both parties. This has frequently been stated by a supposed analogy to the rule of evidence that requires proof of foreign law in a local court, treating it as a fact. Broad statements are sometimes made in appellate opinions, that every statement of foreign law is a statement of fact.

A statement of foreign law may, however, be so clearly an opinion only, that the recipient is not justified in regarding it as an assertion of what the law is, and so is not justified in relying upon it in the absence of some one of the special reasons stated in § 542. To take an extreme example, "I believe the law of Brazil to be thus and so, but I am not at all certain of it," cannot reasonably be regarded as asserting the state of the Brazilian law. In determining whether the statement is one of opinion, the fact that the maker does or does not reside or habitually do business in the foreign jurisdiction, and so may or may not be expected to have superior knowledge and to be asserting it, is important; but it is not necessarily controlling, since other circumstances may make it clear that he is or is not stating only his opinion.

§ 545A   Contributory Negligence

One who justifiably relies upon a fraudulent misrepresentation is not barred from recovery by his contributory negligence in doing so.

Comment:

a.   A fraudulent misrepresentation is an intentional tort. As in the case of other intentional harm, as stated in § 481, the plaintiff's recovery is not barred by his own negligence which has contributed to his loss. He is, in other words, not required in all cases to exercise the care of a reasonable man for his own protection. A different rule is applied when the misrepresentation is merely a negligent one. (See § 552A).

b.   Although the plaintiff's reliance on the misrepresentation must be justifiable, as that term is used in §§ 537 to 545, this does not mean that his conduct must conform to the standard of the reasonable man. Justification is a matter of the qualities and characteristics of the particular plaintiff, and the circumstances of the particular case, rather than of the application of a community standard of conduct to all cases. Negligent reliance and action sometimes will not be justifiable, and the recovery will be barred accordingly; but this is not always the case. There will be cases in which a plaintiff may be justified in relying upon the representation, even though his conduct in doing so does not conform to the community standard of knowledge, intelligence, judgment or care. Thus, under the rule stated in § 540, the recipient of a fraudulent misrepresentation is not required to investigate its truth, even when a reasonable man of ordinary caution would do so before taking action; and it is only when he knows of the falsity or it is obvious to him that his reliance is not justified. (See § 541). When he proceeds in the face of this knowledge, his conduct is more analogous to assumption of risk than to contributory negligence.

Cases frequently arise in which negligent reliance is justified, when the defendant knows of the plaintiff's incapacity to conform to the standard of conduct f a reasonable man, or of his credulity, gullibility or other tendency to depart from it, and deliberately practices upon the deficiencies of the plaintiff in order to deceive him. (Compare Clauses (b), (c) and (d) of § 542). Thus one who presents a document to an illiterate man, misrepresenting its contents, and invites him to sign it, knowing that he cannot read it, cannot be heard to say that he is negligent in doing so. The same may be true when there is a relation of trust and confidence between the parties or the defendant has made successful efforts to win the confidence of the plaintiff and then takes advantage of it to deceive him.

Illustrations:

1.   A is the owner of a roadhouse of ill repute, and is seeking to sell it to B, a young man whom A knows to be entirely inexperienced and especially gullible. A endeavors to, and does, win B's confidence by establishing cordial relations in A's home. Although the roadhouse is practically worthless, A tells B that its value is $35,000, and advises B not to make inquiries of others, because if he does so they will make higher offers and B will lose the bargain. Relying upon the representation, B buys the roadhouse from A for $35,000. B's recovery from A is not barred by his contributory negligence in relying upon the misrepresentation.

2.   A is a believer in spiritualism; B purports to be a spiritualist medium. In order to induce A to purchase worthless mining stock, B stages a spiritualist seance for the benefit of A, goes into a purported trance and evokes the "spirit" of A's deceased husband, which advises A to buy the stock. A is induced to do so and suffers pecuniary loss. A is not barred from recovery by her contributory negligence.

3.   A, having paid accident insurance to B, tenders B a promissory note for twice the amount, telling B that it is a receipt. B is a foreigner, unfamiliar with American customs and documents and unable to read English. B signs the note without making inquiry of those in the vicinity who could inform him as to its character and as a result suffers pecuniary loss. B is not barred from recovery by his contributory negligence.

Title D. Causation

§546 Causation in Fact

The maker of a fraudulent misrepresentation is subject to liability for pecuniary loss suffered by one who justifiably relies upon the truth of the matter misrepresented, if his reliance is a substantial factor in determining the course of conduct that results in his loss.

Comment:

a. The rule stated in this Section deals only with the question of causation in fact. It is concerned with the question of whether the misrepresentation made by the defendant has caused the plaintiff's loss at all. The further question, as to whether the misrepresentation is a legal cause of the loss that has in fact resulted, for which the maker will be legally responsible, is covered in § 548A.

If the misrepresentation has not in fact been relied upon by the recipient in entering into a transaction in which he suffers pecuniary loss, the misrepresentation is not in fact a cause of the loss under the rule stated in this Section. If the misrepresentation has in fact induced the recipient to enter into the transaction, there is causation in fact of the loss suffered in the transaction; and the question becomes one of whether the loss is of a kind for which the maker is legally responsible. The latter question is covered in § 548A.

b. For a misrepresentation to be a cause in fact of the pecuniary loss that results from the plaintiff's action or inaction, the plaintiff must have relied upon the misrepresentation in incurring the loss. It is not, however, necessary that his reliance upon the truth of the fraudulent misrepresentation be the sole or even the predominant or decisive factor in influencing his conduct. It is not even necessary that he would not have acted or refrained from acting as he did unless he had relied on the misrepresentation. (Compare § 432). It is enough that the representation has played a substantial part, and so has been a substantial factor, in influencing his decision. Thus it is immaterial that he is influenced by other considerations, such as similar misrepresentations from third persons, if he is also substantially influenced by the misrepresentation in question.

Illustrations:

1. A, B and C all make the same misrepresentation to D in order to induce him to buy land. D buys the land. In deciding to do so, he is substantially influenced by all three representations, although any two of them would have been sufficient to induce him to act. A, B and C are all subject to liability to D for pecuniary loss that he suffers through the purchase of the land.

2. A makes fraudulent misrepresentation to B in order to induce B to buy land. Although he believes A's statements, B wishes to confirm

them and therefore makes an inspection of the land and inquiries of third persons. He then buys the land from A. In doing so, he relies in substantial part upon A's representation, as well as on the results of his investigation and inquiries. A is subject to liability to B for the pecuniary loss that B suffers through the purchase of the land.

    3.   A, seeking to sell land to B, makes two statements to B concerning the land, the one true and the other false and fraudulent. B buys the land from A, relying in substantial part upon the truth of both statements. A is subject to liability to B for pecuniary loss to B from the purchase of the land.

§ 547   Recipient Relying on His Own Investigation

(1) Except as stated in Subsection (2), the maker of a fraudulent misrepresentation is not liable to another whose decision to engage in the transaction that the representation was intended to induce is not caused by his belief in the truth of the representation but is the result of an independent investigation made by him.

(2) The fact that the recipient of a fraudulent misrepresentation is relying upon his own investigation does not relieve the maker from liability if he by false statements or otherwise intentionally prevents the investigation from being effective.

Comment on Subsection (1):

    a.   It is not enough to relieve the maker of a fraudulent misrepresentation from liability that the person to whom it is made makes an investigation of its truth. It is only when he relies upon his investigation and does not rely upon the false statement that he cannot recover. Whether he does rely upon the one or the other or in substantial part upon both (see § 546), is a question of fact and is for the jury to determine, unless the evidence clearly indicates only one conclusion.

    Ordinarily one who makes an investigation will be taken to rely upon it alone as to all facts disclosed to him and all facts that must have been obvious to him in the course of it. Thus one who has fully inspected a house before buying it ordinarily cannot claim that he was deceived by a misrepresentation of the condition of the ceilings that was apparent to any one taking the trouble to look at them. Even if there were in fact reliance, it might not be justifiable under the rule stated in § 541. On the other hand, if the condition is a latent one, which the inspection or investigation could not reasonably be expected to discover, the recipient may still be relying upon the representation as well as the investigation. The circumstances of the case and the language used between the parties may be important evidence indicating whether he does so. It is possible although unusual for the buyer of land or chattels to rely only upon his own investigation even as to latent defects.

Particularly when the investigation produces results that tend to confirm the representation but are still somewhat inconclusive, it may be found that the recipient has relied upon both the investigation and the representation and that the latter has played a substantial part in inducing him to take action.

Illustrations:

1.   A, seeking to sell a house to B, makes fraudulent statements to B that the floors in the house are sound. B inspects the house, and walks over the floors, which are full of large and obvious holes. B then buys the house from A. A is not liable to B.

2.   The same facts as in Illustration 1, except that the floors are apparently sound but have dangerously weakened supports, not discoverable by ordinary examination. A is subject to liability to B.

3.   A, seeking to sell to B a promissory note signed by C, fraudulently informs B that C is a man of considerable wealth, who owns large quantities of oil-producing land in a distant state. B makes inquiries of six persons in his community, all of whom inform him that they believe A's statement to be true, and that what they know of C confirms it, but that they have no definite knowledge as to C's financial status. B buys the note, relying upon A's statement as well as his investigation. A is subject to liability to B.

Comment on Subsection (2):

b.   Even though the recipient is found to act or to refrain from action in reliance only upon his own investigation, the maker of the fraudulent misrepresentation may still be liable if he intentionally frustrates the investigation. When he makes it ineffective by false statements, by misdirection, concealment or other trickery, his original misrepresentation carries through, and he cannot be heard to say that the recipient has relied upon an inquiry that has come to nothing through his own machinations. It is by reason of his conduct that the recipient has been induced to surrender his judgment in reliance upon a frustrated investigation originally set in motion by reason of the misrepresentation.

Illustration:

4.   A, seeking to buy goods from B, fraudulently makes false statements to B concerning his financial status. B asks A where he can obtain information as to A's credit standing. A gives B a list of five references, all of whom are creditors of A, knowing that all of them wish to avoid his bankruptcy and that they will all dishonestly confirm his statements. They do so and in reliance upon their information B sells goods to A on credit. A is subject to liability to B.

§ 548   Reliance on Action for Misrepresentation

The maker of a fraudulent misrepresentation is not liable to one who does not rely upon its truth but upon the expectation that the maker will be held liable in damages for its falsity.

Comment:

a. In order to justify recovery, the recipient of a misrepresentation must rely upon the truth of the misrepresentation itself, and his reliance upon its truth must be a substantial factor in inducing him to act or to refrain from action. (See § 546). It is not enough that, without belief in its truth, he proceeds to enter into the transaction in the expectation that he will be compensated in an action for damages for its falsity.

§ 548A   Legal Causation of Pecuniary Loss

A fraudulent misrepresentation is a legal cause of a pecuniary loss resulting from action or inaction in reliance upon it if, but only if, the loss might reasonably be expected to result from the reliance.

Comment:

a. Causation, in relation to losses incurred by reason of a misrepresentation, is a matter of the recipient's reliance in fact upon the misrepresentation in taking some action or in refraining from it. (See § 546). Not all losses that in fact result from the reliance are, however, legally caused by the representation. In general, the misrepresentation is a legal cause only of those pecuniary losses that are within the foreseeable risk of harm that it creates. There is an analogy here to the rules as to legal causation of physical harm resulting from negligent conduct, stated in §§ 435 to 461.

b. Pecuniary losses that could not reasonably be expected to result from the misrepresentation are, in general, not legally caused by it and are beyond the scope of the maker's liability. This means that the matter misrepresented must be considered in the light of its tendency to cause those losses and the likelihood that they will follow. Thus one who misrepresents the financial condition of a corporation in order to sell its stock will become liable to a purchaser who relies upon the misinformation for the loss that he sustains when the facts as to the finances of the corporation become generally known and as a result the value of the shares is depreciated on the market, because that is the obviously foreseeable result of the facts misrepresented. On the other hand, there is no liability when the value of the stock goes down after the sale, not in any way because of the misrepresented financial condition, but as a result of some subsequent event that has no connection with or relation to its financial condition. There is, for example, no liability when the shares go down because of the sudden death of the corporation's leading officers. Although the misrepresentation has in fact caused the loss, since it has induced the purchase without which the loss would not have occurred, it is not a legal cause of the loss for which the maker is responsible.

In determining what is foreseeable as a result of the misrepresentation, the possibility of intervening events is not to be excluded altogether. Thus, when the financial condition of a corporation is misrepresented and it is subsequently driven into insolvency by reason of the depressed condition of an entire industry, which has no connection with the facts misrepresented, it may still be found that the misrepresentation was a legal cause of the recipient's loss, since it may appear that if the company had been in sound condition it would have survived the depression, and hence that a loss of this kind might reasonably have been expected to follow.

Illustrations:

1. A, seeking to sell to B the municipal bonds of C County, fraudulently tells B that the county has received full payment for the bond issue. B purchases the bonds in reliance upon this statement. Subsequently the county is paid in full, but the bonds are held void by the supreme court of the state on the ground that a court had no jurisdiction to issue certain orders with respect to them. As a result B suffers pecuniary loss. A is not liable to B for the loss.

2. A, seeking to buy bonds for investment, approaches B. B offers A the bonds of X Oil Corporation, fraudulently misrepresenting its financial condition. In reliance upon these statements, A buys the bonds. After his purchase conditions in the oil industry become demoralized and as a result of financial losses the X Oil Corporation becomes insolvent. Because of the insolvency A suffers a pecuniary loss greater than that which would have resulted from the deterioration of conditions in the industry alone. It is found that if the financial condition of the Corporation had been as represented it would probably have weathered the storm and not become insolvent. B is subject to liability to A for the additional pecuniary loss resulting from the insolvency.

c. As to the damages recoverable for fraudulent misrepresentation, see further § 549 and Comments.

Title E. Damages for Fraudulent Misrepresentation

§ 549 Measure of Damages for Fraudulent Misrepresentation

(1) The recipient of a fraudulent misrepresentation is entitled to recover as damages in an action of deceit against the maker the pecuniary loss to him of which the misrepresentation is a legal cause, including

(a) the difference between the value of what he has received in the transaction and its purchase price or other value given for it; and

(b) pecuniary loss suffered otherwise as a consequence of the recipient's reliance upon the misrepresentation.

(2) The recipient of a fraudulent misrepresentation in a business transaction is also entitled to recover additional damages sufficient to give him the benefit of his contract with the maker, if these damages are proved with reasonable certainty.

Comment on Subsection (1):

a. Loss may result from a recipient's reliance upon a fraudulent misrepresentation in a business transaction in one of several ways. The most usual is when the falsity of the representation causes the article bought, sold or exchanged to be regarded as of greater or less value than that which it would be regarded as having if the truth were known. The rule applicable in this situation is that stated in Clause (a). The damages so resulting, being those which normally result from a misrepresentation in such transactions, are often called general damages.

Loss that may be suffered in reliance upon a fraudulent misrepresentation otherwise than as stated in Clause (a) includes two types of situations to both of which the rule stated in Clause (b) applies. The first is when the financial position of a third person is misrepresented for the purpose of inducing the recipient to extend credit to him. In this case the loss for which the plaintiff can recover is that suffered because of the third person's inability to meet the credit extended to him. If the third person pays nothing, the loss recoverable is the entire amount of the credit extended. If the third person pays in part, the loss recoverable is the residue remaining unpaid by him. Here again the situation being a usual one, and the loss one that normally results from the recipient's reliance upon the misrepresentation, the damages are often called general. A second situation in which loss may be sustained otherwise than through difference in value as stated in Clause (a) is when a buyer, in reliance upon the misrepresentation, uses the subject matter of the sale in the belief that it is appropriate for a use for which it is harmfully inappropriate or when he has incurred expenses in preparation for a use of the article for which it would have been appropriate if the representation had been true. In these latter situations the loss depends upon the particular use to which the plaintiff puts the article and is not inherent in the nature of the transaction and the damages are often called special or consequential damages.

Comment on Clause (1)(a):

b. Under the rule stated in Clause (1)(a), the recipient of a fraudulent misrepresentation is entitled to recover from its maker in all cases the actual out-of-pocket loss which, because of its falsity, he sustains through his action or inaction in reliance on it. If, notwithstanding the falsity of the representation, the thing that the plaintiff acquires through the fraudulent transaction is of equal or greater value than the price paid and he has suffered no harm through using it in reliance upon its being as represented, he has suffered no loss and can recover nothing under the rule stated in this

Clause. His recovery, if any, must be upon the basis of the rule stated in Subsection (2).

c.   Value, how ascertained. In a sales or exchange transaction the loss for which the recipient of a fraudulent misrepresentation is entitled to recover is usually the difference between the price paid or the value of the thing given in exchange and the value of the thing acquired. The value of the article is normally determined by the price at which it could be resold in an open market or by private sale if its quality or other characteristics that affect its value were known. However, the price that determines the value of the article is not necessarily the price that it would bring at the time the sale is made. In many cases this price is due to the widespread belief of other buyers in misrepresentations similar to that made to the person seeking recovery, as when market price of securities, such as bonds or shares, is the result of widely spread misrepresentations of those who issue or market them. The fact that the market price is inflated or depressed by the misrepresentations is the important factor making the price fictitious; it is, therefore, immaterial that the inflated or depressed price does or does not result from the misrepresentations of the same person who made the misrepresentation on which the person seeking recovery relied. In this case if the recipient of the misrepresentation, in reliance upon it, retains the securities either as a permanent or temporary investment, their value is determined by their market price after the fraud is discovered when the price ceases to be fictitious and represents the consensus of buying and selling opinion of the value of the securities as they actually are. If the plaintiff has resold the securities in the interim, however, his loss is the difference between the price paid and that received.

To this there is one qualification. One who, having acquired securities, retains them in reliance upon another's fraudulent representation is not entitled to recover from him a loss in the value of the securities that is in no way due to the falsity of the representation but is caused by some subsequent event that has no connection with or relation to the matter misrepresented. (See § 548A). Thus, a shareholder in a bank induced to retain his stock by the fraudulent misrepresentation of its president that "wash" sales were bona fide transactions is not entitled to recover for the depreciation of the shares due solely to the subsequent speculations of the cashier of the bank. On the other hand, the mere fact that the subsequent changes in financial or business conditions are factors which, in conjunction with the falsity of the misrepresentation, contribute to diminish or increase the market price of the securities does not prevent the price from fixing the value that determines the loss for which the person defrauded is entitled to recover. Thus, when a promoter induces an investor to subscribe to shares in a corporation by false statements of the amount of capital subscribed and of its assets, the fact that the insolvency of the corporation was in part due to the depressed condition of the industry in question does not prevent the investor from recovering his entire loss from the promoter, since if the corporation had had the capital and assets that it was represented as having, its chance of surviving the depression would have been greatly increased.

In the majority of stock transactions the person seeking recovery discovers the falsity of the misrepresentations at the same time that it becomes known to the investing public and, therefore, at a time when the price of the stock is no longer inflated or depressed by the same or similar misrepresentations. It may be, however, that he discovers the falsity of the representations either earlier or later than the general public. In the first situation his loss is determined by the actual value of the securities in question shown by their market price after the public discovery of the fraud brings the price into accord with the actual value. In the second situation, where the person seeking recovery does not learn of the falsity of the facts represented until sometime after the general public has discovered it, the value of the securities is fixed by the price at which they are selling at the time of his discovery and not that of the public.

Although the market price of securities is more often affected by the wide dissemination of fraudulent misrepresentations than is the market or resale price of other articles, the same considerations are decisive when the price of the articles is thus inflated or depressed. Thus a piece of land may gain a fictitious appearance of value because of widely spread misrepresentations that oil has been found in its close vicinity. In this case a purchaser induced to buy land by the misrepresentation is entitled to the difference between the price he paid and the amount for which land can be sold after the falsity of the representation has become notorious.

Comment on Clause (1)(b):

d. Although the most usual form of financial loss caused by participation in a financial transaction induced by a fraudulent misrepresentation is the lessened value of the subject matter due to its falsity, the loss may result from a purchaser's use of the article for a purpose for which it would be appropriate if the representation were true but for which it is in fact harmfully inappropriate. So, too, it may be the expense to which he has gone in preparation for a use of the article for which it would have been appropriate if the representation had been true.

These "indirect" or "consequential" damages resulting from the misrepresentation are recoverable if the misrepresentation is a legal cause of them, as stated in § 548A. This means that they must be of a kind that might reasonably be expected to result from reliance upon the misrepresentation.

Illustrations:

1. A induces B to purchase a bull by showing him a fraudulent pedigree representing it to be of pure Guernsey ancestry. Before discovering the falsity of A's representation, B breeds the bull to his Guernsey cows. B is entitled to recover not only the difference between the price paid and the actual value of the bull but also the loss sustained by the inferiority of the calves got by the bull upon his Guernsey cows.

2.   The A Automobile Company puts upon the market cars in part made by itself, in part consisting of parts bought elsewhere and assembled in the cars. B sells to the A Company a quantity of roller bearings by misrepresenting them to be X roller bearings. The X bearings are standard and high class bearings. The bearings sold are in fact inferior and not made by the X Company. After these bearings have been assembled in a number of the cars their true character is discovered and the cars are sold at a lesser price because the bearings are not the X bearings. The A Company is entitled to recover the depreciation in the sales value of its cars because of the inferior bearings.

3.   A sells to B, f.o.b. Detroit, a machine that he fraudulently misrepresents to be of great value in the manufacture of B's product. B pays the freight of the machine to his factory and expends money in preparing for its installation. On the arrival of the machine the falsity of the representation is discovered and the machine is found to be useless for the purpose for which it was bought. B is entitled to recover, as special damages, the freight that he has paid and the expense that he has incurred in the installation of the machine as well as for harm done to his raw material by the machine before its uselessness was discovered.

Comment on Subsection (1):

e.   Alternative remedies. One who is misled by the fraudulent representations of another may rescind the transaction induced by it. In this case, if the other accepts the subject matter of the transaction and returns the purchase price, the person defrauded can, of course, not recover the difference of the value between the thing received and the price paid for it. If the other on rescission refuses to receive the subject matter of the transaction, the person defrauded may dispose of it and maintain an action for the difference between the amount realized at the sale and the price paid by him. In either event the fact of rescission does not prevent the defrauded person from recovering from the other any loss that he has suffered in consequence of any use which, in reliance upon the misrepresentation, he has made of the article prior to his discovery of the fraud. If the subject matter of the transaction has been accepted by the other and the purchase price refunded the action is for that loss and for it only. If the other has refused to accept the subject matter of the sale and the person defrauded has sold it on his account, the loss resulting from its use is recoverable as part of the damages in addition to the difference between the price paid and the amount realized at the sale.

f.   If two persons make fraudulent misrepresentations to the same recipient neither one of which by itself is enough to cause the recipient of them to take the action which results in his loss, but which together are enough to do so, both or either of them is liable at the recipient's election. However, if the recipient by execution or otherwise realizes the amount of a judgment recovered against one of the two, he extinguishes the liability of the other. If only a part of the judgment against one of the two is realized, it operates as an extinguishment pro tanto of the liability of the other.

Comment on Subsection (2):

g.   Subsection (1) states the rules normally applicable to determine the measure of damages recoverable for a fraudulent misrepresentation in a tort action of deceit. If the plaintiff is content with these damages, he can always recover them. The rules stated in Subsection (1) are the logical rules for a tort action, since the purpose of a tort action is to compensate for loss sustained and to restore the plaintiff to his former position, and not to give him the benefit of any contract he has made with the defendant. When the plaintiff has not entered into any transaction with the defendant but has suffered his pecuniary loss through reliance upon the misrepresentation in dealing with a third person, these are the rules that must of necessity be applied.

When the plaintiff has made a bargain with the defendant, however, situations arise in which the rules stated in Subsection (1), and particularly that stated in Clause (a) of that Subsection, do not afford compensation that is just and satisfactory. If the value of what the plaintiff has received from the defendant is fully equal to the price he has paid for it or other value he has parted with and he has suffered no consequential damages, he may be unable to recover at all under the rules stated in Subsection (1). He may nevertheless be left with something acquired under the transaction which, because of the matter misrepresented, he does not want and cannot use. He may have lost the opportunity of acquiring a substitute at the same price and because of his commitments made or expenses incurred or for a variety of other reasons he may find rescission of the transaction and recovery of the price paid an unsatisfactory and insufficient remedy. In this case, under the rules stated in Subsection (1), the defrauding party would escape all liability.

The frequency of these situations has led the great majority of the American courts to adopt a broad general rule giving the plaintiff, in an action of deceit, the benefit of his bargain with the defendant in all cases, and making that the normal measure of recovery in actions of deceit.

The rule adopted in Subsection (2) does not take this position. One reason is that in occasional cases the out-of-pocket measure of damages will actually be more profitable and satisfactory from the point of view of the plaintiff than the benefit-of-the-bargain rule. This would be the case, for example, if the owner of valuable property were induced to sell it for less than its value by a representation that it had defects that made it practically worthless. On the basis of the representations, taken to be true, the seller would have sold worthless property for a substantial price and suffered no loss at all. Another and a more important, reason is that there are many cases in which the value that the plaintiff would have received if the bargain made with him had been performed cannot be proved with any satisfactory degree of certainty, because it must necessarily turn upon the estimated value of something non-existent and never in fact received. In this case the benefit-of-the-bargain harm to the plaintiff becomes mere speculation, and ordinary rules of the law of damages preclude the award.

h. This Section therefore follows a compromise position adopted by some jurisdictions, giving the plaintiff the option of either the out-of-pocket or the benefit-of-the-bargain rule in any case in which the latter measure can be established by proof in accordance with the usual rules of certainty in damages. The comments and illustrations that follow deal with the more common situations in which the plaintiff may wish to elect to receive the benefit of his bargain.

i. Value received equal to value paid. When the value of what the plaintiff has received under the transaction with the defendant is fully equal to the value of what he has parted with, he has suffered no out-of-pocket loss, and under the rule stated in Subsection (1), Clause (a), he could recover no damages. This would mean that the defrauding defendant has successfully accomplished his fraud and is still immune from an action in deceit. Even though the plaintiff may rescind the transaction and recover the price paid, the defendant is enabled to speculate on his fraud and still be assured that he can suffer no pecuniary loss. This is not justice between the parties. The admonitory function of the law requires that the defendant not escape liability and justifies allowing the plaintiff the benefit of his bargain.

Illustration:

4. A, seeking to sell land to B, fraudulently tells B that half of the land is covered with good pine timber. B buys the land from A for $5,000. There is no timber on the land but it is still worth $5,000. Competent evidence establishes that if the representation had been true the land, with the timber, would have been worth $9,000. B may recover $4,000 from A.

Comment:

j. Thing received useless to plaintiff. Although the thing which the plaintiff has received under the transaction with the defendant may have substantial value and may even be sold to others, it may, because of the matter misrepresented, be entirely useless to the plaintiff for his own purposes. In this case, if the plaintiff is limited to his out-of-pocket loss, he is left with something on his hands that he does not want and cannot use and forced to credit its value to the defendant. To be restored to his original position he must be put to the trouble and expense of seeking a purchaser with all of the risk that he will not realize the value, and he must then begin again to seek the thing that he really wants. This becomes all the more clear when there is no immediate or ready market for the thing in question or when the plaintiff will be delayed and his purpose frustrated before he can obtain the thing which he originally bargained for.

Illustrations:

5. A, seeking to sell B a quantity of textiles, fraudulently tells B that they are of a kind and quality suitable for manufacture in B's mill.

B buys the textiles for $10,000. Because of the matters misrepresented, they are in fact worth only $6,000. If they had been as represented they would have been worth $14,000. B is unable to use the textiles in his mill and finding a market for them will involve delay. B is entitled to recover $8,000 from A.

    6. The same facts as in Illustration 5, except that, although the textiles purchased can readily be resold for $6,000, B cannot obtain a supply of suitable textiles without a long delay. The same conclusion.

k. The preceding Comments and Illustrations are not intended to be exclusive. There may be many other types of situations in which particular circumstances may mean that just compensation cannot be given to the plaintiff under the out-of-pocket rule.

l. *Benefit of the bargain.* The damages necessary to give the plaintiff the benefit of the bargain that he has made with the defendant will depend, first of all, upon the nature of the bargain. If the defendant has undertaken to convey property of a certain description to the plaintiff, the plaintiff is entitled to an amount sufficient to give him the value of property of that description. If the defendant has undertaken merely to give the plaintiff accurate information about the property, he is entitled to a sufficient amount to place him in the position he would have occupied if he had had the information. If the defendant has undertaken merely to use care to give accurate information, the plaintiff is entitled only to an amount sufficient to compensate him by placing him in the position he would have occupied if that care had been used.

In order to give the plaintiff the benefit of the bargain, it is not necessary in all cases to give him the value of the thing as represented. He may be fully and fairly compensated if he is given the cost of making it as represented.

Illustrations:

    7. A, seeking to sell a farm to B, fraudulently tells B that there is a well on the farm, with an ample supply of water. B buys the farm for $3,000. There is no well but there is water under the land, and a well can easily and quickly be dug for $250. With the well the land would be worth $5,000. B is entitled to recover $250 from A.

    8. A, seeking to acquire students for his dental college, fraudulently tells B that the college gives a good dental education and awards a degree. B takes the dental course, paying A $1,000. The dental education is a good one and worth $1,000, but at the end of the course B finds that the college is not licensed to award a degree, without which B cannot obtain a license to practice dentistry. B is entitled to recover from A the cost of attendance at a licensed dental college for the additional time necessary to obtain a degree.

m. Situations may arise in which, as a result of the misrepresentation, the plaintiff has been deprived of chattels of fluctuating market exchange value. In these cases the "highest replacement value" rule stated in § 927(1)(b) may be applied.

Topic 2. Concealment and Nondisclosure

§ 550   Liability for Fraudulent Concealment

One party to a transaction who by concealment or other action intentionally prevents the other from acquiring material information is subject to the same liability to the other, for pecuniary loss as though he had stated the nonexistence of the matter that the other was thus prevented from discovering.

Comment:

a. The rule stated in this Section is commonly applied in two types of situations, although it is not limited to them. The first occurs when the defendant actively conceals a defect or other disadvantage in something that he is offering for sale to another. Thus a defendant is subject to liability for a fraudulent misrepresentation if he paints over and so conceals a defect in a chattel or a building that he is endeavoring to sell to the plaintiff, and thus induces the plaintiff to buy it in ignorance of its defective character. So also, he is subject to liability if he reads a contract to the plaintiff and omits a portion of it, or if he so stacks aluminum sheets that he is selling as to conceal defective sheets in the middle of the pile.

Illustration:

1.   A is seeking to sell to B a horse which is a crib-biter and a wind-sucker. In order to conceal these characteristics from B, A hitches the horse up short with its head raised so that it cannot bite its crib and suck wind. B inspects the horse and does not discover its defects. A is subject to liability to B.

b.   The second situation occurs when the defendant successfully prevents the plaintiff from making an investigation that he would otherwise have made, and which, if made, would have disclosed the facts; or when the defendant frustrates an investigation. Sending one in search of information in a direction where it cannot be obtained is a typical illustration of frustration. Even a false denial of knowledge or information by one party to a transaction, who is in possession of the facts, may subject him to liability as fully as if he had expressly misstated the facts, if its effect upon the plaintiff is to lead him to believe that the facts do not exist or cannot be discovered.

§ 551   Liability for Nondisclosure

(1) One who fails to disclose to another a fact that he knows may justifiably induce the other to act or refrain from acting in a business transaction is subject to the same liability to the other as though he had represented the nonexistence of the matter that he has failed to disclose,

if, but only if, he is under a duty to the other to exercise reasonable care to disclose the matter in question.

(2) One party to a business transaction is under a duty to exercise reasonable care to disclose to the other before the transaction is consummated,

> (a) matters known to him that the other is entitled to know because of a fiduciary or other similar relation of trust and confidence between them; and
>
> (b) matters known to him that he knows to be necessary to prevent his partial or ambiguous statement of the facts from being misleading; and
>
> (c) subsequently acquired information that he knows will make untrue or misleading a previous representation that when made was true or believed to be so; and
>
> (d) the falsity of a representation not made with the expectation that it would be acted upon, if he subsequently learns that the other is about to act in reliance upon it in a transaction with him; and
>
> (e) facts basic to the transaction, if he knows that the other is about to enter into it under a mistake as to them, and that the other, because of the relationship between them, the customs of the trade or other objective circumstances, would reasonably expect a disclosure of those facts.

Comment on Subsection (1):

a.   Unless he is under some one of the duties of disclosure stated in Subsection (2), one party to a business transaction is not liable to the other for harm caused by his failure to disclose to the other facts of which he knows the other is ignorant and which he further knows the other, if he knew of them, would regard as material in determining his course of action in the transaction in question. The interest in knowing those facts that are important in determining the advisability of a course of action in a financial or commercial matter is given less protection by the rule stated in this Subsection than is given to the interest in knowing facts that are important in determining the recipient's course of action in regard to matters that involve the security of the person, land or chattels of himself or a third person.

b.   The conditions under which liability is imposed for nondisclosure in an action for deceit differ in one particular from those under which a similar nondisclosure may confer a right to rescind the transaction or to recover back money paid or the value of other benefits conferred. In the absence of a duty of disclosure, under the rule stated in Subsection (2) of this Section, one who is negotiating a business transaction is not liable in deceit because of his failure to disclose a fact that he knows his adversary would regard as material. On the other hand, as is stated in Restatement, Second, Contracts § 303(b) the other is entitled to rescind the transaction if the undisclosed fact is basic; and under Restatement of Restitution, § 8, Comment *e*, and § 28, he would be entitled to recover back any money paid or benefit conferred in consummation of the transaction.

Comment on Subsection (2):

c. A person under the duty stated in this Subsection is required to disclose only those matters that he has reason to know will be regarded by the other as important in determining his course of action in the transaction in hand. He is therefore under no duty to disclose matter that the ordinary man would regard as unimportant unless he knows of some peculiarity of the other that is likely to lead him to attach importance to matters that are usually regarded as of no moment.

d. Under the rule stated in this Subsection the person under a duty of disclosure is not subject to liability merely because he has failed to bring the required information home to the person entitled to it. His duty is to exercise reasonable care to do so. If reasonable care is exercised, the fact that the information does not reach the person entitled to it does not subject him to liability. Thus a trustee whose distant cestui que trust is contemplating a sale of part of his interest in the trust res to a third person and who writes to his cestui que trust communicating certain information which it is material for the latter to know in the transaction in question, is not subject to liability in an action of deceit, if the letter goes astray and therefore does not reach the cestui until the sale is made. On the other hand, if the trustee knows that the consummation of the transaction is immediately imminent, it may not be reasonable for him to communicate by mail rather than by telegraph. However, in the great majority of cases the person owing the duty has so available an opportunity to make the required disclosure that it is rare that the failure to give it can be other than intentional or negligent.

Comment on Clause (a):

e. On the duty of a trustee to disclose all material matters to his beneficiary with whom he is dealing on the trustee's own account, see Restatement, Second, Trusts § 170(2). On the duty of a trustee to disclose to his beneficiary matters important for the beneficiary to know in dealing with third persons, see Restatement, Second, Trusts § 173, Comment *d.* On the duty of an agent to disclose to his principal matters important for the principal to know in dealing with the agent or a third person and the similar duty of the principal to the agent, see Restatement, Second, Agency §§ 381 and 435. It is not within the scope of this Restatement to state the rules that determine the duty of disclosure which under the law of business associations the directors of a company owe to its shareholders.

f. Other relations of trust and confidence include those of the executor of an estate and its beneficiary, a bank and an investing depositor, and those of physician and patient, attorney and client, priest and parishioner, partners, tenants in common and guardian and ward. Members of the same family normally stand in a fiduciary relation to one another, although it is of course obvious that the fact that two men are brothers does not establish relation of trust and confidence when they have become estranged and have not spoken to one another for many years. In addition, certain types of contracts, such as those of suretyship or guaranty, insurance and joint adventure, are recognized as creating in themselves a confidential relation and hence as requiring the utmost good faith and full and fair disclosure of all material facts.

Comment on Clause (b):

g. A statement that is partial or incomplete may be a misrepresentation because it is misleading, when it purports to tell the whole truth and does not. (See § 529). So also may a statement made so ambiguously that it may have two interpretations, one of which is false. (See §§ 527, 528). When such a statement has been made, there is a duty to disclose the additional information necessary to prevent it from misleading the recipient. In this case there may be recovery either on the basis of the original misleading statement or of the nondisclosure of the additional facts.

Comment on Clause (c):

h. One who, having made a representation which when made was true or believed to be so, remains silent after he has learned that it is untrue and that the person to whom it is made is relying upon it in a transaction with him, is morally and legally in the same position as if he knew that his statement was false when made.

Illustrations:

1. A, a stock breeder, tells B, a prospective buyer, that a thoroughbred mare is in foal to a well-known stallion. The mare miscarries. Immediately afterwards B offers $500 for the mare relying, as A knows, upon his statement. A does not inform B of the mare's miscarriage. A is subject to liability to B for the loss that he suffers because the mare is not in foal as originally represented.

2. A, the president of a mercantile corporation, makes a true statement of its financial position to a credit rating company, intending the substance to be published by it to its subscribers. The corporation's financial position becomes seriously impaired, but A does not inform the credit rating company of this fact. The corporation receives goods on credit from B, a subscriber of the rating company, who when the goods are bought is relying, as A knows, on the credit rating based on his statements to the rating company. A is subject to liability in deceit to B.

Comment on Clause (d):

i. One who knowingly makes a misrepresentation without any expectation that the recipient will act upon it may subsequently discover that the other is relying upon it in a transaction then pending between them. If, in this case, he does not exercise reasonable care to inform the other that his misrepresentation is untrue, he is under the same liability as though he had then made it for the purpose of influencing the other's conduct in the transaction in hand.

The rule stated in Clause (d) is not necessarily limited to "a transaction with him." When, for example, the defendant makes a statement to the plaintiff concerning the credit of a third person not expecting it to be acted upon and then discovers that the plaintiff is about to lend money to the third person in reliance upon the statement, it would appear that the duty of disclosure would arise.

Comment on Clause (e):

j. *"Facts basic to the transaction."* The word "basic" is used in this Clause in the same sense in which it is used in Comment *c* under § 16 of the Restatement of Restitution. A basic fact is a fact that is assumed by the parties as a basis for the transaction itself. It is a fact that goes to the basis, or essence, of the transaction, and is an important part of the substance of what is bargained for or dealt with. Other facts may serve as important and persuasive inducements to enter into the transaction, but not go to its essence. These facts may be material, but they are not basic. If the parties expressly or impliedly place the risk as to the existence of a fact on one party or if the law places it there by custom or otherwise the other party has no duty of disclosure. (Compare Restatement, Second, Contracts § 296).

Illustrations:

3. A sells to B a dwelling house, without disclosing to B the fact that the house is riddled with termites. This is a fact basic to the transaction.

4. A sells to B a dwelling house, knowing that B is acting in the mistaken belief that a highway is planned that will pass near the land and enhance its value. A does not disclose to B the fact that no highway is actually planned. This is not a fact basic to the transaction.

5. Having purchased a certain tract of land for $25,000, A hears that B may have a claim to it. He goes to B and offers to purchase B's interest. B does not believe he has a valid legal claim but agrees to give A a quit-claim deed for $250. B's lack of a valid legal claim is not a fact that he is under a duty to disclose.

Comment:

k. *Nondisclosure of basic facts.* The rule stated in Subsection (1) reflects the traditional ethics of bargaining between adversaries, in the absence of any special reason for the application of a different rule. When the facts are patent, or when the plaintiff has equal opportunity for obtaining information that he may be expected to utilize if he cares to do so, or when the defendant has no reason to think that the plaintiff is acting under a misapprehension, there is no obligation to give aid to a bargaining antagonist by disclosing what the defendant has himself discovered. To a considerable extent, sanctioned by the customs and mores of the community, superior information and better business acumen are legitimate advantages, which lead to no liability. The defendant may reasonably expect the plaintiff to make his own investigation, draw his own conclusions and protect himself; and if the plaintiff is indolent, inexperienced or ignorant, or his judgment is bad, or he does not have access to adequate information, the defendant is under no obligation to make good his deficiencies. This is true, in general, when it is the buyer of land or chattels who has the better information and fails to disclose it. Somewhat less frequently, it may be true of the seller.

Illustrations:

6. A is a violin expert. He pays a casual visit to B's shop, where second-hand musical instruments are sold. He finds a violin which, by reason of his expert knowledge and experience, he immediately recognizes as a genuine Stradivarius, in good condition and worth at least $50,000. The violin is priced for sale at $100. Without disclosing his information or his identity, A buys the violin from B for $100. A is not liable to B.

7. The same facts as in Illustration 6, except that the violin is sold at auction and A bids it in for $100. The same conclusion.

8. B has a shop in which he sells second-hand musical instruments. In it he offers for sale for $100 a violin, which he knows to be an imitation Stradivarius and worth at most $50. A enters the shop, looks at the violin and is overheard by B to say to his companion that he is sure that the instrument is a genuine Stradivarius. B says nothing, and A buys the violin for $100. B is not liable to A.

l. The continuing development of modern business ethics has, however, limited to some extent this privilege to take advantage of ignorance. There are situations in which the defendant not only knows that his bargaining adversary is acting under a mistake basic to the transaction, but also knows that the adversary, by reason of the relation between them, the customs of the trade or other objective circumstances, is reasonably relying upon a disclosure of the unrevealed fact if it exists. In this type of case good faith and fair dealing may require a disclosure.

It is extremely difficult to be specific as to the factors that give rise to this known, and reasonable, expectation of disclosure. In general, the cases in which the rule stated in Clause (e) has been applied have been those in which the advantage taken of the plaintiff's ignorance is so shocking to the ethical sense of the community, and is so extreme and unfair, as to amount to a form of swindling, in which the plaintiff is led by appearances into a bargain that is a trap, of whose essence and substance he is unaware. In such a case, even in a tort action for deceit, the plaintiff is entitled to be compensated for the loss that he has sustained. Thus a seller who knows that his cattle are infected with tick fever or contagious abortion is not free to unload them on the buyer and take his money, when he knows that the buyer is unaware of the fact, could not easily discover it, would not dream of entering into the bargain if he knew and is relying upon the seller's good faith and common honesty to disclose any such fact if it is true.

There are indications, also, that with changing ethical attitudes in many fields of modern business, the concept of facts basic to the transaction may be expanding and the duty to use reasonable care to disclose the facts may be increasing somewhat. This Subsection is not intended to impede that development.

Illustrations:

9. A sells B a dwelling house, without disclosing the fact that drain tile under the house is so constructed that at periodic intervals water accumulates under the house. A knows that B is not aware of this fact, that he could not discover it by an ordinary inspection, and that he would not make the purchase if he knew it. A knows also that B regards him as an honest and fair man and one who would disclose any such fact if he knew it. A is subject to liability to B for his pecuniary loss in an action of deceit.

10. A is engaged in the business of removing gravel from the bed of a navigable stream. He is notified by the United States government that the removal is affecting the channel of the stream, and ordered to stop it under threat of legal proceedings to compel him to do so. Knowing that B is unaware of this notice, could not reasonably be expected to discover it and would not buy if he knew, A sells the business to B without disclosing the fact. A is subject to liability to B for his pecuniary loss in an action of deceit.

11. A, who owns an amusement center, sells it to B without disclosing the fact that it has just been raided by the police, and that A is being prosecuted for maintaining prostitution and the sale of marijuana on the premises. These facts have seriously affected the reputation and patronage of the center, and greatly reduced its monthly income. A knows that B is unaware of these facts, could not be expected to discover them by ordinary investigation and would not buy if he knew them. He also knows that B believes A to be a man of high character, who would disclose any serious defects in the business. A is subject to liability to B for his pecuniary loss in an action of deceit.

12. A sells a summer resort to B, without disclosing the fact that a substantial part of it encroaches on the public highway. A knows that B is unaware of the fact and could not be expected to discover it by ordinary inquiry, and that B trusts him to disclose any such facts. A is subject to liability to B for his pecuniary loss in an action of deceit.

m. Court and jury. Whether there is a duty to the other to disclose the fact in question is always a matter for the determination of the court. If there are disputed facts bearing upon the existence of the duty, as for example the defendant's knowledge of the fact, the other's ignorance of it or his opportunity to ascertain it, the customs of the particular trade, or the defendant's knowledge that the plaintiff reasonably expects him to make the disclosure, they are to be determined by the jury under appropriate instructions as to the existence of the duty.

Topic 3.   Negligent Misrepresentation

§ 552   Information Negligently Supplied for the Guidance of Others

who can be a defendant

who can be a plaintiff

(1)   One who, in the course of his business, profession or employment, or in any other transaction in which he has a pecuniary interest, supplies false information for the guidance of others in their business transactions, is subject to liability for pecuniary loss caused to them by their justifiable reliance upon the information, if he fails to exercise reasonable care or competence in obtaining or communicating the information.

(2)   Except as stated in Subsection (3), the liability stated in Subsection (1) is limited to loss suffered

>   (a)   by the person or one of a limited group of persons for whose benefit and guidance he intends to supply the information or knows that the recipient intends to supply it; and

>   (b)   through reliance upon it in a transaction that he intends the information to influence or knows that the recipient so intends or in a substantially similar transaction.

(3)   The liability of one who is under a public duty to give the information extends to loss suffered by any of the class of persons for whose benefit the duty is created, in any of the transactions in which it is intended to protect them.

Comment:

a.   Although liability under the rule stated in this Section is based upon negligence of the actor in failing to exercise reasonable care or competence in supplying correct information, the scope of his liability is not determined by the rules that govern liability for the negligent supplying of chattels that imperil the security of the person, land or chattels of those to whom they are supplied (see §§ 388–402), or other negligent misrepresentation that results in physical harm. (See § 311). When the harm that is caused is only pecuniary loss, the courts have found it necessary to adopt a more restricted rule of liability, because of the extent to which misinformation may be, and may be expected to be, circulated, and the magnitude of the losses which may follow from reliance upon it.

The liability stated in this Section is likewise more restricted than that for fraudulent misrepresentation stated in § 531. When there is no intent to deceive but only good faith coupled with negligence, the fault of the maker of the misrepresentation is sufficiently less to justify a narrower responsibility for its consequences.

The reason a narrower scope of liability is fixed for negligent misrepresentation than for deceit is to be found in the difference between the obligations of honesty and of care, and in the significance of this difference to the reasonable expectations of the users of information that is supplied in connection with commercial transactions. Honesty requires only that the maker of a representation speak in good faith and without consciousness of a lack of any basis for belief in the truth or accuracy of what he says. The standard of honesty is unequivocal and ascertainable without regard to the character of the transaction in which the information will ultimately be relied upon or the situation of the party relying upon it. Any user of commercial information may reasonably expect the observance of this standard by a supplier of information to whom his use is reasonably foreseeable.

On the other hand, it does not follow that every user of commercial information may hold every maker to a duty of care. Unlike the duty of honesty, the duty of care to be observed in supplying information for use in commercial transactions implies an undertaking to observe a relative standard, which may be defined only in terms of the use to which the information will be put, weighed against the magnitude and probability of loss that might attend that use if the information proves to be incorrect. A user of commercial information cannot reasonably expect its maker to have undertaken to satisfy this obligation unless the terms of the obligation were known to him. Rather, one who relies upon information in connection with a commercial transaction may reasonably expect to hold the maker to a duty of care only in circumstances in which the maker was manifestly aware of the use to which the information was to be put and intended to supply it for that purpose.

By limiting the liability for negligence of a supplier of information to be used in commercial transactions to cases in which he manifests an intent to supply the information for the sort of use in which the plaintiff's loss occurs, the law promotes the important social policy of encouraging the flow of commercial information upon which the operation of the economy rests. The limitation applies, however, only in the case of information supplied in good faith, for no interest of society is served by promoting the flow of information not genuinely believed by its maker to be true.

b. The rule stated in this Section applies not only to information given as to the existence of facts but also to an opinion given upon facts equally well known to both the supplier and the recipient. Such an opinion is often given by one whose only knowledge of the facts is derived from the person who asks it. As to the care and competence that the recipient of such an opinion is justified in expecting, see Comment *e.*

Comment on Subsection (1):

c. *Pecuniary interest in the transaction.* The rule stated in Subsection (1) applies only when the defendant has a pecuniary interest in the transaction in which the information is given. If he has no pecuniary interest and the information is given purely gratuitously, he is under no duty to exercise reasonable care and competence in giving it. The situation is analogous to that of one who gratuitously lends or otherwise supplies a chattel, whose duty is only to disclose any facts he knows that may make it unsafe for use. (See § 405).

Illustrations:

1. A, seeking information as to the will of B, asks C Trust Company for a copy of the will. C Trust Company is not in the business of supplying copies of wills, and has no interest in giving this one to A, but gratuitously agrees to supply the copy as a favor to A. By a negligent mistake but in good faith it gives A a copy of the will of another person of the same name as B. In reliance on the copy A incurs pecuniary loss. C Trust Co. is not liable to A.

2. The A Newspaper negligently publishes in one of its columns a statement that a certain proprietary drug is a sure cure for dandruff. B, who is plagued with dandruff, reads the statement and in reliance upon it purchases a quantity of the drug. It proves to be worthless as a dandruff cure and B suffers pecuniary loss. The A Newspaper is not liable to B.

d. The defendant's pecuniary interest in supplying the information will normally lie in a consideration paid to him for it or paid in a transaction in the course of and as a part of which it is supplied. It may, however, be of a more indirect character. Thus the officers of a corporation, although they receive no personal consideration for giving information concerning its affairs, may have a pecuniary interest in its transactions, since they stand to profit indirectly from them, and an agent who expects to receive a commission on a sale may have such an interest in it although he sells nothing.

The fact that the information is given in the course of the defendant's business, profession or employment is a sufficient indication that he has a pecuniary interest in it, even though he receives no consideration for it at the time. It is not, however, conclusive. But when one who is engaged in a business or profession steps entirely outside of it, as when an attorney gives a casual and offhand opinion on a point of law to a friend whom he meets on the street, or what is commonly called a "curbstone opinion," it is not to be regarded as given in the course of his business or profession; and since he has no other interest in it, it is considered purely gratuitous. The recipient of the information is not justified in expecting that his informant will exercise the care and skill that is necessary to insure a correct opinion and is only justified in expecting that the opinion will be an honest one.

e.   Reasonable care and competence. Since the rule of liability stated in Subsection (1) is based upon negligence, the defendant is subject to liability if, but only if, he has failed to exercise the care or competence of a reasonable man in obtaining or communicating the information. (See §§ 283, 288 and 289). What is reasonable is, as in other cases of negligence, dependent upon the circumstances. It is, in general, a matter of the care and competence that the recipient of the information is entitled to expect in the light of the circumstances and this will vary according to a good many factors. The question is one for the jury, unless the facts are so clear as to permit only one conclusion.

The particulars in which the recipient of information supplied by another is entitled to expect the exercise of care and competence depend upon the character of the information that is supplied. When the information concerns a fact not known to the recipient, he is entitled to expect that the supplier will exercise that care and competence in its ascertainment which the supplier's business or profession requires and which, therefore, the supplier professes to have by engaging in it. Thus the recipient is entitled to expect that such investigations as are necessary will be carefully made and that his informant will have normal business or professional competence to form an intelligent judgment upon the data obtained. On the other hand, if the supplier makes no pretense to special competence but agrees for a reward to furnish information that lies outside the field of his business or profession, the recipient is not justified in expecting more than that care and competence that the nonprofessional character of his informant entitles him to expect. When the information consists of an opinion upon facts supplied by the recipient or otherwise known to him, the recipient is entitled to expect a careful consideration of the facts and competence in arriving at an intelligent judgment. In all of these cases the recipient of the information is entitled to expect reasonable conversance with the language employed to communicate the information in question and reasonable care in its use, unless he knows that his informant is ignorant of the language in question or peculiarly careless in its use.

Illustration:

3.   XYZ Corporation seeks a credit of $100,000 from F & Co., a factoring concern. Because the latest XYZ financial statements, audited by A & Co., a partnership of certified public accountants, are dated as of the last fiscal year-end of XYZ Corporation which fell some eight months previously, F & Co., requests that A & Co. be retained to provide unaudited financial statements for the current interim period. A & Co., knowing the statements are being prepared for the consideration of F & Co. in connection with XYZ Corporation's request for the $100,000 credit, prepares financial statements from the books of the corporation without performing any tests of the accuracy of the entries themselves or respecting the transactions represented to underlie them. The statements, furnished under A & Co.'s letterhead, are labeled "unaudited" on each page and accompanied by a written representation

that they have not been audited and that, accordingly, A & Co. is not in a position to express an opinion upon them. Nothing comes to the attention of A & Co. in the course of preparing the statements to indicate that they were incorrect, but because the books from which they were prepared were, unknown to A & Co., in error, the financial statements materially misstate the financial position of XYZ Corporation and its results of operations for the period subsequent to the preceding fiscal year-end. F & Co., because it extends the credit in reliance upon the statements, suffers substantial pecuniary loss. A & Co. is not subject to liability to F & Co.

f.   The care and competence that the supplier of information for the guidance of others is required under the rule stated in this Section to exercise in order that the information given may be correct, must be exercised in the following particulars. If the matter is one that requires investigation, the supplier of the information must exercise reasonable care and competence to ascertain the facts on which his statement is based. He must exercise the competence reasonably expected of one in his business or professional position in drawing inferences from facts not stated in the information. He must exercise reasonable care and competence in communicating the information so that it may be understood by the recipient, since the proper performance of the other two duties would be of no value if the information accurately obtained was so communicated as to be misleading.

Comment on Subsection (2):

g.   *Information supplied directly and indirectly.* The person for whose guidance the information is supplied is often the person who has employed the supplier to furnish it, in which case, if it is supplied for a consideration paid by that person, he has at his election either a right of action under the rule stated in this Section or a right of action upon the contract under which the information is supplied. In many cases, however, the information is supplied directly to the person who is to act upon it although it is paid for by the other party to the transaction. Thus, when a vendor of beans employs a public weigher to weigh beans, the weigher, who gives to the vendee a certificate which through his carelessness overstates the weight of the beans, is subject to liability to the vendee for the amount that he overpays in reliance upon the certificate. However, direct communication of the information to the person acting in reliance upon it is not necessary. In the situation above the liability of the weigher would not be affected by his giving the certificate to the vendor for communication to the vendee.

h.   *Persons for whose guidance the information is supplied.* The rule stated in this Section subjects the negligent supplier of misinformation to liability only to those persons for whose benefit and guidance it is supplied. In this particular his liability is somewhat more narrowly restricted than that of the maker of a fraudulent representation (see § 531), which extends to any person whom the maker of the representation has reason to expect to act in reliance upon it.

Under this Section, as in the case of the fraudulent misrepresentation (see § 531), it is not necessary that the maker should have any particular person in mind as the intended, or even the probable, recipient of the information. In other words, it is not required that the person who is to become the plaintiff be identified or known to the defendant as an individual when the information is supplied. It is enough that the maker of the representation intends it to reach and influence either a particular person or persons, known to him, or a group or class of persons, distinct from the much larger class who might reasonably be expected sooner or later to have access to the information and foreseeably to take some action in reliance upon it. It is enough, likewise, that the maker of the representation knows that his recipient intends to transmit the information to a similar person, persons or group. It is sufficient, in other words, insofar as the plaintiff's identity is concerned, that the maker supplies the information for repetition to a certain group or class of persons and that the plaintiff proves to be one of them, even though the maker never had heard of him by name when the information was given. It is not enough that the maker merely knows of the ever-present possibility of repetition to anyone, and the possibility of action in reliance upon it, on the part of anyone to whom it may be repeated.

Even when the maker is informed of the identity of a definite person to whom the recipient intends to transmit the information, the circumstances may justify a finding that the name and identity of that person was regarded by the maker, and by the recipient, as important only because the person in question was one of a group whom the information was intended to reach and for whose guidance it was being supplied. In many situations the identity of the person for whose guidance the information is supplied is of no moment to the person who supplies it, although the number and character of the persons to be reached and influenced, and the nature and extent of the transaction for which guidance is furnished may be vitally important. This is true because the risk of liability to which the supplier subjects himself by undertaking to give the information, while it may not be affected by the identity of the person for whose guidance the information is given, is vitally affected by the number and character of the persons, and particularly the nature and extent of the proposed transaction. On the other hand, the circumstances may frequently show that the identity of the person for whose guidance the information is given is regarded by the person supplying it, and by the recipient, as important and material; and therefore the person giving the information understands that his liability is to be restricted to the named person and to him only. Thus when the information is procured for transmission to a named or otherwise described person, whether the maker is liable to another, to whom in substitution the information is transmitted in order to influence his conduct in an otherwise identical transaction, depends upon whether it is understood between the one giving the information and the one bringing about its transmission, that it is to be given to the named individual and to him only.

Illustrations:

4. A, having lots for sale, negligently supplies misinformation concerning the lots to a real estate board, for the purpose of having the information incorporated in the board's multiple listing of available lots, which is distributed by the board to approximately 1,000 prospective purchasers of land each month. The listing is sent by the board to B, and in reliance upon the misinformation B purchases one of A's lots and in consequence suffers pecuniary loss. A is subject to liability to B.

5. A is negotiating with X Bank for a credit of $50,000. The Bank requires an audit by independent public accountants. A employs B & Company, a firm of accountants, to make the audit, telling them that the purpose of the audit is to meet the requirements of X Bank in connection with a credit of $50,000. B & Company agrees to make the audit, with the express understanding that it is for transmission to X Bank only. X Bank fails, and A, without any further communication with B & Company, submits its financial statements accompanied by B & Company's opinion to Y Bank, which in reliance upon it extends a credit of $50,000 to A. The audit is so carelessly made as to result in an unqualified favorable opinion on financial statements that materially misstates the financial position of A, and in consequence Y Bank suffers pecuniary loss through its extension of credit. B & Company is not liable to Y Bank.

6. The same facts as in Illustration 5, except that nothing is said about supplying the information for the guidance of X Bank only, and A merely informs B & Company that he expects to negotiate a bank loan, for $50,000, requires the audit for the purpose of the loan, and has X Bank in mind. B & Company is subject to liability to Y Bank.

7. The same facts as in Illustration 5, except that A informs B & Company that he expects to negotiate a bank loan, but does not mention the name of any bank. B & Company is subject to liability to Y Bank.

8. A, wishing to sell his car to B, writes to C, an expert mechanic, asking him to inspect the car and forward to A a letter stating its condition, in order that A may give the letter to B, who, as A tells C, is a prospective purchaser. Nothing is said about using the information only for B. C may be found to have supplied the information for the guidance of B only, or for the guidance either of B or of any other purchaser whom A may find.

9. The City of A is about to ask for bids for work on a sewer tunnel. It hires B Company, a firm of engineers, to make boring tests and provide a report showing the rock and soil conditions to be encountered. It notifies B Company that the report will be made available to bidders as a basis for their bids and that it is expected to be used by the successful bidder in doing the work. Without knowing the identity of any of the contractors bidding on the work, B Company

negligently prepares and delivers to the City an inaccurate report, containing false and misleading information. On the basis of the report C makes a successful bid, and also on the basis of the report D, a subcontractor, contracts with C to do a part of the work. By reason of the inaccuracy of the report, C and D suffer pecuniary loss in performing their contracts. B Company is subject to liability to C and to D.

10. A, an independent public accountant, is retained by B Company to conduct an annual audit of the customary scope for the corporation and to furnish his opinion on the corporation's financial statements. A is not informed of any intended use of the financial statements; but A knows that the financial statements, accompanied by an auditor's opinion, are customarily used in a wide variety of financial transactions by the corporation and that they may be relied upon by lenders, investors, shareholders, creditors, purchasers and the like, in numerous possible kinds of transactions. In fact B Company uses the financial statements and accompanying auditor's opinion to obtain a loan from X Bank. Because of A's negligence, he issues an unqualifiedly favorable opinion upon a balance sheet that materially misstates the financial position of B Company, and through reliance upon it X Bank suffers pecuniary loss. A is not liable to X Bank.

11. A Bank receives an inquiry from B Bank respecting the creditworthiness of C Corporation, a customer of A Bank. B Bank informs A Bank that the reason for the inquiry is that D & Co., an advertising agency, has been approached by C Corporation with a request that it manage a $200,000 advertising campaign for C Corporation on the local television station; that under the terms of its customary arrangement with the television station, D & Co. would be guarantor of any amount owing the station, and that D & Co. has requested its bank to ascertain from C Corporation's bank whether C Corporation is sufficiently creditworthy to incur and satisfy a liability of $200,000. A Bank, without checking C Corporation's account, and without a disclaimer of liability for its answer, replies that it believes C Corporation to be good for such an obligation. D & Co. arranges for the advertising campaign and shortly thereafter C Corporation enters bankruptcy. A Bank is subject to liability for negligence to D & Co.

12. In 1934, A Company, a firm of surveyors, contracts with B to make a survey and description of B's land. A Company is not informed of any intended use of the survey report but knows that survey reports are customarily used in a wide variety of real estate transactions and that it may be relied upon by purchasers, mortgagees, investors and others. The survey is negligently made and misstates the boundaries and extent of the land. In 1958 C, relying upon the report that B exhibits to him, purchases the land from B, and in consequence suffers pecuniary loss. A Company is not liable to C.

Comment:

i. Comparison with other Sections. When a misrepresentation creates a risk of physical harm to the person, land or chattels of others, the liability of the maker extends, under the rules stated in §§ 310 and 311, to any person to whom he should expect physical harm to result through action taken in reliance upon it. When a misrepresentation is fraudulent and results in pecuniary loss, the liability of the maker extends, under the rule stated in § 531, to any of the class of persons whom he intends or should expect to act in reliance upon it, and to loss suffered by them in any of the general type of transactions in which he intends or should expect their conduct to be influenced.

Under the rule stated in Subsection (2) of this Section, when the misrepresentation is merely negligent and results in pecuniary loss, the scope of the liability is narrower. The maker of the negligent misrepresentation is subject to liability to only those persons for whose guidance he knows the information to be supplied, and to them only for loss incurred in the kind of transaction in which it is expected to influence them, or a transaction of a substantially similar kind. There is an exception, as stated in Subsection (3), when there is a public duty to give the information. (See Comment *k*, below).

j. Transactions for guidance in which the information is supplied. The rule stated in Clause (2)(b) is somewhat more narrowly restricted than in the case of the liability of the maker of a fraudulent representation stated in § 531, Clause (b). The liability of the maker of the fraudulent representation extends to all transactions of the type or kind that the maker intends or has reason to expect. Under this Section, the liability of the maker of a negligent misrepresentation is limited to the transaction that he intends, or knows that the recipient intends, to influence, or to a substantially similar transaction.

Thus independent public accountants who negligently make an audit of books of a corporation, which they are told is to be used only for the purpose of obtaining a particular line of banking credit, are not subject to liability to a wholesale merchant whom the corporation induces to supply it with goods on credit by showing him the financial statements and the accountant's opinion. On the other hand, it is not necessary that the transaction in which the opinion is relied on shall be identical in all of its minute details with the one intended. It is enough that it is substantially the same transaction or one substantially similar. Thus, in the situation above stated, if the corporation, finding that at the moment it does not need the credit to obtain which the audit was procured, uses it a month later to obtain the same credit from the same bank, the accountants will remain subject to liability to the bank for the loss resulting from its extension of credit, unless the financial condition of the corporation has materially changed in the interim or so much time has elapsed that the bank cannot justifiably rely upon the audit.

There may be many minor differences that do not affect the essential character of the transaction. The question may be one of the extent of the departure that the maker of the representation understands is to be expected. If he is told that the information that he supplies is to be used in applying to a particular bank for a loan of $10,000, the fact that the loan is made by that bank for $15,000 will not necessarily mean that the transaction is a different one. But if the loan is for $500,000, the very difference in amount would lead the ordinary borrower or lender to regard it as a different kind of transaction. The ordinary practices and attitudes of the business world are to be taken into account, and the question becomes one of whether the departure from the contemplated transaction is so major and so significant that it cannot be regarded as essentially the same transaction. It is also possible, of course, that more than one kind of transaction may be understood as intended.

Illustrations:

13. A negligently furnishes to a title insurance company a letter praising its facilities and operation, for the purpose of aiding it in selling title insurance. The company exhibits the letter to B, who relies on it in taking out title insurance with the company, and is also induced by the letter to purchase stock in the company. The company proves to be insolvent and B suffers pecuniary loss. A is subject to liability to B for his loss on the title insurance but not for his loss on the purchase of the stock.

14. A, an independent public accountant, negligently conducts an audit for B Corporation, and issues an unqualified favorable opinion on its financial statements, although it is in fact insolvent. A knows that B Corporation intends to exhibit the balance sheet to C Corporation, as a basis for applying for credit for the purchase of goods. In reliance upon the balance sheet, C Corporation buys the controlling interest in the stock of B Corporation and as a result suffers pecuniary loss. A is not liable to C Corporation.

15. The same facts as in Illustration 14, except that A is informed that C Corporation will be asked to extend credit for the purchase of washing machines, and credit is extended instead for the purchase of electric refrigerators. A is subject to liability to C Corporation.

Comment on Subsection (3):

k. *Public duty to give information.* When there is a public duty to supply the information in question, an exception arises to the rule stated in Subsection (2), and the maker of the negligent misrepresentation becomes subject to liability to any of the class of persons for whose benefit the duty is created and for their pecuniary losses suffered in any of the general type of transactions in which they are intended to be protected.

The usual case in which the exception arises is that of a public officer who, by his acceptance of his office, has undertaken a duty to the public to furnish information of a particular kind. Typical is the case of a recording clerk, whose duty it is to furnish certified copies of the records under his control. The rule stated is not, however, limited to public officers, and it may apply to private individuals or corporations who are required by law to file information for the benefit of the public.

The scope of the defendant's duty to others in these cases will depend upon the purpose for which the information is required to be furnished. The purpose may be found to be to protect only a particular and limited class of persons, as when a statute requiring insurance companies to file information concerning their finances with a state insurance commissioner is found to be only for the protection of those buying insurance. In such a case the liability of the company when it negligently gives false information extends only to those who take out insurance policies and only to losses suffered through taking out the policy. On the other hand, the group protected may be a much broader one and may include any one who may reasonably be expected to rely on the information and suffer loss as a result.

Illustrations:

16. A, a notary public, in the performance of his official duties, negligently takes an acknowledgment of a signature on a deed, and certifies that it is that of B. In fact the person signing is not B and the signature is a forgery. The deed is recorded, and in reliance upon the record C purchases the land from D, and as a result suffers pecuniary loss. A is subject to liability to C.

17. A, a county tax clerk, in the performance of his official duties, negligently gives B a certificate stating that the taxes on B's land have been paid. In reliance upon the certificate, C buys the land from B and as a result suffers pecuniary loss when he is compelled to pay the taxes. A is subject to liability to C.

18. A, a United States government food inspector, in the performance of his official duties, negligently stamps a quantity of B's beef as "Grade A." In fact the beef is of inferior quality. In reliance upon the stamps, C buys the beef from D, and suffers pecuniary loss as a result. A is subject to liability to C.

§ 552A   Contributory Negligence

The recipient of a negligent misrepresentation is barred from recovery for pecuniary loss suffered in reliance upon it if he is negligent in so relying.

Comment

a. The recipient of a fraudulent misrepresentation who justifiably relies upon it is not barred from recovery by his contributory negligence in doing so. (See § 545A). But when the misrepresentation is not fraudulent but only negligent, the action is founded solely upon negligence, and the ordinary rules as to negligence liability apply. Therefore the contributory negligence of the plaintiff in relying upon the misrepresentation will bar his recovery. This means that the plaintiff is held to the standard of care, knowledge, intelligence and judgment of a reasonable man, even though he does not possess the qualities necessary to enable him to conform to that standard. (See § 464.)

   b.   With respect to physical harms caused by negligence, the old rule that contributory negligence is a complete bar to liability based on negligence is yielding to a trend toward comparative negligence. It is debatable whether this development should affect liability for pecuniary harm as well. Precedents to date have not made this extension.

§ 552B   Damages for Negligent Misrepresentation

(1) The damages recoverable for a negligent misrepresentation are those necessary to compensate the plaintiff for the pecuniary loss to him of which the misrepresentation is a legal cause, including

   (a) the difference between the value of what he has received in the transaction and its purchase price or other value given for it; and

   (b) pecuniary loss suffered otherwise as a consequence of the plaintiff's reliance upon the misrepresentation.

(2) the damages recoverable for a negligent misrepresentation do not include the benefit of the plaintiff's contract with the defendant.

Comment:

   a.   The rule stated in this Section applies, as the measure of damages for negligent misrepresentation, the rule of out-of-pocket loss that is stated as to fraudulent misrepresentations in Subsection (1) of § 549. Comments *a* to *f* under § 549 are therefore applicable to this Section, so far as they are pertinent.

   b.   This Section rejects, as to negligent misrepresentation, the possibility that, in a proper case, the plaintiff may also recover damages that will give him the benefit of his contract with the defendant, which is stated, as to fraudulent misrepresentations, in Subsection (2) of § 549. This position is consistent with that taken, in § 766C, that there is as a general rule no liability for merely negligent conduct that interferes with or frustrates a contract interest or an expectancy of pecuniary advantage. The considerations of policy that have led the courts to compensate the plaintiff for the loss of his bargain in order to make the deception of a deliberate defrauder unprofitable to him, do not apply when the defendant has had honest intentions but has merely failed to exercise reasonable care in what he says or does.

Topic 4. Innocent Misrepresentation

§ 552C   Misrepresentation in Sale, Rental
or Exchange Transaction

(1) One who, in a sale, rental or exchange transaction with another, makes a misrepresentation of a material fact for the purpose of inducing the other to act or to refrain from acting in reliance upon it, is subject to liability to the other for pecuniary loss caused to him by his justifiable reliance upon the misrepresentation, even though it is not made fraudulently or negligently.

(2) Damages recoverable under the rule stated in this section are limited to the difference between the value of what the other has parted with and the value of what he has received in the transaction.

Caveat:

The Institute expresses no opinion as to whether there may be other types of business transactions, in addition to those of sale, rental and exchange, in which strict liability may be imposed for innocent misrepresentation under the conditions stated in this Section.

Comment on Subsection (1):

a. History. The rule developed by the English courts, following the leading case of Derry v. Peek (1889) 14 A.C. 337, was that there was no liability for a misrepresentation causing only pecuniary loss unless the misrepresentation was fraudulent, as that term is defined in § 526. This rule received wide application in the United States. As to the extent to which it has been modified to permit recovery for misrepresentation that is not fraudulent but merely negligent, see § 552 and Comments. The rule stated in this Section represents a further modification reflected in the decisions of a number of American jurisdictions, some of which, in the case of bargaining transactions, rejected the rule of Derry v. Peek or never really accepted the holding of that case despite some judicial language seemingly to the contrary. It is a rule of strict liability for innocent misrepresentation of a material fact, made to another in a sale, rental or exchange transaction.

The courts that apply this rule have expressed it in differing ways. Some have imposed upon a party to a bargaining transaction a "duty" to know. Others have held that an unqualified statement of fact, which is susceptible of personal knowledge and which turns out to be false, is fraudulent insofar as there was no disclaimer of personal knowledge; and this view seems to have been taken without regard to whether the other party was actually deceived by the absence of the disclaimer. Although these courts use the language of scienter, their decisions actually constitute the imposition of liability for innocent misrepresentation.

More significantly, other courts have utilized the rule originating in equity that when a party seeks rescission of a transaction on the ground of a misrepresentation of a material fact by the other party relief will be granted even though the misrepresentation was innocent (just as rescission is also granted for mutual mistake). (See, generally, Restatement of Restitution, §§ 6, 8; Restatement, Second, Contracts §§ 304, 306). This rule of the law of restitution has also been regularly applied in actions at law, at least in situations in which the plaintiff is seeking to recover money paid and has already effected a rescission, so that a decree establishing the rescission is not required. (See Restatement of Restitution, § 28). Under similar circumstances a number of courts have permitted a tort action for damages without regard to the requirement that the transaction be completely rescinded, either by the plaintiff or by the court, and without limiting the action to the restitutionary concept of recovery of money paid.

b. *Relationship to action for restitution or breach of warranty.* The remedy provided in this Section is very similar to that afforded under the law of restitution. It differs, however, in a material respect. The plaintiff is permitted to retain what he has received and recover damages, rather than rescind and seek restitution, in which case he must return what he received. The tort action for damages may have a definite advantage to the plaintiff in cases in which he is unable to restore what he received in its original condition; when he has made improvements or for other reasons finds it desirable to keep what he has received rather than return it; when he is barred from rescission by delay or has so far committed himself that he has lost the remedy by an election; or when for some other reason, such as the defendant's change of position, restitution is not available to him. It may even in many cases be a better solution from the point of view of the defendant himself, since it permits the transaction to stand, rather than be upset at a later date.

In view of the many similarities of the rule set forth in this Section to the restitutionary remedy, it is difficult to say with certainty whether this rule should be regarded as one of strict liability in the law of torts, eliminating the requirement of intent or negligence in making the representation, or one of the law of restitution, eliminating the requirement of rescinding and restoring the status quo. Under either classification the rule of this Section retains its usefulness.

It should be added that in cases involving the sale of goods, and probably in other transactions, a somewhat similar remedy has been available in the action for breach of warranty. The latter action, despite its historic relationship to tort, has been subject to important contract defenses, notably among them the parol evidence rule. This is made explicit by the Uniform Commercial Code. (See U.C.C. § 2–202). Further, in cases involving the sale of goods, most of the innocent misrepresentations made actionable by this Section would also be actionable under the Code on the theory of breach of warranty. But it does not necessarily follow that actions for damages founded upon innocent misrepresentation are preempted by the Code. The measure of damages provided by this Section differs from the traditional measure of damages for breach of warranty (now embodied in the Code). Under this

Section, damages are solely restitutionary in character. In contrast, the measure of damages for breach of warranty includes compensation for benefit of the bargain and for consequential losses. This difference argues for viewing the tort action under this Section as unburdened by contract (or Code) defenses. However, this issue has gone virtually unnoticed in the jurisdictions that give damages in tort for innocent misrepresentation. In a case in which, as a practical matter, the amount recoverable under this Section is substantially the same as the amount recoverable for breach of warranty, the argument against recognition of defenses traditional to the warranty action loses much of its force.

c. *Sale, rental or exchange.* The cases to which the rule of strict liability for innocent misrepresentation stated in this Section has been applied thus far have generally been confined to sale, rental or exchange transactions between the plaintiff and the defendant. This includes any sale, rental or exchange of land, chattels, securities or anything else of value, such as copyrights, patents and other valuable intangible rights. As to possible application of the rule to other types of business transactions, see the Caveat, and Comment g below.

d. *Parties.* The rule stated is limited to the immediate parties to the sale, rental or exchange transaction itself. It does not apply in favor of a third person who is not a party to the transaction, even though he acts according to expectations in taking action or refraining from it in reliance upon the misrepresentation. The third person may recover only if the misrepresentation is fraudulent or negligent, and thus is within a rule stated in §§ 531 or 552. The same is true of one to whom the misrepresentation is made directly, but who is induced by it to incur loss in a transaction with a third person.

e. *Misrepresentation.* In order for the rule stated in this Section to apply there must be a misrepresentation of fact, express or implied. The rule of this Section does not apply to misrepresentations of opinion, intention or law, except as they may imply misrepresentations of fact. (See §§ 542–545). The fact misrepresented must be one that is material to the transaction and of sufficient consequence to justify reliance upon it in entering into the transaction. The representation must be made for the purpose of inducing the plaintiff to rely upon it in acting or refraining from action as a part of the transaction. He must in fact so rely and his reliance must be justifiable under the circumstances. In these respects the rules stated in §§ 531 to 548 are applicable to this Section, so far as they are pertinent.

Comment on Subsection (2):

f. *Damages.* The damages given under this Section are restitutionary in nature. In the traditional restitution action, the plaintiff returns what he has received in the transaction, and recovers what he has parted with, so that he is in effect restored to the pecuniary position in which he stood before the transaction. A similar and yet different result is achieved by the rule of this Section, in that the plaintiff recovers the difference between the value of what he parted with and the value of what he has received and still retains. Since the defendant's misrepresentation is an innocent one, he is not held liable for other damages; specifically, he is not liable for benefit of the bargain or for consequential damages.

Comment on Caveat:

g. Under the rule stated in this Section, the strict liability for innocent misrepresentation is limited to sale, rental or exchange transactions between the plaintiff and the defendant. There have, however, been occasional decisions in which the same rule has been applied to other types of business transactions, such as the issuance of an insurance policy or the inducement of an investment or a loan. In a few other instances agents selling for their principals have been held to the strict liability for innocent misrepresentation, when they have received a commission or had some other pecuniary interest in the transaction. The law appears to be still in a process of development, and the ultimate limits of the liability are not yet determined. The Caveat therefore leaves open the question of whether there may be other types of transactions to which the rule stated here may be applied.

Chapter 23. Fraudulent Misrepresentation and Nondisclosure in Miscellaneous Transactions

§ 557A Fraudulent Misrepresentations Causing Physical Harm

One who by a fraudulent misrepresentation or nondisclosure of a fact that it is his duty to disclose causes physical harm to the person or to the land or chattel of another who justifiably relies upon the misrepresentation, is subject to liability to the other.

Comment:

a. The rule as to liability for a fraudulent misrepresentation that involves an unreasonable risk of physical harm to another is stated in § 310. The liability there stated is negligence liability and is enforced in an ordinary negligence action. The rule here stated permits a tort action of deceit to be maintained, when there is physical harm to person, land or chattels of a person who justifiably relies on it. This liability also extends to the economic loss resulting from the physical harm.

The action of deceit is subject to the rules stated for fraudulent misrepresentations in §§ 525 to 551, including particularly those as to justifiable reliance of the plaintiff and legal causation of the resulting harm. An exception is § 548A; in the case of physical harm, the case is governed by the ordinary rules as to legal cause.

Illustration:

1.   A, seeking to sell B a shotgun, fraudulently tells B that it is in good condition, although he knows that there is an obstruction in the barrel. B, in reliance on the misrepresentation, buys the gun from A, and discharges it. The gun explodes and B is injured. A is subject to liability to B in an action for deceit.

Division Five.   Defamation
Chapter 24.   Invasions of Interest in Reputation
Topic 1.   Elements of a Cause of Action for Defamation

§ 558   Elements Stated

To create liability for defamation there must be:

(a)   a false and defamatory statement concerning another;

(b)   an unprivileged publication to a third party;

(c)   fault amounting at least to negligence on the part of the publisher; and

(d)   either actionability of the statement irrespective of special harm or the existence of special harm caused by the publication.

Topic 5.   Defamation Actionable Irrespective of Special Harm (Defamation Actionable Per Se)

§ 569   Liability Without Proof of Special Harm—Libel

One who falsely publishes matter defamatory of another in such a manner as to make the publication a libel is subject to liability to the other although no special harm results from the publication.

§ 570   Liability Without Proof of Special Harm—Slander

One who publishes matter defamatory to another in such a manner as to make the publication a slander is subject to liability to the other although no special harm results if the publication imputes to the other

(a)   a criminal offense, as stated in § 571, or

(b)   a loathsome disease, as stated in § 572, or

(c)   matter incompatible with his business, trade, profession, or office, as stated in § 573, or

(d)   serious sexual misconduct, as stated in § 574.

Chapter 25. Defenses to Actions for Defamation
Topic 2. Absolute Privileges
Title A. Consent

§ 583 General Principle

Except as stated in § 584, the consent of another to the publication of defamatory matter concerning him is a complete defense to his action for defamation.

Title B. Absolute Privilege Irrespective of Consent

§ 585 Judicial Officers

A judge or other officer performing a judicial function is absolutely privileged to publish defamatory matter in the performance of the function if the publication has some relation to the matter before him.

§ 586 Attorneys at Law

An attorney at law is absolutely privileged to publish defamatory matter concerning another in communications preliminary to a proposed judicial proceeding, or in the institution of, or during the course and as a part of, a judicial proceeding in which he participates as counsel, if it has some relation to the proceeding.

§ 587 Parties to Judicial Proceedings

A party to a private litigation or a private prosecutor or defendant in a criminal prosecution is absolutely privileged to publish defamatory matter concerning another in communications preliminary to a proposed judicial proceeding, or in the institution of or during the course and as a part of, a judicial proceeding in which he participates, if the matter has some relation to the proceeding.

§ 588 Witnesses in Judicial Proceedings

A witness is absolutely privileged to publish defamatory matter concerning another in communications preliminary to a proposed judicial proceeding or as a part of a judicial proceeding in which he is testifying, if it has some relation to the proceeding.

§ 589 Jurors

A member of a grand or petit jury is absolutely privileged to publish defamatory matter concerning another in the performance of his function as a juror, if the defamatory matter has some relation to the proceedings in which he is acting as juror.

§ 590   Legislators

A member of the Congress of the United States or of a State or local legislative body is absolutely privileged to publish defamatory matter concerning another in the performance of his legislative functions.

§ 590A   Witnesses in Legislative Proceedings

A witness is absolutely privileged to publish defamatory matter as part of a legislative proceeding in which he is testifying or in communications preliminary to the proceeding, if the matter has some relation to the proceeding.

§ 592   Husband and Wife

A husband or a wife is absolutely privileged to publish to the other spouse defamatory matter concerning a third person.

Topic 3.   Conditional Privileges
Title A.   Occasions Making a Publication
Conditionally Privileged
Subtitle III.   Abuse of Privilege

§ 599   General Principle

One who publishes defamatory matter concerning another upon an occasion giving rise to a conditional privilege is subject to liability to the other if he abuses the privilege.

§ 600   Knowledge of Falsity or Reckless Disregard as to Truth

Except as stated in § 602, one who upon an occasion giving rise to a conditional privilege publishes false and defamatory matter concerning another abuses the privilege if he

    (a)   knows the matter to be false, or

    (b)   acts in reckless disregard as to its truth or falsity.

Division Six.   Injurious Falsehood
Chapter 28.   Injurious Falsehood (Including Slander
of Title and Trade Libel)
Topic 1.   General Principle

§ 623A   Liability for Publication of Injurious Falsehood—General Principle

One who publishes a false statement harmful to the interests of another is subject to liability for pecuniary loss resulting to the other if

(a) he intends for publication of the statement to result in harm to interests of the other having a pecuniary value, or either recognizes or should recognize that it is likely to do so, and

(b) he knows that the statement is false or acts in reckless disregard of its truth or falsity.

Caveats:

The Institute takes no position on the questions of:

(1) Whether, instead of showing the publisher's knowledge or reckless disregard of the falsity of the statement, as indicated in Clause (b), the other may recover by showing that the publisher had either

(a) a motive of ill will toward him, or

(b) an intent to interfere in an unprivileged manner with his interests; or

(2) Whether either of these alternate bases, if not alone sufficient, would be made sufficient by being combined with a showing of negligence regarding the truth or falsity of the statement.

Topic 2. Disparagement of Property in or Quality of Land, Chattels and Intangible Things

§ 624   Disparagement of Property—Slander of Title

The rules on liability for the publication of an injurious falsehood stated in § 623A apply to the publication of a false statement disparaging another's property rights in land, chattels or intangible things, that the publisher should recognize as likely to result in pecuniary harm to the other through the conduct of third persons in respect to the other's interests in the property.

§ 626   Disparagement of Quality—Trade Libel

The rules on liability for the publication of an injurious falsehood stated in § 623A apply to the publication of matter disparaging the quality of another's land, chattels or intangible things, that the publisher should recognize as likely to result in pecuniary loss to the other through the conduct of a third person in respect to the other's interests in the property.

§ 629   Disparagement Defined

A statement is disparaging if it is understood to cast doubt upon the quality of another's land, chattels or intangible things, or upon the existence or extent of his property in them, and

(a) the publisher intends the statement to cast the doubt, or

(b) the recipient's understanding of it as casting the doubt was reasonable.

Topic 3.   Rules Applicable to All Publication of Injurious Falsehood

§ 630   Publication

Publication of an injurious falsehood is its communication intentionally or by a negligent act to someone other than the person whose interest is affected.

§ 632   Legal Causation of Pecuniary Loss

The publication of an injurious falsehood is a legal cause of pecuniary loss if

(a) it is a substantial factor in bringing about the loss, and

(b) there is no rule of law relieving the publisher from liability because of the manner in which the publication has resulted in the loss.

§ 633   Pecuniary Loss

(1) The pecuniary loss for which a publisher of injurious falsehood is subject to liability is restricted to

(a) the pecuniary loss that results directly and immediately from the effect of the conduct of third persons, including impairment of vendibility or value caused by disparagement, and

(b) the expense of measures reasonably necessary to counteract the publication, including litigation to remove the doubt cast upon vendibility or value by disparagement.

(2) This pecuniary loss may be established by

(a) proof of the conduct of specific persons, or

(b) proof that the loss has resulted from the conduct of a number of persons whom it is impossible to identify.

Comment:

h. Widely disseminated injurious falsehood may, however, cause serious and genuine pecuniary loss by affecting the conduct of a number of persons whom the plaintiff is unable to identify and so depriving him of a market that he would otherwise have found. When this can be shown with reasonable certainty, the rule requiring the identification of specific purchasers is relaxed and recovery is permitted for the loss of the market. As in analogous cases involving the loss of profits of an established business, as the result of other torts or of breach of contract, this may be proved by circumstantial evidence showing that the loss has in fact occurred, and eliminating other causes.

Thus a tradesman whose goods are denounced by a newspaper as adulterated can prove the pecuniary loss necessary to recovery by showing that after the publication the sales of his goods, theretofore constant or increasing, have fallen off and by eliminating all other reasonably likely causes, such as new competition, a general decline in the market for such goods or defects in the goods themselves. So likewise, when a real estate development company is prevented from selling a particular lot of land by wide publication of the statement that its title to that lot is defective, it may be able to establish its loss by showing that similar lots held for sale by the company and its competitors were readily marketable, and by eliminating other explanations. Whether particular evidence of this kind is sufficient to sustain the plaintiff's burden of proof as to his loss is a question of fact and is not within the scope of this Restatement.

Illustration:

1. A publishes in his magazine an untrue statement that a particular method of canning foods used by B is dangerous because it is likely to render the food unwholesome. B proves that the magazine was widely circulated; that prior to the publication his annual sales of the foods were constant at a volume of $500,000 a year; that immediately after the publication his sales began to decline, and during the year following amounted to only $200,000; that the market for the foods in general remained steady and there was no change in competition or in the sales methods of B; and that the foods themselves were in no way changed or defective. Upon this evidence it may be found that the publication has caused B a pecuniary loss of the profits he would have made on sales of $300,000.

i. Consequential damages. The damages recoverable under the rule stated in Clause (1)(a) of this Section are restricted to the pecuniary loss that results directly and immediately from the effect of the injurious falsehood in influencing the conduct of third persons. They do not include any loss resulting from the plaintiff's failure to make an advantageous use of money that he would have made if a prospective sale had been consummated, since this is not the direct and immediate consequence of the injurious falsehood but depends upon the situation of the disappointed vendor and the particular purposes for which it would have been necessary or advantageous for him to apply the purchase money.

Similarly, an owner of land who is refused a mortgage loan by his bank because of disparagement of his title can not recover for the loss of his intended use of the money he was seeking to borrow. On the other hand, if it can be proved with reasonable certainty that he could obtain another loan only at a higher rate of interest, the loss of the favorable interest rate is a result directly and immediately caused by the disparagement and is recoverable.

Illustrations:

2. A's business is in a precarious financial position. In order to protect himself from bankruptcy, A offers land to B at $20,000. B is about to accept this offer but is prevented from doing so by C's false statement that A's title to the land is bad. In consequence of A's failure to consummate the sale and receive the agreed price his business goes into bankruptcy. A can not recover from C the loss that he has sustained by the bankruptcy of his business.

3. The facts are identical with those stated in Illustration 2, except that A offers the land for $20,000 in order to put himself in funds to buy an oil lease. The sale being prevented, he is unable to purchase the lease. Oil is subsequently found in large quantities on the land for which the lease is given. C is not liable to A for his failure to obtain the gain that would have resulted had he been in funds to purchase the lease.

4. The facts are identical with those stated in Illustration 2, except that in consequence of B's failure to purchase the land, A for the protection of his business is forced to sell securities on a temporarily and artificially depressed market. C is not liable to A for the loss that A sustains through the sale of these securities.

§ 634   Truth

The publisher of a statement injurious to another is not liable for injurious falsehood if the facts stated, or implied as justification for an opinion stated, are true.

Comment:

b. Matter generally or specifically disparaging. Another's title to land or other thing may be disparaged by a statement that he does not have the title to the thing in question that he claims to have or by the statement that there is a particular defect in his title. When the disparagement consists in a general attack upon another's title without specifying in what particulars it is defective, the other must as plaintiff establish that his title is as he claims it to be. Thus if the defendant says that the plaintiff's title to a particular piece of land is not good, the plaintiff must prove that his title is marketable since the test of a good title is its marketability. If, on the other hand, the disparagement consists of a statement that there is a particular defect in the other's title, the other as plaintiff need only show that his title is free from that defect. Thus, if A states that B's land is mortgaged for $5,000 to C, B is required to prove that C owns no mortgage on the land or that the mortgage that C holds is for less than $5,000. He need not prove that the land is free from other incumbrances as, for example, a lien for unpaid taxes.

A statement disparaging the quality of a thing may be general or specific in its disparagement. If the defendant says that the plaintiff's product is bad or worthless, as if he implies that it will not wear in use, the plaintiff must prove that it is so constructed as to do so. If, on the other hand, the statement is that the product has a particular defect, as if the statement is that the brakes of a particular make of car are bad, the plaintiff need only prove that the brakes are such as are generally regarded as sufficient.

Topic 4. Privileges to Publish Injurious Falsehood

§ 635 Absolute Privileges

The rules on absolute privilege to publish defamatory matter stated in §§ 583 to 592A apply to the publication of an injurious falsehood.

§ 646A Conditional Privileges

The rules on conditional privileges to publish defamatory matter stated in §§ 594 to 598A and on the special privileges stated in §§ 611 and 612 apply to the publication of an injurious falsehood.

§ 647 Conditional Privilege of Rival Claimant

A rival claimant is conditionally privileged to disparage another's property in land, chattels or intangible things by an assertion of an inconsistent legally protected interest in himself.

Comment:

b. This Section states an added conditional privilege, applicable only to the publication of injurious falsehood and not to defamation. It differs from the conditional privilege stated in § 594 in that it goes further and permits the publisher to assert a claim to a legally protected interest of his own provided that the assertion is honest and in good faith, even though his belief is neither correct nor reasonable.

d. *Belief in validity of claim.* One may disparage another's property in land, chattels or intangible things by asserting a legally protected interest in one's self that is inconsistent with the other's property in the land or other thing in question. Under the rule stated in this Section a rival claimant is privileged to assert the inconsistent interest unless a trier of fact is persuaded that he did not believe in the possible validity of his claim. It is not necessary that the person asserting the claim should believe in its certain or even probable validity. It is enough if he believes in good faith that there is a substantial chance of its being sustained. Bad faith is treated as an abuse of the privilege stated in this Section. (See § 650A).

§ 649   Conditional Privilege of Competitors

A competitor is conditionally privileged to make an unduly favorable comparison of the quality of his own land, chattels or other things, with the quality of the competing land, chattels or other things of a rival competitor, although he does not believe that his own things are superior to those of the rival competitor, if the comparison does not contain false assertions of specific unfavorable facts regarding the rival competitor's things.

Comment:

c.   Although one who dishonestly makes an unfavorable comparison of a competitor's things with his own competing things to a certain extent disparages the quality of his competitor's things by asserting the superiority of his own, he does not assert that the quality of the competitor's things is bad but only that they are less good than his own. These statements have a strong analogy to the "sales talk" or "puffing" that a vendor is permitted to indulge in without liability to a purchaser who alleges that he was thereby misled. (See § 542). In both cases the practice of vendors to make consciously exaggerated claims for their goods is so well known that little or no importance is attached to the statements. In addition, courts are properly reluctant to permit a lawsuit to be used as a means by which producers may obtain advertisement by a verdict that declares a rival's claim to superiority to be unfounded. So long as nothing more is done than to exaggerate dishonestly the merits of the publisher's goods as compared with those of his competitor the publisher is not liable. If, however, he goes further and makes a direct attack upon the quality of his competitor's things by stating specific unfavorable facts even though he does so to supply a reason for his claim that his own things are superior, he cannot successfully claim a privilege under the rule stated in this Section. Thus a manufacturer who advertises that his goods are the best in the market or that they have an efficiency for certain important purposes superior to that of any other product, is not liable to a competitor whose product the publisher knows to be superior to his own. If, however, he goes further and says that his own product is superior because of the bad material put into that of his competitor, he has made a statement of a specific fact that directly attacks the quality of his competitor's product.

§ 650A   Abuse of Conditional Privilege

Except as otherwise stated in §§ 647 and 649, a conditional privilege to publish injurious falsehood is abused under circumstances that amount to an abuse of a conditional privilege to publish defamation.

Topic 5. Burden of Proof and Functions of Court and Jury

§ 651 Burden of Proof

(1) In an action for injurious falsehood the plaintiff has the burden of proving, when the issue is properly raised,

(a) the existence and extent of the legally protected interest of the plaintiff affected by the falsehood;

(b) the injurious character of the falsehood;

(c) the falsity of the statement;

(d) publication of the falsehood;

(e) that the circumstances under which the publication was made were such as to make reliance on it by a third person reasonably foreseeable;

(f) the recipient's understanding of the communication in its injurious sense;

(g) the recipient's understanding of the communication as applicable to the plaintiff's interests;

(h) the pecuniary loss resulting from the publication;

(i) the defendant's knowledge of the falsity of the statement or his reckless disregard as to its truth or falsity;

(j) the defendant's motivation of ill will;

(k) the defendant's intent to affect plaintiff's interests in an unprivileged manner; and

(l) abuse of a conditional privilege.

(2) The defendant has the burden of proving, when the issue is properly raised, that the publication was absolutely or conditionally privileged.

Division Nine. Interference with Advantageous Economic Relations
Chapter 37. Interference with Contract or Prospective Contractual Relation

§ 766 Intentional Interference with Performance of Contract by Third Person

One who intentionally and improperly interferes with the performance of a contract (except a contract to marry) between another and a third person by inducing or otherwise causing the third person not to perform the contract, is subject to liability to the other for the pecuniary loss resulting to the other from the failure of the third person to perform the contract.

Comment:

a.   Cross-references. See the Special Note to this Chapter, immediately preceding this Section. In order for the actor to be held liable, this Section requires that his interference be improper. The factors of importance in determining this issue are stated and explained in § 767, which must be read closely with this Section. Sections 768–773 deal with special situations in which the application of these factors has produced more clearly identifiable decisional patterns.

This Section uses the expression, "subject to liability," as defined in § 5, meaning that the actor is liable if his conduct was a legal cause of the interference and he has no defense to the action.

This Section is concerned only with intentional interference with subsisting contracts. It does not cover contracts to marry, which are dealt within § 698. The rule for intentional interference with another's performance of his own contract with a third person is stated in § 766A. The rule for intentional interference with prospective contractual relations not yet reduced to contract is stated in § 766B. The rule for negligent interference with either existing or prospective contractual relations is stated in § 766C.

b.   The rule stated in this Section does not apply to a mere refusal to deal. Deliberately and at his pleasure, one may ordinarily refuse to deal with another, and the conduct is not regarded as improper, subjecting the actor to liability. One may not, however, intentionally and improperly frustrate dealings that have been reduced to the form of a contract. There is no general duty to do business with all who offer their services, wares or patronage; but there is a general duty not to interfere intentionally with another's reasonable business expectancies of trade with third persons, whether or not they are secured by contract, unless the interference is not improper under the circumstances. When the interference is with a contract, an interference is more likely to be treated as improper than in the case of interference with prospective dealings, particularly in the case of competition, as stated in § 768.

c.   Historical development. Historically the liability for tortious interference with advantageous economic relations developed first in cases of intentional prevention of prospective dealings, by violence, fraud or defamation—conduct that was essentially tortious in its nature, either to the third party or to the injured party. (See § 766B, Comment *b*).

In 1853, the decision in Lumley v. Gye, 2 El. & Bl. 216, 118 Eng.Rep. 749, began the development of inducement of breach of contract as a separate tort. In that case a singer under contract to sing at the plaintiff's theatre was induced by the defendant, who operated a rival theatre, to break her contract with the plaintiff in order to sing for the defendant. No violence, fraud or defamation by the defendant was alleged. The decision in favor of the plaintiff was rested largely on the analogy of the rules relating to enticement of another's servants. This case differed from earlier cases in that the means of inducement used by the defendant were not tortious toward the singer. Subsequent cases extended the rule of Lumley v. Gye to contracts other than contracts of service and to interference with advantageous business relations even when they were not cemented by a contract.

After Lumley v. Gye, some cases dealing with the liability for intentional interference in contractual relations by inducing breach of contract or refusal to deal in absence of contract tended largely to build on that case as if it were the foundation. But the foundation is further back. The significance of Lumley v. Gye lies in its extension of the rule of liability to nontortious methods of inducement. Particularly in view of subsequent interpretations of that case in England, it established no rule peculiar to contracts.

The liability for inducing breach of contract is now regarded as but one instance, rather than the exclusive limit, of protection against improper interference in business relations. The added element of a definite contract may be a basis for greater protection; but some protection is appropriate against improper interference with reasonable expectancies of commercial relations even when an existing contract is lacking. The improper character of the actor's conduct and the harm caused by it may be equally clear in both cases. The differentiation between them relates primarily to the scope of the justification or the kind and amount of interference that is not improper in view of the differences in the facts.

Likewise, the importance of the means of inducement relates primarily to the issue of whether the interference is improper or not. The predatory means in the early cases, intimidation and fraud, were tortious toward the plaintiff because they were calculated to, and did, affect the conduct of third persons to the plaintiff's damage. (See § 766A, Comment *b*). But other means may be equally calculated and effective to produce that result; and primarily the plaintiff is concerned with that result rather than with the means by which the third persons were caused to act. The plaintiff's interest in his contractual rights and expectancies must be weighed, however, against the defendant's interest in freedom of action. If the defendant's conduct is predatory the scale on his side may weigh very lightly, but if his conduct is not predatory it may weigh heavily. The issue is whether in the given circumstances his interest and the social interest in allowing the freedom claimed by him are sufficient to outweigh the harm that his conduct is designed to produce. In deciding this issue, the nature of his conduct is an important factor. (See § 767).

d. *Types of contract.* The leading case of Lumley v. Gye involved the inducement of the breach of a contract of employment. Early decisions in the American courts, cautious in their acceptance of what was regarded as a new principle, declined to extend it beyond service contracts. In nearly all jurisdictions these decisions have now been repudiated, and the rule stated in this Section is applied to any type of contract, except a contract to marry. On the special rule applicable to contracts to marry, see § 698.

e. Illegal agreements. On illegal agreements and those in violation of public policy, see § 774.

f. Voidable contracts. The word "contract" connotes a promise creating a duty recognized by law. (See Restatement, Second, Contracts § 1). The particular agreement must be in force and effect at the time of the breach that the actor has caused; and if for any reason it is entirely void, there is no liability for causing its breach. Furthermore, it must be applicable to the particular performance that the third person has been induced or caused not to discharge. It is not, however, necessary that the contract be legally enforceable against the third person. A promise may be a valid and subsisting contract even though it is voidable. (See Restatement, Second, Contracts § 13). The third person may have a defense against action on the contract that would permit him to avoid it and escape liability on it if he sees fit to do so. Until he does, the contract is a valid and subsisting relation, with which the actor is not permitted to interfere improperly. Thus, by reason of the statute of frauds, formal defects, lack of mutuality, infancy, unconscionable provisions, conditions precedent to the obligation or even uncertainty of particular terms, the third person may be in a position to avoid liability for any breach. The defendant actor is not, however, for that reason free to interfere with performance of the contract before it is avoided.

g. Contracts terminable at will. A similar situation exists with a contract that, by its terms or otherwise, permits the third person to terminate the agreement at will. Until he has so terminated it, the contract is valid and subsisting, and the defendant may not improperly interfere with it. The fact that the contract is terminable at will, however, is to be taken into account in determining the damages that the plaintiff has suffered by reason of its breach. (See § 774A).

One's interest in a contract terminable at will is primarily an interest in future relations between the parties, and he has no legal assurance of them. For this reason, an interference with this interest is closely analogous to interference with prospective contractual relations. (See § 766B). If the defendant was a competitor regarding the business involved in the contract, his interference with the contract may be not improper. (See § 768, especially Comment *i*).

h. Inducing or otherwise causing. The word "inducing" refers to the situations in which A causes B to choose one course of conduct rather than another. Whether A causes the choice by persuasion or by intimidation, B is free to choose the other course if he is willing to suffer the consequences. Inducement operates on the mind of the person induced. The phrase "otherwise causing" refers to the situations in which A leaves B no choice, as, for example, when A imprisons or commits such a battery upon B that he cannot perform his contract with C, or when A destroys the goods that B is about to deliver to C. This is also the case when performance by B of his contract with C necessarily depends upon the prior performance by A of his contract with B and A fails to perform in order to disable B from performing for C. The rule stated in this Section applies to any intentional causation whether by inducement or otherwise. The essential thing is the intent to cause the result. If the actor does not have this intent, his conduct does not subject him to liability under this rule even if it has the unintended effect of deterring the third person from dealing with the other. (On purpose and intent, see Comment *j*).

i.   Actor's knowledge of other's contract. To be subject to liability under the rule stated in this Section, the actor must have knowledge of the contract with which he is interfering and of the fact that he is interfering with the performance of the contract. Although the actor's conduct is in fact the cause of another's failure to perform a contract, the actor does not induce or otherwise intentionally cause that failure if he has no knowledge of the contract. But it is not necessary that the actor appreciate the legal significance of the facts giving rise to the contractual duty, at least in the case of an express contract. If he knows those facts, he is subject to liability even though he is mistaken as to their legal significance and believes that the agreement is not legally binding or has a different legal effect from what it is judicially held to have.

j.   Intent and purpose. The rule stated in this Section is applicable if the actor acts for the primary purpose of interfering with the performance of the contract, and also if he desires to interfere, even though he acts for some other purpose in addition. The rule is broader, however, in its application than to cases in which the defendant has acted with this purpose or desire. It applies also to intentional interference, as that term is defined in § 8A, in which the actor does not act for the purpose of interfering with the contract or desire it but knows that the interference is certain or substantially certain to occur as a result of his action. The rule applies, in other words, to an interference that is incidental to the actor's independent purpose and desire but known to him to be a necessary consequence of his action.

The fact that this interference with the other's contract was not desired and was purely incidental in character is, however, a factor to be considered in determining whether the interference is improper. If the actor is not acting criminally nor with fraud or violence or other means wrongful in themselves but is endeavoring to advance some interest of his own, the fact that he is aware that he will cause interference with the plaintiff's contract may be regarded as such a minor and incidental consequence and so far removed from the defendant's objective that as against the plaintiff the interference may be found to be not improper. (See § 767, especially Comment *d*).

k.   Means of interference. There is no technical requirement as to the kind of conduct that may result in interference with the third party's performance of the contract. The interference is often by inducement. The inducement may be any conduct conveying to the third person the actor's desire to influence him not to deal with the other. Thus it may be a simple request or persuasion exerting only moral pressure. Or it may be a statement unaccompanied by any specific request but having the same effect as if the request were specifically made. Or it may be a threat by the actor of physical or economic harm to the third person or to persons in whose welfare he is interested. Or it may be the promise of a benefit to the third person if he will refrain from dealing with the other.

On the other hand, it is not necessary to show that the third party was induced to break the contract. Interference with the third party's performance may be by prevention of the performance, as by physical force, by depriving him of the means of performance or by misdirecting the performance, as by giving him the wrong orders or information.

l.   Inducement by refusal to deal. A refusal to deal is one means by which a person may induce another to commit a breach of his contract with a third person. Thus A may induce B to break his contract with C by threatening not to enter into, or to sever, business relations with B unless B does break the contract. This situation frequently presents a nice question of fact. While, under the rule stated in this Section, A may not, without some justification induce B to break his contract with C, A is ordinarily free to refuse to deal with B for any reason or no reason. The difficult question of fact presented in this situation is whether A is merely exercising his freedom to select the persons with whom he will do business or is inducing B not to perform his contract with C. That freedom is not restricted by the relationship between B and C; and A's aversion to C is as legitimate a reason for his refusal to deal with B as his aversion to B. If he is merely exercising that freedom, he is not liable to C for the harm caused by B's choice not to lose A's business for the sake of getting C's.

On the other hand, if A, instead of merely refusing to deal with B and leaving B to make his own decision on what to do about it, goes further and uses his own refusal to deal or the threat of it as a means of affirmative inducement, compulsion or pressure to make B break his contract with C, he may be acting improperly and subject to liability under the rule stated in this Section.

Illustrations:

1.   Upon hearing of B's contract with C, A ceases to buy from B. When asked by B to explain his conduct, A replies that his reason is B's contract with C. Thereupon B breaks his contract with C in order to regain A's business. A has not induced the breach and is not subject to liability to C under the rule stated in this Section.

2.   Upon hearing of B's contract with C, A writes to B as follows: "I cannot tolerate your contract with C. You must call it off. I am sure that our continued relations will more than compensate you for any payment you may have to make to C. If you do not advise me within ten days that your contract with C is at an end, you may never expect further business

from me." Thereupon B breaks his contract with C. A has induced the breach and is subject to liability under the rule stated in this Section.

m.   Inducement by offer of better terms. Another method of inducing B to sever his business relations with C is to offer B a better bargain than that which he has with C. Here, as in the situation dealt with in Comment *l*, a nice question of fact is presented. A's freedom to conduct his business in the usual manner, to advertise his goods, to extol their qualities, to fix their prices and to sell them is not restricted by the fact that B has agreed to buy similar goods from C. Even though A knows of B's contract with C, he may nevertheless send his regular advertising to B and may solicit business in normal course. This conduct does not constitute inducement of breach of the contract. The illustration below is a case of solicitation that does constitute inducement.

Illustration:

3.   A writes to B: "I know you are under contract to buy these goods from C. Therefore I offer you a special price way below my cost. If you accept this offer, you can break your contract with C, pay him something in settlement and still make money. I am confident that you will find it more satisfactory to deal with me than with C." As a result of this letter, B breaks his contract with C. A has induced the breach.

n.   Making agreement with knowledge of the breach. One does not induce another to commit a breach of contract with a third person under the rule stated in this Section when he merely enters into an agreement with the other with knowledge that the other cannot perform both it and his contract with the third person. (Compare Comment *m*). For instance, B is under contract to sell certain goods to C. He offers to sell them to A, who knows of the contract. A accepts the offer and receives the goods. A has not induced the breach and is not subject to liability under the rule stated in this Section. In some cases, however, B may be enjoined at the suit of C from performing for A, or B may be compelled specifically to perform the contract with C. (On the normal availability of injunctive relief, see Comment *u*). In some cases, too, as in the case of a contract for the sale of land, the purchaser acquires an equitable interest good against subsequent transferees of the vendor who are not bona fide purchasers. The rules relating to the protection of this interest against subsequent transferees are not within the scope of this Restatement.

o.   Causation. The question whether the actor's conduct caused the third person to break his contract with the other raises an issue of fact. The reasonableness of the claimed reaction of the third person to the actor's conduct is material evidence on this issue, but it is not conclusive. Thus the fact that only a coward or a fool would have been influenced by the defendant's conduct is evidence that may warrant a finding that the third person was not in fact influenced by it. On the other hand, if other evidence establishes that the actor did in fact induce the third person's conduct, the actor is liable even though the third person was cowardly or foolish or otherwise unreasonable in permitting himself to be so influenced and is himself liable for his own misconduct. (See §§ 546–548).

p.   *The person protected.* The person protected by the rule stated in this Section is the specified person with whom the third person had a contract that the actor caused him not to perform. To subject the actor to liability under this rule, his conduct must be intended to affect the contract of a specific person. It is not enough that one has been prevented from obtaining performance of a contract as a result of the actor's conduct. (Cf. § 766A). Thus, if A induces B to break a contract with C, persons other than C who may be harmed by the action as, for example, his employees or suppliers, are not within the scope of the protection afforded by this rule, unless A intends to affect them. Even then they may not be able to recover unless A acted for the purpose of interfering with their contracts. (See § 767, Comment *h*). The rule does not require, however, that the person who loses the performance of the contract as a result of the conduct of the actor should be specifically mentioned by name. It is sufficient that he is identified in some manner,— that he is the person intended by the actor and understood by those whom the actor seeks to induce. Thus inducement to break a contract to purchase an identified brand of cigarettes, "Saspan," may subject the inducer to liability to the commercial source identified by that trade symbol, the "Russo–Germanic Alliance Co.," but not to other distributors who sell the product.

In some cases the expression of one's general opinions or advice may cause persons not to perform their contracts with another. Thus a prominent person's opinion that economic opportunities are greater in the West than in the East and his advice to young men in general that they "go West" may cause some young man to leave an existing employment in breach of his contract and seek new fortune in the West. Again a person's lecture on the perils of eating meat may cause another to break his contract and cease buying meat from his butcher; or in a public lecture or private conversation, one may persuade others not to buy foreign or union made goods. The rule stated in this Section does not afford protection against harm thus caused. Only when the actor's conduct is intended to affect a specific person is the actor subject to liability under this rule.

q.   *Persons intended to be induced.* When inducement of a breach of contract is involved, the situation is ordinarily one in which a single person is induced to commit a breach of a single contract. However, the situation may be one in which many persons are induced to act. Thus a boycott campaign may be intended to induce numerous persons to break their contracts with the plaintiff.

r.   *Ill will.* Ill will on the part of the actor toward the person harmed is not an essential condition of liability under the rule stated in this Section. He may be liable even when he acts with no desire to harm the other. But the freedom to act in the manner stated in this Section may depend in large measure on the purposes of his conduct. Although the actor is acting for the purpose of advancing an interest of his own, that interest may not be of sufficient importance to make his interference one that is not improper and avoid liability. Satisfying one's spite or ill will is not an adequate basis to justify an interference and keep it from being improper. The presence or absence of ill will toward the person harmed may clarify the purposes of the actor's conduct and may be, accordingly, an important factor in determining whether the interference was improper.

s.   *"Malice."* There are frequent expressions in judicial opinions that "malice" is requisite for liability in the cases treated in this Section. But the context and the course of the decisions make it clear that what is meant is not malice in the sense of ill will but merely "intentional interference without justification." Malicious conduct may be an obvious type of this interference, but it is only one of several types. Compare Introductory Note to Chapter 29 (Wrongful Prosecution of Criminal Proceedings). If the plaintiff is required to show malicious interference in this latter sense, however, it is sometimes held to impose upon him the burden of alleging and proving "lack of justification." (See § 767, Comment *k*).

t.   *Damages.* On the elements of damages, see § 774A. The cause of action is for pecuniary loss resulting from the interference. Recovery may be had also for consequential harms for which the interference was a legal cause. (See § 774A).

u.   *Equitable relief.* In appropriate circumstances under the general rules relating to equitable relief (see §§ 933–951), one may be enjoined from conduct that would subject him to liability under the rule stated in this section.

v.   *Relation to action for breach of contract.* The fact that the plaintiff has an available action for breach of contract against the third person does not prevent him from maintaining an action under the rule stated in this Section against the person who has induced or otherwise caused the breach. The two are both wrongdoers, and each is liable to the plaintiff for the harm caused to him by the loss of the benefits of the contract. (Compare § 875). Even a judgment obtained against the third person for the breach of contract will not bar the action under this Section so long as the judgment is not satisfied. Payments made by the third person in settlement of the claim against him must, however, be credited against the liability for causing the breach and so go to reduce the damages for the tort. (See § 774A(2)).

§ 766A   Intentional Interference with Another's Performance of His Own Contract

One who intentionally and improperly interferes with the performance of a contract (except a contract to marry) between another and a third person, by preventing the other from performing the contract or causing his performance to be more expensive or burdensome, is subject to liability to the other for the pecuniary loss resulting to him.

Comment:

a.   Cross-references. See the Special Note to this Chapter, immediately preceding § 766. In order for the actor to be held liable, this Section requires that his interference be improper. The factors of importance in determining this issue are stated and explained in § 767, which must be read closely with this Section. Sections 768–773 deal with special situations in which application of these factors has produced more clearly identifiable decisional patterns.

This Section uses the expression, "subject to liability," as defined in § 5, meaning that the actor is liable if his conduct was a legal cause of the interference and he has no defense to the action.

This Section is concerned only with the actor's intentional interference with the plaintiff's performance of his own contract, either by preventing that performance or making it more expensive or burdensome. It is to be contrasted with § 766, which states the rule for the actor's intentional interference with a third person's performance of his existing contract with the plaintiff. The rule for the actor's intentional interference with the plaintiff's prospective contractual relations not yet reduced to contract is stated in § 766B. The rule for negligent interference with either a contract or a prospective contractual relation is stated in § 766C.

b.   Historical development. The tort of intentional interference with business relations developed first in the form of interference with prospective advantage. The steps in this development are described in § 766B, Comment *b*. In 1853, with the decision of Lumley v. Gye, 2 El. & Bl. 216, 118 Eng.Rep. 749, liability was extended to inducing a third party to break his existing contract with the plaintiff, even though the means of inducement was not otherwise tortious. See the exposition in § 766, Comment *c*. Later cases extended this latter form of the tort beyond inducing a party to break a contract—meaning persuading him by operating on his mind and thus causing him to choose to break the contract—to causing him not to perform the contract by preventing his performance by some means other than influencing his mental choice. (See § 766, Comment *h*). The form of the tort stated in this Section is similar to this last development, except that the conduct preventing the performance operates on the injured party himself, rather than the third person. No single case has been identified as constituting the origin of this form of the tort, but it is now consistently recognized.

c.   Rationale. This Section and § 766 both involve interference with an existing contract. Under § 766, the plaintiff's interest in obtaining performance of the contract is interfered with directly. Under this Section the interference is indirect, in that the plaintiff is unable to obtain performance of the contract by the third person because he has been prevented from performing his part of the contract and thus from assuring himself of receiving the performance by the third person. But the interference with receiving the benefits of obtaining the performance is just as real as in a case coming under § 766.

The next logical step has also been taken. If the plaintiff's performance has intentionally been made more burdensome or more expensive by the actor, the cost that he incurs in order to obtain the performance by the third party has increased, and the net benefit from the third person's performance has been correspondingly diminished. This Section covers that loss, too.

d.   *Kinds of contracts.* If an agreement is void or illegal or against public policy, this Section does not apply. (See § 774). It does apply, however, to voidable contracts or contracts terminable at will. The discussion in § 766, Comments *f* and *g* has application here.

e.   *Intent and purpose.* The intent required for this Section is that defined in § 8A. The interference with the other's performance of his contract is intentional if the actor desires to bring it about or if he knows that the interference is certain or substantially certain to occur as a result of his action. (See § 766, Comment *j*).

The interference, however, must also be improper. The factors to be considered in determining whether an interference is improper are stated in § 767. One of them is the actor's motive and another is the interest sought to be advanced by him. Together these factors mean that the actor's purpose is of substantial significance. If he had no desire to effectuate the interference by his action but knew that it would be a mere incidental result of conduct he was engaging in for another purpose, the interference may be found to be not improper. Other factors come into play here, however, particularly the nature of the actor's conduct. If the means used is innately wrongful, predatory in character, a purpose to produce the interference may not be necessary. Again, if the sole purpose of the actor is to vent his ill will, the interference may be improper although the means are less blameworthy. For a more complete treatment see § 767, especially Comment *d*.

f.   *Malice and ill will.* On this, see § 766, Comments *r* and *s*.

g.   *Means of interference.* One may be prevented from performing his contract in numerous ways. Thus he may be physically restrained or intimidated or be excluded from the place where the contract must be performed or be deprived of the necessary equipment or labor. Other means of interfering with a contract by affecting the third party are treated in § 766, Comments *h, i, k, l* and *m*. They have application here. It is also sufficient that the performance of the contract to which the plaintiff is obligated is made more expensive to him, so that he loses all or part of the profits that he would otherwise have obtained, or is subjected to a financial loss. Thus if the plaintiff is under a contract to keep a highway in repair, a defendant who intentionally inflicts additional expense upon him by damaging the highway is subject to liability under this Section.

h.   *Causation.* On this, see § 766, Comment *o*.

i.   Damages and equitable relief. On these, see § 766, Comments *t* and *u.*

§ 766B   Intentional Interference with Prospective Contractual Relation

One who intentionally and improperly interferes with another's prospective contractual relation (except a contract to marry) is subject to liability to the other for the pecuniary harm resulting from loss of the benefits of the relation, whether the interference consists of

(a) inducing or otherwise causing a third person not to enter into or continue the prospective relation or

(b) preventing the other from acquiring or continuing the prospective relation.

Comment:

a.   Cross-references. See the Special Note to this Chapter, immediately preceding § 766. In order for the actor to be held liable, this Section requires that his interference be improper. The factors of importance in determining this issue are stated and explained in § 767, which must be read closely with this Section. In addition, § 768 deals specifically with the question of an interference by a competitor with a prospective contractual relation and when it is improper; it, too, must be read closely with this Section. Sections 769–773 deal with special situations in which application of these factors has produced more clearly identifiable decisional patterns.

This Section uses the expression, "subject to liability," as defined in § 5, meaning that the actor is liable if his conduct was a legal cause of the interference and he has no defense to the action.

This Section is concerned only with intentional interference with prospective contractual relations, not yet reduced to contract. The rule for the actor's intentional interference with a third person's performance of his existing contract with the plaintiff is stated in § 766. The rule for the actor's intentional interference with the plaintiff's performance of his own contract with a third person is stated in § 766A. The rule for negligent interference with either a contract or prospective contractual relations is stated in § 766C.

One other Section dealing with interference with prospective pecuniary benefit is closely related to this Section. It is § 774B, which concerns intentional interference with a legacy or gift.

b.   Historical development and rationale. As early as 1621 the court of King's Bench held one liable to another in an action on the case for interfering with his prospective contracts by threatening to "mayhem and vex with suits" those who worked for or bought from him, "whereby they durst not work or buy." Garrett v. Taylor, Cro.Jac. 567, 79 Eng.Rep. 485. In 1793, the same court held one similarly liable who shot at some African natives in order to prevent them from trading with the plaintiff until the debts claimed by the defendant were paid. Tarleton v. McGawley, Peake N.P. 205, 170 Eng.Rep. 153. Precedent for these decisions is found as early as the fifteenth century, and even earlier. Thus in 1410 it was said that "if the comers to my market are disturbed or beaten, by which I lose my toll, I shall have a good action of trespass on the case." 11 Hen. IV 47; see also (1356) 29 Edw. III 18. An action for threatening plaintiff's tenants in life and limb "so that they departed from their tenures to the plaintiff's damage" was not uncommon, and there was a special writ adapted to this complaint. See (1494) 9 Hen. VII 7, and Reg.Brev. III—quare tenentibus de vita et mutilatione membrorum suorum comminatus. In Keeble v. Hickeringill, (1706) 11 East 574, 103 Eng.Rep. 127, Holt, C.J., explains the "reason" and "principle" upon which liability in these cases was based and illustrates the application of the rule to a variety of situations.

In another line of cases liability was imposed upon one who diverted another's business by fraudulently palming off his own goods as those of the other, or by infringing another's trade mark or trade name. Liability was later extended to cases in which the diversion of business was accomplished by fraudulent misrepresentations of different types. Again, in an independent development, liability was imposed for loss of business caused by defamation of another in his business or profession or by disparagement of his goods. (See §§ 623A–629).

In all of these cases liability was imposed for interference with business expectancies and was not limited to interference with existing contracts; but in all of them the actor's conduct was characterized by violence, fraud or defamation, and was tortious in character.

In 1853 the decision in Lumley v. Gye, 2 El. & Bl. 216, 118 Eng.Rep. 749, which involved inducement of the breach of an existing contract, imposed liability when the means of inducement were not tortious in themselves, and it was the intentional interference with the relation that was the basis of liability. (See § 766, Comment b). Later English decisions, and notably Temperton v. Russell, [1893] 1 Q.B. 715, extended the same principle to interference with business relations that are merely prospective and potential.

c.   *Type of relation.* The relations protected against intentional interference by the rule stated in this Section include any prospective contractual relations, except those leading to contracts to marry (see § 698), if the potential contract would be of pecuniary value to the plaintiff. Included are interferences with the prospect of obtaining employment or employees, the opportunity of selling or buying land or chattels or services, and any other relations leading to potentially profitable contracts. Interference with the exercise by a third party of an option to renew or extend a contract with the plaintiff is also included. Also included is interference with a continuing business or other customary relationship not amounting to a formal contract. In many respects, a contract terminable at will is closely analogous to the relationship covered by this Section. (See § 766, Comment *g* and § 768, Comment *i*).

The expression, prospective contractual relation, is not used in this Section in a strict, technical sense. It is not necessary that the prospective relation be expected to be reduced to a formal, binding contract. It may include prospective quasi-contractual or other restitutionary rights or even the voluntary conferring of commercial benefits in recognition of a moral obligation.

On interference with noncommercial expectancies involving pecuniary loss, see § 774B and the Special Note following it. Of course, interference with personal, social and political relations is not covered in either Section.

    d. Intent and purpose. The intent required for this Section is that defined in § 8A. The interference with the other's prospective contractual relation is intentional if the actor desires to bring it about or if he knows that the interference is certain or substantially certain to occur as a result of his action. (See § 766, Comment *j*).

The interference, however, must also be improper. The factors to be considered in determining whether an interference is improper are stated in § 767. One of them is the actor's motive and another is the interest sought to be advanced by him. Together these factors mean that the actor's purpose is of substantial significance. If he had no desire to effectuate the interference by his action but knew that it would be a mere incidental result of conduct he was engaging in for another purpose, the interference may be found to be not improper. Other factors come into play here, however, particularly the nature of the actor's conduct. If the means used is innately wrongful, predatory in character, a purpose to produce the interference may not be necessary. On the other hand, if the sole purpose of the actor is to vent his ill will, the interference may be improper although the means are less blameworthy. For a more complete treatment see § 767, especially Comment *d*.

    e. Inducing or otherwise causing. The cause of action arising under the rule stated in this Section closely parallels that covered by § 766, and Comments *h, k, l* and *m* under that Section are applicable here so far as they are pertinent. The fact that the interference is not with a subsisting contract but only with a prospective relation not yet reduced to contract form is, however, important in determining whether the actor was acting properly in pursuing his own purposes. (See §§ 767 and 768). If the means of interference is itself tortious, as in the case of defamation, injurious falsehood, fraud, violence or threats, there is no greater justification to interfere with prospective relations than with existing contracts; but when the means adopted is not innately wrongful and it is only the resulting interference that is in question as a basis of liability, the interference is more likely to be found to be not improper.

    f. Malice and ill will. On this, see § 766, Comments *r* and *s*.

g.   Damages and equitable relief. On these, see § 766, Comments *t* and *u.*

§ 766C   Negligent Interference with Contract or Prospective Contractual Relation

One is not liable to another for pecuniary harm not deriving from physical harm to the other, if that harm results from the actor's negligently

(a)   causing a third person not to perform a contract with the other, or

(b)   interfering with the other's performance of his contract or making the performance more expensive or burdensome, or

(c)   interfering with the other's acquiring a contractual relation with a third person.

Comment:

a.   Liability for interference with contracts and prospective contractual relations developed in the field of intentional torts. Sections 766, 766A and 766B all involve intentional torts. Thus far there has been no general recognition of any liability for a negligent interference, whether it is interference with a third person's performance of his contract with the plaintiff (cf. § 766), with the plaintiff's performance of his own contract (cf. § 766A) or with the plaintiff's acquisition of prospective contractual relations. (Cf. § 766B). The explanation usually given by the courts, when one is given at all, is that the harm is too "remote" for negligence liability and that the defendant's conduct is not the "proximate cause." In most of the cases in which recovery has been denied, the defendant has had no knowledge of the contract or prospective relation and no reason to foresee any harm to the plaintiff's interests; and the decision sometimes has been explained under the rule as to unforeseeable plaintiffs stated in § 281. It seems more likely, however, that it is the character of the contract or prospective interest itself that has led the courts to refuse to give it protection against negligent interference. They apparently have been influenced by the extremely variable nature of the relations, the fear of an undue burden upon the defendant's freedom of action, the probable disproportion between the large damages that might be recovered and the extent of the defendant's fault, and perhaps in some cases the difficulty of determining whether the interference has in fact resulted from the negligent conduct. Whatever the reason may be, there is as yet no general recognition of liability for negligent interference with an existing contract or with a prospective contractual relation, although a number of cases, scattered through the years, have held that liability should be imposed.

Illustrations:

1.   A has contracted to tow a barge owned by B between two ports. Before the contract can be performed, C negligently sinks the barge, and

A is prevented from towing it and so deprived of the profit to be made out of the towage fees. C is not liable to A.

2. A has insured a barge owned by B against loss. C negligently sinks the barge, making A liable to B under the terms of the insurance policy. Except as to any subrogation rights, C is not liable to A.

3. A is under contract with a county to maintain a bridge and keep it in repair. B, negligently driving a truck, damages the bridge and A suffers pecuniary loss in performing his contract by repairing the bridge. B is not liable to A.

4. A contracts with a telephone company for the insertion of A's business advertisement in its telephone directory. Through the negligence of B, who prints the directory for the company, the advertisement is omitted and as a result A suffers pecuniary loss. B is not liable to A for tortiously interfering with contractual relations.

b. *Physical harm to the other.* The rule stated in this Section applies when the plaintiff suffers only pecuniary loss, such as the loss of the financial benefits of a contract or of prospective trade or financial loss through being put to additional expense. If there is physical harm to the person or land or chattels of the plaintiff, the rule stated in this Section does not apply and there may be recovery for negligence that results in physical harm because of the nonperformance of a contract with the plaintiff. (Cf. §§ 435B, 499). This recovery is of course subject to the usual rules governing liability for negligence. When recovery is allowed, the loss of expected profits or other pecuniary loss may, in an appropriate case, be recovered as "parasitic" compensatory damages.

Illustration:

5. A is engaged in the business of producing and selling mushrooms. Under a contract with B Power Company, he is supplied with electric power to keep his mushroom cellars at a uniform temperature. C, installing a pole for a telephone line near the power line of B Company, negligently allows the pole to fall on the power line and break it. Before the line can be repaired, A's mushrooms are killed by freezing. In an action for harm to the mushrooms, C is subject to liability to A for their value, and also for pecuniary loss to A's business, if the loss is proved with reasonable certainty.

c. *Relationship of principal and agent.* On liability to a principal for loss of services caused by negligent infliction of bodily harm to an agent, see Restatement, Second, Agency § 316(2), including the caveat referring to the relationship of master and servant.

d. *Recklessness.* This Restatement recognizes a form of tortious conduct, called reckless disregard for safety, lying in between negligence and intentional infliction of injury. (See § 500). It is confined, however, to reckless disregard of physical safety of another, and there is little reason to anticipate that the courts will develop a category of reckless disregard for pecuniary loss to another from conduct interfering with his contractual relations and impose liability for it when it would not be imposed for negligent interference.

e.   Duty of care to prevent pecuniary loss. Outside the scope of this Section are certain cases in which the actor renders a service or has some other contractual relationship in which he owes a duty to use reasonable care to avoid a risk of pecuniary loss to the person with whom he is directly dealing, and that same duty is held to extend to another person whom he knows to be pecuniarily affected by the service rendered. Most of the cases coming within this category are covered by § 552, involving information negligently supplied for the guidance of others. Other cases, involving other services than the supplying of information, may not fall within the exact provisions of § 552 but are covered by the general principle underlying it. Representative cases include the attorney who negligently prepares an invalid will and is held liable to the intended beneficiary, the telegraph company that negligently transmits a message and is held liable for pecuniary loss caused to the addressee and the surveyor who negligently surveys a tract of land for the vendor and is held liable for pecuniary loss caused to the vendee. In all of these cases the defendant may be liable for a breach of duty of care that he owes to the plaintiff as such, and the cases do not fall within the scope of this Section.

§ 767   Factors in Determining Whether Interference is Improper

In determining whether an actor's conduct in intentionally interfering with a contract or a prospective contractual relation of another is improper or not, consideration is given to the following factors:

(a)   the nature of the actor's conduct,

(b)   the actor's motive,

(c)   the interests of the other with which the actor's conduct interferes,

(d)   the interests sought to be advanced by the actor,

(e)   the social interests in protecting the freedom of action of the actor and the contractual interests of the other,

(f)   the proximity or remoteness of the actor's conduct to the interference and

(g)   the relations between the parties.

Comment:

a.   Significance of section. The tort of interference with existing or prospective contractual relations includes interference with an existing contract either by causing a third party not to perform his contract with the plaintiff (as in § 766) or by preventing the plaintiff from performing his own contract or making that performance more expensive or burdensome (as in § 766A); it also includes interference with prospective contractual relationships (as in § 766B). In each of these forms there is a requirement that the interference be both intentional and improper. See the Special Note to this Chapter, treating the basis of liability for the tort of interference and the terminology used in this Chapter, located immediately preceding § 766.

This Section applies to each form of the tort as stated in §§ 766–766B and indicates the factors to be taken into consideration in determining whether the interference is improper or not, through an appraisal of the several factors and an evaluation of their comparative weight. In the three forms of the tort, the weight carried by these factors may vary considerably and the determination of whether the interference is improper may also vary; but the listed factors are nevertheless important in each form. It is in the application of this Section that the most frequent and difficult problems of the tort of interference with a contract or prospective contractual relation arise.

Section 768, following this Section, deals specifically with the question of whether competition is a proper or improper interference with contractual relations, either existing or prospective. Sections 769–773 deal with other special situations in which application of the factors enumerated in this Section have produced more clearly identifiable decisional patterns. The specific applications in these Sections therefore supplant the generalization expressed in this Section.

b.   Privilege to interfere, or interference not improper. Unlike other intentional torts such as intentional injury to person or property, or defamation, this branch of tort law has not developed a crystallized set of definite rules as to the existence or non-existence of a privilege to act in the manner stated in §§ 766, 766A or 766B. Because of this fact, this Section is expressed in terms of whether the interference is improper or not, rather than in terms of whether there was a specific privilege to act in the manner specified. The issue in each case is whether the interference is improper or not under the circumstances; whether, upon a consideration of the relative significance of the factors involved, the conduct should be permitted without liability, despite its effect of harm to another. The decision therefore depends upon a judgment and choice of values in each situation. This Section states the important factors to be weighed against each other and balanced in arriving at a judgment; but it does not exhaust the list of possible factors. The comments in the Section deal with the significance of each of the listed factors.

Since the determination of whether an interference is improper is under the particular circumstances, it is an evaluation of these factors for the precise facts of the case before the court; and, as in the determination of whether conduct is negligent, it is usually not controlling in another factual situation. On the other hand, factual patterns develop and judicial decisions regarding them also develop patterns for holdings that begin to evolve crystallized privileges or rules defining conduct that is not improper. The rules stated in §§ 768–774 shows the results of the balancing process in some specific situations that have been the subject of judicial decision; but they do not constitute an exhaustive list of situations in which it has been determined that an intentional interference with contractual relations is not improper.

Ambiguity as to the scope of the privileges available for the tort of intentional interference with an existing or prospective contractual relation has meant that at least some of the factors listed in this Section are sometimes treated as going to the culpability of the actor's conduct in the beginning, rather than to the determination of whether his conduct was justifiable as an affirmative defense. This bears on the issues of whose responsibility it is to raise the question of culpability or justification—that is, whether the interference was improper or not—in the pleadings and who has the burden of proof in the sense of the risk of nonpersuasion. Justification is generally treated as a matter of defense, but not always in the tort of interference with contractual relations. Thus a court that calls the tort "malicious interference" and defines this as interference without justification, often decides that it is a part of the plaintiff's case to plead and prove lack of justification. (See § 766, Comment s). A plaintiff is therefore well advised, when the matter is unclear, to include in suitable form in his complaint the allegation that the interference is improper and not justified. On the other hand, even though the particular matter may be held to be one of defense, the complaint may itself show that a defense is applicable and thus not stand against a demurrer or motion to dismiss.

Comment on Clause (a):

c. *Nature of actor's conduct.* The nature of the actor's conduct is a chief factor in determining whether the conduct is improper or not, despite its harm to the other person. The variety of means by which the actor may cause the harm are stated in § 766, Comments k to n. Some of them, like fraud and physical violence, are tortious to the person immediately affected by them; others, like persuasion and offers of benefits, are not tortious to him. Under the same circumstances interference by some means is not improper while interference by other means is improper; and, likewise, the same means may be permissible under some circumstances while wrongful in others. The issue is not simply whether the actor is justified in causing the harm, but rather whether he is justified in causing it in the manner in which he does cause it. The propriety of the means is not, however, determined as a separate issue unrelated to the other factors. On the contrary, the propriety is determined in the light of all the factors present. Thus physical violence, fraudulent misrepresentation and threats of illegal conduct are ordinarily wrongful means and subject their user to liability even though he is free to accomplish the same result by more suitable means. A, C's competitor for B's business, may justifiably induce B by permissible means not to buy from C (see § 768); he is not justified in doing so by the predatory means stated above. Yet even these means are not always forbidden. The relation between the actor and the person induced, and the object sought to be accomplished by the actor, may be such as to warrant even physical violence. For example, C operates a gambling den in the rear room of his ice cream parlor. B's parent, A, having the privilege of corporal punishment, may exercise that privilege in order to cause B not to patronize C's ice cream parlor. This may also be the case between an institution and its inmates. The nature of the means is, however, only one factor in determining whether the interference is improper. Under some circumstances the interference is improper even though innocent means are employed.

Physical violence. Threats of physical violence were the means employed in the very early instances of liability for intentional interference with economic relations; and interference by physical violence is ordinarily improper. The clearest example is the case in which the violence exerted or threatened is violence to the person sought to be induced and is actionable by him. The actor is subject to liability also when the third person is threatened with physical violence to his children or other persons in whom he is interested, or to property in which he is interested. And the actor is subject to liability whether the violence is actually exerted or is threatened imminently or in the future. The issue is simply whether the actor induces the third person's conduct or prevents the injured party's performance of his own contract by putting him in fear of physical violence.

Misrepresentations. Fraudulent misrepresentations are also ordinarily a wrongful means of interference and make an interference improper. A representation is fraudulent when, to the knowledge or belief of its utterer, it is false in the sense in which it is intended to be understood by its recipient. (See § 527). In some circumstances one who is liable to another for intentional interference with economic relations by inducing a third person by fraudulent misrepresentation not to do business with the other may also be liable under other rules of the law of torts. Thus if the representation is also defamatory of the other, the actor may be liable under the rules relating to defamation. (See §§ 558–581). Or, if the representation disparages the other's goods, the actor may be liable under the rules relating to injurious falsehood. (See §§ 624–652). Or, if the representation seeks to pass off the actor's goods for those of the other, the actor may be liable under the rules relating to fraudulent marketing. Or the misrepresentation may subject the actor to liability for false advertising. The tort of intentional interference thus overlaps other torts. But it is not coincident with them. One may be subject to liability for intentional interference even when his fraudulent representation is not of such a character as to subject him to liability for the other torts. And, on the other hand, one may be liable for the other torts as for a defamatory statement negligently believed by him to be true, without being liable for intentional interference because of his good faith.

Prosecution of civil suits. In a very early instance of liability for intentional interference, the means of inducement employed were threats of "mayhem and suits," and both types of threats were deemed tortious. Litigation and the threat of litigation are powerful weapons. When wrongfully instituted, litigation entails harmful consequences to the public interest in judicial administration as well as to the actor's adversaries. The use of these weapons of inducement is ordinarily wrongful if the actor has no belief in the merit of the litigation or if, though having some belief in its merit, he nevertheless institutes or threatens to institute the litigation in bad faith, intending only to harass the third parties and not to bring his claim to definitive adjudication. (See §§ 674–681B). A typical example of this situation is the case in which the actor threatens the other's prospective customers with suit for the infringement of his patent and either does not believe in the merit of his claim or is determined not to risk an unfavorable judgment and to rely for protection upon the force of his threats and harassment.

Criminal suits. Threats of criminal prosecutions, even more than threats of civil suits, enlist the powers of government on the side of the actor and prejudice the public interest in public administration as well as unduly influence the person threatened. (See §§ 653–673). Causing or threatening to cause, in bad faith, the institution of criminal prosecution is ordinarily a wrongful method of interference under the rules stated in §§ 766–766B.

Unlawful conduct. Conduct specifically in violation of statutory provisions or contrary to established public policy may for that reason make an interference improper. This may be true, for example, of conduct that is in violation of antitrust provisions or is in restraint of trade or of conduct that is in violation of statutes, regulations, or judicial or administrative holdings regarding labor relations.

Economic pressure. Economic pressure of various types is a common means of inducing persons not to deal with another, as when A refuses to deal with B if B enters into or continues a relation with C, or when A increases his prices to B or induces D not to deal with B on the same condition. Or the pressure may consist of the refusal to admit B to membership into a trade association or a professional organization, as a medical or legal association. The question whether this pressure is proper is answered in the light of the circumstances in which it is exerted, the object sought to be accomplished by the actor, the degree of coercion involved, the extent of the harm that it threatens, the effect upon the neutral parties drawn into the situation, the effects upon competition, and the general reasonableness and appropriateness of this pressure as a means of accomplishing the actor's objective.

Business ethics and customs. Violation of recognized ethical codes for a particular area of business activity or of established customs or practices regarding disapproved actions or methods may also be significant in evaluating the nature of the actor's conduct as a factor in determining whether his interference with the plaintiff's contractual relations was improper or not.

Other aspects of actor's conduct. It is often important whether the defendant was acting alone or in concert with others to accomplish his purpose. In a case in which other factors are otherwise evenly balanced, less censurable aspects of the actor's conduct may sometimes tip the scales. Thus the manner of presenting an inducement to the third party may be significant. There is an easily recognized difference between (1) A's merely routine mailing to B of an offer to sell merchandise at a reduced price, even though A knows that B is bound by an existing contract to purchase the goods from C, and (2) A's approaching B in person and offering expressly to sell the merchandise at such a low price that B can "pay any costs of getting out of his contract with C and still profit." The question of who was the moving party in the inducement may also be important. A's active solicitation of B's business is more likely to make his interference improper than his mere response to an inquiry from B.

Comment on Clause (b):

d. The actor's motive. Since interference with contractual relations is an intentional tort, it is required that in any action based upon §§ 766, 766A or 766B the injured party must show that the interference with his contractual relations was either desired by the actor or known by him to be a substantially certain result of his conduct. (See § 8A). Intent alone, however, may not be sufficient to make the interference improper, especially when it is supplied by the actor's knowledge that the interference was a necessary consequence of his conduct rather than by his desire to bring it about. In determining whether the interference is improper, it may become very important to ascertain whether the actor was motivated, in whole or in part, by a desire to interfere with the other's contractual relations. If this was the sole motive the interference is almost certain to be held improper. A motive to injure another or to vent one's ill will on him serves no socially useful purpose.

The desire to interfere with the other's contractual relations need not, however, be the sole motive. If it is the primary motive it may carry substantial weight in the balancing process and even if it is only a casual motive it may still be significant in some circumstances. On the other hand, if there is no desire at all to accomplish the interference and it is brought about only as a necessary consequence of the conduct of the actor engaged in for an entirely different purpose, his knowledge of this makes the interference intentional, but the factor of motive carries little weight toward producing a determination that the interference was improper.

Motive as a factor is often closely interwoven with the other factors listed in this Section, so that they cannot be easily separated. There is obviously a very intimate relation between the factors of motive and of the interests that the actor is trying to promote by his conduct. So close is the relationship that the two factors might well be merged into a single one. The basis for the separation in this Section is that the factor of motive is concerned with the issue of whether the actor desired to bring about the interference as the sole or a partial reason for his conduct, while the factor of the actor's interests is concerned with the individual and social value or significance of any interests that he is seeking to promote.

The relation of the factor of motive to that of the nature of the actor's conduct is an illustration of the interplay between factors in reaching a determination of whether the actor's conduct was improper. If the conduct is independently wrongful—as, for example, if it is illegal because it is in restraint of trade or if it is tortious toward the third person whose conduct is influenced—the desire to interfere with the other's contractual relations may be less essential to a holding that the interference is improper. On the other hand, if the means used by the actor are innocent or less blameworthy, the desire to accomplish the interference may be more essential to a holding that the interference is improper.

A similar interplay exists between the factor of motive and that of the proximity of the actor's conduct to the actual interference. If the relationship is direct and immediate, as when A induces B to sell a particular article to him, knowing that B is under contract to sell it to C, it makes no difference that A did not desire to have the contract broken between B and C or that he is quite sorry that this was a necessary consequence of his action. On the other hand, if in the same situation A also knows that C has contracted to sell the chattel to D and that his conduct will also prevent that contract from being carried out, this result is so consequential and indirect that a motive or purpose to accomplish that interference may be necessary to a finding that the interference was improper.

Comment on Clause (c):

e. *The interests of the other with which the actor's conduct interferes.* Some contractual interests receive greater protection than others. Thus, depending upon the relative significance of the other factors, the actor's conduct in interfering with the other's prospective contractual relations with a third party may be held to be not improper, although his interference would be improper if it involved persuading the third party to commit a breach of an existing contract with the other. (See, for example, § 768). The result in the latter case is due in part to the greater definiteness of the other's expectancy and his stronger claim to security for it and in part to the lesser social utility of the actor's conduct. Again, the fact that a contract violates public policy, as, for example, a contract in unreasonable restraint of trade, or that its performance will enable the party complaining of the interference to maintain a condition that shocks the public conscience (see § 774), may justify an inducement of breach that, in the absence of this fact, would be improper. Even with reference to contracts not subject to these objections, however, it may be found to be not improper to induce breach when the inducement is justified by the other factors stated in this Section. (See, for example, § 770).

Comment on Clause (d):

f. *The actor's interest.* The correlative of the interest with which the actor interferes (see Comment *e*) is the interest that his conduct is intended to promote. Both are important in determining whether the interference is improper. And both are to be appraised in the light of the social interests that would be advanced by their protection.

Usually the actor's interest will be economic, seeking to acquire business for himself. An interest of this type is important and will normally prevail over a similar interest of the other if the actor does not use wrongful means. (See § 768). If the interest of the other has been already consolidated into the binding legal obligation of a contract, however, that interest will normally outweigh the actor's own interest in taking that established right from him. Of course, the interest in gratifying one's feeling of ill will toward another carries no weight. Some interests of the actor that do carry weight are depicted in §§ 770–773.

In some cases the actor may be seeking to promote not solely an interest of his own but a public interest. The actor may believe that certain practices used in another's business are prejudicial to the public interest, as, for example, his maintenance of a gambling den in the rear room of his cigar store and in plain sight of his patrons, or his despoiling the environment by polluting a stream or strip-mining an area without restoring the natural conditions, or his racial or sexual discrimination in his employment policy. If the actor causes a third person not to perform a contract or not to enter into or continue a contractual relation with the other in order to protect the public interest affected by these practices, relevant questions in determining whether his interference is improper are: whether the practices are actually being used by the other, whether the actor actually believes that the practices are prejudicial to the public interest, whether his belief is reasonable, whether he is acting in good faith for the protection of the public interest, whether the contractual relation involved is incident or foreign to the continuance of the practices and whether the actor employs wrongful means to accomplish the result.

Comment on Clause (e):

g.   The social interests. Appraisal of the private interests of the persons involved may lead to a stalemate unless the appraisal is enlightened by a consideration of the social utility of these interests. Moreover, the rules stated in §§ 766–766B deal with situations affecting both the existence and the plan of competitive enterprise. The social interest in this enterprise may frequently require the sacrifice of the claims of the individuals to freedom from interference with their pursuit of gain. Thus it is thought that the social interest in competition would be unduly prejudiced if one were to be prohibited from in any manner persuading a competitor's prospective customers not to deal with him. On the other hand, both social and private interests concur in the determination that persuasion only by suitable means is permissible, that predatory means like violence and fraud are neither necessary nor desirable incidents of competition. (See further § 768).

Comment on Clause (f):

h. Proximity or remoteness of actor's conduct to interference. One who induces a third person not to perform his contract with another interferes directly with the other's contractual relation. The interference is an immediate consequence of the conduct, and the other factors need not play as important a role in the determination that the actor's interference was improper. The actor's conduct need not be predatory or independently tortious, for example, and mere knowledge that this consequence is substantially certain to result may be sufficient.

If, however, A induces B to sell certain goods to him and thereby causes him not to perform his contract to supply the goods to C, this may also have the effect of preventing C from performing his contractual obligations to supply them to D and E. C's failure to perform his contracts is a much more indirect and remote consequence of A's conduct than B's breach of his contract with C, even assuming that A was aware of all of the contractual obligations and the interference can be called intentional. This remoteness conduces toward a finding that the interference was not improper. The weight of this factor, however, may be controverted by the factor of motive if it was the actor's primary purpose to interfere with C's obligation to D and E, or perhaps by the factor of the actor's conduct if that conduct was inherently unlawful or independently tortious. Similar results follow in cases in which the person whose contract was the subject of the initial interference has contracts of his own with his employees, his subcontractors or his suppliers, which he is now unable to perform.

Recovery for A's interference with B's obtaining performance of a contract by C by preventing B from performing himself and thus becoming entitled to C's performance may also be affected by this factor. The injury to B is his failure to obtain the benefit of C's performance. That consequence is an indirect one and if it was not a part of A's motivation but a mere incidental result of his conduct and if that conduct was not independently tortious or unlawful, the interference will ordinarily be held not to be improper.

Comment on Clause (g):

i. Relations between the parties. The relation between the parties is often an important factor in determining whether an interference is proper or improper. In a case where A is the actor, B is the injured party and C is the third party influenced by A's conduct, the significant relationship may be between any two of the three parties. Thus A and B may be competitors, and A's conduct in inducing C not to deal with B may be proper, though it would have been improper if he had not been a competitor. (See § 768). Or, if A is C's business advisor, it is proper for him to advise C, in good faith and within the scope of C's request for advice, that it would be to his financial advantage to break his contract with B, while it would be improper if he were a volunteer. (See § 772). Again, it is important whether the relationship between B and C is that of a prospective contract, an existing contract or a contract terminable at will. (See § 768).

j. Determination of whether the actor's conduct is improper or not. The weighing process described in this Section does not necessarily reach the same result in regard to each of the three forms of interference with business relations stated in §§ 766, 766A and 766B. As indicated in Comment *e*, for example, greater protection is given to the interest in an existing contract than to the interest in acquiring prospective contractual relations, and as a result permissible interference is given a broader scope in the latter instance. (See § 768). In some situations the process of weighing the conflicting factors set forth in this Section has already been performed by the courts, and incipient privileges and rules defining conduct as not improper are developing. When this has been accomplished and the scope of the more or less crystallized rule or privilege has been indicated by the decisions, the responsibility in the particular case is simply to apply it to the facts involved; and there is no need to go through the balancing process afresh. Some of the situations in which this development has occurred are stated in §§ 769–773.

When no crystallized pattern is applicable, however, the balancing process must be followed for the individual case. Though consideration must be given to the factors stated in this Section, generalizations utilizing a standard are sometimes offered. Thus, it has been suggested that the real question is whether the actor's conduct was fair and reasonable under the circumstances. Recognized standards of business ethics and business customs and practices are pertinent, and consideration is given to concepts of fair play and whether the defendant's interference is not "sanctioned by the 'rules of the game.' " The determination is whether the actor's interference is "improper" or not. But an attempt to apply these broad, general standards is materially helped by breaking the conflicting elements into the factors stated in this Section.

k. Burden of proof. As indicated previously, particularly in the Special Note to this Chapter, immediately preceding § 766, the intentional tort of interference with contractual relations differs from most other intentional torts, which have rather clearly defined requirements for establishing a prima facie case and for setting up an affirmative defense based upon a privilege. This tort has not fully developed to this stage and some of the factors stated in this Section may be significant in ascertaining whether the actor's conduct is to be regarded as initially wrongful or culpable in nature. This tort is sometimes treated like the tort of negligence, with the result that it is a part of the plaintiff's case to show all of the factors making the defendant's interference improper. This is especially true in jurisdictions where the courts speak of malicious interference and define it as meaning intentional interference without justification. (See Comment *b*).

The result is that there is little consensus on who has the burden of raising the issue of whether the interference was improper or not and subsequently of proving that issue; and it can not be predicted with accuracy what rule will ultimately develop. Instead of laying down a categoric rule for one position or the other, therefore, it seems appropriate to draw a more particularized line depending upon whether the precise matter goes more specially to the culpability of the actor's conduct in general or to its justification under the specific facts. (Cf. § 870). Thus the question of whether the actor was competing with the other for the prospective business of a third person might be treated as a matter of culpability (cf. § 768), for which the burden of pleading and proving would be on the plaintiff, while the question of whether there was a special relation existing between the actor and the third party making it appropriate for the actor to advise freely with the third party might be treated as a matter of justification for which the burden would be on the defendant. (Cf. § 770).

l. Function of court and jury. The jury determines whether the defendant's interference with the plaintiff's advantageous relation was intentional or not. But the cases fail to indicate clearly whether the judge or the jury makes the decision of whether the conduct was improper, or whether the function varies, depending upon the circumstances. In the case of most intentional torts, crystallized privileges have been established; and the court determines the circumstances under which a privilege exists and the jury determines what the actual circumstances are.

A similar approach is usually followed for the tort of interference with contractual relations under circumstances in which a more or less established privilege has been formulated, as indicated, for example, in §§ 770–773. Even under certain other circumstances recurrent factual patterns may have developed, reflecting identifiable standards of business ethics or recognized community customs as to acceptable conduct and leading the court to feel that the determination of whether the interference was improper should be made as a matter of law, similar to negligence per se. (Cf. § 285, Comment *e*). The analogy to negligence continues to hold in the situations where no recognized privilege has been formulated. Here, as with negligence, when there is room for different views, the determination of whether the interference was improper or not is ordinarily left to the jury, to obtain its common feel for the state of community mores and for the manner in which they would operate upon the facts in question.

§ 768 Competition as Proper or Improper Interference

(1) One who intentionally causes a third person not to enter into a prospective contractual relation with another who is his competitor or not to continue an existing contract terminable at will does not interfere improperly with the other's relation if

    (a) the relation concerns a matter involved in the competition between the actor and the other and

    (b) the actor does not employ wrongful means and

(c) his action does not create or continue an unlawful restraint of trade and

(d) his purpose is at least in part to advance his interest in competing with the other.

(2) The fact that one is a competitor of another for the business of a third person does not prevent his causing a breach of an existing contract with the other from being an improper interference if the contract is not terminable at will.

Comment:

a. *In general.* This Section differentiates between interference with an existing contract (see §§ 766, 766A) and interference with a prospective contractual relation. (See § 766B). Under the conditions stated in Clauses (a) through (d) of Subsection (1), competition is not an improper basis for interference in the latter situation. If one party is seeking to acquire a prospective contractual relation, the other can seek to acquire it too. Even an option to renew or extend a contract is prospective while not exercised. But an existing contract, if not terminable at will, involves established interests that are not subject to interference on the basis of competition alone. However, the fact that the actor is not justified on the basis of competition is not conclusive of his liability. His action may be justified for other reasons.

Like § 767, this Section speaks of an interference that is improper or not, rather than of a specific privilege because there is no consensus that engaging in competition is an affirmative defense to be raised and proved by the defendant or is instead simply not improper conduct inconsistent with the American system of free enterprise. In either event the provisions of this Section are applicable. (See § 767, Comments *b* and *k*; and also the Special Note to this Chapter, immediately preceding § 766).

Comment on Subsection (1):

b. *Basis of the rule in this Section.* The rule stated in this Section is a special application of the factors determining whether an interference is improper or not, as stated in § 767. One's privilege to engage in business and to compete with others implies a privilege to induce third persons to do their business with him rather than with his competitors. In order not to hamper competition unduly, the rule stated in this Section entitles one not only to seek to divert business from his competitors generally but also from a particular competitor. And he may seek to do so directly by express inducement as well as indirectly by attractive offers of his own goods or services. The only limitations upon this are those stated in Clauses (a) to (d).

c. *Competition between actor and the person harmed.* The rule stated in this Section applies whether the actor and the person harmed are competing as sellers or buyers or in any other way, and regardless of the plane on which they compete. Thus the rule applies whether the actor and the other are competing manufacturers or wholesalers or retailers or competing banks, newspapers or brokers. It applies when they are competing for the purchase of a farmer's tobacco crop or cattle as well as when they are competing for the sale of the crop or cattle. It applies also to the indirect competition between a manufacturer whose goods are marketed by independent retailers and a retailer who markets the competing goods of another manufacturer.

Comment on Clause (a):

d.   The diverted business. The rule stated in this Section applies only in the situation in which the business diverted from the competitor relates to the competition between him and the actor. It does not apply when the business diverted by the actor does not relate to his competition with his competitor.

Illustrations:

1.   A and B are competing distributors of shoes. A induces prospective customers of B to buy shoes from A instead of from B. A's interference with B's prospective business is not improper under the conditions stated in this Section.

2.   A and B are competing distributors of shoes. A induces C not to purchase B's dwelling. A's interference with B's prospective business is improper under the rule stated in this Section.

3.   A is B's employer and C is the carrier of A's employer's liability insurance. B, having been injured in the course of his employment, presents his claim. He rejects an offer of settlement made by C on the ground of its inadequacy and brings suit on his claim. C informs B that unless he will accept the settlement he will lose his job with A. Upon B's refusal, C causes A to discharge B by threatening to cancel all A's insurance with C. C is subject to liability to B and the interference is improper under the rule stated in this Section.

B and C, in Illustration 3, are in a bargaining struggle resembling competition. But their competition has no relation to B's continued employment by A. Other reasons may also make for a holding that the interference was improper under these circumstances. C's conduct may contravene the public policy expressed in worker's compensation legislation, or, in view of the relative positions of C and B, C's conduct may be deemed otherwise unduly oppressive and unreasonable. The case might be different if the reason for C's procuring B's discharge were that B was a hypochondriac and a chronic claimant of work accident compensation. (See § 769).

Comment on Clause (b):

e.   Means of inducement. If the actor employs wrongful means, he is not justified under the rule stated in this Section. The predatory means discussed in § 767, Comment *c*, physical violence, fraud, civil suits and criminal prosecutions, are all wrongful in the situation covered by this Section. On the other hand, the actor may use persuasion and he may exert limited economic pressure. Subject to Clause (c) (see Comment *f*), he may refuse to deal with the third persons in the business in which he competes with the competitor if they deal with the competitor. Or he may refuse other business transactions with the third person relating to that business.

The rule stated in this Section rests on the belief that competition is a necessary or desirable incident of free enterprise. Superiority of power in the matters relating to competition is believed to flow from superiority in efficiency and service. If the actor succeeds in diverting business from his competitor by virtue of superiority in matters relating to their competition, he serves the purposes for which competition is encouraged. If, however, he diverts the competitor's business by exerting a superior power in affairs unrelated to their competition there is no reason to suppose that his success is either due to or will result in superior efficiency or service and thus promote the interest that is the reason for encouraging competition. For this reason economic pressure on the third person in matters unrelated to the business in which the actor and the other compete is treated as an improper interference.

Comment on Clause (c):

f.   Illegal restraint of competition. The actor's interference is improper under the rule stated in this Section if his conduct is intended illegally to restrain competition. One who refuses to deal with another in order to establish or maintain an illegal monopoly is subject to liability to the other. Obviously he is subject to liability if for the same purpose he intentionally causes third persons not to deal with the other. Federal legislation and statutes in many States prohibit inducement not to deal with competitors for the purpose or with the effect of unreasonably restraining competition. Thus § 3 of the Clayton Act, 15 U.S.C. § 14, declares that "it shall be unlawful for any person . . . to lease or make a sale or contract for sale of goods . . . or fix a price charged therefor . . . on the condition, agreement or understanding that the lessee or purchaser thereof shall not use or deal in the goods . . . of a competitor or competitors of the lessor or seller, where the effect of such lease, sale, or contract for sale or such condition, agreement or understanding may be to substantially lessen competition or tend to create a monopoly in any line of commerce."

Other pertinent federal legislation includes the Sherman Act, 15 U.S.C. §§ 1–7, especially § 2, and the Federal Trade Commission Act, 15 U.S.C. §§ 41–58, especially § 45.

All of this legislation and the very extensive case law that has developed as a gloss upon it are pertinent to a great number of the cases in which this Section may be applicable. While there is therefore interplay between that law and the law of tortious interference with prospective contractual relations, that law is so involved and is so primarily concerned with areas of public law only tangentially related to tort law that it must be regarded as outside the scope of the Restatement of Torts.

Comment on Clause (d):

g. The actor's purpose. The rule stated in this Section developed to advance the actor's competitive interest and the supposed social benefits arising from it. If his conduct is directed, at least in part, to that end, the fact that he is also motivated by other impulses, as, for example, hatred or a desire for revenge is not alone sufficient to make his interference improper. But if his conduct is directed solely to the satisfaction of his spite or ill will and not at all to the advancement of his competitive interests over the person harmed, his interference is held to be improper. The limitation stated in Clause (d) overlaps that stated in Clause (a). If the business diverted by the actor relates to his competition with his competitor, his conduct will ordinarily be directed, at least in part, to the improvement of his position in the competition. And if his conduct is directed to some other end, the diverted business will ordinarily not be related to that competition. (Compare § 767, Comment *d*).

Comment on Subsection (2):

h. Inducing breach of contract. The rule that competition is not an improper interference with prospective contractual relations as stated in Subsection (1) does not apply to inducement of breach of contract. When B is legally free to deal either with C or with A, freedom to engage in competition implies a privilege on the part of A to induce B to deal with him rather than with C. But when B is legally obligated to deal with C, A is not justified by the mere fact of competition in inducing B to commit a breach of his legal duty. Under the general rule stated in § 767, the social interest in the security of transactions and the greater definiteness of C's expectancy outweigh the interests in A's freedom of action in this situation. But the rule stated in Subsection (2) is limited to the case in which A's claim that his interference is not improper rests solely on the fact of competition and his purpose to advance his interest in that competition, as stated in Subsection (1). His interference may be proper because of other circumstances including the fact of competition. (See § 769). That fact does not negative the existence of a justification appropriate on other grounds.

i. Contracts terminable at will. The rule stated in Subsection (1) that competition may be an interference that is not improper also applies to existing contracts that are terminable at will. If the third person is free to terminate his contractual relation with the plaintiff when he chooses, there is still a subsisting contract relation; but any interference with it that induces its termination is primarily an interference with the future relation between the parties, and the plaintiff has no legal assurance of them. As for the future hopes he has no legal right but only an expectancy; and when the contract is terminated by the choice of the third person there is no breach of it. The competitor is therefore free, for his own competitive advantage, to obtain the future benefits for himself by causing the termination. Thus he may offer better contract terms, as by offering an employee of the plaintiff more money to work for him or by offering a seller higher prices for goods, and he may make use of persuasion or other suitable means, all without liability.

An employment contract, however, may be only partially terminable at will. Thus it may leave the employment at the employee's option but provide that he is under a continuing obligation not to engage in competition with his former employer. Under these circumstances a defendant engaged in the same business might induce the employee to quit his job, but he would not be justified in engaging the employee to work for him in an activity that would mean violation of the contract not to compete.

§ 769   Actor Having Financial Interest in Business of Person Induced

One who, having a financial interest in the business of a third person intentionally causes that person not to enter into a prospective contractual relation with another, does not interfere improperly with the other's relation if he

(a)   does not employ wrongful means and

(b)   acts to protect his interest from being prejudiced by the relation.

Comment:

a.   This Section is a special application of the general test for determining whether an interference with a prospective contractual relation is improper or not, as stated in §§ 766B and 767. Comments to those Sections may be relevant here.

b.   *Breach of contract.* The rule stated in this Section does not apply to the causing of a breach of contract. (See § 766). This does not imply, however, that the actor's interference is necessarily improper in such a case under the general principle stated in § 767.

c.   *Financial interest.* The financial interest in another's business requisite for the rule stated in this Section is an interest in the nature of an investment. A part owner of the business, as for example, a partner or stockholder, has at least an interest of this nature. A bondholder or other creditor may also have it. On the other hand, the interest of a person who looks to a third person for business and will lose business opportunities if that person enters into the business relations involved is not a financial interest under the rule stated in this Section.

Illustrations:

1.   A provides the financial backing for B's theatrical production. The arrangement is in the form of a loan for the purposes of the production. While B undertakes to repay the loan in any event, in fact the chances of repayment depend upon the success of the play. B is about to engage C to play the leading role. Under the conditions stated in

Clauses (a) and (b), A's interference with the prospective relation by causing B not to have C play that role is not improper.

2.   A is employed by B Corporation under contract to invent a machine. He does so, and submits it to the corporation. C, a stockholder in the corporation, believes that the machine is unfit for the purpose, and that its adoption by the corporation will lead to heavy financial loss. For the protection of his interest in the corporation, he persuades its officers to reject the machine. C's interference is not improper.

3.   A customarily supplies B with raw materials for B's business. B is legally free to buy the materials elsewhere but has never done so. A does not have a financial interest in B's business under the rule stated in this Section.

d.   *Wrongful means.* The predatory means discussed in § 767, Comment c, are usually tortious to the person directly affected by them, and wrongful under the rule stated in this Section. Also wrongful is the use of unlawful means such as an illegal boycott or conduct in restraint of competition or productive of an illegal monopoly. And this is true of conduct in abuse of a fiduciary relationship to the person influenced, such as that of a corporate director or officer, or of a minority stockholder in threatening a frivolous stockholder's suit for purposes of harassment. As indicated in § 874, violation of a fiduciary duty is a tort. In determining whether other means are wrongful, the nature of the actor's interest and of his relation to the person induced are factors to be considered.

e.   *Intention to protect interest.* The rule stated in this Section applies for the purpose of protecting the actor's interest. If his conduct is directed to that end, it is immaterial that he also takes a malicious delight in the harm caused by his action; if his conduct is not so directed and is designed solely for some other aim, such as the gratification of his ill will, he is not entitled to the protection of the rule in this Section. Whether the conduct is so intended is a question of fact. If the actor does not believe that his interest will be endangered by the relation that he seeks to prevent, his purpose in seeking to prevent it is not the protection of that interest.

§ 770   Actor Responsible for Welfare of Another

One who, charged with responsibility for the welfare of a third person, intentionally causes that person not to perform a contract or enter into a prospective contractual relation with another, does not interfere improperly with the other's relation if the actor

(a)   does not employ wrongful means and

(b)   acts to protect the welfare of the third person.

Comment:

a. This Section is a special application of the general test for determining whether an interference with an existing or prospective contractual relation is improper or not as stated in §§ 766–766B and 767. Comments to those Sections may be relevant here.

b. *Relation between actor and person induced.* The rule stated in this Section deals with cases in which, by ordinary standards of decent conduct, one is charged with some responsibility for the protection of the welfare of another. It does not apply to an officious assumption of responsibility. The welfare that is the subject of the actor's responsibility may be physical, moral or economic welfare. The responsibility may exist in such relationships as those of parent, or person standing in loco parentis, and child, of minister and member of his congregation, attorney and client, teacher and pupil or of employer and employee. The rule stated is frequently applicable to those who stand in a fiduciary relation toward another, as in the case of agents acting for the protection of their principals, trustees for their beneficiaries or corporate officers acting for the benefit of the corporation.

Illustrations:

1. A's child attends a private school. B, a child with a contagious disease, attends the school. For the protection of his child, A persuades the school authorities to dismiss B from the school until he is well. A's action is not improper.

2. A operates a private school. B operates a store near the school, in which he sells the children large quantities of inferior candy, which in a number of instances affects their health. For the protection of the children, A announces a school regulation forbidding them to patronize B's store under penalty of dismissal. A's action is not improper.

3. The A Corporation conducts a business dealing with the public. B, an employee of the corporation, repeatedly appears on duty in an intoxicated condition, in a manner damaging to its business relations. C, another employee, for the protection of the corporation, reports this to the manager and urges him to discharge B. He does so. C's action is not improper.

c. *Requested or volunteered advice.* The privilege stated in this Section extends to cases in which the actor volunteers his advice as well as to those in which his advice is requested. For the privilege to advise in other relationships, see § 772.

Illustration:

4. A is employed by B to represent B in Asia for a period of six months. C is a friend of A and has been his personal physician for many years. C learns of A's employment. Fearing that the sojourn in Asia might be fatal to A in view of his health, C telephones A, informs him of this belief and the reasons for it and urges him to give up the job, even in

breach of his contract. C's action is not improper under the rule stated in this Section.

d.   Nature of means. As in other cases, the rule stated in this Section allows the use of means that are not wrongful. Persuasion is not wrongful. The predatory means discussed in § 767, Comment *c* are ordinarily wrongful unless the relation between the parties is such as to permit the use of the means for purposes of discipline, as for example, in the case of parent and minor child. In determining whether the means are wrongful, the extent of the danger threatened to the welfare of the person induced, the relation between him and the actor and the consequent extent of the actor's interest are important factors.

e.   Actor's purpose. The rule stated in this Section applies to protect the welfare of the person induced. If the actor's conduct is not directed to this end, he is not protected by this rule. His conduct is not so directed if he does not believe that danger to that welfare is threatened by the relation that he seeks to sever or prevent.

§ 771   Inducement to Influence Another's Business Policy

One who intentionally causes a third person not to enter into a prospective contractual relation with another in order to influence the other's policy in the conduct of his business does not interfere improperly with the other's relation if

(a)   the actor has an economic interest in the matter with reference to which he wishes to influence the policy of the other and

(b)   the desired policy does not unlawfully restrain trade or otherwise violate an established public policy and

(c)   the means employed are not wrongful.

Comment:

a.   This Section is a special application of the general test for determining whether an interference with a prospective contractual relation is improper or not, as stated in §§ 766B and 767. Comments to those Sections may be relevant here.

b.   Breach of contract. The rule stated in this Section does not apply to the causing of a breach of contract. (See § 766). This does not imply, however, that the actor's interference is necessarily improper in such a case under the general principle stated in § 767.

c.   Actor's purpose. The rule stated in this Section applies to protect the actor's interest in the business policy of the person harmed. Accordingly, his conduct is not protected by this rule if his purpose is something else. But if he has the proper purpose, the fact that he also delights in the incidental harm caused to the other is not controlling.

The purpose required under the rule stated in this Section is, then, a purpose to alter the other's policy in the conduct of his business, such as his hours of business, his wage policy, his sales policy, his employment or credit policy and so forth. Thus if A induces B not to sell to C in order to influence C not to cut his prices below his purchase price, or not to employ child labor, or not to be open for business on Wednesday afternoon during the summer, and if the conditions stated in Clauses (a), (b) and (c) are satisfied, A's conduct is not improper.

d. Actor's interest. The rule stated in this Section applies whether or not the actor and the person harmed are competitors. If they are competitors, the actor's conduct may also be justified under the rule stated in § 768. When they are competitors, the actor's interest in the business policy of the other that affects their competition is apparent. Even when they are not competitors, the actor may have an interest in the other's business policy. All retailers in a community, whether competitors or not, may have an interest in each other's policy relative to hours of business. A wholesale grocer has an interest in the food manufacturer's marketing policy with respect to direct marketing to retailers, or discounts to chain stores, and so forth. And the employees of one retailer may have an economic interest in the hours of employment maintained by a competing retailer.

e. Unlawful policy. If the business policy that the actor seeks to have the other person adopt is unlawful, the actor is not protected in his effort to achieve the adoption. The law does not prohibit the policy and at the same time protect a person in his efforts to impose it on others. The policy may be unlawful because it violates a defined policy against restraint of competition. Or it may be unlawful because it violates some other policy defined by legislation or judicial decision, as, for example, the payment of wages below established minima or the use of gambling devices or submission to racketeering.

f. Nature of means. As to the wrongful character of the means of inducement, see § 767, Comment *c.* The extent of the actor's interest, the nature of the desired business policy and the amount of pressure exerted are factors in determining the wrongfulness of the means.

g. Concerted action. The rule stated in this Section applies to action by one person or to action by several in concert. The effects of federal or state antitrust legislation dealing with the situations to which this rule is applicable are not within the scope of this Restatement. (Cf. § 768, Comment *f*).

§ 772   Advice as Proper or Improper Interference

One who intentionally causes a third person not to perform a contract or not to enter into a prospective contractual relation with another does not interfere improperly with the other's contractual relation, by giving the third person

(a) truthful information, or

(b) honest advice within the scope of a request for the advice.

Comment:

a. This Section is a special application of the general test for determining whether an interference with an existing or prospective contractual relation is improper or not, as stated in §§ 766–766B and 767. Comments to those Sections may be relevant here.

b. *Truthful information.* There is of course no liability for interference with a contract or with a prospective contractual relation on the part of one who merely gives truthful information to another. The interference in this instance is clearly not improper. This is true even though the facts are marshaled in such a way that they speak for themselves and the person to whom the information is given immediately recognizes them as a reason for breaking his contract or refusing to deal with another. It is also true whether or not the information is requested. Compare § 581A, on the effect of truth in an action for defamation.

c. *Honest advice.* The rule as to honest advice applies to protect the public and private interests in freedom of communication and friendly intercourse. In some instances the rule protects the public and private interests in certain professions or businesses. Thus the lawyer, the doctor, the clergyman, the banker, the investment, marriage or other counselor, and the efficiency expert need this protection for the performance of their tasks. But the rule protects the amateur as well as the professional adviser. The only requirements for its existence are (1) that advice be requested, (2) that the advice given be within the scope of the request and (3) that the advice be honest. If these conditions are present, it is immaterial that the actor also profits by the advice or that he dislikes the third person and takes pleasure in the harm caused to him by the advice. If one or more of the three stated conditions are lacking, the rule stated in this Section does not apply. But the actor may be protected by some other rule, as for example, that stated in § 770, which applies to volunteered as well as requested advice.

d. *Advice within scope of request.* The fact that one asks another for advice on one matter does not entitle the other, under the rule stated in this Section, to advise him on some other matter unrelated to the request. Thus, a doctor who is asked for advice about the probable effect of a contemplated employment on his patient's health cannot invoke the rule stated in this Section to protect advice he gives on the financial aspects of the employment. His relation to the patient may be such that he is protected by the rule stated in § 770. That rule is based upon the actor's interest in the welfare of the person induced. The rule stated in this Section applies even when the actor and that person are total strangers whose acquaintance with one another is limited to the one occasion on which the advice is given. Request for advice is, therefore, a condition for application of this rule, though not of the rule stated in § 770.

Whether the advice is within the scope of the request is a question of fact under the circumstances to be determined in the light of the total transaction between the adviser and the person advised. The initial request may be limited to a specific phase of a problem and remain so limited to the end. Or it may be broadened in the course of the conversation to include one or more other phrases. Or it may initially be broad enough to embrace the whole problem. Past and present relations of the adviser and the advisee may be helpful in determining the scope of the request.

e.   *Honesty and reasonable care.* It is sufficient for the application of this rule that the actor gave honest advice within the scope of the request made. Whether the advice was based on reasonable grounds and whether the actor exercised reasonable diligence in ascertaining the facts are questions important only in determining his good or bad faith. But no more than good faith is required. In some cases the nature of the actor's employment and the extent of the foreseeable reliance on his advice are such that he may be under a duty to the third person to exercise reasonable care in the giving of the advice. There may be circumstances in which this duty to exercise reasonable care is held, despite the lack of privity, to extend beyond the advisee to a person affected by the advisee's conduct taken by him in reliance upon the advice. Compare § 552 on liability to a third party for negligent misrepresentation; and see § 774B, Comment *a.* But any tort liability that may exist in that situation is based upon a duty owed directly to the plaintiff rather than upon violation of a Section within this Chapter. (See § 766C, Comment *e*).

§ 773   Asserting Bona Fide Claim

One who, by asserting in good faith a legally protected interest of his own or threatening in good faith to protect the interest by appropriate means, intentionally causes a third person not to perform an existing contract or enter into a prospective contractual relation with another does not interfere improperly with the other's relation if the actor believes that his interest may otherwise be impaired or destroyed by the performance of the contract or transaction.

Comment:

a.   The rule stated in this Section gives to the actor a defense for his legally protected interest. It is of narrow scope and protects the actor only when (1) he has a legally protected interest, and (2) in good faith asserts or threatens to protect it, and (3) the threat is to protect it by appropriate means. Under these circumstances his interference is not improper although he knows that his conduct will cause another to break his contract or otherwise refuse to do business with a third person. If any of these elements is lacking, the rule stated in this Section, does not apply but he may have some other justification. The actor's claim may be either against the person induced or against the one harmed and it may be an interest in rem or an interest in personam.

Illustrations:

1.   A enters into a contract to buy Blackacre from B. C honestly believes that he has a right of way over Blackacre. With knowledge of the contract, C in good faith informs A of his interest and threatens to enforce it by legal proceedings if, as and when the owner of Blackacre should deny his claim. A thereupon refuses to perform his contract with B. C's interference is not improper under the rule stated in this Section.

2.   The same facts as in Illustration 1, except that C threatens to shoot A or any member of his family on sight if A denies C's claim. C's interference is improper under the rule stated in this Section.

3.   A and B both have contracts with C for the purchase of the same horse from C. When C is about to deliver the horse to A, B in good faith demands delivery under his contract and threatens to sue C for damages if delivery is not made. C thereupon makes delivery to B and is disabled from performing the contract with A. B's interference is not improper under the rule stated in this Section.

§ 774   Agreement Illegal or Contrary to Public Policy

One who by appropriate means causes the nonperformance of an illegal agreement or an agreement having a purpose or effect in violation of an established public policy is not liable for pecuniary harm resulting from the nonperformance.

Comment:

a.   An agreement may be clearly illegal, as when it is forbidden by statute. There are other types of agreements that violate a definite public policy recognized by the courts, such as contracts for life employment in control of a corporation or agreements that a lawsuit will not be settled without the consent of one not a party to it. A common type of contract regarded as contrary to public policy is a contract tending to monopoly or undue restraint of trade. In some cases this result may be the avowed purpose of the agreement in question; in others this may be the effect in view of the administration of the agreement or other circumstances, whether or not it is the purpose. It is not enough, however, that the contract or agreement restricts the actor's business opportunities. Every contract limits in some degree the opportunities of persons who are not party to it. This type of restriction is ordinarily deemed desirable in both public and private interest. If, however, the restriction works prejudice to both interests by tending to create a monopoly or by unduly restraining trade, it is regarded as in violation of a clear public policy.

b.   Illegal agreements and those in violation of public policy are commonly held to be entirely void and so not contracts at all. On that basis they are simply not within the rules stated in §§ 766 and 766A on liability for interference with the performance of contracts and there is no liability for causing their breach. The contract, however, may not be void and may be merely voidable by one party or the other or enforceable by one of them. To the extent that an agreement is not void but is a subsisting contract, the actor may properly cause its breach by means that are not wrongful and under the rule stated in this Section is still not liable.

Illustrations:

1. A makes a bet with B on a horse race. By statute a gambling transaction like this is illegal. A loses the bet and C persuades him not to pay it. C is not liable to B.

2. A makes a usurious loan to B. By statute a usurious contract is illegal. C persuades B not to repay the loan to A. C is not liable to A.

3. A, by bribery, induces a United States government officer to arrange a sale to him of land that is restricted by federal statute to ownership and use by American Indians. C persuades other government officers to revoke the sale. C is not liable to A.

4. A, a cinema exhibitor in the town of X has a contract with the chief cinema producers that they will not permit any first-run pictures to be shown in X except at his theatre. B builds a cinema theatre in X. He is not liable for inducing one or more of the producers to license him for a first-run cinema in breach of the contract with A, if he does not use wrongful means.

5. Under the applicable law, any person may enter the business of distributing electricity in the city of X if he first procures a contract from 50 per cent. of the householders in X to purchase their electricity from him when he is ready to sell. A, who operates the sole distribution system in X, has these contracts with 70 per cent. of the householders. Subsequently, B desires to enter the business. B is not liable for soliciting these householders for the required contracts.

6. A, a textile manufacturer, makes a contract with B, another textile manufacturer, that neither will employ members of C, a labor union of textile operatives. C is not liable for causing A to employ its members in violation of the contract, if he does not use wrongful means.

§ 774A Damages

(1) One who is liable to another for interference with a contract or prospective contractual relation is liable for damages for

(a) the pecuniary loss of the benefits of the contract or the prospective relation;

(b) consequential losses for which the interference is a legal cause; and

(c) emotional distress or actual harm to reputation, if they are reasonably to be expected to result from the interference.

(2) In an action for interference with a contract by inducing or causing a third person to break the contract with the other, the fact that the third person is liable for the breach does not affect the amount of damages awardable against the actor; but any damages in fact paid by the third person will reduce the damages actually recoverable on the judgment.

Comment:

a. This Section states only the rules applicable to the recovery of compensatory damages. Since the tort is an intentional one, punitive damages are recovered in these actions under appropriate circumstances. On the rules governing the award of punitive damages, see §§ 908 and 909.

b. Whether the interference is with an existing contract or with a prospective contractual relation, one who becomes liable for it is liable for damages for the pecuniary loss of the benefits of the contract or the relation. In the case in which a third person is prevented from performing a contract with the plaintiff, the plaintiff may recover for the loss of profits from the contract. When it is the plaintiff himself who is prevented from performance of his contract with a third person, he may recover for expenses to which he is put or for other pecuniary losses incurred in making his performance good. And when the defendant's interference is with prospective contractual relations, the plaintiff may recover for the loss of profits to be made out of the expected contracts.

c. A major problem with damages of this sort is whether they can be proved with a reasonable degree of certainty. This matter is discussed in general in § 912; see Comments *d* and *f* for specific discussion of loss of profits and chances for gain. If the question is whether the plaintiff would have succeeded in attaining a prospective business transaction in the absence of defendant's interference, the court may, in determining whether the proof meets the requirement of reasonable certainty, give due weight to the fact that the question was "made hypothetical by the very wrong" of the defendant. Sometimes, when the court is convinced that damages have been incurred but the amount cannot be proved with reasonable certainty, it awards nominal damages.

d. The action for interference with contract is one in tort and damages are not based on the contract rules, and it is not required that the loss incurred be one within the contemplation of the parties to the contract itself at the time it was made. The plaintiff can also recover for consequential harms, provided they were legally caused by the defendant's interference.

The tests for legal causation for the tort of interference with a contract of prospective contractual relation, like the tests for determining when an interference is improper (see § 767), have not been reduced to precise rules. By analogy to the rules for legal causation for negligent physical injury, it is sometimes held that the particular loss need not be contemplated, expected or foreseen by the defendant. (Compare § 435). At other times, it is held that the loss must be expectable, by analogy to legal causation for the tort of deceit. (See § 548A). It seems likely that the issue in a particular case may be affected by some of the factors listed in § 767. Emphasis may be given, for example, to the means used (i.e., physical force or oral persuasion) and to the motive (e.g., intent in broad sense of knowledge of result, or sole purpose motivated by ill will).

Recovery for emotional distress is allowable if it was reasonably to be expected to result from the interference. The same is true of actual harm to reputation.

e. The fact that the plaintiff may have a cause of action against the person who has broken his contract does not prevent recovery against the defendant who has induced or otherwise caused the breach, or reduce the damages recoverable from him. The defendant and the contract breaker are both wrongdoers (compare § 875), and each is liable for the entire loss that he has caused. Even a judgment obtained for breach of the contract if it is not satisfied does not bar or reduce recovery from the one who has caused the breach. But since the damages recoverable for breach of the contract are common to the actions against both, any payments made by the one who breaks the contract or partial satisfaction of the judgment against him must be credited in favor of the defendant who has caused the breach.

Conversely, an action or judgment against the one who causes the breach without satisfaction will not bar or reduce recovery from the one who breaks the contract; but to the extent that there is duplication of the damages any payments made by the tortfeasor must be credited in favor of one who has broken the contract.

f. In appropriate circumstances injunctive relief may be granted against future violation of §§ 766–766B. On the rules involved, see §§ 933–951.

Division Eleven. Miscellaneous Rules
Chapter 43. Rules Applicable to Certain Types of Conduct

§ 874   Violation of Fiduciary Duty

One standing in a fiduciary relation with another is subject to liability to the other for harm resulting from a breach of duty imposed by the relation.

Comment:

a. A fiduciary relation exists between two persons when one of them is under a duty to act for or to give advice for the benefit of another upon matters within the scope of the relation. (See Restatement, Second, Trusts, § 2).

b.   A fiduciary who commits a breach of his duty as a fiduciary is guilty of tortious conduct to the person for whom he should act. The local rules of procedure, the type of relation between the parties and the intricacy of the transaction involved, determine whether the beneficiary is entitled to redress at law or in equity. The remedy of a beneficiary against a defaulting or negligent trustee is ordinarily in equity; the remedy of a principal against an agent is ordinarily at law. However, irrespective of this, the beneficiary is entitled to tort damages for harm caused by the breach of duty arising from the relation, in accordance with the rules stated in §§ 901–932. In addition to or in substitution for these damages the beneficiary may be entitled to restitutionary recovery, since not only is he entitled to recover for any harm done to his legally protected interests by the wrongful conduct of the fiduciary, but ordinarily he is entitled to profits that result to the fiduciary from his breach of duty and to be the beneficiary of a constructive trust in the profits. Further, when there is a contract between the parties or when there has been an assumption of duty by a trustee, guardian or executor, the beneficiary may be entitled to what the fiduciary should have made in the prosecution of his duties. Special application of these rules of agents and trustees respectively is made in the Restatement, Second, Agency, §§ 401–407 and in the Restatement, Second, Trusts, §§ 197–226A. See also Restatement of Restitution, §§ 138 and 190. The same underlying principles apply to the liability of other fiduciaries, such as administrators and guardians; the liability is not dependent solely upon an agreement or contractual relation between the fiduciary and the beneficiary but results from the relation.

c.   A person who knowingly assists a fiduciary in committing a breach of trust is himself guilty of tortious conduct and is subject to liability for the harm thereby caused. (See § 876). The measure of his liability, however, may be different from that of the fiduciary since he is responsible only for harm caused or profits that he himself has made from the transaction, and he is not necessarily liable for the profits that the fiduciary has made nor for those that he should have made. Specific applications of the rule are made in the Restatement, Second, Agency, §§ 312 and 313 and in the Restatement, Second, Trusts, §§ 280–326. The same principles are applicable when one has colluded with other types of fiduciaries.

Chapter 44. Contributing Tortfeasors

§ 876   Persons Acting in Concert

For harm resulting to a third person from the tortious conduct of another, one is subject to liability if he

(a) does a tortious act in concert with the other or pursuant to a common design with him, or

(b) knows that the other's conduct constitutes a breach of duty and gives substantial assistance or encouragement to the other so to conduct himself, or

(c) gives substantial assistance to the other in accomplishing a tortious result and his own conduct, separately considered, constitutes a breach of duty to the third person.

Caveat:

The Institute takes no position on whether the rules stated in this Section are applicable when the conduct of either the actor or the other is free from intent to do harm or negligence but involves strict liability for the resulting harm.

Comment on Clause (a):

a. Parties are acting in concert when they act in accordance with an agreement to cooperate in a particular line of conduct or to accomplish a particular result. The agreement need not be expressed in words and may be implied and understood to exist from the conduct itself. Whenever two or more persons commit tortious acts in concert, each becomes subject to liability for the acts of the others, as well as for his own acts. The theory of the early common law was that there was a mutual agency of each to act for the others, which made all liable for the tortious acts of any one.

Illustrations:

1. A, B, C and D come together to E's house at night to rob. A breaks in E's front door, B ties E up, C beats E and D steals and carries away E's jewelry. A, B, C and D are all subject to liability to E for all damages caused by the trespass to land, the false imprisonment, the battery and the conversion.

2. A and B are driving automobiles on the public highway. A attempts to pass B. B speeds up his car to prevent A from passing. A continues in his attempt and the result is a race for a mile down the highway, with the two cars abreast and both travelling at dangerous speed. At the end of the mile, A's car collides with a car driven by C and C suffers harm. Both A and B are subject to liability to C.

b. The same rule is applicable, in general, to tortious acts done pursuant to a common design or plan for cooperation in a tortious line of conduct or to accomplish a tortious end. It is in connection with these common designs or plans that the word "conspiracy" is often used. The mere common plan, design or even express agreement is not enough for liability in itself, and there must be acts of a tortious character in carrying it into execution. When both parties engage in the acts, each becomes subject to liability for the cars of the other.

c. In order for the rule stated in Clause (a) to be applicable, it is essential that the conduct of the actor be in itself tortious. One who innocently, rightfully and carefully does an act that has the effect of furthering the tortious conduct or cooperating in the tortious design of another is not for that reason subject to liability.

Illustration:

3.   A is drunk and disorderly on the public street. B, C and D, who are all police officers, attempt to arrest A for the misdemeanor committed in their presence. A resists arrest. B and C take hold of A, using no more force than is reasonable under the circumstances. A breaks away and attempts to escape. D draws a pistol and shoots A in the back. B and C are not liable to A for the shooting.

Comment on Clause (b):

d.   Advice or encouragement to act operates as a moral support to a tortfeasor and if the act encouraged is known to be tortious it has the same effect upon the liability of the adviser as participation or physical assistance. If the encouragement or assistance is a substantial factor in causing the resulting tort, the one giving it is himself a tortfeasor and is responsible for the consequences of the other's act. This is true both when the act done is an intended trespass (see Illustrations 4 and 5) and when it is merely a negligent act. (See Illustration 6). The rule applies whether or not the other knows his act is tortious. (See Illustrations 7 and 8). It likewise applies to a person who knowingly gives substantial aid to another who, as he knows, intends to do a tortious act.

The assistance of or participation by the defendant may be so slight that he is not liable for the act of the other. In determining this, the nature of the act encouraged, the amount of assistance given by the defendant, his presence or absence at the time of the tort, his relation to the other and his state of mind are all considered. (See Illustration 9). Likewise, although a person who encourages another to commit a tortious act may be responsible for other acts by the other (see Illustration 10), ordinarily he is not liable for other acts that, although done in connection with the intended tortious act, were not foreseeable by him. (See Illustration 11). In determining liability, the factors are the same as those used in determining the existence of legal causation when there has been negligence (see § 442) or recklessness. (See § 501).

Illustrations:

4.   A and B participate in a riot in which B, although throwing no rocks himself, encourages A to throw rocks. One of the rocks strikes C, a bystander. B is subject to liability to C.

5.   A, a policeman, advises other policemen to use illegal methods of coercion upon B. A is subject to liability to B for batteries committed in accordance with the advice.

6.   A and B are members of a hunting party. Each of them in the presence of the other shoots across a public road at an animal, which is

negligent toward persons on the road. A hits the animal. B's bullet strikes C, a traveler on the road. A is subject to liability to C.

7. A persuades B, who is not an officer, to arrest C for a crime which A tells B was committed by C but which he knows has not been committed by anyone. A is subject to liability to C.

8. A sells to B for resale a gun known by him to be dangerously defective. B negligently fails to examine the gun before selling it to C, who is hurt while attempting to discharge it. A is subject to liability to C.

9. A is employed by B to carry messages to B's workmen. B directs A to tell B's workmen to tear down a fence that B believes to be on his own land but that in fact, as A knows, is on the land of C. A delivers the message and the workmen tear down the fence. Since A was a servant used merely as a means of communication, his assistance is so slight that he is not liable to C.

10. A and B conspire to burglarize C's safe. B, who is the active burglar, after entering the house and without A's knowledge of his intention to do so, burns the house in order to conceal the burglary. A is subject to liability to C, not only for the conversion of the contents of the safe but also for the destruction of the house.

11. A supplies B with wire cutters to enable B to enter the land of C to recapture chattels belonging to B, who, as A knows, is not privileged to do this. In the course of the trespass upon C's land, B intentionally sets fire to C's house. A is not liable for the destruction of the house.

Comment on Clause (c):

e. When one personally participates in causing a particular result in accordance with an agreement with another, he is responsible for the result of the united effort if his act, considered by itself, constitutes a breach of duty and is a substantial factor in causing the result, irrespective of his knowledge that his act or the act of the other is tortious. Thus each of a number of trespassers who are jointly excavating a short ditch is liable for the entire harm done by the ditch, although each reasonably believes that he is not trespassing.

In a large undertaking to which the services of many persons contribute, the contribution to the enterprise of one individual may be so small as not to constitute substantial assistance within the meaning of the rule stated in this Section. Thus a workman who tortiously excavates for the foundation of one of a series of buildings to be used by a manufacturing plant is not necessarily a co-tortfeasor with other workmen simultaneously tortiously excavating for other buildings upon the same premises.

It is to be noted that a person may be privileged, and hence be committing no breach of duty, in assisting another who is committing or who later commits a tort. Thus one who reasonably believes that he is defending another against an aggressor may not be liable although the other is in fact the aggressor. (See § 76). Further, one who assists in doing an act that from his standpoint does not involve elements of undue risk is not liable merely because another with whom he co-operates is negligent. (See Illustration 12). Likewise one who supplies another with the means of committing a tort is not liable if he has no reason to suppose that a tort will be committed. (See Illustrations 13 and 14). In none of these cases is the defendant committing a breach of duty to the injured person.

Illustrations:

12. A and B hunt together but not in the prosecution of a joint enterprise. It is not negligent to hunt where they are, and neither of them has reason to believe that the other will be negligent. Under the unreasonable belief that it is an animal, A shoots at a moving object that proves to be a man. B is not liable for A's negligent act.

13. A sells to B a second-hand gun, knowing that it is defective but reasonably believing that B, who also knows of the defect, will repair it before it is used. B, however, uses it without repairs and C is harmed by the resulting explosion. A is not liable to C.

14. A supplies B with wrecking tools, knowing that B is going to use them on a specific tract of land but having no reason to know that B is planning to burglarize a building on the land. A is not liable to C, the owner of the building burglarized by B through the use of the wrecking tools.

Comment on Caveat:

f. On the liability for the escape of animals and for abnormally dangerous conduct for which there is strict liability, see §§ 504–524. Liability in these cases is imposed, not on the ground that the conduct upon which it is based is wrongful, but on the ground that the conduct, although lawful because of the importance of the enterprise to the community, creates such great risk of harm to third persons that it is fair that the one conducting the enterprise should be required to compensate for the harm caused by it.

Illustrations:

15. In a state in which there is strict liability for harm resulting from the intentional explosion of dynamite, A and B are employees of C and make preparations for exploding dynamite at a place where it is not negligent to do so. Debris from the explosion strikes D. The Institute takes no position on the liability of A and B.

16. A is B's servant, employed to feed and care for the animals in a menagerie. Without fault on A's part, one of the wild animals escapes and harms C. Assuming that A was not a possessor of the animal and hence not liable as such, the Institute takes no position on A's liability to C.

III. RESTATEMENT (THIRD) OF TORTS

(Selected Sections)

■ ■ ■

Table of Sections

Chapter 1. Unintentional Infliction of Economic Loss

Section

Chapter 2. Liability in Tort for Fraud

Chapter 1. Unintentional Infliction of Economic Loss

§ 1 Liability for the Unintentional Infliction of Economic Loss: General Principles

(a) An actor has no general duty to avoid the unintentional infliction of economic loss on another.

(b) Duties to avoid the unintentional infliction of economic loss are recognized in the circumstances set forth in §§ X–Y.

Comment:

a. *Scope.* An actor ordinarily has a duty of care when engaged in any activity that creates a risk of physical harm to others. See Restatement

Third, Torts: Liability for Physical and Emotional Harm § 7. Duties to avoid the negligent infliction of economic loss are notably narrower. They do not arise merely because an act creates a risk of economic loss to another; they require a more specific rationale. This Section explains how such duties of care generally are identified. The Sections that follow describe the principal duties thus far recognized and rules of limitation that accompany them. Section 2 discusses the definition of economic loss.

b.   *Relation to "economic loss rule."* A minority of courts have stated an "economic loss rule" to the effect that there is generally no liability in tort for causing pure economic loss to another. This Restatement does not use the expression in that manner or describe the law in that way. Subsection (a) states a more limited principle: not that liability for economic loss is generally precluded, but that duties of care with respect to economic loss are not general in character; they are recognized in specific circumstances according to the principles stated in Comment *c.* The difference between these formulations is narrow but significant. Stating the absence of a duty as a general rule can create confusion by seeming to threaten well-established causes of action, by leaving behind an uncertain and unwieldy number of exceptions, and by implying a needless presumption against the existence of a duty on facts not yet considered. The rule of this Section creates no such presumption. It merely means that duties to avoid causing economic loss require justification on more particular grounds than duties to avoid causing physical harm.

Section 3 of this Chapter does recognize an "economic loss rule" that is more precise and robust than the broader version described a moment ago: it precludes tort liability for economic loss caused by negligence in the negotiation or performance of a contract between the parties.

c.   *Rationale.* An economic loss or injury, as the term is used here, means a financial loss not arising from injury to the plaintiff's person or from physical harm to the plaintiff's property. See § X. Economic injuries may be no less important than injuries of other kinds; a pure but severe economic loss might well be worse for a plaintiff than a more modest personal injury, and the difference between economic loss in itself and economic loss resulting from property damage may be negligible from the victim's standpoint. For several reasons, however, courts impose tort liability for economic loss more selectively than liability for other types of harms.

(1). Indeterminate and disproportionate liability. Economic losses proliferate more easily than losses of other kinds. Physical forces that cause injury ordinarily spend themselves in predictable ways; their exact courses may be hard to predict, but their lifespan and power to harm are limited. A badly driven car threatens physical harm only to others nearby. Economic harm is not self-limiting in this way. A single negligent utterance can cause economic loss to thousands of people who rely on it, those losses may produce additional losses to those who were relying on the first round of victims, and so on. Consequences of this sort may be at least generally foreseeable to the

person who commits the negligent act. Defendants in such cases thus might face liabilities that are indeterminate and out of proportion to their culpability. Those liabilities may in turn create an exaggerated pressure to avoid an activity altogether.

(2). Deference to contract. Risks of economic loss tend to be especially well suited to allocation by contract. First, economic injuries caused by negligence often result from a decision by the victim to rely on a defendant's words or acts when entering some sort of transaction—an investment in a company, the purchase of a house, and so forth. A potential plaintiff making such a decision has a full chance to consider how to manage the risks involved, whether by inspecting the item or investment, obtaining insurance against the risk of disappointment, or making a contract that assigns the risk of loss to someone else. Second, money is a complete remedy for an economic injury. Insurance benefits, indemnification by agreement, or other replacements of money payments are just as good as the money lost in a transaction that turns out badly. This fungibility makes those other ways of managing risk—insurance, indemnity, and the like—more attractive than they might be to a party facing a prospect of personal injury.

Those same points often will make it hard for a court to know what allocation of responsibility for economic loss would best serve the interests of the parties to a risky situation. A contract that settles responsibility for such a risk will therefore be preferable in most cases to a judicial assignment of liability after harm is done. The contract will better reflect the preferences of the parties and help prevent the need for speculation and litigation later. Contracts also are governed by a body of commercial law that has been developed to address economic loss, and thus will often be better suited for that task than the law of torts. In short, contracts to manage the risk of economic loss are more often possible, and more often desirable, than contracts to manage risks of other types of injury. As a result, courts generally do not recognize tort liability for economic losses caused by the breach of a contract between the parties (see § 3), and often restrict the role of tort law in other circumstances in which protection by contract is available.

d. Recognized duties. Courts recognize duties of care to prevent economic loss when the rationales stated in Comment *c* are weak or absent. Most of those duties, and some more precise rules of limitation, are stated in the subsequent Sections of this Chapter. A summary of those rules and limits, and of their relationship to the rationales just discussed, may be useful here.

(1). Professional negligence. Section 3 states a general rule of no liability in tort for economic losses that arise from negligence in the negotiation or performance of a contract between the parties. Section 4 recognizes an exception to that rule when a client sues a professional for malpractice, because the rationales stated in this Section are not present in that context. First, the professional sued for malpractice by a client who has suffered economic loss is not likely to face an unusual risk of indeterminate or

disproportionate liability. Second, the imbalance of knowledge between the typical professional and client makes contracts between them less trustworthy and important than usual: less trustworthy because one side is not in a position to negotiate effectively with the other, and less important because the right allocation of responsibility between the parties is clear enough as a matter of public policy.

(2). Invited reliance. Sections 5 and 6 recognize a duty of care when a defendant speaks or acts for the purpose of providing a basis for reliance by the plaintiff. The risk of indeterminate liability is controlled by rule: both Sections provide that liability runs only to limited classes of parties for limited purposes. The role of contract is respected by excluding liability when the defendant speaks or acts in performance of a contract with the plaintiff. Indeed, liability under §§ 5 and 6 typically serves as a substitute for a contract between two parties who cannot conveniently write one, and whose affairs will be made simpler and more efficient if the party who invites the reliance has enforceable obligations to the party who accepts the invitation. In some cases under §§ 5 and 6 the parties could have made a contract but did not; the law nevertheless supplies a remedy in tort because the appropriate allocation of responsibility between them is particularly clear.

(3). [Rules about harm resulting to plaintiffs from injury to others, or to property they do not own: fisherman's rule, public nuisance, wrongful death.]

e. Residual duties. The rules summarized in Comment *d*, and elaborated in the Sections that follow, cover the most commonly recurring types of claims for the unintentional infliction of economic loss. On occasion, claims arise outside the scope of those general rules. Such residual claims are decided by application of the principles stated in Comment *b*. Courts consider, first, whether recognizing a duty of care would expose the defendant to indeterminate or disproportionate liability. They consider as well whether parties in the plaintiff's position can reasonably be expected to protect themselves against the loss by contract. An affirmative answer to either question results in no liability, which is the typical result when a plaintiff seeks to recover for economic loss in tort outside the recognized headings of this Chapter. In some such cases, however, the scope of a defendant's liability for economic loss is no more troubling than it would be in cases of physical harm: the set of potential plaintiffs is compact, and the size of the potential liability to them is clear and proportionate to the defendant's culpability. In some cases, too, the plaintiff is in a poor position to allocate the risk of economic loss by contract, whether directly or indirectly. Where those conditions hold, a duty of care may reasonably be found. A court should not labor under a presumption against liability when the rationales for restricting it are absent.

Illustrations:

1. Lawyer prepares will for Client. Lawyer negligently concludes that no witnesses are required to make the will effective so long as it is notarized. After Client's death, the will is found to be invalid because

Client's signature lacked sufficient witnesses. Daughter, who would have inherited Client's entire estate under the will, instead inherits 1/8 of it by intestate succession. Daughter sues Lawyer. Since Daughter was not a client of Lawyer and did not rely on Lawyer, liability from Lawyer to Daughter under §§ 4–6 of this Chapter is not available. A duty running from Lawyer to Daughter may be found, however, under the principles underlying this Section. Because Client has died, Lawyer may not be sufficiently answerable for his negligence by contract, and the scope of Lawyer's liability presents no special problems of clarity or proportionality.

2. Impostor applies to Bank for credit card in Victim's name. Bank issues card without any effort to verify Impostor's identity. Impostor runs up extensive charges, then disappears without paying them. Victim's credit record is impaired as a result, causing him economic losses. Since Victim was not a client of Bank and did not rely on Bank, liability from Bank to Victim under §§ 4–6 of this Chapter is not available. A duty running from Bank to Victim may be found, however, under the principles underlying this Section. Bank may have to absorb Impostor's charges, but no contract will bring home to Bank the cost of its negligence to Victim. Bank's potential liability if a duty is recognized may be somewhat uncertain in dollar amount, but it is limited to the individual in whose name a card is issued. Bank is subject to liability to Victim.

3. Owner operates a restaurant at an airport in space leased from County. County hires Contractor to renovate the restaurant's ventilation system. Contractor's negligence causes the work to take longer than is customary. The delay causes business losses to Owner. Owner has no tort claim against Contractor under § 6 of this Chapter, because Contractor's purpose was not to provide a basis for Owner's reliance. The general principles of this Section likewise yield no duty. Owner can readily enough seek protection against the cost of delays in its contract with County or by other means.

4. Contractor supplies gravel for Town's construction project. Consultant hired by Town negligently states that Contractor's gravel is of an inferior grade and should be rejected. Acting in reliance on Consultant's advice, Town rejects Contractor's gravel and Contractor replaces it with a new batch. Contractor cannot sue Consultant for negligent misrepresentation under § 5, because Consultant's purpose was not to provide a basis for Contractor's reliance. The general principles of this Section likewise yield no duty. Contractor can readily enough seek protection against improper rejection of its work in its contract with Town.

5. Charterer leases vessel from foreign Owner, and is obliged to make payments to Owner by the end of each month. In late May, Charterer orders Domestic Bank to wire payment to Owner. Domestic

Bank transmits the request to Swiss Bank. Swiss Bank negligently delays payment. Owner does not receive payment on time, and thus cancels the lease. Charterer cannot find a replacement lease at the same good price. Charterer seeks to recover from Swiss Bank. Since Charterer was not a client of Swiss Bank and Swiss Bank did not act to provide a basis for reliance by Charterer, liability from Swiss Bank to Charterer under §§ 4–6 of this Chapter is not available. The general principles of this Section likewise yield no duty. Owner can readily enough seek protection against loss from delay by contractual or other means; liability for Swiss Bank would be indeterminate, since Swiss Bank cannot know the stakes of the transfers it is asked to make; and the best allocation of the risk at issue is not clear, since Charterer is in a better position than Swiss Bank to foresee the consequences of a mishap and to gauge the extent of the precautions or insurance that are appropriate in response.

§ 2　Economic Loss Defined

For purposes of this Restatement, "economic loss" is pecuniary damage not arising from injury to the plaintiff's person or from physical harm to the plaintiff's property.

Comment:

a.　Definitional note. Courts often refer to the losses defined by this Section as "purely" economic, but this Restatement will generally omit that qualifier unless the purity of the economic loss calls for particular emphasis; thus "economic loss" in this Restatement normally means "pure economic loss." The black letter refers to "physical" harm to the plaintiff's property because some cases discussed in this Chapter might be viewed as involving harm to a plaintiff's intangible property—the loss of a legal claim, for example, or the reduced value of securities. When this Restatement refers to "property damage," it generally means damage to tangible property.

Usually the distinction between physical injury and pure economic loss is easy to draw, though it occasionally causes confusion when relatively minor damage to person or property leads to monetary losses on a large scale. It may then seem tempting to describe the plaintiff's losses as purely economic in character. They are not. The property damage at the root of such a loss brings the case within the scope of Restatement Third, Torts: Liability for Physical and Emotional Harm, and the rules stated there. Economic loss that accompanies even minor injury to the plaintiff's person or property does not tend to raise the same considerations found when a plaintiff's losses are economic alone. See § 1.

Wrongs that might seem to cause only economic loss are sometimes regarded otherwise because the law takes an expansive view of what counts as a personal injury. Defamation, for example, is regarded as inflicting a kind of personal injury: harm to the plaintiff's reputation. If a defendant inflicts emotional harm on the plaintiff, and causes the plaintiff to suffer consequent pecuniary loss, it is likewise a case of personal injury covered not here but in Restatement Third, Torts: Liability for Physical and Emotional Harm.

b. *Other property.* Defining economic loss is most challenging when property the plaintiff has bought causes damage to itself. The problem can arise when the plaintiff buys a house from a builder and later finds that defects in one part of it lead to damage in another: leaks in a roof ruin the rafters, or a defective foundation causes cracks in the walls. The result is damaged property in a literal sense, but the law typically regards such cases as involving economic loss alone. This view evolved from earlier cases in which buyers of products sued the sellers when the products did not work. Courts held that a product's failure to operate was a matter best addressed by the law of warranty rather than tort, and the analysis was the same when the product failed because one of its components damaged another. Liability in tort was recognized only when a product damaged other property besides itself.

The reasoning just stated has since been extended to cases that involve the sale of real property, which typically fall beyond the coverage of the law of products liability as a formal matter. Thus the buyer of a house who discovers that its rafters are rotting may have contractual remedies against the builder; and the claim should not become a matter of tort just because the cause of the rot is found to be a leak in the roof. Though the rot might then be construed as a kind of property damage caused by negligence in building the house, it is more apt to say the house was not properly constructed and disappointed the buyer's economic expectations.

Whether a defect in a house has caused damage to "other property" or only to the house itself is sometimes a matter of controversy. The answer generally depends on whether the property causing the harm and the property receiving it were sold to the plaintiff as a single unit under a common warranty and as the benefit of a common bargain. Compare Illustrations 1 and 2. More detailed guidance on the meaning of "other property" can be found in the law of products liability, where the distinction has been developed more fully. See Restatement Third, Torts: Products Liability § 21. This Chapter does not govern claims that arise from defective products, but it seeks consistency with the separate Restatement of that topic.

Illustrations:

1. Buyer purchases a house from Developer. The house includes defective windows that Developer installed after obtaining them from Manufacturer. Leaks from the windows damage the interior walls of the house. Buyer sues Manufacturer in tort, claiming the faulty windows caused damage to other property: the walls. The court finds that the windows and walls were part of an integrated product bought and sold as a single unit. Buyer's losses therefore are purely economic in character; under the rules of this Chapter, Buyer's protections lie not in tort but in whatever warranties Developer may have provided.

2.   Manufacturer builds a warehouse and sells it to Firm. Defects in the warehouse resulting from Manufacturer's negligence cause it to collapse, destroying inventory that Firm stored there. Firm's tort claim to collect for damage to its inventory does not seek recovery for economic loss as the term is used in this Restatement, because the defects in the warehouse caused damage to other property: the inventory placed inside it after purchase. At the time the parties made their contract, damage to Firm's inventory if the warehouse were to collapse may have been a foreseeable risk; this does not change the result. Manufacturer may be subject to liability in tort under the principles of Restatement Third, Torts: Liability for Physical and Emotional Harm.

§ 3   Preclusion of Tort Liability Arising from Contract (Economic Loss Rule)

Except as provided elsewhere in this Restatement, there is no liability in tort for economic loss caused by negligence in the performance or negotiation of a contract between the parties.

Comment:

a.   Terminology. Courts have used the expression "economic loss rule" to refer to a variety of propositions. As noted in § 1, a minority have used it to mean that there is, in general, no liability in tort for causing pure economic loss to another. This Restatement does not endorse that formulation because its breadth is potentially misleading. This Section instead states an economic loss rule that is narrower and more robust, and that is followed by a majority of courts. It is limited to parties who have contracts. This version of the rule hews closer than the broader one to the rationale that courts state for the rule in any of its forms: the need to separate matters best left to contract from those properly resolved by the law of tort. If two parties have a contract, the argument for limiting tort claims between them is most powerful. See Comment *b.*

The narrower scope of the rule stated here also ties it more clearly to its origins in cases that involve products liability. A buyer of a product disappointed by its performance cannot sue its maker in tort for negligence. Courts have long recognized that the law of warranty is better suited than the law of torts to address such cases, and that contracts between the parties determine the allocation of economic losses that arise from the transaction. See Restatement Third, Torts: Products Liability § 21. The rule recognized by this Section generalizes that principle to economic injuries arising from the breach of other sorts of contracts.

b.   Rationale. An actor whose negligence causes personal injury or physical harm to the property of another can be held liable in tort regardless of whether the negligence occurs in the performance of a contract between the parties. The result is different, however, in cases of economic loss; if a plaintiff and defendant have a valid contract, monetary harm caused by the

146

defendant's negligent performance of it is not generally actionable in tort. Nor does tort law provide a remedy for economic loss caused by negligent statements that parties make during efforts to form a contract. When a party's negligence in performing or negotiating a contract causes economic loss to the counterparty, remedies are determined by other bodies of law: principally the law of contract, though sometimes also the law of restitution or relevant statutes. The law of contract and the law of restitution have been developed for the specific purpose of allocating economic losses that result from the negotiation and performance of contracts. They provide a more extensive and finely tuned apparatus for the purpose than the law of torts, which has developed primarily to address injuries that occur outside contractual relationships.

The rule of this Section serves several purposes. When a dispute arises, the rule protects the bargain the parties have made against disruption by a tort suit. Seen from an earlier point in the life of a transaction, the rule allows parties to make dependable allocations of financial risk without fear that tort law will be used to undo them later. Viewed in the long run, the rule prevents the erosion of contract doctrines by the use of tort law to work around them. The rule also reduces the confusion that can result when a party brings suit on the same facts under contract and tort theories that are largely redundant in practical effect. For more general discussion of the value of contract in allocating responsibility for economic loss, see § 1, Comment c.

c. *Scope of preclusion.* A contract precludes common-law tort claims for financial loss based on negligent conduct that the contract regulates. See Illustrations 1–3. It does not foreclose tort claims based on conduct outside the contract's scope. See Illustration 4. Close cases can arise when an act of negligence occurs at the fringe of a contract's coverage. The important question then is whether allowing the tort claim creates a risk of interference with an allocation of risk made by the parties. A contract can allocate a risk without mentioning it explicitly; silence may itself serve as an allocation if the risk falls within the scope of activity the contract governs. On the other hand, the purpose of this Section is to protect the bargain the parties made, not to penalize the plaintiff for failing to make a broader one. Navigating between these points may require study of the transaction and its logic. See Illustration 5. The extent to which a contract precludes liability in tort for economic loss is a question for the court.

Illustrations:

1. Town hires Firm to lay sewer pipe. Town later incurs costs of repair after finding that Firm laid the pipe negligently. Town's contract with Firm provided a one-year warranty, and Town discovered the defective work two years after the pipe was laid; Town therefore determines that it has no contract claim against Firm. Town instead brings a timely tort claim against Firm, alleging that Firm was negligent in laying the pipe. Firm is not liable in tort to Town. Town's rights are determined by the contract and the law that governs it.

2.   Developer makes preliminary agreement to buy land from Seller. Before closing the sale, Developer hires Inspector to examine the property. Inspector informs Developer that most of the property consists of wetlands unsuitable for development. Developer declines to go through with the sale. Developer later observes another buyer extensively developing the same property; Developer finds on investigation that Inspector's earlier report was incorrect. Developer sues Inspector in tort. Court finds that Inspector's alleged negligence came in the performance of a contract with Developer, and that Inspector is not a professional within the meaning of § 4 of this Chapter. Inspector therefore is not liable in tort to Developer; Developer's remedies, if any, are those provided by his contract with Inspector.

3.   Owner hires Mechanic to examine airplane. Mechanic negligently overlooks defects in the plane's landing gear. Owner sells plane to Buyer. Buyer discovers the problems in the landing gear, orders repairs, and sues Mechanic in tort to recover the costs. The rule of this Section is not an obstacle to Buyer's suit because Mechanic and Buyer had no contract. Whether Mechanic is liable to Buyer is determined by the principles of §§ 5 and 6 (see, e.g., § 5, Illustration 9).

4.   In the course of planning his retirement, Employee asks Employer when he must exercise stock options that he has accumulated. Employer negligently advises Employee that he has five years to exercise the options after leaving the firm. In fact the stock plan requires the options to be exercised within three years. Acting in reliance on Employer's statements, Employee retires, waits too long to exercise the stock options, and forfeits them. The court finds that while a contract of employment existed between the parties, Employer's statements were not a breach of it; the discussion about the stock options was outside the scope of Employer's contractual performance. Employer may be liable in tort to Employee for negligent misrepresentation under § 5 despite the contract between them.

5.   Owner of mineral lease makes a contract that gives Driller rights to extract oil. During a meeting at the office of Owner after the contract is formed, Driller asks whether Owner's insurance covers Driller's interests in the project. Owner negligently asserts that it has insurance against a blowout and that the policy covers Driller's interests. Driller's oil well suffers a blowout. Driller then learns that its interests are not covered by Owner's insurance policy. After examining the parties' contract, the court concludes that their discussion about insurance did not overlap with their obligations of performance; permitting liability in tort would not interfere with any allocation of risk the contract made. Owner may be liable in tort to Driller for negligent misrepresentation under § 5 despite the contract between them.

d.   *Negligent inducement of contract.*   Some courts have used Restatement Second, Torts § 552—the predecessor to § 5 of this Chapter—to hold sellers liable for negligent misrepresentations that cause buyers to enter into contracts with them. The rule of this Section eliminates the tort claim in that circumstance. A seller's negligent misrepresentations are addressed sufficiently by the law of contract and restitution. Such misrepresentations may give the buyer a claim for breach of warranty, for rescission and incidental damages, or for breach of contract accompanied by a claim of estoppel. In other cases, the language of the contract and the parol evidence rule may foreclose claims based on statements made before the contract was signed. In either event, adding a tort claim to the analysis interferes with the operation of those contract doctrines and creates confusion without offsetting gains. Liability under §5 of this Chapter is thus limited to negligent misrepresentations that were not made in the performance or negotiation of a contract.

In a familiar instance of this pattern, the plaintiff buys a house and then discovers that the seller negligently vouched for a feature of it that turned out to be defective. The contract between the parties, coupled with the jurisdiction's parol evidence rule, precludes any claim for contract damages based on statements the seller made before the contract was signed. Pressure to find a tort claim arises because the stakes are high and the plaintiff's position is sympathetic: if the contract contained an integration clause, it may have been boilerplate that the plaintiff did not read; and the contract itself might have been a form drafted by real-estate brokers. But if denying relief to the plaintiff seems to produce an injustice on those grounds, a better response is to reconsider the application of the parol evidence rule or the other doctrines of contract law that are responsible for the result. Using tort law to bypass those doctrines weakens them and retards their development. It also interferes with the ability of others to make reliable agreements in the future. In the alternative, a result unappealing on its equities may call for a statutory solution. Statutes can impose responsibility on sellers for certain risks without distorting widely applicable legal principles to reach the desired outcome.

Fraudulent inducement to enter a contract, unlike a claim of negligent misrepresentation, can in some circumstances give a plaintiff a viable tort claim. When two parties negotiate over a contract, the amount of care they are expected to show for each other's interests will often be unclear or significantly less than the care expected in a situation involving strangers or the risk of physical injury. That is among the reasons why the duties of care between parties who negotiate contracts are not governed by the law of tort. Expectations of honesty are more regular, however, and the disappointment of them may call for remedies not customarily available from the law of contract or restitution. Liability in tort may therefore be recognized in such circumstances. See Sections [§§ XX, in a later Chapter].

Illustration:

6. Purchasers enter contract to buy house from Seller. Seller negligently states that the septic system is in good working order. Acting

partly in reliance on that assurance, Purchasers buy house. Purchasers then discover that the septic system is not in good working order. Purchasers' remedies are determined by their contract with Seller and the rules of contract law that apply to it. Thus, Purchasers may have a claim for rescission and restitution based on mutual mistake or misrepresentation. They may have a claim for breach of warranty, depending on the relationship between the language in the contract, the Seller's statements outside the contract, and the jurisdiction's parol evidence rule. Whatever the outcome may be under those theories, Purchaser has no tort claim against Seller.

Restatement Second, Torts § 552C recognized liability in tort for innocent misrepresentation. The liability applied when one party made a material but innocent misrepresentation to another in a sale, rental, or exchange transaction. For the reasons just discussed, this Restatement does not recognize tort liability under those circumstances. All such cases involve the negotiation and performance of a contract; if a plaintiff was induced to enter into an exchange with the defendant by the defendant's innocent misrepresentation, the plaintiff has recourse under the law of restitution, warranty, and estoppel. See Restatement Third, Restitution and Unjust Enrichment §§ 13 and 54.

e. Contracts never concluded. A party may be injured by reliance on another's negligent statements in the course of negotiating a contract that is never concluded. This Section treats the resulting claims for relief as matters for other bodies of law to resolve. It therefore eliminates tort claims based on a defendant's negligent statements of intent to make a contract, predictions about the likelihood of a contract, or mistaken suggestions that a contract has been formed. Detailed doctrines in the law of contract, of restitution, and of estoppel have developed to provide relief in such cases where necessary. If those bodies of law fall short, the appropriate response again is to reform them, not to use the law of tort to supply their deficiencies.

Illustration:

7. Agent for Firm negligently misinforms Applicant that Firm will award him a grocery store franchise if he buys land where the store can be built. Applicant buys the land but never receives the franchise. The doctrine of promissory estoppel may give Applicant a remedy against Agent or Firm. Applicant has no claim in tort against either of them.

f. Parties indirectly linked by contract. Sometimes a plaintiff and defendant who had no contract with each other both had contracts with the same third party. In some cases of this type, it would have been possible for the plaintiff and defendant to work out their obligations to each other in advance by carefully writing their contracts with the party who stood between them. This Section does not extend its rule to those cases, however; it does not foreclose claims between plaintiffs and defendants who are only indirectly linked by contract. Whether the plaintiff has a good claim in such a case is determined by other rules of this Chapter.

Illustration:

8.   City hires Engineer to test soil conditions at a site where it plans to erect a large building. City explains that Engineer's report will be distributed to prospective building contractors for use in estimating their costs. Engineer negligently submits an inaccurate report. Contractor wins the right to perform the construction, having relied on Engineer's report in preparing its bid. Engineer's errors cause Contractor to suffer losses in performing its contract with City. The contracts between Contractor and City, and between City and Engineer, do not preclude a claim by Contractor against Engineer under § 5 or § 6 of this Chapter. Engineer remains potentially liable to Contractor under either of those Sections.

In Illustration 8, a contract between Contractor and Engineer might not have been feasible. But Contractor could have insisted that City guarantee the soundness of Engineer's report, and City could have insisted that Engineer indemnify City for claims brought against it by Contractor. In effect, those contracts would have protected Contractor against the risk of errors by Engineer, and would have ensured that Engineer would bear the costs of its negligence. The pattern of Illustration 8 is thus one of many circumstances in which two parties might be able to settle their obligations to each other through a chain of contracts, and may or may not do so in practice.

The significance of a missed opportunity to assign responsibility by contract bears clarification. Such missed opportunities do not trigger this Section's rule against recovery in tort; only an actual contract has that effect. Missed opportunities to make contracts also do not bar a plaintiff from recovery under § 5 or § 6 [or § X]. Courts have concluded that in the circumstances addressed by those Sections, liability is appropriate even if the parties might have proceeded by contract but did not. But if a plaintiff argues for recognition of a duty outside the well-recognized categories stated in this Chapter, missed opportunities to seek protection by contract do become relevant. Where contracts might readily have been used to allocate the risk of a loss, a duty to avoid the loss is unlikely to be recognized in tort—not because the economic loss rule applies, but simply because courts prefer, in general, that economic losses be allocated by contract where feasible. See § 1, Comment *e*.

g.   Exceptions. Some well-established exceptions to the rule of this Section are addressed in subsequent parts of this Restatement. The most prominent is the tort liability of professionals to their clients despite (and alongside) any contract between them. See § 4. Fiduciaries likewise have duties recognized in tort notwithstanding the terms of contracts to which they may be subject. See Chapter X. In certain circumstances, an insurer may be held liable in tort for its rejection of an offer to settle a suit brought against its insured by a third party; that, too, may be considered an exception to the rule of this Section, and is discussed in Chapter Y along with other problems involving breach of contract by an insurer.

Common carriers and other bailees are sometimes said to have duties of care independent of their contracts, thus entitling an aggrieved bailor to recover against them in tort. Those statements typically are made, however, in the setting of claims to recover for damaged or lost property, not claims for pure economic loss. Economic loss alone, even in the setting of a bailment, may well be most appropriately allocated by contract, as is common. The extensive regulation of many bailments by the Uniform Commercial Code and other statutes provides additional reason to hesitate before recognizing a role for tort law in such a case. In view of the limited authority on the question, however, the right of a bailor to recover in tort for economic loss is left to developing case law.

h.   Relation to other Sections. This Section precludes liability under §§ 5 and 6 when the defendant's negligent conduct occurs in the performance of a contract with the plaintiff. Sections 5 and 6 recognize liability when a defendant acts to provide a basis for reliance by the plaintiff, and the plaintiff in turn relies. The purpose of such liability is usually to provide a substitute for a contract where the parties have not made one and the appropriate allocation of risk between them is clear. Once parties do make a contract, it displaces the obligations of §§ 5 and 6; the contract alone determines the parties' responsibility for economic loss caused by negligence in performing it.

§ 5   Negligent Misrepresentation

(1) One who, in the course of his business, profession, or employment, or in any transaction in which he has a pecuniary interest, supplies false information for the guidance of others, is subject to liability for pecuniary loss caused to them by their reliance upon the information, if he fails to use reasonable care in obtaining or communicating it.

(2) Except as stated in Subsection (3), the liability stated in Subsection (1) is limited to loss suffered

    (a) by the person or one of a limited group of persons for whose guidance the actor intends to supply the information, or for whose guidance he knows the recipient intends to supply it; and

    (b) through reliance upon the information in a transaction that the actor intends to influence, or that he knows the recipient intends to influence, or in a substantially similar transaction.

(3) The liability of one who is under a public duty to supply the information extends to loss suffered by any of the class of persons for whose benefit the duty is created, in any of the transactions in which it is intended to protect them.

(4) A plaintiff's recovery under this Section is subject to the same principles of comparative responsibility that apply to other claims of negligence.

(5) This Section does not recognize liability for negligent misrepresentations made in the course of negotiating or performing a contract between the parties.

Comment:

a.   Relation to § 6. This Section and § 6 state rules that govern liability for economic loss resulting from a plaintiff's reliance on a defendant's statements or services. The two Sections have been kept as parallel as the subject matter of each will permit. Both are based on the logic of Restatement Second, Torts § 552, which a majority of states have adopted. The black letter of this Section, which covers liability for negligent statements, repeats § 552 with small changes. Section 6 adapts the same principles to services that a defendant performs. The general theory of liability is the same under both Sections. A plaintiff's reliance alone, even if foreseeable, is not a sufficient basis for recovery; under either Section a defendant generally must act with the apparent purpose of providing a basis for the reliance. It may be useful to say that a defendant held liable under either Section must "invite reliance" by the plaintiff, so long as the expression is understood to refer to the defendant's apparent purpose and not to a temptation incidentally created by the defendant's words or acts.

Reliance on statements and on services can give rise to different complications, as the Comments to this Section and § 6 will reflect. The two categories overlap, however, and the separation of them into two Sections should be understood as a convenience. No substantive differences are intended between the rules the Sections state; no plaintiff should recover under both Sections on the same facts, and no claim should be dismissed for relying on one Section when the other would have been a better fit.

b.   Rationale. Liability under this Section depends on the same standard of care familiar from other cases of negligence. See Comment *i.* The defendant's duty here is limited, however, in various ways that the elements of this Section detail. The limits each reflect specific policies but are also supported by several shared concerns. Like the economic forces discussed in § 1, words do not spend themselves in the way that physical forces do. They often can be circulated to one person or to thousands with little difference in cost and no reduction in their power to do economic harm when others rely on them. Liabilities that expand as easily as words travel would therefore become indeterminate and unduly widespread in many cases. Secondly, when a defendant's words are actionable under this Section, they do not overtake their victims by surprise. They do harm when someone decides to rely on them. This usually gives potential victims of negligent statements opportunities to protect themselves, whether through their own investigations or by making a contract with the party offering the statement. This Section thus recognizes duties only in a limited set of cases where the parties have no contract on point (see § 3), where the defendant nevertheless undertook to provide the plaintiff with a basis for reliance, and where holding the defendant accountable will produce a liability that is reasonably predictable and proportional to the defendant's culpability.

    c.   *Pecuniary interest.* For liability to arise under this Section, the defendant must act "in the course of his business, profession, or employment, or in any transaction in which he has a pecuniary interest." This requirement serves several purposes. First, it helps confine liability to cases where information is offered in a sufficiently serious spirit to make the plaintiff's reliance reasonable. Second, liability for those who speak gratuitously would tend to discourage them from speaking at all; the speech would then amount to the assumption of an economic burden (the risk of liability) without any offsetting gain that they are able to capture. Defendants who receive economic benefits for offering advice, by contrast, may well choose to speak despite the risk of liability for being wrong. They can treat that potential liability as a cost of doing business and charge accordingly or consider buying insurance against it. The "pecuniary interest" element of the tort should be interpreted flexibly to give effect to these purposes that the requirement serves.

    Common questions that recur concerning this element involve, first, whether defendants act in the course of their business when they supply information on occasions that are incidental to their main line of work. The requirement tends to be satisfied when the plaintiff and defendant are in a commercial relationship. Thus, employers who give information about retirement benefits to their employees have duties of care; they speak in the course of their business, even if not in performance of any particular contracts they may have with their employees. The result is the same if the plaintiff and defendant are in a joint commercial venture. The economic framework that surrounds the parties' dealings is then enough to lend a pecuniary interest to statements they make to each other that satisfy the other elements of this Section. See § 3, Illustrations 4 and 5; in both, the defendant has a sufficient pecuniary interest to support liability.

    In another set of cases, the defendant makes representations to a plaintiff without any direct commercial relationship between the parties, as when a firm responds to a request for information from an outsider who does not propose to pay for it. The important question then is whether speaking will redound to the defendant's economic benefit in some reasonably clear way, perhaps because it helps another party with whom the defendant has a contract. Compare Illustrations 1 and 2.

Illustrations:

    1.   Buyer, seeking to buy furniture on credit from Seller, offers Bank as a credit reference. Seller contacts Bank and is told that Buyer has a substantial account there and a good record as a borrower. Acting in reliance on these statements, Seller sends furniture to Buyer. Buyer goes bankrupt before paying for the furniture. Seller discovers that Bank's statements were false and made without reasonable investigation into the status of Buyer's accounts. Bank is liable to Seller for negligent

misrepresentation. Though Seller did not pay for Bank's reply, Bank had an indirect pecuniary interest because providing a credit reference is a valuable service to its customers; the bank would be less attractive to them if it refused. (If Seller had paid Bank to supply the information, liability under this Section would be foreclosed by § 3; Seller's rights against Bank would then be determined by their contract.)

2. Husband and Wife agree to separate. Wife seeks to learn whether she continues to be covered by an automobile insurance policy that Husband owns. Mother-in-law of Wife claims to be familiar with the policy and to understand it. She negligently misadvises Wife that the policy does provide coverage for her. Wife relies on Mother-in-law's statements. Wife is then injured in an automobile accident and discovers that in fact she has no coverage. Wife sues Mother-in-law for negligent misrepresentation. Mother-in-law is not liable because she had no pecuniary interest in the matter on which she spoke.

3. Patient seeks treatment from Hospital. Hospital asks Insurer to confirm that patient has coverage. Insurer negligently provides confirmation, but in fact Patient does not have a valid policy. Hospital treats Patient. Insurer refuses to pay. Court finds that Hospital and Insurer have no contract on point. Insurer is liable to Hospital for negligent misrepresentation.

A final difficulty involves the defendant who speaks without being paid but normally requires a fee. No rule can be stated for such cases, but liability tends not to be found in them; the professional who usually gets paid to speak is, when speaking without pay, typically found to have acted gratuitously. Conversely, a business that supplies information without charge on a regular basis is more likely to be held responsible for it. The regularity suggests that providing certain advice for "free" is part of the defendant's business, not an isolated favor with unconsidered implications. Thus, a lawyer who offers advice to a client in an unpaid initial consultation will be held liable when the advice is negligent, because consultations of that kind are a regular and necessary part of a lawyer's professional work. By contrast, an appraiser who normally charges for an opinion may be found to act outside the course of business when offering an occasional unpaid comment on the value of a painting.

d. *False information.* Liability attaches under this Section to the supply of "false information." This generally means that a claim must be based on a defendant's statements of fact, not on opinions or predictions. This element of the tort might be viewed as a rule that reliance on an opinion or prediction ordinarily is unreasonable as a matter of law. An opinion or prediction may be actionable after all, however, if it falsely implies that the speaker has facts that form the basis of it, or knows of no facts to the contrary. In addition, defendants who hold themselves out as having expertise in rendering opinions or predictions, as appraisers and auditors often do, may be held liable for negligence in forming or communicating them. (Liability for the fraudulent statement of predictions or opinions is considered in Chapter X.)

Illustration:

    4.   Builder constructs house and hires Expert to satisfy Buyer that the house is structurally sound. Without making an appropriate investigation, Expert tells Buyer that no water will collect in the cellar. Acting in reliance on Expert's statements, Buyer purchases house. The house has structural defects that cause water to collect in the cellar. Though Expert's statement might appear to be a prediction or opinion, Expert can be held liable to Buyer for negligent misrepresentation on either of two theories. Expert's prediction was reasonably understood by Buyer to imply a factual claim: that the house was so constructed as to prevent water from entering the cellar. And because Expert invited Buyer to rely on his specialized knowledge of home construction, his opinions can support a claim if not formed with reasonable care.

e.   *Omissions.* A failure to speak, by itself, does not create liability under this Section. (Silence may be actionable under another Chapter of this Restatement if the defendant is a fiduciary. See § X.) This Section does recognize liability, however, if a defendant chooses to speak and negligently makes an omission that misleads the plaintiff. A plaintiff may be misled, for example, if a defendant tells part of the truth but negligently fails to add qualifications or other information necessary to avoid conveying a false impression.

Illustration:

    5.   Firm hires Lawyer to produce an opinion letter for distribution to potential investors. The letter concerns the tax consequences of investing in Firm. Acting in reliance on the letter, Investor invests in Firm, then suffers losses when the tax advantages do not materialize. Court finds that while the statements in Lawyer's letter were accurate, the letter negligently failed to qualify its claims in important ways. The omissions caused the letter, taken as a whole, to be misleading. Lawyer is subject to liability to Investor.

f.   *Limited group; known party and transaction.* Liability under this Section is confined to plaintiffs who may be described as a "limited group." This element of the tort helps to prevent a defendant's potential liability from becoming indeterminate and unduly widespread. Sometimes the intended audience for a statement is vast; it might include the general public or all possible investors in the stock market. Potential liability to members of such a large audience would make a speaker's exposure hard to gauge. Moreover, a speaker whose words reach a general audience will not usually be compensated by all those who benefit from hearing them. If speakers were nevertheless held liable to everyone injured by reliance on statements circulated so widely, the result would be an incentive not to speak at all. The "limited group" corrects for these possibilities by permitting liability only to discrete classes of plaintiffs.

Illustrations:

6.   Newspaper's table of bond prices negligently misstates the terms on which Company's bonds traded on the previous day. Acting in reliance on Newspaper's listing, Investor buys Company's bonds and suffers losses. Investor is one of many newspaper readers who saw the erroneous listing. Newspaper is not liable to Investor for negligent misrepresentation.

7.   Company hires Accountant to perform an audit and issue a report. The purpose of the audit, as Company makes clear, is to satisfy potential investors that Company's condition is sound. Accountant further understands that its evaluation will be made available to the general public. Accountant negligently issues a report indicating that Company is in good financial condition. Company makes the report generally available. Acting in reliance on the report, Investors buy high-yield, high-risk bonds issued by Company. Company goes bankrupt. Investors sue Accountant for negligent misrepresentation, claiming that they qualify as a limited class because the market for bonds of the kind they bought is small and specialized. Because Accountant's report was public and Company bonds were sold on the open market, Investors' claim fails.

8.   Same facts as Illustration 7, but Company tells Accountant that the audit report will be distributed to a series of unnamed venture capital firms that may be interested in investing in Company. Plaintiff, one such venture capital firm, receives the negligent report, invests in Company in reliance on it, and suffers losses when Company goes bankrupt. Accountant is liable to Plaintiff for negligent misrepresentation.

g.   For the guidance of others; intended influence. To be held liable under this Section, a defendant must supply information for the guidance of the plaintiff. Liability is also limited to losses produced by reliance in a transaction that the defendant intended to influence. Both requirements make clear that liability is not established by evidence that the plaintiff's reliance on the defendant's information was merely foreseeable. See Illustrations 9 and 12. These elements, like those discussed in Comment *f*, help keep the defendant's exposure to liability clear and determinate. The defendant's purpose or intent is measured objectively; in other words, the question is what the defendant's statements and behavior reasonably indicated, not what the defendant thought privately.

Cases arising under this Section often involve a defendant who is paid by another to provide information for the benefit of the plaintiff. A common example is an accountant hired by a firm to produce an audit report; the firm then distributes the report to potential investors. This pattern can raise questions about whether the accountant had the necessary intent to supply information "for the guidance" of those investors; for the accountant supplied the information not to the investors but to the client, who only then passed it on to others. Language in Subsection (2)(a) ("or for whose guidance he knows the recipient intends to supply it") makes clear, however, that the intent required for liability under this Section can belong to the party who has hired the defendant, if the defendant knows that party's purpose and acquiesces in it. Thus, accountants are routinely held liable for negligence in cases that follow the pattern just described.

The requirement that an accountant or similar defendant know how the information that it supplies will be used by the final recipient is subject to refinement in the following respects.

(1) If a defendant clearly states that its guidance is supplied for the benefit of a specific recipient and no other, the defendant cannot be held liable to a similar but different recipient who relies on the information later. See Illustration 10. A defendant likewise may state that its work is meant to serve as a basis for reliance in a particular transaction and no other. If no such limiting understandings are in place, however, this Section does not require the class of parties or the transaction at issue to be the very same ones the defendant expected. See Illustration 11. In close cases, the test for substantial similarity should be kept functional: it is whether the use made of the information, if understood in advance, would likely have changed the defendant's perception of the risks taken by speaking and caused the defendant to take measures in response—such as more care, more disclaimers, higher charges, or more insurance.

(2) Courts sensibly interpret what a defendant "knew" to encompass as well what the defendant should have known—in other words, what the defendant reasonably should have expected the client's use of the information to be. Otherwise a defendant's negligent assessment of that use would serve to reduce its own duty of care. The knowledge held by such defendants, or charged to them, may be derived from custom and business practice as well as from the client directly.

(3) On the other hand, even a defendant's actual knowledge of a client's intentions does not, by itself, subject the defendant to liability for losses that result when the intentions are carried out. The defendant must act for the purpose of enabling the type of use the recipient makes. Thus, in Illustration 11, liability is intact because the defendant's purpose is to provide information for uses such as those the client makes, though the defendant lacks knowledge of certain specific details. In Illustration 12, by contrast, the defendant may have exact knowledge of those to whom the client will pass the information, but nevertheless is not liable to them. Providing advice for distribution to the client's friends is no part of the defendant's purpose; in the absence of such a purpose, recovery would be founded on nothing more than foreseeability to the defendant that others might choose to rely on his statements. That is not a sufficient basis for liability under this Section.

Illustrations:

9. Owner of a machine hires Mechanic to regularly inspect and service it. Mechanic makes negligent entries in the machine's maintenance records, incorrectly stating that all repair work is up to date. Owner later sells machine to Buyer, whose decision to go through with the purchase is made partly in reliance on the incorrect records. Buyer suffers financial losses when he discovers that unexpected repairs need to be done. It was foreseeable to Mechanic that a later purchaser of the machine might someday rely on the maintenance records, but Mechanic nevertheless acted for the sole purpose of assisting Owner, and Buyer could not reasonably have interpreted the records otherwise. Mechanic is not liable to Buyer for negligent misrepresentation.

10. Borrower hires Accountant to audit its books. Borrower states that the audit's purpose is to satisfy the requirements of Lender, from whom Borrower hopes to obtain a credit line of $5 million. Accountant performs the audit and issues a report with the express understanding that it is for transmission to Lender only. Lender declines the requested line of credit. Borrower, without further communication with Accountant, submits Accountant's report to Second Choice Bank, which in reliance upon the report extends $5 million in credit to Borrower. Accountant's audit was negligent. In consequence, Second Choice Bank suffers pecuniary loss through its extension of credit. Accountant is not liable to Second Choice Bank.

11. Same facts as Illustration 10, except that nothing is said about supplying the information for the guidance of Lender only. Borrower merely informs Accountant that he expects to negotiate a loan for $5 million, requires the audit for this purpose, and has Lender in mind. Accountant is subject to liability to Second Choice Bank.

12. Adviser negligently recommends bad investments to Client, misstating their tax advantages. Adviser knows that Client is in the habit of passing such recommendations on to various friends, but Adviser does not speak for the purpose of providing those friends with a basis for reliance, and does nothing to suggest such an intent. Adviser is not liable to Client's friends for negligent misrepresentation.

In some cases, a plaintiff suffers economic loss not from reliance on a defendant's negligent statements, but because the statements are relied upon by a third party; the negligent statements affect judgments the third party makes about the plaintiff. Courts routinely reject tort liability on these facts for the party who made the misrepresentation. The result can be explained by noting the plaintiff's lack of reliance, or by observing that the defendant's purpose was not to supply information for the plaintiff's benefit or guidance. See Illustration 13 below, and § 1, Illustration 4. Liability on such facts occasionally may be established on theories outside this Section. See discussion in § 1, Comment *e*.

Illustrations:

13. Buyer makes preliminary agreement to purchase house from Seller, pending outcome of appraisal ordered by Buyer. Appraiser's report negligently understates the value of Seller's house. Acting in reliance on the report, Buyer refuses to close the deal. Seller has no claim against Appraiser for negligent misrepresentation. The result may be explained by pointing out that Seller did not rely on Appraiser's report; he may have "relied" in the sense that he was counting on Appraiser to do a competent job, but he did not change position in reliance on anything that Appraiser said. The result also may be explained on the ground that Appraiser was not supplying information for the purpose of guiding Seller.

h. Business transactions. Under Restatement Second, Torts § 552, liability depended on a showing that the guidance furnished by the defendant applied to "business transactions." This Restatement omits that requirement. Though the Comments to § 552 did not explain the rationale for the rule, it might have been thought a helpful way to identify cases in which the defendant's advice was seriously offered and received, or in which damages would be straightforward to calculate. Subsequent case law has shown, however, that other elements of the tort adequately secure those ends, and that cases not involving business transactions sometimes are compelling candidates for liability.

Illustration:

14. Friend asks Photographer to film Friend's intimate encounters with various women without their knowledge. Photographer hesitates. Lawyer hired by Friend negligently assures Photographer that the filming is lawful. Acting in reliance on this advice, Photographer performs the filming as an unpaid favor to Friend. The women who have been filmed discover this and sue Photographer. Photographer settles those cases, then sues Lawyer to recover his losses. Photographer was not a client of Lawyer, and Photographer's filming of Friend's encounters cannot reasonably be classified as a business decision. Lawyer nevertheless is liable to Photographer for negligent misrepresentation. (For the possibility of a deduction based on the plaintiff's fault, see Comment *j*.)

i. Traditional elements of the tort. Most provisions of this Section amount to rules about when and to whom a defendant owes a duty of care. Once that duty is settled, the other elements of the tort—the standard of care, factual causation, and scope of liability (or proximate cause)—are generally governed by the same principles that would apply to an ordinary negligence case. This Comment summarizes how those principles apply in the context of this Section. For more detailed discussion of the principles at issue, see the relevant provisions of Restatement Third, Torts: Liability for Physical and Emotional Harm.

(1). Due care. The applicable standard of care under this Section is the familiar one from negligence law: reasonableness, in view of the size and probability of the harms risked and the costs of being more careful. See Restatement Third, Torts: Liability for Physical and Emotional Harm § 3. The standard applies to all aspects of the defendant's supply of the information: the steps taken in obtaining it, and the care used in communicating it. A defendant who claims to have specialized knowledge, typically by virtue of membership in a profession or trade, must exercise the skill normally expected of specialists; a professional is held to a professional standard of care. Often a plaintiff will need expert testimony to prove that a professional failed to meet that standard, but not always. It depends on whether lay jurors can judge the adequacy of the defendant's care for themselves. See § 4, Comment *c*.

(2). Factual causation. The plaintiff generally has the burden of showing that the harm would not have occurred but for the defendant's negligent misrepresentation. Sometimes this showing will be made naturally in the course of proving that the plaintiff relied on what the defendant said. If the defendant's negligent misstatements persuaded the plaintiff to make a bad purchase or investment, for example, it might be evident that the plaintiff's financial losses would not have occurred otherwise. Strictly speaking, however, the defendant's statements must be a "but for" cause of the plaintiff's loss, not just of the plaintiff's decision to enter into the damaging transaction. Those two points occasionally may be distinct, as when accurate statements by the defendant would have caused the plaintiff to enter into a different transaction with results that were no better. See Illustration 16.

The treatment of factual causation under this Section follows the general principles in Restatement Third, Torts: Liability for Physical and Emotional Harm §§ 26 and 27. Some classic problems of causation treated in Chapter 5 of that Restatement, such as multiple sufficient causes of harm, have not arisen often enough in claims for negligent misrepresentation to call for separate restatement of their application here.

Illustrations:

15. Buyer has misgivings about purchasing house from Seller because the roof looks infirm. Inspector hired by Seller negligently certifies that the roof is in good condition. Buyer purchases the house. The roof fails, costing Buyer $20,000 to repair. If Inspector had competently identified the roof's defects, Buyer probably would not have purchased the house or would have obtained a price reduction equal to the cost of the needed repairs. Inspector's negligence is a cause in fact of Buyer's $20,000 loss.

16. Investor wants to invest in an oil-and-gas venture and has narrowed the field to two candidates: Company A and Company B. Investor chooses to invest in Company A. Company A collapses, causing Investor to suffer economic losses. Investor sues Accountant hired by

Company A, claiming that an audit report prepared by Accountant, and read by Investor before investing, negligently understated Company A's liabilities. Court finds that Accountant's report did contain negligent misrepresentations, but that Investor would likely have invested in Company A even if Accountant's report had been free from error; an accurate report still would have caused Company A to seem a sound investment and to appear superior to Company B along all metrics relevant to Investor. Accountant's negligence is not a cause in fact of Investor's injuries.

17. Investor wants to invest in an oil-and-gas venture and has narrowed the field to two candidates: Company A and Company B. Investor chooses to invest in Company A, relying on a negligent report issued by Company A's Accountant. Sharp declines in the oil-and-gas market cause large losses to Investor, who then withdraws his investment and sues Accountant for negligent misrepresentation. Investor would not have invested in Company A if Accountant had issued a competent report. The court finds, however, that Investor would instead have invested in Company B, which also was wiped out by the collapse of the market. Since Investor would have suffered the same losses in any event, Accountant is not liable to Investor. Accountant's negligence was a cause in fact of Investor's decision to enter the damaging transaction, but Accountant's negligence did not cause Investor's damages.

(3). Scope of liability (proximate cause). The various limitations on a defendant's duty of care under this Section do some of the work that might be performed by rules of proximate cause elsewhere in the law of torts. For example, the requirement that the defendant intend to provide guidance to the plaintiff partly displaces an inquiry into foreseeability of harm that a court might otherwise make. Once the elements of this Section are satisfied, however, the remaining questions about the scope of a defendant's liability— that is, the harms for which the defendant is answerable—are decided in conventional fashion. A defendant generally is liable for harm if it arises from the risks that made the negligent conduct a breach of duty. See Restatement Third, Torts: Liability for Physical and Emotional Harm §§ 29 and 30. If a defendant's misrepresentation had a comparatively small role in producing the plaintiff's injury, that point can be captured by other elements of this Section. See the earlier discussion in this Comment, and Comments *j* and *l*.

Illustration:

18. Firm hires Accountant to prepare financial statements for the benefit of Insurer to whom Firm has applied for coverage. Accountant negligently fails to report objections that a state regulatory agency made to one of Firm's dividend payments. Acting in reliance on Accountant's work, Insurer writes coverage for Firm. One of Firm's officers then embezzles a large share of Firm's assets. Insurer is obliged to cover Firm's losses, and seeks to recover from Accountant for negligent

misrepresentation. Court finds that Insurer would not have written policy for Firm if it had known of the objections raised by the state agency. Court also finds, however, that the agency's objections were entirely unrelated to the risk of embezzlement that caused Firm's losses; the chance that Firm would be looted by one of its officers was not among the risks that made the audit negligent. Accountant is not liable to Insurer.

j. Comparative responsibility; justifiable reliance. Restatement Second, Torts § 552 required that a plaintiff seeking to recover for negligent misrepresentation must show "justifiable reliance" on the information supplied by the defendant. This Section omits the word "justifiable" and instead adds the language of Subsection (4), treating the plaintiff's responsibility for a loss as a question of comparative fault. "Justifiable reliance" has the sound of an all-or-nothing inquiry, which is how it tends to be treated in other settings. This made sense at the time § 552 was adopted, because the Second Restatement viewed contributory negligence as a complete defense to a claim under that Section. Comparative responsibility has since become a standard principle in negligence cases, however, and courts have extended it to claims of negligent misrepresentation. Confusion has thus arisen concerning the relationship between those principles and a requirement of "justifiable" reliance; treating judgments about a plaintiff's reliance as an all-or-nothing matter, while every other type of plaintiff's negligence is a matter of degree, creates hard problems in separating those categories. The same conduct by a plaintiff can often be described as imprudent reliance or as negligence of some other kind. This Section resolves the tension in favor of comparative responsibility. Liability under this Section is a species of liability for negligence, though with restrictions on the defendant's duty and scope of liability. The plaintiff's share of blame for a loss can be analyzed as it would be in any other negligence case. See generally Restatement Third, Torts: Apportionment of Liability.

Comparative responsibility can become an issue under this Section when a plaintiff may have relied on the defendant's statements too heavily, omitting additional precautions that ordinary prudence would have suggested. Due care does not normally require a plaintiff to duplicate precautions that the defendant should have taken before speaking. Negligence on the plaintiff's part, rather, means omitting precautions that due care would require even if the defendant had spoken carefully. But the plaintiff may have some independent obligation to investigate, even redundantly, if the stakes are high enough, or the defendant's assumption of responsibility unclear enough, to make exclusive reliance on the defendant's statements imprudent. Compare Illustrations 19 and 20.

Comparative responsibility also becomes important when the plaintiff had access to information that counseled against relying on what the defendant said, such as a writing that was inconsistent with the defendant's oral statements or that disclaimed their reliability. Disclaimers a defendant makes in a contract with the plaintiff are not usually important under this

Section, because claims arising from a contract between the parties are matters resolved by contract law or, on occasion, by the law of professional malpractice. See §§ 3 and 4 and Comment *m* below. Between parties who have no contract, however, a disclaimer the defendant has made may bear significantly on liability under this Section. It may show that providing a basis for reliance by the plaintiff was no part of the defendant's purpose, or make the plaintiff's reliance unreasonable in other respects. See Illustrations 21 and 22.

Though the plaintiff's share of responsibility for a loss is ordinarily a question for a jury, the court retains its usual power to decide the issue as a matter of law if considerations of policy call for it. In the context of this Section, promoting certainty in commercial transactions is a prominent policy of that kind. Thus, a court may decide that a plaintiff's reliance was of a kind that should be protected against any reduction of recovery for the sake of commercial stability. See Illustration 19. Conversely, summary judgment may be appropriate when a plaintiff relied on a defendant's words despite a clear written warning not to do so; a court may reasonably conclude that a defendant who offers an appropriate and enforceable disclaimer before speaking should have protection against the risk and expense of a jury trial. See Illustrations 21 and 22.

Illustrations:

19. Farmer seeking loan from Bank offers farm machinery as collateral. Bank asks Farmer for a letter from a lawyer certifying that the machinery is not already subject to liens. Lawyer for Farmer so certifies without due investigation. Bank makes loan to Farmer; Farmer then goes bankrupt. Security interests held by other creditors make it impossible for Bank to collect from Farmer. Bank sues Lawyer for negligent misrepresentation. Lawyer argues that Bank's reliance was not reasonable because Bank easily could have made its own search for liens on the machinery and knew enough about Farmer's finances to make its own search advisable. Bank's reliance nevertheless was reasonable as a matter of law. Bank was entitled to assume that Lawyer would not issue a certificate without making a careful search, in which case another search for liens would have been redundant.

20. Buyers propose to buy tract of timberland from Farmer and turn it into residential real estate. Farmer gives Buyers documents bearing on the property. The documents include a report by Appraiser, prepared for the benefit of potential purchasers, stating that the land is zoned in a manner that permits residential development. Without further investigation, Buyers purchase the land from Farmer for $10,000,000. Buyers then discover that the land is not zoned for residential development. Buyers sue Appraiser for negligent misrepresentation. In view of the size of the transaction, Buyers might have been imprudent in making the purchase without further

investigation. The allocation of fault between the two sides is a question for the jury.

21. Buyers are interested in purchasing a house. Broker, who works for the owners of the house and not for Buyers, provides a listing sheet negligently stating that the house contains 3500 square feet of space. Acting in reliance on this statement, Buyers purchase the property. Buyers then discover that the house contains only 3000 square feet. Buyers sue Broker for negligent misrepresentation. The listing sheet contained a disclaimer stating that the square footage described was "deemed reliable but not guaranteed" and adding, "If exact square footage is important to you, measure, measure!" Buyers' reliance on the statement in the listing sheet was unreasonable as a matter of law. Broker is not liable to Buyers.

22. Buyers of house apply to Bank for financing. Bank hires Appraiser to determine the fair market value of the house. Appraiser negligently states that the house is worth $300,000. Bank agrees to make loan to Buyers; in the course of the transaction, Bank supplies Buyers with a copy of Appraiser's report. Acting partly in reliance on the report, Buyers complete their purchase of the house. They then discover that the fair market value of the house is $200,000. Buyers sue Appraiser for negligent misrepresentation. The appraisal report stated in an appropriately visible location that it was "intended for use by Bank for a mortgage finance transaction only." In view of this language, Buyers' reliance on the report was unreasonable as a matter of law. Appraiser is not liable to Buyers. The same result might be reached by observing that the report was not intended for the guidance of Buyers.

k. *Public duties.* Subsection (3) relaxes the strictures of Subsection (2) when a statute or regulation obliges a defendant to speak. The court does not then have its usual role in defining the defendant's duty. The duty has been defined by a legislature or agency. The negligent defendant is presumptively liable to anyone the statute was meant to protect, and for losses sustained in whatever transactions the statute was meant to cover. The presumption is rebuttable. Analysis of the statute's purpose and the consequences of liability may suggest that the legislature did not intend to create civil liability after all, or likely would not have intended it if the question had been foreseen. If applying Subsection (3) would create indeterminate liability, it is particularly unsafe to assume that liability follows from the defendant's obligation to speak. In that case, a court should not find a duty unless it is clear that the statute was meant to provide a right of action to a party in the plaintiff's position.

Illustrations:

23. Buyer applies for a loan from Bank to purchase car from Dealer. Before releasing funds, Bank requires submission of a "report of sale," a document that Dealer is required by statute to produce for each car sold. The report lists any security interests in the vehicle; Bank

wants to ensure that it is named for that purpose. Dealer issues a report that is satisfactory but negligent: Bank is named, but in fact Dealer has failed to record Bank's interest. Buyer obtains the loan and fails to repay it. Upon discovering that it cannot collect from Buyer, Bank sues Dealer for negligent misrepresentation. Court finds that Bank is among the parties for whose benefit the legislature imposed a duty to create an accurate report of sale. Dealer is liable to Bank.

24. Applicant applies to Agency for a permit to open a car dealership. Agency requires Applicant to produce certification from City's zoning official that the dealership will be located at an appropriate site. Zoning official negligently provides the certification. Agency awards Applicant a permit. Applicant spends time and money establishing the dealership, then discovers that zoning rules forbid the operation of such a business at its chosen location. Applicant suffers financial losses and sues City for negligent misrepresentation. Although a statute makes City liable for the torts of its agents, Court finds that City's zoning official spoke in fulfillment of a regulation that was intended to assist Agency in its decisions, not to protect the interests of those seeking permits. City is not liable to Applicant.

l.   *Damages.* Damages under this Section aim to restore the plaintiff to the financial position that the plaintiff would have occupied if the defendant had spoken carefully. This is often known as an "out of pocket" measure of recovery. Damages do not attempt to restore a plaintiff to the position that would have resulted if the false statements the defendant made had in fact been true. That would amount to an expectation or "loss of bargain" measure of recovery of the kind familiar from contract law and available in some cases of fraud. Damages here follow the usual logic of recovery for negligence. They are meant to bring home to defendants the costs of their mistakes, not to hold them to what they negligently said. See Illustration 25. For comparison to recovery in cases of fraudulent misrepresentation, see Chapter 2, § X.

The distinction just drawn is most often relevant when a defendant's misstatement causes the plaintiff to enter into a transaction that is expected to be profitable but turns out badly. If the defendant's negligent advice causes the plaintiff to buy property for the sake of investment, for example, damages are not measured by the difference between the actual value of the property and the value that the defendant said it had. Damages are measured by the difference between the price the plaintiff paid for the property and the value it would have been understood to have if the defendant had used due care. The measurement is made as of the time of the transaction, not by examining how the purchase turned out later, in order to separate the harm caused by the defendant's misstatement from other influences that may affect the performance of an investment after it is made. See Illustration 26.

A plaintiff also can collect for certain other losses beyond the "out of pocket" measure. These are sometimes called consequential damages, though that term can invite confusion with the law of contract; "special" damages may be a better way to refer to them in tort. Either term is meant to separate the immediate losses the plaintiff took on a transaction from less direct losses also caused by reliance on what the defendant said. Whether a plaintiff can recover for the less direct losses is governed, first, by the rules on scope of liability noted in Comment *i*. Second, the losses must be proven to a reasonable degree of certainty. Damages under this heading may include wasted expenditures the plaintiff made in reliance on the expectations the defendant created.

The principles stated in this Comment are meant as guides to decision, not as rigid categories. The notion of "out of pocket" recovery, for example, sometimes may be an awkward or unsatisfactory fit to an unusual set of facts. In that case, a court reasonably will recur to first principles and seek a measure of recovery that restores the position the plaintiff would have occupied if the tort had not been committed.

Illustrations:

25. Firm hires Accountant to prepare audit report for the benefit of specified potential Investor. Accountant negligently certifies financial statements indicating that Firm is in excellent condition with reliable expectations of profits. In fact, Firm is near bankruptcy. Investor, acting in reliance on Accountant's report, invests $100,000 in Firm. Firm goes bankrupt. Investor's damages are the $100,000 that Investor lost out of pocket, not the amount the investment would have produced if Accountant's statements had been true and Firm had been profitable.

26. Firm hires Accountant to prepare audit report for the benefit of specified potential Investor. Accountant negligently understates Firm's liabilities. Acting in reliance on Accountant's statements, Buyer purchases Firm. A year later, Buyer sells Firm at a loss. Firm's value decreased during Buyer's ownership for several reasons, including a decline in the demand for Firm's products. There is a fair basis for estimating the market value that Firm would have had at the time of the acquisition if Buyer and other potential acquirers had received a competent account of Firm's liabilities. Accountant is liable for the difference between that amount and the price Buyer paid for Firm. Accountant is not liable for losses Buyer suffered in excess of that sum on account of the decline in demand for Firm's products.

m. Significance of contract. Restatement Second, Torts § 552 was addressed primarily to cases in which the parties did not have a contract. Comment *g* of that Section stated, however, that its liability extended to cases in which the plaintiff had directly hired the defendant to speak. The tort claim in those circumstances is now eliminated by § 3 and by Subsection (5) here, however, which both reflect the judicial consensus against the use of tort suits to recover for economic losses that arise from a breach of contract.

Section 4 of this Chapter recognizes an exception to the economic loss rule of § 3 for malpractice claims against professionals. Such claims may be used to recover for economic loss even when the professional has a contract with the plaintiff. Sometimes those acts of malpractice may seem to involve "negligent misrepresentations," but a client who sues a professional proceeds under § 4, not this Section.

§ 6   Negligent Performance of Services

(1) One who, in the course of his business, profession, or employment, or in any other transaction in which he has a pecuniary interest, performs a service for the benefit of others, is subject to liability for pecuniary loss caused to them by their reliance upon the service, if he fails to exercise reasonable care in performing it.

(2) The liability stated in Subsection (1) is limited to loss suffered

     (a) by the person or one of a limited group of persons for whose benefit the actor performs the service; and

     (b) through reliance upon it in a transaction that the actor intends to influence.

(3) A plaintiff's recovery under this Section is subject to the same rules of comparative responsibility that apply to other claims of negligence.

(4) This Section does not recognize liability for negligence in the course of negotiating or performing a contract between the parties.

Comment:

a. Analogies to negligent misrepresentation. This Section and § 5 are complementary. Section 5 recognizes liability when a defendant negligently supplies information for the guidance of others. This Section recognizes liability when a defendant negligent performs a service for the benefit of others. In either case, the defendant intends the plaintiff's reliance, and in either case, the plaintiff does rely. As explained in § 5, Comment *a*, some cases can be described as involving either the supply of information or the performance of a service. Nothing should depend on that characterization, or on a plaintiff's choice to proceed under the rule of this Section or the rule of the previous one.

The close relationship between this Section and § 5 can be seen in cases that are similar in all respects except the form of the defendant's negligence: statements in § 5, services here. Thus § 5 recognizes liability when an accountant makes negligent misrepresentations about a firm and invites reliance on them by investors. See, e.g., § 5, Illustration 25. An accountant can likewise be held liable under this Section when the facts are the same but the negligence takes the form of a careless oversight in the accountant's inspection, rather than a misstatement afterwards. See Illustration 1 below.

This Section also provides most of the same safeguards as § 5 against indeterminate or disproportionate liability: the requirement that the service be rendered in the course of the defendant's business, or that the defendant have a pecuniary interest of some other sort; the objective measurement of the defendant's intent; the requirement that the plaintiff be part of a limited group the defendant meant to benefit; and application of principles of comparative responsibility to account for the plaintiff's own contribution to the loss. The longer discussion of these and other points in § 5 can be carried over to this Section where necessary. Liability under this Section, like liability under § 5, is unavailable when the defendant's negligence occurs in the performance of a contract with the plaintiff.

Liabilities under this Section should be extended by cautious analogy to case law under § 5 and its predecessor. The principal function of this Section is simply to permit the logic of § 5 to operate where the policies behind that provision are engaged but where it is difficult to describe the defendant's negligent act as a misrepresentation.

Illustrations:

1. Limited Partnership hires Accountant to perform auditing services. Accountant negligently fails to examine transactions made by general partners that would have been of concern to the limited partners. The resulting report from Accountant contains no misrepresentations, but it fails to discuss matters that should have been noted. The limited partners rely on the accountant's work and suffer losses as a result. Accountant's contract was with the partnership, not the partners, but its assistance was provided for the partners' benefit and with the understanding that they would rely on it. Accountant is liable to the limited partners under the rule of this Section.

2. Owner of tavern agrees to sell it to Buyer. Buyer hires Lawyer to handle the closing; Owner does not retain counsel. All parties understand that Lawyer works for Buyer. With Buyer's consent, however, Lawyer tells Owner that he will protect Owner's interests as well when drawing up the contract documents. Lawyer negligently fails to include customary safeguards of Owner's rights in the contact. As a result, Owner ends up an unsecured creditor of Buyer and suffers losses when Buyer later defaults on payments. Lawyer is liable to Owner under this Section. The result is otherwise if Lawyer does not tell Owner that he will represent Owner's interests.

3. Potential Buyer of house asks Realtor to have the furnace inspected. Realtor works for Seller, not for Buyer, but agrees to arrange for an inspection. Realtor negligently hires Amateur for the purpose, and Amateur declares the furnace to be in good condition. Buyer purchases the house. The furnace fails. Buyer sues Realtor for negligently selecting Amateur to perform the inspection. Realtor is subject to liability under this Section. Amateur is subject to liability under § 5.

4. Buyer borrows money from Bank to finance construction of a new house by Contractor. Buyer's agreement with Bank gives Bank the right to inspect the construction before issuing payments to Contractor.

Bank negligently inspects Contractor's work, overlooks various errors in it, and disburses payments. Buyer sues Bank. Bank knew that Buyer was out of town and unable to inspect the construction himself, but Bank's purpose in inspecting the work was not to benefit Buyer. It was to protect Bank's security interest in the house. Bank is not liable to Buyer.

5.   Owner of a machine hires Mechanic to service it. Owner later sells the machine to Buyer. Buyer then discovers that Mechanic's work was negligent and that the machine's engine is wearing out prematurely as a result. Buyer sues Mechanic to recover the cost of repairs. Mechanic is not liable to Buyer, because Mechanic did not act for Buyer's benefit. Mechanic would be subject to liability under this Section if Owner had hired him to service the machine for the purpose of satisfying Buyer and closing the sale.

b.   *Three-cornered construction disputes.* An important class of case under this Section involves litigation between a contractor hired to erect a building and the architect who designed it. Both are hired by the project's owner, but they have no contract with each other. A mistake in the architect's plans imposes costs on the builder, who sues the architect to recover. Sometimes the negligence of the architect or other design professional takes the form of a misrepresentation. In other cases, it may amount to a nonverbal misjudgment or other lack of care. This Restatement recognizes tort liability on such facts. See § 3, Illustration 8, in which liability may be found under the rule of this Section or the previous one. The plans drawn by the architect are intended to serve as a basis for reliance by the contractor who forms a bid on the basis of them and is then hired to carry them out. The architect's plans are analogous to the audit report that an accountant supplies to a client for distribution to potential investors—a standard case of liability under § 5. In either instance, the defendant's work is meant to provide a basis for reliance by another party, and does. If this allocation of responsibility is not congenial to the parties, they are free to change it in the contracts that link them.

There is no liability in tort, by contrast, when the owner of a construction project sues a subcontractor for negligence resulting in economic loss; nor is liability found when one subcontractor is sued by another because the negligence of the first drives up the costs of the second. A subcontractor's negligence in either case is viewed just as a failure in the performance of its obligations to its contractual partner, not as the breach of a duty in tort to other subcontractors on the same job, or to the owner of the project. This way of describing the subcontractor's role is not inevitable in all cases. General rules are favored in this area of the law, however, because their clarity allows parties to do business on a surer footing. In this setting, a rule of no liability is made especially attractive by the number and intricacy of the contracts that define the responsibilities of subcontractors on many construction projects. That web of contracts would be disrupted by tort suits between subcontractors or suits brought against them by a project's owner. Allowing a suit against the architect of a project by a party who made a bid in reliance on a defective plan does not create comparable problems.

    c.   *Subsequent purchasers of property.* Another recurring case under this Section arises when a plaintiff buys a house, discovers a hidden defect that is expensive to repair, and sues the architect who designed the house or the contractor who built it. The plaintiff has no contract with either of those parties; their contracts were with a previous owner of the house. This Restatement does not recognize tort liability in that circumstance. Liability fails as a doctrinal matter because the defendant did not act for the purpose of providing a basis for reliance by the plaintiff. In the cases discussed in the prior Comment, the architect knows that the plans commissioned by the owner are meant to serve as a basis for a bid, and thus as a basis for reliance, by a contractor. In the cases considered here, the contractor builds the house and supplies warranties for the owner, not primarily for subsequent purchasers—though of course the contractor may well foresee that other purchasers will someday exist.

    The denial of liability on the facts considered here is also supported by the policies stated in § 1 of this Chapter. The buyer of a house has other ways to manage the risk of economic loss from latent defects: inspection, insurance, or negotiations with the seller (who might, in turn, have been able to negotiate with the builder for a transferable warranty). The result stated here is also most consistent with the law of products liability. No tort liability is recognized when a product fails to perform or causes damage to itself in a manner that produces pure economic loss. The plaintiff's remedies are left to contract. This Comment resolves claims arising from the defective construction of a house according to the same principles. Such cases are made difficult principally by the plight of the buyer for whom the house represents a great investment. But as often is true in cases under this Chapter, the question is not whether the buyer is entitled to a remedy. The question is the theory on which the remedy is best pursued. Many states provide relief to plaintiffs on the facts considered here on theories of implied warranty or by statute. Those sources of law provide a better basis for relief than the law of torts when a house disappoints a buyer's economic expectations. They can be fashioned to address the specific problem and its equities without creating a principle of uncertain reach.

Illustration:

    6.   Buyer purchases house from Seller. Buyer then discovers that the chimney is pulling away from the rest of the house and has inadequate support in the ground. The defects cause no personal injuries and no damage to other property besides the house itself, but they will be expensive to fix. Buyer sues Builder, who negligently constructed the house for Seller. Builder is not liable in tort to Buyer.

§ 7 Economic Loss from Injury to a Third Person or to Property Not Belonging to the Claimant

Except as provided elsewhere in this Restatement, a claimant cannot recover for economic loss caused by

(a) unintentional injury to another person; or

(b) unintentional injury to property in which the claimant has no proprietary interest.

Comment:

a. Scope. The two limits on recovery stated in this Section are related applications of the same principle, and they apply to facts that usually have certain features in common. The plaintiff and defendant typically are strangers. The defendant commits a negligent act that injures a third party's person or property, and indirectly though perhaps foreseeably—causes various sorts of economic loss to the plaintiff: lost income or profits, missed business opportunities, expensive delays, or other disruption. The plaintiff may suffer losses, for example, because the defendant injured someone with whom the plaintiff had a contract and from whom the plaintiff had been expecting performance, such as an employee or supplier. See Illustration 1. Or the plaintiff may be unable to make new contracts with others, such as customers who cannot conveniently reach the plaintiff's business because the defendant's negligence has damaged property that now blocks the way. See Illustration 4. The common law of tort does not recognize a plaintiff's claim in such circumstances.

Illustrations:

1. Driver negligently runs over Goalie, who has a contract to play for Employer's hockey team. As a result of the accident, Goalie is unable to perform for the rest of the season, and Employer suffers lost revenues from ticket sales. Employer has no tort claim against Driver.

2. Owner buys a policy from Insurer to cover the risk of damage or loss to Owner's barge. Tortfeasor negligently sinks the barge, forcing Insurer to pay Owner under the terms of the policy. Insurer seeks to recover those sums from Tortfeasor. Insurer may be entitled to restitution as subrogee of the rights of Owner. Insurer does not have a right to collect from Tortfeasor in an action for negligence.

3. Carrier delivering toxic chemicals to Factory negligently spills them on Factory's property. The spill forces Factory to shut down for a week, during which time Employees of Factory go unpaid. Employees have no tort claim against Carrier for their lost wages.

4. Builder negligently constructs a building for Client. The building collapses as a result, forcing the closure of adjacent streets for several weeks. Delicatessen, which operates next door to the collapsed building, suffers no physical damage but loses profits because customers

cannot reach the entrance while the street is closed. Delicatessen has no tort claim for negligence against Builder for lost profits.

Many state statutes allow a plaintiff to recover for economic loss that results from the wrongful death of another. Common law in some jurisdictions may provide such a right to recover for loss of consortium, which this Restatement does not classify as economic injury. Those rights of action are outside the scope of this Restatement, and they are not affected by the rule of this Section. Liability for intentional interference with contractual relations is addressed in Chapter [X].

b. Rationale. The rule of this Section is justified by several considerations. The first, as noted in § 1, is that economic losses can proliferate long after the physical forces at work in an accident have spent themselves. A collision that sinks a ship will cause a well-defined loss to the ship's owner; but it also may foreseeably cause economic losses to wholesalers who had expected to buy the ship's cargo, then to retailers who had expected to buy from the wholesalers, and then to suppliers, employees, and customers of the retailers, and so on. Recognizing claims for those sorts of losses would greatly increase the number, complexity, and expense of potential lawsuits arising from many accidents. In some cases, recognition of such claims would also result in liabilities that are indeterminate and out of proportion to the culpability of the defendant. These costs do not seem likely to be justified by comparable benefits. Courts doubt that threats of open-ended liability would usefully improve the incentives of parties to take precautions against accidents or would make a material contribution to the cause of fairness.

At the same time, the victims of economic injury often can protect themselves effectively by means other than a tort suit. They may be able to obtain first-party insurance against their losses, or recover in contract from those who do have good claims against the defendant. Those contractual lines of protection against economic loss, where available, are considered preferable to judicial assignments of liability in tort. See discussion in § 1.

The rationales just stated are general, and no one of them is conclusive. They prevail by their cumulative force. And while they do not apply equally to every claim that arises under this Section, most courts reject such claims categorically. They have concluded that distinctions allowing some plaintiffs to recover but not others, based on a case-by-case inquiry into the policies at issue, cannot be made in a sufficiently principled manner. Denying claims by rule undeniably works a hardship on plaintiffs with claims that fall outside the policies that make the rule attractive—claims that do not lend themselves to solution by contract, for example, or that present no problems of indeterminacy. But a rule against recovery has other advantages: predictability, clarity, and economy of application for courts, lawyers, and those attempting to plan their affairs and anticipate their liabilities. In this area, those values have been thought to outweigh the benefits of occasionally providing relief. Where exceptions are appropriate, they are best established by statute, as was done in the Oil Pollution Act of 1990.

 c. Proprietary interests. A claimant with a proprietary interest in property can recover for economic losses that result when the property is damaged. Simple ownership is the most familiar example of a proprietary interest, but there are other kinds as well. Proprietary interests can be divided into two types: those that arise from mere possession of property, and those that arise from ownership interests without need of possession. If a claimant possesses property without owning it, courts decide whether the resulting interest is "proprietary" by using a functional test. They ask whether the claimant has control of the property and is responsible for its maintenance and repair. Thus the law frequently allows a lessee or bailee of property to recover for damage to it, but does not allow recovery by a claimant who occupies or holds property under a license that confers less extensive powers and responsibilities.

 If the claimant does not possess the damaged property, then any proprietary interest must arise from a formal right of ownership in it. Common examples of parties with rights in property they do not possess include a lessor, a remainderman, a bailor, and the holder of an easement. These parties' rights are regarded as proprietary interests, so they can recover for economic losses they suffer when the property is damaged while out of their possession. By contrast, a claimant who does not possess the property and has a merely contractual interest in it, such as an option to purchase or a contract for future delivery, cannot recover in tort when the property is damaged. The rights of the buyer and seller in such a case are defined by their contracts.

Illustrations:

 5. Company hires Contractor to build an underground pipeline. Unrelated Excavator negligently damages the pipeline while it is under construction. Contractor has control of the pipeline at the time the incident occurs, and is responsible for repair of any damage to the work until the project is completed. Contractor can recover its losses from Excavator.

 6. Vessel negligently damages a bridge that Railroad has a right to use. The bridge is owned and maintained by another. The damage forces Railroad to send its trains by an alternate route that is more expensive than using the bridge. Railroad cannot recover its losses from owner of Vessel.

 7. Manufacturer hires Factory to add dye to fabric. While Factory is performing the work, Contractor negligently severs a power line that is owned by a local utility company and that carries power to Factory's machines. The fabric is ruined as a result. The court finds that Factory was acting as bailee of the fabric. Factory may recover in tort against Contractor.

 d. Damage to property. As already noted, economic loss can be recovered as an ordinary item of damages when it results from actionable physical harm to the claimant or the claimant's property. But a plaintiff whose property suffers some harm does not necessarily gain the right to recover for economic loss that results from other features of the same general incident. Courts require a causal connection between the physical harm and the economic loss; the plaintiff must show a reduction in the value of the physical property at issue or a reduction in the ability to exploit it.

Illustrations:

8.   Contractor negligently severs a power line running from Utility to Factory where steel is being melted. The resulting loss of power causes Factory to suffer three types of losses. (a) Factory has to pour molten metal out of its furnace to prevent the furnace from being destroyed during the outage; this causes a reduction in the metal's quality and value. (b) Factory loses the profit that it would have made from selling the metal if it had not been poured out of the furnace and thus reduced in quality. (c) Factory loses profits on other work that it could have performed but did not attempt during the hours when power was unavailable. Contractor is subject to liability for loss (a) because it is a claim for physical damage to property. Contractor is subject to liability for loss (b) because it is a claim for economic loss resulting from physical damage to property. Contractor is not subject to liability for loss (c) because it is a claim for economic loss unconnected to damage to property. Categories (a) and (b) must be measured in a fashion that avoids double recovery for the same loss of value.

9.   Barge Operator negligently causes an oil spill that forces the closure of a harbor and requires Contractor to delay work on a construction project there. The spilled oil also ruins an expensive piece of Contractor's machinery, but the machinery can be swiftly replaced and is not the cause of Contractor's delay. Contractor can recover from Barge Operator for the ruined machinery but not for the costs occasioned by the delay of the project, unless the rule of § 8 applies.

e.   Fishermen. Commercial fishermen have sometimes prevailed on claims that appear inconsistent with the rules of this Section. Those results occur in two different kinds of cases, and they are best considered separately.

(a)   In the first pattern, a defendant's negligence damages a ship, typically by collision. The accident causes economic losses to fishermen hired to work on the ship, and who were to be paid a percentage of the profits from the voyage—a so-called "lay agreement," which might be viewed as a type of joint venture with the owner. It is understood, as a background matter, that the owner likely can sue the tortfeasor for profits that were expected from the ship's voyage and were lost because of delays caused by the accident. It is further understood that the owner is liable in restitution to the fishermen for their share of any such recovery; the judgment in favor of the owner can be accompanied on the spot by recognition of a constructive trust in favor of the fishermen. In these circumstances, courts have alternatively given fishermen the option of skipping the middleman and suing the tortfeasor directly.

Why fishermen are allowed this direct option is a matter of occasional debate. The same privilege is not extended to other parties who suffer economic harm when they have contracts with those whose property is damaged. The difference is probably best explained by the unusually clear and precise nature of the fishermen's entitlement: though they do not own the damaged property, they are joint venturers with the party who does own it. Payment from the tortfeasor, if made to the owner, passes through to the fishermen in a manner that is unusually regular, clear-cut, and automatic. Allowing the fishermen to sue in their own right thus amounts to a convenient shortcut, not an expansion of substantive rights. Nobody is made worse off by it, since the tortfeasor merely pays one party rather than another.

Describing this state of affairs as a "fishermen's exception," or explaining it on the ground that fishermen are "favorites of admiralty," is unfortunate and best avoided. Those phrases imply that fishermen are, by virtue of their trade, exempt from the rules of this Section and able to collect whenever they suffer economic harm on account of a defendant's negligence. That is not so. In the well-reasoned cases, only certain fishermen have been subject to distinctive treatment: those who have lay agreements with the owner of a damaged ship. The distinctive treatment is justified not because the plaintiffs catch fish but because features of their commercial arrangement make it unusually efficient to let them collect directly rather than indirectly. The difference is procedural in character. The allowance is not properly used to provide fishermen with a greater recovery than they would have received in the end without it, or to make a defendant pay more than would have been due without it.

(b) In a second pattern, a defendant causes harm to a natural resource, typically by spilling oil or other chemicals into a body of water that serves as a fishing ground. The affected fishermen sue and often win damages, although they had no proprietary interest in the contaminated waters or the uncaught fish. These cases are usually, and correctly, understood as suits to remedy a public nuisance. See § 8, which sometimes allows a plaintiff to recover for damage to a natural resource if the plaintiff's injury differs from the injuries suffered by the community in general. Fishermen often qualify as plaintiffs under that rule, as may various others. Referring to the result as a "fisherman's exception" to the rule of this Section is again misleading. The right to sue belongs to anyone who satisfies the principles of § 8.

f. *Judge and jury.* Most courts express the rule of this Section by describing it as a limitation of the defendant's duty. Other courts have occasionally stated the principle as a matter of causation, or scope of liability, or as a rule about damages. The labeling of the issue usually is of no consequence so long as the rule's applicability is understood to be a matter of law for the court, not a question for the jury. Treating the rule as a limitation on the defendant's duty will generally be the clearest way to establish that distribution of labor.

§ 8 Public Nuisance Resulting in Economic Loss

An actor whose wrongful conduct harms or obstructs a public resource or public property is subject to liability for resulting economic loss if the claimant's losses are distinct in kind from those suffered by members of the affected community in general.

Comment:

a. Scope. This Section addresses the liability in tort of a defendant who creates a public nuisance that results only in economic loss to the plaintiff. This Section does not seek to restate the substantive law of public nuisance except as necessary to explain those cases that produce liability in tort for economic loss. Many public nuisances are not of that character; they cause physical harm, as when a defendant negligently leaves an obstruction in a road and the plaintiff collides with it, or as when a defendant's pollution causes damage to property that the plaintiff owns. Those cases are outside the scope of this Section.

In addition to the common-law claims recognized here, public officials may bring civil or criminal actions against a defendant who creates a public nuisance. An action of that type is the most common response to a defendant's invasion of a public right. The definition of "public nuisance" for those purposes is widely a matter of statute, and tends to be considerably broader than the common-law definition recognized by this Section as a basis for a private suit. Statutes also may provide citizens with rights of recovery more expansive than those recognized by the common law.

b. General principles; rationale. A public nuisance arises when a defendant's wrongful act causes harm to a public right: a right held in common by all members of the community. The wrongfulness may be established by showing that the defendant's conduct violated a statute (and thus was a public nuisance "per se"), or by showing that the conduct was intentional and unprivileged, that it was unreasonable, or that it was subject to strict liability. When a public nuisance is thus established, a private plaintiff generally can sue only to redress a distinctive or "special" injury distinct in kind from the harm suffered by all members of the affected community.

The propositions just stated are widely accepted, but are phrased at a level of generality that has sometimes caused confusion about their scope. Any dangerous act by a defendant might, in the abstract, be described as invading the rights of the public, and this way of speaking has occasionally caused unsound claims of public nuisance to be brought on facts outside the traditional ambit of the tort. See Comment *g*. The actual scope of tort liability for economic loss caused by a public nuisance has generally and appropriately been confined to the more limited circumstances stated in the black letter of this Section and discussed in the Comments.

Private liability for creation of a public nuisance is an exception to the rule of § 7, which ordinarily prevents a plaintiff from recovering for economic loss caused by damage to property that the plaintiff does not own. That background rule is justified in part because redress may more appropriately be sought from the defendant by a better plaintiff: the owner of the damaged property. When the defendant does harm to resources that have no private owner, however, it may be that no natural plaintiff exists who can be counted upon to seek redress. An action by a public official will commonly lie to abate the nuisance by injunction but may not involve monetary recovery for harm done. The social and private costs of a public nuisance can nevertheless be large. Allowing certain classes of private parties a right of action can then provide appropriate compensation for their losses and usefully deter repetition of the wrong.

c.   *Special injury.* Recovery in tort by everyone who is harmed by a public nuisance would raise the characteristic problems that give rise to the rules of this Section. Defendants would be subject to potentially massive and unpredictable liabilities, and courts would be faced with lawsuits large and unwieldy in number and in character. In response to these concerns, courts recognize liability for a public nuisance in tort only to a plaintiff who has suffered a "special injury" distinct in kind from the harm suffered by all members of the affected community.

What injuries are "special," or "distinct in kind," is unavoidably a matter of judgment rather than rule. Courts have reduced some of those judgments to the patterns explained in Comments *d* and *e*. In cases arising outside those patterns, decisions about recovery are best made by asking if liability would cause the problems that the requirement of special injury is meant to address: whether permitting the plaintiff's claim would multiply the amount of litigation or the defendant's liabilities unduly, and whether plaintiffs who are allowed to sue can be separated in a principled fashion from those who are not.

d.   *Harm to public resources.* A public nuisance involving harm to a natural resource most often arises from contamination of waterways, as when a defendant spills toxic chemicals into the sea and thus causes economic injury to those who depend on it for commercial or recreational purposes. Courts typically recognize fishermen as a class of plaintiffs who suffer special injury in those circumstances and allow them to recover in tort. As an original matter it might be questioned whether the injuries suffered by such fishermen are clearly distinct from the injuries suffered by the many other parties who are affected by a spill but whose claims tend to be denied. That conclusion is nevertheless repeated often, probably because it provides a familiar and convenient answer to a hard question.

The pattern just described is sometimes confused with the practice of allowing fishermen who work on lay agreements to recover when a defendant negligently damages the ship they are using. Courts occasionally view these patterns together and infer the existence of a "fishermen's rule" exempting that class from the usual rules governing recovery for economic loss. The inference is faulty. Fishermen recover in the two circumstances for distinct reasons. The rationale for recognizing the claims of fishermen on lay agreements are explained in § 7, Comment *e*. When claims by fishermen to recover for public nuisance are allowed, it is on a different rationale, or should be: they are the class of victims most immediately and obviously affected by contamination of a waterway, and can be separated with tolerable clarity from other classes of affected plaintiffs. But claims by fishermen need not be allowed when they do not satisfy the criteria just noted, nor is there any impediment to recognizing claims by other groups who may satisfy the criteria in any given case.

Illustrations:

1. Carrier negligently spills toxic chemicals into a bay. Hotel located on a nearby beach sues to recover for economic losses it suffers when its customers, after hearing of the spill, cancel their reservations. The court finds that Carrier created a public nuisance, but that Hotel's injuries are similar in kind to injuries shared by all businesses in the area. Carrier is not liable to Hotel.

2. Same facts as Illustration 1, but Carrier is sued by fishermen and clam diggers for economic losses that result from their inability to carry on their work as a result of the contamination of the bay. The court finds that these plaintiffs are directly prevented from exercising their right to catch fish and dig for clams. The court also finds that the fishermen and clam diggers have suffered injuries distinct in kind from those suffered by individuals and businesses in the area generally, and that permitting these plaintiffs to recover will not result in liabilities that are indeterminate in scale. Carrier is subject to liability to the fishermen and clam diggers for economic harm caused by the public nuisance it created.

e. Obstruction of public property. A public nuisance that causes economic harm can also involve the obstruction of public property or similar interference with access to it, as when the defendant's negligent conduct blocks a road. An obstruction of that kind may cause economic loss to plaintiffs who were accustomed to using the road for commercial purposes or who relied on it as a means of access for their customers. Suits to recover for such losses most often fail because the plaintiff cannot show a sufficiently distinctive injury. The courts typically conclude that the hardships the plaintiff has suffered are similar to those suffered by others, and that recovery by none of them is a lesser evil than recovery by all. Courts have been willing to recognize such claims in certain narrow circumstances, however, as when the defendant's wrongful conduct affects the plaintiff more severely than others. Compare Illustrations 3 and 4.

The requirement that the plaintiff show a "special injury," here as elsewhere in this Section, is a placeholder for the policies described in Comment *c*. Courts usually decline to impose liability for economic losses caused by obstruction of a public way because they see no end to it. Countless businesses might show that a given disruption to nearby traffic reduced the number of visits they received from customers. On the other hand, liability may be unobjectionable and useful if the plaintiff can show an injury that is sufficiently distinct to allow principled separation of the resulting claim from the claims that others might bring.

Illustrations:

3.   Builder negligently constructs a building for Client. The building collapses as a result, forcing the closure of adjacent streets for several weeks. Delicatessen, which operates next door to the collapsed building, suffers no physical damage but loses profits because customers cannot reach the entrance while the street is closed. Delicatessen sues Builder on a theory of public nuisance to recover the profits it lost during the closure. The court finds that Delicatessen's injuries are indistinguishable in kind from injuries suffered by large numbers of other businesses in the area. Builder is not liable in tort to Delicatessen.

4.   Restaurant on the bank of a river provides a dock where customers can arrive by boat. Logger wrongfully floats logs down the river in a loose manner that allows them to become stuck near Restaurant and block access to its dock. Restaurant sues Logger on a theory of public nuisance to recover profits it lost as a result of the blockage. The court finds that Logger created a public nuisance and that Restaurant suffered special damage as a result. Logger is subject to liability to Restaurant in tort.

f.   Abatement. A plaintiff may seek an injunction to abate a public nuisance that causes economic loss. The usual requirement that such a plaintiff show a special injury applies here as well, and again it may be satisfied by plaintiffs who can show no personal injury or property damage. In some cases, a plaintiff seeking injunctive relief may be found to satisfy the requirement of "special injury" more easily than a plaintiff seeking to recover money, because the concerns in the background of the inquiry are different. An injunction does not subject a defendant to indeterminate liabilities or threaten the court with an avalanche of lawsuits. See Illustration 5, where the types of injuries stated by the injunction-seeking residents would not be enough to support liability if they were businesses seeking to recover for lost profits.

Illustration:

5.   Company opens a granite quarry near a residential area. Residents sue to enjoin Company's operations, claiming that Company has created a public nuisance. On the basis of evidence supplied by Residents, the court finds that the trucks Company uses to serve the quarry violate size and weight limits specified by ordinance for adjoining roads. The court further finds that the trucks cause noise and damage to the roads that affects Residents more than others in the community,

because Residents use the roads to come and go from their homes. Residents have a sufficiently special injury in prospect to allow them to sue, and to permit the court to enjoin Company's use of the trucks at their request.

g. *Products.* Tort suits seeking to recover for public nuisance have occasionally been brought against the makers of products that have caused harm, such as tobacco, firearms, and lead paint. These cases vary in the theory of damages on which they seek recovery, but often involve claims for economic losses the plaintiffs have suffered on account of the defendant's activities; they may include the costs of removing lead paint, for example, or of providing health care to those injured by smoking cigarettes. Liability on such theories has been rejected by most courts, and is excluded by this Section, because the common law of public nuisance is an inapt vehicle for addressing the conduct at issue. Mass harms caused by dangerous products are better addressed through the law of products liability, which has been developed and refined with sensitivity to the various policies at stake. Claims for reimbursement of expenses made necessary by a defendant's products might also be addressed by the law of warranty or restitution. If those bodies of law do not supply adequate remedies or deterrence, the best response is to address the problems at issue through legislation that can account for all the affected interests.

As noted in Comment *b*, problems caused by dangerous products might once have seemed to be matters for the law of public nuisance because the term "public nuisance" has sometimes been defined in broad language that appears to encompass anything injurious to public health and safety. The traditional office of the tort, however, has been narrower than those formulations suggest, and contemporary case law has made clear that its reach remains more modest. The rules stated in this Section and Comment reflect that modesty.

Chapter 2. Liability in Tort for Fraud

§ 9   Fraud

One who fraudulently makes a material misrepresentation of fact, opinion, intention, or law, for the purpose of inducing another to act or refrain from acting, is subject to liability for economic loss caused by the other's justifiable reliance on the misrepresentation.

Comment:

a. *Scope.* This Section states the general rule of liability for the tort of fraud, or deceit. The Comments below discuss foundational matters such as the scope of the tort and its relation to other causes of action. They also address the standard of proof and the requirement of materiality. The immediately subsequent Sections address the principal remaining elements of fraud: scienter (§ 10), justifiable reliance (§ 11), and the scope of the defendant's liability (§ 12). Later Sections explain variations on the basic tort: liability for nondisclosure (§ 13), liability for false statements of opinion (§ 14), and liability for promises that the maker does not intend to keep (§ 15). The measurement of damages in these and other tort cases may be the subject of a separate Restatement.

The word "fraud" has two general meanings in law. It may refer to a knowing misrepresentation without reference to the law of tort. Indeed, a fraudulent statement has consequences under many other branches of law— most notably the law of contract, the law of restitution, and criminal law. "Fraud" also may refer more specifically to the cause of action addressed by this Chapter. The distinction is worth noting because the best legal response to the act of fraud is not necessarily a claim in tort for fraud. Fraud most often does harm by causing a plaintiff to enter into a transaction and suffer losses as a result. The law of contract and the law of restitution supply remedies in such a case that may be superior to those provided in tort and that have traditionally been a plaintiff's first line of response. Thus many Illustrations in this Section that result in liability might also have been pressed as other sorts of claims. In Illustration 2, for example, Seller's fraud might serve as a defense against a claim for payment, as a reason for rescinding the transaction, or as a basis for a suit for breach of warranty.

The availability of other remedies for fraud, however, is no impediment to a plaintiff's ability to recover in tort. As discussed in § 2, the economic-loss rule generally forecloses tort liability for negligence in the negotiation or performance of a contract, but it does not impair the claims of fraud discussed in this Chapter. The economic-loss rule is meant to protect contractual allocations of risk against interference by the law of tort. Claims for fraud rarely cause such interference because parties to a contract do not usually treat the chance that they are lying to each other as a subject for their contract to allocate. They regard honesty as an assumed backdrop to their negotiations. (For treatment of cases in which the parties may be understood to allocate risks of dishonesty, see § 11, Comment *e*.) Liability in tort for fraud thus helps to protect the integrity of the contractual process and sometimes furnishes useful remedies that the law of contract does not as readily provide. For a comparison of the remedies available for fraud under the law of tort, contract, and restitution, see Comment *b*.

Actionable fraud may also be committed, of course, by a party who did not attempt to make a contract with the plaintiff, and in that case tort liability may be the plaintiff's only recourse. This pattern can occur, for example, when misrepresentations are made by an agent for a principal with whom the plaintiff has contractual relations. The agent may not be a party to the contract; the agent nevertheless can be held liable, perhaps along with the principal, in tort. See, e.g., § 11, Illustration 3.

b. Relation to restitutionary and contract remedies. As noted in Comment *a*, fraudulent statements that induce a plaintiff to enter into a contract may be addressed simultaneously by the law of tort, the law of contract, and the law of restitution. It may be useful to summarize the differences between the remedies typically available to a plaintiff under those three theories.

(1). Restitution. Rescission is a remedy for fraud available under the law of restitution and contract, not tort. Both sides give back whatever they received from the other, to the extent such a return is feasible. Rescission is not always available because it requires that a reasonably complete restoration of performance be possible between both parties. These acts of restoration can be supplemented by awards of incidental damages to make up for value that cannot be fully returned, or to reflect costs that the defrauded party incurred in reliance on the transaction. Some jurisdictions allow a plaintiff to recover punitive damages in conjunction with rescission in an appropriate case. See generally Restatement Third, Restitution and Unjust Enrichment §§ 13, 54.

The law of restitution may also require a defendant to disgorge consequential gains from a transaction. If fraud results in profits for the defendant that exceed the loss to the plaintiff, restitution (measured by the defendant's wrongful gain) may yield a larger recovery than tort or contract damages and may leave the plaintiff better off than if the fraud had never occurred. See Restatement Third, Restitution and Unjust Enrichment §§ 13, 51.

(2). Contract. The law of contract responds to fraud in several ways.

First, a court may find that the fraud prevented a contract from being formed at all, and so leave the parties to their remedies under the law of restitution.

Second, a contract procured by fraud may be treated as voidable; in other words, the victim of the fraud can elect either to affirm and enforce the contract despite the fraud that induced it or to disaffirm the contract and seek rescission. Rescission as a contract remedy is functionally indistinguishable from the remedy of the same name in restitution.

Third, if one party has obtained the other's assent by fraud to a writing that does not reflect their actual agreement, the contract may be reformed to reflect their true intentions and then be enforced on its new terms. See Restatement Second, Contracts § 166.

Finally, a misrepresentation, whether fraudulent or not, may amount to a warranty that goes unfulfilled, and in that case will entitle a plaintiff to contract damages. The original and strongest examples come from the law of sales. Except for "dealer talk" of the kind represented by Illustration 6, a seller's representations to a buyer about the qualities of a good sold will generally become part of the bargain and be enforceable as warranties. Damages for breach of warranty give the buyer the difference between the value of the goods as warranted and their value as delivered (or sometimes the cost of putting nonconforming goods into their promised condition). Courts allow recovery by the same logic in some settings that do not involve goods. The plaintiff recovers because the defendant gave an assurance and is held to it, whether it was fraudulent or honest.

As this statement of options shows, fraud in itself gives a plaintiff no claim to damages under the law of contract. If a party is induced to enter a contract by fraud, the fraud will typically allow the party to escape the contract or have it reformed. And if the fraudulent statement amounted to a promise, it can be enforced to the same extent as any other promise. But the law of contract does not otherwise enable a victimized party to both enforce a contract and also seek additional sums that would have been received if the defendant's fraudulent statement had been true. A plaintiff seeking that result might most closely achieve it by making a claim for punitive damages, which are available for breach of contract in some jurisdictions when the breach also amounts to tortious misconduct—a criterion satisfied if the defendant has engaged in fraud. See Restatement Second, Contracts § 355.

(3). Tort. A tort claim, unlike the other types of suit just described, permits recovery of damages for fraud as such and without reference to the validity of any contract between the parties. The plaintiff can leave the contract in place but seek damages for harm done by the defendant's misrepresentation.

Damages awarded in tort for fraud may be measured on an "out of pocket" basis: the difference between the value of what the plaintiff paid and received, along with other sums needed to restore the position the plaintiff would have occupied if the defendant had not committed the fraud. Such damages resemble a combination of reliance and consequential damages in the law of contract. Many states also let a plaintiff seek damages on a "loss of bargain" theory that resembles expectation damages in a contract case. See Restatement Second, Torts § 549. A limitation to out-of-pocket recovery in most cases is probably more consistent with the approach of this Restatement, which seeks to distinguish clearly between contract and tort theories of recovery.

Punitive damages also may be available as a remedy for intentional misconduct. This is the most common reason why a plaintiff who might have sued for breach of warranty sues instead, or in addition, in tort. The tort claim may be no easier to prove, but it often provides an easier route to punitive damages and sometimes may supply incidental advantages such as a longer statute of limitations due to particular facts of the case.

A plaintiff may allege a right to recover under multiple theories, but cannot be compensated more than once. The pursuit of multiple remedies may also be subject to rules of election. Rescission is obviously inconsistent with an effort to enforce a contract, such as a claim for expectation damages. Less obviously, perhaps, the remedy of rescission for fraud is often held to be inconsistent with a claim for tort damages, possibly because rescission should accomplish the same restoration of position that a tort claim would. Claims for breach of contract and for tort damages are not inconsistent with one another, however, and so usually may be advanced together at trial without an election between them so long as it is clear that the plaintiff can recover under one theory or the other, but not both.

Illustration:

1.   Buyer offers to purchase Seller's business for two installment payments of $450,000 spaced six months apart. Buyer is to receive half of Seller's shares in the company in return for each payment. After paying the first installment, Buyer discovers that Seller fraudulently misrepresented the value of the business: he made it appear to be worth $1.5 million, but its actual value was $500,000. Buyer can rescind the contract, returning Seller's shares and recouping his $450,000 payment. If Buyer instead affirms the contract and brings a tort claim for fraud, he owes Seller the remaining installment payment of $450,000, but can collect (or subtract), as out-of-pocket damages, the $400,000 difference between what he agreed to pay for the business ($900,000) and what it was worth ($500,000). If Buyer wishes to collect the $1 million difference between what the Seller said the business was worth and what it was worth in fact, Buyer must pursue that sum as a contract remedy for breach of warranty or as punitive damages for the tort claim. (Some states would allow recovery of the $1 million as compensatory damages in tort.) Buyer cannot collect both out-of-pocket damages in tort and expectation damages in contract.

c.   *Types of misrepresentations.* Fraud in its most common form involves misrepresentations of fact, as when the seller of a house falsely states that the roof does not leak. But the tort can also extend to some situations outside that pattern. First, a misrepresentation need not take the form of a statement. It may arise from conduct rather than words, as when the seller of a car turns back its odometer. Second, a misrepresentation can be implied rather than explicit. A statement of opinion may falsely imply, for example, that its holder knows of no facts to the contrary; liability then attaches to that false implication, not to the opinion or prediction in itself. Doubtful cases are best resolved by asking whether the defendant's statements included or implied any assertions that are capable of being proven false. See Illustration 2. (Liability for false statements of opinion as such, apart from any facts they might imply, is addressed in § 11.)

Liability also may be found under this Section for ambiguous statements and half-truths. Thus a speaker may make a statement and know that it is open to two interpretations, one true and one false. The statement is actionable if the speaker intends that it be understood in its false sense or is indifferent to which way the statement is taken; a speaker who knowingly makes an ambiguous statement is obliged to take reasonable steps to ensure that the statement is understood accurately. See Illustration 3. Liability may likewise be found if a speaker believes a statement is true as far as it goes but knows that it is misleading because it is incomplete or not duly qualified. See Illustration 4. On the other hand, a statement is not necessarily fraudulent merely because the speaker is aware of some facts contrary to it.

Much depends on the context of the representation and the surrounding customs. The author and recipient of a legal opinion letter may both understand that its conclusions represent the author's best judgment after considering facts and authorities in both directions, even if the author does not belabor that qualification explicitly.

However involved their details may become, the ultimate issue in all the cases just discussed is the same: a defendant who knowingly misleads another is subject to liability in damages for fraud.

Illustrations:

2. Buyer of a building asks Seller what material lies behind the structure's interior walls. Seller replies that it's "not a problem." Seller later discovers asbestos behind the walls and is required to spend large sums remediating it. Buyer sues Seller for fraud. Seller admits that he was aware of the asbestos, that he knew it might be expensive to remove, and that he knew it might have affected Buyer's decision to purchase the property. Seller claims that his statement that the material was "not a problem" was merely an opinion and so was not actionable. The trier of fact finds that Seller's statement falsely implied knowledge of facts to support the opinion and that Buyer justifiably relied on it. Seller is subject to liability for fraud.

3. Seller promises to deliver "new" specialty batteries to Buyer. Buyer later discovers that the batteries already had been used, and sues Seller for fraud. Buyer claims that Seller's description of the batteries as "new" meant that the batteries had never been used before. Seller contends that "new" meant the batteries were the most recent model of their kind, and not part of an earlier series. The trier of fact finds that the word "new" was ambiguous, and that Seller knew Buyer was relying on an interpretation that Seller did not share. Seller's failure to dispel the ambiguity subjects him to liability for fraud.

4. Retailer agrees to sell specialty cars made by Manufacturer. Retailer worries that its rights will not be exclusive; in response, Manufacturer represents that it has no intention of marketing the same specialty car through Rival, another dealership nearby. Two months later, Manufacturer opens a new dealership down the street from Retailer to sell the same specialty car. Manufacturer admits that it had long intended to open the new dealership and deliberately hid its plans from Retailer, but points out that its statement to Retailer was technically accurate: it never did intend to market the specialty car through Rival. The trier of fact finds that Manufacturer's representation, while not false on its face, was misleading because it caused Retailer to reasonably believe that Manufacturer intended to give Retailer exclusive rights. Manufacturer may be held liable for fraud.

d. Materiality. Liability for fraud attaches only to misrepresentations that are material. A misrepresentation is material if a reasonable person would give weight to it in deciding whether to enter into the relevant transaction, or if the defendant knew that the plaintiff would give it weight (whether reasonably or not). The question, in effect, is whether the defendant knew or should have known that the misrepresentation would matter to the plaintiff. If not, the plaintiff cannot collect damages in tort, though any resulting contract may still be voidable upon a showing that the plaintiff relied on the misrepresentation. See Restatement Second, Contracts § 164. This element of the tort is most likely to be important when one party to a negotiation makes false statements to the other about a matter collateral to the immediate subject of the bargain. Compare Illustrations 5 and 6. The materiality requirement also excludes liability for statements amounting to "puffery"—that is, a seller's broad and predictably exaggerated statements about the quality of an item, as distinct from particular claims of fact. (Claims based on such statements may be dismissed, in the alternative, for want of justifiable reliance.)

Illustrations:

5. Contractor on a building project in an unincorporated area approaches neighboring Town to negotiate the purchase of a water supply. Town tells Developer that it lacks the capacity to provide all the water that Developer needs; Town agrees to meet Developer's requirements only if Developer decreases the size of the project. Developer does so. Developer later learns that Town spoke falsely in the negotiations: Town did have the capacity to provide the water that Developer wanted, but preferred to allocate it elsewhere rather than to him. Developer sues Town for fraud. Developer's claim fails because Town's misrepresentation was not material. A reasonable person would not be expected to assign weight to the details of Town's reasons for its bargaining position, and Town had no reason to believe that Contractor regarded those details as important to his consent.

6. Buyer purchases a car from Seller. Seller tells Buyer during negotiations that the car is "top of the line" and provides an "outstanding ride." Buyer later determines that the car is mediocre and provides a poor ride. Buyer sues Seller for fraud. Buyer's claim fails because the court finds that Seller's claims were puffery; even if they were misrepresentations, they cannot be considered material. The same conclusion might also be explained by saying that a buyer cannot justifiably rely on obvious "dealer's talk."

e. Standard of proof. The elements of a tort claim ordinarily must be proven by a preponderance of the evidence, but most courts have required clear and convincing evidence to establish some or all of the elements of fraud. They reason that a claim of fraud is easy to allege and often has damaging side effects; it may injure the reputation of the defendant and entitle the plaintiff to seek punitive damages. Those points may be accurate, but in themselves they do not fully explain the higher standard of proof because they are true of many other intentional torts as well. The special treatment of fraud is better understood as a protection against encroachment into the law of contract by the law of tort. An allegation of fraud often arises from an exchange between the parties. The claim may allow the plaintiff to obtain more aggressive remedies in tort than contract law would provide. The law generally prefers that disputed transactions be resolved by the law of contract, and so makes escape from that body of law somewhat more difficult than the assertion of a tort claim that has no other legal home. Granted, some claims of fraud arise outside contractual settings; those patterns are less common, however, and the rules about the standard of proof have been devised for the typical case.

A majority of courts apply the clear-and-convincing standard of proof to all elements of a claim for fraud. A minority apply it to scienter and perhaps to certain other elements of the tort, but not to damages. This Restatement favors application of the heightened standard of proof only as far as the rationale for it will carry. The rationale is convincing when applied to an assertion that the defendant made a false statement knowingly, because that element of the tort—scienter—distinguishes a fraud claim from a claim of negligence that would be extinguished by a contract between the parties. See § 3. Once a defendant's culpable state of mind has been proven, however, it is difficult to see why the plaintiff should be put to a harder task in proving causation than would be necessary if the defendant were merely negligent. Applying a more demanding standard to the proof of damages is still harder to support. The best justification is that a jury might be confused by different standards of proof for different elements of a fraud claim, but juries are assigned more demanding tasks often enough. Because these issues have yet received only occasional judicial attention, this Restatement leaves to developing case law the details of when clear and convincing proof ought to be required. It recommends, however, that the heightened standard be applied sparingly and be justified by good and specific reasons whenever it is used.

§ 10   Scienter

A misrepresentation is fraudulent if the maker of it

(a)   knows or believes that the matter is not as he represents it to be,

(b)   knows that he does not have the confidence in the accuracy of his representation that he states or implies, or

(c)   knows that he does not have the basis for the representation that he states or implies.

Comment:

a.   Scienter generally. To prevail on a claim of fraud, a plaintiff must prove that the defendant made a misrepresentation knowingly; in other words, the plaintiff must prove scienter. This requirement is the most important difference between cases of fraud and cases of negligent misrepresentation or breach of contract. The legal tests for negligence or breach of contract are both objective in character. They do not depend on whether the defendant consciously committed a wrong. Fraud depends on a subjective test. The defendant must be shown to have had a culpable state of mind. The motive for making the statement is not relevant, but liability for fraud does require a conscious discrepancy between some feature of a defendant's representation and the truth. Thus a party who makes a false statement carelessly, but in good faith, is not liable for fraud, but may be liable for negligent misrepresentation under the rule of § 5. A party who promises an act but then decides not to carry it out may be liable for breach of contract or on a theory of promissory estoppel, but is not liable for fraud unless the statement of intention was false when made. See § 15. In short, the law of fraud is concerned with various sorts of lies, not with mistakes or broken promises.

b. *Implied representations.* A statement often includes several components to which the rule of this Section, and the requirement of scienter, might apply: the literal truth of the matter stated (the number of square feet in a house, the financial condition of a company), but also implied claims about the speaker's confidence in the statement and basis for asserting it. These latter points are representations in their own right, even if they are not explicit. They can be true or false, just as the literal substance of the claim can be true or false. Thus a speaker may offer a statement as certain despite having doubts about it, or imply that a claim is founded on personal observation when it is based on hearsay. In such cases, the speaker may think the substance of the claim is true, yet still commit a knowing misrepresentation with respect to the basis for the claim or the confidence it warrants. The speaker then has the necessary state of mind to support liability for fraud if the other elements of the tort are satisfied.

Illustrations:

1.   Buyer negotiates a purchase of property from Seller. Seller firmly states that the property consists of 130 acres. Seller believes this statement of the acreage is more likely true than false, but knows that he has not conducted a sufficient investigation of the point to support the sense of certainty that he implies. Buyer completes the purchase of the property in justifiable reliance on Seller's claims, then discovers that the property consists of 90 acres. Seller is subject to liability to Buyer for fraud.

2.   Entrepreneur invites Investor to buy stock in his company. In the course of their negotiations, Entrepreneur grossly understates the company's liabilities. Investor purchases stock in reliance on Entrepreneur's false statements and suffers losses as a result. The trier of fact finds that Entrepreneur, while negligent, believed that his statements were true and well-founded; Entrepreneur had examined the relevant balance sheets but misunderstood them. Investor has no tort claim for fraud against Entrepreneur. Nor does Investor have a claim for

negligent misrepresentation; the economic-loss rule precludes it, because Investor's complaint arises from Entrepreneur's negligence in the negotiation or performance of a contract. Investor may have a good common-law claim for breach of warranty, or for rescission, restitution, and incidental damages. He may also have a claim against Entrepreneur under federal statutes bearing on the case.

c.   Recklessness. It is sometimes said that a statement is fraudulent if its maker believes it to be false or is reckless as to its truth or falsity. This last possibility must be treated with care because "reckless" has a range of meanings in law. The recklessness sufficient to support a claim of fraud occurs when a speaker acts in conscious disregard of a risk that a statement is false, as by offering it without qualification while knowing that it may well be untrue. Such cases can be described as matters of recklessness if the word is found convenient, but they also can be viewed as straightforward cases of liability under the language of this Section. They involve knowingly false representations, perhaps implied, about the speaker's confidence in the statement or basis for making it. In other legal settings, recklessness may be defined to resemble gross negligence, but a statement reckless in that sense does not subject its maker to liability under this Chapter. However negligent it may be, an utterance is not fraudulent if made in the belief that it is true and that it accurately reflects whatever confidence and basis for belief the speaker may possess.

d.   Proof. Scienter is often difficult to prove directly in a suit for fraud. Mere evidence of a false or negligent statement, without more, generally is not enough to support an inference of scienter; from either of those showings, no presumption arises that the speaker knew the statement was false when made or lacked the confidence in the statement or basis for it that was implied. Successful claims of fraud typically are supported, rather, by evidence that the defendant knew the truth and made a statement inconsistent with it. Compare Illustrations 3 and 4.

Whether the defendant had the necessary state of mind is ordinarily a question for the trier of fact. Like any such question, however, it may be decided by the court if it can be reasonably resolved in only one way.

Illustrations:

3.   Buyer negotiates the purchase of a hotel from Seller. Seller provides documents to Buyer showing that the hotel has high occupancy rates and provides consistent stated revenues. Buyer completes the purchase of the hotel in reliance on Seller's documents. Buyer then examines the hotel's internal records, which were personally maintained by Seller. Buyer discovers that the hotel's actual occupancy rates and revenues were half those claimed by Seller during the period in question. A trier of fact may infer from this discrepancy between Seller's records and statements that Seller made knowing misrepresentations to Buyer.

4. Buyer negotiates a purchase of land from Seller. Buyer negotiates solely with Broker who serves as Seller's agent. Broker provides a listing sheet and brochure stating that the land consists of "20 acres, more or less." Buyer completes the purchase of the land in reliance on these statements. Buyer then discovers that the land consists of 15 acres. Buyer sues Seller. Broker testifies at trial that Seller provided the statement of acreage that was passed on to Buyer. Seller is elderly and infirm and is not called to testify, nor is any other evidence provided to establish Seller's relationship to the property or actual knowledge of it. Buyer's tort claim for fraud fails because Buyer's evidence of scienter is insufficient as a matter of law. Seller's negligent and material misrepresentation may support other lines of redress, such as a suit for breach of warranty or a suit seeking rescission, restitution, and incidental damages.

§ 11   Factual Causation; Justifiable Reliance

The recipient of a fraudulent misrepresentation can recover against its maker for economic loss only if

(a) the misrepresentation causes the loss,

(b) the recipient relies on the misrepresentation in acting or refraining from action, and

(c) the reliance is justifiable.

Comment:

a. Reliance and causation. A successful claim for fraud requires proof that the plaintiff relied on the defendant's misrepresentation. The element of reliance overlaps with (and may be considered a form of) the usual requirement in tort that a defendant's wrong be a factual or "but for" cause of the harm that the plaintiff suffered. The plaintiff may have been influenced by several sources, or by multiple statements—some true, some false—made by the same party. Liability is nevertheless intact if the defendant's fraud made a necessary contribution to the plaintiff's loss, typically by inducing the plaintiff to enter a damaging transaction. If the plaintiff was subject to multiple influences that each would have been sufficient to cause the resulting loss, the defendant whose fraud was among those influences may be held liable even though it may appear that the fraud was not a "but for" cause of the harm. See Illustration 4.

On the other hand, there can be no recovery if the plaintiff did not believe the defendant's misrepresentation, or was not aware of it until after the transaction was complete, or if the plaintiff would have been legally obliged to follow the same course regardless of what the defendant said. In those cases, the claim fails because the plaintiff did not act in reliance on the defendant's statement. A claim likewise fails if the plaintiff suffered harm as a result of the defendant's fraud but without relying on it. In that case, the plaintiff's loss may have been caused by the defendant's conduct, but the plaintiff's interest in receiving truthful information—the interest protected by the tort of fraud—was not invaded. See Illustration 5.

For additional discussion of factual causation apart from the element of reliance, see § 5, Comment *i*, which discusses the requirement in cases of negligent misrepresentation. The relevant points are the same in a case of fraud, and follow the general principles set forth in Restatement Third, Torts: Liability for Physical and Emotional Harm §§ 26–27.

Illustrations:

1.   Buyer makes an investment in Firm. After the purchase, Buyer discovers that Firm's disclosure statement contained misleading information. Buyer sues Firm for fraud. The trier of fact finds that Buyer did not read Firm's disclosure statement, and was not directly or indirectly aware of the claims it contained, until after making the investment. Buyer's claim fails for want of reliance.

2.   Buyer negotiates the purchase of an antique car from Seller. The car is advertised as having 500 miles of wear. Buyer does not believe the claimed mileage is accurate but wishes it were. Seller says that if the claimed mileage turns out to be wrong, he will allow Buyer to return the car and will give Buyer his money back. Buyer purchases the car, then determines that the claimed mileage was wrong. Buyer sues Seller for fraud. Buyer's claim fails because he did not rely on Seller's claims about mileage. Buyer doubted the claims were true, and was compensated for the doubts by Seller's promise to undo the transaction if the claims were false. That promise is enforceable, but Buyer has no claim in tort.

3.   Firm, acting through Manager, hires Worker to manage a department. Manager makes several representations that cause Worker to leave his previous job and accept this one: a promised salary, attractive benefits, and an assurance that Firm will soon expand in ways that will provide Worker with new opportunities. Worker later learns that the last representation was fraudulent; Firm never intended to expand, and Manager knew it. Worker sues Firm and Manager for fraud. The trier of fact finds that while all of Firm's assurances, true and false, were relevant to Worker, the fraudulent promise of expansion was necessary to his decision. Firm and Manager are both subject to liability for fraud.

4.   Same facts as Illustration 3, but the trier of fact finds that the promised salary, promised benefits, and assurances of expansion would each have been sufficient by themselves to induce Worker to leave his prior job and join Firm. Firm and Manager are both subject to liability for fraud.

5.   Dealer offers to sell a painting to Collector and fraudulently assures Collector that the painting is genuine. Dealer and Collector settle on a price of $15,000. The bill is sent to Collector's Mother, who

pays it as a gift to Collector; she is unaware of Dealer's misrepresentations. The painting is later revealed to be a forgery. Collector has a good claim for fraud against Dealer, but Mother does not. She was injured by Dealer's fraudulent statements but was not misled by them. Whatever the other theories Mother may be able to pursue, her claim for fraud fails for want of reliance.

b. Fraud on the market. The requirement of actual reliance excludes liability at common law for "fraud on the market"—that is, for claims that a defendant's misrepresentations pushed up the price of a stock, causing the plaintiff to pay too much for it without ever hearing what the defendant said. To recover under this Section, a plaintiff's reliance may be indirect; in other words, the plaintiff may in some cases rely on a statement received second-hand. See § 12, Comment *b.* Directly or indirectly, however, plaintiffs who sue for fraud must show that they themselves relied on what the defendant said, not that they were injured by the reliance of others. The result is different in claims brought under federal statutes regulating securities. See Basic, Inc. v. Levinson, 485 U.S. 224 (1988).

c. Holder claims. Some special problems of causation are posed by "holder" claims, in which a plaintiff is persuaded by the defendant's fraudulent statements not to sell shares of stock or other assets. There is no reason in principle why a plaintiff may not recover on those facts; no immunity arises from the happenstance that a defendant's lies move the plaintiff to inaction rather than action. The problems are matters of proof. A plaintiff may claim to have thought about selling, to have told nobody, and to have had a change of mind after reading something the defendant wrote. The defendant may then be peculiarly unable to argue the point, because the facts consist entirely of mental states in the plaintiff that produced no action and to which no one else was privy. (The problem is similar if the plaintiff claims to have thought about buying stock but to have decided against it.) To protect against false claims of this sort, the law requires plaintiffs who base their suits on transactions not made to provide more than a recounted train of thought as proof of reliance. Typically, there must be evidence of direct efforts by the defendant to dissuade the plaintiff from entering into a particular transaction, or evidence of action that corroborates the account the plaintiff gives of the decision—contemporaneous writings or conversations, for example, that show the terms of a sale the plaintiff would have made if not for the defendant's fraud.

d. Justifiable reliance. Principles of comparative negligence do not apply to a claim of fraud, but liability does require a showing that the plaintiff's reliance on what the defendant said was "justifiable." Justifiable reliance is an element of the plaintiff's cause of action; its absence is not an affirmative defense that the defendant must assert.

Justifiable reliance amounts to freedom from recklessness: plaintiffs who close their eyes to a known or obvious danger that a statement is fraudulent cannot recover losses they suffer from reliance on it. See Illustration 6; cf.

Restatement Third, Torts: Liability for Physical and Emotional Harm § 2. The rules also differ because reasonableness is measured against community standards of behavior. Justifiable reliance has a personalized character. It is measured by reference to the plaintiff's capabilities and knowledge; a plaintiff's sophistication may affect a court's judgments about what dangers were fairly considered obvious. Compare Illustrations 7 and 8. Finally, the justifiable reliance required by this Section does not call for a comparison of the fault attributable to the plaintiff and defendant. It is a threshold requirement; if it is satisfied, incremental doubts about the plaintiff's degree of care will not reduce the resulting recovery from the intentional tortfeasor.

Requiring justifiable reliance creates some tension with the usual rule that contributory negligence is no defense to an intentional-tort claim. The requirement serves partly to bolster the element of actual reliance; if a plaintiff claims to have relied on the defendant's statements in the face of obvious indications that the statements were false, one may doubt that the plaintiff meaningfully relied at all. See Illustration 6. The requirement does not impose a duty of active investigation on a plaintiff, and does not entitle a defendant to exploit a plaintiff's foolishness with impunity; if the defendant has deliberately preyed on the plaintiff's inattention, that inattention should not be considered an instance of unjustifiable reliance.

Whether a plaintiff's reliance was justifiable is ordinarily a question for the trier of fact. It may be decided as a matter of law when reasonable minds could reach only one conclusion.

Illustrations:

6. Buyer purchases a house from Seller. During their negotiations, Seller asserts that he "never had water problems in the house." Buyer orders an inspection prior to closing. The inspector informs Buyer that there is clear evidence of recent water damage in the basement. Buyer nevertheless goes through with the purchase. Buyer then discovers that the basement leaks. Buyer sues Seller for fraud. Buyer's claim fails as a matter of law because Buyer's reliance on Seller's statements was not justifiable in view of the findings in the inspection report. It may also be possible to conclude that Buyer did not rely on what Seller said.

7. Insurer sells a life-insurance policy to Consumer. Insurer misrepresents the effect of the policy, falsely assuring Consumer that the policy can serve as a vehicle for retirement savings. Consumer later discovers that the policy cannot function as described. Consumer sues Insurer for fraud. Insurer claims that Consumer's reliance on its statements was unjustifiable because a reading of the written policy would have made its limits clear to her. Consumer did not read the relevant part of the policy. The trier of fact may reasonably conclude that Consumer's reliance was nevertheless justifiable.

8. Investor and Director of Company both sign a guaranty in which each agrees to be personally liable for repayment of Bank's loan to Company if Company defaults. The agreement states prominently that Bank can collect the entire amount from either guarantor. Company defaults; Director is insolvent; Bank recovers the whole of the debt from Investor, who has no effective recourse against Director as co-surety. Investor sues Bank for fraud. Investor claims that during negotiations over the loan, an officer of Bank said that Investor would not be held responsible for more than half of it in the event of default. The court finds that Investor was a sophisticated and experienced party represented by counsel, that the liability of Investor for the full amount was a carefully negotiated term of the agreement, and that the guaranty contract forbade Bank's officer to alter its terms. Investor's claim fails as a matter of law because his reliance on the alleged oral assurances from the Bank's officer was unjustifiable.

e. No-reliance clauses. Sometimes a plaintiff claims to have been induced to sign a contract by false statements that the defendant made during their negotiations. The parol-evidence rule, as a doctrine of contract law, is not an impediment to a tort claim based on such facts. The contract itself, however, may contain language that is inconsistent with the plaintiff's theory of recovery. It might include an integration clause stating that the written contract is the exclusive statement of the parties' entire agreement, or it might contain a disclaimer of reliance on representations made outside the four corners of the document. Language of either type may undermine a plaintiff's claim to have relied on fraudulent statements made before the contract was signed. Disclaimers of either sort can serve a useful commercial purpose, not by shielding parties who lie but by protecting both parties from costly litigation about whether they lied. Disclaimers also may allow parties to usefully allocate responsibility for determining the truth about the subject of a transaction. But disclaimers also can serve as traps for parties who are content to treat a written contract as final but do not mean to assume the risk that the other side has committed fraud. The effect of a "no-reliance" clause on a tort claim for fraud thus depends on two considerations: the specificity of its wording and the sophistication of the parties.

First, an ordinary integration clause, written in general language, will not be read to foreclose a claim that the plaintiff's consent to a contract was procured by fraud. Nor is such a claim barred by a broad statement in the contract that neither party is relying on statements made by the other outside the contract. More specific disclaimers may effectively negate an element of the plaintiff's claim, however, as when the plaintiff signs a writing that denies reliance on particular statements or on assurances the defendant has made about a particular topic. See Illustration 9.

Second, a disclaimer of reliance will ordinarily be enforced only against a sophisticated party. Sophistication, for these purposes, typically means that the plaintiff was represented by counsel and was a commercial actor rather than a consumer (or for other reasons had extensive experience with such transactions). The considerations just noted may bear on one another: the more sophisticated the plaintiff, the less specific the disclaimer need be to foreclose a claim. When close questions arise about whether a contract was specific enough, or a plaintiff sophisticated enough, to justify enforcement of a no-reliance clause, they may be resolved by reference to the policies that lie behind the requirements. The purpose of the requirements is generally to limit enforcement to cases in which the disclaimer was a deliberate choice made for considered reasons, not a piece of boilerplate that the plaintiff would be surprised to find had effected a waiver of the right to honesty from the other party to the agreement.

Whether to give effect to a disclaimer of reliance is a question of law for the court unless it depends on factual disputes on which reasonable minds could differ.

Illustrations:

9.   Commercial Purchaser of real estate makes a contract to buy a building from Seller. The contract between the parties states, "Seller makes no representations as to the expenses, operation or any other matter related to the premises, except as herein specifically set forth. Purchaser acknowledges that no such representations have been made or are relied upon." Purchaser sues Seller some months after the transaction is completed, stating that Seller had made fraudulent oral representations about the operating expenses of the building that were inconsistent with those set forth in the written contract. Purchaser seeks damages for fraud measured by the difference in value between the building as allegedly described by Seller and its value as is. Purchaser's tort claim fails because, in view of the contractual language, he cannot show that he justifiably relied on any oral representations the Seller might have made about the expenses of operating the building.

10. Homeowner buys a security system from Company. Homeowner relies on assurances offered orally by Company's Agent that the system will operate even after a general power failure affecting the house. Homeowner later discovers that Company's assurance was fraudulent and incurs expenses to have the system replaced by another firm. The contract between Homeowner and Company did not mention the system's ability to withstand a power failure, and the contract contained an integration clause stating that the written agreement was a complete expression of the parties' understandings. Homeowner's tort claim for fraud nevertheless survives because he is not a sophisticated party and because the contract did not specifically disclaim reliance on Agent's assurances.

§ 12   Scope of Liability

An actor who makes a fraudulent misrepresentation is subject to liability for harm only if the risk of the harm was foreseeably increased by the fraud.

Comment:

a. Scope of liability generally. This Section addresses the issue sometimes known as "proximate" causation: the scope of a defendant's liability for injuries that are a factual or "but for" result of a misrepresentation. Briefly stated, a plaintiff can recover only for the types of losses that might reasonably have been expected to result from the defendant's fraud. This generally means that the fraud must have foreseeably increased the risk of the kind of harm that the plaintiff suffered. Thus no liability results when a defendant's lie causes the plaintiff to make an investment that fails for reasons entirely unrelated to what the defendant said. See Illustration 1. On the other hand, a lie that caused a small increase in the likelihood of the loss that the plaintiff suffered is sufficient to support liability. See Illustration 2. The requirement of a causal connection between the subject of the misrepresentation and the source of plaintiff's loss is a notable difference between the remedies that tort law provides for fraud and the remedies supplied by the law of restitution or contract. See Illustration 1.

Illustrations:

1. Investor buys shares in Company. Investor is persuaded to make the purchase by Director's false assurance that Company is in compliance with various state regulations. Six months later, Company fails due to a decline in the demand for its products. Company's failure to comply with the regulations raised the risk that Company would be subject to various civil penalties, but did not raise the risk that Company would fail in the way that it did. The losses that Investor suffered as a result of Company's failure are outside Director's scope of liability for fraud in tort. Director's misrepresentation might nevertheless entitle Investor to rescind the transaction—that is, to recover his purchase price upon restoration of the shares—despite the lack of causal connection between the matter misrepresented and the source of the loss. See Restatement Third, Restitution and Unjust Enrichment § 13, Comment *h*.

2. Investor buys shares in Company. Investor is persuaded to make the purchase by Director's false assurance that he will invest in Company to a comparable extent. Six months later, Company fails due to a decline in the demand for its products and a lack of vigor in marketing them. Company might have failed even if Director had invested as heavily as he promised. Investor sought Director's assurances, however, because the commitment they reflected would have reduced the risk that Company would fail for the reason that it did. Investor's losses are within Director's scope of liability for fraud.

b. The purpose of the representation. Liability for fraud requires a showing that the defendant spoke for the purpose of influencing the plaintiff or a class of parties in which the plaintiff was included. The liability, in turn, extends to damage suffered by those whose reliance the defendant intended to induce. It also includes damage suffered by others who the defendant had reason to expect would rely on a statement. The plaintiff need not have dealt directly with the defendant. It is enough if the defendant had reason to expect that the plaintiff would receive the statement and rely on it. Nor need the defendant know the specific identities of those who were likely to rely; awareness of a class of potential victims is sufficient. If the defendant's statement is embedded in a commercial document—a product label, for example, or a security—then reliance on it by any who deal with the document in the ordinary course of business is regarded as expectable. The same general principles apply to the types of decisions affected by the defendant's statements: liability extends to transactions of the kind the defendant meant to influence by the fraudulent statement, or had reason to believe would be influenced by it. If a statute requires a defendant to provide information, a defendant who speaks falsely may be held liable for losses suffered by those people, and in those types of transactions, that the statute was meant to protect.

The principles just stated require more than just foreseeability of a risk that the plaintiff might someday rely on what the defendant says. They require, rather, that the defendant have reason to consider that reliance likely, even if the plaintiff's identity is indistinct. It might seem peculiar to place such limits on the liability of a defendant who, by hypothesis, has acted with a culpable state of mind. But the limits reflect a reasonable solicitude for the potential defendant who commits no fraud but speaks often, or who employs others who speak often. Even when speaking truthfully, such a party may wish to prepare for (and insure against) the risk of litigation, with its attendant expenses, risk of error, and other hardships. The limits explained here help such defendants measure their potential exposure in advance and act accordingly.

Illustrations:

3. Seller, considering a business arrangement with Buyer, asks Bank that holds Buyer's account for an opinion of Buyer's financial stability. Bank replies that Buyer is "sound." Seller enters into a transaction with Buyer 18 months later; Buyer goes bankrupt soon thereafter. Seller sues Bank, claiming that its assurance of Buyer's soundness was fraudulent. The trier of fact finds that Buyer's business was highly volatile, that the soundness of an enterprise in its field will often change over the course of a few months, and that Bank could not reasonably have expected a statement it made to become the basis of reliance by Seller over a year later. Seller's claim against Bank fails as a matter of law for this reason, even if the other elements of the tort could be established.

4. Accountant produces an audit report for Company 1. Company 1 then merges with Company 2, and the shareholders of both companies receive Accountant's report. Investor decides a few months later to buy bonds that had been issued by Company 2 before the merger. Investor relies in part on Accountant's audit of Company 1; the report satisfies

Investor that, with the companies now merged, the bonds issued by Company 2 are safe. The merged company soon fails and the bonds become worthless. Investor sues Accountant in tort for fraud. The court finds that Accountant prepared its audit of Company 1 to satisfy shareholders who would be approving the merger, and that Accountant had no reason to expect reliance on the report by someone buying Company 2's bonds. Investor's claim fails as a matter of law.

5. Buyer negotiates to purchase Rancher's cattle. Rancher gives Buyer written assurances that the cattle are healthy; in fact, Rancher knows that the cattle are diseased. Buyer takes Rancher's assurances to Bank to obtain financing for the purchase. Bank provides it. Buyer acquires the cattle, they all die from their preexisting disease, and Buyer goes bankrupt. Bank sues Rancher for fraud. The trier of fact finds that Rancher knew Buyer would seek financing from a bank, even if Rancher did not know which one, and that Rancher knew Buyer was likely to provide the bank with Rancher's assurances that the cattle were healthy. Rancher is subject to liability to Bank.

§ 13 Duties to Disclose; Tacit Misrepresentation

A failure to disclose material information may result in liability if the actor has a duty to speak. Such a duty exists where

(a) the actor has made a prior statement and knows that it will likely mislead another if not amended, even if it was not misleading when made; or

(b) the actor is in a fiduciary or confidential relationship with another that obliges the actor to make disclosures; or

(c) the actor knows that the other party to a transaction is mistaken about a basic assumption behind it, and that the other party, because of the relationship between them, the customs of the trade, or other circumstances, would reasonably expect disclosure of what the actor knows.

Comment:

a. Scope; other actions compared. Liability for fraud ordinarily arises from affirmative statements, not from silence. That is so because one party to a transaction has no general duty to make disclosures to the other. On occasions discussed in this Section, however, a party does have such a duty. In those cases, silence may be considered a form of deceit, and the nondisclosure of a fact treated the same as an assertion of its nonexistence.

This Section is best understood as detailing when silence can satisfy the "misrepresentation" element of § 9. A statement that is misleading if not properly qualified may support liability under § 9 without reference to the principles stated here. This Section, rather, recognizes liability at common law for nondisclosure as such—that is, for a failure to disclose unaccompanied by any statement that would support liability itself. The discussion in § 9 of other elements of liability for fraud, such as materiality and causation, continues to be relevant to a claim that meets the requirements of this Section.

On liability for omissions under a theory of negligent misrepresentation, see § 5, Comment *e*. If the cases treated in this Section were found to involve negligence rather than a more culpable state of mind, most of them would not be candidates for liability under § 5. The reason is that liability under § 5 cannot arise from negligence in the performance or negotiation of a contract; such claims are eliminated by the economic-loss rule of § 2. Thus § 5 generally involves negligent misrepresentations between parties who do not have contracts. The claims treated in this Section, by contrast, typically do arise from the performance or negotiation of contracts. They survive the economic-loss rule because they are varieties of deceit to which the rule does not apply. It follows that if a defendant lacks the state of mind needed to support a claim under this Section, the plaintiff's likely fallback is not a negligence claim. It is a claim based on contract or restitution. Those bodies of law provide rules that allow plaintiffs, on terms more liberal than those found here, to rescind a transaction and seek recovery of any benefits conferred because the defendant failed to disclose information material to a bargain the parties made. See Restatement Third, Restitution and Unjust Enrichment §§ 5 and 34; Restatement Second, Contracts §§ 163–164 and §§ 372 and 376. The plaintiff may also have statutory remedies in some of the cases discussed in this Section.

b.   Prior speech. Nondisclosure can amount to deceit if the defendant has spoken other words, or performed other acts, that may not have been culpable at the time but will become so if the defendant remains silent. Thus a defendant may make a statement and believe it to be true but later discover that it is false or misleading. See Illustrations 1 and 2. Or a defendant may make a false statement in the reasonable belief that it will not elicit justifiable reliance but later discover that it has. See Illustration 3. In these cases, the defendant may be obliged to update the earlier statements to prevent them from having fraudulent effect. Here as in § 9, however, these general principles must be applied in a manner that is sensitive to context and custom. An accountant who issues an audit report on a firm, for example, may not have an obligation to update it upon learning of new facts that are contrary to the report's conclusions. Whether such an obligation exists will depend on what is expected by the report's audience, and on the author's reasonable understanding of those expectations. See Illustration 4.

Illustrations:

1.   Seller of property tells prospective Buyer that the property's septic system is in good working order. Seller's statement is true when he makes it, but Seller learns a week later that the septic system has

failed. Seller signs a contract of sale with Buyer without disclosing the failure of the system. Seller is subject to liability to Buyer for fraud.

2. Executive offers to leave his job at Company and join Rival. Executive tells Rival that he can bring clients from Company to Rival if he moves there. Executive's statements are true when made. Two weeks later, Company offers Executive a severance contract that requires him not to take Company's clients elsewhere. Executive signs the agreement, then joins Rival without disclosing it. Executive immediately gains an equity stake in Rival. Rival later discovers that Executive cannot bring clients from Company as he had described. Rival fires Executive and sues him in tort for fraud. Executive is subject to liability to Rival.

3. Retailer enters into a six-month contract to distribute Manufacturer's products. Manufacturer offers a friendly assurance that he hopes to work with Retailer for years to come. The statement is false, but Manufacturer has no reason to expect Retailer to rely on it. Retailer later informs Manufacturer that he plans to reject an alternative supplier in favor of the long-term relationship that Manufacturer has proposed. Manufacturer says nothing, but has no interest in a long-term relationship and ends its dealings with Retailer a few months later. Manufacturer did not commit fraud when he first spoke, but had a duty to modify his statement when he learned that Retailer was relying on it. Manufacturer is subject to liability to Retailer.

4. Accountant issues a favorable audit report on Firm. Accountant later learns that Firm's condition has deteriorated and that the favorable conclusions it reached are no longer accurate, but does not publish an update of its report. Investor relies on the report in buying Firm's shares, then suffers losses and sues Accountant for fraud. The court finds that Accountant's report was accurate when published, and that customs of the profession do not call upon accountants to update their reports in light of later developments. Accountant is not subject to liability to Investor. (Accountant would likely have been obliged to issue an update if it had discovered that its report was misleading when published because it was based on false information.)

c. *Special relationships.* Strangers cannot generally expect one another to volunteer all that they know about the subject matter of an arm's-length transaction between them. Silence may amount to deceit, however, if it occurs against the backdrop of a special relationship between the parties that causes one of them to count on the other to be forthcoming. A defendant in a fiduciary relationship with the plaintiff, for example, is expected to disclose anything the plaintiff might consider material to a transaction between them. "Confidential" relationships are defined less formally than fiduciary relationships but have similar consequences under this Section. They arise when one party is bound to act in good faith for the benefit of the other because they have a relationship of trust; typically one of the parties has gained a position of substantial influence over the other. Such relationships often develop within families. See Restatement Third, Restitution and Unjust Enrichment § 15, Comment *b* and Reporter's Note thereto. The influential party is obliged to disclose to the dependent party any facts material to their dealings.

Illustrations:

5. Partner A and Partner B enter into a partnership to buy Blackacre. They own equal shares. Later Investor approaches Partner A and offers to buy Blackacre on generous terms. Partner A does not tell Partner B about the offer; instead Partner A offers to buy Partner B's interest in Blackacre. Partner B agrees to sell his interest to Partner A for $10,000. Partner A then sells Blackacre to Investor for $300,000. Partner B sues Partner A for fraud, claiming that Partner A had a duty to disclose the offer from Investor before Partner B sold him his interest in Blackacre. The court finds that the parties had a fiduciary relationship. Partner A is subject to liability to Partner B.

6. Tenant 1 and Tenant 2 hold a parcel of property as tenants in common. They agree to partition the property. Tenant 1, who has possession of the parcel, does not disclose to Tenant 2 that he has harvested most of the timber on the part of the land that Tenant 2 will receive. Tenant 2 later discovers that the timber is gone and sues Tenant 1. The court finds that Tenant 1's possession of the land gave rise to a relationship of trust and confidence with Tenant 2, which in turn created a duty to disclose facts material to the proposed transaction. The court further finds that Tenant 1 did not disclose the information to Tenant 2 because he thought that it would affect Tenant 2's willingness to consent to the deal. Tenant 1 may be held liable in tort for fraud. (In the alternative, Tenant 2 may pursue a claim for rescission.)

7. Driller 1 owns a lease to extract minerals from tribal lands. Worker for tribe discovers that mineral deposits on the lands are more extensive than Driller 1 knows. Worker joins Driller 2 and passes on his knowledge. Driller 2 buys Driller 1's mineral rights. Driller 1 then discovers that it sold the rights for much less than they were worth, and sues Worker and Driller 2 for fraud. The court finds that Worker obtained his knowledge lawfully, that Driller 1 and Driller 2 were engaged in an arm's-length transaction, and that neither Worker nor Driller 2 had any obligation to disclose their knowledge to Driller 1. Driller 1's fraud claim fails.

d. Superior knowledge. One party often knows more than the other about the subject of an exchange between them. That difference, without more, creates no obligation of disclosure. Better information is a legitimate advantage at the bargaining table, and the law encourages its acquisition. In some cases, however, an imbalance of knowledge creates a duty in the better-informed party to disclose it. Liability on this theory requires, first, a showing that the fact at issue was basic to the transaction. Second, the plaintiff must have a legitimate reason to rely on an adversary to supply the information.

Part of that reason usually is a difference in each side's access to the facts. If one party knows something that the other cannot find out, letting the other suffer for its ignorance may not usefully encourage the discovery of knowledge and may offend ordinary standards of fairness. Even when two parties have different access to basic facts, however, rules to govern the defendant's obligations are hard to state. Liability on this basis typically arises from conduct that represents a clear violation of business ethics. Such conclusions depend in significant part on commercial customs, which vary in different settings.

Illustrations:

8. Buyer purchases a house from Seller. Buyer then discovers serious defects in the foundation that Seller did not disclose. The court finds that Seller knew of the defects before the sale, knew they would be of great importance to Buyer, and knew they were not discoverable by the use of reasonable care; Buyer had obtained a customary and competent inspection, and the defects were not found. Seller is subject to liability to Buyer for fraud.

9. Employee and Employer negotiate a compensation agreement. After each side has reviewed the resulting document many times, Employer inserts a change without telling Employee. Employee signs the document, discovers the change a week later, and brings suit for fraud. The court finds that the transaction was made at arm's length and that Employee had a full opportunity to reread the contract just before signing it. The court also finds, however, that Employer knew its last-minute change was important, and that Employee would not expect it and was not aware of it. Employer may be held liable in tort for fraud. Reformation of the contract is another natural possibility.

10. Wholesaler has an ongoing agreement to buy cereals from Producer for resale to various grocers. Producer decides to start selling its cereals to grocers directly, but does not disclose this plan to Wholesaler. The parties renew their contract. Wholesaler then discovers that it can no longer resell most of the cereals it has purchased because grocers are buying them directly from Producer. The court finds that when the parties renewed their contract, Producer knew that Wholesaler expected to resell the cereals but would no longer be able to do so; that Producer knew that Wholesaler would consider Producer's new plans important in deciding whether to renew; and that Wholesaler had no way to learn of Producer's plans if Producer did not disclose them. Producer is subject to liability for fraud.

11. Buyer purchases house from Seller, then discovers that its driveway encroaches on a neighbor's property. The court finds that Seller knew of the encroachment and did not disclose it to Buyer. The court also finds, however, that the encroachment could have been discovered by a survey or by inspection of public records, neither of which Buyer performed. Seller had no obligation to disclose the

encroachment to Buyer and is not liable for fraud. Other rights and remedies may be available to Buyer by statute.

In Illustration 8, denying recovery would give future buyers an incentive to invest in more expensive inspections that would rarely be worth the cost. It is more efficient to require the seller to reveal what he knows in the sales contract. In Illustration 11, by contrast, requiring each side to inform itself of the facts—or even just requiring the buyer to put direct questions to the seller—is not unduly burdensome, and is consistent with the commercial customs that govern real-estate transactions.

e.   Judge and jury. Liability under this Section requires a finding that the defendant had a duty to speak. The existence of that duty is a question for the court. If disputed facts bear on the existence of the duty, they are appropriately submitted to the trier of fact for resolution. Examples may include one side's knowledge of a fact, the other's ignorance of it, the customs of a commercial situation, or the defendant's knowledge that the plaintiff expected disclosure.

§ 14   Liability for Misrepresentations of Opinion

A false statement of opinion may result in liability only if

(a)   the parties are in a fiduciary or confidential relationship, or

(b)   the defendant claims to have expertise or other knowledge not accessible to the plaintiff, and offers the opinion to provide a basis for reliance by the plaintiff.

Comment:

a.   Generally. A statement of opinion may imply that its maker has knowledge of facts to support it. In either case, that factual implication, if known by the speaker to be false, can support liability for fraud under the rule of § 9 without reference to the rules stated in this Section. This Section addresses a separate question: the liability of a defendant for the false statement of an opinion as such, and without reference to any implications of fact.

Statements traditionally classified as opinions include judgments about the quality or value of a thing sold and views about the future likelihood of events. False statements of pure opinion ordinarily are not actionable. The reason is not that statements of opinion are incapable of being true or false; when a speaker claims to hold an opinion but does not, the claim is as contrary to the truth as any other lie. The reason for the rule, rather, is that reliance on another party's opinion is regarded in most cases as unjustifiable as a matter of law. It is better practice, and more consistent with commercial custom, for parties to rely just on statements of fact made by others and to form their own opinions on the basis of them. That rule is relaxed when there is unusually good reason for the plaintiff to defer to the defendant's judgment (as explained in Comment *b*), but a typical buyer is not entitled to rely on the opinions of a typical seller.

If a defendant offers an opinion in circumstances that can support liability under the rules of this Section, the other traditional elements of fraud must still be satisfied: the requirement of scienter, the requirement of materiality, the requirement of justifiable reliance, and so forth. See §§ 9–12.

Illustrations:

1. Buyer negotiates the purchase of a used car from Seller. Buyer relies on Seller's statement that the car is in good condition. Buyer soon discovers that the car's engine is in poor repair and will be expensive to fix, and that other interior components have rotted. Buyer sues Seller for fraud. The court finds that Seller's statement of the car's condition was an opinion, but that it implied that Seller knew of facts to support it and had no knowledge of facts that made it false. The court finds that Seller knew of the car's problems at the time he made the claim. Seller may be held liable for fraud under the principles of § 9 without resort to this Section. The liability is not for Seller's false statement of opinion as such. It is for the false factual implications of what Seller said. In the alternative, Buyer may recover for breach of warranty.

2. Buyer negotiates the purchase of a restaurant from Seller. Seller accurately states the restaurant's revenues to date and gives Buyer complete access to his business records. Seller tells Buyer that on the basis of those records he thinks the restaurant will produce gross revenues of $10,000 per day going forward. Buyer finds, after acquiring the restaurant, that it produces revenues of $5000 per day. Buyer sues Seller for fraud, claiming that Seller's statements about the restaurant's future earnings were wrong and that Seller knew they would be. Buyer's claim fails because Seller's statements about the future were matters of opinion and implied no knowledge of facts that Buyer did not have.

It often is clear that a statement is an opinion, as when the defendant says that a company has great prospects or that a car is the best-looking one on the lot. But difficult cases can arise at the boundary between opinion and fact. They are best resolved by recalling that the distinction is drawn not for its own sake but to identify cases in which reliance by one party on the claims of another is categorically unjustifiable. The inquiry serves a practical policy: enabling parties to rely on each other's words when it saves time and trouble or is otherwise commercially useful, and discouraging them from such reliance when they should form their own judgments for themselves. If the classification of a statement as opinion or fact is a matter on which reasonable minds could differ, it is an appropriate matter for decision by jury.

b. Circumstances justifying reliance. False statements of opinion can support a claim for fraud in two general circumstances. The first arises when parties have a fiduciary or confidential relationship. A fiduciary has a legal obligation to act for the benefit of another. The obligation arises automatically from certain formally recognized relationships, such as attorney and client or trustee and beneficiary. A confidential relationship produces similar obligations but is less formal. It arises from circumstances in which the parties are not on equal footing; one has influence over the other, and the stronger party is trusted to act in good faith for the benefit of the weaker. See § 13, Comment *c*. In a relationship of either of these types, it may be appropriate for the dependent party to rely on the opinions of the other.

Second, a claim of fraud may be supported by a false statement of opinion when the defendant purports to be an expert or otherwise invites deference by claiming access to knowledge that the plaintiff cannot readily duplicate. Relying on the defendant's opinion in such a case may well be reasonable and more efficient than collecting facts and forming an opinion of one's own. The law protects the plaintiff's right to so rely by imposing liability if the opinion is falsely stated and offered for the purpose of providing the plaintiff with a basis for reliance.

The conditions stated in this Comment define the circumstances in which a plaintiff may generally be justified in relying on the opinion of another. A successful claim still requires, however, a showing that the plaintiff's reliance was justifiable on the facts of the case—for example, that the plaintiff did not ignore obvious reasons to doubt the accuracy of what the defendant said.

Illustrations:

3. Buyer negotiates purchase of ranch from Seller. The value of the property depends in part on how long three companies will continue to conduct strip-mining activities there. Seller sends Buyer a letter during their negotiation stating that "I think the three mines operating on the ranch at the present time will be winding down their operations these next 4–6 years." Buyer relies on this statement in purchasing the ranch. The mines do not wind down. Buyer sues Seller for fraud. The court finds that Seller's statement about the mines was an opinion and was not based on special expertise or access to facts that Buyer could not duplicate. Seller is not liable to Buyer.

4. Professional Realtor produces a report appraising a house at $300,000. Buyer relies on Realtor's report in deciding to purchase the house. Buyer later discovers that the market value of the house was below $200,000. Buyer sues Realtor for fraud. Buyer's evidence shows that Realtor was party to a scheme to acquire houses at low prices and then knowingly offer inflated opinions of their value to prospective buyers. The court finds that Realtor's appraisal was an opinion, but also finds that Realtor held himself out as an expert whose opinions could be trusted. Realtor is subject to liability to Buyer for fraud.

c. *Statements of law.* It is sometimes said that assertions of law are matters of opinion that cannot serve as the basis for a claim of fraud. While that is often true, false legal claims sometimes have implications that are actionable or may be the subject of justifiable reliance by another party. They are best handled according to the logic of this Section: they subject their makers to liability if they imply untrue facts, or if the parties have a relationship that makes it reasonable for the plaintiff to rely on the defendant's opinions. They are not actionable if they amount to judgments based on facts available to both sides and on which the plaintiff can reasonably be expected to arrive at an independent view.

A claim of law can imply facts of various kinds. It may imply the existence of ordinary and nonlegal facts that justify the speaker's conclusions. Thus an assertion that one mortgage has priority over another may imply that one was made or at least recorded before the other; and a claim that a corporation has the right to do business in a state may imply that it has taken all steps necessary to be duly qualified. A claim of law also may imply the existence of legal facts: that a regulation has been passed or repealed, or that a piece of property was zoned for commercial use or not. A defendant who knowingly misleads the plaintiff with respect to any of these sorts of facts may be held liable for fraud if the other elements stated in § 9 are satisfied. Often they will not be satisfied. Justifiable reliance typically is hard to show when the defendant's claim might easily have been checked against public records. In all events, any liability in such a case arises not from the defendant's false statement of opinion per se, but from the facts it implies.

On the other hand, no liability arises when one adversary in a negotiation offers another a view about the best interpretation of legal language—for example, the wording of a contract or a statute—that is equally visible to both. The defendant's statement then is a true matter of opinion, and a claim of fraud founded on it fails as a matter of law unless the rules of this Section are satisfied. They are satisfied when an attorney falsely states an opinion to a client, because an attorney and client have a fiduciary relationship. And if a party claims to have special expertise and invites reliance by the plaintiff, a plaintiff again may recover if falsely stated opinions of law follow and the other elements of liability for fraud are satisfied.

Illustrations:

5. Tenant negotiates the rental of property from Landlord. Landlord tells tenant that local zoning rules will permit Tenant's business to operate on the premises. Landlord dissuades Tenant from seeking to confirm this, assuring Tenant that "we know the area." Acting in reliance on these assurances, Tenant signs a contract with Landlord. The assurances turn out to be false, and Tenant suffers losses as a result. Tenant produces evidence that Landlord knew the assurances were false when he made them. Landlord is subject to liability for fraud.

6. Buyer negotiates the purchase of property from Seller. Seller makes a claim about the meaning of language in the proposed contract. Seller says the language is best understood to give Buyer exclusive use

of a walkway adjacent to the property. Acting in reliance on these assurances, Buyer signs the contract with Seller. A court later finds that a neighboring tenant has a right to use the walkway as well. Buyer sues Seller for fraud, proposing to show that Seller knew his reading of the lease was infirm. Buyer's claim fails because Seller's interpretation of the language in the contract was a matter of opinion, the basis for which was equally visible to both sides, and the parties were in an arm's-length relationship that did not entitle Buyer to rely on Seller's opinions.

§ 15   Promissory Fraud

A statement of a speaker's intention to perform a promise is a fraudulent misrepresentation if the intention does not exist at the time the statement is made.

Comment:

a.   *Generally.* A statement of intention is false if the intention does not exist. A false statement of the intent to do something, or not to do something, is actionable like any other misrepresentation if the elements of §§ 9–12 are satisfied. In practice, most allegations of this form of deceit involve one problematic type of intent in particular: the defendant is alleged to have made a promise without intending to keep it, and so is said to have committed "promissory fraud." Such a claim can cause confusion because it may closely resemble a claim of promissory estoppel or breach of contract. See Restatement Second, Contracts § 90. A claim of promissory fraud differs from a claim of promissory estoppel because the plaintiff adds an assertion that the promisor did not intend to carry out the promise at the time it was made. The plaintiff who makes such a claim typically receives two practical benefits in return. First, a claim of fraud may permit the plaintiff to obtain an award of punitive damages that would not be available on other theories. Second, a suit for promissory fraud may allow a plaintiff to avoid doctrinal obstacles that would defeat claims for breach of contract or promissory estoppel. See Comment *c.*

Since it is not tortious to break a promise, it may seem surprising that it can be tortious to make a promise while not intending to keep it. But the recipient of a promise typically values the promisor's intention to perform, and would not do business as readily, or at all, with a promisor whose intentions were known to be otherwise. A tort claim for fraud under this Section thus protects rights of the promisee in a way that a suit for breach of contract does not.

b.   *Proof.* A claim of promissory fraud must be supported by evidence that the defendant made a misrepresentation of intent. The statement of intent need not be explicit. Ordinarily, a contract itself will suffice as a representation of the defendant's intent to perform; a party who signs a contract presumptively represents, at least by implication, an intent to do what the contract requires. But that description may not apply to every case.

Both parties to a contract might understand that a breach of it is likely if various contingencies arise; the purpose of the agreement may just be to make clear who pays for the resulting damages in that event. There is no liability for fraud if those facts are shown. Liability arises only when the promisor misleads the promisee.

A plaintiff typically must use circumstantial evidence to prove that the defendant did not intend to keep a promise at the time it was made. No such inference can be drawn from a mere failure to perform the promise later. A plaintiff's case may be helped, however, by evidence of plans the defendant had at the time of the promise that were inconsistent with it; or by evidence that the promise was impossible to keep for reasons the defendant knew (and the plaintiff did not); or by evidence that the defendant made and broke other promises routinely, and so must have expected to break this one as well. Other facts may tend to support the innocence of the defendant's intentions: evidence that the defendant partially performed the promise, for example, or that changed circumstances make the defendant's promise costlier to honor than had originally appeared. See Illustrations 1 and 2.

Illustrations:

1.   Corporation promises to supply Seller with products. Seller promises to distribute them in Montana. The term of the agreement is five years. Two years later, Corporation announces that it is withdrawing from Montana and cancels its agreement with Seller. Seller discovers internal memoranda from Corporation showing that at the time the agreement was signed, Corporation had already made a decision, not disclosed to Seller, to end all operations in Montana after two years. Corporation is subject to liability for fraud.

2.   Employee is dismissed by Employer. Employee brings a lawsuit alleging that during his term of employment he performed extra services after hours, that Employer promised him payment for those services, and that Employer made the promise without ever intending to keep it. Employer denies making such a promise at all. Employee's only proof of fraud is his evidence that Employer made the promise, that Employer now falsely denies having made it, and that Employer stood to benefit financially by inducing Employee to work without paying him. Employee may have a valid claim for breach of contract, but his evidence of fraud is insufficient as a matter of law. He has no proof of scienter.

c.   *Relation to the Statute of Frauds and parol-evidence rule.* Claims under this Section are not impaired by a jurisdiction's statute of frauds. A statute of frauds extinguishes contract claims, not tort claims; it prevents the enforcement of a promise under certain circumstances if the promise is not evidenced in a writing signed by the promisor. Liability under this Section does not result in the enforcement of a promise. It results in compensation for losses suffered by a plaintiff who relied on a promise. The law of tort protects defendants against unfounded claims of deceit not with the Statute of Frauds but by the use of a heightened standard of proof with respect to the defendant's state of mind. See § 9, Comment *e*.

Courts likewise state as a matter of course that the parol-evidence rule does not impede claims of fraud. See Restatement Second, Contracts § 214. The application of that principle to claims of promissory fraud may be explained in more particular terms. Thus two parties may sign a contract with an integration clause stating that the writing is the complete expression of their agreement; later the plaintiff might offer extrinsic evidence that the promisor never intended to perform the promise that the agreement contained. The plaintiff in such a case is not adding terms to the written contract or varying them. The plaintiff is proving, rather, that a representation implicit in the contract was false. Neither the parol-evidence rule nor an integration clause is an obstacle to such a showing.

A related problem arises when the parties have a written agreement and the plaintiff claims that the defendant made a separate false promise that was not reflected in the writing. The parol-evidence rule may preclude enforcement of the separate promise as a matter of contract law. The plaintiff nevertheless may assert a claim in tort that the second promise—the one outside the written contract—was made with no intention that it would be kept. It might seem odd that a promise the parol-evidence rule would otherwise extinguish becomes enforceable just because it was made by a promisor who never planned to keep it. Again, however, liability for fraud does not cause the promise to be enforced; rather, the plaintiff collects for damage caused by reliance on it.

While the parol-evidence rule does not obstruct claims of promissory fraud, the existence of a contract may suggest that the plaintiff was not justified in relying on an earlier promise that was inconsistent with it. That conclusion is especially likely to be drawn, of course, if the contract contains language expressly disavowing reliance on a promise such as the one at issue. For discussion of when a no-reliance clause defeats a claim of fraud, see § 11, Comment *e*.

Illustration:

3.   Company hires Accountant, then fires him six months later. Accountant sues Company for fraud. He offers to prove that Company originally promised to retain him for at least a year, that he relied on the promise, and that Company never intended to keep it. Company argues that Accountant's claim fails because their written contract allows Company to fire him at any time, and because the parol-evidence rule forbids claims based on promises made outside the writing that are inconsistent with it. The parol-evidence rule may prevent Accountant from bringing a successful contract claim to enforce the promise that he says Company made. Accountant nevertheless may pursue a claim in tort to collect damages he suffered in reliance on Company's false assurances.

IV. RESTATEMENT (THIRD) OF RESTITUTION & UNJUST ENRICHMENT

(Selected Sections)

■ ■ ■

Table of Sections

Part II. Liability in Restitution
Chapter 2. Transfers Subject to Avoidance
Topic 2. Defective Consent or Authority

§ 13   Fraud and Misrepresentation

(1) A transfer induced by fraud or material misrepresentation is subject to rescission and restitution. The transferee is liable in restitution as necessary to avoid unjust enrichment.

(2) A transfer induced by fraud is void if the transferor had neither knowledge of, nor reasonable opportunity to learn, the character of the resulting transfer or its essential terms. Otherwise the transferee obtains voidable title.

Comment:

a.   General principles and scope; relation to other sections. Fraud is one of the principal grounds for restitution and one of the principal sources of unjust enrichment. The consequences of these related propositions are largely but not entirely coextensive.

Fraud is one of the most common grounds of rescission. A person whose consent to a transfer has been obtained by fraud is entitled to revoke it, if the remaining requirements of the rescission remedy can be met (§ 54). Rescission is unquestionably a form of restitution, but it is not in every instance a remedy for unjust enrichment. A transfer induced by fraud will usually be a source of unjust enrichment to the transferee, but this is not always the case; the claimant's right to avoid a transfer based on defective consent does not depend on showing that the transfer was a source of benefit to the transferee. See Comment e.

A conclusion that one party has obtained benefits from another by fraud is also one of the most recognizable sources of unjust enrichment. Rescission of the transaction may also reverse the unjust enrichment, but rescission is not always available; even if available, rescission by itself may not suffice to avoid the unjust enrichment of the fraudulent party at the expense of the claimant. Fraud gives the injured party a claim in restitution as necessary to avoid unjust enrichment, whether relief takes the form of rescission or not. See Illustration 1.

Illustration:

1. A notices a "For Sale" sign on Blackacre and mentions to B that he would be interested in purchasing the property. B represents falsely that he is acting as agent for C, the owner of Blackacre, and offers to transmit A's offer to C. A offers to pay $100,000 for Blackacre. B approaches C and offers $80,000 to purchase the property himself; C accepts. B informs A that A's offer to C has been accepted. B then manipulates the transaction to give A the impression he is purchasing Blackacre from C, when in reality B has purchased the property with A's money and resold to A at $20,000 profit. The fair market value of Blackacre is $100,000. By the law of the jurisdiction, B has neither undertaken nor breached any fiduciary or confidential duty to A. Although B has committed the tort of deceit, A is not entitled to damages because B's fraudulent misstatements have not caused A economic injury (as defined by local law). On the other hand, B has been unjustly enriched in consequence of his fraudulent conduct toward A, whether or not A can establish quantifiable injury. A may recover $20,000 from B by the rule of this section.

The proposition that a defendant is liable in restitution for benefits obtained by fraud recurs frequently in this Restatement. To the extent that a particular defendant's conduct might be characterized as fraudulent, every example of liability under the more specific rules of Chapter 2, Topic 1 (Benefits Conferred by Mistake), Chapter 5 (Restitution for Wrongs), and Chapter 6 (Benefits Conferred by a Third Person) might also serve as an instance of liability by the general rule of this section.

b.   Relation to contract law. Because most transfers are made pursuant to contract, rules that determine when such a transfer is subject to rescission for fraudulent inducement necessarily coincide with rules that determine when the agreement itself is subject to avoidance. In the case of a contractual transfer, therefore, the consequences of fraudulent inducement may be simultaneously a part of contract law and of the law of restitution. The rules here stated are intended to be fully consistent with the rules stated in Restatement Second, Contracts §§ 163–164, 372, and 376.

Where contract is concerned with the effectiveness of an agreement, the focus of restitution is on the effectiveness of any resulting transfer. Although many issues of fraudulent inducement are simultaneously a question of contract and of restitution, the overlap between the subjects at this point is not complete. Avoidance of a wholly executory contract, whether the reason is fraud or something else, presents no issue of restitution. Reversal of a completed exchange—whatever the basis of invalidity—is squarely within the province of restitution, while it is explained only awkwardly as a liability in contract. See Illustration 2.

Illustration:

2.   Buyer purchases a one-half interest in the mineral rights to Blackacre for $100,000, paying $10,000 down and promising to pay the balance in installments. In negotiating the contract, both parties rely on a report of Engineer to the effect that Blackacre contains approximately 50,000 tons of magnesite. They subsequently learn that the appraisal reflects an error in computation: properly interpreted, Engineer's findings indicate the presence of only 5000 tons of magnesite. Engineer's misrepresentation is not fraudulent, but it is material. Contract law permits Buyer to avoid his executory obligations to Seller. The rule of this section entitles Buyer to recover the $10,000 already paid. (If the case is analyzed as one of mutual mistake, the same relief is available by the rule of § 34.)

c.   Law of misrepresentation; causation; materiality. This Restatement does not describe the substantive law of misrepresentation. Accordingly, it does not state rules to govern such matters as the elements of fraud; the test of materiality; the circumstances in which concealment or nondisclosure is treated as assertion; or the plaintiff's right to rely upon misrepresentations of particular kinds, notably statements of intention, expressions of opinion, and misstatements of law. The law of misrepresentation is voluminous, and its function within the law of restitution, while indispensable, is by no means unique. See the sources indicated in the Reporter's Note.

A transfer is not subject to invalidation for misrepresentation, fraudulent or otherwise, unless the misrepresentation induced the transfer. Subject to this test of causation, a transfer induced by fraud is subject to rescission without regard to materiality; whereas a transfer induced by innocent misrepresentation is subject to rescission only if the misrepresentation was material.

Cases in which the claimant confers benefits as the result of another's innocent (but material) misrepresentation will usually be characterized as cases of mistake. The distinction makes no difference to the analysis or to the outcome. See Illustrations 3–4.

Illustrations:

3.   Brother and Sister are sole heirs of their father's estate. Executor informs them (as he honestly believes) that the estate comprises, in addition to Blackacre, an insignificant amount of personal property. Brother delivers to Sister a quitclaim deed to Blackacre and disclaims in favor of Sister his share in the personal property. The personal property of the estate proves to be substantial; Executor's misrepresentation was innocent but material. Brother is entitled to restitution of his share of the personal property by rescission of the disclaimer. (Because the gift of the realty was not induced by the misrepresentation, Brother has no right to rescind the deed.) Rights and remedies are identical, whether restitution is explained by reference to Executor's misrepresentation (by the rule of this section) or to Brother's mistake (as in § 11, Illustration 12).

4.   County appoints public defender to represent Defendant charged with burglary, relying on Defendant's affidavit of indigence. It transpires that Defendant owns substantial property. County is entitled to recover from Defendant the reasonable value of the services provided. If Defendant's misrepresentation was innocent, the case—while still within the rule of this section—is likely to be analyzed in terms of County's mistake.

d.   Void and voidable transfers. The law recognizes degrees of fraudulent inducement. Section 13(2) describes the circumstances, traditionally referred to as "fraud in the execution" or "fraud in the factum," in which a transfer will be treated on rescission not merely as voidable but as void ab initio. As between transferor and transferee, the distinction between void and voidable transfers is rarely of any consequence. The difference normally becomes relevant only when property that the defrauded transferor seeks to recover has come into the hands of a bona fide purchaser (or when a negotiable instrument obtained by fraud has been transferred to a holder in due course), because a purchaser cannot acquire a legal title that his grantor does not hold (§ 66). See Illustrations 5–6.

Illustrations:

5.   Father conveys Blackacre to Son, induced by Son's fraudulent misrepresentation of his personal circumstances. Son thereafter borrows money on the security of Blackacre, giving a mortgage to Bank. On discovery of the fraud, Father is entitled to rescind the transfer to Son. The mortgage is not subject to avoidance, however, if Bank establishes that it took the mortgage as a bona fide purchaser (§ 66). The outcome is

that title to Blackacre is revested in Father, subject to the mortgage in favor of Bank.

6. Same facts as Illustration 5, except that Father has no ability to read or write English; Son procures Father's signature on the deed by representing the document to be a will. Discovering the fraud, Father is entitled to rescind the transfer to Son. The mortgage to Bank is likewise invalid, Son's title to Blackacre being void and not merely voidable, although the purported mortgage (if valid) would have made Bank a bona fide purchaser.

e. *No requirement of injury or enrichment.* Rescission of a transfer induced by fraud or material misrepresentation requires no showing either that the transferor has suffered economic injury (the requirement in tort) or that the transferee has realized a benefit at the transferor's expense (the standard condition of unjust enrichment). See Comment *a*. Restitution via rescission under §§ 13 and 54 protects the claimant against an involuntary dispossession. If the defendant has induced a transfer by fraud, it is no answer to show that the transaction did the claimant no harm, or that it resulted in no gain to the defendant. See Illustrations 7–9.

By contrast, a claimant who seeks restitution of unjust enrichment realized as a result of fraud or material misrepresentation—instead of, or in addition to, restitution via rescission—must establish the amount of the defendant's unjust enrichment as in every other case.

Illustrations:

7. A sells Blackacre to B at its fair market value. Two weeks later B reconveys to C, a neighbor with whom A has a notorious and longstanding dispute and to whom A has repeatedly refused to sell. B and C have acted by prearrangement to procure a transfer from A to C. If the court finds that B's conduct was fraudulent as to A, and that C took the property with notice of the fraud, A is entitled to recover Blackacre from C. The result might be reached by cancellation of both deeds, or by a decree that C holds Blackacre in constructive trust for A.

8. Parishioner pledges to give Blackacre to Church for the construction of a new rectory. Parishioner's stated intention is to convey a defeasible fee, reverter to Parishioner when the property ceases to be used for church purposes. Church causes to be prepared for Parishioner's signature a deed conveying a fee simple absolute, then fraudulently represents to Parishioner that the document gives effect to Parishioner's true intentions. On learning the effect of the deed after it has been executed and recorded, Parishioner seeks to rescind the transfer and recover the property. Pointing to Parishioner's donative intent and to Church's use of the property as intended, Church's lawyers deny that Church has been "enriched" at the expense of Parishioner; but the case is one in which Parishioner is entitled to rescission and restitution without regard to Parishioner's loss or Church's gain.

9. Following protracted negotiations over price, Buyer pays Seller $25,000 for a fur coat having a fair market value of $30,000, then makes a gift of the coat to Friend. Unknown to Buyer, Seller has secretly agreed to accept $5000 toward the price from Friend. This deception allows Seller to make a sale, Buyer to acquire the coat at a price he considers a bargain, and Friend to acquire a valuable coat for a modest outlay. Although the joint fraud of Seller and Friend has caused Buyer no pecuniary loss, Buyer is entitled to rescind the gift as against Friend and the sale as against Seller.

f. Gratuitous transfers. Gratuitous transfers, whether induced by the fraud of the transferee or of a third party, furnish numerous examples of the rule of this section. When a gratuitous transfer is made by a donor judged to be particularly susceptible (as in Illustrations 10–11), the facts that justify rescission for fraud may simultaneously support rescission for duress, undue influence, or incapacity. Because these overlapping grounds of liability yield the same legal consequences, there is little significance to the choice between them. See §§ 14–16.

The closely-related problem of fraud in the inducement of testamentary dispositions (or analogous provisions under will substitutes) is addressed by Restatement Third, Property (Wills and Other Donative Transfers) § 8.3.

Illustrations:

10. A, characterized by the court as "a gullible, foolish old man," is persuaded "by various types of suggestions" to convey realty without consideration to B, "an adventuress of world-wide experience." The court finds that A's gift was induced by B's fraudulent misrepresentations. The transfer is subject to rescission.

11. Son and daughter-in-law park their mobile home on a ranch belonging to elderly and infirm Mother. Within a few months, Mother gives the ranch, all her cattle, and two cashier's checks to Son. The court finds that these gifts were induced by Son's fraudulent assertions that Mother would lose her property if it were not transferred to him. Mother is entitled to recover land, cattle, and money by whatever remedies are most convenient, including rescission, cancellation, and constructive trust.

g. Misrepresentation by third party. A transfer induced by fraud or material misrepresentation is subject to restitution, whether the representation is made by the transferee or by a third party. Because the defendant in third-party cases is not primarily at fault, the availability of restitution will frequently turn on affirmative defenses.

Rescission of a transfer induced by the fraud of a third party is not available against an immediate transferee who takes the property for value, without notice of the fraud. See Illustration 16. Although such a case is not strictly within the rule of bona fide purchase, the transferee is protected by analogy. Compare § 66, Illustration 8. When a transfer is induced by the fraud of a third party, an innocent transferee (not for value) may also be protected by the affirmative defense of change of position. See § 65, Illustration 5.

Illustrations:

12. A is induced by the fraud of B to make gifts of $5000 each to B and C. Although C has no notice of B's fraud, C is liable in restitution (as is B) because C takes A's money as donee.

13. Corporation pays $45 million in bonuses to its President, based on its reported net income during a five-year period. It is subsequently revealed that Corporation's net income for the period was artificially inflated, in consequence of an accounting fraud perpetrated by certain officers and directors. (Corporation was actually operating at a loss.) Corporation has a claim in restitution against President to recover $45 million plus interest. Restitution from President does not depend on proof that President participated in the fraud, or that President had notice that earnings were overstated. President is protected as a bona fide payee only to the extent that Corporation's payment reduced the amount of a valid obligation, and on the facts supposed there was none. Compare § 67, Illustration 10.

14. A is induced by B's fraud to convey Blackacre to B. B reconveys to C, who purchases with notice of B's fraud. A is entitled to recover Blackacre from C. One way to achieve this result is via cancellation of both deeds.

15. Same facts as Illustration 14, except that C takes Blackacre as a bona fide purchaser, giving B his note and mortgage. A is not entitled to restitution from C, but A is entitled to a decree that B holds C's note and mortgage and the proceeds thereof in constructive trust for A.

16. A is induced by B's fraud to sell her house to C, who purchases for value without notice of B's fraud. A is not entitled to restitution from C. If the transaction results in any benefit to B, A is entitled to restitution from B.

Claims between banks in the aftermath of a check-kiting scheme may be viewed as attempts to recover payments made by mistake, or as payments induced by the fraud of a third party. See Illustration 17. Such claims are decided, not by the Uniform Commercial Code, but by general principles of restitution. See U.C.C. § 3–418, Official Comment 3 (rev. 1990). Characterizing the transaction as a mistaken payment is unsatisfactory, given that the payor/claimant is necessarily aware that it is honoring a draft on uncollected funds. On the other hand, the payor's decision to do so is plainly influenced by the fraud of a third party, its customer. So long as both payor and payee bank are unaware of their customer's deception, restitution will be foreclosed by the payee's status as bona fide payee (§ 67). As in Illustration 17, however, a payor bank seeking restitution will ordinarily attempt to recover only the *last* payments in the sequence: those made when the payee had become aware of the fraud and the payor had not. Notice of fraud or mistake makes the defense of § 67 unavailable to the payee/defendant.

Substantial reasons of policy nevertheless support a rule that denies restitution between banks victimized by a check-kiting scheme, so long as the bank obtaining payment has not done so by means of fraudulent misrepresentations to the payor. If restitution is denied, the rationale consistent with the principles of this section is that the decision to pay checks drawn against uncollected funds—an indispensable element of any check-kiting scheme—is primarily a credit decision on the part of the payor. The payor bank in such circumstances assumes the risk of noncollection and, to that extent, extends credit to its customer. If it is appropriate for policy reasons to regard this credit decision as the primary cause of the payor's loss, the court may conclude that the payor bank should bear the losses to which its business practices make it subject.

Illustration:

17. Bank A and Bank B are victims of a check-kiting scheme operated by C. A (having detected the fraud) obtains payment of a final batch of checks drawn by C on B and deposited with A, while dishonoring at the last possible moment other checks drawn by C on A and presented by B. Although B is still unaware of C's fraudulent scheme, B is necessarily aware that it is paying checks drawn by C against uncollected funds. B has a potential claim in restitution against A, based either on mistaken payment (§ 6) or on the fraud of C within the rule of this section. A's knowledge of C's fraud, at the time of B's payment, precludes the assertion by A of the usual affirmative defense to B's restitution claim (§ 67). Restitution will nevertheless be denied if the court concludes (i) that A's conduct was not fraudulent toward B, and (ii) that by electing to pay checks drawn against uncollected funds, B has knowingly extended credit to its customer and assumed the risk of noncollection.

h. *Restitution versus damages.* Frequently, a claimant who seeks restitution on the basis of the defendant's misrepresentation might have sued for damages instead, whether in contract for breach of warranty or in tort for deceit. Remedies in restitution may offer important advantages over a remedy in damages, depending on the circumstances of the particular case.

The remedies suggested by the remaining Illustrations to this section are not limited to cases of fraud, though some of them are available only against a defendant whose actions—as in cases of fraud—are consciously wrongful. Remedies in restitution are described in detail in §§ 49–61; the numerous Illustrations to those sections include many further examples of restitution for fraud within the rule of § 13. A sampling of restitutionary remedies for fraud is included at this point because a fraud victim (unlike many other plaintiffs with valid restitution claims) is likely to have alternative damage claims on a variety of theories, making the comparison of restitution and damages especially pertinent.

A fraud victim may choose restitution rather than damages to obtain the immediate advantages of specific over substitutionary relief (see Illustrations 18–19); or of specific relief supplemented by a money judgment eliminating the defendant's unjust enrichment (see Illustration 20). Restitution and rescission may be superior to damages for deceit merely because it is easier for the claimant to show the price that was paid (and to reverse the transaction) than to prove the amount of the resulting injury. See Illustration 21; compare § 54, Illustration 8. When a fraudulent transaction has been profitable to the defendant, restitution allows the claimant to obtain disgorgement of the defendant's consequential gains—and thereby to recover more than the claimant's loss. See Illustrations 1 and 22; compare § 51, Illustration 10.

Illustrations:

18. A is induced by B's fraudulent misrepresentations to trade horses with B. Rescission and restitution (§ 54) permits A to recover his own horse on restoration of B's horse. A might alternatively recover damages for B's breach of warranty or B's deceit, but rescission and restitution for B's fraud is likely to offer more effective relief.

19. H and W participate in a ceremony of marriage after W fraudulently represents that she has been divorced from her husband, A. H thereafter purchases Blackacre from O, taking title in W's name at her suggestion. On subsequently learning of W's marriage to A, H is entitled to recover Blackacre from W. The court will declare that W holds the property in constructive trust for H.

20. A is induced by B's fraudulent misrepresentations to lease valuable mineral rights to C and D, B's confederates. On discovery of the fraud A is entitled to restitution of the mineral rights (via cancellation of the lease) and to restitution of the profits obtained in the interim by C and D.

21. A is induced by B's fraudulent misrepresentations to purchase securities that are worth less than the price paid. By choosing to rescind the transaction, A can recover the purchase price plus interest without proving damages.

22. Manager purchases 10 shares of closely-held Corporation from Employee at $5000 per share, fraudulently representing that Employee is required to relinquish his shareholding on retirement and that Corporation itself is the purchaser. In fact Manager acquires the shares for himself. The value of the stock at the time of the sale to Manager is $10,000 per share. Some years later, after Employee has died, Manager disposes of his entire interest in Corporation at $75,000 per share; Employee's Estate learns of the fraud and sues Manager to rescind the original sale. The court may decree that Manager holds the traceable

proceeds of Employee's shares ($750,000) in constructive trust for Estate, subject to Estate's repayment to Manager of $50,000 plus interest.

Sometimes a transaction induced by fraud proves disadvantageous to the claimant for reasons unrelated to the fraud. Rescission for misrepresentation may permit the claimant to shift this loss to the defendant, although the defendant's misrepresentation—not being the legal cause of the plaintiff's injury—would not support a claim for damages in tort. See Illustration 23; compare § 54, Illustration 9. In other cases, the advantage of rescission and restitution is simply that it allows the claimant to escape relatively unfavorable contract terms: for example, to recover in quantum meruit (in other words, at market value) for goods or services previously supplied on contract terms favorable to the transferee. See Illustration 24.

Illustrations:

23. Trustee informs Broker that it wishes to purchase corporate bonds of specified quality and maturity. Broker is informed, moreover, that because of limits to its investment powers, Trustee can only purchase listed securities. Broker sells bonds to Trustee at a price of $975 each, confirming that they are listed on the New York Stock Exchange. In fact the issue is not listed on any exchange. Acting promptly after discovery of the facts, Trustee tenders the bonds and demands return of the price paid. Interest rates rose sharply after the initial transaction, with the result that the bonds are now trading at $925; the price of comparable, listed securities has fallen to the same extent. Trustee is entitled to rescission whether Broker's misrepresentation was innocent or fraudulent.

24. Psychiatrist provides professional services to elderly Patient at nominal charge, relying on Patient's representation that she is impoverished. Patient dies, leaving an estate of $100,000; her misrepresentation of financial status, which may have been innocent, was in any event material. Psychiatrist is entitled to recover from Patient's estate the amount of his reasonable and customary fee, less the amounts previously collected.

Most importantly, a claimant who is entitled to avoid (rather than enforce) a contract induced by fraud may be able to avoid becoming the creditor of an insolvent defendant. See § 55, Illustration 9; § 60, Illustrations 3, 4, and 6. A claim to recover money or other property obtained by fraud benefits from the full range of remedies that achieve restitution via rights in identifiable property, reaching assets obtained by the defendant as the product of, or in exchange for, the property of which the claimant was originally deprived. See § 58. A claimant who can assert rights of ownership or security in property so obtained obtains an effective priority over unsecured creditors (including lien creditors) of the defendant. Relief of this kind is most often achieved through the device of constructive trust. In particular circumstances, the appropriate remedy may be described in terms of equitable lien or subrogation. See Illustrations 25–27.

Illustrations:

25. Victim loses $100,000 to Embezzler. After discovering the fraud, Victim is able to establish that Embezzler used Victim's money to purchase Blackacre. Because Blackacre qualifies as Embezzler's homestead, it would be exempt from execution on a judgment for damages. Restitution gives Victim ownership of Blackacre, rather than a judgment to be satisfied from property of Embezzler. Relief will usually take the form of a decree that Embezzler holds Blackacre in constructive trust for Victim.

26. Same facts as Illustration 25, except that (before Victim discovers the facts) the United States has recorded a lien against Blackacre for Embezzler's unpaid federal income tax. Victim is entitled to a decree that Embezzler holds Blackacre in constructive trust for A, free of the tax lien. A lien creditor does not have the rights of a bona fide purchaser (§ 60(1)), and a lien for Embezzler's taxes cannot attach to what is, in legal contemplation, the property of Victim.

27. A lends $10,000 to B, taking as security a purported mortgage of property B does not own. After discovering the fraud, A is able to establish that B used A's money to discharge a valid first mortgage on Blackacre, which B does own. A is entitled to be subrogated to the rights of the discharged mortgagee, as security for A's restitution claim for $10,000.

Part III. Remedies
Chapter 7. Remedies
Topic 1. Restitution Via Money Judgment:
The Measure of Unjust Enrichment

§ 51 Enrichment by Misconduct; Disgorgement; Accounting

(1) As used in this section, the term "misconduct" designates an actionable interference by the defendant with the claimant's legally protected interests for which the defendant is liable under §§ 13–15 or §§ 39–46 of this Restatement.

(2) The value for restitution purposes of benefits obtained by the misconduct of the defendant, culpable or otherwise, is not less than their market value. Market value may be identified, where appropriate, with the reasonable cost of a license.

(3) A "conscious wrongdoer" is a defendant who is enriched by misconduct and who acts

(a) with knowledge of the underlying wrong to the claimant, or

(b) despite a known risk that the conduct in question violates the rights of the claimant.

(4) Unless the rule of subsection (2) imposes a greater liability, the unjust enrichment of a conscious wrongdoer, or of a defaulting fiduciary without regard to notice or fault, is the net profit attributable to the underlying wrong. The object of restitution in such cases is to eliminate profit from wrongdoing while avoiding, so far as possible, the imposition of a penalty. Restitution remedies that pursue this object are often called "disgorgement" or "accounting."

(5) In determining net profit the court may apply such tests of causation and remoteness, may make such apportionments, may recognize such credits or deductions, and may assign such evidentiary burdens, as reason and fairness dictate, consistent with the object of restitution as specified in subsection (4). The following rules apply unless modified to meet the circumstances of a particular case:

(a) Profit includes any form of use value, proceeds, or consequential gains (§ 53) that is identifiable and measurable and not unduly remote.

(b) A conscious wrongdoer or a defaulting fiduciary who makes unauthorized investments of the claimant's assets is accountable for profits and liable for losses.

(c) A conscious wrongdoer or a defaulting fiduciary may be allowed a credit for money expended in acquiring or preserving the property or in carrying on the business that is the source of the profit subject to disgorgement. By contrast, such a defendant will ordinarily be denied any credit for contributions in the form of services, or for expenditures incurred directly in the commission of a wrong to the claimant.

(d) A claimant who seeks disgorgement of profit has the burden of producing evidence permitting at least a reasonable approximation of the amount of the wrongful gain. Residual risk of uncertainty in calculating net profit is assigned to the defendant.

Comment:

a. General principles and scope; relation to other sections. The present section employs the term "misconduct" to encompass any form of actionable wrongdoing by the defendant for which the defendant is liable in restitution by the rules of §§ 13–15 or §§ 39–46. Strict liability in tort creates the possibility of actionable wrongdoing without culpability: the unjust enrichment of tortfeasors without fault—such as innocent converters or trespassers, or unwitting infringers—is accordingly measured by the rule of § 51(2), not by the rule of § 50. See Comment *c.* (By contrast, a defendant without fault who is unjustly enriched by the misconduct of a third person may be an innocent recipient, whose unjust enrichment is measured by the rule of § 50 rather than the rule of this section.)

Outside the particular scope of § 39, breach of contract does not constitute "misconduct" for purposes of this section. See § 44, Comment *a*. The alternative remedies for breach described in §§ 37–38 are not directed at unjust enrichment, and they do not implicate the rules for measuring enrichment that are the subject of the present Topic.

The principal focus of § 51 is on cases in which unjust enrichment is measured by the defendant's profits, where the object of restitution is to strip the defendant of a wrongful gain (§§ 3, 49(4)). This profit-based measure of unjust enrichment determines recoveries against conscious wrongdoers and defaulting fiduciaries. Recovery so measured may potentially exceed any loss to the claimant. Rules and objectives that guide the measurement of enrichment in such cases are stated in subsections (3) and (4).

Restitution measured by the defendant's wrongful gain is frequently called "disgorgement." Other cases refer to an "accounting" or an "accounting for profits." Whether or not these terms are employed, the remedial issues in all cases of conscious wrongdoing are the same. They concern the identification and measurement of those gains to the defendant that should be regarded as unjust enrichment, in that they are properly attributable to the defendant's interference with the claimant's legally protected rights. Recurring problems in measuring the profits for which a defendant should be liable in restitution are examined in Comments *e* through *i*.

Status as a conscious wrongdoer is established in most cases by showing "knowledge of the underlying wrong to the claimant," but there are contexts in which—although the risk of liability is known—the legal conclusion that a wrong has been committed may not be reached until after the fact. See § 3, Comment *e*. Subsection (3)(b) makes clear that one who chooses to act in such circumstances bears the risk of liability by a disgorgement measure.

b.   Relation to the asset-based remedies in restitution. Section 51 describes the extent of enrichment for which a wrongdoer is liable in restitution on the assumption that the claimant's remedy is a simple money judgment (§§ 49(1), 49(4)). Such a remedy involves no claim to particular assets and no requirement of tracing by the rules of §§ 58–59. The resulting judgment, to be satisfied from the defendant's available assets, ranks equally with the rights of competing claimants and unsecured creditors. See Illustration 1.

A claimant who could require the defendant to disgorge profits as a conscious wrongdoer might also be able to establish that particular assets in the defendant's hands—besides being the fruits of wrongdoing and the natural measure of the defendant's profits—are the traceable product of assets to which the claimant has a paramount claim of ownership. Such a case is one in which the rules of § 51 (which aim to strip the defendant of a wrongful gain) coincide with the rules of Chapter 7, Topic 2 (which preserve the claimant's property against wrongful dispossession).

There are cases in which a proprietary or asset-based remedy in restitution offers the most convenient resolution of a simple two-party contest. If the defendant's wrongful gain may be identified with the defendant's interest in particular property, restitution is achieved without the need to measure unjust enrichment—or to reduce it to a money judgment—by a remedy that strips the defendant of the interest in question and awards it to the claimant. See Illustration 2; compare § 55, Comment *c*. More frequently, the significance of the asset-based restitution remedies in such cases (and of their associated tracing requirements) is that rights so established have priority over the claims of the defendant's general creditors. See Illustration 3. See also § 55, Comment *d*; § 58, Comment *b*; § 60, Comment *b*.

Illustrations:

1.   Infringer violates Owner's copyright, realizing net profits of $50,000. Although the amount of Infringer's liability will sometimes be described as the amount of profits "traceable to the infringement," Owner is required only to identify the net profits that are properly *attributable* to the infringement. In other words, there is no requirement of tracing or following assets from Owner's hands into Infringer's bank account (or other assets) by the rules of §§ 58–59. Without the ability to trace, on the other hand, Owner's remedy is limited to a money judgment for $50,000, to be satisfied from Infringer's general assets. Such a judgment ranks equally with the claims of Infringer's unsecured creditors.

2.   Embezzler uses $100,000 of Employer's money to purchase Blackacre, an investment Embezzler would not otherwise have been able to make. Property values have increased, and by the time the embezzlement comes to light the value of Blackacre is more than $150,000. By the rule of § 51(4), Employer would be entitled to a money judgment against Embezzler for the present value of Blackacre, thereby stripping Embezzler of the gain attributable to the wrong. Embezzler's assets (including Blackacre) are more than adequate to satisfy such a judgment. On the other hand, a judgment giving Employer title to Blackacre may be a more convenient remedy than a money judgment against Embezzler, because it avoids the need to prove the value of the property and may be easier to enforce. Since Employer is able to trace the embezzled funds into the property (§ 58), Employer may obtain a remedy by constructive trust (§ 55) in preference to a simple money judgment.

3.   Same facts as Illustration 2, except that the claims of Embezzler's unsecured creditors far exceed Embezzler's assets. Although Employer would be entitled to a money judgment of at least $150,000 against Embezzler by the rule of § 51(4), Employer would recover only a

small fraction of such a judgment from an insolvent defendant. Employer's ability to trace the embezzled funds into the property means that Employer can assert an interest in Blackacre that is paramount to the interest of Embezzler's unsecured creditors (§ 60(1)). On the other hand, the rule that prohibits a profitable recovery in restitution at the expense of unpaid creditors means that Employer, on the facts supposed, will not be permitted to recover more than the amount of his loss (§ 61). Employer is entitled to an equitable lien on Blackacre securing his claim to $100,000 plus interest (§ 56(4)).

c.   Liability without fault. Persons who are without fault are frequently liable in restitution, but their unjust enrichment is measured in ways that tend to protect them from prejudice. The passive recipient of benefits conferred by mistake—or of benefits obtained from the claimant by the wrongdoing of a third person—will likely qualify as an "innocent recipient" whose enrichment is measured by the protective rules of § 50. Section 51(2) is relevant to a different category of liability without fault, typically arising in the context of the strict-liability property torts. Persons such as innocent converters, unconscious trespassers, and unwitting infringers are liable in restitution for the market value of the rights they have "taken," even if this measure of enrichment exceeds any value actually realized by the defendant. (It is the latter qualification that distinguishes the liability of these unconscious tortfeasors from the liability of "innocent recipients." Compare § 51(2) with § 50(2)(a).) Liability of the nonculpable tortfeasor in restitution thus parallels the liability in tort from the same transaction, from which it may be indistinguishable as a practical matter. See Illustrations 4–5. Even if the measure of liability in restitution is identical to tort damages for the same interference, it may be important to distinguish the alternative theories of recovery, because they are likely to be governed by different periods of limitation. See § 70, Comment *e.*

A defendant who commits no misconduct by the rule of § 51(1) may yet bear responsibility for the transaction that leads to the defendant's unjust enrichment (§ 52). Liability will then be measured in a manner more protective of the claimant—in some cases, as if the recipient were a conscious wrongdoer. See Illustration 6 and the Illustrations to § 52.

Conversely, a defendant who is enriched by misconduct but who is not at fault in the underlying transaction is not liable for consequential gains, or for proceeds not constituting unjust enrichment (§ 53(3)). In the classic example, an innocent converter who improves the converted property and resells it at a profit is liable to the owner for the value of the original property (§ 51(2)) but not for the profit realized thereafter. See § 40, Illustration 13.

Illustrations:

4.   A purchases coal from B at $5 per ton, unaware that B has stolen it from C. Because A is entitled under contract with D to obtain his requirements of coal at $5.50 per ton, the value of C's coal in advancing A's purposes is not more than $5.50 per ton. The market price

of coal is $6 per ton. A burns the coal before the facts come to light. Because A (as an innocent converter) is guilty of misconduct, albeit without fault, A's liability to C in restitution (§ 40) is measured at $6 per ton (§ 51(2)).

5.   B sells coal to C at the market price of $6 per ton but delivers it by mistake to A. A is entitled under contract with D to obtain his requirements of coal at $5.50 per ton. A burns the coal before the facts come to light. A's liability to B in restitution (§ 9) is measured at $5.50 per ton (§§ 49(3)(a), 50(2)(a)).

6.   Same facts as Illustration 5, except that B's mistake is attributable in substantial part to A's carelessness in accepting delivery. If the court finds that A's negligence is a principal cause of A's unjust enrichment, A's liability will be measured more liberally, to avoid or mitigate the loss to B (§ 52(2)(b)).

d.   *Liability not less than market value.* The use of market value to fix a minimum liability in restitution is most often pertinent in cases involving conscious wrongdoers, but it applies to any case in which enrichment results from misconduct, with or without culpability, on the part of the defendant. Enrichment from benefits wrongfully obtained is not discounted to reflect some lesser value actually realized in advancing the purposes of the defendant. See Illustrations 7–8; compare the contrasting treatment of innocent recipients under § 50(2). So long as benefits wrongfully obtained have an ascertainable market value, that value is the minimum measure of the wrongdoing defendant's unjust enrichment, even if the transaction produces no ascertainable injury to the claimant and no ascertainable benefit to the defendant. Reasonable rental value or a reasonable royalty will often supply such a measure, as in Illustration 9; see also § 42, Illustrations 5–6.

Illustrations:

7.   By the legal tariff, a telephone call from the United States to Guyana requires payment to Guyana Telecom of 85 cents per minute. (U.S. carriers operating legally charge their customers at least $1.25 per minute, of which they remit 85 cents to Guyana Telecom.) Florida Telecom fraudulently transmits one million minutes of calls without payment to Guyana Telecom, charging its customers only 25 cents per minute. Damages from the fraud to Guyana Telecom cannot exceed $350,000, because Guyana Telecom is obliged to pay unrelated parties a "commission" of 50 cents per minute on calls originating in the U.S. Profits from the fraud to Florida Telecom cannot exceed its total revenues of $250,000. Florida Telecom is liable in restitution to Guyana Telecom for the market value of the benefit wrongfully obtained, or $850,000.

8.   A employs B to dig a well on A's land, on an agreement that B is to be paid only if water is found. A represents that no efforts to find water have been made in the past. In fact, as A knows, many attempts

have been made, all of them unsuccessful. B is entitled to the market value of his services although he also is unsuccessful in finding water.

9.   Without obtaining permission, Orchestra uses a photograph of Artist's sculpture to illustrate one page of a brochure advertising season subscriptions. It is conceded that this use of the image is an infringement of Artist's copyright. Artist is entitled to recover Orchestra's profits attributable to the infringement, but he is unable to produce any evidence of what these might have been (if any). Artist is likewise entitled to recover damages, but he is unable to show that he suffered any. Nevertheless, Orchestra is liable in restitution for the value of what it has obtained in violation of Artist's rights: in this case, the use it made of the photograph in question. The court determines that the reasonable price of a license permitting such use is $1000. Orchestra is liable to Artist in restitution (whether characterized as "damages" or "profits" under the Copyright Act) in the amount of $1000.

e.   *Disgorgement; accounting for profits; the general problem of attribution.* The object of the disgorgement remedy—to eliminate the possibility of profit from conscious wrongdoing-is one of the cornerstones of the law of restitution and unjust enrichment. See § 3. While its purpose is easily stated and readily understandable, the application of the remedy involves well-known, sometimes intractable difficulties.

The profit for which the wrongdoer is liable by the rule of § 51(4) is the net increase in the assets of the wrongdoer, to the extent that this increase is attributable to the underlying wrong. Profit results in some cases from the avoidance of an otherwise necessary expenditure. See, e.g., § 40, Illustration 6 (saving from willful trespass); § 40, Illustration 17 (saving from willful conversion). More commonly, the claimant seeks profits in the form of net income or appreciated property value.

Calculation of profits is simplest when the whole of the wrongdoer's unjust enrichment is captured in the ownership, possession, or disposition of specific property. See Illustration 2, supra (claimant's property used by defendant to acquire other property); compare § 40, Illustration 12 (enrichment measured by proceeds of defendant's sale of claimant's property). Elsewhere the application of the disgorgement remedy turns on problems of *attribution*, as the court attempts to decide what portion of the defendant's assets or income is properly attributable to the underlying wrong to the claimant. See § 42, Comment *h* (introducing issues of attribution in the context of infringement).

The question of attribution will sometimes have a simple answer. Observable facts concerning the defendant's activities may support a direct inference about the proportion of the defendant's overall business profits, or the increase over profits that would otherwise have been realized, attributable to the defendant's interference with the claimant's interests. See, e.g., § 40, Illustration 5 (where 15 percent of defendant's underground storage capacity is situated on claimant's property, 15 percent of defendant's profits from underground storage are attributable to defendant's trespass); § 40, Illustration 17 (where defendant's unauthorized use of claimant's machine saved 500 hours of labor at $5 per hour, defendant's profit from wrongdoing is $2500).

The task of attribution is frequently more difficult, however, and many such calculations are to a large extent the product of presumptions. This is because—in important recurring settings—the question of what is properly attributable tends to escape specification by objective rules. Even if all relevant facts can be ascertained, the problem of attribution may involve questions that facts cannot answer. Such questions include:

How far to follow a chain of causation before deciding that a particular element of profit is too remote from the underlying wrong to be subject to restitution.

What proportion of the defendant's overall profits to treat as the product of the underlying wrong; conversely, what proportion of the profits would have been realized had the wrong not been committed.

What credit to allow on account of the defendant's contributions of property or services in calculating the net profit for which the defendant is liable.

The question whether specific elements of defendant's profit are properly attributable to the underlying wrong to the claimant is multifaceted. To facilitate analysis, the following Comments and their accompanying Illustrations address four principal aspects of the general problem of attribution: questions of causation and remoteness (Comment *f*), questions of apportionment (Comment *g*), questions of deductions and credits (Comment *h*), and questions of proof (Comment *i*). This subdivision is merely approximate, and it is not intended to suggest a nonexistent precision in deciding the overall problem of attribution. Few of the questions are susceptible to resolution by rule, and the answers given will be visibly influenced by the court's view of the broader context in which the question is presented—including the defendant's degree of culpability, the importance of the claimant's protected interest, and the remedial alternatives available as a practical matter.

f. Causation and remoteness. Sections 51(5) and 53 refer to the possibility that a court may deny recovery of particular elements of profit on the ground of remoteness. Characterization of profit as "remote" implies that the causal connection with wrongdoing is unduly attenuated, although (on closer analysis) issues of causation may not be strictly involved. The usage is retained in this Restatement, not only because it is ingrained, but because it summarizes in intuitive fashion a variety of concerns that are potentially relevant to the ultimate issue of unjust enrichment.

To say that a profit is directly attributable to the underlying wrong, or (as sometimes expressed) that the profit is the "proximate consequence" of the wrong, does not mean that the defendant's wrong is the exclusive or even

228

the predominant source of the defendant's profit. Indeed, because the disgorgement remedy is usually invoked when the defendant's profits exceed the claimant's provable loss, it should be possible in almost every case to identify additional *causes* of the profit for which the defendant is liable. So if the defendant embezzles $100 and invests the money in shares that he later sells for $500, the $500 that the claimant recovers is largely the result of causes independent of the wrong: favorable market conditions and the defendant's investment acumen or simply luck. The determination in this easy case that the embezzler's profit is properly attributable to the underlying wrong rests on a number of related judgments. The first, evidently a matter of causation, is a finding (or a presumption) that the defendant would not have made the investment (and realized the profit) but for the wrong. But causation in this sense gives only part of the answer. The conclusion that the defendant's profit is properly attributable to the defendant's wrong depends equally on an implicit judgment that the claimant, rather than the wrongdoer, should in these circumstances obtain the benefit of the favorable market conditions, acumen, or luck, as the case may be. The conclusion draws further support from another implicit judgment, that there would be an incentive to embezzlement if the defendant were permitted to retain the profits realized in such a transaction.

Judgment that a particular item of profit is not recoverable in restitution, being unduly "remote" from the wrong, sometimes reflects a contrary conclusion about causation. A finding that the defendant would have realized the profit in any event may support a judicial conclusion that principles of unjust enrichment do not require that the profit in question be surrendered to the victim of the wrong.

But neither the presence nor the absence of a causal link between the defendant's wrongdoing and the defendant's profit will be conclusive in all cases on the ultimate issue of unjust enrichment. Absence of but-for causation does not necessarily exonerate the wrongdoer, because a finding that the defendant would have realized the profit in any event does not compel the conclusion that the defendant, under the circumstances, has not been unjustly enriched. To take an obvious example, a trustee who makes a profit from the personal use of trust assets could not escape liability in restitution by proving that he could have (and would have) made the same profit legitimately, supposing that his access to the trust assets had been hindered in some way. Nor does the existence of but-for causation compel the conclusion in every case that the proper measure of unjust enrichment is the whole of the defendant's traceable gains. See Illustration 11; compare § 43, Illustration 36, and § 53, Illustration 8 (suggesting limits in terms of remoteness on how far to pursue consequential gains).

Where causation is not the issue, an objection that profits are "remote" may mean simply that they are impossible to measure with sufficient accuracy; or that they are the product of legitimate contributions by the defendant that should not, in justice, be awarded to the claimant; or that liability for the profits so designated would be unacceptably punitive, being unnecessary to accomplish the object of the disgorgement remedy in restitution.

A court's decision that one item of profit is properly attributable to the defendant's wrongdoing, while another is unduly remote, depends finally on its assessment of these and other factors affecting not only justice between the parties but the incentives to be created for others. A court that denies recovery of profits that it characterizes as "remote" has concluded that the defendant may retain them without being unjustly enriched. See Illustrations 11–13; compare § 42, Illustration 19 (representing cases in which "indirect" profits from infringement may be denied on the ground that they are impermissibly speculative or remote).

Illustrations:

10. Corporate Insider purchases from minority Shareholder 10,000 shares of ABC Corp. at a price of $100 per share. To induce the sale, Insider wrongfully withholds material nonpublic information about ABC. Had this information been revealed, the market value of the shares at the time of the sale would have been $125. Twelve months later ABC is dissolved, and its shareholders receive $200 per share on liquidation. Under the law of the jurisdiction, Insider would be liable to former Shareholder in tort (for deceit) for the difference between the value of the shares at the time of the sale and the price paid, or $250,000. Insider is alternatively liable in restitution, based on fraud (§ 13), breach of fiduciary duty (§ 43), or statutory violation (§ 44). On any analysis Insider is a conscious wrongdoer whose unjust enrichment is measured by § 51(4). Insider is liable to former Shareholder for the profit realized in the wrongful transaction: profit in this case includes proceeds of the shares wrongfully acquired (§ 53(2)), whether or not the liquidation of ABC was foreseen at the time of the transaction. Insider's liability in restitution is $1 million.

11. Same facts as Illustration 10, except that the information withheld by Insider becomes public one month after the initial transaction. The shares of ABC are traded on the New York Stock Exchange, where their price moves immediately from $100 to $125. Former Shareholder, now in possession of all the facts, neither purchases ABC shares nor seeks to rescind the sale to Insider. Over the course of the next 11 months, the price of ABC shares increases from $125 to $200 in response to extraneous developments (unrelated to Insider's misrepresentation) and to general market conditions. Insider then sells 10,000 shares at $200, at which point former Shareholder brings an action in restitution seeking disgorgement of $1 million on the theory of Illustration 10. If the court concludes that Insider's further $750,000 profit on the ABC shares is too remote from the wrong to former Shareholder, it may find that Insider's unjust enrichment from the transaction is limited to $250,000 (§ 51(5)(a)). Such a finding is especially appropriate if the court believes that former Shareholder—

who is entitled to recover $250,000 in any event—has delayed asserting a claim in order to speculate on ABC shares at Insider's expense.

12. Director borrows corporate funds to finance the private purchase of property which he subsequently resells to Corporation, realizing from this disloyalty a profit of $300,000. Director thereafter reinvests the $300,000 in an unrelated venture, producing a further gain of $700,000. Director is liable to Corporation for $300,000 in any event. The additional $700,000 is a consequential gain for which Director is also liable to Corporation (§ 53(3)), unless the court finds that the profit from this subsequent transaction is unduly remote from the underlying wrong (§ 51(5)(a)). The causal connection between the wrong to Corporation and Director's consequential gain might be broken, for example, if Director could prove that he had alternative sources of financing from which he both could and would have made the subsequent investment in any event.

13. Edwards discovers on his property an entrance to the Great Onyx Cave, which he explores and develops as a successful tourist attraction. (See § 40, Illustration 4.) As Edwards is aware, 30 percent of the exhibited portion of the cave lies under the adjoining land of Lee. In litigation after these facts come to light, Edwards is held liable to Lee for 30 percent of the net profits realized from exhibiting the cave. Lee seeks, in addition, 30 percent of the net profits from operation of a nearby hotel, built by Edwards to serve visitors to the cave. The court denies recovery of any part of the hotel profits, on the ground that such profits are unduly remote from the underground trespass. The conclusion might be further explained by observing that the hotel profits are visibly and predominantly the product of factors other than the underground trespass, with the consequence that an award to Lee of a share of these profits would subject Edwards to a remedy that was confiscatory rather than restitutionary.

g. *Apportionment.* The general question of attribution may include issues of *apportionment* at one or more levels. If the defendant's business is complex, and the underlying wrong to the claimant affects only one of its various components, threshold apportionment issues may involve (i) the proportion of the firm's overall results properly attributable to the particular business in which the wrong has been committed, and (ii) the proportion of overhead or other common expenses properly charged against these results in determining the net profits of the business in question. Because similar questions need to be addressed for a variety of purposes, unrelated to liability in restitution, it may be possible to find appropriate answers in existing accounting practice.

Once this threshold apportionment has been made, however, the court confronts a further problem of apportionment that ordinary accounting practice has no call to address. When the net profit in question has been realized in part as a result of the wrong to the claimant and in part from the defendant's legitimate activities—so that some part, at least, of the defendant's profit would have been realized in the absence of the wrong—what proportion of the net profit is attributable to the wrong to the claimant? Because precise answers to this part of the apportionment problem are often unattainable, the court will reach the best approximation it can under the circumstances. See Illustrations 14–15.

Illustrations:

14. In violation of Author's copyright, Studio produces a successful film, "Letty Lynton," as described in § 42, Illustration 16. Studio is liable to Author in restitution for the net profits attributable to its conscious interference with Author's rights. Measurement of the profits attributable to the infringement involves a problem of apportionment at several stages. As a threshold matter, the court must determine the proportion of Studio's overall profits that is derived from the production and distribution of "Letty Lynton" as distinct from its other activities. Calculation of the net profit realized from "Letty Lynton" requires, moreover, an apportionment of various items of overhead and general expense between "Letty Lynton" and Studio's other ventures. Despite their complexity, the same apportionments are routinely made in other contexts (for example, in determining Studio's contractual obligations to persons entitled to share in the net profits of particular films). Unless circumstances dictate otherwise, the same apportionment will serve as the starting point for measuring Studio's liability to Author. Once the net profits derived from "Letty Lynton" have been determined, however, the court confronts the further problem of deciding what proportion of those profits is attributable to the unauthorized use of Author's play. Evidence presented at trial would support a range of answers between 25 percent of the total (according to Author's expert) and nil (according to Studio's expert). Weighing all the relevant evidence, the court concludes that the proportion of Studio's profits attributable to the infringement is somewhere between zero and 10 percent; moreover, that the correct answer within these limits is impossible to determine. Because the risk of uncertainty in such an accounting is assigned to the wrongdoer, Author is entitled to 10 percent of the net profits of "Letty Lynton."

15. Edwards exhibits a cave located partially under Lee's property, as described in § 40, Illustration 4, and in Illustration 13, supra. Net profits realized by Edwards from the operation of the cave during the period of the statute of limitations amount to $100,000. The only evidence in the record that would serve as the basis of allocating these profits between Edwards and Lee is the finding that 30 percent of the cave lies under Lee's land. (The most noteworthy features of the cave, judging by the postcards published by Edwards, are situated proportionately on either side of the boundary.) There being no other basis of apportionment, the court concludes that 30 percent of Edwards's net profits are attributable to his conscious violation of Lee's interests.

h. *Deductions and credits.* A recurring issue of the accounting described in § 51(5) is the extent to which the defendant should be allowed a deduction (that is, a credit against liability) for contributions made by the defendant to the gain for which the defendant is liable. As a general rule, the defendant is entitled to a deduction for all marginal costs incurred in producing the revenues that are subject to disgorgement. Denial of an otherwise appropriate deduction, by making the defendant liable in excess of net gains, results in a punitive sanction that the law of restitution normally attempts to avoid. See § 42, Comment *i.* By contrast, the defendant will not be allowed to deduct expenses (such as ordinary overhead) that would have been incurred in any event, if the result would be that defendant's wrongful activities—by defraying a portion of overall expenses—yield an increased profit from defendant's operations as a whole.

(Cases that address issues of deductions and credits are concerned, almost exclusively, with the liability of conscious wrongdoers to disgorge profits; but the principle that limits liability to net gains applies equally to a defendant without fault, such as an innocent converter. See Illustration 16.)

In its allowance of deductions for defendants' contributions to the assets or profits subject to disgorgement, the law of restitution appears to be more solicitous of some conscious wrongdoers than of others. Intentional converters and trespassers are uniformly denied any allowance for improvements made to the claimant's property. See Illustrations 17–18 and § 10, Illustration 5. Yet deliberate infringers who make profitable use of others' intellectual property are liable only for the profits attributable to the infringement— obtaining, in effect, a credit for their legitimate contributions to the end result. See § 42, Illustration 16. Disloyal fiduciaries are uniformly reimbursed for the purchase price of property acquired in conscious breach of their duty of loyalty. See § 43, Illustrations 8, 14, and 21; compare § 63, Illustration 14. Because the defendants in all these cases are conscious wrongdoers, it does not seem possible to explain the contrasting outcomes by comparing their relative blameworthiness.

These divergent results are partially reconciled by observing that the defendants in these cases, in seeking a credit against liability to the claimant, are asserting what is in effect a restitutionary setoff or counterclaim. Although the transactions take various forms, in each case the defendant's implicit counterclaim is an attempt to recover (through a credit against liability) the value to the claimant of benefits conferred without request. The viability of these implicit restitutionary counterclaims appears to depend, to some extent at least, on the same considerations that would be relevant if they were brought as free-standing claims for affirmative relief in restitution.

Because restitution for benefits conferred in money is consistently easier to obtain than restitution for services, it is not surprising that a defendant will more readily obtain credit against a liability in restitution for money spent in acquiring property of which the claimant elects to assert ownership, or for out-of-pocket expenses that the claimant would otherwise have had to bear. By contrast, a defendant's claim to credit or deduction will predictably be denied if allowance of the credit would permit a conscious wrongdoer to force the claimant to pay for unrequested services that the claimant had no opportunity to refuse. See Illustration 17 and § 40, Illustration 1.

The defendant will not be allowed a credit for the direct expenses of an attempt to defraud the claimant, even if these expenses produce some benefit to the claimant. See Illustration 21. By contrast, even a conscious wrongdoer may be allowed a credit for the value of services if the transaction is profitable to the claimant and the alternative would be an unacceptable forfeiture. See Illustration 22.

The defendant is normally denied a credit for income taxes paid. The reason is not to punish wrongdoers (as is sometimes stated), but to avoid a distortion resulting from the effect of the judgment on the defendant's future tax liability. See Illustration 23.

Illustrations:

16. The right to extract natural gas from Blackacre is pooled and apportioned according to ownership of the surface estate. By a mistake as to title for which neither party is responsible, A extracts and sells as his own gas that belongs to A and B in equal shares. A is liable to B in restitution for one-half the market value of the gas (§§ 40, 51(2)), or for one-half the sale proceeds (§ 53(2)), whichever is greater. Either way, A is entitled to a credit for B's share of A's reasonable expenses in producing this income. A has drilled five wells in the course of the transaction at a cost of $100,000 each, but one of these wells turned out to be a dry hole. In the accounting between A and B, A is entitled to a credit of at least $200,000 (representing half the cost of the productive wells). A is not entitled to a credit in respect of the dry hole unless the court is satisfied that the expenditure on the failed well conferred a benefit on B.

17. A enters B's land as a conscious trespasser and removes standing timber having a stumpage value of $5000. By his own labor or at his own expense, A causes the timber to be felled, hauled, sawn, and milled, ultimately receiving $50,000 in cash from the sale of finished veneer. A's liability to B in restitution is $50,000 without deduction. To allow a credit for the value of A's services or expenses would to that extent impose a forced exchange, requiring B not only to pay for logging services for which he did not contract but to acquire them from a thief.

18. Same facts as Illustration 17, except that A enters B's land as an innocent trespasser, relying on a mistaken survey. Under such circumstances A is liable in restitution for the market value of what he has taken from B (the $5000 stumpage value (§ 51(2)), but A is not liable for the profits of the logging operation (§ 50(5)). One way to explain this result is to say that A obtains title to the veneer by the doctrine of accession, subject to B's equitable lien in the amount of $5000. Compare

§ 10, Illustration 28; § 40, Illustration 14; § 58, Illustration 25. On the alternative view that B retains legal title to the veneer as the product of the timber, A may be allowed a claim in restitution as the mistaken improver of B's chattels. On either approach, A's net liability to B in restitution is $5000.

19. Edwards discovers and develops a cave located partially under Lee's property, as described in § 40, Illustration 4, and in Illustrations 13 and 15, supra. Edwards is liable to disgorge 30 percent of the net profits realized from the exhibition of the cave, but the court must decide what deductions to allow from gross revenues in calculating these net profits. In the ensuing accounting, Edwards will typically be allowed a credit for cash outlays necessary to the operation of the business from which the profit has been realized. Under the circumstances, such outlays include the cost of building walkways and installing electric lights, as well as operating expenses such as wages and utilities. No credit is allowed for Edwards's personal services in the discovery, development, and subsequent management of the cave, despite the fact that no profit would have been realized without these contributions.

20. Tenant plants millet in June; his lease expires in August; Landlord harvests the crop in September at a cost of $10,000 and sells it for $50,000. Tenant sues Landlord in restitution, alleging conversion of the millet crop. The court decides the controversy—a close question under local property law—in favor of Tenant. Because Landlord is not regarded as a conscious wrongdoer, his harvesting expenses of $10,000 are properly deducted in determining his liability for net profits of $40,000. (If Tenant's crop had been harvested and sold by a thief, the thief would be liable for $50,000 in proceeds without deduction.)

21. Purchaser retains Agent to locate suitable land at a price of not more than $1 million. Agent eventually recommends that Purchaser acquire Blackacre from Straw for $950,000, which Purchaser agrees to do. In reality, the owner of Blackacre has offered to sell it to Agent for $850,000, and the purported transaction with Straw is a sham to disguise Agent's secret profit. Agent pays $850,000 and acquires title to Blackacre before the fraud is discovered. If Purchaser still wants Blackacre, he is entitled to a decree that Agent holds the land for Purchaser in constructive trust; but relief will be conditioned on reimbursement to Agent of the $850,000 cost of acquisition. If Agent had faithfully represented Purchaser in acquiring Blackacre for $850,000, Agent would have been entitled to a commission of $85,000 plus reimbursement of $15,000 in closing costs. The closing costs are genuine, but the court regards them as "expenditures incurred directly in the commission of the wrong" (as distinct from the cost of acquiring Blackacre). Agent has no claim either to a commission or to reimbursement of $15,000.

22. By fraudulent misrepresentations, A induces B to sell a chain of retail stores at a grossly inadequate price. The transaction is later set aside, and A is ordered to restore to B's successors both the assets of the business (which have substantially increased) and the net profits realized in the interim. A claims a credit against net profits for the reasonable value of the services to the business contributed by A ($300,000 per year) and A's wife ($100,000 per year). The court accepts these values of the services performed. It allows the credit for A's wife's services because she was entirely innocent of the fraud. It allows the credit for A's services, despite A's status as a conscious wrongdoer, because A is being forced to disgorge a much more valuable business than the one he originally acquired from B; because in working so effectively to expand the business, A (although he was not aware of it at the time) was in fact working for B and B's successors; and because an order that not only required A to work for B, but required him to do so without compensation, would in the opinion of the court impose an unacceptable forfeiture.

23. A's conscious interference with B's rights yields net pre-tax profits of $100,000 to A. Both A and B pay income tax at a marginal rate of 30 percent. The amount of B's judgment against A will be taxable to B and deductible by A in the current tax year. Because A has previously paid $30,000 in income tax on his ill-gotten gains, A asks the court to allow a reduction of $30,000 in calculating A's disgorgement liability to B. The credit for income taxes will normally be denied. Under the tax regime supposed, A's liability in restitution after a reduction for tax paid ($70,000) would produce a current-year tax deduction worth $21,000 to A, resulting in a gain to A of $21,000 from the transaction as a whole ($100,000 profit less $30,000 tax paid less $70,000 liability in restitution plus $21,000 current-year tax reduction). By contrast, A's liability in restitution without the reduction ($100,000) strips A of the wrongful gain without imposing a penalty ($100,000 profit less $30,000 tax less $100,000 liability in restitution plus $30,000 current-year tax reduction).

i.   Burden of proof; risk of uncertainty. Disgorgement does not impose a general forfeiture: defendant's liability in restitution is not the whole of the gain from a tainted transaction, but the amount of the gain that is attributable to the underlying wrong. For reasons already mentioned, however, the precise amount of the defendant's unjust enrichment may be difficult or impossible to ascertain. The unusual difficulty of measurement in particular contexts explains why, in applying the disgorgement remedy, courts so often refer to burdens of proof and presumptions.

Burdens of proof become relevant whenever the fact to be determined—here, the net profit attributable to the underlying wrong—cannot be established with certainty. A traditional formula, inherited from trust accounting and enshrined in the Copyright Act (17 U.S.C. § 504(b)), states that the claimant has the burden of proving revenues and the defendant has the burden of proving deductions. This Restatement adopts a more modern and generally useful rule that the claimant has the burden of producing evidence from which the court may make at least a reasonable approximation of the defendant's unjust enrichment. If the claimant has done this much, the defendant is then free (there is no need to speak of "burden shifting") to introduce evidence tending to show that the true extent of unjust enrichment is something less. If the claimant's evidence will not yield even a reasonable approximation, the claim of unjust enrichment is merely speculative, and disgorgement will not be allowed. See Illustration 9, supra.

Yet the claimant's burden of proof, so described, is ordinarily met as soon as the claimant presents a coherent theory of recovery in unjust enrichment. The claimant's case is not merely that the defendant has committed a wrong to the claimant, but that the wrong has proximately resulted in an unjust gain to the defendant. Allegations that the defendant is a wrongdoer, and that the defendant's business is profitable, do not state a claim in unjust enrichment. By contrast, a claimant who is prepared to show a causal connection between defendant's wrongdoing and a measurable increase in the defendant's net assets will satisfy the burden of proof as ordinarily understood.

Underlying the rules about evidentiary burdens in these cases is the equitable disposition that resolves uncertainty in favor of the claimant against the conscious wrongdoer. "Reasonable approximation" will suffice to establish the disgorgement liability of a conscious wrongdoer, when the evidence allows no greater precision, because the conscious wrongdoer bears the risk of uncertainty arising from the wrong. The same disposition against the wrongdoer yields the rule that "when damages are at some unascertainable amount below an upper limit and when the uncertainty arises from the defendant's wrong, the upper limit will be taken as the proper amount." Gratz v. Claughton, 187 F.2d 46, 51–52 (2d Cir. 1951) (L. Hand, J.). Supposing, in other words, that the true measure of unjust enrichment is an indeterminable amount not less than 50 and not more than 100, liability in disgorgement will be fixed at 100. See Illustration 14, supra. Conversely, the same disposition against the wrongdoer gives content to the evidentiary standard of "reasonable approximation," since the standard of proof marks the point beyond which it would no longer be equitable to resolve doubts against the wrongdoer.

j. Liability for both profits and losses. A conscious wrongdoer who makes an unauthorized investment of the claimant's property is both accountable for profits and liable for losses, and the claimant is free to pursue the most advantageous remedy in light of the outcome. Thus if the defendant has invested the claimant's funds in a traceable asset of uncertain value, the claimant may obtain either ownership of the asset (when the investment has been profitable) or security in the asset for the misappropriated funds (when it has not), the election to be made after the value has been determined. See Illustration 24. A defendant who has made a profitable investment of funds acquired in breach of duty may not set off losses from other unauthorized investments, where the separate transactions may be distinguished. See Illustration 25.

Illustrations:

24. Trustee uses $100,000 of Trust funds to purchase Blackacre, taking title in his own name. Trust is entitled, at its option, either to Blackacre itself (via constructive trust) or to a judgment against Trustee for $100,000 plus interest, secured by an equitable lien on Blackacre. The court may decree such relief in the alternative, the election to be made after the value of Blackacre has been determined. If Blackacre is now worth $120,000, awarding title to Trust gives effect to Trustee's disgorgement liability under § 51(4). If Blackacre has declined in value to $80,000, an equitable lien on Blackacre in the amount of $100,000 plus interest may be more advantageous than an unsecured money judgment, but it affords Trust only partial relief. In the latter case, Trust can sell Blackacre under the lien and enforce its judgment against Trustee for the deficiency.

25. Administrator of Estate makes two loans from Estate to himself, investing the funds in separate business ventures of his own. The first of these investments returns a substantial profit, from which Administrator repays both loans with interest at market rates. Administrator's personal use of Estate assets is a breach of fiduciary duty giving rise to liability in restitution (§ 43). Administrator will be required to account to Estate for the profit realized in the successful venture. In making this accounting, Administrator may deduct the interest paid for the unauthorized use of Estate funds, but he may not deduct losses incurred on the second, unsuccessful investment of those funds.

k. Punitive or exemplary damages. Disgorgement of wrongful gain is not a punitive remedy. While the remedy will be burdensome to the defendant in practice—in consequence of some issues of deductions and credits (see Comment *h*) and burden of proof (see Comment *i*)—the wrongdoer who is deprived of an illicit gain is ideally left in the position he would have occupied had there been no misconduct.

Precisely because disgorgement, in theory at least, imposes no net loss on the defendant, there are situations in which a court may conclude that the threat of liability to disgorge profits will not adequately deter the misconduct revealed by the case before it. A court that reaches this conclusion will sometimes supplement the defendant's liability in restitution with an award of exemplary damages. See Illustration 26.

The rationale of punitive or exemplary damages is independent of the law of unjust enrichment. The rules that govern such damages are part of the tort law of a given jurisdiction, often fixed by statute, outside the scope of this Restatement. If the defendant's conduct meets the applicable standard for additional liability, there is no intrinsic inconsistency in a judgment that reinforces disgorgement of wrongful gain with an explicitly punitive award.

Illustration:

26. Disloyal Agent induces Client to advance funds for a purported investment in real estate. The transaction is structured in such a way that Agent will take any profits while Client will bear any losses. After the facts come to light, Agent is held liable to Client for the amount of Agent's wrongful gain, without deduction for Agent's incidental expenses. Compare Illustration 21. The court concludes, however, that a potential liability to disgorge profits in those cases where such a fraud might be detected is insufficient, by itself, to deter the misconduct in which Agent has engaged. Agent faces no substantial risk of criminal penalties. A local statute authorizes an award of exemplary damages "in an action for the breach of an obligation not arising from contract, where the defendant has been guilty of oppression, fraud, or malice." (The court holds, correctly, that liability in restitution by the rules of §§ 43 and 51 is not an obligation "arising from contract.") There is no inconsistency with principles of restitution if the court combines a liability in disgorgement with exemplary damages under the local statute.

Topic 2. Restitution Via Rights in Identifiable Property

§ 54 Rescission and Restitution

(1) A person who has transferred money or other property is entitled to recover it by rescission and restitution if

(a) the transaction is invalid or subject to avoidance for a reason identified in another section of this Restatement, and

(b) the further requirements of this section may be satisfied.

(2) Rescission requires a mutual restoration and accounting in which each party

(a) restores property received from the other, to the extent such restoration is feasible,

(b) accounts for additional benefits obtained at the expense of the other as a result of the transaction and its subsequent avoidance, as necessary to prevent unjust enrichment, and

(c) compensates the other for loss from related expenditure as justice may require.

(3) Rescission is limited to cases in which counter-restitution by the claimant will restore the defendant to the status quo ante, unless

(a) the defendant is fairly compensated for any deficiencies in the restoration made by the claimant, or

(b) the fault of the defendant or the assignment of risks in the underlying transaction makes it equitable that the defendant bear any uncompensated loss.

(4) Rescission is appropriate when the interests of justice are served by allowing the claimant to reverse the challenged transaction instead of enforcing it. As a general rule:

(a) If the claimant seeks to reverse a transfer induced by fraud or other conscious wrongdoing, the limitation described in subsection (3) is liberally construed in favor of the claimant.

(b) If the claimant seeks rescission instead of damages as a remedy for material breach of contract (§ 37), the limitation described in subsection (3) is employed to prevent injustice to the defendant from the reversal of a valid and enforceable exchange.

(c) If rescission would prejudice intervening rights of innocent third parties, the remedy will on that account be denied.

(5) Restitution or a tender of restitution by the claimant is not a prerequisite of rescission if affirmative relief to the claimant can be reduced by (or made subject to) the claimant's reciprocal obligation of restitution.

(6) Prejudicial or speculative delay by the claimant in asserting a right of rescission, or a change of circumstances unfairly prejudicial to the defendant, justifies denial of the remedy.

Comment:

a.   *General principles and scope; relation to other sections.* Rescission is the common, shorthand name for a composite remedy (more fully, "rescission and restitution") that combines the avoidance of a transaction and the mutual restoration of performance thereunder. A judicial decree of rescission typically provides for (i) the nullification of a transfer of property between the claimant and the defendant, (ii) the restoration of performance on either side, and (iii) a mutual accounting in which each party pays for benefits received from the other in consequence of the underlying exchange and its subsequent reversal.

A party seeking rescission and restitution must first establish a substantive right to avoidance of the transaction in question. As a further requirement, the proponent of rescission must show that the unwinding of performance (as opposed to a remedy by money judgment) is both feasible and equitable on the facts of the case. Potential grounds for avoidance are identified by other sections of this Restatement, while the special requirements of the rescission remedy are the subject of the present section.

The remedy of rescission is mentioned by name in those sections of this Restatement (§§ 13–17, 34, 37) where the nature of the liability makes it most likely that judges and lawyers will think of a remedy in those terms. The same right to avoidance is implied by the substantive rules of other sections that do not use the word "rescission" in describing the right to restitution, whenever the basis of the restitution claim is a transfer from the claimant to the defendant that the claimant seeks to undo.

Rescission as a remedy for unjust enrichment usually allows the claimant to recover property that has been transferred to the defendant pursuant to contract. Performance may be reversed when the contract proves to be invalid by reason of fraud, duress, undue influence, incapacity, or lack of authority (§§ 13–17), or when it is subject to avoidance on grounds such as mistake (§ 34) or breach of fiduciary duty (§ 43).

In a different set of cases, also arising in a contractual context, rescission and restitution may be available as an alternative to damages for material breach (§ 37). Rescission as a remedy for breach is available only in those circumstances indicated by § 37 (and subject to the express limitation of § 37(2)). In considering the availability of rescission as a remedy for breach of contract, it is essential that §§ 37 and 54 be read together.

The word "rescission" may also be used to describe the avoidance of a transfer when there is no contract to be set aside. Common examples of such rescission permit the recovery of property following transfers induced by fraud, mistake, or undue influence, as authorized by the rules of this Restatement. See, e.g., § 11, Illustration 8 (following mistake in a unilateral conveyance, the remedy known as "cancellation" might also be called "rescission"); § 13, Illustrations 3, 6–9, and 11 (authorizing rescission of noncontractual transfers induced by innocent or fraudulent misrepresentation); § 15, *passim* (authorizing rescission of transfers induced by undue influence, whether or not the transfers were made pursuant to contract). Specific relief in such cases can often be achieved without using the language of rescission: for example, by granting cancellation or reformation of a deed or other instrument, or by making the recipient a constructive trustee of the property transferred (§ 55). Neither the underlying theory of liability, the availability of defenses, nor the outcome of a particular case should depend on the language used to describe the remedy.

The object of rescission in the law of restitution is the reversal of a transfer of property. Accordingly, the Illustrations to this section exclude cases in which the object of an action for "rescission" is to avoid the plaintiff's obligations under an executory contract. The decisive issues in such cases are predominantly a matter of contract law. Such a case will nevertheless involve restitution—governed by the rules of this section—to the extent there has been partial performance of the contract being set aside. See Illustration 1.

Illustration:

1. Employer insures Employee's life for Employer's benefit in the amount of $250,000, paying an initial annual premium of $1000. Unknown to Employer, the application for insurance (completed in part

241

by Employee) states falsely that Employee has never smoked cigarettes. Relying on this misstatement, Insurer issues the policy at its "non-smoker premium rate." The facts come to light on Employee's death 11 months later. Insurer refuses to pay on the policy and seeks rescission for misrepresentation. Employer argues that Insurer should be liable for the $150,000 death benefit that concededly could have been purchased with the same $1000 premium, had Employee's smoking been disclosed. Leaving aside particular questions governed by local insurance law, the argument over "rescission" in this case turns on issues of contract, not restitution: the question is whether Insurer can avoid an executory obligation, not whether Insurer can recover something previously transferred. Rescission under these circumstances nevertheless involves a restitutionary element, consistent with the rules of this section, because Insurer (if permitted to rescind) will be required to restore Employer to the status quo ante—on the facts supposed, by repayment of the $1000 premium plus interest.

"Rescission and restitution" by the rule of this section is in some respects the paradigm mode of specific relief in restitution, alias "restitution via rights in identifiable property," since it effects (so far as possible) a literal restoration of something the claimant previously had and which the claimant is entitled to recover. In other ways, the remedy of rescission makes a poor fit within the present Chapter and Topic. Rescission sometimes permits the claimant to reverse a transfer and recover a performance without any showing that the defendant has been unjustly enriched. See § 13, Illustration 8 (fraud); § 34, Illustration 29 (mistake); § 37, Illustration 2 (breach). Every other section of this Chapter is concerned, in one way or another, with ways to measure and rectify the unjust enrichment of one party at the expense of another.

A second difference is chiefly a matter of usage. The most important characteristic of all the other rules of asset-based restitution (§§ 55–61) is that they permit a claimant, to some extent at least, to assert an interest in property of the defendant that is paramount to the claims of the defendant's creditors. Although "rescission and restitution" might be employed for this purpose in a proper case—in particular, a case in which the ground of rescission is fraud or mistake rather than breach of contract—a claimant who seeks to reacquire an asset in priority to the defendant's creditors will usually ask the court to decree a rescission in conjunction with some further remedy such as constructive trust. See Illustration 2.

This combination of remedies is unsurprising (if somewhat redundant) in cases of fraud or mistake. By contrast, a party injured by a material breach of contract—typically, an unpaid credit seller—may not normally obtain priority over the other creditors of the breaching party by electing rescission rather than damages, or by claiming that property delivered to the breaching party is held in constructive trust (see § 55, Illustration 11). The unpaid seller is usually barred from rescission at the threshold by the rule of § 37(2). Even if the defendant's breach involves something beyond a failure to pay money, a court will refuse to grant the claimant a retroactive priority—to the prejudice of third parties—that might have been acquired by contract, employing the ordinary modes of security. See § 37, Comment *b*.

b. The availability of rescission. A perfect rescission would restore both parties to the status quo ante by specific restitution of property previously transferred, leaving no unjust enrichment, no loss to either party (apart from the defendant's loss of bargain), and no need for the court to place a value on benefits conferred. Rescission becomes complicated when courts must decide how far to depart from this ideal version to accommodate a claimant who is unable to restore in specie the benefits received from the defendant; and when the consequence of rescission, seen in retrospect, is a noncontractual transaction in which one party's temporary possession and subsequent restoration of the other's property may give rise to unjust enrichment and reliance loss on either side. While incidental gains and losses from these sources can be addressed in the parties' mutual accounting, the essence of rescission is specific rather than substitutionary relief. To the extent that the court must determine the money value of nonreturnable benefits, a remedy that attempts to unwind the transaction may be no more equitable (or administratively efficient) than enforcement by an award of damages.

Rescission is usually invoked in a contractual setting, where its effect is to release the claimant—with retroactive effect—from an exchange transaction with the other party. A claimant who is allowed to rescind has usually been given a choice between (i) dealing with the other party on the basis of their agreement, which the claimant was free to ratify and enforce, and (ii) dealing with the other party "off the contract," where benefits that either party may have derived at the expense of the other give rise to a liability in unjust enrichment. The divergence between contractual and extracontractual values means that rescission and damages will often lead to different results. The strategic possibilities of the choice between remedies, and the potential for hardship to the party against whom rescission is sought, explain the elaborate rules and the extensive case law regulating the availability of rescission as a remedial option.

The availability of rescission thus depends partly on the degree to which the parties' performance is capable of restoration in specie, and partly on the grounds of the claimant's entitlement to relief. Rescission will almost certainly be available when the claimant seeks to escape from an agreement that was induced by the other party's fraud or other wrongdoing. Even when a plaintiff seeks rescission as an alternative to damages for breach of a valid and enforceable contract, there are certain simplified situations in which the potential advantages of rescission over damages—in terms of fairness to the plaintiff as well as remedial efficiency—appear so evident that a plaintiff is uniformly permitted to pursue either remedy. Such cases typically involve breach or repudiation by a defendant who has obtained the plaintiff's performance without tendering any return.

By contrast, the complex rules traditionally associated with the remedy of rescission and restitution derive mostly from transactions in which (i) the parties are bound by a valid and enforceable contract, (ii) the claimant prefers rescission to damages, yet (iii) rescission is potentially prejudicial to the other party, costly in terms of judicial resources, or both. Such cases pose the threshold question whether justice will be served by attempting to unwind the transaction instead of enforcing it.

That determination has always been committed to the sound discretion of the court, though certain factors relevant to the decision have traditionally been cast as legal rules. Rescission in equity was explicitly subject to the court's equitable discretion; rescission at law was made subject to formal requirements—ostensibly objective—that effectively reserved to the courts the same judgment about the suitability of rescission in a particular case. Such is the function of the familiar rule that a party seeking rescission at law must tender to the other party, as a precondition of suit, specific restitution of everything received under the contract; with the result that a plaintiff who is unable (and has not merely neglected) to restore the defendant to the status quo ante is barred from rescission. As a practical matter, a rule so stated gives a court of law nearly as much discretion to allow rescission or withhold it as the chancellors enjoyed in equity. Because a requirement of specific restitution by the claimant cannot be applied without a lengthy list of exceptions, and because restitution to the status quo ante is literally impossible in any event, the decision whether the claimant has come close enough to an unattainable standard becomes a decision about the propriety of rescission in the circumstances of the particular case.

Factors relevant to this ultimate question are sometimes addressed directly. Elsewhere they are implicit in a judicial conclusion that rescission would not be equitable under the circumstances, or that it is not possible to place the parties *in statu quo*. Courts naturally consider the circumstances of the transaction; the quality of the parties' conduct; the relative ease or difficulty of compensating the claimant's injury in damages; and the fairness of limiting the claimant to a damage remedy. On the other side of the scale, they consider the difficulty of measuring noncontractual values; the burden to the defendant of being compelled to reverse a contractual exchange; and the extent of windfalls and forfeitures resulting from interim variation in the values being restored.

c. *Restitution as a safeguard against forfeiture.* There is a visible connection between the beneficial uses of the rescission remedy and the traditional test for its availability. A plaintiff who can in fact restore the defendant to the status quo ante by a full restitution in specie will usually be proposing a remedy that is less costly to administer (because it avoids the necessity for judicial valuation of benefits conferred and losses sustained), and moreover is not materially prejudicial to the defendant, who (in theory at least) loses only the benefit of the bargain. To the extent that specific restitution is infeasible in a particular case, these favorable consequences are less likely to be realized.

Rescission of a valid and enforceable contract overturns legitimate contractual expectations on which both parties may have significantly relied. The most notable form of reliance in this context is likely to consist in the defendant's performance (or preparation for performance), resulting in a change of position to the extent that any performance is not capable of restoration and subsequent resale. The consequences of invalidating the contractual exchange will not be adverse to the party seeking rescission, because the remedy is chosen at the claimant's election; but they impose a potential forfeiture on the party in breach, who stands to lose not only the benefit of the bargain but also the sunk costs of performance.

The potentially inequitable consequences of rescission are therefore limited by the traditional requirement that the claimant make counter-restitution of property received under the contract, as a means of restoring both parties to the precontractual status quo. Such a rule reinforces significantly the stability of contractual price terms. If rescission were an optional remedy for any material breach of contract—with no requirement of restoration by the plaintiff—the plaintiff might elect in every case between (i) enforcing the bargain and (ii) dealing with the defendant (in restitution) as if no bargain had ever been made. Such an outcome would expand the implied conditions of the bargain beyond recognized limits, giving the party injured by material breach the right not only to terminate the contract (that is, to cease his own performance and recover damages) but, in the alternative, to set aside the contract whenever it was advantageous to do so. Rescission as an alternative remedy for material breach—if unrestricted by the requirement of counter-restitution—would thus give the plaintiff in effect an option on the defendant's performance, rather than enforceable rights under a bilateral obligation.

As already noted (see § 54(4) and Comment b), the terms on which rescission is available may be seen to differ appreciably—although the applicable rules are usually stated in identical terms—depending on whether the ground of rescission is fraud or mistake, on the one hand, or material breach of contract, on the other. A claimant (such as a fraud victim) who has been an innocent party to a legally defective exchange will ordinarily be able to rescind on making restitution (in specie or in value) of any benefits conferred by the other party. Rescission is available on relatively liberal terms in such cases—especially if the defendant is a conscious wrongdoer—because the underlying exchange is ineffective to determine the parties' respective entitlements. See Comment d. Rescission as a remedy for breach of contract is subject to more restrictive requirements because of its potential to destabilize the contractual exchange, imposing what may be an effective forfeiture as a penalty for breach. See Comment e. Traditional limitations on rescission in such cases, sometimes expressed as absolute preconditions, have been restated more realistically in subsections (3) and (4). See Comment g.

d. *Rescission of defective agreements.* When it extricates the claimant from a defective agreement, rescission reverses a transfer that lacks an adequate legal basis and prevents the unjustified enrichment that would otherwise result on either side. Concern for the stability of the contractual exchange has no relevance to such a case, because there is no valid exchange to protect. Specific restitution is required to the extent feasible, given the relative efficiency of specific over substitutionary relief, but the parties' residual obligations of restitution may be satisfied by any means sufficient to prevent unjust enrichment and to compensate for reliance loss as justice requires.

Unjust enrichment resulting from performance of a defective agreement is frequently remedied without mention of "rescission." If a transfer from the claimant to the recipient has been procured by fraud or other wrongdoing, it may sometimes facilitate an understanding of the remedy to point out that the claimant has made a voidable transfer that is subject to rescission. That explanation may be superfluous once it is understood that the net profits attributable to the wrongful transaction constitute unjust enrichment that the recipient is liable to disgorge (§ 51(4)). Even if the claimant is seeking to recover a specific asset from the defendant's possession, the concept of rescission is easily displaced by alternative descriptions of the same outcome. See Illustration 2. Compare § 12, Illustration 3 (mistaken conveyance remedied by reformation of the deed).

Illustrations:

2. A conveys Blackacre to B in exchange for B's promise to pay $100,000 one year later. B fails to pay, and A discovers that the transaction was induced by B's fraud. A can enforce B's contractual obligation to pay. Alternatively, A may choose to avoid the transaction and recover Blackacre from B (§ 13). Specific restitution to A may be described in terms of "rescission and restitution," or cancellation, or constructive trust, or quieting title in A, or a combination thereof: the language employed makes no difference to the outcome. Whatever the form of specific restitution, moreover, complete relief in restitution will require an accounting for such additional factors as A's claim to interest and rental value and B's claim in respect of improvements. See Comment h and § 55, Comment l.

3. Purchaser buys Blackacre for $300,000, relying on Vendor's fraudulent representation that the house is free of termites. Purchaser discovers termites within a few weeks of moving in, by which point he has already spent $500 on unrelated repairs to the garage. Extermination and repair of the termite damage would cost $5000. Purchaser may keep the house and recover tort damages for deceit. Alternatively, Purchaser may seek rescission and restitution for Vendor's fraud (§ 13). If rescission is granted on the facts supposed, the remedy will involve (i) restitution of Blackacre to Vendor, (ii) restitution of the purchase price to Purchaser, and (iii) restitution of net enrichment from use value on either side (§ 53), in which interest on the purchase price is set against the value of Purchaser's interim occupation. The

accounting on rescission will credit Purchaser with his $500 expenditure on the garage (§ 54(2)(c)).

e.   Rescission as a remedy for breach of contract. The availability of rescission and restitution as an alternative remedy for breach of contract is introduced at § 37. The topic reappears at this point—despite the resulting overlap—because the object of § 54 is to describe the operation of the rescission remedy in general terms, while distinguishing its application to the two most important categories of cases: rescission for fraud and rescission for breach. Sections 37 and 54 should be consulted together on the subject of rescission as a remedy for breach.

When rescission restores a performance rendered under a defective agreement—as when rescission unwinds an exchange that is invalid by reason of mistake, fraud, or duress—it can usually be understood as a remedy for unjust enrichment. By contrast, when rescission affords an alternative remedy for breach of a valid and enforceable contract (as permitted by the rule of § 37)—a breach, in other words, that might be remedied by damages or specific performance—the effect and the justification of the rescission remedy are significantly different. Rescission in such a case permits the injured party to make a fundamental election, choosing to go backward (to the status quo ante) instead of forward (by enforcement of the contractual exchange). The advantages to the party entitled to this remedial election are self-evident, but the court must determine whether rescission in place of enforcement serves the interests of justice. Unlike the case of rescission for fraud or mistake, the justification of rescission as an alternative remedy for breach is not the avoidance of unjust enrichment, but a concern with fairness to the injured party combined with remedial economy.

For representative circumstances in which rescission may be available as an alternative remedy for breach of contract, see § 37, Illustrations 5–9.

Rescission may be denied when its effect would give the claimant a form of security for which the claimant should properly have bargained. See § 37, Illustrations 3–4. Rescission may be limited in some cases by a traditional concern to protect the stability of land titles. See § 37, Illustrations 15–17. The most difficult cases are those in which the competing advantages of rescission and damages—measured either by fairness to the parties or by ease of administration—are the most evenly balanced. See Illustration 4.

Illustration:

4.   Vendor sells Blackacre to Purchaser for payment in installments, retaining title, and Purchaser takes possession. Before payment is completed, one of the buildings on Blackacre is destroyed by fire without the fault of either party. As a result of this loss, which was uninsured, Vendor can no longer convey the property described in the parties' agreement. The contract assigns the risk of such loss to Vendor, but neither the contract nor local law specifies the remedies available to Purchaser in consequence of Vendor's breach. Purchaser seeks rescission

of the transaction; Vendor argues that Purchaser should be limited to damages in the form of a reduction of the purchase price. The court must determine whether rescission rather than enforcement serves the interests of justice under the circumstances of the case (§ 54(4)). Findings by the court that (i) the loss in question is relatively small by comparison with the overall value of Blackacre, (ii) damages are easily calculated, and (iii) benefits from Purchaser's use and occupation of Blackacre would be difficult to value, would all weigh against allowing rescission and in favor of limiting Purchaser to a price adjustment.

f.   Restitution to the claimant. Rescission is a means to recover money or other property that the claimant has previously transferred to the defendant. It has no application to remedies, restitutionary in nature, by which the claimant recovers property from someone with no title (see Illustration 5); nor to a case in which the transaction creating unjust enrichment does not involve a voidable transfer of title by the claimant (see Illustration 6). For related reasons, rescission as an alternative remedy for breach of contract is not a means to recover the value of a performance that by its nature is impossible to restore, such as services or improvements to realty. Recovery of the cost or value of performance in such cases—as an alternative to expectation damages—is available by the rule of § 38.

While there is no logical objection to using the language of rescission and restitution to describe a remedy by which the claimant recovers the *traceable product* of property that the claimant has previously transferred, in practice such a claim will almost certainly be described in the language of constructive trust. For this reason, cases in which claimants obtain legal title to traceable products are presented in this Restatement primarily as illustrations of the rules governing constructive trust and tracing (§§ 55, 58–59). By contrast, the expression "rescission and restitution" aptly describes cases in which the claimant may be restored to the status quo ante by obtaining the *fungible equivalent* of personal property previously transferred to the other party. See Illustrations 8 and 11.

Rescission permits the claimant to escape from a failed transaction without proof of damages. It therefore offers inherent advantages to the claimant whenever damages would be difficult (or merely expensive) to prove, or when specific restitution is attractive to the claimant for reasons other than its relative simplicity (as in transactions involving unique property). A transaction may thus be subject to rescission even if it results in no measurable loss to the claimant. See Illustration 7; compare § 13, Illustrations 7–9. A more common consequence of rescission is to protect the claimant against a loss that is causally related to the grounds for avoidance, without requiring the claimant to establish the amount thereof. See Illustrations 8 and 19.

In some circumstances, rescission will protect the claimant against a loss that is unrelated to the grounds for avoidance. See Illustration 9 and § 13, Illustration 23. The fact that rescission permits the claimant to escape from an unfavorable bargain does not by itself make rescission inequitable, but rescission will be denied if its effect would be the unjust enrichment of the claimant at the expense of the other party. The potential for unjust enrichment is obvious when one party seeks rescission to pursue opportunistic gain, or as a means of speculating at the other's expense. See Illustrations 10 and 31. Restrictions on the strategic use of rescission are generally enforced by the recognition of equitable defenses. See § 54(6) and Comment *k*.

Illustrations:

5.   Acting without authority, A takes possession of B's cattle and B's ranch. B obtains specific restitution of both kinds of property by an action for replevin and ejectment. B's remedies do not involve a rescission, because A never obtained title from B.

6.   A employs B, a minor, at a salary of $50 per week. The reasonable value of B's services is $300 per week. After working for 10 weeks, B disaffirms the contract and sues A to recover the unpaid value of his work. B has a claim in restitution (§ 16) for the amount of A's unjust enrichment ($2500). B's remedy does not involve a rescission by the rule of this section, because B does not seek to recover title to property.

7.   A conveys Blackacre to B, a public utility, for a price equal to its market value. A was induced to sell by B's fraudulent misrepresentations that the property was needed for public purposes and might be acquired by eminent domain. A (having suffered no measurable injury) has no claim for damages, but she is entitled to recover Blackacre on repayment of the price.

8.   Buyer purchases 100 shares of XYZ common stock at $100 per share, induced by Seller's fraudulent statements about the prospects of the company. In fact the shares are worth substantially less. On discovery of the fraud, Buyer is entitled to recover the difference between the actual value of the shares and the price paid: such a claim might be based on tort (Restatement Second, Torts § 549) or unjust enrichment (§ 13). Either approach necessitates proof of the value of the shares, including the identification of a relevant date for valuation purposes. Alternatively, rescission permits Buyer to recover $10,000 on restoring to Seller either the shares originally purchased or any 100 shares of XYZ common as their fungible equivalent.

9.   Buyer purchases 100 shares of XYZ common stock at $100 per share, on Seller's assurance that the shares in question are treasury stock of the newly-formed corporation. Five years later, when XYZ is bankrupt and its common stock almost worthless, Buyer discovers that the shares purchased were in fact the property of Seller. The court determines that Seller's misrepresentations as to the source of the shares sold to Buyer were fraudulent, though if Buyer had purchased

treasury stock of XYZ he would have suffered the same loss. Rescission allows Buyer to recover $10,000 plus interest, on restoration to Seller of the shares originally purchased.

10. Same facts as Illustration 9, except that Buyer sells his XYZ common at $100 per share after holding it for one year. Learning later of Seller's fraud, Buyer reacquires 100 shares of XYZ common at $10 per share and tenders them to Seller, seeking rescission of the transaction and restitution of $10,000 plus interest. Rescission will be denied. Buyer's remedy for Seller's fraud is limited to Buyer's damages or Seller's unjust enrichment, if any.

The function of rescission as a means to obtain specific restitution tends to be self-limiting, since a claimant who cannot identify in the defendant's hands either the same thing that the claimant has previously transferred or its fungible equivalent is unlikely to seek a remedy via rescission. See Illustration 11. Where only part of the claimant's property is identifiable in the defendant's hands, the claimant may obtain specific restitution of that part and restitution of value for the remainder. See Illustration 12.

Illustrations:

11. By fraudulent misrepresentations, A induces B to sell 100 shares of ABC common stock at $50 per share. The value of ABC (which is closely held) is approximately $100 per share at the time of the transaction; by the time B discovers the facts, the value has increased to approximately $150 per share. B is entitled to rescind the sale for A's fraud (§ 13) and to recover from A either (i) the original 100 shares in specie, (ii) any equivalent 100 shares of ABC, or (iii) any traceable product of the original shares (§ 58). (Restitution to B of either the ABC shares or their product might alternatively be described using the language of constructive trust, without changing the outcome.) If specific restitution is unavailable because neither the shares, nor their fungible equivalent, nor their product can be identified in A's hands, B's remedy in restitution is by a claim to money in the amount of A's unjust enrichment (§§ 49, 51), not by rescission under this section.

12. A conveys to B his family house in Arkansas and a one-half interest in a hardware store, in exchange for B's conveyance to A of 40 acres of land in Texas and $10,000. The transaction is induced by B's fraudulent representations about the attributes and value of the Texas land. Promptly after traveling to Texas for the first time, A gives notice to B of his intent to rescind the transaction, offering to restore the 40 acres and $10,000. B has already sold the interest in the hardware store to C, a bona fide purchaser who was A's previous partner in the business. A can obtain specific restitution of the house plus restitution of (i) the value of the interest in the store, or (ii) the price B obtained from C, whichever is greater.

g. *Restitution by the claimant.* The remedy of rescission and restitution is often invoked (and offers particular advantages) when the party who seeks to recover a down payment or other performance has not yet received anything of value in exchange. The claimant who elects rescission under such circumstances gives up only the benefit of the bargain; this is easy to do if the bargain has proven unprofitable in hindsight. See § 37, Illustrations 1–2. More often, the reason to choose rescission rather than damages in such circumstances is simply that the prepaid price exceeds the expected damage award. The relative simplicity of proving the price paid rather than the damages sustained may be a further advantage of the rescission remedy. See Illustration 13.

Most of the law of rescission is concerned with the contrasting case in which the party seeking to set aside the transaction has received at least some part of the defendant's performance. The traditional requirement is that the claimant make specific restitution of everything received from the other party by way of performance. There are cases in which this sort of restitution is straightforward. Sellers return money; buyers return property. Rescission is not forfeiture, and the fact that the basis of rescission may be the defendant's fraud or other wrongdoing does not permit the claimant to recover what has been given without restoring what has been received.

When the claimant is unable to make full restitution in specie, the court must determine whether restitution of value makes an acceptable substitute. The reason to require specific restitution is to avoid undue prejudice to the defendant. See § 54(4) and Comments *b* and *c*. Predictably, therefore, the claimant whose transaction was induced by the other party's fraud has greater latitude in making counter-restitution than the claimant who seeks rescission for nonfraudulent breach. Compare Illustrations 4 and 14.

Subsequent transactions by which third parties acquire an interest in the property transferred may or may not be an obstacle to rescission, depending on the circumstances of a particular case. Compare Illustrations 15–16; see also Comment *l* and Illustrations 34–35.

If the claimant has received benefits not capable of specific restitution, and the court is prepared to allow restitution of value instead, the principal difficulty may be the measurement of the benefits for which the claimant is liable. Answers reflect the same factors that influence any other case in which unjust enrichment is measured for the purpose of awarding a money judgment (§§ 49–53). See Illustrations 17 and 24.

Illustrations:

13. Buyer agrees with Builder on the purchase of a new house and makes a $10,000 down payment. While the house is still under construction, and before title is conveyed, Buyer with Builder's consent invests $9000 in landscaping the property. The house as completed by Builder contains numerous defects, and Buyer refuses to proceed to closing. On Builder's suit to terminate the contract and forfeit Buyer's

down payment, the court finds that the defects in construction constitute a material breach of contract, based on Builder's implied warranties to Buyer. Buyer may enforce the contract by an action for damages (measured either by the difference in value or by the cost of correcting the defects); alternatively, Buyer may elect to rescind the transaction. In the latter case, Buyer is entitled to restitution of $10,000 with interest, plus $9000 to compensate his landscaping expenditure (§ 54(2)(c)). Buyer has no reciprocal obligation of restitution because Buyer has received nothing from Builder.

14. Seller agrees to furnish an oil furnace, with an oil tank and equipment needed for permanent installation, and to install the system in Buyer's premises, for a combined price of $10,000. The furnace meets all specifications, but it is incorrectly installed and never works properly. After several unsuccessful attempts by Seller to resolve the problem, Buyer has a replacement furnace installed by another dealer; this second installation (at a price of $9000) makes use of the tank and fuel lines that were permanently attached by Seller to Buyer's walls. Buyer then sues Seller, asking for rescission. Buyer's theory is that he should be allowed to return the original furnace to Seller and recover his purchase price ($10,000), less the value (as determined by the court) of the usable tank and fuel lines. Rescission on precisely these terms would be allowed if the transaction had been induced by Seller's fraud. If Seller is liable only for nonfraudulent breach of his obligation to install the furnace correctly, rescission will predictably be denied, and Buyer limited to a remedy in damages. (Buyer may or may not be able to establish that his damages from Seller's faulty installation are properly measured by the $9000 cost of a new furnace.) The traditional explanation of the denial of rescission is that Buyer cannot make restitution of everything received from Seller, and that the law does not permit a partial rescission of an indivisible contract. An explanation more consistent with the rule of this section would note, inter alia, that (i) rescission imposes a near-forfeiture on Seller, who would recover a used furnace in place of a new one; (ii) Seller's conduct in the underlying transaction does not make it appropriate that Seller bear a loss in excess of Buyer's damages; and (iii) rescission would not be appreciably easier to administer than the ordinary assessment of contract damages, because it requires a valuation of the benefits retained by Buyer from Seller's performance.

15. A conveys Blackacre to B in exchange for Whiteacre and a restaurant business being operated on Whiteacre. Whiteacre is subject to an existing mortgage to C, which A assumes. On acquiring title, B mortgages Blackacre to D to secure a new loan of $100,000. Two months after the exchange is completed, A discovers that B has misrepresented the restaurant's profitability. A gives B prompt notice of her intent to rescind the transaction and later files suit for this purpose. After B refuses to resume ownership, A takes reasonable steps to close down the business and halt operating losses. While A's suit for rescission is

pending, C forecloses the mortgage on Whiteacre, which neither A nor B takes steps to redeem. The court finds that B's misrepresentation justified A's election to rescind. Under the circumstances, the fact that A cannot restore B to the status quo ante (given the closure of the restaurant and the foreclosure of the C mortgage) does not bar rescission: it would have been inequitable to require that A make any further investment in the transaction, and B had adequate opportunity to protect his own interest. To the extent that either event has resulted in a loss to the owner of Whiteacre, that loss is appropriately assigned to B. If the mortgage to D means that A cannot obtain Blackacre unencumbered, B can be ordered to reconvey Blackacre subject to the mortgage and to pay A the amount necessary to compensate for the encumbrance.

16. Vendor agrees to sell Blackacre to Purchaser for $60,000 cash. Purchaser obtains a $50,000 mortgage loan commitment from Lender, and Lender sells Purchaser's loan to Financer. At the closing (i) Vendor delivers to Purchaser a deed to Blackacre; (ii) Purchaser delivers to Lender a negotiable note and mortgage for $50,000; (iii) Purchaser delivers to Vendor his personal check for $10,000 and Lender's check, payable to Vendor, for $50,000; and (iv) Lender endorses Purchaser's note and delivers it to Financer in exchange for $50,000 (plus an origination fee), paid by wire transfer. The next day, Lender stops payment on its check and files for bankruptcy. Vendor seeks rescission of the sale on the grounds of Lender's fraud (§ 13) and Purchaser's breach (§ 37). If Purchaser's note were still in Lender's hands, rescission would be easily accomplished by repayment to Purchaser of $10,000 and cancellation of the deed, note, and mortgage. The court finds, however, that Financer took the note as a holder in due course. Rescission is not available, because Vendor cannot restore Purchaser to the status quo ante.

17. Assuring him that he has "exceptional potential to be a fine and accomplished dancer," Studio agrees to provide 5000 hours of ballroom-dancing instruction to untalented elderly Pupil in exchange for a one-time payment of $250,000. After 100 hourly lessons the relationship suddenly deteriorates. Pupil sues to rescind the contract and recover the $250,000, variously alleging fraud by Studio (§ 13) and discharge by supervening circumstances as the result of injuries sustained by Pupil in an automobile accident (§ 34). If the agreement was induced by Studio's fraud, Pupil is entitled to recover $250,000 less the value (if any) of 100 lessons in advancing Pupil's purposes (§ 49(3)(a)). If Pupil's injury makes the agreement subject to avoidance in consequence of supervening circumstances—a question of contract law—the court might instead measure Pupil's obligation of counter-restitution by the market value of 100 lessons, or $5000 (§ 50(2)(b)).

The standard requirement of two-way restitution may be an obstacle to rescission if property received by the claimant has been lost, damaged, or disposed of, or has suffered deterioration in value. Traditional statements of the rules governing rescission for breach of contract usually provide that the claimant must make restitution of property "in substantially as good condition as when it was received," then qualify this requirement with a number of exceptions, such as the rule excusing counter-restitution (and thereby permitting rescission) when intervening loss to goods has been "caused by their own defects" or is otherwise attributable to the fault of the other party. See, e.g., Restatement Second, Contracts § 384; U.C.C. § 2–608(2).

Instead of enumerating particular exceptions to govern these cases—most of which, in practice, involve further discussion and qualification—the present section incorporates more general guides to the availability of rescission. The first of these is the explicit recognition that rescission necessarily involves judicial discretion. The second is the explicit recognition that a central concern of the overall inquiry—and the realistic focus of the traditional formula by which courts examine how closely the parties might be restored to the status quo ante—is the risk of undue prejudice to the defendant. Section 54(3) thus incorporates the traditional status quo ante benchmark, modified to reflect the reality that loss in value can often be compensated in money and that uncompensated loss is properly assigned, in certain circumstances, to the party against whom rescission is obtained.

When property subject to restitution by the claimant has declined in value, therefore, § 54(3) allows the court to choose between (i) allowing specific restitution supplemented by money compensation; (ii) denying rescission and leaving the claimant to a damage remedy, on the ground that the shortfall in restoration (by comparison with the status quo ante) would be unfairly prejudicial to the defendant; and (iii) allocating the resulting loss to the defendant, on the ground that it is more appropriately borne by the defendant than by the claimant. The choice between these solutions depends on the grounds for rescission, the source of the loss that must be assigned, and the relation between them.

Illustrations:

18. Vendor conveys Blackacre and promises to deliver a clean abstract of title; Purchaser makes a down payment of $25,000 and gives a note and mortgage for the balance of the price. When the abstract is eventually prepared, it reveals that Vendor's title is seriously deficient. Purchaser seeks to rescind the transaction for Vendor's material breach, offering to restore Blackacre in exchange for repayment of $25,000 and cancellation of the note and mortgage. Agricultural land values have declined significantly, and the market value of Blackacre is only 70 percent of what it was at the time of the sale. Vendor resists rescission on the ground, among others, that specific restitution of Blackacre under these circumstances will not restore her to the status quo ante. Purchaser may nevertheless be permitted to rescind. The loss in market value is appropriately borne by Vendor if the court finds that—had the

parties been aware of the true state of Vendor's title—the transaction would not have taken place, with the result that loss would have been borne by Vendor rather than Purchaser. Compare Illustration 33.

19. An agreement for the purchase and sale of a city lot describes its size as 66 by 22 feet. Purchaser pays $100,000, takes title, and demolishes an existing building in preparation for new construction, before discovering that the size of the tract is only 55 by 22 feet and insufficient for his purposes. If the transaction has been induced by Vendor's fraudulent misrepresentations, Purchaser is entitled to recover $100,000, notwithstanding the removal of the buildings, on reconveyance of the vacant lot. If the discrepancy is the result of a mutual mistake for which neither party is to blame, Purchaser will be allowed to rescind only if Vendor is compensated for the loss of the building.

20. A trades her team of horses for B's span of mules. After one of the mules dies, A seeks rescission of the transaction on the ground that B fraudulently misrepresented the age and soundness of the mules. B defends on the ground, inter alia, that in returning only one of two mules, A will not restore him to the status quo ante. A is entitled to rescission on making restitution of the surviving mule. The uncompensated loss from the transaction is appropriately assigned to B, because it relates directly to the state of affairs that B misrepresented.

21. Owner sells timberland to Logger under a warranty deed. Logger pays $250,000, enters into possession, and removes 150,000 feet of timber before discovering that Owner is unable to convey good title to the entire tract. Rescission and restitution is accomplished by restoring the land to Owner and $250,000 to Logger, less an offset in the amount of the stumpage value of 150,000 feet of timber.

22. Buyer purchases Seller's retail antiques business. In connection with the sale, Seller promises to obtain further inventory and perform other services on which the continued operation of the business depends. Seller fails to perform the executory part of his contract, and Buyer demands rescission. Seller defends on the ground, inter alia, that the parties cannot be restored to the status quo ante: inventory has been sold in the ordinary course of business, and fixtures and equipment have been destroyed in a flood. The impossibility of specific restitution in this case does not threaten the kind of hardship to Seller that would lead the court to deny rescission. Rescission and restitution may be achieved through an accounting in which (i) Buyer is credited with the price paid and the present value of what is restored in specie, and (ii) Seller is credited with the value, at the time of the original transfer, of what Buyer is unable to return.

23. Buyer purchases a used car from Seller for $10,000, making a down payment of $2000 and promising to pay the balance in 30 days. Before payment is due, the car is stolen from Buyer; it is later discovered wrecked and abandoned. When Seller demands the balance of the

purchase price, Buyer announces his intent to rescind the transaction on the ground that Seller misrepresented the car's condition by turning back the odometer. Even if Buyer has acted with reasonable promptness, rescission will be denied. Allowing Buyer to restore a wrecked car would shift to Seller a risk of loss that the contract (as the parties fully understood) assigns to Buyer; moreover, the loss that would be shifted bears no relation to the state of affairs that Seller misrepresented. Had the car not been wrecked, Buyer might have returned the car and recovered $2000, less the value of the interim use of the car.

h. Mutual accounting on rescission. Rescission includes an implicit mutual accounting in which each party makes restitution of any values received in the transaction being set aside that are not capable of specific restitution. Calculation of net liability may include reimbursement of incidental or reliance loss to the claimant, but only to the extent such recovery is consistent with a remedy via rescission. See Comment *i.*

The more characteristic feature of the mutual accounting on rescission relates, however, not to money substitutes for the parties' contractual performance, but to the collateral benefits realized on either side from the parties' temporary exchange and its subsequent reversal. The most common items are well-known forms of supplemental enrichment (§ 53): the seller's liability for interest on the purchase price, and the purchaser's liability for the use or rental value of the property being returned. Additional items derive from the circumstance that each party to the interrupted exchange is revealed—in retrospect—to have been dealing with the other's property as if it were his own, resulting in nonconsensual benefits conferred as classified by various rules of this Restatement. So a vendor who recovers real property on rescission may be liable, inter alia, for property taxes paid in the interim by the purchaser, or for the discharge of an encumbrance on the property recovered, or for the cost of necessary repairs, or for the value added by improvements. Liability of the rescinding vendor in any of these circumstances is not just a matter of "accounting," being directly supported by the principles of §§ 26–27 (or of §§ 7, 8, and 10, if the transaction bears features of mistake).

If the amounts involved are relatively modest, and fault in the underlying transaction is not decisively on one side rather than the other, courts will often find that benefits on either side (such as interest on the purchase price versus rental value of the land) balance each other out. Otherwise, the various items comprised by the parties' mutual accounting on rescission pose the same issues of valuation as when they are asserted as freestanding claims in unjust enrichment. Here as elsewhere, the choice between different measures of benefit is made to protect an innocent recipient—so far as possible—from an unfavorable outcome or a forced exchange. See Illustrations 25–26; compare the general rules stated at §§ 49–53.

Illustrations:

24. On rescission by the Policyholder of an insurance policy for which the premium has been paid in advance, Policyholder is entitled in principle to restitution of the prepaid premium, less the value of the insurance coverage already provided. Valuation of the benefit conferred in such a case will reflect the reasons for rescission. If Policyholder is merely exercising a contractual right of cancellation, the nonreturnable benefit will be measured as a ratable portion of the premium. By contrast, if Policyholder obtains rescission because of the misstatements of Insurer's agent, or because Insurer has committed a material breach of its obligations under the policy (as in § 37, Illustration 13), the court may find that the value of the coverage to Policyholder is something less than a ratable portion of the premium; or that it may properly be set off against the injury to Policyholder caused by Insurer's misconduct.

25. Lawyer sells commercial real estate to Client. After learning of problems that Lawyer had not disclosed, Client obtains rescission of the sale on the ground of Lawyer's breach of fiduciary duty (§ 43). Because of the parties' relationship, issues of valuation in their mutual accounting will be resolved in the manner most protective of Client. For example, Lawyer will be liable for interest on the purchase price from the date of payment, not from the date on which Client gave notice of rescission; while Client will be liable for the reasonable rental value of the premises, or for the income actually derived therefrom, whichever is less. Compare Illustration 26.

26. The completed sale of Blackacre is set aside because of Purchaser's fraud. In this circumstance, issues of valuation in the parties' mutual accounting will be resolved in the manner most protective of Vendor. For example, Vendor's liability for interest on the purchase price may run only from the date Vendor had notice of the grounds for rescission, rather than from the date of payment. Purchaser is liable for the reasonable rental value of the premises or for the income derived therefrom, whichever is more. Purchaser may be credited with payments of taxes, and with the saved cost to Vendor of necessary repairs, but Purchaser has no claim in respect of unsolicited improvements.

i. Incidental or reliance loss. Rescission of the parties' exchange may leave the claimant with losses from related expenditures (as distinct from payment of the price) made in reliance on the transaction that is being set aside. Compensation of such loss by an award of damages is a remedy different in kind from rescission and restitution, but the remedies are not necessarily inconsistent when the claimant's basic entitlement is to be restored to the status quo ante. Damages measured by the claimant's expenditure can be included in the accounting that accompanies rescission, in order to do complete justice in a single proceeding.

Recovery of what are commonly called "incidental damages" may thus be allowed in connection with rescission, consistent with the remedial objective of restoring the claimant to the precontractual position. See Illustration 27. Reimbursement of other forms of reliance expenditure—as distinguished from restitution of the claimant's performance itself, in the form of the price paid—may likewise be included in the parties' accounting on rescission. See Illustration 13, supra, and Illustration 28.

The fact that rescission is consistent with reimbursement of the claimant's reliance expenditures in some cases should not be allowed to obscure the central distinction between avoidance of a contract and enforcement by an action for damages. Rescission contemplates a mutual restoration of performance without the need to compare contract and market values. Its most dramatic applications therefore permit a claimant to recover a prepaid price without proof of damages from the defendant's breach. See § 37, Illustrations 1–2. By contrast, no measure of *damages* for breach of contract—including performance-based damages measured by the claimant's expenditures—can be calculated without reference to contractual expectations. Because a nonfraudulent breach does not make the defendant a guarantor of the profitability of the claimant's bargain, damages measured by unreimbursed expenditures are reduced by losses the claimant would have incurred had there been full performance (§ 38(2)(a)). Accordingly, when the ground of rescission is breach of contract (§ 37), the claimant may not combine rescission with a claim to recover expenditures that would circumvent this fundamental limitation. See § 38, Illustration 8.

Illustrations:

27. Relying on Seller's misleading description, Buyer pays $5000 for a boat lying in 100 feet of water. After spending $500 to raise the boat and finding that it is worthless, Buyer obtains rescission of the transaction based on Seller's fraud. In addition to recovering the $5000 paid, Buyer can recover the $500 spent in raising the boat.

28. Purchaser pays Vendor $500,000 for Blackacre and spends $100,000 on improvements, increasing the value of the property by $85,000. Rescission for Vendor's fraud allows Purchaser to reconvey the property and recover the purchase price without proof of damages. In the parties' mutual accounting, Purchaser will be credited with the $100,000 spent on improvements. This element of Purchaser's recovery represents compensation for Purchaser's reliance expenditure (§ 54(2)(c)) rather than restitution by Vendor of benefits conferred (§ 54(2)(b)).

j.   Tender of restitution not a precondition. Section 54(5) explicitly eliminates previous requirements that the claimant tender restitution to the other party as a precondition of rescission. No distinction is recognized between rescission "at law" and "in equity." The effect of former distinctions to govern the right to jury trial in a suit for rescission is a question outside the scope of this Restatement.

The requirement of a prior tender carried implicit safeguards to the defendant that the present section imposes more directly. It reduced the risk of a one-sided restitution, whereby the defendant might be compelled to restore what had been received in the transaction without obtaining restitution of what had been given. But there is no such danger when a judicial order can make restitution by one party conditional on counter-restitution by the other. Often the problem is resolved because mutual restitution leads to offsets and a net liability on one side only. In particular cases, the court may avoid prejudice to the party who is required to surrender an asset by supplemental devices such as equitable lien and constructive trust. See Illustration 30.

More broadly, the requirement of prior tender imposed a procedural barrier as a proxy for a substantive rule, since it purported to bar from rescission all claimants who were unable (and had not merely neglected) to restore the other party to the status quo ante. This ostensibly simple rule, as already noted, engendered a host of exceptions. Section 54(3)(b) states a more realistic test, requiring the court to determine whether any loss that will be allocated by rescission is appropriately borne by the party against whom rescission is sought.

Rescission of a release or settlement agreement on grounds of fraud or mistake presents particular difficulties that are largely outside the scope of this Restatement, because the key determinations turn on issues of contract law rather than restitution. See § 34, Illustration 21.

Illustrations:

29. By fraudulent misrepresentations, Seller induces Buyer to purchase 100 shares of XYZ common stock at $100 per share. Shortly thereafter, XYZ pays a dividend of $2.50 per share. Learning subsequently of Seller's fraud, Buyer brings an action to rescind the transaction. Buyer need not tender to Seller either the shares or the dividend as a precondition to bringing suit. Buyer's obligation to make restitution of the dividend ($250) can be set off against his claim to restitution of the price; judgment for a net $9750 in favor of Buyer may be made conditional on Buyer's restitution to Seller of the shares or their fungible equivalent.

30. Vendor purportedly conveys to Purchaser, for $100,000 cash, a fee simple interest in Blackacre. In fact Vendor has only a life estate. Under local property law, Vendor's breach of the covenant of title allows Purchaser to rescind the transaction, but Purchaser will not be required to surrender Blackacre before he obtains restitution of the price or adequate security therefor. Vendor has used the $100,000 obtained from Purchaser to purchase Whiteacre, and Vendor has no other assets with which to satisfy a judgment. The court might simultaneously (i) cancel the conveyance of Blackacre and (ii) subject both Blackacre and Vendor's interest in Whiteacre to equitable liens securing Purchaser's claim to $100,000.

k. Equitable defenses to rescission. The possibility of reversing a transfer after a change in underlying values imposes an obvious risk of forfeiture on one side while inviting opportunism on the other. The effect of rescission in shifting losses can be tolerated as an incidental consequence of a remedy whose principal function is to release the claimant from an involuntary exchange, or to achieve remedial economies where the reversal of an exchange is manifestly easier than its enforcement. By contrast, if a claimant were permitted to entertain for any significant period an election between enforcement and avoidance—against a background of potentially fluctuating values—the availability of rescission would give the claimant, in effect, an unpaid option on the defendant's performance. Such a result may be inequitable even if the defendant is guilty of fraud or other conscious wrongdoing.

The opportunistic use of rescission is barred, within traditional doctrine, by a rule that a claimant seeking to rescind must give notice of the election to do so with reasonable promptness after learning of the grounds for rescission. The purpose of such a rule is to protect the defendant against prejudice from the strategic use of the rescission remedy, not to foreclose an otherwise appropriate remedy because of an inadvertent and nonprejudicial delay. There is no need to insist on a formal "election of remedies," nor to require that the claimant decide at once between rescission and enforcement, so long as the claimant's actions are not strategic and the defendant is not prejudiced.

Section 54(6) accordingly refers to "prejudicial or speculative delay" as the circumstance justifying denial of the remedy. This equitable defense to rescission may sometimes be classified as a partial affirmative defense and an example of laches (§ 70). The same consequences might be described by treating the claimant's undue delay as a ratification. In some cases, an intervening change in circumstances may make the effects of rescission unacceptably harsh, even if the claimant acts immediately on learning the relevant facts. See Illustration 10, supra, and Illustrations 31–33.

Illustrations:

31. Vendor owns two tracts of land in a gold-mining region. Purchaser agrees with Vendor to buy one of them. The transaction is carried out by inattentive agents, and the deed describes the wrong tract. On entering the land, Purchaser immediately realizes that a mistake has been made. Instead of notifying Vendor, Purchaser spends several weeks digging exploratory shafts on the property conveyed. When these explorations prove fruitless, Purchaser notifies Vendor of the mistake and demands repayment of the purchase price or reformation of the deed. Rescission and reformation will both be denied because Purchaser has been seeking, in effect, to profit from the mistake by speculating at the expense of Vendor. Furthermore, because Purchaser's unsuccessful explorations have reduced the value of the tract—though in an amount difficult to ascertain—the court might deny

rescission and reformation even if Purchaser had learned of the mistake only after digging the shafts and had given prompt notice thereafter.

32. Vendor and Purchaser agree on the sale of Blackacre for a price of $350,000. Purchaser pays $100,000 down and agrees to pay the balance with interest in annual installments of $10,000. After two years' possession, Purchaser learns that Vendor's title is defective: undisclosed encumbrances affect 20 acres at the margin of the 200–acre tract. Both parties have acted in good faith. On suit by Purchaser, the court determines that the encumbrances reduce the value of Blackacre by $20,000, and (because land values have not changed appreciably in two years) that the parties might be effectively returned to the status quo ante via cancellation, restitution of payments on the price, and a mutual accounting for interest, rental value, taxes, and improvements. Purchaser will be allowed to choose between (i) completing the purchase of Blackacre at an adjusted price of $330,000 and (ii) rescission and restitution.

33. Same facts as Illustration 32, except that the encumbrances come to light five years after the sale. Purchaser immediately notifies Vendor of his intent to rescind. Because of a general decline in land prices, the fair market value of Blackacre has fallen from $330,000 to $250,000. If the court finds that this change of circumstances would make rescission inequitable to Vendor, rescission will be denied, and Purchaser's remedy will be limited to an appropriate reduction in the price. Rescission might be allowed, notwithstanding the intervening decline in market values, if the title defect were more substantial. Rescission would certainly be allowed if Vendor's misrepresentation had been fraudulent.

l.   Rights of third parties. Because the principal effect of rescission and restitution is to reverse any transfer of property made in connection with the transaction being set aside, the propriety of the remedy in a particular case requires consideration of the intervening rights of third parties. See § 54(4)(c). The third party protected by the rule is someone who has acquired an interest in the property, such as a mortgagee or other purchaser for value, through subsequent dealings with the original transferee. A claimant who attempted to recover the property from such a third party directly would potentially encounter the affirmative defense of bona fide purchase (§ 66). The third party is entitled to the same protection if the claimant seeks rescission against the original transferee. See Illustrations 34–35.

Illustrations:

34. A and B agree to dissolve their partnership, and A sells his interest in the partnership assets to B for $250,000. B forms a new partnership with C and D: the BCD partnership proceeds to exploit the business assets of the former AB partnership. Learning thereafter that his interest in the AB assets was worth at least $400,000, A sues B to rescind the sale on the grounds of B's fraud and breach of fiduciary duty

(§§ 13, 43). The intervening rights of C and D preclude rescission of the A–B transaction, unless A can establish that C and D had notice of B's breach of duty to A. If not, A has a claim to restitution measured by B's unjust enrichment ($150,000), but A is not entitled to rescission.

35. Elderly Widow, unable to read or write, owns a one-fifth interest in minerals underlying a 75–acre tract. Widow makes an oral agreement with Grantee to sell 2/15 of her interest for $5000, but Grantee induces Widow to execute a deed that purports to convey the whole of her interest. (Widow's daughter reviewed the deed before its execution and told her mother that she "guessed it was all right.") Grantee makes a partial assignment to A, and A makes a partial assignment to B and C. On discovering the fraud, Widow sues Grantee to rescind the transaction, offering to restore $5000 plus interest in exchange for cancellation of the deed. The initial question presented, given the intervening interests of A, B, and C, is whether Widow's deed is void or merely voidable (§ 13(2)). If Widow's deed is void, rescission is available without difficulty. If the deed is merely voidable, the availability to Widow of specific relief in restitution (whether by rescission or by cancellation of the deed) depends on whether any of the subsequent purchasers took their interests for value and without notice of Grantee's fraud (§ 66).

V. RESTATEMENT (THIRD) OF UNFAIR COMPETITION

(Selected Sections & Comments)

■ ■ ■

Table of Sections

Chapter 1. The Freedom to Compete

Chapter 1.   The Freedom to Compete

§ 1   General Principles

One who causes harm to the commercial relations of another by engaging in a business or trade is not subject to liability to the other for such harm unless:

(a)   the harm results from acts or practices of the actor actionable by the other under the rules of this Restatement relating to:

(1)   deceptive marketing, as specified in Chapter Two;

(2)   infringement of trademarks and other indicia of identification, as specified in Chapter Three;

(3)   appropriation of intangible trade values including trade secrets and the right of publicity, as specified in Chapter Four;

or from other acts or practices of the actor determined to be actionable as an unfair method of competition, taking into account the nature of the conduct and its likely effect on both the person seeking relief and the public; or

(b) the acts or practices of the actor are actionable by the other under federal or state statutes, international agreements, or general principles of common law apart from those considered in this Restatement.

Comment:

a. The freedom to compete. The freedom to engage in business and to compete for the patronage of prospective customers is a fundamental premise of the free enterprise system. Competition in the marketing of goods and services creates incentives to offer quality products at reasonable prices and fosters the general welfare by promoting the efficient allocation of economic resources. The freedom to compete necessarily contemplates the probability of harm to the commercial relations of other participants in the market. The fundamental rule stated in the introductory clause of this Section promotes competition by insuring that neither new entrants nor existing competitors will be subject to liability for harm resulting solely from the fact of their participation in the market.

The freedom to compete implies a right to induce prospective customers to do business with the actor rather than with the actor's competitors. This Section permits a seller to seek to divert business not only from competitors generally, but also from a particular competitor. This Section is applicable to harm incurred by persons with whom the actor directly competes and to harm incurred by other persons affected by the actor's decision to enter or continue in business. Thus, the actor is not subject to liability to indirect competitors or to employees or suppliers of others who may be harmed by the actor's presence in the market. Liability is imposed under this Section, and under this Restatement generally, only in connection with harm resulting from particular methods of competition determined to be unfair.

The principle embodied in this Section is often loosely described as a "privilege" to compete. That characterization, however, is sometimes taken to imply that any intentional interference in the commercial relations of another is prima facie tortious, with the burden on the actor to establish an applicable privilege as an affirmative defense. There is as yet no consensus with respect to the allocation of the burdens of pleading and proof under the general tort of intentional interference with prospective economic relations. See Restatement, Second, Torts § 767, Comment *k.* However, in the case of harm resulting from competition in the marketplace, the privilege rationale appears inconsistent with the basic premise of our free enterprise system. Rather than adopting the view that such harm is prima facie tortious subject to a competitive privilege, this Restatement rejects the privilege rationale in favor of a general principle of non-liability. A person alleging injury through competition must therefore establish facts sufficient to subject the actor to liability under one or more of the rules enumerated in this Section.

This Section does not preclude the imposition of liability when the actor's participation in the market is itself unlawful. One who engages in a particular business or trade in violation of a statute prohibiting such activity, either absolutely or without prescribed permission, may be subject to liability to others engaged in the business or trade if one of the purposes of the enactment is to protect the others against unauthorized competition and the recognition of a private right of action is not inconsistent with the legislative intent. This result is an application of the general principles relating to the imposition of tort liability for violations of legislative enactments that do not explicitly authorize a private cause of action. See Restatement, Second, Torts § 874A.

Intentional interference with another's commercial relations by means other than the actor's participation in the market is not within the scope of this Section. Such conduct may subject the actor to liability under the general rules on interference with prospective economic relations stated in Restatement, Second, Torts § 766B.

Illustrations:

1.   *A*, the owner of a bakery, employs *B*, a baker, and sells products made with ingredients purchased from *C*, a supplier. *D* opens a competing bakery and *A* is compelled to go out of business. *D* is not subject to liability to *A*, *B*, or *C*.

2.   *A* and *B* are competing distributors of shoes. *A* induces *C* not to purchase *B*'s house. *A*'s interference is not within the scope of this Restatement. *A* may be subject to liability to *B* for intentionally interfering with *B*'s prospective economic relations under the rule stated in Restatement, Second, Torts § 766B.

3.   A federal statute prohibits *A*, a governmental corporation, from selling electricity outside a designated geographic area. *B*, a private utility company, commences an action seeking to enjoin sales by *A* in localities served by *B* that are outside the designated area. If the court concludes that a purpose of the statute is to protect private utilities from competition by *A* and that the recognition of a private remedy is not inconsistent with the legislative intent, *A* may be subject to liability to *B*.

b.   "Subject to liability"; "harm". This Restatement uses the words "subject to liability" to denote the fact that the actor's conduct is such as to make it liable to another if the conduct is the legal cause of the other's injury and the actor has no defense applicable to the particular claim. See Restatement, Second, Torts § 5. The phrase carries no implications with respect to the remedies available to the injured party. In particular, it does not imply that the injured party is entitled to monetary relief. The word "harm" as used in this Restatement denotes the existence of loss or detriment in fact, whether or not the loss or detriment results from an invasion of a legally protected interest. See *id.*, § 7.

c.   Motives of the actor. Several cases recite, mostly in dicta, that one who engages in competition solely or primarily for the purpose of causing harm to another is subject to liability to the other, apparently without regard to the nature of the actor's business methods. The prior Restatement of this topic incorporated a narrow version of this principle, requiring both a malicious motive and an intention on the part of the actor to terminate the business after the infliction of harm. Restatement of Torts § 709. However, both the case law and the prior Restatement declined to invoke the rule when the actor's conduct was directed at least in part to the advancement of its own competitive interests. This proposition necessitated a distinction between "good faith" competition, which would not subject the actor to liability even if motivated in part by ill will toward the other, and "simulated competition" that was undertaken merely as a means of inflicting harm.

The rule purporting to impose liability upon one who engages in business solely for the purpose of harming another has had little practical effect. When harm results from the actor's participation in a bona fide business or trade, courts are quick to find a concurrent commercial motive sufficient to preclude the imposition of liability even in the face of evidence of genuine ill will. When the rule has been invoked to support the imposition of liability, the actor's conduct has typically involved unfair methods of competition sufficient in themselves to subject the actor to liability. In the absence of such misconduct, the rule invites misuse by affording a colorable claim through which an established business can restrict legitimate competition and harass new entrants in the market. The public benefits derived from competition are independent of the actor's motivation, and even an intention to withdraw from the market will not ordinarily threaten the public interest in light of the opportunity for entry by others. Under the rule stated in this Section, an actor who causes harm to another merely by engaging in a business or trade is not subject to liability regardless of motive. Liability is thus determined by an analysis of the business methods employed by the actor and not by the actor's motivation.

Although a malicious motive is not sufficient in itself to subject an actor to liability, a competitor motivated by ill will may be tempted to pursue impermissible means of competition in order to insure or enhance the harm to another. Evidence of such ill will may therefore justify close scrutiny of the actor's methods under the various rules enumerated in this Section. The actor's motives may also be relevant to the application of rules of liability outside the scope of this Restatement, including state and federal antitrust laws.

Illustration:

4. *A*, a manufacturer of medicines, quarrels with *B*, a newspaper publisher, because of *B*'s articles ridiculing *A*'s medicines. *A*, after threatening to drive *B* out of business, establishes a competing newspaper. *A*'s newspaper is successful and *B* is eventually forced to cease publication. *A* is not subject to liability to *B*.

d.   Deceptive marketing. Competitive markets cannot operate efficiently unless consumers have access to information about the goods and services offered by competing sellers. Much of the information available to prospective purchasers is provided by sellers in the form of advertising. If the message that it communicates is accurate, advertising can function as a convenient, low-cost source of information that assists consumers to choose intelligently among competing products. False or deceptive advertising, however, can result in improvident expenditures or force consumers to spend additional resources in an effort to acquire more reliable information. Deceptive advertising also threatens harm to other sellers who are thereby deprived of the opportunity to compete on the merits of their goods and services. Recognition of a right of action for deceptive marketing in favor of other sellers, however, raises complex issues. It is often difficult to establish a clear nexus between the misrepresentations of one seller and injury to the business relations of another seller. Further, unless the cause of action for deceptive advertising is carefully circumscribed, it may inhibit the dissemination of useful information and function as a barrier to vigorous competition. The scope of liability for deceptive advertising must also reflect the constitutional protection afforded to commercial speech.

The rules stated in Chapter Two describe the circumstances in which a seller may be subject to liability for injuries to the commercial relations of other sellers resulting from the use of deceptive representations in the marketing of goods or services.

e. Trademark infringement. A trademark is a word, name, symbol, device, or other designation used by a manufacturer or seller to identify its goods or services and distinguish them from goods or services manufactured or sold by others. The protection of trademarks and other indicia of origin or sponsorship is a fundamental feature of the law of unfair competition.

By indicating the source or sponsorship of the goods or services with which they are used, trademarks communicate to prospective purchasers information relating to the quality and other characteristics of the product. The deceptive use of another's trademark can be seen as a form of deceptive marketing, and the protection of trademarks thus implicates many of the interests identified in Comment *d*. The recognition of rights in trademarks also serves to protect and encourage investments in good will by insuring the trademark owner an opportunity to capture the benefits of a favorable reputation created through expenditures on quality, service, or promotion.

The rules governing the protection of trademarks must also be responsive to the public interest in fostering vigorous competition. In defining protectable subject matter and in delineating the scope of exclusive rights, the law cannot neglect the legitimate interests of other competitors. In some cases the recognition of exclusive rights in favor of a particular seller may undermine the ability of other sellers to communicate useful information to consumers or deprive competitors of access to product features necessary for effective competition. The scope of exclusive rights in trademarks must also accommodate the interest in free expression.

The rules governing the acquisition and protection of rights in trademarks and related subject matter are stated in Chapter Three.

f. Appropriation of trade values. An important function of the law of unfair competition is to delimit the circumstances in which a person may prohibit the appropriation by another of intangible business assets created through an investment of time, money, or effort. The law of trademarks and the general proscription against passing off, for example, prohibit the appropriation of another's good will through misrepresentations relating to source. Other appropriations can be more direct, as when a competitor utilizes the work-product of another in competition with the creator. The federal patent and copyright statutes offer a complex regime of protection for some intangible assets, but the common law also imposes limitations on the appropriation of intangible assets.

The recognition of rights in intangible business assets generally proceeds from the premise that protection is necessary in order to insure adequate incentive for the investment of resources necessary to produce such assets. This incentive rationale is frequently augmented by references to the perceived unjust enrichment resulting from an appropriation of the fruits of another's investment. The recognition of exclusive rights in intangible business assets, however, must also take account of the anticompetitive consequences inherent in restrictions on the free flow of ideas and information. Thus, in many instances the incentive and unjust enrichment rationales may be outweighed by the advantages of unrestricted imitation and dissemination as embodied in the concept of a public domain. The common law has generally accorded rights against the appropriation of intangible business assets only when the recognition of rights is supported by additional interests justifying protection, and then only when the scope of the resulting rights can be clearly defined. In the case of trade secrets, for example, the owner's rights reflect the protection traditionally accorded confidential relationships as well as the interest in security against wrongful physical intrusions. Appropriation of the commercial value of another's name or likeness implicates interests in privacy and personal autonomy. The recognition of rights in intangible assets must also reflect the appropriate relationship between common law and legislation and the permissible sphere of state authority in light of the extensive regime of federal intellectual property law. Rules relating to the appropriation of intangible business assets, including the protection of trade secrets and the recognition of a right of publicity, are stated in Chapter Four.

g. Unfair methods of competition. A primary purpose of the law of unfair competition is the identification and redress of business practices that hinder rather than promote the efficient operation of the market. Certain recurring patterns of objectionable practices form the basis of the traditional categories of liability specifically enumerated in Subsection (a)(1)–(3). However, these specific forms of unfair competition do not fully exhaust the scope of statutory or common law liability for unfair methods of competition, and Subsection (a) therefore includes a residual category encompassing other business practices determined to be unfair.

It is impossible to state a definitive test for determining which methods of competition will be deemed unfair in addition to those included in the categories of conduct described in the preceding Comments. Courts continue to evaluate competitive practices against generalized standards of fairness and social utility. Judicial formulations have broadly appealed to principles of honesty and fair dealing, rules of fair play and good conscience, and the morality of the marketplace. The case law, however, is far more circumscribed than such rhetoric might indicate, and courts have generally been reluctant to interfere in the competitive process. An act or practice is likely to be judged unfair only if it substantially interferes with the ability of others to compete on the merits of their products or otherwise conflicts with accepted principles of public policy recognized by statute or common law.

As a general matter, if the means of competition are otherwise tortious with respect to the injured party, they will also ordinarily constitute an unfair method of competition. A competitor who interferes with the business of another by acts or threats of violence directed at the other, for example, is subject to liability for unfair competition. So also is one who interferes by instituting or threatening to institute groundless litigation against a competitor. Similarly, if a competitor interferes with the commercial relations of another by engaging in defamation or by establishing or maintaining an unlawful restraint of trade, the conduct also constitutes unfair competition. Liability for unfair competition under the residual rule stated in Subsection (a), however, is not limited to conduct that is otherwise tortious with respect to the party seeking relief. Thus, interference in the commercial relations of a competitor resulting from unlawful threats directed at customers of the competitor will also constitute unfair competition.

In assessing the propriety of the actor's conduct, a primary consideration is the social utility of the conduct as a means of competition. If the conduct is likely to interfere in a substantial manner with the ability of prospective purchasers to choose on the merits of the competing products, it will ordinarily be considered unfair. In some circumstances, for example, a court may conclude that a failure to disclose to prospective consumers particular information that is crucial to an intelligent purchasing decision constitutes unfair competition.

Some applications of the residual rule of liability specified in Subsection (a) can be seen as extensions of the established categories of unfair competition. A competitor who diverts business from another by means of fraudulent misrepresentations or through the wrongful use of confidential information, for example, may in some circumstances be subject to liability for unfair competition even if the conduct is not specifically actionable under the rules relating to deceptive marketing or the appropriation of trade secrets. However, in determining whether it is appropriate to conclude that an act or practice is unfair despite the fact that a restrictive element of traditional doctrine precludes the imposition of liability under an established category of unfair competition, careful consideration must be given to the nature of the restriction. If the restriction expresses an important policy of

270

the law against the imposition of liability in such circumstances, the conduct should not be actionable as unfair competition.

A person seeking relief under the residual rule stated in Subsection (a) bears the burden of establishing that the method of competition employed by the actor is unfair. The use of equitable remedies has contributed to the development of the law by facilitating the condemnation of practices not previously determined to be unlawful. A person likely to be damaged by the unfair competition of another may obtain an injunction against a continuation of the conduct. The court may also award appropriate monetary relief.

Liability at common law for acts of unfair competition has been supplemented by the widespread enactment of the Unfair Trade Practices and Consumer Protection Act, which commonly prohibits "unfair methods of competition and unfair or deceptive acts or practices." See the Statutory Note following this Section. The private right of action available under many of these statutes has been pursued primarily as an alternative to traditional contract and tort actions by disappointed purchasers attracted by the generous remedial provisions of the Act. In a number of jurisdictions, however, competitors also have standing to seek redress under the Act for harm to their commercial relations. Application of the Act in this latter context has thus far been generally limited to conduct falling within the traditional categories of unfair competition law. However, the broad substantive standards embodied in many of these statutes provide a flexible statutory counterpart to the general common law proscription against unfair competition.

Illustrations:

5. *A* manufactures a computer designed for use by school children. *B*, a manufacturer of a competing product, sends letters to wholesalers and distributors stating that *A*'s computer infringes a patent owned by *B*. The letters contain a threat to institute an infringement action against anyone who markets *A*'s product. *B* knows that *A*'s product does not infringe the patent and has no intention of commencing the threatened litigation. *B* is subject to liability to *A*.

6. *A* is the local distributor for a brand of wall paneling. *B*, a builder, makes a contract to install wall paneling in a school being constructed by *C*, a school district. *C* requests *B* to solicit bids for the wall paneling from suppliers. *B* then arranges to become the local distributor for a brand of paneling similar to that sold by *A*. Without informing *A* of this fact, *B* obtains a bid from *A* but alters *A*'s figures to increase the price before submitting *A*'s bid, together with its own lower bid, to *C*. *C* awards the supply contract to *B*. *B* is subject to liability to *A*.

7. *A* is involved in a dispute with *B*, a former licensee, concerning the use by *B* of a trade name similar to *A*'s. *A* files a change of address form under *B*'s name at the local post office, listing its own address as

the new address of *B*'s business. As a result of the diversion of mail, *B* loses the opportunity to bid on several contracts. *A* is subject to liability to *B*.

h.   Liability under other rules. The succeeding Chapters of this Restatement treat the common law and statutory rules governing liability for the specific forms of unfair competition enumerated in Subsection (a)(1)–(3). Other conduct undertaken to advance the competitive interests of the actor may result in liability under the various federal and state statutes regulating aspects of the competitive process beyond those considered in this Restatement. The federal copyright and patent statutes, for example, prohibit the unauthorized appropriation of another's writings and discoveries. Federal and state statutes afford private remedies against price discrimination, and state "sales below cost" statutes subject a seller to liability to competitors for other specified pricing practices. Similarly, if the actor's conduct threatens to reduce or eliminate competition, liability may arise under federal and state antitrust law.

A competitor may also be subject to liability to other participants in the market if its methods of competition violate generally applicable principles of tort and contract law. A seller who seeks to improve its position in the market through physical violence to the person or property of a competitor, for example, may be subject to liability under traditional rules of tort law. If the actor has made an enforceable promise not to compete with another, competition may subject it to liability under general principles of contract law. Unreasonable interference with the use of real property owned by a competitor may be actionable under rules relating to nuisance. Statements derogatory to the personal reputation of a competitor or to the quality of its goods or services may be actionable as defamation or disparagement.

As the other party's economic relations approach the status of formal contract rights, the freedom of a competitor to interfere with those expectancies is also circumscribed by the protection afforded in tort against intentional interference with contracts. See Restatement, Second, Torts §§ 766–774A. The freedom to compete embodied in this Section extends only to interference with prospective economic relations and does not insulate the actor from liability for intentional interference with a competitor's contract rights. The characterization of economic relations as prospective or contractual, however, is itself influenced by the policies underlying recognition of the freedom to compete. Many cases, for example, recognize a right to induce a third person to terminate a contract with a competitor if the agreement is terminable at will.

The rules in this Restatement relating to liability for unfair methods of competition supplement rather than displace these general principles of common law.

272

Illustration:

8.   *A* and *B* are engaged in the sale of gasoline and convenience foods on adjoining properties. In order to block the view of *B*'s premises from a nearby highway, *A* constructs a wall 14 feet in height at the boundary of the properties and places a sign marked "Exit Only" near the entrance to *B*'s property. *A* may be subject to liability to *B* under general principles of tort law relating to nuisance.

Chapter 2.   Deceptive Marketing

§ 2   Deceptive Marketing: General Principle

One who, in connection with the marketing of goods or services, makes a representation relating to the actor's own goods, services, or commercial activities that is likely to deceive or mislead prospective purchasers to the likely commercial detriment of another under the rule stated in § 3 is subject to liability to the other for the relief appropriate under the rules stated in §§ 35–37.

Comment:

a.   Rationale. Unless prospective purchasers can accurately compare the products offered by competing sellers, the free enterprise system cannot operate efficiently. The use of deceptive representations in the marketing of goods and services impairs the ability of purchasers to choose intelligently among competing products. As confidence in the truth of advertising diminishes, prospective purchasers may be forced to expend additional resources in examining and sampling competing products. A seller's misrepresentations may be actionable by deceived purchasers under traditional rules of tort and contract law and also under the various state and federal consumer protection statutes. In many instances, however, the cost of obtaining relief may exceed the purchaser's potential remedy. The use of deceptive representations in the marketing of goods and services may also cause injury to the legitimate commercial interests of other sellers by unfairly depriving them of the opportunity to compete on the merits of their products in the marketplace or by threatening harm to their reputation and good will. The rules of this Chapter are concerned with the protection of these commercial interests. Although the rules are not applicable to actions by deceived purchasers, they function as an indirect form of consumer protection. The rules in this Chapter, however, also reflect the public interest in avoiding unnecessary restrictions on the dissemination of commercial information.

This Section is applicable only to representations made in connection with the marketing of goods or services. The United States Supreme Court has held that the first amendment protects communications promoting the sale of goods or services from unjustified governmental interference, but it has repeatedly affirmed that there is no constitutional prohibition on the imposition of liability in connection with false, deceptive, or misleading commercial speech. The rule of this Section is applicable only to commercial speech.

Illustrations:

1. *A*, a utility company, includes with its monthly bill an insert stating the company's views on nuclear power. The insert states that nuclear power plants are safe, clean, and economical and that use of nuclear energy reduces the nation's dependence on foreign energy sources. The representations, whether true or false, are not within the scope of this Section.

2. *A* and *B* are pharmaceutical companies engaged in the marketing of over-the-counter analgesics. In a television commercial, *A* makes a false representation that its product is more effective than *B*'s for the relief of pain. The representation is within the scope of this Section.

b. Historical development. Liability to other sellers for commercial injuries resulting from an actor's deceptive marketing was initially confined to misrepresentations of source. Thus, use of another's trademark to falsely represent that the actor was the other, or that the actor's goods were manufactured by the other, subjected the actor to liability in an action for trademark infringement. See Chapter Three. Other misrepresentations relating to source were cognizable in an action for unfair competition. See § 4, Comment *b*. Recognition of liability in the absence of a misrepresentation relating to source was retarded by several factors: the seeming complexity of identifying appropriate plaintiffs; the fear that such liability might unduly hamper free enterprise; the development of alternative means of dealing with the problem of deceptive advertising; and the acceptance of precedents as exhaustive rather than illustrative.

During the first half of the 20th century, liability at common law was cautiously expanded beyond misrepresentations of source to misrepresentations concerning other characteristics or qualities of the seller's goods. Relying upon the "passing off" cases, however, courts generally required proof that the misrepresentation had directly diverted trade from the plaintiff to the actor. This requirement effectively precluded relief unless the plaintiff was the sole alternative source of the misrepresented goods. (An exception to this "single source" requirement was a series of cases involving misrepresentations of geographic origin, which were held actionable by a competitor doing business in the locality falsely designated as the origin of the defendant's goods.) The "single source" requirement severely limited the capacity of the common law to respond to the problem of deceptive advertising and it was forcefully criticized by contemporary commentators. The Restatement of Torts proffered a cautious expansion of liability, see § 761, but retained the requirement of proof that the misrepresentation had diverted sales from the plaintiff to the actor.

This limitation on the private right of action may have encouraged the public regulation of advertising. In the early decades of the twentieth century, many state legislatures enacted criminal prohibitions against false advertising (the so-called Printers Ink Statutes), but their impact was blunted by strict construction and sporadic enforcement. Federal legislation undertook to regulate the labeling of a wide variety of specific products. The Federal Trade Commission Act, proscribing "unfair methods of competition" and "unfair or deceptive acts or practices," established a comprehensive regulatory regime encompassing deceptive representations in advertising, but with no provision for private enforcement. More recently, state legislatures, inspired by the Federal Trade Commission's draft of the Unfair Trade Practices and Consumer Protection Act, have enacted "Little FTC Acts" augmenting public regulation at the state level. See the Statutory Note following § 1.

The expansion of the private right of action by competitors for deceptive marketing can be traced to the enactment of the Trademark Act of 1946, 15 U.S.C.A. §§ 1051–1127, commonly known as the Lanham Act. As originally enacted, § 43(a) of the Act, 15 U.S.C.A. § 1125(a), recognized a right of action against "a false designation of origin, or any false description or representation" used in connection with any goods or services in favor of "any person who believes that he is or is likely to be damaged." Some early interpretations confined § 43(a) to misrepresentations relating to source; other interpretations viewed it as a codification of existing common law liability under the "single source" doctrine. Subsequent decisions, however, established the section's general applicability to deceptive advertising and rejected the attempt to engraft the common law limitations onto the statutory tort. The 1988 revision of § 43(a) confirmed its application to both misrepresentations of source and other deceptive representations made in connection with the marketing of goods and services.

State legislation now also recognizes private rights of action in favor of businesses likely to be injured by deceptive marketing on the part of other sellers in the marketplace. A number of states have enacted the Uniform Deceptive Trade Practices Act. See the Statutory Note following this Section. Among the practices proscribed by the Act are deceptive designations of geographic origin; representations that the goods or services have characteristics, ingredients, uses, benefits, or quantities that they do not in fact possess; and false representations that goods are original or new, or are of a particular standard, quality, or grade. Injunctions may be granted under the Uniform Deceptive Trade Practices Act to persons likely to be damaged by the deceptive practice. In addition, in several states, either by express statutory authorization or judicial interpretation, competitors damaged by deceptive practices may also bring private actions under the Unfair Trade Practices and Consumer Protection Act. See § 1, Comment g.

Limitations on the common law cause of action for deceptive marketing have sometimes been ascribed to the potential chilling effect of broader liability and to the prospect of increased litigation. Although the development of private rights of action in favor of businesses injured by deceptive marketing has been achieved largely through legislation, the public policy implications of these statutes, the dearth of modern common law precedents articulating the "single source" limitation, and the persistent expansion of common law rights against other forms of unfair competition support the statement of a general principle of liability. In view of existing statutory rights, the marginal effect of an expansion of liability at common law is minimal. This Section thus recognizes a general principle of liability for deceptive marketing independent of specific statutory authority. The rules embodied in this Section and in the succeeding Sections of this Chapter are therefore applicable to both common law and statutory causes of action.

c.   *Relation to product disparagement.* To be actionable under this Section, the representation must relate to the goods, services, or commercial activities of the actor; representations relating solely to the goods or services marketed by others are not within the scope of the rule as stated here. Liability at common law for misrepresentations that disparage the goods or services of others has long been subject to distinct rules shaped in part by questionable analogies to the law of defamation. The general rules governing product disparagement, or "trade libel" as it is sometimes called, are set forth in Restatement, Second, Torts §§ 623A–652 and are not repeated here. However, under the 1988 revision of § 43(a) of the Lanham Act and under § 2(a)(8) of the Uniform Deceptive Trade Practices Act, an actor who falsely disparages the goods or services of another seller is subject to liability without proof of special damages or of an intent to deceive, thus diminishing the distinctions drawn at common law between disparagement and false advertising. It is also uncertain whether the analogy to defamation will ultimately subject the statutory and common law actions for product disparagement to some or all of the constitutional restrictions that have been imposed on the action for defamation. Since disparaging statements that are made in connection with the marketing of goods or services typically fall within the classification of commercial speech, the full range of constitutional restrictions may not be applicable, but the issue remains unsettled. Although the rule of this Section is expressly limited to misrepresentations relating to the goods, services, or commercial activities of the actor, that limitation is not intended to preclude or discourage the development of a similar rule of liability at common law applicable to misrepresentations relating to the products or commercial activities of another.

The distinctions between representations relating to the goods or services of the actor and representations relating to the goods or services of another is particularly difficult to maintain when the representation is expressly or implicitly comparative. For example, a representation concerning the products of a competitor may imply that the actor's own product is different or superior to the competitor's with respect to the matter represented. Thus, if a representation directed at another's product causes prospective purchasers to infer facts about the actor's own goods or services, the representation is within the scope of this Section.

   d.   Likelihood of deception. In order to subject an actor to liability under this Section, the actor's representation must be likely to deceive or mislead "prospective purchasers." Prospective purchasers include any persons or legal entities to whom the actor's goods or services are marketed, whether by sale, lease, license, or other manner of commercial transaction, or to whom an offer of such a transaction is made. They may be the immediate customers of the actor or the customers of others who market the actor's products. The term "prospective purchasers" also includes persons such as purchasing agents, product consultants, end users, and others who may control or influence the purchasing decisions of others and whose deception is therefore likely to result in commercial detriment to competing sellers under the principles stated in § 3.

   The likelihood that a particular representation will deceive or mislead is determined by the meaning likely to be attributed to the representation by its audience and the relationship between that meaning and the true facts. A representation may be likely to deceive or mislead because it is literally false, such as a claim that furniture is solid mahogany when it has only a mahogany veneer or that what is in fact a cotton textile is 40 percent wool. Representations that are not literally false may nevertheless be likely to deceive or mislead if the audience is likely to infer additional facts that are false. Thus, a statement may be true with respect to the facts stated but fail to include qualifying matter necessary to prevent the implication of further assertions that are false. Such half-truths may be as likely to deceive or mislead as a representation that is wholly false. So also may an ambiguous statement subject to two interpretations, one of which is false.

   The meaning of any statement depends on the context in which it is made. The determination of meaning, and hence of the tendency of a representation to deceive or mislead, must accordingly be made in light of all the circumstances surrounding the representation, including the character and sophistication of the audience and the subject matter of the communication. If the representation is expressed through words alone, the words themselves are the most important evidence of meaning. When the representation is literally false, a court may conclude in the absence of credible evidence to the contrary that the representation is likely to deceive or mislead. When the tendency to deceive or mislead turns instead upon the inferences to be drawn from the representation or upon a choice among several possible interpretations, direct evidence of the meaning attached to the representation by the relevant audience may be necessary to establish a likelihood of deception. Surveys, when properly structured and conducted, can be helpful in ascertaining the meaning likely to be attributed to a representation and hence the likelihood that it will deceive or mislead. Evidence of actual deception, misunderstanding, or confusion, although not required under the rule in this Section, is relevant in determining whether the audience is likely to be deceived or misled.

   The intentions of the speaker are also relevant in assessing the likelihood of deception. Although an intention to deceive is not required in order to subject a seller to liability, evidence that the representation is in fact intended to communicate a false or misleading message may justify the inference that deception is likely, since it is ordinarily appropriate to assume that a speaker who intends to deceive will be successful in doing so.

A person seeking to establish liability under this Section bears the burden of proving that the representation, as it is likely to be understood by the audience, is false or misleading. Thus, the fact that the representation lacks adequate substantiation is not in itself sufficient for the imposition of liability. However, liability may be established by proof that the representation either expressly or by implication includes a claim concerning the nature or degree of substantiation and that such substantiation does not in fact exist.

In many instances a representation may be likely to deceive or mislead only some of the prospective purchasers to whom it is directed. A person is subject to liability under this Section only if the representation is likely to deceive or mislead a significant portion of the audience. As a general matter, if the representation would deceive a reasonably prudent purchaser of the goods or services, it is likely to deceive or mislead under the rule in this Section. If a reasonably prudent purchaser would not be deceived or misled by the representation, the actor is not subject to liability in the absence of other evidence indicating that the representation is nevertheless likely to deceive or mislead a significant portion of its audience.

Imposition of liability in connection with a representation likely to deceive only a portion of the audience necessarily interferes with the communication of non-deceptive speech between the actor and that portion of the audience not likely to be misled. In determining whether the portion of the audience likely to be deceived is "significant," the potential harm to such persons and to the interests of competitors must be weighed against the harm that the imposition of liability and contemplated relief would cause to the actor and the remainder of the audience. It is thus not possible to analyze the issue solely in terms of absolute numbers or percentages. Among the relevant factors are the seriousness of the threatened injury to deceived purchasers and the extent to which the representation could be easily recast to convey the information in a form less likely to deceive or mislead.

Determining the likelihood that a representation will deceive or mislead is closely analogous to determining the likelihood of confusion under the rule governing the infringement of trademarks stated in § 20, and much of the commentary to § 20 is therefore also applicable to the rule stated here.

The fact that a seller has made a representation that is likely to deceive or mislead is not in itself sufficient to subject the seller to liability. Liability may be imposed under this Section only if the deception is also to the likely commercial detriment of the person seeking relief under the rule stated in § 3, which requires proof of both materiality and likelihood of harm.

Illustrations:

3. *A* and *B* manufacture competing non-prescription pain relievers. In a television commercial advertising *A*'s product, an actor wearing a white jacket and holding a stethoscope states that A's product has been "proven faster-acting than any other non-prescription pain reliever." Existing clinical tests comparing *A*'s product to *B*'s are insufficient to establish which of the two products provides faster relief. *A*'s representation is likely to deceive or mislead.

4. *A*, a record distributor, represents that a particular record contains songs played by a well-known musician. In fact, the musician was a mere background player on the recording. If a significant number of prospective purchasers are likely to infer from *A*'s representation that the musician was a principal performer on the record, the representation is likely to deceive or mislead.

e. Non-disclosure. This Section subjects an actor to liability for false or misleading representations; a failure to disclose even material facts is not in itself actionable under the rule stated here. Similarly, the fact that a representation made by the actor would be more useful to prospective purchasers if accompanied by further disclosures is not sufficient to subject the actor to liability. However, in some circumstances the disclosure of additional facts may be necessary to avoid liability for a representation that would be misleading in the absence of further disclosure. In determining whether a representation is misleading because of a failure to make additional disclosures, it may be appropriate to consider the extent to which the information communicated by the representation is valuable to prospective purchasers despite the absence of the additional disclosures. In the absence of a misleading representation, the failure to disclose additional information will not subject the actor to liability under this Section.

On the possibility of liability for non-disclosure of material facts, see § 1, Comment *g.*

Illustration:

5. *A*, a manufacturer of video-recording equipment, fails to disclose to potential purchasers that certain uses of the equipment may subject the user to liability for copyright infringement. The non-disclosure does not subject *A* to liability under the rule stated in this Section.

f. Intent. Liability under this Section turns upon an objective evaluation of the probable consequences of the actor's conduct and not upon a determination of the actor's subjective intent. Although the intent of the actor may be relevant to a number of issues arising under this Section, including the meaning to be attributed to the words or conduct of the actor (see Comment *d*), the materiality of the representation (see § 3, Comment *b*), and the availability of monetary relief (see § 36, Comment *j*; § 37, Comment *e*), an intent to deceive is not a necessary element of liability.

The history of the law of unfair competition reveals a persistent retreat from its initial emphasis on the actor's subjective state of mind. Because the action for trademark infringement arose as an offshoot of the common law action for deceit, an intent to deceive was originally thought to be an essential element of the cause of action. In the case of fanciful or arbitrary trademarks, the natural inference that the defendant's imitation had been adopted with an intent to deceive prospective purchasers eventually crystallized into a conclusive presumption, in effect a rule of law that proof of fraudulent intent is unnecessary. See § 9, Comment *d*. For a time, a distinction was maintained between actions for the infringement of technical "trademarks" and actions for "unfair competition" in which protection was sought for other designations that had acquired source significance. In the latter action, proof of fraudulent intent remained a requirement. The distinction between these actions, however, has been abandoned, and fraud is no longer a necessary element in an action for infringement. See § 20, Comment *c*.

Statutory actions for unfair competition have similarly abandoned the requirement of fraudulent intent. Liability for deceptive marketing under § 43(a) of the Lanham Act is not dependent on the defendant's intent. Under the Uniform Deceptive Trade Practices Act, a person causing confusion as to source, sponsorship, or affiliation, or falsely describing the characteristics, ingredients, or benefits of the goods or services is similarly subject to liability without regard to intent. In keeping with the trend of common law developments and the prevailing statutory formulations, this Section does not require proof of fraudulent intent.

g.   *Form of misrepresentation.* There are no technical requirements as to the form or manner in which the misrepresentation is made. It may be conveyed at the point of sale through labels, packaging, or displays, or it may be contained in brochures, catalogs, or price lists, or in print, radio, or television advertising. The misrepresentation may be written or oral, or it may be conveyed through visual images or inferred from other conduct of the actor. If the misrepresentation is repeated by several actors in the marketing chain, each may be subject to liability under this Section.

Illustrations:

6.   *A* sells a snack food product made from dehydrated potato granules. The packaging describes the product as "potato chips." If prospective purchasers, in the absence of additional disclosures, are likely to interpret that term to refer only to products made from whole, sliced potatoes, *A* has made a representation likely to deceive or mislead.

7.   *A*, a manufacturer of synthetic mink garments, sells its products under the trademark NORMINK. If the use of that trademark is likely to cause prospective purchasers to believe that the garments are made of genuine mink, *A* has made a representation likely to deceive or mislead.

8.   *A* is a manufacturer of dresses. In a magazine advertisement promoting mail order sales, *A* includes a photograph purporting to show one of the dresses. The photograph in fact depicts a dress manufactured by *A*'s competitor *B*, and the dress offered for sale by *A* is not identical to *B*'s dress. *A* has made a representation likely to deceive or mislead.

9.   *A*, a manufacturer of orange juice, broadcasts a television commercial in which an actor is shown squeezing oranges and pouring the freshly-squeezed juice directly into a carton bearing *A*'s name. *A*'s juice is in fact frozen after it is squeezed and later heated to prevent spoilage before being packaged in cartons. If prospective purchasers are likely to interpret the commercial as a statement that *A*'s product contains only freshly-squeezed, unprocessed juice, *A* has made a representation likely to deceive or mislead.

10.   *A* produces wine that it bottles under labels falsely indicating its geographic origin. *A* sells the wine to *B*, a distributor, who sells it to retailers including *C*. *C* offers the wine for sale to the public. *A*, *B*, and *C* have made a representation likely to deceive or mislead.

h.   Remedies. This Section subjects the maker of a representation to liability upon a showing that the representation is *likely* to deceive or mislead prospective purchasers to the *likely* commercial detriment of another; proof of actual deception or actual harm is not required. See § 3, Comment *e*. Thus, injunctive relief may be awarded even though the fact or extent of harm to the party seeking relief is uncertain. Such a remedy does not afford a windfall to the plaintiff and furthers the public interest in preserving the integrity of the marketplace. A person seeking monetary relief, however, bears the additional burden of establishing entitlement to such relief under the rules stated in §§ 36 and 37. Those rules generally require proof of actual deception resulting in demonstrable pecuniary loss to the plaintiff or demonstrable pecuniary gain to the defendant.

§ 3   Commercial Detriment of Another

A representation is to the likely commercial detriment of another if:

(a)   the representation is material, in that it is likely to affect the conduct of prospective purchasers; and

(b)   there is a reasonable basis for believing that the representation has caused or is likely to cause a diversion of trade from the other or harm to the other's reputation or good will.

Comment:

b.   Materiality. The materiality of a representation, like its meaning, must be determined from the perspective of the audience to whom it is directed. If a significant number of prospective purchasers are likely to attach importance to the representation in determining whether to engage in a proposed transaction, the representation is material. It is not necessary that the representation be the sole or predominant factor influencing the conduct of prospective purchasers. Nor is it necessary to demonstrate that purchasers would have acted differently in the absence of the representation. It is sufficient if the representation is likely to influence prospective purchasers to some substantial degree.

The materiality of a representation does not depend upon proof of harm to persons acting in reliance upon it. It is sufficient if the representation is likely to be considered important by prospective purchasers, regardless of whether their reliance causes demonstrable pecuniary harm. It is also unnecessary to prove that the actor foresaw or should have foreseen that the representation would be likely to influence prospective purchasers. Evidence indicating an intent to deceive, however, may justify an inference that the representation is material since a seller will not ordinarily make a fraudulent representation without believing that the representation is likely to influence prospective purchasers.

If a representation is not likely to be relied upon by its audience, it is not a material representation. Unless the circumstances indicate otherwise, however, a court may infer that prospective purchasers are likely to rely on representations that relate to matters that the purchasers ordinarily consider important. In some instances, however, the falsity of the representation will be obvious to prospective purchasers, and there is thus no likelihood of reliance. In other instances, purchasers may be likely to rely on their own investigations or experience rather than on the representations of the seller, and there is again no likelihood of reliance. In these or other circumstances in which reliance is unlikely, the representation is not material.

d.   Puffing. An important application of the principles described in the preceding Comments concerns certain representations by sellers sometimes characterized as "puffing" or "sales talk." The propensity of sellers to exaggerate the advantages of their wares is well known, and to some extent buyers are expected to and do understand that they should discount such claims in evaluating the merits of the proposed bargain. Buyers generally assume, for example, that a seller will make favorable representations concerning the quality of the goods or services offered for sale. Statements of praise in general terms without reference to specific facts are therefore unlikely to affect the conduct of prospective purchasers and are thus not material for purposes of the rule stated in this Section.

A distinction is sometimes drawn between statements in the form of opinion and statements of fact. Although as a general matter purchasers may be less likely to rely on a representation of the seller's opinion, the form of the statement is not controlling. In many circumstances prospective purchasers may reasonably understand a statement of opinion to be more than a mere assertion as to the seller's state of mind. Some representations of opinion may imply the existence of facts that justify the opinion, or at least that there are no facts known to the speaker that are substantially incompatible with the stated opinion. Thus, although consumers may be assumed to make some allowance for the favorable opinions expressed by sellers, they may in some instances rely on an implied representation that the seller knows of no specific facts that make the expressed opinion clearly untenable. In other instances, particularly when the seller is thought to have special knowledge or skill unavailable to the consumer, it may be expected that prospective purchasers will rely directly upon the seller's statement of opinion as to value or quality. The ultimate issue in each case is whether the representation, regardless of form, is likely to affect to some substantial degree the conduct of a significant number of prospective purchasers.

It is sometimes possible, even in instances of obvious hyperbole, to identify specific consumers who have in fact relied on the representation. This Section does not subject the actor to liability, however, unless a significant number of prospective purchasers have or are likely to rely on the representation. If a reasonably prudent purchaser of the goods or services would not rely on the representation, the actor is not subject to liability in the absence of evidence establishing that the representation is nevertheless likely to be relied upon by a significant number of prospective purchasers.

Illustrations:

6. *A*, an automobile manufacturer, states in its advertising that its cars are "the best automobiles made in America." The representation is not material.

7. *A* markets a computer chess game and states in its advertising that the game "is like having a World Champion as your opponent." In the absence of other evidence establishing that the representation is likely to be relied upon by a significant number of prospective purchasers, if the court finds that a reasonably prudent purchaser would not rely upon the representation, the representation is not material.

8. *A* operates a retail jewelry store and represents to prospective customers that the diamonds offered for sale are of "first quality." If a reasonably prudent purchaser, lacking the expertise to judge the quality of diamonds, is likely to rely upon the jeweler's statement, the representation is material.

9. *A* manufactures commemorative plates. In its advertising brochures, *A* states that its plates have all been "good investments." If a reasonably prudent purchaser would interpret *A*'s statement as an assertion that the facts known to *A* are not substantially incompatible with the stated opinion and would be likely to rely upon the statement, the representation is material.

f. Interests protected. If the actor markets goods or services of the same kind as those marketed by the person seeking relief, reliance by prospective purchasers on the actor's misrepresentation is likely to cause harm to the complainant by diverting sales to the actor. If the goods are not of the same kind, the other person may establish a likelihood of harm through evidence indicating that a significant number of consumers are nevertheless likely to substitute purchase of the actor's product for that of its own. Reliance on the misrepresentation is also likely to cause harm to another who, although not in competition with the actor, nevertheless has a direct pecuniary interest in the sale of competing products, such as the owner of a royalty interest measured by the sales of goods that compete with the actor's. The asserted injury, however, must be direct; derivative injury such as harm suffered by a competitor's employees or suppliers is not within the scope of this Section. In deciding whether the complainant's interest is sufficiently direct to justify protection, an important factor is the presence or absence of harm to a less remote party whose self-interest would normally motivate the party to vindicate the public interest by exposing the actor's deceptive representation.

The commercial harm cognizable under this Section is not limited to direct diversions of trade, and an actor may thus be subject to liability to a person with whom it does not compete. (See the similar rules regarding liability for misrepresentations of source and trademark infringement: § 4, Comment *f*; § 21, Comment *b*.) Commercial detriment sufficient to subject an actor to liability may be found in a threat of harm to the business reputation or good will of another. In determining the existence of likely commercial detriment, the dispositive question is whether the party seeking relief has a reasonable interest to be protected against the deceptive marketing of the actor.

Non-profit entities such as charitable, educational, governmental, fraternal, and religious organizations may also experience threatened or actual detriment cognizable under this Section, such as the disruption of economically valuable relations with present or potential donors, members, or customers.

Illustrations:

10. *A* manufactures solid walnut furniture; *B* manufactures walnut veneer furniture. *C* manufactures walnut veneer furniture that it falsely represents to be solid walnut. The representation by *C* is to the likely commercial detriment of both *A* and *B*.

11. *A*, a manufacturer of a depilatory product, falsely represents that a new ingredient in its product has a moisturizing effect on the skin. *B* manufactures lotions sometimes used as moisturizers after the use of depilatories. If a significant number of prospective purchasers acting in reliance on *A*'s representation are likely to refrain from using *B*'s product, the representation by *A* is to the likely commercial detriment of *B*.

12. *A*, an importer, sells sweaters manufactured in Ireland by *B*. *C* sells sweaters made in the United States, falsely representing that they are manufactured in Ireland. The representation by *C* is to the likely commercial detriment of both *A* and *B*.

13. *A* is the exclusive United States distributor of watches made in Switzerland by *B*. *C* sells watches in the United States, falsely representing that they are manufactured by *B*. The representation by *C* is to the likely commercial detriment of both *A* and *B*.

14. *A* and *B* manufacture microwave ovens; *C* publishes a magazine containing information and advice relating to consumer products. *C* publishes an article on microwave ovens that contains a favorable report on *B*'s products. Two years later, *C* publishes another article on the same topic that is highly critical of *B*'s products. *B*, in its advertising, subsequently quotes and attributes the favorable commentary from the first article with no mention of the second article. The representation by *B* is to the likely commercial detriment of both *A* and *C*.

15. *A*, the owner of master recordings featuring *B*, a well-known musician, grants to *C*, a record company, a license to produce tapes and discs embodying the recordings in exchange for royalties based on *C*'s sales. *D*, a competing record company, offers for sale a recording made 10 years earlier by *B*. *D* places a recent photograph of *B* on the cover of its recording in order to suggest that the songs reflect *B*'s current performing style. The representation by *D* is to the likely commercial detriment of *A*, *B*, and *C*.

§ 4 Misrepresentations Relating to Source: Passing Off

One is subject to liability to another under the rule stated in § 2 if, in connection with the marketing of goods or services, the actor makes a representation likely to deceive or mislead prospective purchasers by causing the mistaken belief that the actor's business is the business of the other, or that the actor is the agent, affiliate, or associate of the other, or that the goods or services that the actor markets are produced, sponsored, or approved by the other.

Comment:

d. Intent. Liability for passing off was originally imposed through the common law action for deceit, and thus proof of the actor's fraudulent intent was an essential element of the plaintiff's case. Subsequent developments, however, eroded the emphasis on the actor's subjective state of mind. The requirement of fraud was first discarded in connection with misrepresentations of source accomplished through the infringement of fanciful or arbitrary trademarks. It was later abandoned in cases involving the unauthorized use of other designations that had acquired source significance. See § 9, Comment *d*. State and federal legislation, including § 43(a) of the Lanham Act and the Uniform Deceptive Trade Practices Act, have also dispensed with the necessity of establishing an intent to deceive in connection with misrepresentations of source or other misrepresentations concerning the actor's goods or services. See § 2, Comment *f*. Liability under this Section is determined by an evaluation of the probable consequences of the actor's conduct and does not depend upon the actor's subjective intent.

Although an intent to deceive is not an element of the cause of action under this Section, evidence that the representation was in fact intended to mislead prospective purchasers with respect to the identity of the actor or the source, sponsorship, or approval of the goods or services may justify an inference that deception is likely. When such evidence is adduced, the burden may properly shift to the actor to demonstrate that deception is unlikely despite the attempt to deceive. The subjective intent of the actor is also relevant to an award of monetary relief under the rules stated in §§ 36 and 37.

Illustrations:

1. *A* and *B* are plumbing firms. *A* has a contract to provide plumbing services to the University of Nebraska. *B* falsely represents to prospective customers that it is the firm that does the plumbing work for the University. *B* is subject to liability to *A*.

2. *A*, a cereal company, manufactures by means of a patented process a breakfast cereal that it sells under the generic name "shredded wheat." Upon expiration of the patent, *B* begins to manufacture the same product, which it sells in packages similar in appearance to *A*'s and which prominently display the words "The Original Shredded Wheat." *B* is subject to liability to *A*.

3. *A* designs dresses and sells the designs to dress manufacturers. *B*, a dress manufacturer, *C*, a wholesaler, and *D*, a retailer, sell dresses to their respective customers with the false representation that the dresses were designed by *A*. *B*, *C*, and *D* are subject to liability to *A*.

4. The facts being otherwise as stated in Illustration 3, the evidence establishes that *D* was unaware that the dresses were not in fact designed by *A*. *D* is nevertheless subject to liability to *A*, although the remedy may properly be limited to injunctive relief. See §§ 36 and 37.

5. *A* manufactures baseball gloves. In its advertising, *A* uses without consent a photograph of *B*, a famous baseball player, in a manner that falsely implies that *B* endorses *A*'s product. *A* is subject to liability to *B* under the rule stated in this Section. *A* is also subject to liability to *B* for infringement of *B*'s right of publicity under the rule stated in § 46.

§ 5   Misrepresentations Relating to Source: Reverse Passing Off

One is subject to liability to another under the rule stated in § 2 if, in marketing goods or services manufactured, produced, or supplied by the other, the actor makes a representation likely to deceive or mislead prospective purchasers by causing the mistaken belief that the actor or a third person is the manufacturer, producer, or supplier of the goods or services if the representation is to the likely commercial detriment of the other under the rule stated in § 3.

§ 6 Misrepresentations in Marketing the Goods or Services of Another

One is subject to liability to another under the rule stated in § 2 if, in marketing goods or services of which the other is truthfully identified as the manufacturer, producer, or supplier, the actor makes a representation relating to those goods or services that is likely to deceive or mislead prospective purchasers to the likely commercial detriment of the other under the rule stated in § 3.

Comment:

b.   Types of misrepresentations. There are no technical limitations as to the nature or form of the misrepresentations actionable under this Section. However, the representation must be likely to deceive or mislead prospective purchasers with respect to a matter that relates to goods or services marketed by the actor and truthfully identified as originating from the person seeking relief. It is sufficient if the representation is likely to deceive or mislead a significant portion of its audience. See § 2, Comment *d*. The misrepresentation may be express or implied, and proof of actual deception or of an intention to deceive is not required.

The misrepresentations described in this Section are typically made in an attempt to sell goods that the actor has on hand and are thus generally laudatory rather than derogatory. A seller may assert, for example, that the goods are fresh when in fact they are stale or deteriorated, that they are the manufacturer's latest style or highest quality when in fact they are outdated or seconds, or that they are warranted by the manufacturer in respects that exceed the manufacturer's actual undertaking. If the misrepresentation is derogatory, as is the case in "bait and switch" advertising, the actor may also be subject to liability for product disparagement under the rule stated in Restatement, Second, Torts § 626.

§ 7 Contributory Liability of Printers, Publishers, and Other Suppliers

(1) One who, by supplying materials or rendering services to a third person, directly and substantially assists the third person in making a representation that subjects the third person to liability to another for deceptive marketing under the rules stated in §§ 2–6 is subject to liability to that other for contributory deceptive marketing.

(2) If an actor subject to contributory liability under the rule stated in Subsection (1) acted without knowledge that the actor was assisting the

third person in making a representation likely to deceive or mislead, the actor is subject only to appropriate injunctive relief.

§ 8   Contributory Liability of Manufacturers and Distributors

One who markets goods or services to a third person who further markets the goods or services in a manner that subjects the third person to liability to another for deceptive marketing under the rules stated in §§ 2–6 is subject to liability to that other for contributory deceptive marketing if:

(a) the actor intentionally induces the third person to engage in such conduct; or

(b) the actor fails to take reasonable precautions against the occurrence of the third person's conduct in circumstances in which that conduct can be reasonably anticipated.

Chapter 3.   The Law of Trademarks
Topic 1.   Subject Matter of Trademark Law

§ 9   Definitions of Trademark and Service Mark

A trademark is a word, name, symbol, device, or other designation, or a combination of such designations, that is distinctive of a person's goods or services and that is used in a manner that identifies those goods or services and distinguishes them from the goods or services of others. A service mark is a trademark that is used in connection with services.

Comment:

f. "Trademark"; "Trade name"; "Service mark". The term "trademark" as originally employed at common law described only inherently-distinctive designations such as fanciful or arbitrary marks. The term "trade name" was used to denote other designations such as descriptive terms or personal names that through use had come to identify the goods of a particular seller. During the first half of the 20th century the substantive rules governing the protection of "trademarks" and "trade names" became essentially identical, and the significance of the distinction diminished. Passage of the Lanham Act in 1946 hastened the abandonment of the former terminology. The statutory definition of "trademark" subsumes all designations that are distinctive of the user's goods. The term "trade name" as defined in the Lanham Act denotes the name of a business or other enterprise. See § 12. The Model State Trademark Bill incorporates similar definitions, and modern common law usage now reflects these statutory formulations. The definition of "trademark" adopted in this Section thus includes all designations that identify the source of goods or services. The requirement of distinctiveness as elaborated in § 13 preserves the substantive distinction between inherently-distinctive marks and other potential trademarks.

The Lanham Act and the Model State Trademark Bill limit the term "trademark" to marks used to identify the source of goods. A mark used to identify the source of services is denominated a "service mark." The substantive rules applicable to both types of marks are fundamentally identical, however, and the term "trademark" is generally understood to include marks used in the marketing of either goods or services. The definitions in this Section adopt this convenient usage. The term "service mark" as defined here thus denotes a specific type of trademark.

g.   *Subject matter.* The subject matter of trademark law was initially limited to fanciful or arbitrary words and symbols. This limitation excluded not only descriptive words and symbols, but also other devices that could identify the source of goods, such as the physical appearance of the goods or the appearance of labels, wrappers, containers, or advertising materials that accompany the goods in the marketplace. When such features in fact served to distinguish the goods of a particular producer, they were protected, together with descriptive marks, in an action for unfair competition. As the distinctions between the actions for trademark infringement and unfair competition diminished, the law of trademarks eventually subsumed descriptive designations that had acquired significance as indications of source. Although the protection of product and packaging designs that are indicative of source remains subject to special limitations not applicable to other marks, they too have now been subsumed under the law of trademarks. See §§ 16 and 17.

The definition of "trademark" adopted in this Section does not incorporate any technical limitations on the nature of the subject matter that may qualify for protection. Words remain the most common type of trademark, such as the word FORD used in connection with the sale of automobiles or KODAK used in connection with cameras. Numbers, letters, and slogans are also eligible for protection as trademarks, as are pictures, symbols, characters, sounds, graphic designs, product and packaging features, and other matter capable of identifying and distinguishing the goods or services of the user. See §§ 13 and 14. Limitations on the recognition of trademark rights in "functional" subject matter are considered in § 17. For other public policy limitations, see § 32.

Statutory Note

Every state has enacted legislation providing for the registration and protection of trademarks. All but a few of these statutes are derived from the Model State Trademark Bill drafted by the United States Trademark Association in 1949, as revised in 1964 and 1992. . . .

§ 10   Definition of Collective Mark

A collective mark is a word, name, symbol, device, or other designation, or a combination of such designations, that is distinctive of a cooperative, association, organization, or other collective group and that is used by members of the collective group in a manner that:

(a) identifies the goods or services of members and distinguishes them from the goods or services of nonmembers; or

(b) indicates membership in the collective group.

Comment:

a. Nature of collective marks. A collective mark that is used in connection with the sale of goods or services to indicate that the goods or services originate from a member of the collective group is called a "collective trademark." See Comment *b*. A collective mark that is used to indicate that a person or entity is a member of the collective group is called a "collective membership mark." See Comment *c*. Although collective marks are used by the members of an organization to indicate a connection with the collective group, the organization, by virtue of its control over the use of the mark through its power to determine membership, is ordinarily the owner of the collective mark.

The group or organization to which a collective mark refers may be any group of persons or entities brought together in an organized manner. The sole requirement is that the group functions or exists as a collective body of individual members. The organization may be commercial in nature, such as a business cooperative, trade association, or labor union. It may also be noncommercial, such as a fraternal organization, service club, or other organized social group.

A designation that is used by the collective organization itself to identify goods or services produced or rendered by the organization, as distinguished from its individual members, is not a collective mark under the rule stated in this Section. Such a designation is instead eligible for protection as a trademark under the rule stated in § 9. On the distinction between collective marks and certification marks, see § 11, Comment *a*. Although the characterization of a designation as a trademark, trade name, collective mark, or certification mark is legally significant in connection with registration of the mark under the Lanham Act, rights at common law may exist whenever a designation is used in a manner consistent with any of the various categories of marks protected under the rules in this Chapter.

The general requirements applicable to the protection of trademarks, including the rules relating to distinctiveness (see § 13) and acquisition of rights (see § 18), also apply to collective marks, although application of these criteria must take account of the special function of a collective mark. The principles of law governing trademark infringement are similarly applicable to collective marks. See § 20. On the federal registration of collective marks, see § 4 of the Lanham Act, 15 U.S.C.A. § 1054.

b. Collective trademarks. When a collective mark is used by members to identify their goods or services, the mark indicates source in a manner analogous to a trademark. Such "collective trademarks," however, signify that the goods or services originate with a member of the group rather than with a specific individual. The rationales justifying the protection of trademarks (see § 9, Comment *c*) also apply to the protection of collective trademarks.

Illustrations:

1. A is an unincorporated association consisting of numerous independent bus companies. Members of the association use the designation BYWAYS to indicate to prospective customers that their transportation services are rendered by a member of the association. The designation is a collective trademark under the rule stated in this Section.

2. A is a membership corporation incorporated under the name "Sunshine Inns United." A derives its revenue from dues paid by members who operate motels throughout the United States. A prepares and distributes guidebooks listing the names of motels operated by its members and engages in other advertising and promotional activities. To identify their lodging services as those of a member of A, individual members prominently display the designation SUNSHINE INN at each motel. The designation is a collective trademark under the rule stated in this Section.

c. Collective membership marks. A collective mark may be used by a person to indicate membership in an organization. The mark may be used, for example, on membership cards, plaques, certificates, or jewelry. Trade and professional associations, cooperatives, and labor unions are typical owners of "collective membership marks." Such marks are also employed by noncommercial entities such as fraternal, religious, and educational organizations. Unlike a collective trademark, a mark used as a collective membership mark is not analogous to a trademark in that it does not indicate the source or sponsorship of goods or services. Membership marks do, however, identify members of the organization and distinguish them from nonmembers. The inclusion of such marks within the scope of trademark law affords protection to organizations that do not use their insignia or symbols on goods or services but that wish to prevent unauthorized use by nonmembers. On the infringement of collective membership marks, including issues relating to noncommercial use, see § 20, Comment *e*.

Illustrations:

3. A, a fraternal organization, adopts as a symbol of membership an emblem that consists of a representation of clasped hands together with geometric designs and letters. The emblem is used by members of A on jewelry, certificates, and other items to indicate membership in the organization. The designation is a collective membership mark under the rule stated in this Section.

4. A manufactures aircraft escape equipment including ejection seats and parachutes. A forms a club, called "The Grasshopper Club," consisting of pilots who have successfully utilized A's equipment. The

words GRASSHOPPER CLUB are used on membership cards and pins. The designation is a collective membership mark under the rule stated in this Section.

5.   A is an association of businesses and individuals active in the electronics industry that operates under the name "Electronics Group." Members of the association are given plaques bearing a distinctive design consisting of the letters EG against a background depicting electron orbits in order to indicate their membership in the association. The designation is a collective membership mark under the rule stated in this Section.

§ 11   Definition of Certification Mark

A certification mark is a word, name, symbol, device, or other designation, or a combination of such designations, that is distinctive of goods or services certified by a person but produced and marketed by others and that is used by the others in a manner that certifies regional origin, composition, quality, method of manufacture, or other characteristics of the goods or services.

§ 12   Definition of Trade Name

A trade name is a word, name, symbol, device, or other designation, or a combination of such designations, that is distinctive of a person's business or other enterprise and that is used in a manner that identifies that business or enterprise and distinguishes it from the businesses or enterprises of others.

Comment:

a.   Subject matter. A "trademark" as defined in § 9 identifies and distinguishes goods or services; a "trade name" as defined in this Section identifies and distinguishes businesses or other enterprises. A trade name may be the real name of the entity operating the business, such as a corporate or personal name. It may also be an assumed name under which business is conducted, such as a name adopted by a sole proprietorship or partnership. The only requirement is that the designation identify the business or other enterprise and distinguish it from the businesses or enterprises of others. See Comment *b.*

Before the enactment of the Lanham Act, the term "trade name" was also used to denote descriptive marks and other non-inherently distinctive designations that had through use acquired significance as indications of the source or sponsorship of goods or services. See § 9, Comment *f.* This Section follows the modern usage adopted in the Lanham Act and the Model State Trademark Bill and confines the term "trade name" to designations used to identify businesses or other enterprises.

Trade names are not limited to designations adopted by commercial entities. A designation that identifies an enterprise conducted by a nonprofit organization is also eligible for protection. Thus, names adopted by charitable, educational, governmental, fraternal, and religious organizations are included within the definition in this Section. These organizations have the same interest in protecting their identities and good will as do profit-seeking enterprises. The public interest in preventing consumer confusion is similarly applicable to nonprofit organizations.

b. Infringement of rights. The rationales justifying the protection of trade names are analogous to those underlying the protection of trademarks. The protection of trade names prevents an unfair diversion of trade to an infringer who seeks to appropriate the identity and good will of another. Even if the parties are not direct competitors, such an appropriation threatens the legitimate interests of the business identified by the trade name by putting its reputation at risk. The protection of trade names also encourages investment in quality, service, and other activities that generate good will by insuring the opportunity to recapture the benefits of a favorable reputation. As in the case of trademarks, the protection of trade names also serves as an indirect form of consumer protection.

A designation is protectable as a trade name only if it symbolizes the identity and good will of a particular enterprise. The common law has long required as a condition of protection that the trade name distinguish the business of the user from businesses operated by others. This requirement of distinctiveness is analogous to the rule applicable to trademarks. See § 13. On the requirements for the acquisition of rights in a trade name, see § 18.

The standard of trade name infringement is analogous to that applicable to trademarks, and the provisions of this Chapter relating to infringement expressly encompass trade names. Protection against the use of confusingly similar trade names has been recognized at common law and under § 43(a) of the Lanham Act as well as under state statutes such as the Uniform Deceptive Trade Practices Act (see the Statutory Note following § 2) and the Unfair Trade Practices and Consumer Protection Act (see the Statutory Note following § 1). Rights in a trade name can also be infringed by its unauthorized use as a trademark, just as a trademark can be infringed by unauthorized adoption as a trade name. See § 20.

c. Legislation affecting trade names. Business Corporation Acts typically preclude incorporation under a name that is "deceptively similar" to that of an existing domestic corporation or a foreign corporation authorized to transact business in the state. Such restrictions offer an indirect measure of protection to the first person to incorporate under a particular name by preventing others from incorporating under deceptively similar names. Incorporation under a name, however, does not in itself create substantive rights in the name. Substantive rights in a trade name derive from public use, see § 18, and the right of a corporation to obtain relief against the use of a similar trade name by another is determined under the rules in this

Chapter relating to infringement. Similarly, in permitting incorporation under a particular name, the state does not pass upon the applicant's right to use the name in business. Thus, the fact of incorporation under the name is not a defense if the corporation's use of the name otherwise subjects it to liability for infringement. Because administrative determinations of deceptive similarity for purposes of incorporation cannot take account of the multitude of factors relevant to the likelihood of confusion (see § 21), administrative acceptance of a corporate name is generally entitled to little or no weight in subsequent infringement litigation.

Many states require the registration of assumed or fictitious names under which individuals or commercial entities conduct business. (See the Statutory Note following this Section.) The primary purpose of these statutes is to assist others in identifying the owners of the businesses with whom they deal. In several states these trade name acts forbid the registration of names that are deceptively similar to a previously-registered name, thus providing a degree of administrative protection to the initial registrant. In the absence of a specific statutory grant of substantive rights, however, registration of a trade name does not expand the registrant's right to prevent use of the name by others. Similarly, registration is not a defense to an infringement claim brought against the registrant by another user. Trade name registration statutes in a few states, however, specifically grant the registrant the right to enjoin the use of the name by another, although some expressly preserve rights previously acquired by others at common law. In addition, the antidilution provisions that are part of many state trademark registration acts often extend protection to trade names as well as trademarks. See § 25.

Trade names are not eligible for registration under the Lanham Act. Rights previously established in a trade name, however, can prevent registration by another of a confusingly similar trademark. 15 U.S.C.A. § 1052(d). If a trade name is also used as a trademark, it is on that basis eligible for registration under the Act.

Illustrations:

1.   A is a business incorporated under the name "Lawyer's Title Guaranty Company." Although it uses this name for internal purposes, it conducts all its public business under another name. B, a foreign corporation, begins to conduct business in A's locality under a name that is similar to A's corporate name. Because A's corporate name has not been "used" as a trade name under the rule stated in § 18, A has not acquired rights in the trade name despite incorporation under the name. B is thus not subject to liability for infringement.

2.   A is a domestic corporation incorporated under the name "Indian Oil Company." B is a foreign corporation that has previously used a similar designation as its trade name. In an infringement action brought by B, A's incorporation under the name does not prevent the imposition of injunctive or monetary relief against A if A is otherwise

subject to liability for infringement of B's trade name under the rules stated in this Chapter.

3. A is a charitable organization operating under the name "Cancer Research Institute." A's principal activity is raising funds to support research in the prevention and treatment of cancer. Because of A's extensive activities, the name "Cancer Research Institute" is understood by the public to identify A's organization. B begins to solicit contributions for medical research through an organization that uses the name "Cancer Research Society." If the evidence establishes that B's use of the name is likely to cause prospective contributors to confuse the two organizations, B is subject to liability for infringement of A's trade name under the rules stated in this Chapter.

§ 13 Distinctiveness; Secondary Meaning

A word, name, symbol, device, or other designation, or a combination of such designations, is "distinctive" under the rules stated in §§ 9–12 if:

(a) the designation is "inherently distinctive," in that, because of the nature of the designation and the context in which it is used, prospective purchasers are likely to perceive it as a designation that, in the case of a trademark, identifies goods or services produced or sponsored by a particular person, whether known or anonymous, or in the case of a trade name, identifies the business or other enterprise of a particular person, whether known or anonymous, or in the case of a collective mark, identifies members of the collective group or goods or services produced or sponsored by members, or in the case of a certification mark, identifies the certified goods or services; or

(b) the designation, although not "inherently distinctive," has become distinctive, in that, as a result of its use, prospective purchasers have come to perceive it as a designation that identifies goods, services, businesses, or members in the manner described in Subsection (a). Such acquired distinctiveness is commonly referred to as "secondary meaning."

Comment:

a. Requirement of distinctiveness. Under the rules stated in §§ 9–12, a designation is protectable as a trademark, trade name, collective mark, or certification mark only if the designation is "distinctive." This Section states the criteria governing that requirement. On the distinctiveness of descriptive, geographic, and personal name designations, see § 14. On generic designations, see § 15.

A designation is distinctive only if it functions as a symbol of identification. To be eligible for protection as a trademark or trade name, the designation must identify the goods, services, or business of the person asserting rights in the designation. See § 9, Comment *f*; § 12, Comment *b*. Collective marks must identify the members of the collective group or the goods or services of members, and certification marks must identify the certified goods or services. See § 10, Comment *a*; § 11, Comment *b*.

The person claiming rights in a mark or name bears the burden of proving that the designation is inherently distinctive or that it has become distinctive by acquiring secondary meaning. A trademark registration on the principal register of the Lanham Act is prima facie evidence of the validity of the registered mark. 15 U.S.C.A. §§ 1057(b), 1115(a). This has been interpreted as creating a rebuttable presumption of either inherent distinctiveness or secondary meaning, depending upon the basis of the registration. If the registration has become "incontestable" under the provisions of 15 U.S.C.A. § 1065 applicable to marks in continuous use for five years subsequent to registration, the presumption is conclusive and the mark cannot be challenged as a descriptive designation lacking secondary meaning. See 15 U.S.C.A. § 1115.

b. Inherently distinctive designations. Certain designations by their nature are likely to be perceived by prospective purchasers as symbols of identification that indicate an association with a particular source. These designations are "inherently distinctive." A word with no existing meaning coined to identify the products of a particular manufacturer, for example, is inherently distinctive because its lack of lexicographic significance makes it likely that the designation will be perceived as a symbol of identification. See Comment *c*. If the recognition of trademark rights in a particular designation is likely to diminish the ability of other sellers to communicate information about their own goods or services or is otherwise likely to undermine a legitimate interest in unrestricted access to the designation, it will not ordinarily be considered inherently distinctive.

Inherently distinctive designations are eligible for protection immediately upon use. See § 18. They are also eligible for registration under state and federal trademark statutes without further evidence of distinctiveness.

c. Fanciful, arbitrary, and suggestive terms. Fanciful terms that are coined by a user to identify itself or its goods or services are inherently distinctive. Because a fanciful term has no meaning other than as an identifying symbol, prospective purchasers can be expected to view it as an indication of source or other association with a particular user. In addition, the recognition of trademark rights in fanciful terms does not diminish the vocabulary available to other sellers of similar products.

A designation that consists of an existing word whose lexicographic meaning has no apparent application to the particular product or business with which it is used, such as SHELL used in connection with petroleum products, is also inherently distinctive. Prospective purchasers are likely to perceive such "arbitrary" designations as symbols of identification.

Restrictions on the use of arbitrary designations are also unlikely to hinder communication by competitors.

Both the likely reaction of prospective purchasers and the potential impact on other sellers are less certain when the ordinary lexicographic meaning of a designation is relevant to the specific goods, services, or business to which it is applied. If the ordinary meaning of the word only indirectly or tangentially applies to the product or business, consumers remain likely to place primary emphasis on its identifying rather than its lexicographic significance. Restrictions on the use of terms that are only marginally related to the goods, service, or business with which they are used are also unlikely to interfere with the ability of other sellers to convey information about competing products. Thus, words that are merely suggestive of the nature or characteristics of the product or business are also considered inherently distinctive and eligible for protection without additional proof of distinctiveness. As the designation becomes more clearly descriptive of the goods, service, or business, however, it is more likely to be perceived by consumers in its ordinary lexicographic sense rather than as a symbol of identification. Recognition of trademark rights in descriptive terms also presents a more substantial threat to the legitimate interests of competitors in accurately and prominently describing their own products or business. Thus, if the designation is not merely suggestive but actually describes the nature or characteristics of the product or business of the user, the recognition of trademark rights requires proof of actual distinctiveness under the rule stated in Subsection (b). The distinction between "suggestive" and "descriptive" terms is considered in § 14, Comment *b*.

Illustrations:

1. A, a manufacturer of steel girders, prominently places the coined word TRAQ on its goods as an indication of source. The designation is a fanciful term that is inherently distinctive.

2. The facts being otherwise as stated in Illustration 1, A instead places the word LION on its girders. The designation is an arbitrary term that is inherently distinctive.

3. The facts again being otherwise as stated in Illustration 1, A instead places the word HERCULES on its girders. The designation is a suggestive term that is inherently distinctive.

4. The facts again being otherwise as stated in Illustration 1, A instead places the word RIGID on its girders. The designation is a descriptive term that is not inherently distinctive. See § 14.

d. Symbols, graphic designs, and colors. Symbols and graphic designs are eligible for protection as trademarks under the same principles applicable to other designations. Inherently distinctive symbols and graphic designs are protectable as trademarks under the rule stated in Subsection (a); other symbols and graphic designs are protectable only if the user establishes that the designation has become distinctive of its goods or services under the rule stated in Subsection (b).

A symbol or graphic design is not inherently distinctive unless the nature of the designation and the manner of its use make it likely that prospective purchasers will perceive the designation as an indication of source. Commonplace symbols and designs are not inherently distinctive since their appearance on numerous products makes it unlikely that consumers will view them as distinctive of the goods or services of a particular seller. Thus, unless the symbol or design is striking, unusual, or otherwise likely to differentiate the products of a particular producer, the designation is not inherently distinctive. Recognition of exclusive rights in symbols or designs that are inherently distinctive is also unlikely to inhibit the legitimate activities of competitors.

The manner in which a symbol or design is used also is relevant to the likelihood that it will be perceived as an indication of source. In some instances a design is likely to be viewed as mere ornamentation rather than as a symbol of identification. Colored stripes on socks, for example, or a floral design on cookware may be seen merely as ornamental features of the product and not as the trademark of a particular manufacturer. Similarly, a series of white concentric rings applied to automobile tires might be seen merely as a pleasing variation of the standard white-wall tire. Protection is available in such cases only upon proof that, in addition to its ornamental significance, the design has acquired secondary meaning as an indication of source.

A background design used in connection with other trademarks can be protected as a separate mark only if the design functions independently as a trademark. Thus, unless the design creates a separate and distinctive impression on prospective purchasers, it will not be recognized as an independent trademark.

Color can be protected as an element of a trademark when used as part of a design, pattern, or combination of colors that as a whole is inherently distinctive or has acquired secondary meaning. Thus, a seller may acquire trademark rights in a yellow octagonal design placed on shoe soles or in a particular combination of colors used on a toy puzzle. Some cases have also recognized trademark rights in a product's color per se.

On the application of the doctrine of functionality to graphic designs and colors, see § 17, Comment *c*. On the protection of distinctive packaging and product features, see § 16.

e.   Secondary meaning. A designation that is not inherently distinctive, such as a word that describes the nature of the product on which it appears, nevertheless may become, as a result of its use by a specific person, uniquely associated with that person's goods, services, or business. Such acquired distinctiveness is called "secondary meaning." Secondary meaning does not connote a subordinate or rare meaning. It refers instead to a subsequent significance added to the original meaning of the term. Secondary meaning exists only if a significant number of prospective purchasers understand the term, when used in connection with a particular kind of good, service, or business, not merely in its lexicographic sense, but also as an indication of association with a particular, even if anonymous, entity. The concept of secondary meaning is also applicable to designations such as graphic designs, symbols, packaging features, and product designs. In these contexts secondary meaning denotes that the feature, although not inherently distinctive, has come through use to be uniquely associated with a particular source. A designation that has acquired secondary meaning thus distinguishes the goods, services, or business of one person from those of others.

When a designation has become distinctive through the acquisition of secondary meaning, it is protected under the same principles applicable to inherently distinctive designations. Protection extends, however, only to the secondary meaning that has attached to the designation. The trademark owner acquires no exclusive right to the use of the term in its original, lexicographic sense. See § 28. On secondary meaning as it relates to the "strength" of a mark and hence to its scope of protection, see § 21, Comment *i*.

The doctrine of secondary meaning is applicable both at common law and under the various state and federal trademark registration statutes. A designation that is not inherently distinctive is registrable under the Lanham Act and under the Model State Trademark Bill only if it "has become distinctive" of the applicant's goods or services. The doctrine is also applicable to actions for the infringement of unregistered designations under § 43(a) of the Lanham Act.

The existence of secondary meaning is a question of fact, with the burden of proof on the person claiming rights in the designation. See Comment *a*. The sufficiency of the evidence offered to prove secondary meaning should be evaluated in light of the nature of the designation. Highly descriptive terms, for example, are less likely to be perceived as trademarks and more likely to be useful to competing sellers than are less descriptive terms. More substantial evidence of secondary meaning thus will ordinarily be required to establish their distinctiveness. Indeed, some designations may be incapable of acquiring distinctiveness. See § 15. Personal names, on the other hand, although subject to the requirement of secondary meaning (see § 14, Comment *e*), are frequently adopted as trademarks and readily recognized as such by consumers. Their prima facie lack of distinctiveness may thus be overcome more easily than in the case of descriptive terms.

Secondary meaning may be established by either direct or circumstantial evidence. Testimony from individual consumers is clearly relevant to the existence of secondary meaning, but the lack of a representative sample of consumers often undermines its probative value. Surveys of prospective purchasers, if properly formulated and conducted, can be particularly persuasive. Proof of actual consumer confusion caused by another's use of the designation is also evidence of secondary meaning, since if the designation is not distinctive, use by another will not result in confusion.

The required association between the designation and the user may also be established by circumstantial evidence. Secondary meaning may be inferred, for example, from evidence relating to the nature and extent of the public exposure achieved by the designation. Thus, evidence of the volume of sales made under the designation is relevant, particularly for designations such as personal names and marginally descriptive terms that are more likely to be perceived as trademarks than more clearly descriptive designations or ornamental designs. The length of time the designation has been in use is also relevant. Although secondary meaning may sometimes be inferred from evidence of long and continuous use, no particular length of use is required. In some cases distinctiveness is not acquired even after an extended period of time; in others it may be acquired soon after adoption. Section 2(f) of the Lanham Act, 15 U.S.C.A. § 1052(f), permits but does not require the Patent and Trademark Office to accept as prima facie evidence of distinctiveness proof of "substantially exclusive and continuous use" for five years. Advertising and other promotional efforts resulting in increased public exposure for the designation may also support an inference of secondary meaning. It is the likely effect rather than the effort invested in such activities, however, that is determinative, and the expenditure of substantial sums in advertising does not in itself create protectable rights. Advertisements that emphasize the source significance of the designation through prominent use of the term or symbol or that invite consumers to "look for" the designation when selecting goods, for example, are more likely to generate secondary meaning than are more descriptive advertising uses.

The physical manner in which the designation is used with the goods, services, or business can also affect the likelihood that the designation will acquire secondary meaning. A designation that is relatively inconspicuous or that is used only in conjunction with other trademarks may be less likely to acquire secondary meaning than a more prominently displayed designation. Similarly, prominent use of a designation in the manner typical of a trade name, such as its appearance on signs or correspondence, can emphasize its association with the particular business more clearly than less conspicuous uses.

Concurrent use of a term by competitors is relevant as tending to negate the existence of secondary meaning. If the term has been used in a descriptive sense or as part of a trademark or trade name by numerous sellers in the market, it is unlikely to become associated exclusively with a single producer.

The significance of the designation to prospective purchasers may also be demonstrated by the nature of its use in newspapers, popular magazines, or dictionaries, at least when the product is marketed to the general public. The significance of the term to professionals in the trade such as dealers or retailers is also relevant, although it may not be accorded substantial weight if the goods or services are marketed primarily to nonprofessionals.

Proof that a competing seller has intentionally copied a designation previously used by another is often accepted as evidence of secondary meaning on the theory that the copying was motivated by a desire to benefit from confusion with the prior user. The strength of the inference may be diminished, however, by other credible motives for the copying. Thus, if the designation is plainly descriptive and equally applicable to the products of both sellers, or consists of a feature that is functional (see § 17) or that otherwise enhances the value of the product for reasons unrelated to any alleged source significance, evidence of intentional copying may carry little weight on the issue of secondary meaning. See also § 22.

A person attempting to prove the existence of secondary meaning is not required to establish that the designation is recognized as distinctive by all prospective purchasers in the relevant market, nor even by a majority of them. It is sufficient if the designation is distinctive to a significant number of prospective purchasers, taking into account the interest of the user in preventing a misappropriation of its good will, the harm to consumers from potential confusion, and the interest in permitting access to the particular designation by competing sellers.

On the geographic scope of secondary meaning as it relates to issues of priority and infringement, see § 19, Comment b; § 21, Comment l.

Illustration:

5. The facts being otherwise as stated in Illustration 4, the evidence establishes that as a result of A's use of the designation prospective purchasers have come to perceive the term RIGID when displayed on steel girders as a designation that identifies girders manufactured by A. The designation has become distinctive through the acquisition of secondary meaning.

§ 14 Descriptive, Geographic, and Personal Name Designations

A designation that is likely to be perceived by prospective purchasers as merely descriptive of the nature, qualities, or other characteristics of the goods, services, or business with which it is used, or as merely geographically descriptive of their origin or location, or as the personal name of a person connected with the goods, services, or business, is not inherently distinctive under the rule stated in § 13(a). Such a designation is distinctive only if it has acquired secondary meaning under the rule stated in § 13(b).

Comment:

a. Descriptive terms. A person cannot, by mere adoption and use, obtain exclusive rights in words that describe the attributes of the goods, services, or business to which the words are applied. Prospective purchasers are likely to understand such words in their descriptive sense rather than as indications of source. Appropriation of descriptive words can also limit the ability of other sellers to emphasize the characteristics of their own goods, services, or business by restricting the manner in which the descriptive term can be used. Over time, however, the descriptive meaning of a word may become subordinate and the word may become instead primarily a symbol of identification. The threat of confusion or deception resulting from the use of the word by others will then ordinarily outweigh the costs of restricted access, particularly in light of the right of competitors to make "fair use" of the word in its original descriptive sense. See § 28. Protection for descriptive designations is therefore available upon proof that the designation has become distinctive of the goods, services, or business of the user under the rule stated in § 13(b). On the proof of such "secondary meaning," see § 13, Comment *e*.

In general, if a word directly conveys information about the product or business with which it is used, other than information relating to source or association with a particular entity, the word is "descriptive." Thus, words that describe the characteristics of the goods, services, or business are descriptive. So too are words describing the purpose or function of a product, the effect of its use, or the class of intended purchasers. Indications of size, quantity, or capacity are also descriptive, as are laudatory terms such as "premium" or "superior."

Determinations of descriptiveness must be made with reference to the specific goods, services, or business with which the designation is used. The term TRIM may be descriptive when used in connection with hedge clippers, clothing, or hair styling services but arbitrary when used as a trademark for toothpaste, cement, or brokerage services. Thus, CAR–FRESHNER is descriptive of an auto deodorizer, VISION CENTER of an optical clinic, RICH 'N CHIPS of chocolate-chip cookies, and HOMEMAKERS of housekeeping services. Similarly, slogans adopted by sellers to identify their goods and services may be descriptive of the products to which they relate. The slogan EXTRA STRENGTH PAIN RELIEVER used in connection with the marketing of an analgesic, for example, is descriptive and therefore unprotectable as a trademark absent proof of secondary meaning.

Designations adopted by a seller merely to distinguish the various styles, grades, or models of its goods are also descriptive. Even when the lexicographic meaning of the term is "arbitrary" with respect to the goods, its use to describe a particular style or model of the seller's goods undermines the likelihood that the designation will also serve to indicate source. Thus, unless such designations are used in a manner that also emphasizes their source significance, style and model names such as alphanumeric symbols used to denominate machine parts, terms used to designate the colors of cosmetics, and names indicating the patterns on china are descriptive and hence unprotectable absent proof that they have acquired secondary meaning.

Descriptiveness is determined by the commercial impression created by the mark as a whole. A designation consisting of a combination of elements may be inherently distinctive even if some or all of the individual elements are descriptive. Recognition of rights in the composite will not deprive competitors of access to the descriptive components. The combination of a descriptive word with a distinctive design or picture, for example, may produce a composite that is inherently distinctive. Similarly, the combination of two or more words, each of which is descriptive, may result in a composite that is fanciful, arbitrary, or suggestive.

The misspelling or corruption of an otherwise descriptive word will not ordinarily alter the descriptive character of the designation. In many instances the contrivance will not overcome the ordinary meaning of the term, and prospective purchasers will thus continue to understand the designation in a purely descriptive sense. Indeed, in some instances the alteration may go entirely unnoticed by a significant number of consumers. If the altered form is phonetically equivalent to the original word, its aural significance will also remain merely descriptive. Recognition of exclusive rights in variants and corruptions of descriptive words also imposes a risk of liability on subsequent users of the original words. See § 21, Comment c. Thus, unless the alteration is sufficient to avoid encumbering use of the original word, the variation remains descriptive. If the term FLEXIBLE is descriptive of a particular product, for example, so too is the term FLEXITIZED. Similarly, if the designation STEAM is descriptive, the requirement of secondary meaning cannot be avoided by substituting STEEM. Abbreviations recognized as shorthand forms of descriptive terms are also descriptive.

If the descriptive meaning of a designation is generally unknown in the marketplace, it is likely to be perceived as an indication of source. A word is therefore descriptive only if a significant number of prospective purchasers are likely to understand its descriptive connotations. In many instances dictionary definitions are sufficient to establish descriptiveness, but they are not always conclusive. If the descriptive meaning of a term is obsolete or known only to lexicographers or other select groups, the designation is ordinarily not descriptive. The mark L'ORIGAN is thus not necessarily descriptive of a perfume despite the fact that origan is an aromatic mint.

Similar rules apply to words in a foreign language. If a descriptive foreign word is similar to its English equivalent, prospective purchasers are likely to understand the word in its descriptive sense, and proof of secondary meaning is therefore required to establish trademark rights. Thus, OPTIQUE for eyeglasses and SELECTA as the Spanish equivalent of "select" for beer are descriptive. The same is true for foreign words generally understood by English-speaking consumers, such as BLANC used on white wine. For other foreign words, the test remains whether a significant number of prospective purchasers are likely to understand the word merely in its descriptive sense. The multilingual character of the purchasing public and the increasing exposure to foreign terms on imported goods justify general adherence to the "doctrine of foreign equivalents" under which the descriptiveness of a foreign word is determined according to its English translation. The doctrine applies to words from major foreign languages and to other foreign words used on products marketed to groups familiar with the language from which the word is taken. A word from a little-known or dead language, however, although literally descriptive, will typically be perceived by consumers as fanciful and thus protectable without proof of secondary meaning.

Illustrations:

1.   A, a manufacturer of audio equipment, displays on its products a designation consisting of the words "Stereo–Fidelity" and a stylized depiction of two stereo speakers connected by lines representing sound waves bounded by a hyperbola. The composite mark is inherently distinctive because taken as a whole it is not merely descriptive of the goods.

2.   A markets pasta and meats under the designation SAPORITO, which in Italian means "tasty" or "delicious." Because a significant number of prospective purchasers of the goods are likely to perceive the designation as describing the attributes of the products, the designation is descriptive and thus not distinctive absent proof of secondary meaning.

b.   Suggestive versus descriptive terms. Terms that are descriptive of the nature, qualities, or other characteristics of the goods, services, or business with which they are used were not historically protected as trademarks at common law even if they had acquired secondary meaning. Relief against the unauthorized use of such designations was available only through an action for "unfair competition" rather than through the less onerous action for "trademark infringement" available for inherently distinctive marks. See § 9, Comment *d*. Registration under federal law also was generally unavailable for descriptive marks prior to the enactment of the Lanham Act. Judicial attempts to expand the common law and statutory protection of trademarks eventually resulted in a distinction between terms that are directly descriptive and terms that instead merely suggest some quality or characteristic of the goods, services, or business with which they are used. These "suggestive" marks were not classified as "descriptive" and thus were protected under the same rules applicable to fanciful and arbitrary marks. The distinction retains significance under modern law since unlike descriptive designations, suggestive designations are registrable and protectable without proof of secondary meaning. See § 13, Comment *c*.

The distinction between suggestive and descriptive designations is an aspect of the more general distinction between designations that are treated as inherently distinctive of source and designations for which actual proof of source significance is required. See § 13. The classification of a designation as either suggestive or descriptive thus depends upon both the likelihood that prospective purchasers will perceive it as an indication of source and the potential effect on competitors of its appropriation as a trademark by a particular seller. Both factors are often evaluated indirectly by considering the degree of imagination required to extract from the designation information concerning the nature, qualities, or other characteristics of the product or business. If the lexicographic meaning of the term is only remotely or subtly related to the product or business with which it is used, consumers are unlikely to view the designation as a mere description, and the designation is also unlikely to be needed by other merchants selling similar products. Thus, COPPERTONE is merely suggestive of a tanning lotion, CYCLONE of wire fencing, WRANGLER of jeans, and GOBBLE GOBBLE of turkey meat. Such suggestive terms are considered to be inherently distinctive. If the term is more directly informative, consumers are more likely to perceive it solely in a descriptive sense and it is also more likely to be useful to other sellers marketing similar goods or services. It is also appropriate to consider the extent to which the same or similar terms have been used by others in connection with comparable goods. If the term has been frequently employed by other sellers, an inference of descriptiveness may be justified.

§ 15   Generic Designations

(1) A designation that is understood by prospective purchasers to denominate the general category, type, or class of the goods, services, or business with which it is used is a generic designation. A user cannot acquire rights in a generic designation as a trademark, trade name, collective mark, or certification mark.

(2) If prospective purchasers have come to perceive a trademark, trade name, collective mark, or certification mark primarily as a generic designation for the category, type, or class of the goods, services, or business with which it is used, the designation is no longer eligible for protection as a trademark, trade name, collective mark, or certification mark.

Comment:

a. Rationale. A generic designation is a term that denominates a general type or class of goods, services, or business. Thus, "camera" is a generic designation for a type of good, "computer programming" for a type of service, and "bank" for a type of business. A term that denominates a subcategory of a more general class, such as "light" used with beer or "diet" with cola, is also generic. As in the case of descriptive designations, abbreviations or misspellings that are recognized as shorthand or corrupted forms of generic words retain the character of the original term, and words in foreign languages are generally characterized according to their English translations. See § 14, Comment *a.* Generic designations are not subject to appropriation as trademarks at common law and are ineligible for registration under federal and state trademark registration statutes.

The recognition of trademark rights in generic designations could significantly impede competition in the market for the goods or services denominated by the generic term. Competitors denied access to a term that denominates the goods or services to prospective purchasers would be at a distinct disadvantage in communicating information regarding the nature or characteristics of their product. Consumers would be forced either to expend additional time and money investigating the characteristics of competing goods or to pay a premium price to the seller with trademark rights in the accepted generic term.

The rule stated in this Section prohibits the recognition of exclusive rights in generic designations. See Comment *b*. It also prohibits the continued recognition of rights in formerly distinctive designations that have become generic. See Comment *c*. Thus, use of a generic term will not subject a subsequent user to liability for trademark infringement. However, this Section does not preclude relief under other rules relating to misrepresentations of source or deceptive advertising. See Comment *d*.

   c.   Loss of distinctiveness. The rule precluding protection for generic terms also applies to designations originally perceived as indications of source or sponsorship but that later come to be understood by prospective purchasers as generic. A designation formerly distinctive of the goods or services of a particular seller may lose its significance as a trademark and become instead the generic name applied to a particular product category regardless of source. This loss of distinctiveness occurs most frequently in connection with trademarks used on new categories of goods initially available only from a single source. A designation adopted as a trademark for such a product may become incorporated into the language as the generic name for the product itself. "Aspirin," for example, although initially a fanciful term applied to the product of a single manufacturer, came instead to be understood by prospective purchasers as the generic name for a type of medicine. The principle is applicable, however, to any trademark ultimately adopted by consumers as a generic term. Other designations found to have lost their distinctiveness as indications of source include "cellophane," "escalator," and "thermos." In addition to the loss of common law rights, a registration under the Lanham Act is subject to cancellation if the mark becomes a generic term for the goods or services. If a designation used on several different products becomes a generic name for only one of the products, trademark rights are not lost in connection with its use on the remaining products.

The rule in Subsection (1) prohibiting the acquisition of trademark rights in existing generic terms operates against users who have chosen to adopt as a mark a term that may already be generic. The risk created by such a choice is appropriately borne by the user, and evidence of any significant generic usage is sufficient to preclude the recognition of trademark rights. See Comment *b*. Equity and public policy dictate a more cautious approach in the case of a valid trademark that is alleged to have become a generic term. The public interest in access to generic terms will outweigh the residual good will associated with the designation and its value to consumers as an indication of source only if the designation has acquired substantial generic significance. Under the rule stated in Subsection (2), trademark rights are not lost unless the generic meaning becomes the primary or principal significance of the designation to prospective purchasers. The burden of proof may be properly placed on the person alleging such a loss of distinctiveness. Although the difficulties of quantitative measurement and the possibility of multiple meanings often preclude analysis in terms of percentages, if majority usage is established as a fact, it will generally be determinative of the designation's primary significance.

The fact that a trademark is used by consumers as the name of a product does not necessarily establish that the designation has become generic. In the case of products advertised as unique or otherwise distinguishable from competing goods, it is customary to adopt the trademark as the name for the product itself. Thus, a consumer may state that he drives a FORD, drinks COCA–COLA, or washes laundry with TIDE. Use of a designation to denominate only the product of a specific manufacturer, whether known or anonymous, is not a generic use. A designation is used generically only if it is used to denominate a type of good or service irrespective of source.

Consumers who are aware of the trademark significance of a designation may nevertheless use it on occasion in a purely generic sense. A person who understands the designation DICTAPHONE as the trademark of a particular manufacturer, for example, may nevertheless employ it in a generic sense in casual conversation. It is the use and understanding of the term in the context of purchasing decisions, however, that determines the primary significance of a designation.

A designation challenged as generic will often have significance as a trademark to some prospective purchasers and significance as a generic term to other prospective purchasers. The status of the designation as a trademark is determined by the primary or principal significance in the market as a whole. Although surveys can provide important evidence of the significance of a designation to prospective purchasers, the nature of the relevant factual inquiry creates difficult problems of formulation and interpretation. Survey questions focusing on use of the designation as the name of a product, for example, must be sufficiently sophisticated to distinguish use to denominate only the goods of a specific producer from truly generic usage. Questions emphasizing an association between the designation and a single source must permit a distinction between true trademark significance and the mere association of a generic term with a sole or principal producer of that type of product.

The primary significance of a designation also may be established by indirect evidence of the understanding of prospective purchasers. The manner in which the designation has been used by the person claiming trademark rights, for example, is evidence of the likely significance of the designation to consumers. A pattern of use that emphasizes the source significance of the term may support an inference that the designation has not become generic. Use of the designation with accompanying generic terms or with indications of trademark status such as the prescribed notice of federal registration or the notations "TM" or "brand" is thus evidence of continuing distinctiveness. Consistent use of the term by the claimant to denominate the product itself, however, may support an inference that the public perceives the designation as a generic name for the goods, particularly when the product has no other well-known generic name.

The manner in which the term is used by third persons in publications likely to reflect or influence the understanding of the relevant consumers, such as magazine and newspaper articles or technical journals and texts, also is probative of the current status of the designation. Dictionary entries, although relevant, must be discounted to the extent that they reflect the protective efforts of trademark owners rather than the independent judgment of lexicographers. Substantial policing efforts undertaken to preserve distinctiveness such as infringement actions, letters to the media regarding improper use, and educational advertising are themselves some evidence that the designation retains its source significance.

The effect on competition resulting from the continued recognition of trademark rights in the designation is also relevant in determining genericness, particularly if the primary significance of the designation to prospective purchasers is unclear. If alternative generic designations for the product are well-known to consumers, or if the nature of the product permits a simple investigation of its characteristics, the harm to competition from the recognition of trademark rights in the disputed designation may be relatively minor. The risk of confusion and the threatened loss of good will may then justify continued protection. Even when trademark rights persist, however, others remain free to employ the mark in a non-infringing manner such as use in comparative advertising. See § 20, Illustration 3.

Illustration:

3.   A develops a new toy consisting of a ball containing weights that cause the ball to curve when thrown through the air. A markets the product in packages that prominently display the phrase "WHIZ BALL." When B, a competing toy manufacturer, begins to market a similar product in boxes bearing the words "whiz ball," A commences an action against B for trademark infringement. Surveys introduced by B establish that a majority of prospective purchasers understand the term "whiz ball" to denominate any curving ball regardless of source. A cannot prevent the use of the term by B. Whether A is entitled to other relief is determined by the principles discussed in Comment *d*.

§ 16   Configurations of Packaging and Products: Trade Dress and Product Designs

The design of elements that constitute the appearance or image of goods or services as presented to prospective purchasers, including the design of packaging, labels, containers, displays, decor, or the design of a product, a product feature, or a combination of product features, is eligible for protection as a mark under the rules stated in this Chapter if:

(a) the design is distinctive under the rule stated in § 13; and

(b) the design is not functional under the rule stated in § 17.

Comment:

a.   Scope. The freedom to engage in business and to compete for the patronage of prospective purchasers generally includes, in the absence of a patent or copyright, the freedom to copy the goods and marketing methods of others. However, the freedom to copy is qualified by the law of trademarks to the extent necessary to prevent confusion as to the source or sponsorship of goods or services.

The law of trademarks deals primarily with designations consisting of words or other symbols used to indicate the source of goods or services. However, the manner in which the goods or services are presented to prospective purchasers, or the physical features of the product itself, may also serve as an indication of source. Source significance may attach, for example, to the overall appearance of a product or its packaging, or to some specific element or aspect of that appearance. The appearance then functions as a trademark, distinguishing the goods or services of one seller from those of others.

The term "trade dress" is often used to describe the overall appearance or image of goods or services as offered for sale in the marketplace. "Trade dress" traditionally includes the appearance of labels, wrappers, and containers used in packaging a product as well as displays and other materials used in presenting the product to prospective purchasers. The design features of the product itself are also sometimes included within the meaning of "trade dress," although the substantive rules applicable to the protection of product designs differ in some respects from those applicable to packaging and related subject matter. See Comments *b* and *c*.

Although not originally classified as "trademarks," distinctive packaging and product designs were afforded protection through the common law action for "unfair competition." See § 9, Comment *d*. With the abandonment of the distinction between technical "trademarks" and other indicia of source, the protection of distinctive packaging and product designs has been incorporated into the general law of trademarks. A nonfunctional design feature of a product or its packaging that is identified with a particular source is thus protectable as a trademark under the rules stated in this Chapter. Nonfunctional packaging and product features are eligible for registration as trademarks under the Lanham Act, and unregistered features are protectable under § 43(a) of the Act. The recognition of trademark rights in packaging and product features under state law is discussed in Comment *c*.

The scope of the rights recognized in packaging features and product designs protected under the rule in this Section is determined according to the general principles relating to infringement as stated in § 20. Thus, if another seller markets a product incorporating a protected packaging or product feature in a manner that is likely to cause confusion as to the source of the product, the seller is subject to liability for trademark infringement. Similarly, use of the protected feature by another in advertising or samples can subject the user to liability if the use is likely to confuse prospective purchasers as to the source of the product offered for sale. At least with respect to product designs, however, the public interest in access may in some cases influence the choice of appropriate relief by encouraging consideration of alternatives to an injunction against imitation, such as mandatory labeling or other precautionary measures. See § 35, Comment *d*.

b. Distinctiveness. The freedom to copy product and packaging features is limited by the law of trademarks only when the copying is likely to confuse prospective purchasers as to the source or sponsorship of goods or services. The imitation or even complete duplication of another's product or packaging will not create a risk of confusion unless some aspect of the duplicated appearance is identified with a particular source. Thus, unless a feature is distinctive under the rule stated in § 13, it is ineligible for protection as a trademark. A further restriction that prohibits protection for functional features is discussed in Comment *d* and in § 17. Rigorous application of the requirements of distinctiveness and nonfunctionality is necessary in order to avoid undermining the carefully circumscribed statutory regimes for the protection of useful and ornamental designs under federal patent and copyright law.

Many of the cases adjudicating trademark rights in product and packaging designs recite that proof of secondary meaning is a prerequisite for protection. At least with respect to packaging and related features, however, it is now recognized that trade dress can be inherently distinctive. This Section, through reference to the rules stated in § 13, recognizes both inherent and acquired distinctiveness, thus assimilating trade dress within the general rules applicable to other trademarks. If the trade dress used by a particular seller differs in significant respects from that employed by others, consumers may be expected to utilize the trade dress as an indication of source. The wide range of designs available for labels and packaging generally permits the recognition of exclusive rights without significantly hindering competition. Trade dress that is unique and prominent can thus be inherently distinctive. If the trade dress is descriptive (see § 14), or inconspicuous, or not sufficiently different from that used by others to justify a conclusion of inherent distinctiveness, trademark rights will depend upon proof of distinctiveness through evidence of secondary meaning.

This Section is also applicable to the recognition of trademark rights in the distinctive design features of the goods themselves. As a practical matter, however, it is less common for consumers to recognize the design of a product or product feature as an indication of source. Product designs are more likely to be seen merely as utilitarian or ornamental aspects of the goods. In addition, the competitive interest in copying product designs is more substantial than in the case of packaging, containers, labels, and related subject matter. Product designs are therefore not ordinarily considered inherently distinctive and are thus normally protected only upon proof of secondary meaning.

The methods of proving secondary meaning for words and symbols (see § 13, Comment e) are also applicable to packaging and product designs. Thus, length and exclusivity of use, sales volume, and promotional efforts that focus on the source significance of the design are relevant, as is direct evidence of consumer recognition through surveys or testimony from prospective purchasers. The source significance, however, must attach to the design feature itself, independent of other trademarks that may accompany the product in the marketplace. Evidence that the packaging or product design was intentionally copied by a competitor can support an inference of secondary meaning if the circumstances indicate an intent to benefit from the good will of the prior user through confusion. An inference of secondary meaning may not be justified, however, if the descriptiveness or other inherent value of the design affords an alternative explanation for the copying. See also § 22.

Illustrations:

1.   A manufactures ice cream products. One of A's products is a square, chocolate-covered ice cream bar. Each bar is wrapped in pebbled foil with a silver background featuring a white polar bear and a sunburst design outlined in blue. The trademark KLONDIKE appears below the design. The bars are sold in six-packs consisting of a double layer of three bars wrapped in clear plastic. At the time A adopted the wrapper design, no other manufacturer used a similar design. A court may properly conclude that A's wrapper design is inherently distinctive and protectable as a trademark apart from A's independent rights in the KLONDIKE trademark.

2.   A produces wine that it sells in a glass decanter. Although designed by A, the appearance of the decanter is not sufficiently different from that used by other producers to qualify as inherently distinctive. A offers no evidence that wine consumers identify the decanter design with wine produced by A. Since the decanter design is not distinctive under the rules stated in § 13, the design is not protectable as a trademark.

3.   A manufactures a liquid drain opener. The product is marketed in a unique and eye-catching container formed in the shape of the pipe trap commonly found below household sinks. A court may properly conclude that the container shape is inherently distinctive.

4.   A, a manufacturer of prestige automobiles, has for more than 50 years incorporated into its product a square-framed, vertically-louvered front grill. As a result of long use and extensive publicity, the

appearance of the grill has come to be identified with automobiles manufactured by A. The design of the grill is distinctive under the rules stated in § 13 and it is protectable as a trademark unless it is determined to be functional under the rule stated in § 17.

5.   A has for many years manufactured steel vacuum bottles. The exterior of the cylindrical bottle is made of stainless steel, with an additional encircling ring of steel at the top and bottom. A steel cup lined with black plastic screws onto the upper portion of the bottle. A's trademark appears on both the bottle and the carton in which it is sold. Although the product has been commercially successful, the appearance of the bottle, apart from the accompanying trademark, is not recognized by consumers as an indication of source. Since the design of the bottle is not distinctive under the rules stated in § 13, the design is not protectable as a trademark.

§ 17 Functional Designs

A design is "functional" for purposes of the rule stated in § 16 if the design affords benefits in the manufacturing, marketing, or use of the goods or services with which the design is used, apart from any benefits attributable to the design's significance as an indication of source, that are important to effective competition by others and that are not practically available through the use of alternative designs.

Comment:

a.   Exclusion from trademark protection. The freedom to copy goods and services that have proven successful in the marketplace is fundamental to the operation of a competitive economy. When the public interest in permitting copying is outweighed by the need to insure adequate incentive for investments in innovation, the freedom to copy may be temporarily interrupted by a federal patent or copyright. In other instances the public interest in copying may conflict with the interest in preventing confusion as to the source or sponsorship of goods and services. The rule excluding functional designs from the subject matter of trademark law is an attempt to identify situations in which the public and private interest in avoiding confusion is outweighed by the anticompetitive consequences of trademark protection. Thus, in determining whether a particular design is "functional" and therefore ineligible for protection as a trademark, the ultimate inquiry is whether a prohibition against copying will significantly hinder competition by others.

If a design is functional under the rule stated in this Section, it is ineligible for protection regardless of its inherent or acquired distinctiveness. Competitors thus remain free, in the absence of a patent or copyright, to copy functional designs regardless of any association with a particular source. The public interest in avoiding confusion must then be pursued through requirements relating to labeling and other precautionary measures (see § 16, Comment *d*) rather than through prohibitions against copying.

b. *Functionality.* A packaging or product feature is not functional merely because the feature serves a utilitarian purpose. The recognition of trademark rights is precluded only when the particular design affords benefits that are not practically available through alternative designs. A bottle, for example, is a utilitarian element of the packaging for wine, but the design of a particular wine bottle is not functional under the rule of this Section unless the shape or other aspects of the bottle provide significant benefits that are not practically obtainable through the use of alternative bottle designs.

In general, a functional design is one that is costly to do without. Thus, the benefits afforded by a particular design do not themselves determine whether that design is functional; a design is functional only if those benefits cannot practically be duplicated through the use of other designs. The availability of alternative designs that satisfy the utilitarian requirements or that otherwise afford similar advantages is therefore decisive in determining functionality. If a particular design affords benefits that are superior to those of any practical alternative design, it is functional if the benefits are important to effective competition.

The exclusion of functional designs from the subject matter of trademark law is intended to insure effective competition, not just by the defendant, but also by other existing and potential competitors. Thus, a design may be functional if it is one of a limited number of superior designs. The range of alternative designs sufficient to preclude a finding of functionality depends on the particular facts of each case.

The benefit conferred by a particular packaging or product design may take various forms. The benefit may lie, for example, in greater economy in manufacturing, shipping, or handling, in increased utility or durability, or in enhanced effectiveness or ease of use. (On aesthetic benefits, see Comment *c*.) If the benefit afforded by the design resides solely in its association with a particular source, however, the design is not functional; the extent to which others may use such a design is determined by the rules of this Chapter governing trademark infringement. See § 20.

Any evidence that relates to the advantages inherent in a particular design is relevant to the issue of functionality. Functionality may thus be inferred from evidence of advertising or other promotional efforts by the plaintiff that emphasize the benefits of the design. Benefits claimed in pursuit of a utility patent may be particularly persuasive evidence of functionality. Discussions of the design in textbooks or trade literature and engineering analysis of its utilitarian aspects are also relevant. The fact that other manufacturers familiar with the design have rejected it in favor of other designs is evidence that the design is not functional.

When the matter claimed as a trademark consists of the overall design of a product or its packaging, or the design of a combination or arrangement of features, eligibility for trademark protection is determined by the functionality of the claimed design as a whole. The fact that the overall design or combination contains individual features that are themselves functional does not preclude protection for the composite. The issue is whether trademark protection should be recognized in the particular combination or arrangement of features, and the functionality of the combination or arrangement as a whole is determinative. If the overall shape of a bottle is distinctive and nonfunctional, for example, the shape may be protected as a trademark despite the inclusion of a top that is functionally configured to accept a standard bottle cap. Protection of the overall design, however, will not preclude others from adopting the functional constituents. If the overall design of a product or package is otherwise functional, however, the addition of minor nonfunctional elements will not render the overall design protectable; trademark rights will be limited to only the nonfunctional elements.

A design that is nonfunctional may be protected as a trademark upon proof that it is distinctive under the rule stated in § 13. Possible limitations on the protection of product features under state law are discussed in § 16, Comment *c*.

Illustrations:

1. A manufactures china plates intended for commercial use. The undersides of A's plates have a circular rib located midway between the rim and base of the plate. When the product was first introduced A obtained a now-expired utility patent on the rib design, citing as advantages of the design its ability to reduce breakage by evenly distributing vibrational stress and its contribution to ease of handling by providing a finger hold on the underside of the plate. The rib design is functional under the rule stated in this Section.

2. A manufactures a breakfast cereal consisting of strands of wheat formed into pillow-shaped biscuits. The evidence establishes that the cost of producing the biscuits would increase and their quality would decrease if another form was substituted for the pillow shape. The pillow-shape design is functional under the rule stated in this Section. See § 16, Illustration 6.

3. A, a fishing reel manufacturer, markets a spin-cast reel with a front cover in the shape of a 40–degree cone ending in a fishing-line guide at its narrow front end. The evidence establishes that various shapes can accommodate the utilitarian functions performed by the cover and that numerous other shapes are used by competing manufacturers. In the absence of other evidence relating to the benefits of the cover shape, the design is not functional under the rule stated in this Section, and it is protectable as a trademark if the design is distinctive under the rules stated in § 13.

4. A manufactures chocolate candy in the form of a six-sided bar with sloping ends. The bars are wrapped with an inner layer of silver foil covered by an outer white paper wrapper that leaves a significant portion of the foil visible at both ends of the bar. The packaging retains the shape of the enclosed chocolate bar. The evidence establishes that chocolate bars can be shaped and wrapped in a variety of forms and styles. In the absence of evidence indicating that A's overall design affords benefits not practically available through the use of other designs, the design is not functional under the rule stated in this Section, and it is protectable as a trademark if the design is distinctive under the rules stated in § 13.

c. *"Aesthetic" functionality.* When aesthetic considerations play an important role in the purchasing decisions of prospective consumers, a design feature that substantially contributes to the aesthetic appeal of a product may qualify as "functional." As with utilitarian design features, however, the fact that the design performs a function by contributing to the aesthetic value of the product does not in itself render the design ineligible for protection as a trademark. A manufacturer thus does not forfeit trademark rights simply because prospective purchasers find the design aesthetically pleasing. A design is functional because of its aesthetic value only if it confers a significant benefit that cannot practically be duplicated by the use of alternative designs. Because of the difficulties inherent in evaluating the aesthetic superiority of a particular design, a finding of aesthetic functionality ordinarily will be made only when objective evidence indicates a lack of adequate alternative designs. Such evidence typically is available only when the range of alternative designs is limited either by the nature of the design feature or by the basis of its aesthetic appeal. The ultimate test of aesthetic functionality, as with utilitarian functionality, is whether the recognition of trademark rights would significantly hinder competition.

Illustrations:

5. A manufactures a line of lightweight luggage. Each bag is made of parachute nylon trimmed with matching cotton tape and matching straps of cotton webbing. The bags have zippers with hollow rectangular metal pulls that are similarly color coordinated. Each bag is covered with the repetitive printing of A's logo enclosed in a small ellipse. The background within the ellipse contrasts with the color of the bag. The evidence establishes that although A's bags are aesthetically attractive to prospective purchasers, the number of alternative designs is virtually unlimited. In the absence of evidence establishing that similarly attractive designs are unavailable to competing manufacturers, the overall design of A's luggage is not functional under the rule stated in this Section, and it is protectable as a trademark if the design is distinctive under the rules stated in § 13.

6. A manufactures china. Among the products marketed by A is a set of china bearing a particular floral pattern covering the entire

surface of each plate. Evidence establishes that aesthetic factors play an important role in the purchase of china, that A's design is attractive to a significant number of consumers, and that the number of alternative floral patterns for china is virtually unlimited. In the absence of evidence establishing that similarly attractive patterns are unavailable to competing manufacturers, A's design is not functional under the rule stated in this Section, and it is protectable as a trademark if the design is distinctive under the rules stated in § 13.

7.   The facts being otherwise as stated in Illustration 6, A's design consists solely of the placement of various gemstones around the rim of each plate. Evidence establishes that the rim design is attractive to a significant number of consumers. Because of the limited number of alternative designs available to satisfy the aesthetic desires of these prospective purchasers, a court may properly conclude that the design is functional under the rule stated in this Section.

8.   A is the first seller to market candy intended for Valentine's Day in heart-shaped boxes. Evidence establishes that the shape of the box is an important factor in the appeal of the product to a significant number of consumers. Because there are no alternative designs capable of satisfying the aesthetic desires of these prospective purchasers, the design of the box is functional under the rule stated in this Section.

9.   A manufactures outdoor lighting fixtures intended for mounting on the walls of commercial buildings to illuminate adjacent areas. The evidence establishes that architectural compatibility with the building is an important factor in the purchase of such fixtures and that A's product is considered to be aesthetically compatible with contemporary architecture. The evidence also establishes that only a limited number of designs are considered compatible with the type of buildings on which A's product is used. Because of the limited range of alternative designs available to competitors, a court may properly conclude that the design of the lighting fixture is functional under the rule stated in this Section.

Topic 3.   Infringement of Rights

§ 20   Standard of Infringement

(1) One is subject to liability for infringement of another's trademark, trade name, collective mark, or certification mark if the other's use has priority under the rules stated in § 19 and in identifying the actor's business or in marketing the actor's goods or services the actor uses a designation that causes a likelihood of confusion:

(a) that the actor's business is the business of the other or is associated or otherwise connected with the other; or

(b) that the goods or services marketed by the actor are produced, sponsored, certified, or approved by the other; or

(c) that the goods or services marketed by the other are produced, sponsored, certified, or approved by the actor.

(2) One is also subject to liability for infringement of another's collective membership mark if the other's use has priority under the rules stated in § 19 and the actor uses a designation that causes a likelihood of confusion that the actor is a member of or otherwise associated with the collective group.

§ 21 Proof of Likelihood of Confusion: Market Factors

Whether an actor's use of a designation causes a likelihood of confusion with the use of a trademark, trade name, collective mark, or certification mark by another under the rule stated in § 20 is determined by a consideration of all the circumstances involved in the marketing of the respective goods or services or in the operation of the respective businesses. In making that determination the following market factors, among others, may be important:

(a) the degree of similarity between the respective designations, including a comparison of

(i) the overall impression created by the designations as they are used in marketing the respective goods or services or in identifying the respective businesses;

(ii) the pronunciation of the designations;

(iii) the translation of any foreign words contained in the designations;

(iv) the verbal translation of any pictures, illustrations, or designs contained in the designations;

(v) the suggestions, connotations, or meanings of the designations;

(b) the degree of similarity in the marketing methods and channels of distribution used for the respective goods or services;

(c) the characteristics of the prospective purchasers of the goods or services and the degree of care they are likely to exercise in making purchasing decisions;

(d) the degree of distinctiveness of the other's designation;

(e) when the goods, services, or business of the actor differ in kind from those of the other, the likelihood that the actor's prospective purchasers would expect a person in the position of the other to expand its marketing or sponsorship into the product, service, or business market of the actor;

(f)   when the actor and the other sell their goods or services or carry on their businesses in different geographic markets, the extent to which the other's designation is identified with the other in the geographic market of the actor.

§ 22   Proof of Likelihood of Confusion: Intent of the Actor

(1)   A likelihood of confusion may be inferred from proof that the actor used a designation resembling another's trademark, trade name, collective mark, or certification mark with the intent to cause confusion or to deceive.

(2)   A likelihood of confusion should not be inferred from proof that the actor intentionally copied the other's designation if the actor acted in good faith under circumstances that do not otherwise indicate an intent to cause confusion or to deceive.

Comment:

a.   Scope. This Section describes the role of the actor's intent in determining whether the use of a designation creates a likelihood of confusion under the rule stated in § 20. The intent of the actor may also be relevant in determining priority, see § 19, and in fashioning appropriate relief, see §§ 35–37.

b.   Relation to other factors. Use of a designation that is likely to cause confusion with another's trademark, trade name, collective mark, or certification mark is an infringement regardless of whether the actor knows of the other's prior use or intends to confuse prospective purchasers. Thus, proof of an intent to deceive is not required in order to subject the actor to liability. However, in deciding whether a use is likely to cause confusion, the intent of the subsequent user is widely regarded as relevant and is often included in the enumeration of factors that determine the likelihood of confusion. Intent differs, however, from the factors listed in § 21, which relate to the market context in which the designations are used. The similarity of the competing marks, the methods by which the goods or services are marketed, the distinctiveness of the prior user's mark, the care likely to be exercised by purchasers, and the relationship of the parties' goods or services all contribute to the manner in which the subsequent user's mark is likely to be perceived by prospective purchasers. The subsequent user's intent, on the other hand, does not itself affect the impression created by the use of the designation since the user's intent is generally unknown to prospective purchasers.

c.   Intent as proof of likelihood of confusion. Although the actor's intent does not affect the perceptions of prospective purchasers, it may be appropriate to assume that an actor who intends to cause confusion will be successful in doing so. Proof of an intent to confuse may thus create an inference that confusion is likely, although the inference can be overcome by other evidence indicating that, notwithstanding such an intent, consumers are unlikely to be widow confused.

It is the intent to cause confusion or to deceive that may justify an inference that confusion is likely. Proof that the actor adopted a similar designation with knowledge of the other's prior use, or even that the actor intentionally copied all or part of the other's designation, is not necessarily sufficient to establish an intent to confuse. For example, if the actor reasonably believes that the other's designation is functional or that the actor's use is on goods sufficiently unrelated to the other's goods that confusion is unlikely, proof that the actor intentionally copied the other's designation does not justify an inference of confusion. Copying another's trademark for the purpose of parody or for use as ornamentation on goods such as clothing or jewelry also does not in itself support an inference that confusion is likely. The issue in such cases is whether the actor's use in fact creates a likelihood of confusion, and resolution of that issue is not affected by the existence of intentional copying. On the other hand, if there is proof of intentional copying with no alternative explanation, an intent to benefit from the other's good will through confusion may be inferred.

Even if an actor believes in good faith that the copying of another's designation is justified, an inference that confusion is likely may arise from other circumstances that suggest an intent to confuse, such as a failure to take reasonable steps to minimize the risk of confusion. For example, although the actor may reasonably believe that the copied element is functional and therefore unprotectable, an intent to confuse may be inferred if the actor fails to label or otherwise distinguish its goods or services from those of the other. See § 16, Comment *d*. What steps are reasonable will depend upon the circumstances of each case, and there may be situations in which no reasonable precautions against confusion are available. The issue is whether the actor's failure to take precautions fairly demonstrates an intent to confuse.

Illustrations:

1. A sells lawn chemicals using a distinctive trade dress consisting of bottles with labels that prominently display a particular pattern of red and yellow stripes. B, knowing of A's prior use, begins to sell similar products in bottles with labels bearing the same pattern and colors but with a different brand name. There is evidence that B instructed its marketing staff to "get as close to A's label as the law allows." In the absence of any alternative explanation for the copying of A's distinctive trade dress, a likelihood of confusion may be inferred.

2. A, a credit card company, has acquired trademark rights in the overall appearance of its credit card. As a parody of A's slogan, "Don't leave home without it," B manufacturers and sells packages of condoms that closely resemble A's credit card. The intentional copying by B does

not necessarily indicate an intent to confuse and thus does not justify an inference that confusion is likely.

3.   A uses a printed advertisement for its plumbing service that includes a map of the city divided into service areas in order to assist consumers in locating the service center nearest to their home or business. The advertisement has become distinctive of A's business under the rule stated in § 13. B begins to use an advertisement for its competing business that includes a map copied from A's advertisement. If B in good faith believed that the map is functional under the rule stated in § 17, B's intentional copying does not justify an inference that confusion is likely unless B has failed to take reasonable steps to minimize the risk of confusion.

§ 23   Proof of Likelihood of Confusion: Evidence of Actual Confusion

(1) A likelihood of confusion may be inferred from proof of actual confusion.

(2) An absence of likelihood of confusion may be inferred from the absence of proof of actual confusion if the actor and the other have made significant use of their respective designations in the same geographic market for a substantial period of time, and any resulting confusion would ordinarily be manifested by probable facts.

§ 25   Liability Without Proof of Confusion: Dilution and Tarnishment

(1) One may be subject to liability under the law of trademarks for the use of a designation that resembles the trademark, trade name, collective mark, or certification mark of another without proof of a likelihood of confusion only under an applicable antidilution statute. An actor is subject to liability under an antidilution statute if the actor uses such a designation in a manner that is likely to associate the other's mark with the goods, services, or business of the actor and:

(a) the other's mark is highly distinctive and the association of the mark with the actor's goods, services, or business is likely to cause a reduction in that distinctiveness; or

(b) the association of the other's mark with the actor's goods, services, or business, or the nature of the actor's use, is likely to disparage the other's goods, services, or business or tarnish the images associated with the other's mark.

(2) One who uses a designation that resembles the trademark, trade name, collective mark, or certification mark of another, not in a manner that is likely to associate the other's mark with the goods, services, or business of the actor, but rather to comment on, criticize, ridicule, parody,

or disparage the other or the other's goods, services, business, or mark, is subject to liability without proof of a likelihood of confusion only if the actor's conduct meets the requirements of a cause of action for defamation, invasion of privacy, or injurious falsehood.

Comment:

c. Interests protected. The antidilution statutes have been invoked against two distinct threats to the interests of a trademark owner. First, a mark may be so highly distinctive and so well advertised that it acts as a powerful selling tool. Such a mark may evoke among prospective purchasers a positive response that is associated exclusively with the goods or services of the trademark owner. To the extent that others use the trademark to identify different goods, services, or businesses, a dissonance occurs that blurs this stimulant effect of the mark. The antidilution statutes protect against this dilution of the distinctiveness and selling power of the mark.

The selling power of a trademark also can be undermined by a use of the mark with goods or services such as illicit drugs or pornography that "tarnish" the mark's image through inherently negative or unsavory associations, or with goods or services that produce a negative response when linked in the minds of prospective purchasers with the goods or services of the prior user, such as the use on insecticide of a trademark similar to one previously used by another on food products.

Tarnishment and dilution of distinctiveness, although conceptually distinct, both undermine the selling power of a mark, the latter by disturbing the conditioned association of the mark with the prior user and the former by displacing positive with negative associations. Thus, tarnishment and dilution of distinctiveness reduce the value of the mark to the trademark owner.

The rule stated in this Section distinguishes between those cases in which the actor uses another's designation to identify the actor's own goods or services and those cases in which the actor uses the other's designation in some other manner. The protection accorded by the law of trademarks is limited to the exploitation of a designation as an identifying symbol. Although the antidilution statutes extend protection to certain nonconfusing uses, they remain part of the general law of trademarks and should be applicable only to disputes involving the concurrent use of similar designations to identify goods, services, or businesses. Subsection (1) states the rules applicable to cases within the scope of the antidilution statutes. Subsection (2) states the rule applicable to cases in which the value of a trademark is undermined by a use other than as an identifying symbol for the actor's own goods, services, or business.

d. Designations protected. The antidilution statutes are applicable to both registered or unregistered marks. Although most of the case law involves word marks, the statutes are also generally applicable to slogans, trade dress, and other symbols that qualify for protection as a trademark.

However, the protection of product designs from non-confusing use by others raises special problems in light of the preemptive effect of federal copyright and patent law. Courts have sometimes justified trademark protection for product designs on the rationale that trademark law protects only against confusion and does not create a property interest that competes or interferes with the rights conferred by copyright or patent. See § 16, Comment *c*. Application of the antidilution statutes to prohibit the use of another's product design without proof of a likelihood of confusion may thus be preempted, but a definitive statement of the law is not possible from the existing cases.

Topic 4.   Defenses and Limitations on Relief

§ 28   Descriptive Use (Fair Use)

In an action for infringement of a trademark, trade name, collective mark, or certification mark, it is a defense that the term used by the actor is descriptive or geographically descriptive of the actor's goods, services, or business, or is the personal name of the actor or a person connected with the actor, and the actor has used the term fairly and in good faith solely to describe the actor's goods, services, or business or to indicate a connection with the named person.

Comment:

a.   Extent of rights in descriptive terms. Section 14 recognizes trademark rights in descriptive and geographically descriptive terms upon proof that the designation has acquired secondary meaning as a symbol of identification. Trademark rights, however, extend only to the source significance that has been acquired by such terms, not to their original descriptive meanings. The owner of a trademark thus cannot deprive others of the use of the term in its original descriptive sense. Reasonable use of a descriptive term by another solely to describe the nature or characteristics of its own goods or services will not subject the user to liability for infringement. An analogous rule is applicable to personal name designations. A subsequent user is not subject to liability if the name is used solely to indicate truthfully the named person's connection with the goods, services, or business.

The defense recognized in this Section is commonly referred to as the "fair use" defense. However, the defense does not represent a general right of reasonable use of another's trademark equivalent to the fair use defense recognized under the law of copyright. See 17 U.S.C.A. § 107. The defense of fair use under the law of trademarks is limited to use of the original descriptive or personal name significance of a term. This limitation on the scope of the fair use doctrine is sometimes described by stating that the doctrine applies only to use "otherwise than as a trademark," or only to "nontrademark use" of another's mark. When the defendant uses a descriptive term that is another's trademark as an element of a trademark for the defendant's own goods or services, the courts generally decline to recognize a fair use defense. In such cases the appropriate balance between the defendant's interest in access to the original lexicographic meaning of the term and the plaintiff's interest in protection against confusion is ordinarily pursued through the application of the likelihood of confusion standard. See § 20. Descriptive trademarks are accorded a narrower scope of protection under the likelihood of confusion analysis than are arbitrary marks, see id., Comment *g*; § 21, Comments *c* and *i*, and the remedies available for infringement of descriptive marks may be similarly limited. See § 35, Comment *d*. However, in some cases it may be difficult to distinguish use as an element of a trademark from a nontrademark use. Thus, there is not always a clear distinction between cases appropriately analyzed under the rule stated in this Section and cases more properly analyzed under the general standard of likelihood of confusion as stated in § 20.

The fair use defense has been recognized with respect to both registered and unregistered trademarks. Section 33(b)(4) of the Lanham Act recognizes as a defense that the name or term is used, not as a trademark, but "fairly and in good faith only to describe" the user's goods or services. 15 U.S.C.A. § 1115(b)(4). The defense has also been recognized at common law and under § 43(a) of the Lanham Act.

Use of another's trademark for the purpose of identifying goods or services that originate from the owner of the trademark is subject to the rules stated in § 24 rather than to the rules stated here. Similarly, use of another's trademark solely as a means of referring to the trademark owner or to the owner's products or business is not within the scope of this Section. See § 20, Comment *b*; § 25, Comment *i*.

b. Relation to likelihood of confusion. Use of another's trademark subjects the user to liability under § 20 only if the use is likely to cause confusion. In the case of a descriptive trademark, the likelihood of confusion will depend in part on whether prospective purchasers are likely to understand the defendant's use of the term as a mere description of the defendant's goods, services, or business rather than as an indication of source or sponsorship. In some cases the manner of the defendant's use may thus justify an inference that confusion is unlikely. Unless this inference is overcome by other evidence, the defendant is not subject to liability—a result sometimes ascribed to the fair use defense. In such cases, however, fair use is a "defense" only in the sense that evidence relating to the manner of use can rebut a necessary element of the plaintiff's case. The burden of proving likelihood of confusion remains on the trademark owner and application of the rule stated here is unnecessary.

The fair use defense recognized in this Section can be applicable even if the trademark owner presents evidence sufficient to prove a likelihood of confusion. If the manner of use by the defendant is reasonable in light of the commercial justification for the use, the possibility or even certainty that some prospective purchasers will perceive the term as an indication of source despite the reasonableness of the defendant's use is not sufficient to deprive the defendant of the right to employ the term in its descriptive sense. Thus, a defendant who uses a descriptive term fairly and in good faith to describe its goods or services is not liable for infringement even if some residual confusion is likely. However, the strength of the plaintiff's mark and the extent of likely or actual confusion are important factors in determining whether a use is fair. Surveys and other evidence relating to the perceptions of prospective purchasers are thus relevant to the application of the defense, and a use that is likely to create substantial confusion will not ordinarily be considered a fair use. The defendant bears the burden of establishing the defense of fair use under this Section.

c. Manner of use. Fair use is a reasonable and good faith use of a descriptive term that is another's trademark to describe rather than to identify the user's goods, services, or business. Use of a descriptive term in textual commentary or instructions, for example, may be unlikely as a practical matter to create a likelihood of confusion, but in any event it is ordinarily a fair use. More prominent use of a descriptive term can also qualify as a fair use. In some instances the presence of the defendant's own trademark in conjunction with the descriptive term can be sufficient to emphasize that the use is merely descriptive. The physical nature of the use in terms of size, location, and other characteristics in comparison with the appearance of other descriptive matter or other trademarks is also relevant to the fairness of the use. The presence or absence of precautionary measures such as labeling or other devices designed to minimize the risk that the term will be understood in its trademark sense are similarly relevant.

Commercial justification is also important in assessing the fairness of the defendant's use. The scope of use permitted under the fair use defense should reflect the degree to which the descriptive meaning of the term is relevant to the goods, services, or business of the subsequent user. If the original meaning of the term is not in fact descriptive of the attributes of the user's goods, services, or business, the defense is not applicable. If the term is only marginally descriptive or descriptive of only a relatively unimportant characteristic, the scope of fair use will be narrower than for terms that directly describe aspects or features of the goods or services that are of importance to prospective purchasers. Similarly, the absence of alternative terms capable of adequately describing the pertinent characteristic is also relevant in assessing the commercial justification for the use and hence the scope of permissible fair use.

Similar principles are applicable to personal name trademarks, particularly in light of the lack of alternative terms available to others with similar names. Factors relevant in accessing whether a subsequent user has made a reasonable descriptive use of a personal name include the relative importance in the particular industry or market of identifying the individuals who are connected with a business, the strength of the plaintiff's personal name mark, the subsequent user's good faith, and the presence or absence of precautionary measures calculated to minimize the risk of confusion.

d.   Good faith. The fair use defense is applicable only if the descriptive term has been used in good faith. Knowledge of a prior trademark use of the term does not in itself prove a lack of good faith. However, if the evidence establishes that the subsequent user intends to trade on the good will of the trademark owner by creating confusion as to source or sponsorship, the use is not in good faith.

Use by the actor of the precise form of the descriptive term adopted by the trademark owner can be evidence of bad faith when equally useful alternative forms are available. Indeed, if there are other terms equally suited to the legitimate commercial needs of the subsequent user, the prominent use of any form of the particular term in which trademark rights exist may in some circumstances support an inference of bad faith. Similarly, a shift by the actor from other descriptive words to the trademarked term after another's adoption of the term as a trademark can also indicate bad faith. Copying aspects of another's trademark that are unrelated to its descriptive significance, such as lettering style or color, can indicate bad faith, as does evidence of other similarities in labeling or packaging that contribute to the likelihood that the subsequent use will confuse prospective purchasers. A refusal to take reasonable precautions to reduce the risk of confusion can also indicate that the use is not in good faith.

Illustrations:

1.   A has acquired trademark rights in the designation NATURALLY for organically grown frozen vegetables. B markets organically grown frozen vegetables and other products under the trademark "B's PREMIER." B's trademark prominently appears in stylized script on the packaging of B's goods. Below the trademark is a photograph of the cooked product. Beneath the photograph is a generic description of the product preceded by the words "Naturally Grown," such as "Naturally Grown Baby Lima Beans." In the absence of evidence establishing that B has not acted in good faith, B's use of the term "naturally" is a fair use under the rule stated in this Section.

2.   The facts being otherwise as stated in Illustration 1, B instead markets its products under the trademark FROM B, NATURALLY. Below the trademark in smaller letters is a generic description of the product, such as "Lima Beans." A photograph of the cooked product occupies the rest of the package. A court may properly conclude that B's use of the term "naturally" is not a use solely to describe B's product and is thus not a fair use under the rule stated in this Section. B is then subject to liability for infringement if A establishes that it has priority under the rule stated in § 19 and that, despite the descriptive connotations of the term, B's use creates a likelihood of confusion under the rule stated in § 20.

§ 31   Unreasonable Delay (Laches)

If the owner of a trademark, trade name, collective mark, or certification mark unreasonably delays in commencing an action for infringement or otherwise asserting the owner's rights and thereby causes prejudice to another who may be subject to liability to the owner under the rules stated in this Chapter, the owner may be barred in whole or in part from the relief that would otherwise be available under §§ 35–37.

Topic 6.   Remedies

§ 35   Injunctions: Trademark Infringement and Deceptive Marketing

(1) Unless inappropriate under the rule stated in Subsection (2), injunctive relief will ordinarily be awarded against one who is liable to another for:

(a)   deceptive marketing under the rules stated in §§ 2–8; or

(b)   infringement of the other's trademark, trade name, collective mark, or certification mark under the rule stated in § 20; or

(c)   dilution of the other's trademark, trade name, collective mark, or certification mark under the rule stated in § 25.

(2) The appropriateness and scope of injunctive relief depend upon a comparative appraisal of all the factors of the case, including the following primary factors:

(a)   the nature of the interest to be protected;

(b)   the nature and extent of the wrongful conduct;

(c)   the relative adequacy to the plaintiff of an injunction and of other remedies;

(d)   the relative harm likely to result to the legitimate interests of the defendant if an injunction is granted and to the legitimate interests of the plaintiff if an injunction is denied;

(e)   the interests of third persons and of the public;

(f)   any unreasonable delay by the plaintiff in bringing suit or otherwise asserting its rights;

(g)   any related misconduct on the part of the plaintiff; and

(h)   the practicality of framing and enforcing the injunction.

§ 36 Damages: Trademark Infringement and Deceptive Marketing

(1) One who is liable to another for deceptive marketing under the rules stated in §§ 2–8 or for infringement of the other's trademark, trade name, collective mark, or certification mark under the rule stated in § 20 is liable for the pecuniary loss to the other caused by the deceptive marketing or infringement, unless an award of damages for such pecuniary loss is prohibited by statute or is otherwise inappropriate under the rule stated in Subsection (3).

(2) The pecuniary loss for which damages may be recovered under this Section includes:

(a) loss resulting to the plaintiff from sales or other revenues lost because of the actor's conduct;

(b) loss resulting from sales made by the plaintiff at prices that have been reasonably reduced because of the actor's conduct;

(c) harm to the market reputation of the plaintiff's goods, services, business, or trademark; and

(d) reasonable expenditures made by the plaintiff in order to prevent, correct, or mitigate the confusion or deception of prospective purchasers resulting from the actor's conduct.

(3) Whether an award of damages for pecuniary loss is appropriate depends upon a comparative appraisal of all the factors of the case, including the following primary factors:

(a) the degree of certainty with which the plaintiff has established the fact and extent of the pecuniary loss caused by the actor's conduct;

(b) the relative adequacy to the plaintiff of other remedies, including an accounting of the actor's profits;

(c) the intent of the actor and the extent to which the actor knew or should have known that the conduct was unlawful;

(d) the role of the actor in bringing about the infringement or deceptive marketing;

(e) any unreasonable delay by the plaintiff in bringing suit or otherwise asserting its rights; and

(f) any related misconduct on the part of the plaintiff.

§ 37 Accounting of Defendant's Profits: Trademark Infringement and Deceptive Marketing

(1) One who is liable to another for deceptive marketing under the rules stated in §§ 2–8 or for infringement of the other's trademark, trade name, collective mark, or certification mark under the rule stated in § 20 is liable for the net profits earned on profitable transactions resulting from the unlawful conduct, but only if:

(a) the actor engaged in the conduct with the intention of causing confusion or deception; and

(b) the award of profits is not prohibited by statute and is otherwise appropriate under the rule stated in Subsection (2).

(2) Whether an award of profits is appropriate depends upon a comparative appraisal of all the factors of the case, including the following primary factors:

(a) the degree of certainty that the actor benefitted from the unlawful conduct;

(b) the relative adequacy to the plaintiff of other remedies, including an award of damages;

(c) the interests of the public in depriving the actor of unjust gains and discouraging unlawful conduct;

(d) the role of the actor in bringing about the infringement or deceptive marketing;

(e) any unreasonable delay by the plaintiff in bringing suit or otherwise asserting its rights; and

(f) any related misconduct on the part of the plaintiff.

Chapter 4. Appropriation of Trade Values
Topic 1. Misappropriation

§ 38 Appropriation of Trade Values

One who causes harm to the commercial relations of another by appropriating the other's intangible trade values is subject to liability to the other for such harm only if:

(a) the actor is subject to liability for an appropriation of the other's trade secret under the rules stated in §§ 39–45; or

(b) the actor is subject to liability for an appropriation of the commercial value of the other's identity under the rules stated in §§ 46–49; or

(c) the appropriation is actionable by the other under federal or state statutes or international agreements, or is actionable as a breach of contract, or as an infringement of common law copyright as preserved under federal copyright law.

Comment:

b.   Misappropriation. Protection against the misappropriation of intangible trade values insures an incentive to invest in the creation of intangible assets and prevents the potential unjust enrichment that may result from the appropriation of an investment made by another. However, the recognition of exclusive rights in intangible trade values can impede access to valuable information and restrain competition. Unlike appropriations of physical assets, the appropriation of information or other intangible asset does not ordinarily deprive the originator of simultaneous use. The recognition of exclusive rights may thus deny to the public the full benefits of valuable ideas and innovations by limiting their distribution and exploitation. In addition, the principle of unjust enrichment does not demand restitution of every gain derived from the efforts of others. A small shop, for example, may freely benefit from the customers attracted by a nearby department store, a local manufacturer may benefit from increased demand attributable to the promotional efforts of a national manufacturer of similar goods, and a newspaper may benefit from reporting on the activities of local athletic teams. Similarly, the law has long recognized the right of a competitor to copy the successful products and business methods of others absent protection under patent, copyright, or trademark law.

Achieving a proper balance between protection and access is often a complicated and difficult undertaking. Because of the complexity and indeterminacy of the competing interests, rights in intangible trade values such as ideas, innovations, and information have been created primarily through legislation. The patent and copyright statutes illustrate the intricacy required to harmonize the competing public and private interests implicated in the recognition of rights in intangible trade values. Both statutes contain elaborate mechanisms intended to balance the interests in protection and access. Protection under the patent act, for example, is limited to innovations that are new, useful, and non-obvious to persons having ordinary skill in the art. The copyright act grants rights in works of authorship subject to a complex system of exemptions and limitations. Both statutes grant rights only for a limited term, after which the discovery or writing enters the public domain and may be freely appropriated by others.

The common law of unfair competition has generally recognized rights against the appropriation of intangible trade values only when the recognition of such rights is supported by other interests that justify protection, and then only when the scope of the resulting rights can be clearly defined. The protection of trade secrets, for example, reflects the established interests in preserving confidential relationships and promoting physical security. See §§ 39–45. Protection against an appropriation of the commercial value of a person's identity implicates interests in privacy, reputation, and personal autonomy. See §§ 46–49. In the absence of such additional interests, the common law has resisted the recognition of general rights against the appropriation of information and other intangible trade values.

In 1918, the United States Supreme Court in International News Service v. Associated Press, 248 U.S. 215, 39 S.Ct. 68, 63 L.Ed. 211 (1918), recognized a common law tort of "misappropriation" that afforded protection against the appropriation by a competitor of commercially valuable information otherwise in the public domain. Although the decision has been frequently cited, it has been sparingly applied. Notwithstanding its longevity, the decision has had little enduring effect. See Comment *c*. In many cases it has been invoked when narrower rules of unfair competition would have achieved the same result. In most of the areas in which it has been expansively applied, its application has now been supplanted by legislation.

The rule stated in this Section limits common law tort liability for appropriations of intangible trade values to cases involving an appropriation of trade secrets, an appropriation of the commercial value of another's identity, or an appropriation of a work of authorship that is not fixed in a tangible medium of expression and thus protectable under common law copyright. See Comment *d*. Although courts have occasionally invoked the *INS* decision on an ad hoc basis to grant relief against other commercial appropriations, they have not articulated coherent principles for its application. It is clear that no general rule of law prohibits the appropriation of a competitor's ideas, innovations, or other intangible assets once they become publicly known. In addition, the federal patent and copyright statutes now preempt a considerable portion of the domain in which the common law tort might otherwise apply. See Comment *e*. The better approach, and the one most likely to achieve an appropriate balance between the competing interests, does not recognize a residual common law tort of misappropriation.

   c.   International News Service v. Associated Press. In International News Service v. Associated Press, 248 U.S. 215, 39 S.Ct. 68, 63 L.Ed. 211 (1918), the United States Supreme Court recognized a cause of action under federal common law for the misappropriation of a competitor's intangible trade values. The International News Service had copied information from Associated Press news dispatches published in eastern newspapers and transmitted news stories based on the information to INS-affiliated newspapers on the west coast for publication in competition with western members of the Associated Press. Although acknowledging the public's right to copy the uncopyrighted news reports, the Supreme Court held that the appropriation of news by a competitor for use in direct competition with the originator was actionable as unfair competition:

   In doing this defendant, by its very act, admits that it is taking material that has been acquired by complainant as the result of organization and the expenditure of labor, skill, and money, and which is salable by complainant for money, and that defendant in appropriating it and selling it as its own is endeavoring to reap where it has not sown, and by disposing of it to newspapers that are competitors of complainant's members is appropriating to itself the harvest of those who have sown. Stripped of all disguises, the process amounts to an unauthorized interference with the normal operation of complainant's legitimate business precisely at the point where the profit is to be reaped, in order to divert a material portion of the profit from those who have earned it to those who have not; with special advantage to defendant in the competition because of the fact that it is not burdened with any part of the expense of gathering the news. The transaction speaks for itself, and a court of equity ought not to hesitate long in characterizing it as unfair competition in business.

248 U.S. at 239–40, 39 S.Ct. at 72–73, 63 L.Ed. at 221.

Although the decision appears to rest on a rationale of unjust enrichment potentially applicable to a wide range of competitive conduct, subsequent decisions have recognized that broad application of the unjust enrichment rationale in a competitive marketplace would unreasonably restrain competition and undermine the public interest in access to valuable information. The facts of the *INS* decision are unusual and may serve, in part, to limit its rationale. The originator of valuable information or other intangible assets normally has an opportunity to exploit the advantage of a lead time in the market. This can provide the originator with an opportunity to recover the costs of development and in many cases is sufficient to encourage continued investment. However, the appropriation in *INS* deprived Associated Press of any lead-time advantage, at least on the West Coast. Associated Press thus faced a direct threat to its primary market by a competitor who had incurred none of the development costs associated with collecting the news. Such circumstances present the most compelling case for protection against appropriation, although even on these facts Justice Brandeis argued persuasively in dissent that the proper balance between protection and access could be drawn only through legislation.

The limited extent to which the *INS* rationale has been incorporated into the common law of the states indicates that the decision is properly viewed as a response to unusual circumstances rather than as a statement of generally applicable principles of common law. Many subsequent decisions have expressly limited the *INS* case to its facts. In addition, in many of the decisions that invoke the misappropriation doctrine, other principles of unfair competition law are more directly applicable. For example, some courts have invoked the misappropriation doctrine to impose liability in trademark and trade dress cases notwithstanding proof of a likelihood of confusion sufficient to establish liability under traditional principles of trademark law. Similarly, some cases have invoked the doctrine against appropriations involving breaches of confidence or other improper conduct actionable under the rules protecting trade secrets.

In most of the small number of cases in which the misappropriation doctrine has been determinative, the defendant's appropriation, like that in *INS*, resulted in direct competition in the plaintiff's primary market. Several cases, for example, invoke the doctrine to impose liability for an appropriation of news on facts more or less analogous to those in the *INS* case. Similarly, the misappropriation doctrine for a time played a significant role in restraining the unauthorized reproduction and sale of musical performances and sound recordings. Injunctions based on the misappropriation doctrine were granted against the sale of unauthorized recordings of radio broadcasts in competition with authorized recordings and against record and tape pirates selling unauthorized copies of popular sound recordings in competition with the originals. These decisions are now effectively superseded by the protection available under the 1976 Copyright Act to sound recordings and to broadcasts that are simultaneously recorded upon transmission. Even with respect to directly competitive appropriations, however, the implementation of enduring and appropriately circumscribed protection is generally best achieved through legislation rather than common law adjudication.

Appeals to the misappropriation doctrine are almost always rejected when the appropriation does not intrude upon the plaintiff's primary market. Only rarely have courts applied the doctrine to appropriations of intangible trade values for use in secondary or derivative markets. Absent proof of consumer confusion or a violation of other recognized principles of unfair competition law, such results go beyond even the broad rationale of the *INS* case.

Topic 2.   Trade Secrets

§ 39   Definition of Trade Secret

A trade secret is any information that can be used in the operation of a business or other enterprise and that is sufficiently valuable and secret to afford an actual or potential economic advantage over others.

Comment:

a.   Rationale for protection. The protection of confidential business information dates at least to Roman law, which afforded relief against a person who induced another's employee to divulge secrets relating to the master's commercial affairs. The modern law of trade secrets evolved in England in the early 19th century, apparently in response to the growing accumulation of technical know-how and the increased mobility of employees during the industrial revolution. In the United States the protection of trade secrets was recognized at common law by the middle of the 19th century, and by the end of the century the principal features of contemporary trade secret law were well established.

The protection of trade secrets advances several interests. Early cases emphasized the unfairness inherent in obtaining a competitive advantage through a breach of confidence. The imposition of liability for the appropriation of a trade secret protects the plaintiff from unfair competition and deprives the defendant of unjust enrichment attributable to bad faith. The development of rules protecting trade secrets formed part of a more general attempt to articulate standards of fair competition. More recently, the protection of trade secrets has been justified as a means to encourage investment in research by providing an opportunity to capture the returns from successful innovations. The rules protecting trade secrets also promote the efficient exploitation of knowledge by discouraging the unproductive hoarding of useful information and facilitating disclosure to employees, agents, licensees, and others who can assist in its productive use. Finally, the protection afforded under the law of trade secrets against breaches of confidence and improper physical intrusions furthers the interest in personal privacy.

The subject matter and scope of trade secret protection is necessarily limited by the public and private interest in access to valuable information. The freedom to compete in the marketplace includes, in the absence of patent, copyright, or trademark protection (see §§ 16 and 17), the freedom to copy the goods, methods, processes, and ideas of others. The freedom to copy, however, does not extend to information that is inaccessible by proper means. Liability for the appropriation of a trade secret thus rests on a breach of confidence or other wrongful conduct in acquiring, using, or disclosing secret information.

b. Doctrinal development. Early trade secret cases, responding to requests for injunctive relief against breaches of confidence, frequently supported the exercise of equity jurisdiction by describing the plaintiff's interest in the trade secret as a property right, often said to derive from the discovery of valuable information. Similar characterizations sometimes appear in the modern case law. The property rationale emphasizes the nature of the appropriated information, especially its value and secrecy. Even the earliest cases, however, also include an examination of the propriety of the defendant's conduct. The plaintiff's property right was effective only against defendants who used or acquired the information improperly. No exclusive rights were recognized against those who acquired the information by proper means. Other cases, choosing to begin their analysis with an examination of the defendant's behavior, concluded that the essence of a trade secret action is a breach of confidence or other improper conduct, sometimes explicitly disavowing any property dimension to a trade secret. The influential formulation in § 757 of the Restatement of Torts (1939), reporting that the property conception "has been frequently advanced and rejected," concluded that the prevailing theory of liability rests on "a general duty of good faith." *Id.*, Comment *a*. Both the former Restatement and the supporting case law, however, also require that the information qualify for protection as a trade secret, thus incorporating the elements of secrecy and value that underlie the property rationale.

The dispute over the nature of trade secret rights has had little practical effect on the rules governing civil liability for the appropriation of a trade secret. The cases generally require that the plaintiff establish both the existence of a trade secret under the principles described in this Section and the fact of misconduct by the defendant under the rules stated in § 40. Many cases acknowledge that the primary issue is the propriety of the defendant's conduct as a means of competition. The substantive scope of the rights recognized under the law of trade secrets thus reflects the accommodation of numerous interests, including the trade secret owner's claim to protection against the defendant's bad faith or improper conduct, the right of competitors and others to exploit information and skills in the public domain, and the interest of the public in encouraging innovation and in securing the benefits of vigorous competition.

In 1979, the National Conference of Commissioners on Uniform State Laws promulgated the Uniform Trade Secrets Act. The Prefatory Note states that the "Uniform Act codifies the basic principles of common law trade secret protection." The original Act or its 1985 revision has been adopted in a majority of the states. (See the Statutory Note following this Section.) Except as otherwise noted, the principles of trade secret law described in this Restatement are applicable to actions under the Uniform Trade Secrets Act as well as to actions at common law. The concept of a trade secret as defined in this Section is intended to be consistent with the definition of "trade secret" in § 1(4) of the Act.

Some states have adopted criminal statutes specifically addressed to the appropriation of trade secrets. In other states, more general criminal statutes have been interpreted to reach such appropriations. In some circumstances the appropriation of a trade secret may also violate the federal wire and mail fraud statutes (18 U.S.C.A. §§ 1341, 1343) and the National Stolen Property Act (18 U.S.C.A. § 2314). The definition of a trade secret contained in this Section, however, is directly applicable only to the imposition of civil liability under the rules stated in § 40. It does not apply, other than by analogy, in actions under criminal statutes or in other circumstances not involving civil liability for the appropriation of a trade secret, such as the protection of trade secrets from disclosure under the Freedom of Information Act (5 U.S.C. § 552).

c.   *Relation to patent and copyright law.* Federal patent law offers protection to "any new and useful process, machine, manufacture, or composition of matter," 35 U.S.C.A. § 101, unless the invention "would have been obvious at the time the invention was made to a person having ordinary skill in the art to which said subject matter pertains." 35 U.S.C.A. § 103. Federal design patents protect "any new, original and ornamental design for an article of manufacture," again subject to the requirement of non-obviousness. 35 U.S.C.A. § 135. Unlike the limited protection against improper acquisition, disclosure, and use accorded to the owner of a trade secret under the rules stated in § 40, the holder of a patent enjoys a general right to exclude others from making, using, or selling the patented invention, 35 U.S.C.A. § 271, enforceable even against persons relying on independent discovery or reverse engineering. An application for a patent must include a specification containing "a written description of the invention, and of the manner and process of making and using it," and "the best mode contemplated by the inventor of carrying out" the invention. 35 U.S.C.A. §§ 111 and 112. Upon issuance of a patent, the specification and other materials comprising the patent file become available for public inspection. 37 C.F.R. § 1.11. Thus, for matter disclosed in the patent, issuance terminates the secrecy required for continued protection as a trade secret, even if the patent is subsequently declared invalid. See Comment *f*. Pending, denied, and abandoned patent applications, however, are not generally open to public inspection. 35 U.S.C.A. § 122; 37 C.F.R. § 1.14. Thus, the filing of a patent application does not in itself preclude continued protection of the invention as a trade secret.

The United States Supreme Court in Kewanee Oil Co. v. Bicron Corp., 416 U.S. 470, 94 S.Ct. 1879, 40 L.Ed.2d 315 (1974), held that federal patent law does not preempt the protection of inventions and other information under state trade secret law. The Court concluded that the requirement of secrecy fundamental to the protection of trade secrets (see Comment *f*) avoids interference with the federal patent policy of access to information in the public domain. It also concluded that the limitations on the scope of state trade secret protection (see § 40) make it unlikely that the federal policy of inducing public disclosure in exchange for the protection of a patent will be significantly undermined by reliance on trade secret protection for patentable inventions. In a subsequent decision, however, the Supreme Court emphasized that any rule of state law that substantially interferes with the use of information that has already been disclosed to the public or that is readily ascertainable from public sources is preempted. Bonito Boats, Inc. v. Thunder Craft Boats, Inc., 489 U.S. 141, 109 S.Ct. 971, 103 L.Ed.2d 118 (1989).

Federal copyright law protects "original works of authorship fixed in any tangible medium of expression," 17 U.S.C.A. § 102(a), against unauthorized reproduction, use in the preparation of derivative works, distribution, public performance, or public display. 17 U.S.C.A. § 106. Protection is limited, however, to the manner in which the authorship is expressed and does not extend to "any idea, procedure, process, system, method of operation, concept, principle, or discovery" embodied in the work. 17 U.S.C.A. § 102(b). Copyright protection subsists from the creation of a work and is not contingent upon public dissemination. See 17 U.S.C.A. § 302. A claim of federal copyright is thus not in itself inconsistent with a claim to trade secret protection for information contained in the work. Although § 301 of the Copyright Act preempts the recognition under state law of "rights that are equivalent to any of the exclusive rights" of copyright in works "within the subject matter" of the statute, the protection afforded to trade secrets under the rules stated in § 40 has been held to lie outside the preemptive scope of the Copyright Act.

Registration of a copyright is not a condition of copyright protection. 17 U.S.C.A. § 408. The registration of a copyright claim in an unpublished work ordinarily requires the deposit of a complete copy of the work, 17 U.S.C.A. § 408(b)(1), which is then open to public inspection. 17 U.S.C.A. § 705. However, the regulations of the Copyright Office permit the deletion of material constituting trade secrets from deposits made in connection with computer programs and also authorize the granting of special relief from the normal deposit requirements in other cases. The status as a trade secret of information contained in a work that is the subject of a copyright registration is determined under the general principles governing secrecy and accessibility described in Comment *f*.

d.   Subject matter. A trade secret can consist of a formula, pattern, compilation of data, computer program, device, method, technique, process, or other form or embodiment of economically valuable information. A trade secret can relate to technical matters such as the composition or design of a product, a method of manufacture, or the know-how necessary to perform a particular operation or service. A trade secret can also relate to other aspects of business operations such as pricing and marketing techniques or the identity and requirements of customers (see § 42, Comment *f*). Although rights in trade secrets are normally asserted by businesses and other commercial enterprises, nonprofit entities such as charitable, educational, governmental, fraternal, and religious organizations can also claim trade secret protection for economically valuable information such as lists of prospective members or donors.

The prior Restatement of this topic limited the subject matter of trade secret law to information capable of "continuous use in the operation of a business," thus excluding information relating to single events such as secret bids and impending business announcements or information whose secrecy is quickly destroyed by commercial exploitation. See Restatement of Torts § 757, Comment *b* (1939). Both the case law and the prior Restatement, however, offered protection against the "improper" acquisition of such short-term information under rules virtually identical to those applicable to trade secrets. See *id.* § 759, Comment *c*. The Restatement, Second, of Agency in § 396 similarly protects both trade secrets and "other similar confidential matters" from unauthorized use or disclosure following the termination of an agency relationship. The definition of "trade secret" adopted in the Uniform Trade Secrets Act does not include any requirement relating to the duration of the information's economic value. See Uniform Trade Secrets Act § 1(4) and the accompanying Comment. The definition adopted in this Section similarly contains no requirement that the information afford a continuous or long-term advantage.

A person claiming rights in a trade secret bears the burden of defining the information for which protection is sought with sufficient definiteness to permit a court to apply the criteria for protection described in this Section and to determine the fact of an appropriation. In the case of technical information, a physical embodiment of the information in the form of a specific product, process, or working model often provides the requisite definition. However, there is no requirement that the information be incorporated or embodied in a tangible form if it is otherwise sufficiently delineated. The degree of definiteness required in a particular case is also properly influenced by the legitimate interests of the defendant. Thus, a court may require greater specificity when the plaintiff's claim involves information that is closely integrated with the general skill and knowledge that is properly retained by former employees. See § 42, Comment *d*.

An agreement between the parties that characterizes specific information as a "trade secret" can be an important although not necessarily conclusive factor in determining whether the information qualifies for protection as a trade secret under this Section. As a precaution against disclosure, such an agreement is evidence of the value and secrecy of the information, see Comments *e* and *f*, and can also supply or contribute to the definiteness required in delineating the trade secret. The agreement can also be important in establishing a duty of confidence. See § 41. However, because of the public interest in preserving access to information that is in the public domain, such an agreement will not ordinarily estop a defendant from contesting the existence of a trade secret. (On the protection of information by contract, see § 41, Comment *d*.)

It is not possible to state precise criteria for determining the existence of a trade secret. The status of information claimed as a trade secret must be ascertained through a comparative evaluation of all the relevant factors, including the value, secrecy, and definiteness of the information as well as the nature of the defendant's misconduct.

e.   Requirement of value. A trade secret must be of sufficient value in the operation of a business or other enterprise to provide an actual or potential economic advantage over others who do not possess the information. The advantage, however, need not be great. It is sufficient if the secret provides an advantage that is more than trivial. Although a trade secret can consist of a patentable invention, there is no requirement that the trade secret meet the standard of inventiveness applicable under federal patent law.

The value of information claimed as a trade secret may be established by direct or circumstantial evidence. Direct evidence relating to the content of the secret and its impact on business operations is clearly relevant. Circumstantial evidence of value is also relevant, including the amount of resources invested by the plaintiff in the production of the information, the precautions taken by the plaintiff to protect the secrecy of the information (see Comment *g*), and the willingness of others to pay for access to the information.

The plaintiff's use of the trade secret in the operation of its business is itself some evidence of the information's value. Identifiable benefits realized by the trade secret owner through use of the information are also evidence of value. Some early cases elevated use by the trade secret owner to independent significance by establishing such use as an element of the cause of action for the appropriation of a trade secret. Such a "use" requirement, however, imposes unjustified limitations on the scope of trade secret protection. The requirement can deny protection during periods of research and development and is particularly burdensome for innovators who do not possess the capability to exploit their innovations. See Comment *h*. The requirement also places in doubt protection for so-called "negative" information that teaches conduct to be avoided, such as knowledge that a particular process or technique is unsuitable for commercial use. Cases in many jurisdictions expressly renounce any requirement of use by the trade secret owner. It is also rejected under the Uniform Trade Secrets Act. See the Comment to § 1 of the Act. Use by the person asserting rights in the information is not a prerequisite to protection under the rule stated in this Section.

f. Requirement of secrecy. To qualify as a trade secret, the information must be secret. The secrecy, however, need not be absolute. The rule stated in this Section requires only secrecy sufficient to confer an actual or potential economic advantage on one who possesses the information. Thus, the requirement of secrecy is satisfied if it would be difficult or costly for others who could exploit the information to acquire it without resort to the wrongful conduct proscribed under § 40. Novelty in the patent law sense is not required. Although trade secret cases sometimes announce a "novelty" requirement, the requirement is synonymous with the concepts of secrecy and value as described in this Section and the correlative exclusion of self-evident variants of the known art.

Information known by persons in addition to the trade secret owner can retain its status as a trade secret if it remains secret from others to whom it has potential economic value. Independent discovery by another who maintains the secrecy of the information, for example, will not preclude relief against an appropriation by a third person. Similarly, confidential disclosures to employees, licensees, or others will not destroy the information's status as a trade secret. Even limited non-confidential disclosure will not necessarily terminate protection if the recipients of the disclosure maintain the secrecy of the information.

Information that is generally known or readily ascertainable through proper means (see § 43) by others to whom it has potential economic value is not protectable as a trade secret. Thus, information that is disclosed in a patent or contained in published materials reasonably accessible to competitors does not qualify for protection under this Section. Similarly, information readily ascertainable from an examination of a product on public sale or display is not a trade secret. Self-evident variations or modifications of known processes, procedures, or methods also lack the secrecy necessary for protection as a trade secret. However, it is the secrecy of the claimed trade secret as a whole that is determinative. The fact that some or all of the components of the trade secret are well-known does not preclude protection for a secret combination, compilation, or integration of the individual elements.

The theoretical ability of others to ascertain the information through proper means does not necessarily preclude protection as a trade secret. Trade secret protection remains available unless the information is readily ascertainable by such means. Thus, if acquisition of the information through an examination of a competitor's product would be difficult, costly, or time-consuming, the trade secret owner retains protection against an improper acquisition, disclosure, or use prohibited under the rules stated in § 40. However, any person who actually acquires the information through an examination of a publicly available product has obtained the information by proper means and is thus not subject to liability. See § 43. Similarly, the theoretical possibility of reconstructing the secret from published materials containing scattered references to portions of the information or of extracting it from public materials unlikely to come to the attention of the appropriator will not preclude relief against the wrongful conduct proscribed under § 40, although one who actually acquires the secret from such sources is not subject to liability.

Circumstantial evidence is admissible to establish that information is not readily ascertainable through proper means and hence is eligible for protection as a trade secret. Precautions taken by the claimant to preserve the secrecy of the information (see Comment g), the willingness of licensees to pay for disclosure of the secret, unsuccessful attempts by the defendant or others to duplicate the information by proper means, and resort by a defendant to improper means of acquisition are all probative of the relative accessibility of the information. When a defendant has engaged in egregious misconduct in order to acquire the information, the inference that the information is sufficiently inaccessible to qualify for protection as a trade secret is particularly strong. See § 43, Comment d.

Although courts have recognized that trade secret rights may not be asserted in information that is in the public domain, the cases disagree on the consequences of a loss of secrecy that occurs between the time of a defendant's confidential receipt of the trade secret and the defendant's subsequent unauthorized use or disclosure. Some decisions refuse to consider the availability of the information from public domain sources at the time of the alleged appropriation, at least when the defendant's knowledge derives from the confidential disclosure rather than from the public sources. Other decisions, more narrowly construing the obligations attendant upon a confidential disclosure, hold that protection against unauthorized use or disclosure is not available after the information has ceased to be a secret. (On the remedial consequences of a loss of secrecy occurring after a defendant's appropriation, see § 44, Comment f; § 45, Comment h.) However, in many of the cases that refuse as a matter of law to take into account a loss of secrecy, the information was in fact only theoretically rather than readily ascertainable from the public domain at the time of the defendant's use or disclosure, thus justifying relief under either rule.

When information is no longer sufficiently secret to qualify for protection as a trade secret, its use should not serve as a basis for the imposition of liability under the rules stated in § 40. If the information has become readily ascertainable from public sources so that no significant benefit accrues to a person who relies instead on other means of acquisition, the information is in the public domain and no longer protectable under the law of trade secrets. Even those courts that decline to take into account a loss of secrecy following a confidential disclosure to the defendant often assert in dicta that no liability attaches if the defendant actually extracts the information from public sources. When the information is readily ascertainable from such sources, however, actual resort to the public domain is a formality that should not determine liability. The public interest in avoiding unnecessary restraints on the exploitation of valuable information supports the conclusion that protection as a trade secret terminates when the information is no longer secret. The defendant remains liable, however, for any unauthorized use or disclosure that occurred prior to the loss of secrecy. This position is consistent with the language and policy of the Uniform Trade Secrets Act. Section 1(2) of the Act defines "misappropriation" as the improper acquisition, disclosure, or use of a "trade secret," and § 1(4) excludes from the definition of "trade secret" information "generally known . . . or readily ascertainable by proper means." Termination of trade secret rights upon a loss of secrecy is also consistent with the limitations on injunctive and monetary relief in §§ 2 and 3 of the Act (and in §§ 44 and 45 of this Restatement) applicable to appropriations occurring prior to the loss of secrecy.

Illustrations:

1.   *A*, a pharmaceutical company, develops a more efficient process for the production of a particular drug. *A* discloses the process in confidence to an engineering firm in order to facilitate the construction of a new manufacturing plant and later discloses the process to specific employees involved in the production of the drug. *A* also discloses the process in confidence to *B*, another pharmaceutical company, under a licensing agreement. *C*, a third pharmaceutical company, independently discovers and secretly implements the process. *D*, a fourth pharmaceutical company, bribes an employee of *A* to disclose the process. If the process otherwise remains unknown and not readily ascertainable through proper means, it is sufficiently secret to be protected as a trade secret. *D* is thus subject to liability to *A* for the appropriation of *A*'s trade secret under the rules stated in § 40. *C* is not subject to liability to *A* because *C*'s acquisition of the trade secret was not improper. See § 43.

2.   *A*, a company in the business of selling building maintenance supplies to large commercial users, employs *B* as a general manager. After termination of the employment, *B* starts a competing business and solicits some of *A*'s customers whose identities *B* learned while employed by *A*. If the identities of the customers solicited by *B* are readily ascertainable in the trade as prospective purchasers of the types of products sold by *A* and *B*, the customer identities are not protectable as a trade secret. See § 42, Comment *f*.

3.   The facts being otherwise as stated in Illustration 2, *B* also copies files prepared by *A* containing detailed data on the requirements, past purchases, and key personnel of individual customers. *B* uses information from the files in soliciting the customers. If a court concludes that the compiled data is valuable and not readily ascertainable from other sources, the information is protectable as a trade secret. *B* is then subject to liability to *A* for the appropriation of *A*'s trade secrets under the rules stated in § 40.

4.   *A* confidentially discloses a trade secret to *B* during negotiations concerning a possible licensing agreement. *A* and *B* eventually terminate the negotiations without reaching agreement, and *B* refrains from all use of the information. Later, the secret is revealed in an article published by *A*, and *B* subsequently begins to use the information. The information is no longer protectable as a trade secret, and *B* is not subject to liability to *A* regardless of whether *B* actually extracted the information from the published article or relied on the prior confidential disclosure.

5.   *A* manufactures heavy-duty centrifugal blowers. Drawings containing dimensions and specifications for components of the blowers are taken without authorization by *B*, a former employee of *A*, and used to manufacture a competing product. Although the approximate dimensions and specifications of *A*'s products can be determined by measuring blowers sold by *A* on the open market, the evidence establishes that the information resulting from such measurements would be less accurate than the drawings taken by *B* and less valuable in manufacturing competing products. The acquisition of information as accurate as that contained in the drawings taken by *B* would require a statistical analysis of measurements taken from a large number of *A*'s blowers. The court may properly conclude that the information contained in the drawings is not readily ascertainable by proper means and is thus sufficiently secret to be protected as a trade secret. *B* is thus subject to liability to *A* for the appropriation of *A*'s trade secrets under the rules stated in § 40.

g.   Precautions to maintain secrecy. Precautions taken to maintain the secrecy of information are relevant in determining whether the information qualifies for protection as a trade secret. Precautions to maintain secrecy may take many forms, including physical security designed to prevent unauthorized access, procedures intended to limit disclosure based upon the "need to know," and measures that emphasize to recipients the confidential nature of the information such as nondisclosure agreements, signs, and restrictive legends. Such precautions can be evidence of the information's value (see Comment *e*) and secrecy (see Comment *f*). The prior Restatement of this topic included the precautions taken to maintain the secrecy of the information as one of a number of factors relevant in determining the existence of a trade secret. See Restatement of Torts § 757, Comment *b* (1939). The Uniform Trade Secrets Act requires a trade secret to be "the subject of efforts that are reasonable under the circumstances to maintain its secrecy." Section 1(4)(ii). Whether viewed as an independent requirement or as an element to be considered with other factors relevant to the existence of a trade secret, the owner's precautions should be evaluated in light of the other available evidence relating to the value and secrecy of the information. Thus, if the value and secrecy of the information are clear, evidence of specific precautions taken by the trade secret owner may be unnecessary.

The precautions taken by the trade secret owner are also relevant to other potential issues in an action for the appropriation of a trade secret. They can signal to employees and other recipients that a disclosure of the information by the trade secret owner is intended to be in confidence. See § 41. They can also be relevant in determining whether a defendant possessed the knowledge necessary for the imposition of liability under the rules stated in § 40 (see § 40, Comment *d*), whether particular means of acquisition are improper under the rule stated in § 43 (see § 43, Comment *c*), and whether an accidental disclosure results in the loss of trade secret rights (see § 40, Comment *e*).

h. "Law of ideas." Cases involving the submission of ideas by employees, customers, inventors, and others to businesses capable of reducing the idea to practice are sometimes analyzed under separate rules referred to as the "law of ideas." Idea submission cases often arise in the context of suggestions for new or improved products submitted to manufacturers, or in connection with programming and other ideas submitted to the entertainment industries. Plaintiffs seeking compensation for their ideas typically rely on contract claims alleging an express or implied-in-fact promise by the recipient to pay for the submitted idea. In some cases, however, compensation is sought through tort or restitutionary claims. These non-contractual claims are generally resolved through an analysis of the nature of the information and the circumstances of the submission that is fundamentally indistinguishable from the rules governing trade secrets. Some decisions explicitly incorporate such claims within the scope of trade secret law.

To sustain a claim in tort for the appropriation of an idea, most courts require the submitted idea to be "novel" in the sense of not being generally known (cf. Comment *f*) and sufficiently "concrete" to permit an assessment of its value and the fact of its use by the recipient (cf. Comment *d*). The courts also examine the circumstances of the disclosure to determine whether the recipient is bound by an obligation of confidentiality. Factors such as the relationship between the submitter and recipient, prior dealings between the parties, the customs of the industry, and the recipient's solicitation or opportunity to refuse the disclosure are relevant in determining the recipient's obligations. Cf. § 41.

With the rejection under the Uniform Trade Secrets Act and under this Section of any requirement of use by the owner of a trade secret, see Comment e, there is no longer a formal distinction between trade secrets and the ideas that form the subject matter of the idea submission cases. The developing rules governing the rights of submitters and recipients of ideas in the absence of an express or implied-in-fact contract can thus be understood as specific applications of the general rules stated here. The rules in this Restatement relating to the protection of trade secrets are therefore applicable, either directly or by analogy, to claims in tort alleging the appropriation of ideas.

Since the public and private interests favoring access to information that is in the public domain are also relevant in analyzing contractual claims, many jurisdictions require proof of novelty and concreteness for the enforcement of express or implied-in-fact contracts to pay for submitted ideas. Thus, the rules stated here may also be helpful in analyzing contractual liability in idea submission cases.

§ 40 Appropriation of Trade Secrets

One is subject to liability for the appropriation of another's trade secret if:

(a) the actor acquires by means that are improper under the rule stated in § 43 information that the actor knows or has reason to know is the other's trade secret; or

(b) the actor uses or discloses the other's trade secret without the other's consent and, at the time of the use or disclosure,

(1) the actor knows or has reason to know that the information is a trade secret that the actor acquired under circumstances creating a duty of confidence owed by the actor to the other under the rule stated in § 41; or

(2) the actor knows or has reason to know that the information is a trade secret that the actor acquired by means that are improper under the rule stated in § 43; or

(3) the actor knows or has reason to know that the information is a trade secret that the actor acquired from or through a person who acquired it by means that are improper under the rule stated in § 43 or whose disclosure of the trade secret constituted a breach of a duty of confidence owed to the other under the rule stated in § 41; or

(4) the actor knows or has reason to know that the information is a trade secret that the actor acquired through an accident or mistake, unless the acquisition was the result of the other's failure to take reasonable precautions to maintain the secrecy of the information.

Comment:

a.   Scope. The rules stated in this Section are applicable to common law actions in tort or restitution for the appropriation of another's trade secret, however denominated, including actions for "misappropriation," "infringement," or "conversion" of a trade secret, actions for "unjust enrichment" based on the unauthorized use of a trade secret, and actions for "breach of confidence" in which the subject matter of the confidence is a trade secret. Except as otherwise noted, the rules governing trade secrets as stated in this Restatement are also intended to be consistent with and applicable to actions under the Uniform Trade Secrets Act. This Section does not govern the imposition of liability for conduct that infringes other protected interests such as interference with contractual relations (see Restatement, Second, Torts §§ 766–774A (1979)), breach of the duty of loyalty owed by an employee or other agent (see Restatement, Second, Agency §§ 387–398 (1958)), or a breach of confidence not involving a trade secret (see § 41, Comment *c*).

The rules stated in this Section are not applicable to actions for breach of contract, including breach of a promise not to use or disclose a trade secret or a promise not to compete with the owner of a trade secret. Such agreements are governed by the rules generally applicable to the formation and enforcement of contracts, including the limitations on the enforcement of contracts in restraint of trade stated in Restatement, Second, Contracts §§ 186–188 (1981). The rules stated in this Chapter, however, can be useful in interpreting and implementing the principles embodied in those limitations. See § 41, Comment *d*. The existence of an express or implied-in-fact contract protecting trade secrets does not preclude a separate cause of action in tort under the rules in this Section. The terms of the contract may be relevant to a number of issues in such an action, including the existence of a protectable trade secret (see § 39, Comment *d*) and the creation of a duty of confidence (see § 41, Comment *b*).

In an action for the appropriation of a trade secret, the plaintiff bears the burden of proving both a proprietary interest in information that qualifies for protection as a trade secret under the rule stated in § 39 and an acquisition, use, or disclosure of the information by the defendant in violation of the rules stated here. A proprietary interest sufficient for relief under this Section can arise through the discovery of a trade secret or through the acquisition of rights in a trade secret discovered by another. On the rights of an employer in trade secrets discovered by an employee, see § 42, Comment *e*. Since neither novelty nor absolute secrecy is a prerequisite for protection as a trade secret, see § 39, Comment *f*, each of several independent discoverers can have a proprietary interest in the same information.

b. Improper acquisition. The prior Restatement of this topic imposed liability only for the wrongful use or disclosure of another's trade secret. Improper acquisition of a trade secret was not independently actionable. See Restatement of Torts § 757 (1939). Wrongful use or disclosure is also frequently recited in the case law as an element of the cause of action for trade secret appropriation. The cases requiring proof of wrongful use or disclosure, however, typically involve information that has been acquired by the defendant through a confidential disclosure from the trade secret owner. In such cases the acquisition of the secret is not improper; only a subsequent use or disclosure in breach of the defendant's duty of confidence is wrongful. Even in these circumstances the courts have recognized a plaintiff's right to obtain relief prior to any wrongful use or disclosure if such misconduct by the defendant is sufficiently likely. See § 44, Comment *c*. A defendant's willingness to resort to improper means in order to acquire a trade secret is itself evidence of a substantial risk of subsequent use or disclosure. Subsection (a) of this Section follows the rule adopted in § 1(2)(i) of the Uniform Trade Secrets Act, which imposes liability for the acquisition of a trade secret by improper means. Thus, a person who obtains a trade secret through a wiretap or who induces or knowingly accepts a disclosure of the secret in breach of confidence is subject to liability. See § 43, Comment *c*. Subsequent use or disclosure of a trade secret that has been improperly acquired constitutes a further appropriation under the rule stated in Subsection (b)(2) of this Section. The relief available to the trade secret owner in such circumstances, however, may be more extensive than that available prior to any use or disclosure of the secret by the defendant.

Illustration:

1. *A* and *B* are competitors. *B* knows that *A* has a secret process that substantially reduces manufacturing costs. *C*, an employee of *A* who learned the secret through a confidential disclosure by *A*, offers to sell *A*'s secret to *B*. *B* knows that *C* is employed by *A* and that a disclosure by *C* would be a breach of *C*'s duty of confidence. If *B* purchases the trade secret from *C*, *B* is subject to liability to *A* under the rule stated in Subsection (a) of this Section. If *B* subsequently uses or discloses the secret, *B* is also subject to liability to *A* under the rule stated in Subsection (b)(2) of this Section.

c. Improper use or disclosure. There are no technical limitations on the nature of the conduct that constitutes "use" of a trade secret for purposes of the rules stated in Subsection (b). As a general matter, any exploitation of the trade secret that is likely to result in injury to the trade secret owner or enrichment to the defendant is a "use" under this Section. Thus, marketing goods that embody the trade secret, employing the trade secret in manufacturing or production, relying on the trade secret to assist or accelerate research or development, or soliciting customers through the use of information that is a trade secret (see § 42, Comment *f*) all constitute "use." The nature of the unauthorized use, however, is relevant in determining appropriate relief. See §§ 44 and 45.

The unauthorized use need not extend to every aspect or feature of the trade secret; use of any substantial portion of the secret is sufficient to subject the actor to liability. Similarly, the actor need not use the trade secret in its original form. Thus, an actor is liable for using the trade secret with independently created improvements or modifications if the result is substantially derived from the trade secret. The extent to which the actor's sales or other benefits are attributable to such independent improvements or modifications, however, can affect the computation of monetary relief. See § 45, Comment *f*. However, if the contribution made by the trade secret is so slight that the actor's product or process can be said to derive from other sources of information or from independent creation, the trade secret has not been "used" for purposes of imposing liability under the rules stated in Subsection (b). Although the trade secret owner bears the burden of proving unauthorized use, proof of the defendant's knowledge of the trade secret together with substantial similarities between the parties' products or processes may justify an inference of use by the defendant.

The owner of a trade secret may be injured by unauthorized disclosure of a trade secret as well as by unauthorized use. A public disclosure injures the trade secret owner by destroying the secrecy necessary for continued protection of the information as a trade secret. See § 39, Comment *f*. A private disclosure can increase the likelihood of both unauthorized use and further disclosure. An actor may thus be subject to liability under the circumstances described in Subsection (b) in connection with either a public or private disclosure of a trade secret. To subject the actor to liability, the unauthorized disclosure need not be express. Any conduct by the actor that enables another to learn the trade secret, including the sale or transfer of goods or other tangible objects from which the trade secret can be obtained, is a "disclosure" of the secret under the rules stated in this Section.

The unauthorized disclosure of a trade secret ordinarily occurs as part of an attempt to exploit the commercial value of the secret through use in competition with the trade secret owner or through a sale of the information to other potential users. The scope of liability at common law and under the Uniform Trade Secrets Act for disclosures that do not involve commercial exploitation of the secret information is unclear. If the trade secret is disclosed primarily for the purpose of causing harm to the trade secret owner, a court may properly conclude that the actor is subject to liability despite an absence of commercial exploitation. Thus, a former employee who publicly discloses trade secrets of the former employer in retaliation for a termination of the employment is subject to liability under this Section. In other circumstances, however, the disclosure of another's trade secret for purposes other than commercial exploitation may implicate the interest in freedom of expression or advance another significant public interest. A witness who is compelled by law to disclose another's trade secret during the course of a judicial proceeding, for example, is not subject to liability. The existence of a privilege to disclose another's trade secret depends upon the circumstances of the particular case, including the nature of the information, the purpose of the disclosure, and the means by which the actor acquired the information. A privilege is likely to be recognized, for example, in connection with the disclosure of information that is relevant to public health or safety, or to the commission of a crime or tort, or to other matters of substantial public concern.

d.   Knowledge of wrongful possession. The owner of a trade secret is protected under Subsection (b) of this Section only against a use or disclosure of the trade secret that the actor knows or has reason to know is wrongful. If the actor has not acquired the information through a confidential disclosure from the trade secret owner, see Subsection (b)(1), use or disclosure of the information will not subject the actor to liability unless the actor knew or had reason to know that the use or disclosure was wrongful due to the manner in which the actor acquired the trade secret. See Subsection (b)(2)–(4). Thus, if an actor acquires a trade secret by improper means, such as by inducing or knowingly accepting a disclosure of the information from a third person that is in breach of a duty of confidence, the actor is subject to liability for any subsequent use or disclosure of the secret. See Subsection (b)(2). However, an actor who acquires a trade secret from a third person without notice of that person's breach of confidence has not acquired the information by improper means and is not subject to liability for use or disclosure unless the actor subsequently receives notice that its possession of the information is wrongful. See Subsection (b)(3).

To subject an actor to liability under the rules stated in Subsection (b)(2)–(4), the owner need not prove that the actor knew that its possession of the trade secret was wrongful; it is sufficient if the actor had reason to know. Thus, if a reasonable person in the position of the actor would have inferred that he or she was in wrongful possession of another's trade secret, the actor is subject to liability for any subsequent use or disclosure. A number of cases also subject an actor to liability if, based on the known facts, a reasonable person would have inquired further and learned that possession of the information was wrongful. Studious ignorance of the circumstances surrounding the acquisition of the information thus will not necessarily avoid liability under this Section. Among the facts relevant in establishing the actor's actual or constructive knowledge are the actor's knowledge of any precautions against disclosure taken by the trade secret owner, the actor's familiarity with industry customs or practices that would justify an assumption that a disclosure to the actor by a third person was unauthorized, information known to the actor regarding the nature of the relationship between the trade secret owner and the person from whom the actor acquired the secret, and any direct communications to the actor from the trade secret owner. The actor's reliance on claims of ownership or other assurances given by the person from whom the actor acquired the information is sufficient to avoid liability only if the actor's reliance is reasonable under the circumstances.

If an actor possesses the actual or constructive knowledge required under Subsection (b)(2)–(4) of this Section at the time of the initial acquisition of the secret, the actor is subject to liability for all use or disclosure of the trade secret. If the actor obtains such knowledge after acquisition of the trade secret, the actor is subject to liability for any use or disclosure occurring subsequent to receipt of the requisite knowledge, but is not liable for prior use or disclosure. However, although receipt of the requisite knowledge is sufficient to subject the actor to liability for subsequent conduct, the relief available to the trade secret owner may be limited by the equities of the case. Thus, if before receiving the required knowledge the actor has in good faith paid value for the trade secret, undertaken significant investment in equipment or research relating to the secret, or otherwise substantially changed its position in reliance on the information, the imposition of particular remedies for subsequent use or disclosure may be inappropriate. See § 44, Comment *b*; § 45, Comment *b*.

Illustrations:

2.   *A*, a manufacturer of paints, developed a secret process for the production of exterior house paint. The process was revealed to *B*, a laboratory assistant in *A*'s research department, after *B* agreed not to disclose the information to unauthorized persons. Upon leaving the employment with *A*, *B* accepted a position in the research department of *C*, a competing paint manufacturer. *C* had tried unsuccessfully for several years to duplicate *A*'s process and was aware of *B*'s prior employment in *A*'s laboratory. Three weeks after joining *C*'s research staff, *B* submitted a report to *C* describing a process that produced paints identical to *A*'s. The process was immediately implemented by *C*. A court may properly conclude that *C* knew or had reason to know that *B* had made an unauthorized disclosure of *A*'s trade secret and that *C* is therefore subject to liability to *A* under the rule stated in Subsection (b)(3) of this Section.

3.   *A*, the owner of computer software containing trade secrets relating to the efficient operation of assembly lines, discloses the software in confidence to *B*, a computer consultant. *B* subsequently offers to sell the software to *C*, a manufacturer. *C* neither knows nor has reason to know that the software contains trade secrets belonging to *A*. *C* purchases the software from *B* for $100,000 and substantially modifies its computer system and assembly line to accommodate the new software. After *C* has used the software for one year, *A* learns of the improper disclosure by *B* and notifies *C* of the circumstances surrounding *B*'s acquisition of the software. *C* is not subject to liability to *A* for use of the software prior to the receipt of *A*'s notice. *C* is subject to liability to *A* for any use of the software subsequent to the notice, but the relief available to *A* may be limited because of *C*'s good faith purchase

and subsequent expenditures in implementing the system. See § 44, Comment *b*; § 45, Comment *b*.

§ 41 Duty of Confidence

A person to whom a trade secret has been disclosed owes a duty of confidence to the owner of the trade secret for purposes of the rule stated in § 40 if:

(a) the person made an express promise of confidentiality prior to the disclosure of the trade secret; or

(b) the trade secret was disclosed to the person under circumstances in which the relationship between the parties to the disclosure or the other facts surrounding the disclosure justify the conclusions that, at the time of the disclosure,

(1) the person knew or had reason to know that the disclosure was intended to be in confidence, and

(2) the other party to the disclosure was reasonable in inferring that the person consented to an obligation of confidentiality.

Comment:

b. Confidential disclosures. A duty of confidence enforceable under the rules stated in § 40 can be created by an express promise of confidentiality made by the recipient of the disclosure. A duty of confidence may also be inferred from the relationship between the parties and the circumstances surrounding the disclosure. However, no duty of confidence will be inferred unless the recipient has notice of the confidential nature of the disclosure. Although no specific form of notice is required, the circumstances must indicate that the recipient knew or had reason to know that the disclosure was intended as confidential. In addition, the circumstances must justify the other party's belief that the recipient has consented to the duty of confidence. Thus, a disclosure to one who has indicated an unwillingness to accept the confidence or who has no opportunity prior to the disclosure to object to the imposition of the confidence will not create an obligation of confidentiality in the recipient.

In some cases the customs of the particular business or industry may be sufficient to indicate to the recipient that a particular disclosure is intended as confidential. The customary expectations surrounding the disclosure of information in noncommercial settings may differ from those arising in connection with disclosures in commercial contexts. The customary expectations regarding the confidentiality of information disclosed within the research facilities of an industrial firm, for example, may differ from those regarding disclosures in a nonprofit research laboratory. Precautions undertaken by the trade secret owner to maintain the secrecy of the information, if known to the recipient, can be evidence that the recipient knew or had reason to know of the owner's expectation of confidentiality. Solicitation of the disclosure by the recipient can also contribute to an inference of confidentiality, particularly if the disclosure is prompted by a misrepresentation or other improper conduct on the part of the recipient. In some cases an express agreement regarding the confidentiality of particular information may be evidence of the parties' expectations regarding the confidentiality of other information not within the scope of the agreement.

If the owner of a trade secret discloses information for a limited purpose that is known to the recipient at the time of the disclosure, the recipient is ordinarily bound by the limitation unless the recipient has indicated an unwillingness to accept the disclosure on such terms. During negotiations with prospective buyers, customers, or licensees, for example, it is sometimes necessary to disclose trade secrets in order to permit the other party to evaluate the merits of the proposed transaction. The law of trade secrets provides the necessary assurance that the limited purpose of such disclosures will be respected.

In the absence of an agreement to the contrary, the sale of a product embodying a trade secret is not ordinarily regarded as a confidential disclosure. The purchaser is thus free to exploit any information acquired through an examination or analysis of the product. However, a transaction such as a lease or a bailment may be more likely to support an inference of confidentiality if the parties understand the transfer to be for a limited purpose. The transfer of a machine embodying trade secrets for the purpose of repair, for example, does not ordinarily authorize the transferee to use or disclose trade secrets learned as a result of the transaction.

Courts frequently recognize an obligation to refrain from the unauthorized use or disclosure of information that is communicated between parties in a so-called "confidential relationship." Certain business relationships such as employer-employee and licensor-licensee are sometimes characterized as "confidential." The fact that the parties are engaged in such an on-going relationship is relevant in determining whether a specific disclosure creates a duty of confidence, but not every disclosure made in the context of a particular relationship is properly treated as confidential. Even within a relationship generally characterized as "confidential," the purpose of the disclosure, the past practice of the parties, the customs of the industry, and the other circumstances of the disclosure remain relevant in determining the recipient's obligations. Thus, although the disclosure to a licensee of a secret formula that is the subject of a license is normally regarded as confidential, a disclosure of other information to a licensee with no indication that the information is confidential may not give rise to a duty of confidence. The special considerations applicable to disclosures within an employment relationship are considered in § 42.

Illustrations:

1.   *A*, a manufacturer, develops a new food-processing machine that incorporates innovations eligible for protection as trade secrets. *B*,

an engineering professor at a local university, asks permission from A to inspect the machine. A grants permission without expressing any need or desire for confidentiality. B subsequently uses information acquired during the inspection to design a competing machine. In the absence of evidence establishing that B knew or had reason to know that the inspection was intended by A to be for a limited purpose or was otherwise intended as confidential, B is not subject to liability under the rules stated in § 40.

2. A and B are negotiating for the sale of A's soft drink business to B. A discloses the secret formula used to produce the soft drink in order to permit B to assess the value of A's business. B subsequently terminates the negotiations and begins to use the formula. B is subject to liability to A under the rules stated in § 40 since B knew or had reason to know that the disclosure was for the limited purpose of enabling B to evaluate the merits of the proposed transaction.

3. The facts being otherwise as stated in Illustration 2, during the negotiations for A's business A also discloses to B plans for a chain of fast-food restaurants that A intends to open after the soft drink business is sold. B subsequently opens several restaurants modeled after those described by A. Since the disclosure was not made for a limited purpose apparent from the nature of the parties' business relationship, B is not subject to liability to A under the rules stated in § 40 unless other evidence establishes that B knew or had reason to know that A intended the disclosure to be confidential and that A was reasonable in believing that B consented to the duty of confidence.

c. *Breach of confidence as a separate tort.* Some courts have recognized liability in tort for the unauthorized disclosure of confidential business information found to be ineligible for protection as a trade secret. In some cases the claim is designated as one for "breach of confidence," while in others it is described as one for "unfair competition." Many of these cases rest on a narrow definition of "trade secret" that excludes non-technical information such as customer identities or information that is not subject to continuous, long-term use. Such information is now subsumed under the broader definition of "trade secret" adopted in § 39. In other cases the imposition of liability for breach of confidence may be justified by interests other than the protection of valuable commercial information, such as the interests that prompt recognition of the general duty of loyalty owed by an employee to an employer, see § 42, Comment *b*, or the special duties of confidence owed in particular relationships such as attorney and client or doctor and patient. However, in the absence of interests justifying broader duties, the plaintiff should be required to demonstrate that the information qualifies for protection as a trade secret under the rule stated in § 39. The recognition of more extensive rights against the use or disclosure of commercial information can restrict access to knowledge that is properly regarded as part of the public domain. Cf. § 39, Comment *f*.

§ 42   Breach of Confidence by Employees

An employee or former employee who uses or discloses a trade secret owned by the employer or former employer in breach of a duty of confidence is subject to liability for appropriation of the trade secret under the rule stated in § 40.

Comment:

d.   General skill, knowledge, training, and experience. Information that forms the general skill, knowledge, training, and experience of an employee cannot be claimed as a trade secret by a former employer even when the information is directly attributable to an investment of resources by the employer in the employee. The Statute of Apprentices enacted in England in 1562, 5 Eliz. I, ch. 4, which mandated a seven-year period of apprenticeship to a master, was in part an early attempt to reconcile the interest of employers in capturing the benefits of their investment in the training of employees and the interest of employees in a competitive market for their services. The modern balance relies primarily on the recognition of a duty of loyalty during the period of employment, see Comment *b*, the ability of employers and employees in most states to contract for reasonable restrictions on the employee's freedom to compete with the employer after termination of the employment, see § 41, Comment *d*, and the recognition of rights in specific information that is eligible for protection as a trade secret. Thus, absent an enforceable covenant not to compete, a former employee may utilize in competition with the former employer the general skills, knowledge, training, and experience acquired during the employment, but the employee remains obligated to refrain from using or disclosing the employer's trade secrets.

Whether particular information is properly regarded as a trade secret of the former employer or as part of the general skill, knowledge, training, and experience of the former employee depends on the facts and circumstances of the particular case. An employer who is asserting rights in information against a former employee bears the burden of proving the existence and ownership of a trade secret. Trade secret rights are more likely to be recognized in specialized information unique to the employer's business than in information more widely known in the industry or derived from skills generally possessed by persons employed in the industry. The relative contribution of the employer and employee to the development of the information can also be relevant. The fact that other competitors have been unsuccessful in independent attempts to develop the information may suggest that the information qualifies for protection as a trade secret. Courts are also more likely to conclude that particular information is a trade secret if the employee on termination of the employment appropriates some physical embodiment of the information such as written formulas, blueprints, plans, or lists of customers. However, although information that is retained in the employee's memory may be less likely to be regarded as a trade secret absent evidence of intentional memorization, the inference is not conclusive.

The distinction between trade secrets and general skill, knowledge, training, and experience is intended to achieve a reasonable balance between the protection of confidential information and the mobility of employees. If the information is so closely integrated with the employee's overall employment experience that protection would deprive the employee of the ability to obtain employment commensurate with the employee's general qualifications, it will not ordinarily be protected as a trade secret of the former employer.

§ 43   Improper Acquisition of Trade Secrets

"Improper" means of acquiring another's trade secret under the rule stated in § 40 include theft, fraud, unauthorized interception of communications, inducement of or knowing participation in a breach of confidence, and other means either wrongful in themselves or wrongful under the circumstances of the case. Independent discovery and analysis of publicly available products or information are not improper means of acquisition.

Comment:

b.   Proper means of acquisition. Unless a trade secret has been acquired under circumstances giving rise to a duty of confidence, a person who obtains the trade secret by proper means is free to use or disclose the information without liability. Unlike the holder of a patent, the owner of a trade secret has no claim against another who independently discovers the secret. Similarly, others remain free to analyze products publicly marketed by the trade secret owner and, absent protection under a patent or copyright, to exploit any information acquired through such "reverse engineering." A person may also acquire a trade secret through an analysis of published materials or through observation of objects or events that are in public view or otherwise accessible by proper means.

Illustrations:

1.   *A* sells a drug compounded from a secret formula. *B*, a competing drug manufacturer, purchases a quantity of *A*'s drug on the open market and learns the formula through scientific analysis. *B* then begins to market a similar product. *B* has not acquired *A*'s trade secret by improper means.

2.   *A*, a chemical company, discovers a new process for producing methanol and begins construction of a manufacturing plant incorporating the process. Although the construction site is clearly visible from a major highway that adjoins the site, *A* takes no precautions to prevent passersby from observing construction of the plant. *B*, a competing chemical company, sends several of its engineers

to observe *A*'s construction site. The engineers take photographs of the partially-completed plant from the adjoining highway. Subsequent analysis of the photographs reveals *A*'s new process. *B* has not acquired *A*'s trade secret by improper means.

c. *Improper means of acquisition.* It is not possible to formulate a comprehensive list of the conduct that constitutes "improper" means of acquiring a trade secret. If a trade secret is acquired through conduct that is itself a tortious or criminal invasion of the trade secret owner's rights, the acquisition ordinarily will be regarded as improper. Thus, a person who obtains a trade secret by burglarizing the offices of a competitor acquires the secret by improper means. So also does one who obtains a trade secret by wiretapping the owner's telephone or by employing fraudulent representations to induce the owner to disclose the trade secret. A person who obtains a trade secret by inducing or knowingly accepting a disclosure from a third person who has acquired the secret by improper means, or who induces or knowingly accepts a disclosure from a third person that is in breach of a duty of confidence owed by the third person to the trade secret owner, also acquires the secret by improper means.

The acquisition of a trade secret can be improper even if the means of acquisition are not independently wrongful. The propriety of the acquisition must be evaluated in light of all the circumstances of the case, including whether the means of acquisition are inconsistent with accepted principles of public policy and the extent to which the acquisition was facilitated by the trade secret owner's failure to take reasonable precautions against discovery of the secret by the means in question. Among the factors relevant to the reasonableness of the trade secret owner's precautions are the foreseeability of the conduct through which the secret was acquired and the availability and cost of effective precautions against such an acquisition, evaluated in light of the economic value of the trade secret.

Illustrations:

3. The facts being otherwise as stated in Illustration 2, *B*'s engineers are unable to photograph *A*'s plant from the adjoining highway because of a large fence erected by *A* to prevent observation of the construction site from the surrounding area. However, because of the size of the site and the nature of the plant, it would be difficult and expensive for *A* to maintain a temporary roof over the site during construction. *B* hires a pilot who flies over the site in a small airplane while *B*'s engineers photograph portions of the partially-completed facility. Subsequent analysis of the photographs reveals *A*'s new process. A court may conclude that *A* has taken reasonable precautions against the discovery of the process and that *B* has acquired *A*'s trade secret by improper means.

4. *A*, a large manufacturing company, employs *B* as an engineer. Angered by a termination of the employment, *B* makes unauthorized photocopies of engineering drawings depicting trade secrets used in the

machines that manufacture A's most successful product. B offers to provide the photocopies to C, a competing manufacturer. C accepts the photocopies from B with knowledge that B is a former employee of A. C has acquired A's trade secrets by improper means.

5. A manufactures a computer system for the transmission, display, and storage of medical data. The system has been licensed for use in several large hospitals under agreements that require the licensees to maintain the confidentiality of trade secrets embodied in A's system. B is hired as a consultant by one of A's licensees and is informed of the confidential nature of A's system. B decides to design and market a competing system. After normal working hours and without the permission of the licensee, B spends a substantial number of hours subjecting A's system to a series of electronic tests in order to learn the trade secrets. B has acquired A's trade secrets by improper means.

§ 44 Injunctions: Appropriation of Trade Secrets

(1) If appropriate under the rule stated in Subsection (2), injunctive relief may be awarded to prevent a continuing or threatened appropriation of another's trade secret by one who is subject to liability under the rule stated in § 40.

(2) The appropriateness and scope of injunctive relief depend upon a comparative appraisal of all the factors of the case, including the following primary factors:

(a) the nature of the interest to be protected;

(b) the nature and extent of the appropriation;

(c) the relative adequacy to the plaintiff of an injunction and of other remedies;

(d) the relative harm likely to result to the legitimate interests of the defendant if an injunction is granted and to the legitimate interests of the plaintiff if an injunction is denied;

(e) the interests of third persons and of the public;

(f) any unreasonable delay by the plaintiff in bringing suit or otherwise asserting its rights;

(g) any related misconduct on the part of the plaintiff; and

(h) the practicality of framing and enforcing the injunction.

(3) The duration of injunctive relief in trade secret actions should be limited to the time necessary to protect the plaintiff from any harm attributable to the appropriation and to deprive the defendant of any economic advantage attributable to the appropriation.

Comment:

f.　Duration of injunctive relief. Injunctions are appropriate in trade secret cases to protect the plaintiff from further harm caused by the use or disclosure of the trade secret and to deprive the defendant of further unjust gain. However, the law of trade secrets does not afford protection against losses or gains that are not attributable to the defendant's appropriation. This principle establishes the appropriate duration of injunctive relief in trade secret cases. Thus, injunctive relief should ordinarily continue only until the defendant could have acquired the information by proper means. Injunctions extending beyond this period are justified only when necessary to deprive the defendant of a head start or other unjust advantage that is attributable to the appropriation. See Uniform Trade Secrets Act § 2(a). More extensive injunctive relief undermines the public interest by restraining legitimate competition.

The issuance of a patent or other public disclosure renders the disclosed information ineligible for continued protection as a trade secret. See § 39, Comment *f.* Some courts, however, have issued or continued injunctions after public disclosure of the trade secret against defendants who appropriated the information while it was still secret. Other courts hold that public disclosure precludes the subsequent issuance of an injunction and justifies termination of an injunction previously granted. When the trade secret is publicly disclosed by the plaintiff or a third person after the defendant's appropriation, the proper inquiry is whether injunctive relief remains necessary to protect against future injury to the plaintiff or future unjust enrichment to the defendant that is attributable to the defendant's wrongful actions prior to the public disclosure. Whether an injunction remains appropriate thus depends on the facts of the particular case. For example, early access to information subsequently disclosed in a patent may allow the defendant to bring to market or reduce to practice the teachings of the patent more quickly than otherwise possible. Similarly, the public disclosure may not encompass all aspects of the information appropriated by the defendant. Limited injunctive relief may thus remain appropriate to eliminate an improper economic advantage that would otherwise be retained by the defendant after the public disclosure of the trade secret. If the public disclosure results from the defendant's own unauthorized conduct, injunctive relief may remain appropriate until the information would have become readily ascertainable to the defendant through proper means. However, if the defendant's public disclosure results in extensive use of the information by others, a continuing injunction against the defendant may yield little benefit to the plaintiff. It may also be difficult to determine the appropriate duration of such an injunction. Since the defendant is subject to liability for the pecuniary loss to the plaintiff resulting from the destruction of the trade secret and for its own pecuniary gain derived from the unauthorized disclosure, see § 45, in some cases a court may properly conclude that monetary relief is a sufficient remedy.

An injunction also should not ordinarily extend beyond the time when the defendant could have properly acquired and implemented the information through reverse engineering or independent discovery. Subsequent use by the defendant does not subject the plaintiff to harm that is attributable to the appropriation of the trade secret. In some cases this duration may be measured by the time it would take a person of ordinary skill in the industry to discover the trade secret by independent means or to obtain the trade secret through the reverse engineering of publicly marketed products. The opinions of experts familiar with the particular industry are thus relevant in determining an appropriate duration. The experience of other competitors in attempting to acquire the information by proper means is also relevant in determining the time it would have taken the defendant to acquire the information in the absence of the appropriation. The defendant may also show that because of a comparative advantage unrelated to the appropriation, the period of lawful development would have been shorter than that for others in the industry. The duration of the injunction, however, should be sufficient to deprive the defendant of any head start or other economic advantage attributable to the appropriation. In some cases courts have issued injunctions for a specific period reflecting the time when the defendant could have acquired the information by proper means. In other cases courts have awarded unlimited injunctions, with the burden on the defendant to seek a modification of the injunction when the commercial advantage from the appropriation has ended. The most efficient procedure depends on the ease and certainty with which the appropriate duration of relief can be determined in advance. In either case the defendant remains liable for any expenses of reverse engineering or independent development that the defendant has saved as a result of the appropriation. See § 45, Comment *f*.

Illustrations:

1. *A* produces a chemical through a process eligible for protection as a trade secret. *B*, a former employee of *A* who learned the process in confidence, establishes a competing business to produce the chemical using the secret process. *C*, a research chemist at a major university, later independently discovers the process and describes it in an article published in a prominent chemistry journal. An injunction against *B*'s use or disclosure of the process should not extend beyond the time of the public disclosure by *C* and any additional period necessary to eliminate any economic advantage to *B* resulting from *B*'s head start in exploiting the information prior to the public disclosure.

2. *A*, a manufacturer, initiates a research project intended to produce a precision tape recorder. *B* works as an engineer on the project through its successful completion and subsequently leaves the employment with *A* to establish a competing business using trade secrets learned during the former employment. Before *B* begins marketing the product, *A* brings an action in which *B* is found liable for appropriating *A*'s trade secrets. The evidence indicates that it would take six months to

acquire the trade secrets through reverse engineering of the tape recorders that *A* has begun to market and to embody the secrets in a finished product. If an injunction is otherwise appropriate, the court may properly conclude that *B* should be enjoined from use or disclosure of the trade secrets for six months following the commencement of sales by *A*. Alternatively, the court may properly conclude that *B* should be enjoined from use or disclosure of the trade secrets for an unlimited time, subject to *B*'s right to apply for a termination of the injunction upon proof that the period required for successful reverse engineering and implementation has passed. *B* is also subject to liability to *A* for any costs associated with reverse engineering that have been saved by *B* as result of the appropriation. See § 45, Comment *f*.

§ 45   Monetary Relief: Appropriation of Trade Secrets

(1) One who is liable to another for an appropriation of the other's trade secret under the rule stated in § 40 is liable for the pecuniary loss to the other caused by the appropriation or for the actor's own pecuniary gain resulting from the appropriation, whichever is greater, unless such relief is inappropriate under the rule stated in Subsection (2).

(2) Whether an award of monetary relief is appropriate and the appropriate method of measuring such relief depend upon a comparative appraisal of all the factors of the case, including the following primary factors:

(a) the degree of certainty with which the plaintiff has established the fact and extent of the pecuniary loss or the actor's pecuniary gain resulting from the appropriation;

(b) the nature and extent of the appropriation;

(c) the relative adequacy to the plaintiff of other remedies;

(d) the intent and knowledge of the actor and the nature and extent of any good faith reliance by the actor;

(e) any unreasonable delay by the plaintiff in bringing suit or otherwise asserting its rights; and

(f) any related misconduct on the part of the plaintiff.

Comment:

e. Relief measured by plaintiff's loss. A frequent element of loss resulting from the appropriation of a trade secret is the lost profit that the plaintiff would have earned in the absence of the use by the defendant. The plaintiff may prove lost profits by identifying specific customers diverted to the defendant. The plaintiff may also prove lost profits through proof of a general decline in sales or a disruption of business growth following the commencement of use by the defendant, although the presence of other market factors that may affect the plaintiff's sales bears on the sufficiency of the plaintiff's proof. If the evidence justifies the conclusion that the sales made by the defendant would have instead been made by the plaintiff in the absence of the appropriation, the plaintiff may establish its lost profits by applying its own profit margin to the defendant's sales. Upon sufficient proof, the plaintiff may also recover lost profits on sales of spare parts, service, supplies, or other items normally purchased from the original seller. In some cases it may be appropriate to measure the plaintiff's loss by a reasonable royalty on the sales made by the defendant. See Comment g.

A plaintiff may also recover any other proven pecuniary loss attributable to the appropriation. Courts have permitted recovery of the costs of remedial efforts such as promotional expenses undertaken to recapture customers lost as a result of the defendant's appropriation. The plaintiff is also entitled to recover losses associated with sales of its own goods at reduced prices resulting from the wrongful competition of the defendant.

Damages resulting from the unauthorized disclosure of a trade secret are frequently more difficult to measure than damages caused by unauthorized use. For example, in some cases a defendant's unauthorized disclosure to one competitor of the plaintiff may cause the trade secret to become known to other competitors or to enter the public domain, thus destroying the value of the secret. The appropriate measure of relief may then be the fair market value of the trade secret at the time of the appropriation. This measure can depend upon a variety of factors, including the likelihood that the trade secret would have become known in the absence of the defendant's appropriation. See Comment h. If the destroyed trade secret is a central asset of the plaintiff's business, the plaintiff can in some cases measure damages by the reduction in the capital value of the business caused by the appropriation.

f. *Relief measured by defendant's gain.* The traditional form of restitutionary relief in an action for the appropriation of a trade secret is an accounting of the defendant's profits on sales attributable to the use of the trade secret. The general rules governing accountings of profits are applicable in trade secret actions. The plaintiff is entitled to recover the defendant's net profits. The plaintiff has the burden of establishing the defendant's sales; the defendant has the burden of establishing any portion of the sales not attributable to the trade secret and any expenses to be deducted in determining net profits. The rules governing the deductibility of expenses and the allocation of overhead are analogous to those stated in § 37, Comments g and h, on accountings in actions for trademark infringement. The defendant must account not only for profits earned on sales of products incorporating the trade secret, but also on other sales dependent on the appropriation. For example, profits on the sale of consumable supplies used in a machine embodying the trade secret or profits on spare parts and service may be included in the accounting to the extent that such profits were made possible by the defendant's sale of the original product.

If the trade secret accounts for only a portion of the profits earned on the defendant's sales, such as when the trade secret relates to a single component of a product marketable without the secret, an award to the plaintiff of defendant's entire profit may be unjust. The royalty that the plaintiff and defendant would have agreed to for the use of the trade secret made by the defendant may be one measure of the approximate portion of the defendant's profits attributable to the use. See Comment g.

If the benefit derived by the defendant consists primarily of cost savings, such as when the trade secret is a more efficient method of production, the "standard of comparison" measure that determines relief based on the savings achieved through the use of the trade secret may be the most appropriate measure of relief. The standard of comparison measure determines the defendant's gain by comparing the defendant's actual costs with the costs that the defendant would have incurred to achieve the same result without the use of the appropriated trade secret. When it would have been possible for the defendant to acquire the trade secret by proper means such as reverse engineering or independent development, the appropriate comparison may be between the costs of such acquisition and the cost of using the appropriated information. In determining the costs of proper acquisition, the court may consider the actual development costs of the plaintiff and, if available, the development or reverse engineering costs of third persons. When acquisition of the trade secret by proper means is unlikely, the appropriate comparison may be between the costs of using the trade secret and the costs of alternative methods available to the defendant to achieve the same result.

Under the principles discussed in § 44, Comment f, it is often appropriate to enjoin the defendant's use of a trade secret only for the period of time that would have been required for the defendant to acquire the information by proper means. In such cases, however, the defendant remains liable for any development or reverse engineering costs saved as a result of the appropriation that are not otherwise accounted for through an award of the defendant's profits or other monetary relief.

Illustrations:

2.   A and B are competing manufacturers of poultry vaccines. A spends $400,000 to develop a secret process for the production of a new vaccine. B appropriates the trade secret and begins to produce the vaccine in competition with A. B earns $50,000 in net profits on sales of the vaccine. In the absence of evidence indicating loss to A in excess of $50,000, A may recover B's $50,000 profit in addition to the award of an injunction prohibiting further use of the process by B.

3.   The facts being otherwise as stated in Illustration 2, B establishes that other competitors have already succeeded in duplicating A's secret process by analyzing samples of A's vaccine and that B would have been similarly successful. The cost of such an analysis is $150,000. The court may properly conclude that an injunction against B's use of

the process would be inappropriate and that an award to *A* of $150,000 representing *B*'s savings in analysis costs and $50,000 representing the net profits earned by *B* prior to the time it would have been able to market the vaccine in the absence of the appropriation is an appropriate remedy.

4.   *A*, a shipper, invents several techniques and devices to improve efficiency in the unloading of ships. *B*, a former employee of *A*, discloses the trade secrets to *C*, a competing shipper, in breach of a duty of confidence. *C*, with notice of *B*'s breach of confidence, adopts the techniques and devices in its business. In addition to appropriate injunctive relief, *A* may recover from *C* any savings that have resulted from *C*'s use of *A*'s trade secrets.

g.   Reasonable royalty. A reasonable royalty measure of relief awards to the plaintiff the price that would be set by a willing buyer and a willing seller for the use of the trade secret made by the defendant. However, the royalty agreed to in an actual market transaction reflects a price at which both parties gain from the transaction. To the extent that a court-awarded reasonable royalty accurately reflects the marketplace, the royalty may compensate the plaintiff for loss but it does not necessarily deprive the defendant of the full gain attributable to the appropriation. Since the imposition of a reasonable royalty requires the defendant to pay only the amount it would have paid had it fairly bargained for use of the plaintiff's secret, it may not adequately discourage the appropriation of trade secrets.

There are at least three situations in which the reasonable royalty measure of relief has been applied. First, when the defendant has made a substantial good faith investment in the trade secret prior to receiving notice of the plaintiff's claim, it may be inequitable to require the relinquishment of all profits earned by the defendant after notice. An award of damages measured by a reasonable royalty for use subsequent to the notice and an injunction conditioning future use on the payment of a reasonable royalty gives the plaintiff the market value of the trade secret but protects the defendant's good faith reliance. Second, when the plaintiff's loss, although difficult to measure, is apparently greater than any gain acquired by the defendant, a reasonable royalty may be the most appropriate measure of relief. For example, if the defendant's inefficiency results in little or no profit from the exploitation of the trade secret and the loss to the plaintiff cannot otherwise be established, a reasonable royalty may be the best available approximation of the plaintiff's loss. Third, in cases in which the defendant's gain from the trade secret is difficult to measure but apparently exceeds the plaintiff's loss, a reasonable royalty may be the best means of approximating the defendant's unjust enrichment.

The purpose for which the reasonable royalty measure is invoked and the equities of the particular case may properly influence the calculation of the appropriate royalty. To insure adequate deterrence and to prevent unjust enrichment, a court may resolve issues relating to the amount of the royalty against a defendant who has willfully appropriated the trade secret.

Illustration:

5.   The facts being otherwise as stated in Illustration 4, *C* has no notice of *B*'s breach of confidence until after *C* has invested in equipment designed to implement the trade secrets in its business. A court may properly conclude that the appropriate remedy is a monetary award measured by a reasonable royalty for use of the trade secret by *C* subsequent to the notice of *B*'s breach of confidence and an injunction conditioning future use by *C* on the payment of a reasonable royalty.

VI. LANHAM ACT
(15 U.S.C. §§ 1051–1052, 1064, 1114–1117, 1119, 1125, 1127)

■ ■ ■

Table of Sections

Section

---

§ 1051.   Application for registration; verification (Lanham Act § 1)

(a) Application for use of trademark

(1) The owner of a trademark used in commerce may request registration of its trademark on the principal register hereby established by paying the prescribed fee and filing in the Patent and Trademark Office an application and a verified statement, in such form as may be prescribed by the Director, and such number of specimens or facsimiles of the mark as used as may be required by the Director.

(2) The application shall include specification of the applicant's domicile and citizenship, the date of the applicant's first use of the mark, the date of the applicant's first use of the mark in commerce, the goods in connection with which the mark is used, and a drawing of the mark.

(3) The statement shall be verified by the applicant and specify that—

(A) the person making the verification believes that he or she, or the juristic person in whose behalf he or she makes the verification, to be the owner of the mark sought to be registered;

(B) to the best of the verifier's knowledge and belief, the facts recited in the application are accurate;

(C) the mark is in use in commerce; and

(D) to the best of the verifier's knowledge and belief, no other person has the right to use such mark in commerce either in the identical form thereof or in such near resemblance thereto as to be likely, when used on or in connection with the goods of such other person, to cause confusion, or to cause mistake, or to deceive, except that, in the case of every application claiming concurrent use, the applicant shall—

    (i) state exceptions to the claim of exclusive use; and

    (ii) shall specify, to the extent of the verifier's knowledge—

        (I) any concurrent use by others;

        (II) the goods on or in connection with which and the areas in which each concurrent use exists;

        (III) the periods of each use; and

        (IV) the goods and area for which the applicant desires registration.

(4) The applicant shall comply with such rules or regulations as may be prescribed by the Director. The Director shall promulgate rules prescribing the requirements for the application and for obtaining a filing date herein.

(b) Application for bona fide intention to use trademark

(1) A person who has a bona fide intention, under circumstances showing the good faith of such person, to use a trademark in commerce may request registration of its trademark on the principal register hereby established by paying the prescribed fee and filing in the Patent and Trademark Office an application and a verified statement, in such form as may be prescribed by the Director.

(2) The application shall include specification of the applicant's domicile and citizenship, the goods in connection with which the applicant has a bona fide intention to use the mark, and a drawing of the mark.

(3) The statement shall be verified by the applicant and specify—

(A) that the person making the verification believes that he or she, or the juristic person in whose behalf he or she makes the verification, to be entitled to use the mark in commerce;

(B) the applicant's bona fide intention to use the mark in commerce;

(C) that, to the best of the verifier's knowledge and belief, the facts recited in the application are accurate; and

(D) that, to the best of the verifier's knowledge and belief, no other person has the right to use such mark in commerce either in the identical form thereof or in such near resemblance thereto as to be likely, when used on or in connection with the goods of such other person, to cause confusion, or to cause mistake, or to deceive.

Except for applications filed pursuant to section 1126 of this title, no mark shall be registered until the applicant has met the requirements of subsections (c) and (d) of this section.

(4) The applicant shall comply with such rules or regulations as may be prescribed by the Director. The Director shall promulgate rules prescribing the requirements for the application and for obtaining a filing date herein.

(c) Amendment of application under subsection (b) to conform to requirements of subsection (a)

At any time during examination of an application filed under subsection (b) of this section, an applicant who has made use of the mark in commerce may claim the benefits of such use for purposes of this chapter, by amending his or her application to bring it into conformity with the requirements of subsection (a) of this section.

(d) Verified statement that trademark is used in commerce

(1) Within six months after the date on which the notice of allowance with respect to a mark is issued under section 1063(b)(2) of this title to an applicant under subsection (b) of this section, the applicant shall file in the Patent and Trademark Office, together with such number of specimens or facsimiles of the mark as used in commerce as may be required by the Director and payment of the prescribed fee, a verified statement that the mark is in use in commerce and specifying the date of the applicant's first use of the mark in commerce and those goods or services specified in the notice of allowance on or in connection with which the mark is used in commerce. Subject to examination and acceptance of the statement of use, the mark shall be registered in the Patent and Trademark Office, a certificate of registration shall be issued for those goods or services recited in the statement of use for which the mark is entitled to registration, and notice of registration shall be published in the Official Gazette of the Patent and Trademark Office. Such examination may include an examination of the factors set forth in subsections (a) through (e) of section 1052 of this title. The notice of registration shall specify the goods or services for which the mark is registered.

(2) The Director shall extend, for one additional 6–month period, the time for filing the statement of use under paragraph (1), upon written request of the applicant before the expiration of the 6–month period provided in paragraph (1). In addition to an extension under the preceding sentence, the Director may, upon a showing of good cause by the applicant, further extend the time for filing the statement of use under paragraph (1) for periods aggregating not more than 24 months, pursuant to written request of the applicant made before the expiration of the last extension granted under this paragraph. Any request for an extension under this paragraph shall be accompanied by a verified statement that the applicant has a continued bona fide intention to use the mark in commerce and specifying those goods or services identified in the notice of allowance on or in connection with which the applicant has a continued bona fide intention to use the mark in commerce. Any request for an extension under this paragraph shall be accompanied by payment of the prescribed fee. The Director shall issue regulations setting forth guidelines for determining what constitutes good cause for purposes of this paragraph.

(3) The Director shall notify any applicant who files a statement of use of the acceptance or refusal thereof and, if the statement of use is refused, the reasons for the refusal. An applicant may amend the statement of use.

(4) The failure to timely file a verified statement of use under paragraph (1) or an extension request under paragraph (2) shall result in abandonment of the application, unless it can be shown to the satisfaction of the Director that the delay in responding was unintentional, in which case the time for filing may be extended, but for a period not to exceed the period specified in paragraphs (1) and (2) for filing a statement of use.

(e) Designation of resident for service of process and notices

If the applicant is not domiciled in the United States the applicant may designate, by a document filed in the United States Patent and Trademark Office, the name and address of a person resident in the United States on whom may be served notices or process in proceedings affecting the mark. Such notices or process may be served upon the person so designated by leaving with that person or mailing to that person a copy thereof at the address specified in the last designation so filed. If the person so designated cannot be found at the address given in the last designation, or if the registrant does not designate by a document filed in the United States Patent and Trademark Office the name and address of a person resident in the United States on whom may be served notices or process in proceedings affecting the mark, such notices or process may be served on the Director.

§ 1052. Trademarks registrable on principal register; concurrent registration (Lanham Act § 2)

No trademark by which the goods of the applicant may be distinguished from the goods of others shall be refused registration on the principal register on account of its nature unless it—

(a) Consists of or comprises immoral, deceptive, or scandalous matter; or matter which may disparage or falsely suggest a connection with persons, living or dead, institutions, beliefs, or national symbols, or bring them into contempt, or disrepute; or a geographical indication which, when used on or in connection with wines or spirits, identifies a place other than the origin of the goods and is first used on or in connection with wines or spirits by the applicant on or after one year after the date on which the WTO Agreement (as defined in section 3501(9) of Title 19) enters into force with respect to the United States.

(b) Consists of or comprises the flag or coat of arms or other insignia of the United States, or of any State or municipality, or of any foreign nation, or any simulation thereof.

(c) Consists of or comprises a name, portrait, or signature identifying a particular living individual except by his written consent, or the name, signature, or portrait of a deceased President of the United States during the life of his widow, if any, except by the written consent of the widow.

(d) Consists of or comprises a mark which so resembles a mark registered in the Patent and Trademark Office, or a mark or trade name previously used in the United States by another and not abandoned, as to be likely, when used on or in connection with the goods of the applicant, to cause confusion, or to cause mistake, or to deceive: *Provided,* That if the Director determines that confusion, mistake, or deception is not likely to result from the continued use by more than one person of the same or similar marks under conditions and limitations as to the mode or place of use of the marks or the goods on or in connection with which such marks are used, concurrent registrations may be issued to such persons when they have become entitled to use such marks as a result of their concurrent lawful use in commerce prior to (1) the earliest of the filing dates of the applications pending or of any registration issued under this chapter; (2) July 5, 1947, in the case of registrations previously issued under the Act of March 3, 1881, or February 20, 1905, and continuing in full force and effect on that date; or (3) July 5, 1947, in the case of applications filed under the Act of February 20, 1905, and registered after July 5, 1947. Use prior to the filing date of any pending application or a registration shall not be required when the owner of such application or registration consents to the grant of a concurrent registration to the applicant. Concurrent registrations may also be issued by the Director when a court of competent jurisdiction has finally determined that more than one person is entitled to use the same or similar marks in commerce. In issuing concurrent registrations, the Director shall prescribe conditions and limitations as to the mode or place of use of the mark or the goods on or in connection with which such mark is registered to the respective persons.

(e) Consists of a mark which (1) when used on or in connection with the goods of the applicant is merely descriptive or deceptively misdescriptive of them, (2) when used on or in connection with the goods of the applicant is primarily geographically descriptive of them, except as indications of regional origin may be registrable under section 1054 of this title, (3) when used on or in connection with the goods of the applicant is primarily geographically deceptively misdescriptive of them, (4) is primarily merely a surname, or (5) comprises any matter that, as a whole, is functional.

(f) Except as expressly excluded in subsections (a), (b), (c), (d), (e)(3), and (e)(5) of this section, nothing in this chapter shall prevent the registration of a mark used by the applicant which has become distinctive of the applicant's goods in commerce. The Director may accept as prima facie evidence that the mark has become distinctive, as used on or in connection with the applicant's goods in commerce, proof of substantially exclusive and continuous use thereof as a mark by the applicant in commerce for the five years before the date on which the claim of distinctiveness is made. Nothing in this section shall prevent the registration of a mark which, when used on or in connection with the goods of the applicant, is primarily geographically deceptively misdescriptive of them, and which became distinctive of the applicant's goods in commerce before December 8, 1993.

A mark which would be likely to cause dilution by blurring or dilution by tarnishment under section 1125(c) of this title, may be refused registration only pursuant to a proceeding brought under section 1063 of this title. A registration for a mark which would be likely to cause dilution by blurring or dilution by tarnishment under section 1125(c) of this title, may be canceled pursuant to a proceeding brought under either section 1064 of this title or section 1092 of this title.

§1064. Cancellation of registration
(Lanham Act § 14)

A petition to cancel a registration of a mark, stating the grounds relied upon, may, upon payment of the prescribed fee, be filed as follows by any person who believes that he is or will be damaged, including as a result of a likelihood of dilution by blurring or dilution by tarnishment under section 1125(c) of this title, by the registration of a mark on the principal register established by this chapter, or under the Act of March 3, 1881, or the Act of February 20, 1905:

(1) Within five years from the date of the registration of the mark under this chapter.

(2) Within five years from the date of publication under section 1062(c) of this title of a mark registered under the Act of March 3, 1881, or the Act of February 20, 1905.

(3) At any time if the registered mark becomes the generic name for the goods or services, or a portion thereof, for which it is registered, or is functional, or has been abandoned, or its registration was obtained fraudulently or contrary to the provisions of section 1054 of this title or of subsection (a), (b), or (c) of section 1052 of this title for a registration under this chapter, or contrary to similar prohibitory provisions of such prior Acts for a registration under such Acts, or if the registered mark is being used by, or with the permission of, the registrant so as to misrepresent the source of the goods or services on or in connection with which the mark is used. If the registered mark becomes the generic name for less than all of the goods or services for which it is registered, a petition to cancel the registration for only those goods or services may be filed. A registered mark shall not be deemed to be the generic name of goods or services solely because such mark is also used as a name of or to identify a unique product or service. The primary significance of the registered mark to the relevant public rather than purchaser motivation shall be the test for determining whether the registered mark has become the generic name of goods or services on or in connection with which it has been used.

(4) At any time if the mark is registered under the Act of March 3, 1881, or the Act of February 20, 1905, and has not been published under the provisions of subsection (c) of section 1062 of this title.

(5) At any time in the case of a certification mark on the ground that the registrant (A) does not control, or is not able legitimately to exercise control over, the use of such mark, or (B) engages in the production or marketing of any goods or services to which the certification mark is applied, or (C) permits the use of the certification mark for purposes other than to certify, or (D) discriminately refuses to certify or to continue to certify the goods or services of any person who maintains the standards or conditions which such mark certifies:

Provided, That the Federal Trade Commission may apply to cancel on the grounds specified in paragraphs (3) and (5) of this section any mark registered on the principal register established by this chapter, and the prescribed fee shall not be required.

Nothing in paragraph (5) shall be deemed to prohibit the registrant from using its certification mark in advertising or promoting recognition of the certification program or of the goods or services meeting the certification standards of the registrant. Such uses of the certification mark shall not be grounds for cancellation under paragraph (5), so long as the registrant does not itself produce, manufacture, or sell any of the certified goods or services to which its identical certification mark is applied.

§ 1114.   Remedies; infringement; innocent infringement by printers and publishers
(Lanham Act § 32)

(1) Any person who shall, without the consent of the registrant—

(a) use in commerce any reproduction, counterfeit, copy, or colorable imitation of a registered mark in connection with the sale, offering for sale, distribution, or advertising of any goods or services on or in connection with which such use is likely to cause confusion, or to cause mistake, or to deceive; or

(b) reproduce, counterfeit, copy, or colorably imitate a registered mark and apply such reproduction, counterfeit, copy, or colorable imitation to labels, signs, prints, packages, wrappers, receptacles or advertisements intended to be used in commerce upon or in connection with the sale, offering for sale, distribution, or advertising of goods or services on or in connection with which such use is likely to cause confusion, or to cause mistake, or to deceive,

shall be liable in a civil action by the registrant for the remedies hereinafter provided. Under subsection (b) hereof, the registrant shall not be entitled to recover profits or damages unless the acts have been committed with knowledge that such imitation is intended to be used to cause confusion, or to cause mistake, or to deceive.

As used in this paragraph, the term "any person" includes the United States, all agencies and instrumentalities thereof, and all individuals, firms, corporations, or other persons acting for the United States and with the authorization and consent of the United States, and any State, any instrumentality of a State, and any officer or employee of a State or instrumentality of a State acting in his or her official capacity. The

United States, all agencies and instrumentalities thereof, and all individuals, firms, corporations, other persons acting for the United States and with the authorization and consent of the United States, and any State, and any such instrumentality, officer, or employee, shall be subject to the provisions of this chapter in the same manner and to the same extent as any nongovernmental entity.

(2) Notwithstanding any other provision of this chapter, the remedies given to the owner of a right infringed under this chapter or to a person bringing an action under section 1125(a) or (d) of this title shall be limited as follows:

(A) Where an infringer or violator is engaged solely in the business of printing the mark or violating matter for others and establishes that he or she was an innocent infringer or innocent violator, the owner of the right infringed or person bringing the action under section 1125(a) of this title shall be entitled as against such infringer or violator only to an injunction against future printing.

(B) Where the infringement or violation complained of is contained in or is part of paid advertising matter in a newspaper, magazine, or other similar periodical or in an electronic communication as defined in section 2510(12) of Title 18, the remedies of the owner of the right infringed or person bringing the action under section 1125(a) of this title as against the publisher or distributor of such newspaper, magazine, or other similar periodical or electronic communication shall be limited to an injunction against the presentation of such advertising matter in future issues of such newspapers, magazines, or other similar periodicals or in future transmissions of such electronic communications. The limitations of this subparagraph shall apply only to innocent infringers and innocent violators.

(C) Injunctive relief shall not be available to the owner of the right infringed or person bringing the action under section 1125(a) of this title with respect to an issue of a newspaper, magazine, or other similar periodical or an electronic communication containing infringing matter or violating matter where restraining the dissemination of such infringing matter or violating matter in any particular issue of such periodical or in an electronic communication would delay the delivery of such issue or transmission of such electronic communication after the regular time for such delivery or transmission, and such delay would be due to the method by which publication and distribution of such periodical or transmission of such electronic communication is customarily conducted in accordance with sound business practice, and not due to any method or device adopted to evade this section or to prevent or delay the issuance of an injunction or restraining order with respect to such infringing matter or violating matter.

(D)(i)(I) A domain name registrar, a domain name registry, or other domain name registration authority that takes any action described under clause (ii) affecting a domain name shall not be liable for monetary relief or, except as provided in subclause (II), for injunctive relief, to any person for such action, regardless of whether the domain name is finally determined to infringe or dilute the mark.

(II) A domain name registrar, domain name registry, or other domain name registration authority described in subclause (I) may be subject to injunctive relief only if such registrar, registry, or other registration authority has—

(aa) not expeditiously deposited with a court, in which an action has been filed regarding the disposition of the domain name, documents sufficient for the court to establish the court's control and authority regarding the disposition of the registration and use of the domain name;

(bb) transferred, suspended, or otherwise modified the domain name during the pendency of the action, except upon order of the court; or

(cc) willfully failed to comply with any such court order.

(ii) An action referred to under clause (i)(I) is any action of refusing to register, removing from registration, transferring, temporarily disabling, or permanently canceling a domain name—

(I) in compliance with a court order under section 1125(d) of this title; or

(II) in the implementation of a reasonable policy by such registrar, registry, or authority prohibiting the registration of a domain name that is identical to, confusingly similar to, or dilutive of another's mark.

(iii) A domain name registrar, a domain name registry, or other domain name registration authority shall not be liable for damages under this section for the registration or maintenance of a domain name for another absent a showing of bad faith intent to profit from such registration or maintenance of the domain name.

(iv) If a registrar, registry, or other registration authority takes an action described under clause (ii) based on a knowing and material misrepresentation by any other person that a domain name is identical to, confusingly similar to, or dilutive of a mark, the person making the knowing and material misrepresentation shall be liable for any damages, including costs and attorney's fees, incurred by the domain name registrant as a result of such action. The court may also grant injunctive relief to the domain name registrant, including the reactivation of the domain name or the transfer of the domain name to the domain name registrant.

(v) A domain name registrant whose domain name has been suspended, disabled, or transferred under a policy described under clause (ii)(II) may, upon notice to the mark owner, file a civil action to establish that the registration or use of the domain name by such registrant is not unlawful under this chapter. The court may grant injunctive relief to the domain name registrant, including the reactivation of the domain name or transfer of the domain name to the domain name registrant.

(E) As used in this paragraph—

(i) the term "violator" means a person who violates section 1125(a) of this title; and

(ii) the term "violating matter" means matter that is the subject of a violation under section 1125(a) of this title.

(3)(A) Any person who engages in the conduct described in paragraph (11) of section 110 of Title 17, and who complies with the requirements set forth in that paragraph is not liable on account of such conduct for a violation of any right under this chapter. This subparagraph does not preclude liability, nor shall it be construed to restrict the defenses or limitations on rights granted under this chapter, of a person for conduct not described in paragraph (11) of section 110 of Title 17, even if that person also engages in conduct described in paragraph (11) of section 110 of such title.

(B) A manufacturer, licensee, or licensor of technology that enables the making of limited portions of audio or video content of a motion picture imperceptible as described in subparagraph (A) is not liable on account of such manufacture or license for a violation of any right under this chapter, if such manufacturer, licensee, or licensor ensures that the technology provides a clear and conspicuous notice at the beginning of each performance that the performance of the motion picture is altered from the performance intended by the director or copyright holder of the motion picture. The limitations on liability in subparagraph (A) and this subparagraph shall not apply to a manufacturer, licensee, or licensor of technology that fails to comply with this paragraph.

(C) The requirement under subparagraph (B) to provide notice shall apply only with respect to technology manufactured after the end of the 180–day period beginning on April 27, 2005.

(D) Any failure by a manufacturer, licensee, or licensor of technology to qualify for the exemption under subparagraphs (A) and (B) shall not be construed to create an inference that any such party that engages in conduct described in paragraph (11) of section 110 of Title 17 is liable for trademark infringement by reason of such conduct.

§ 1115.　Registration on principal register as evidence of exclusive right to use mark; defenses
(Lanham Act § 33)

(a)　Evidentiary value; defenses

Any registration issued under the Act of March 3, 1881, or the Act of February 20, 1905, or of a mark registered on the principal register provided by this chapter and owned by a party to an action shall be admissible in evidence and shall be prima facie evidence of the validity of the registered mark and of the registration of the mark, of the registrant's ownership of the mark, and of the registrant's exclusive right to use the registered mark in commerce on or in connection with the goods or services specified in the registration subject to any conditions or limitations stated therein, but shall not preclude another person from proving any legal or equitable defense or defect, including those set forth in subsection (b) of this section, which might have been asserted if such mark had not been registered.

(b)　Incontestability; defenses

To the extent that the right to use the registered mark has become incontestable under section 1065 of this title, the registration shall be conclusive evidence of the validity of the registered mark and of the registration of the mark, of the registrant's ownership of the mark, and of the registrant's exclusive right to use the registered mark in commerce. Such conclusive evidence shall relate to the exclusive right to use the mark on or in connection with the goods or services specified in the affidavit filed under the provisions of section 1065 of this title, or in the renewal application filed under the provisions of section 1059 of this title if the goods or services specified in the renewal are fewer in number, subject to any conditions or limitations in the registration or in such affidavit or renewal application. Such conclusive evidence of the right to use the registered mark shall be subject to proof of infringement as defined in section 1114 of this title, and shall be subject to the following defenses or defects:

> **(1)**　That the registration or the incontestable right to use the mark was obtained fraudulently; or
>
> **(2)**　That the mark has been abandoned by the registrant; or
>
> **(3)**　That the registered mark is being used by or with the permission of the registrant or a person in privity with the registrant, so as to

misrepresent the source of the goods or services on or in connection with which the mark is used; or

(4) That the use of the name, term, or device charged to be an infringement is a use, otherwise than as a mark, of the party's individual name in his own business, or of the individual name of anyone in privity with such party, or of a term or device which is descriptive of and used fairly and in good faith only to describe the goods or services of such party, or their geographic origin; or

(5) That the mark whose use by a party is charged as an infringement was adopted without knowledge of the registrant's prior use and has been continuously used by such party or those in privity with him from a date prior to (A) the date of constructive use of the mark established pursuant to section 1057(c) of this title, (B) the registration of the mark under this chapter if the application for registration is filed before the effective date of the Trademark Law Revision Act of 1988, or (C) publication of the registered mark under subsection (c) of section 1062 of this title: *Provided, however,* That this defense or defect shall apply only for the area in which such continuous prior use is proved; or

(6) That the mark whose use is charged as an infringement was registered and used prior to the registration under this chapter or publication under subsection (c) of section 1062 of this title of the registered mark of the registrant, and not abandoned: *Provided, however,* That this defense or defect shall apply only for the area in which the mark was used prior to such registration or such publication of the registrant's mark; or

(7) That the mark has been or is being used to violate the antitrust laws of the United States; or

(8) That the mark is functional; or

(9) That equitable principles, including laches, estoppel, and acquiescence, are applicable.

§ 1116.   Injunctive relief
(Lanham Act § 34)

(a) Jurisdiction; service

The several courts vested with jurisdiction of civil actions arising under this chapter shall have power to grant injunctions, according to the principles of equity and upon such terms as the court may deem reasonable, to prevent the violation of any right of the registrant of a mark registered in the Patent and Trademark Office or to prevent a violation under subsection (a), (c), or (d) of section 1125 of this title. Any such injunction may include a provision directing the defendant to file with the court and serve on the plaintiff within thirty days after the service on the defendant of such injunction, or such extended period as the court may direct, a report in writing under oath setting forth in detail the manner and form in which the defendant has complied with the injunction. Any such injunction granted upon hearing, after notice to the defendant, by any district court of the United States, may be served on the parties against whom such injunction is granted anywhere in the United States where they may be found, and shall be operative and may be enforced by proceedings to punish for contempt, or otherwise, by the court by which such injunction was granted, or by any other United States district court in whose jurisdiction the defendant may be found.

(b) Transfer of certified copies of court papers

The said courts shall have jurisdiction to enforce said injunction, as provided in this chapter, as fully as if the injunction had been granted by the district court in which it is sought to be enforced. The clerk of the court or judge granting the injunction shall, when required to do so by the court before which application to enforce said injunction is made, transfer without delay to said court a certified copy of all papers on file in his office upon which said injunction was granted.

(c) Notice to Director

It shall be the duty of the clerks of such courts within one month after the filing of any action, suit, or proceeding involving a mark registered under the provisions of this chapter to give notice thereof in writing to the Director setting forth in order so far as known the names and addresses of the litigants and the designating number or numbers of the registration or registrations upon which the action, suit, or proceeding has been brought, and in the event any other registration be subsequently included in the action, suit, or proceeding by amendment, answer, or other pleading, the clerk shall give like notice thereof to the Director, and within one month after the judgment is entered or an appeal is taken the clerk of the court shall give notice thereof to the Director, and it shall be the duty of the Director on receipt of such notice forthwith to endorse the same upon the file wrapper of the said registration or registrations and to incorporate the same as a part of the contents of said file wrapper.

(d) Civil actions arising out of use of counterfeit marks

(1)(A) In the case of a civil action arising under section 1114(1)(a) of this title or section 220506 of Title 36 with respect to a violation that consists of using a counterfeit mark in connection with the sale, offering for sale, or distribution of goods or services, the court may, upon ex parte application, grant an order under subsection (a) of this section pursuant to this subsection providing for the seizure of goods and counterfeit marks involved in such violation and the means of making such marks, and records documenting the manufacture, sale, or receipt of things involved in such violation.

(B) As used in this subsection the term "counterfeit mark" means—

    (i) a counterfeit of a mark that is registered on the principal register in the United States Patent and Trademark Office for such goods or services sold, offered for sale, or distributed and that is in use, whether or not the person against whom relief is sought knew such mark was so registered; or

    (ii) a spurious designation that is identical with, or substantially indistinguishable from, a designation as to which the remedies of this chapter are made available by reason of section 220506 of Title 36;

but such term does not include any mark or designation used on or in connection with goods or services of which the manufacture[r] or producer was, at the time of the manufacture or production in question authorized to use the mark or designation for the type of goods or services so manufactured or produced, by the holder of the right to use such mark or designation.

(2) The court shall not receive an application under this subsection unless the applicant has given such notice of the application as is reasonable under the circumstances to the United States attorney for the judicial district in which such order is sought. Such attorney may participate in the proceedings arising under such application if such proceedings may affect evidence of an offense against the United States. The court may deny such application if the court determines that the public interest in a potential prosecution so requires.

(3) The application for an order under this subsection shall—

    (A) be based on an affidavit or the verified complaint establishing facts sufficient to support the findings of fact and conclusions of law required for such order; and

    (B) contain the additional information required by paragraph (5) of this subsection to be set forth in such order.

(4) The court shall not grant such an application unless—

    (A) the person obtaining an order under this subsection provides the security determined adequate by the court for the payment of such damages as any person may be entitled to recover as a result of a wrongful seizure or wrongful attempted seizure under this subsection; and

    (B) the court finds that it clearly appears from specific facts that—

(i) an order other than an ex parte seizure order is not adequate to achieve the purposes of section 1114 of this title;

(ii) the applicant has not publicized the requested seizure;

(iii) the applicant is likely to succeed in showing that the person against whom seizure would be ordered used a counterfeit mark in connection with the sale, offering for sale, or distribution of goods or services;

(iv) an immediate and irreparable injury will occur if such seizure is not ordered;

(v) the matter to be seized will be located at the place identified in the application;

(vi) the harm to the applicant of denying the application outweighs the harm to the legitimate interests of the person against whom seizure would be ordered of granting the application; and

(vii) the person against whom seizure would be ordered, or persons acting in concert with such person, would destroy, move, hide, or otherwise make such matter inaccessible to the court, if the applicant were to proceed on notice to such person.

(5) An order under this subsection shall set forth—

(A) the findings of fact and conclusions of law required for the order;

(B) a particular description of the matter to be seized, and a description of each place at which such matter is to be seized;

(C) the time period, which shall end not later than seven days after the date on which such order is issued, during which the seizure is to be made;

(D) the amount of security required to be provided under this subsection; and

(E) a date for the hearing required under paragraph (10) of this subsection.

(6) The court shall take appropriate action to protect the person against whom an order under this subsection is directed from publicity, by or at the behest of the plaintiff, about such order and any seizure under such order.

(7) Any materials seized under this subsection shall be taken into the custody of the court. For seizures made under this section, the court shall enter an appropriate protective order with respect to discovery and use of any records or information that has been seized. The protective order shall provide for appropriate procedures to ensure that confidential, private, proprietary, or privileged information contained in such records is not improperly disclosed or used.

(8) An order under this subsection, together with the supporting documents, shall be sealed until the person against whom the order is directed has an opportunity to contest such order, except that any person against whom such order is issued shall have access to such order and supporting documents after the seizure has been carried out.

(9) The court shall order that service of a copy of the order under this subsection shall be made by a Federal law enforcement officer (such as a United States marshal or an officer or agent of the United States Customs Service, Secret Service, Federal Bureau of Investigation, or Post Office) or may be made by a State or local law enforcement officer, who, upon making service, shall carry out the seizure under the order. The court shall issue orders, when appropriate, to protect the defendant from undue damage from the disclosure of trade secrets or other confidential information during the course of the seizure, including, when appropriate, orders restricting the access of the applicant (or any agent or employee of the applicant) to such secrets or information.

(10)(A) The court shall hold a hearing, unless waived by all the parties, on the date set by the court in the order of seizure. That date shall be not sooner than ten days after the order is issued and not later than fifteen days after the order is issued, unless the applicant for the order shows good cause for another date or unless the party against whom such order is directed consents to another date for such hearing. At such hearing the party obtaining the order shall have the burden to prove that the facts supporting findings of fact and conclusions of law necessary to support such order are still in effect. If that party fails to meet that burden, the seizure order shall be dissolved or modified appropriately.

(B) In connection with a hearing under this paragraph, the court may make such orders modifying the time limits for discovery under the Rules of Civil Procedure as may be necessary to prevent the frustration of the purposes of such hearing.

(11) A person who suffers damage by reason of a wrongful seizure under this subsection has a cause of action against the applicant for the order under which such seizure was made, and shall be entitled to recover such relief as may be appropriate, including damages for lost profits, cost of materials, loss of good will, and punitive damages in instances where the seizure was sought in bad faith, and, unless the court finds extenuating circumstances, to recover a reasonable attorney's fee. The court in its discretion may award prejudgment interest on relief recovered under this paragraph, at an annual interest rate established under section 6621(a)(2) of Title 26, commencing on the date of service of the claimant's pleading setting forth the claim under this paragraph and ending on the date such recovery is granted, or for such shorter time as the court deems appropriate.

§ 1117.   Recovery for violation of rights
(Lanham Act § 35)

(a) Profits; damages and costs; attorney fees

When a violation of any right of the registrant of a mark registered in the Patent and Trademark Office, a violation under section 1125(a) or (d) of this title, or a willful violation under section 1125(c) of this title, shall have been established in any civil action arising under this chapter, the plaintiff shall be entitled, subject to the provisions of sections 1111 and 1114 of this title, and subject to the principles of equity, to recover (1) defendant's profits, (2) any damages sustained by the plaintiff, and (3) the costs of the action. The court shall assess such profits and damages or cause the same to be assessed under its direction. In assessing profits the plaintiff shall be required to prove defendant's sales only; defendant must prove all elements of cost or deduction claimed. In assessing damages the court may enter judgment, according to the circumstances of the case, for any sum above the amount found as actual damages, not exceeding three times such amount. If the court shall find that the amount of the recovery based on profits is either inadequate or excessive the court may in its discretion enter judgment for such sum as the court shall find to be just, according to the circumstances of the case. Such sum in either of the above circumstances shall constitute compensation and not a penalty. The court in exceptional cases may award reasonable attorney fees to the prevailing party.

(b) Treble damages for use of counterfeit mark

In assessing damages under subsection (a) for any violation of section 1114(1)(a) of this title or section 220506 of Title 36, in a case involving use of a counterfeit mark or designation (as defined in section 1116(d) of this title), the court shall, unless the court finds extenuating circumstances, enter judgment for three times such profits or damages, whichever amount is greater, together with a reasonable attorney's fee, if the violation consists of

> **(1)** intentionally using a mark or designation, knowing such mark or designation is a counterfeit mark (as defined in section 1116(d) of

this title), in connection with the sale, offering for sale, or distribution of goods or services; or

(2) providing goods or services necessary to the commission of a violation specified in paragraph (1), with the intent that the recipient of the goods or services would put the goods or services to use in committing the violation.

In such a case, the court may award prejudgment interest on such amount at an annual interest rate established under section 6621(a)(2) of Title 26, beginning on the date of the service of the claimant's pleadings setting forth the claim for such entry of judgment and ending on the date such entry is made, or for such shorter time as the court considers appropriate.

(c) Statutory damages for use of counterfeit marks

In a case involving the use of a counterfeit mark (as defined in section 1116(d) of this title) in connection with the sale, offering for sale, or distribution of goods or services, the plaintiff may elect, at any time before final judgment is rendered by the trial court, to recover, instead of actual damages and profits under subsection (a) of this section, an award of statutory damages for any such use in connection with the sale, offering for sale, or distribution of goods or services in the amount of—

(1) not less than $1,000 or more than $200,000 per counterfeit mark per type of goods or services sold, offered for sale, or distributed, as the court considers just; or

(2) if the court finds that the use of the counterfeit mark was willful, not more than $2,000,000 per counterfeit mark per type of goods or services sold, offered for sale, or distributed, as the court considers just.

(d) Statutory damages for violation of section 1125(d)(1)

In a case involving a violation of section 1125(d)(1) of this title, the plaintiff may elect, at any time before final judgment is rendered by the trial court, to recover, instead of actual damages and profits, an award of statutory damages in the amount of not less than $1,000 and not more than $100,000 per domain name, as the court considers just.

(e) Rebuttable presumption of willful violation

In the case of a violation referred to in this section, it shall be a rebuttable presumption that the violation is willful for purposes of determining relief if the violator, or a person acting in concert with the violator, knowingly provided or knowingly caused to be provided materially false contact information to a domain name registrar, domain name registry, or other domain name registration authority in registering, maintaining, or renewing a domain name used in connection with the violation. Nothing in this subsection limits what may be considered a willful violation under this section.

§ 1119.   Power of court over registration
(Lanham Act § 37)

In any action involving a registered mark the court may determine the right to registration, order the cancelation of registrations, in whole or in part, restore canceled registrations, and otherwise rectify the register with respect to the registrations of any party to the action. Decrees and orders shall be certified by the court to the Director, who shall make appropriate entry upon the records of the Patent and Trademark Office, and shall be controlled thereby.

§ 1125.   False designations of origin, false descriptions, and dilution forbidden
(Lanham Act § 43)

(a) Civil action

(1) Any person who, on or in connection with any goods or services, or any container for goods, uses in commerce any word, term, name, symbol, or device, or any combination thereof, or any false designation of origin, false or misleading description of fact, or false or misleading representation of fact, which—

(A) is likely to cause confusion, or to cause mistake, or to deceive as to the affiliation, connection, or association of such person with another person, or as to the origin, sponsorship, or approval of his or her goods, services, or commercial activities by another person, or

(B) in commercial advertising or promotion, misrepresents the nature, characteristics, qualities, or geographic origin of his or her or another person's goods, services, or commercial activities,

shall be liable in a civil action by any person who believes that he or she is or is likely to be damaged by such act.

(2) As used in this subsection, the term "any person" includes any State, instrumentality of a State or employee of a State or instrumentality of a State acting in his or her official capacity. Any State, and any such instrumentality, officer, or employee, shall be subject to the provisions of this chapter in the same manner and to the same extent as any nongovernmental entity.

(3) In a civil action for trade dress infringement under this chapter for trade dress not registered on the principal register, the person who asserts trade dress protection has the burden of proving that the matter sought to be protected is not functional.

(b) Importation

Any goods marked or labeled in contravention of the provisions of this section shall not be imported into the United States or admitted to entry at any customhouse of the United States. The owner, importer, or consignee of goods refused entry at any customhouse under this section may have any recourse by protest or appeal that is given under the customs revenue laws or may have the remedy given by this chapter in cases involving goods refused entry or seized.

(c) Dilution by blurring; dilution by tarnishment

(1) Injunctive relief

Subject to the principles of equity, the owner of a famous mark that is distinctive, inherently or through acquired distinctiveness, shall be entitled to an injunction against another person who, at any time after the owner's mark has become famous, commences use of a mark or trade name in commerce that is likely to cause dilution by blurring or dilution by tarnishment of the famous mark, regardless of the presence or absence of actual or likely confusion, of competition, or of actual economic injury.

(2) Definitions

(A) For purposes of paragraph (1), a mark is famous if it is widely recognized by the general consuming public of the United States as a designation of source of the goods or services of the mark's owner. In determining whether a mark possesses the requisite degree of recognition, the court may consider all relevant factors, including the following:

(i) The duration, extent, and geographic reach of advertising and publicity of the mark, whether advertised or publicized by the owner or third parties.

(ii) The amount, volume, and geographic extent of sales of goods or services offered under the mark.

(iii) The extent of actual recognition of the mark.

(iv) Whether the mark was registered under the Act of March 3, 1881, or the Act of February 20, 1905, or on the principal register.

(B) For purposes of paragraph (1), "dilution by blurring" is association arising from the similarity between a mark or trade name and a famous mark that impairs the distinctiveness of the famous mark. In determining whether a mark or trade name is likely to cause dilution by blurring, the court may consider all relevant factors, including the following:

(i) The degree of similarity between the mark or trade name and the famous mark.

(ii) The degree of inherent or acquired distinctiveness of the famous mark.

(iii) The extent to which the owner of the famous mark is engaging in substantially exclusive use of the mark.

(iv) The degree of recognition of the famous mark.

(v) Whether the user of the mark or trade name intended to create an association with the famous mark.

(vi) Any actual association between the mark or trade name and the famous mark.

(C) For purposes of paragraph (1), "dilution by tarnishment" is association arising from the similarity between a mark or trade name and a famous mark that harms the reputation of the famous mark.

(3) Exclusions

The following shall not be actionable as dilution by blurring or dilution by tarnishment under this subsection:

(A) Any fair use, including a nominative or descriptive fair use, or facilitation of such fair use, of a famous mark by another person other than as a designation of source for the person's own goods or services, including use in connection with—

(i) advertising or promotion that permits consumers to compare goods or services; or

(ii) identifying and parodying, criticizing, or commenting upon the famous mark owner or the goods or services of the famous mark owner.

(B) All forms of news reporting and news commentary.

(C) Any noncommercial use of a mark.

(4) Burden of proof

In a civil action for trade dress dilution under this chapter for trade dress not registered on the principal register, the person who asserts trade dress protection has the burden of proving that—

(A) the claimed trade dress, taken as a whole, is not functional and is famous; and

(B) if the claimed trade dress includes any mark or marks registered on the principal register, the unregistered matter, taken as a whole, is famous separate and apart from any fame of such registered marks.

(5) Additional remedies

In an action brought under this subsection, the owner of the famous mark shall be entitled to injunctive relief as set forth in section 1116 of this title. The owner of the famous mark shall also be entitled to the remedies set forth in sections 1117(a) and 1118 of this title, subject to the discretion of the court and the principles of equity if—

(A) the mark or trade name that is likely to cause dilution by blurring or dilution by tarnishment was first used in commerce by the person against whom the injunction is sought after October 6, 2006; and

(B) in a claim arising under this subsection—

(i) by reason of dilution by blurring, the person against whom the injunction is sought willfully intended to trade on the recognition of the famous mark; or

(ii) by reason of dilution by tarnishment, the person against whom the injunction is sought willfully intended to harm the reputation of the famous mark.

(6) Ownership of valid registration a complete bar to action

The ownership by a person of a valid registration under the Act of March 3, 1881, or the Act of February 20, 1905, or on the principal register under this chapter shall be a complete bar to an action against that person, with respect to that mark, that—

(A) is brought by another person under the common law or a statute of a State; and

(B)(i) seeks to prevent dilution by blurring or dilution by tarnishment; or

(ii) asserts any claim of actual or likely damage or harm to the distinctiveness or reputation of a mark, label, or form of advertisement.

(7) Savings clause

Nothing in this subsection shall be construed to impair, modify, or supersede the applicability of the patent laws of the United States.

(d) Cyberpiracy prevention

(1)(A) A person shall be liable in a civil action by the owner of a mark, including a personal name which is protected as a mark under this section, if, without regard to the goods or services of the parties, that person—

(i) has a bad faith intent to profit from that mark, including a personal name which is protected as a mark under this section; and

(ii) registers, traffics in, or uses a domain name that—

(I) in the case of a mark that is distinctive at the time of registration of the domain name, is identical or confusingly similar to that mark;

(II) in the case of a famous mark that is famous at the time of registration of the domain name, is identical or confusingly similar to or dilutive of that mark; or

(III) is a trademark, word, or name protected by reason of section 706 of Title 18 or section 220506 of Title 36.

(B)(i) In determining whether a person has a bad faith intent described under subparagraph (A), a court may consider factors such as, but not limited to—

(I) the trademark or other intellectual property rights of the person, if any, in the domain name;

(II) the extent to which the domain name consists of the legal name of the person or a name that is otherwise commonly used to identify that person;

(III) the person's prior use, if any, of the domain name in connection with the bona fide offering of any goods or services;

(IV) the person's bona fide noncommercial or fair use of the mark in a site accessible under the domain name;

(V) the person's intent to divert consumers from the mark owner's online location to a site accessible under the domain name that could harm the goodwill represented by the mark, either for commercial gain or with the intent to tarnish or disparage the mark, by creating a likelihood of confusion as to the source, sponsorship, affiliation, or endorsement of the site;

(VI) the person's offer to transfer, sell, or otherwise assign the domain name to the mark owner or any third party for financial gain without having used, or having an intent to use, the domain name in the bona fide offering of any goods or services, or the person's prior conduct indicating a pattern of such conduct;

(VII) the person's provision of material and misleading false contact information when applying for the registration of the domain name, the person's intentional failure to maintain accurate contact information, or the person's prior conduct indicating a pattern of such conduct;

(VIII) the person's registration or acquisition of multiple domain names which the person knows are identical or confusingly similar to marks of others that are distinctive at the time of registration of such domain names, or dilutive of famous marks of others that are famous at the time of registration of such domain names, without regard to the goods or services of the parties; and

(IX) the extent to which the mark incorporated in the person's domain name registration is or is not distinctive and famous within the meaning of subsection (c) of this section.

(ii) Bad faith intent described under subparagraph (A) shall not be found in any case in which the court determines that the person believed and had reasonable grounds to believe that the use of the domain name was a fair use or otherwise lawful.

(C) In any civil action involving the registration, trafficking, or use of a domain name under this paragraph, a court may order the forfeiture or cancellation of the domain name or the transfer of the domain name to the owner of the mark.

(D) A person shall be liable for using a domain name under subparagraph (A) only if that person is the domain name registrant or that registrant's authorized licensee.

(E) As used in this paragraph, the term "traffics in" refers to transactions that include, but are not limited to, sales, purchases, loans, pledges, licenses, exchanges of currency, and any other transfer for consideration or receipt in exchange for consideration.

(2)(A) The owner of a mark may file an in rem civil action against a domain name in the judicial district in which the domain name registrar, domain name registry, or other domain name authority that registered or assigned the domain name is located if—

(i) the domain name violates any right of the owner of a mark registered in the Patent and Trademark Office, or protected under subsection (a) or (c) of this section; and

(ii) the court finds that the owner—

(I) is not able to obtain in personam jurisdiction over a person who would have been a defendant in a civil action under paragraph (1); or

(II) through due diligence was not able to find a person who would have been a defendant in a civil action under paragraph (1) by—

(aa) sending a notice of the alleged violation and intent to proceed under this paragraph to the registrant of the domain name at the postal and e-mail address provided by the registrant to the registrar; and

(bb) publishing notice of the action as the court may direct promptly after filing the action.

(B) The actions under subparagraph (A)(ii) shall constitute service of process.

(C) In an in rem action under this paragraph, a domain name shall be deemed to have its situs in the judicial district in which—

(i) the domain name registrar, registry, or other domain name authority that registered or assigned the domain name is located; or

(ii) documents sufficient to establish control and authority regarding the disposition of the registration and use of the domain name are deposited with the court.

(D)(i) The remedies in an in rem action under this paragraph shall be limited to a court order for the forfeiture or cancellation of the domain name or the transfer of the domain name to the owner of the mark. Upon receipt of written notification of a filed, stamped copy of a complaint filed by the owner of a mark in a United States district court under this paragraph, the domain name registrar, domain name registry, or other domain name authority shall—

(I) expeditiously deposit with the court documents sufficient to establish the court's control and authority regarding the disposition of the registration and use of the domain name to the court; and

(II) not transfer, suspend, or otherwise modify the domain name during the pendency of the action, except upon order of the court.

(ii) The domain name registrar or registry or other domain name authority shall not be liable for injunctive or monetary relief under this paragraph except in the case of bad faith or reckless disregard, which includes a willful failure to comply with any such court order.

(3) The civil action established under paragraph (1) and the in rem action established under paragraph (2), and any remedy available under either such action, shall be in addition to any other civil action or remedy otherwise applicable.

(4) The in rem jurisdiction established under paragraph (2) shall be in addition to any other jurisdiction that otherwise exists, whether in rem or in personam.

§ 1127.   Construction and definitions; intent of chapter
(Lanham Act § 45)

In the construction of this chapter, unless the contrary is plainly apparent from the context—

The United States includes and embraces all territory which is under its jurisdiction and control.

The word "commerce" means all commerce which may lawfully be regulated by Congress.

The term "principal register" refers to the register provided for by sections 1051 to 1072 of this title, and the term "supplemental register" refers to the register provided for by sections 1091 to 1096 of this title.

The term "person" and any other word or term used to designate the applicant or other entitled to a benefit or privilege or rendered liable under the provisions of this chapter includes a juristic person as well as a natural person. The term "juristic person" includes a firm, corporation, union, association, or other organization capable of suing and being sued in a court of law.

The term "person" also includes the United States, any agency or instrumentality thereof, or any individual, firm, or corporation acting for the United States and with the authorization and consent of the United States. The United States, any agency or instrumentality thereof, and any individual, firm, or corporation acting for the United States and with the authorization and consent of the United States, shall be subject to the provisions of this chapter in the same manner and to the same extent as any nongovernmental entity.

The term "person" also includes any State, any instrumentality of a State, and any officer or employee of a State or instrumentality of a State acting in his or her official capacity. Any State, and any such instrumentality, officer, or employee, shall be subject to the provisions of this chapter in the same manner and to the same extent as any nongovernmental entity.

The terms "applicant" and "registrant" embrace the legal representatives, predecessors, successors and assigns of such applicant or registrant.

The term "Director" means the Under Secretary of Commerce for Intellectual Property and Director of the United States Patent and Trademark Office.

The term "related company" means any person whose use of a mark is controlled by the owner of the mark with respect to the nature and quality of the goods or services on or in connection with which the mark is used.

The terms "trade name" and "commercial name" mean any name used by a person to identify his or her business or vocation.

The term "trademark" includes any word, name, symbol, or device, or any combination thereof—

(1) used by a person, or

(2) which a person has a bona fide intention to use in commerce and applies to register on the principal register established by this chapter,

to identify and distinguish his or her goods, including a unique product, from those manufactured or sold by others and to indicate the source of the goods, even if that source is unknown.

The term "service mark" means any word, name, symbol, or device, or any combination thereof—

(1) used by a person, or

(2) which a person has a bona fide intention to use in commerce and applies to register on the principal register established by this chapter,

to identify and distinguish the services of one person, including a unique service, from the services of others and to indicate the source of the services, even if that source is unknown. Titles, character names, and other distinctive features of radio or television programs may be registered as service marks notwithstanding that they, or the programs, may advertise the goods of the sponsor.

The term "certification mark" means any word, name, symbol, or device, or any combination thereof—

(1) used by a person other than its owner, or

(2) which its owner has a bona fide intention to permit a person other than the owner to use in commerce and files an application to register on the principal register established by this chapter,

to certify regional or other origin, material, mode of manufacture, quality, accuracy, or other characteristics of such person's goods or services or that the work or labor on the goods or services was performed by members of a union or other organization.

The term "collective mark" means a trademark or service mark—

(1) used by the members of a cooperative, an association, or other collective group or organization, or

(2) which such cooperative, association, or other collective group or organization has a bona fide intention to use in commerce and applies to register on the principal register established by this chapter,

and includes marks indicating membership in a union, an association, or other organization.

The term "mark" includes any trademark, service mark, collective mark, or certification mark.

The term "use in commerce" means the bona fide use of a mark in the ordinary course of trade, and not made merely to reserve a right in a mark. For purposes of this chapter, a mark shall be deemed to be in use in commerce—

    (1) on goods when—

        (A) it is placed in any manner on the goods or their containers or the displays associated therewith or on the tags or labels affixed thereto, or if the nature of the goods makes such placement impracticable, then on documents associated with the goods or their sale, and

        (B) the goods are sold or transported in commerce, and

    (2) on services when it is used or displayed in the sale or advertising of services and the services are rendered in commerce, or the services are rendered in more than one State or in the United States and a foreign country and the person rendering the services is engaged in commerce in connection with the services.

A mark shall be deemed to be "abandoned" if either of the following occurs:

    (1) When its use has been discontinued with intent not to resume such use. Intent not to resume may be inferred from circumstances. Nonuse for 3 consecutive years shall be prima facie evidence of abandonment. "Use" of a mark means the bona fide use of such mark made in the ordinary course of trade, and not made merely to reserve a right in a mark.

    (2) When any course of conduct of the owner, including acts of omission as well as commission, causes the mark to become the generic name for the goods or services on or in connection with which it is used or otherwise to lose its significance as a mark. Purchaser motivation shall not be a test for determining abandonment under this paragraph.

The term "colorable imitation" includes any mark which so resembles a registered mark as to be likely to cause confusion or mistake or to deceive.

The term "registered mark" means a mark registered in the United States Patent and Trademark Office under this chapter or under the Act of March 3, 1881, or the Act of February 20, 1905, or the Act of March 19, 1920. The phrase "marks registered in the Patent and Trademark Office" means registered marks.

The term "Act of March 3, 1881", "Act of February 20, 1905", or "Act of March 19, 1920", means the respective Act as amended.

A "counterfeit" is a spurious mark which is identical with, or substantially indistinguishable from, a registered mark.

The term "domain name" means any alphanumeric designation which is registered with or assigned by any domain name registrar, domain name registry, or other domain name registration authority as part of an electronic address on the Internet.

The term "Internet" has the meaning given that term in section 230(f)(1) of Title 47.

Words used in the singular include the plural and vice versa.

The intent of this chapter is to regulate commerce within the control of Congress by making actionable the deceptive and misleading use of marks in such commerce; to protect registered marks used in such commerce from interference by State, or territorial legislation; to protect persons engaged in such commerce against unfair competition; to prevent fraud and deception in such commerce by the use of reproductions, copies, counterfeits, or colorable imitations of registered marks; and to provide rights and remedies stipulated by treaties and conventions respecting trademarks, trade names, and unfair competition entered into between the United States and foreign nations.

VII. FEDERAL TRADE COMMISSION ACT
(15 U.S.C. § 45)

■ ■ ■

Table of Sections

---

§ 45.　Unfair methods of competition unlawful; prevention by Commission
(Federal Trade Commission Act § 5)

(a) Declaration of unlawfulness; power to prohibit unfair practices; inapplicability to foreign trade

(1) Unfair methods of competition in or affecting commerce, and unfair or deceptive acts or practices in or affecting commerce, are hereby declared unlawful.

(2) The Commission is hereby empowered and directed to prevent persons, partnerships, or corporations, except banks, savings and loan institutions described in section 57a(f)(3) of this title, Federal credit unions described in section 57a(f)(4) of this title, common carriers subject to the Acts to regulate commerce, air carriers and foreign air carriers subject to part A of subtitle VII of Title 49, and persons, partnerships, or corporations insofar as they are subject to the Packers and Stockyards Act, 1921, as amended [7 U.S.C.A. § 181 et seq.], except as provided in section 406(b) of said Act [7 U.S.C.A. § 227(b)], from using unfair methods of competition in or affecting commerce and unfair or deceptive acts or practices in or affecting commerce.

(3) This subsection shall not apply to unfair methods of competition involving commerce with foreign nations (other than import commerce) unless—

(A) such methods of competition have a direct, substantial, and reasonably foreseeable effect—

(i) on commerce which is not commerce with foreign nations, or on import commerce with foreign nations; or

(ii) on export commerce with foreign nations, of a person engaged in such commerce in the United States; and

(B) such effect gives rise to a claim under the provisions of this subsection, other than this paragraph.

If this subsection applies to such methods of competition only because of the operation of subparagraph (A)(ii), this subsection shall apply to such conduct only for injury to export business in the United States.

(4)(A) For purposes of subsection (a) of this section, the term "unfair or deceptive acts or practices" includes such acts or practices involving foreign commerce that—

(i) cause or are likely to cause reasonably foreseeable injury within the United States; or

(ii) involve material conduct occurring within the United States.

(B) All remedies available to the Commission with respect to unfair and deceptive acts or practices shall be available for acts and practices described in this paragraph, including restitution to domestic or foreign victims.

(b) Proceeding by Commission; modifying and setting aside orders

Whenever the Commission shall have reason to believe that any such person, partnership, or corporation has been or is using any unfair method of competition or unfair or deceptive act or practice in or affecting commerce, and if it shall appear to the Commission that a proceeding by it in respect thereof would be to the interest of the public, it shall issue and serve upon such person, partnership, or corporation a complaint stating its charges in that respect and containing a notice of a hearing upon a day and at a place therein fixed at least thirty days after the service of said complaint. The person, partnership, or corporation so complained of shall have the right to appear at the place and time so fixed and show cause why an order should not be entered by the Commission requiring such person, partnership, or corporation to cease and desist from the violation of the law so charged in said complaint. Any person, partnership, or corporation may make application, and upon good cause shown may be allowed by the Commission to intervene and appear in said proceeding by counsel or in person. The testimony in any such proceeding shall be reduced to writing and filed in the office of the Commission. If upon such hearing the Commission shall be of the opinion that the method of competition or the act or practice in question is prohibited by this subchapter, it shall make a report in writing in which it shall state its findings as to the facts and shall issue and cause to be served on such person, partnership, or corporation an order requiring such person, partnership, or corporation to cease and desist from using such method of competition or such act or practice. Until the expiration of the time allowed for filing a petition for review, if no such petition has been duly filed within such time, or, if a petition for review has been filed within such time then until the record in the proceeding has been filed in a court of appeals of the United States, as hereinafter provided, the Commission may at any time, upon such notice and in such manner as it shall deem proper, modify or set aside, in whole or in part, any report or any order made or issued by it under this section. After the expiration of the time allowed for filing a petition for review, if no such petition has been duly filed within such time, the Commission may at any time, after notice and opportunity for hearing, reopen and alter, modify, or set aside, in whole or in part, any report or order made or issued by it under this section, whenever in the opinion of the Commission conditions of fact or of law have so changed as to require such action or if the public interest shall so require, except that (1) the said person, partnership, or corporation may, within sixty days after service upon him or it of said report or order entered after such a reopening, obtain a review thereof in the appropriate court of appeals of the United States, in the manner provided in subsection (c) of this section; and (2) in the case of an order, the Commission shall reopen any such order to consider whether such order (including any affirmative relief provision contained in such order) should be altered, modified, or set aside, in whole or in part, if the person, partnership, or corporation involved files a request with the Commission which makes a satisfactory showing that changed conditions of law or fact require such order to be altered, modified, or set aside, in whole or in part. The Commission shall determine whether to alter, modify, or set aside any order of the Commission in response to a request made by a person, partnership, or corporation under paragraph (2) not later than 120 days after the date of the filing of such request.

(c) Review of order; rehearing

Any person, partnership, or corporation required by an order of the Commission to cease and desist from using any method of competition or act or practice may obtain a review of such order in the court of appeals of the United States, within any circuit where the method of competition or the act or practice in question was used or where such person, partnership, or corporation resides or carries on business, by filing in the court, within sixty days from the date of the service of such order, a written petition praying that the order of the Commission be set aside. A copy of such petition shall be forthwith transmitted by the clerk of the court to the Commission, and thereupon the Commission shall file in the court the record in the proceeding, as provided in section 2112 of Title 28. Upon such filing of the petition the court shall have jurisdiction of the proceeding and of the question determined therein concurrently with the Commission until the filing of the record and shall have power to make and enter a decree affirming, modifying, or setting aside the order of the Commission, and enforcing the same to the extent that such order is affirmed and to issue such writs as are ancillary to its jurisdiction or are necessary in its judgement to prevent injury to the public or to competitors pendente lite. The findings of the Commission as to the facts, if supported by evidence, shall be conclusive. To the extent that the order of the Commission is affirmed, the court shall thereupon issue its own order commanding obedience to the terms of such order of the Commission. If either party shall apply to the court for leave to adduce additional evidence, and shall show to the satisfaction of the court that such additional evidence is material and that there were reasonable grounds for the failure to adduce such evidence in the proceeding before the Commission, the court may order such additional evidence to be taken before the Commission and to be adduced upon the hearing in such manner and upon such terms and conditions as to the court may seem proper. The Commission may modify its findings as to the facts, or make new findings, by reason of the additional evidence so taken, and it shall file such modified or new findings, which, if supported by evidence, shall be conclusive, and its recommendation, if any, for the modification or setting aside of its original order, with the return of such additional evidence. The judgment and decree of the court shall be final, except that the same shall be subject to review by the Supreme Court upon certiorari, as provided in section 1254 of Title 28.

(d) Jurisdiction of court

Upon the filing of the record with it the jurisdiction of the court of appeals of the United States to affirm, enforce, modify, or set aside orders of the Commission shall be exclusive.

(e) Exemption from liability

No order of the Commission or judgement of court to enforce the same shall in anywise relieve or absolve any person, partnership, or corporation from any liability under the Antitrust Acts.

(f) Service of complaints, orders and other processes; return

Complaints, orders, and other processes of the Commission under this section may be served by anyone duly authorized by the Commission, either (a) by delivering a copy thereof to the person to be served, or to a member of the partnership to be served, or the president, secretary, or other executive officer or a director of the corporation to be served; or (b) by leaving a copy thereof at the residence or the principal office or place of business of such person, partnership, or corporation; or (c) by mailing a copy thereof by registered mail or by certified mail addressed to such person, partnership, or corporation at his or its residence or principal office or place of business. The verified return by the person so serving said complaint, order, or other process setting forth the manner of said service shall be proof of the same, and the return post office receipt for said complaint, order, or other process mailed by registered mail or by certified mail as aforesaid shall be proof of the service of the same.

(g) Finality of order

An order of the Commission to cease and desist shall become final—

(1) Upon the expiration of the time allowed for filing a petition for review, if no such petition has been duly filed within such time; but the Commission may thereafter modify or set aside its order to the extent provided in the last sentence of subsection (b).

(2) Except as to any order provision subject to paragraph (4), upon the sixtieth day after such order is served, if a petition for review has been duly filed; except that any such order may be stayed, in whole or in part and subject to such conditions as may be appropriate, by—

(A) the Commission;

(B) an appropriate court of appeals of the United States, if (i) a petition for review of such order is pending in such court, and (ii) an application for such a stay was previously submitted to the Commission and the Commission, within the 30–day period beginning on the date the application was received by the Commission, either denied the application or did not grant or deny the application; or

(C) the Supreme Court, if an applicable petition for certiorari is pending.

(3) For purposes of subsection (m)(1)(B) of this section and of section 57b(a)(2) of this title, if a petition for review of the order of the Commission has been filed—

(A) upon the expiration of the time allowed for filing a petition for certiorari, if the order of the Commission has been affirmed or the petition for review has been dismissed by the court of appeals and no petition for certiorari has been duly filed;

(B) upon the denial of a petition for certiorari, if the order of the Commission has been affirmed or the petition for review has been dismissed by the court of appeals; or

(C) upon the expiration of 30 days from the date of issuance of a mandate of the Supreme Court directing that the order of the Commission be affirmed or the petition for review be dismissed.

(4) In the case of an order provision requiring a person, partnership, or corporation to divest itself of stock, other share capital, or assets, if a petition for review of such order of the Commission has been filed—

(A) upon the expiration of the time allowed for filing a petition for certiorari, if the order of the Commission has been affirmed or the petition for review has been dismissed by the court of appeals and no petition for certiorari has been duly filed;

(B) upon the denial of a petition for certiorari, if the order of the Commission has been affirmed or the petition for review has been dismissed by the court of appeals; or

(C) upon the expiration of 30 days from the date of issuance of a mandate of the Supreme Court directing that the order of the Commission be affirmed or the petition for review be dismissed.

(h) Modification or setting aside of order by Supreme Court

If the Supreme Court directs that the order of the Commission be modified or set aside, the order of the Commission rendered in accordance with the mandate of the Supreme Court shall become final upon the expiration of thirty days from the time it was rendered, unless within such thirty days either party has instituted proceedings to have such order corrected to accord with the mandate, in which event the order of the Commission shall become final when so corrected.

(i) Modification or setting aside of order by Court of Appeals

If the order of the Commission is modified or set aside by the court of appeals, and if (1) the time allowed for filing a petition for certiorari has expired and no such petition has been duly filed, or (2) the petition for certiorari has been denied, or (3) the decision of the court has been affirmed by the Supreme Court, then the order of the Commission rendered in accordance with the mandate of the court of appeals shall become final on the expiration of thirty days from the time such order of the Commission was rendered, unless within such thirty days either party has instituted proceedings to have such order corrected so that it will accord with the mandate, in which event the order of the Commission shall become final when so corrected.

(j) Rehearing upon order or remand

If the Supreme Court orders a rehearing; or if the case is remanded by the court of appeals to the Commission for a rehearing, and if (1) the time allowed for filing a petition for certiorari has expired, and no such petition has been duly filed, or (2) the petition for certiorari has been denied, or (3) the decision of the court has been affirmed by the Supreme Court, then the order of the Commission rendered upon such rehearing shall become final in the same manner as though no prior order of the Commission had been rendered.

(k) "Mandate" defined

As used in this section the term "mandate", in case a mandate has been recalled prior to the expiration of thirty days from the date of issuance thereof, means the final mandate.

(l) Penalty for violation of order; injunctions and other appropriate equitable relief

Any person, partnership, or corporation who violates an order of the Commission after it has become final, and while such order is in effect, shall forfeit and pay to the United States a civil penalty of not more than $10,000 for each violation, which shall accrue to the United States and may be recovered in a civil action brought by the Attorney General of the United States. Each separate violation of such an order shall be a separate offense, except that in a case of a violation through continuing failure to obey or neglect to obey a final order of the Commission, each day of continuance of such failure or neglect shall be deemed a separate offense. In such actions, the United States district courts are empowered to grant mandatory injunctions and such other and further equitable relief as they deem appropriate in the enforcement of such final orders of the Commission.

(m) Civil actions for recovery of penalties for knowing violations of rules and cease and desist orders respecting unfair or deceptive acts or practices; jurisdiction; maximum amount of penalties; continuing violations; de novo determinations; compromise or settlement procedure

(1)(A) The Commission may commence a civil action to recover a civil penalty in a district court of the United States against any person, partnership, or corporation which violates any rule under this chapter respecting unfair or deceptive acts or practices (other than an interpretive rule or a rule violation of which the Commission has provided is not an unfair or deceptive act or practice in violation of subsection (a)(1) of this section) with actual knowledge or knowledge fairly implied on the basis of objective circumstances that such act is unfair or deceptive and is prohibited by such rule. In such action, such person, partnership, or corporation shall be liable for a civil penalty of not more than $10,000 for each violation.

(B) If the Commission determines in a proceeding under subsection (b) of this section that any act or practice is unfair or deceptive, and issues a final cease and desist order, other than a consent order, with respect to such act or practice, then the Commission may commence a civil action to obtain a civil penalty in a district court of the United States against any person, partnership, or corporation which engages in such act or practice—

(1) after such cease and desist order becomes final (whether or not such person, partnership, or corporation was subject to such cease and desist order), and

(2) with actual knowledge that such act or practice is unfair or deceptive and is unlawful under subsection (a)(1) of this section.

In such action, such person, partnership, or corporation shall be liable for a civil penalty of not more than $10,000 for each violation.

(C) In the case of a violation through continuing failure to comply with a rule or with subsection (a)(1) of this section, each day of continuance of such failure shall be treated as a separate violation, for purposes of subparagraphs (A) and (B). In determining the amount of such a civil penalty, the court shall take into account the degree of culpability, any history of prior such conduct, ability to pay, effect on ability to continue to do business, and such other matters as justice may require.

(2) If the cease and desist order establishing that the act or practice is unfair or deceptive was not issued against the defendant in a civil penalty action under paragraph (1)(B) the issues of fact in such action against such defendant shall be tried de novo. Upon request of any party to such an action against such defendant, the court shall also review the determination of law made by the Commission in the proceeding under subsection (b) of this section that the act or practice which was the subject of such proceeding constituted an unfair or deceptive act or practice in violation of subsection (a) of this section.

(3) The Commission may compromise or settle any action for a civil penalty if such compromise or settlement is accompanied by a public statement of its reasons and is approved by the court.

(n) Standard of proof; public policy consideration

The Commission shall have no authority under this section or section 57a of this title to declare unlawful an act or practice on the grounds that such act or practice is unfair unless the act or practice causes or is likely to cause substantial injury to consumers which is not reasonably avoidable by consumers themselves and not outweighed by countervailing benefits to consumers or to competition. In determining whether an act or practice is unfair, the Commission may consider established public policies as evidence to be considered with all other evidence. Such public policy considerations may not serve as a primary basis for such determination.

VIII. COPYRIGHT ACT OF 1976
(17 U.S.C. § 301)

■ ■ ■

Table of Sections

Section

301. Preemption with respect to other laws

---

§ 301. Preemption with respect to other laws

(a) On and after January 1, 1978, all legal or equitable rights that are equivalent to any of the exclusive rights within the general scope of copyright as specified by section 106 in works of authorship that are fixed in a tangible medium of expression and come within the subject matter of copyright as specified by sections 102 and 103, whether created before or after that date and whether published or unpublished, are governed exclusively by this title. Thereafter, no person is entitled to any such right or equivalent right in any such work under the common law or statutes of any State.

(b) Nothing in this title annuls or limits any rights or remedies under the common law or statutes of any State with respect to—

(1) subject matter that does not come within the subject matter of copyright as specified by sections 102 and 103, including works of authorship not fixed in any tangible medium of expression; or

(2) any cause of action arising from undertakings commenced before January 1, 1978;

(3) activities violating legal or equitable rights that are not equivalent to any of the exclusive rights within the general scope of copyright as specified by section 106; or

(4) State and local landmarks, historic preservation, zoning, or building codes, relating to architectural works protected under section 102(a)(8).

(c) With respect to sound recordings fixed before February 15, 1972, any rights or remedies under the common law or statutes of any State shall not be annulled or limited by this title until February 15, 2067. The preemptive provisions of subsection (a) shall apply to any such rights and remedies pertaining to any cause of action arising from undertakings commenced on and after February 15, 2067. Notwithstanding the provisions of section 303, no sound recording fixed before February 15, 1972, shall be subject to copyright under this title before, on, or after February 15, 2067.

(d) Nothing in this title annuls or limits any rights or remedies under any other Federal statute.

(e) The scope of Federal preemption under this section is not affected by the adherence of the United States to the Berne Convention or the satisfaction of obligations of the United States thereunder.

(f)(1) On or after the effective date set forth in section 610(a) of the Visual Artists Rights Act of 1990, all legal or equitable rights that are equivalent to any of the rights conferred by section 106A with respect to works of visual art to which the rights conferred by section 106A apply are governed exclusively by section 106A and section 113(d) and the provisions of this title relating to such sections. Thereafter, no person is entitled to any such right or equivalent right in any work of visual art under the common law or statutes of any State.

(2) Nothing in paragraph (1) annuls or limits any rights or remedies under the common law or statutes of any State with respect to—

    (A) any cause of action from undertakings commenced before the effective date set forth in section 610(a) of the Visual Artists Rights Act of 1990;

    (B) activities violating legal or equitable rights that are not equivalent to any of the rights conferred by section 106A with respect to works of visual art; or

    (C) activities violating legal or equitable rights which extend beyond the life of the author.

IX. UNIFORM TRADE SECRETS ACT

■ ■ ■

Table of Sections

PREFATORY NOTE

A valid patent provides a legal monopoly for seventeen years in exchange for public disclosure of an invention. If, however, the courts ultimately decide that the Patent Office improperly issued a patent, an invention will have been disclosed to competitors with no corresponding benefit. In view of the substantial number of patents that are invalidated by the courts, many businesses now elect to protect commercially valuable information through reliance upon the state law of trade secret protection. *Kewanee Oil Co. v. Bicron Corp.*, 416 U.S. 470 (1974), which establishes that neither the Patent Clause of the United States Constitution nor the federal patent laws pre-empt state trade secret protection for patentable or unpatentable information, may well have increased the extent of this reliance.

The recent decision in *Aronson v. Quick Point Pencil Co.*, 99 S.Ct. 1096, 201 USPQ 1 (1979) reaffirmed *Kewanee* and held that federal patent law is not a barrier to a contract in which someone agrees to pay a continuing royalty in exchange for the disclosure of trade secrets concerning a product.

Notwithstanding the commercial importance of state trade secret law to interstate business, this law has not developed satisfactorily. In the first place, its development is uneven. Although there typically are a substantial number of reported decisions in states that are commercial centers, this is not the case in less populous and more agricultural jurisdictions. Secondly, even in states in which there has been significant litigation, there is undue uncertainty concerning the parameters of trade secret protection, and the appropriate remedies for misappropriation of a trade secret. One commentator observed:

> "Under technological and economic pressures, industry continues to rely on trade secret protection despite the doubtful and confused status of both common law and statutory remedies. Clear, uniform trade secret protection is urgently needed. . . ."

Comment, "Theft of Trade Secrets: The Need for a Statutory Solution", 120 U.Pa.L.Rev. 378, 380–81 (1971).

In spite of this need, the most widely accepted rules of trade secret law, § 757 of the Restatement of Torts, were among the sections omitted from the Restatement of Torts, 2d (1978).

The Uniform Act codifies the basic principles of common law trade secret protection, preserving its essential distinctions from patent law. Under both the Act and common law principles, for example, more than one person can be entitled to trade secret protection with respect to the same information, and analysis involving the "reverse engineering" of a lawfully obtained product in order to discover a trade secret is permissible. *Compare* Uniform Act, Section 1(2) (misappropriation means acquisition of a trade secret by means that should be known to be improper and unauthorized disclosure or use of information that one should know is the trade secret of another) *with Miller v. Owens–Illinois, Inc.,* 187 USPQ 47, 48 (D.Md.1975) (alternative holding) (prior, independent discovery a complete defense to liability for misappropriation) *and Wesley–Jessen, Inc., v. Reynolds*, 182 USPQ 135, 144–45, (N.D.Ill.1974) (alternative holding) (unrestricted sale and lease of camera that could be reversed engineered in several days to reveal alleged trade secrets preclude relief for misappropriation).

For liability to exist under this Act, a Section 1(4) trade secret must exist and either a person's acquisition of the trade secret, disclosure of the trade secret to others, or use of the trade secret must be improper under Section 1(2). The mere copying of an unpatented item is not actionable.

Like traditional trade secret law, the Uniform Act contains general concepts. The contribution of the Uniform Act is substitution of unitary definitions of trade secret and trade secret misappropriation, and a single statute of limitations for the various property, quasi-contractual, and violation of fiduciary relationship theories of noncontractual liability utilized at common law. The Uniform Act also codifies the results of the better reasoned cases concerning the remedies for trade secret misappropriation.

The History of the Special Committee on the Uniform Trade Secrets Act

On February 17, 1968, the Conference's subcommittee on Scope and Program reported to the Conference's Executive Committee as follows:

"14. Uniform Trade Secrets Protection Act.

This matter came to the subcommittee from the Patent Law Section of the American Bar Association from President Pierce, Commissioner Joiner and Allison Dunham. It appears that in 1966 the Patent Section of the American Bar Association extensively discussed a resolution to the effect that 'the ABA favors the enactment of a uniform state law to protect against the wrongful disclosure or wrongful appropriation of trade secrets, know-how or other information maintained in confidence by another.' It was decided, however, not to put such a resolution to a vote at that time but that the appropriate Patent Section Committee would further consider the problem. In determining what would be appropriate for the Conference to do at this juncture, the following points should be considered:

(1) At the present much is going on by way of statutory development, both federally and in the states.

(2) There is a fundamental policy conflict still unresolved in that the current state statutes that protect trade secrets tend to keep innovations secret, while our federal patent policy is generally designed to encourage public disclosure of innovations. It may be possible to devise a sensible compromise between these two basic policies that will work, but to do so demands coordination of the statutory reform efforts of both the federal government and the states.

(3) The Section on Patents, the ABA group that is closest to this problem, is not yet ready to take a definite position.

It is recommended that a special committee be appointed to investigate the question of the drafting of a uniform act relating to trade secret protection and to establish liaison with the Patent Law Section, the Corporation, Banking and Business Law Section, and the Antitrust Law Section of the American Bar Association."

The Executive Committee, at its Midyear Meeting held February 17 and 18, 1968, in Chicago, Illinois, "voted to authorize the appointment of a Special Committee on Uniform Trade Secrets Protection Act to investigate the question of drafting an act on the subject with instructions to establish liaison with the Patent Law Section, the Corporation,

Banking and Business Law Section, and the Antitrust Law Section of the American Bar Association." Pursuant to that action, a Special Committee was appointed, which included Professor Richard Cosway of Seattle, Washington, who is the only original Committee member to serve to the present day. The following year saw substantial changes in the membership of the Committee. Professor Richard F. Dole, Jr., of Iowa City, Iowa, became a member then and has served as a member ever since.

The work of the Committee went before the Conference first on Thursday afternoon, August 10, 1972, when it was one of three Acts considered on first reading. Thereafter, for a variety of reasons, the Committee became inactive, and, regrettably, its original Chairman died on December 7, 1974. In 1976, the Committee became active again and presented a Fifth Tentative Draft of its proposed bill at the 1978 Annual Meeting of the National Conference of Commissioners on Uniform State Laws.

Despite the fact that there had previously been a first reading, the Committee was of the opinion that, because of the lapse of time, the 1978 presentation should also be considered a first reading. The Conference concurred, and the bill was proposed for final reading and adoption at the 1979 Annual Meeting.

On August 9, 1979, the Act was approved and recommended for enactment in all the states. Following discussions with members of the bar and bench, the Special Committee proposed amendments to Sections 2(b), 3(a), 7 and 11 that clarified the intent of the 1979 Official Text. On August 8, 1985, these four clarifying amendments were approved and recommended for enactment in all the states.

SECTION 1.   DEFINITIONS.

As used in this [Act], unless the context requires otherwise:

(1) "Improper means" includes theft, bribery, misrepresentation, breach or inducement of a breach of a duty to maintain secrecy, or espionage through electronic or other means;

(2) "Misappropriation" means:

    (i) acquisition of a trade secret of another by a person who knows or has reason to know that the trade secret was acquired by improper means; or

    (ii) disclosure or use of a trade secret of another without express or implied consent by a person who

        (A) used improper means to acquire knowledge of the trade secret; or

(B) at the time of disclosure or use, knew or had reason to know that his knowledge of the trade secret was

(I) derived from or through a person who had utilized improper means to acquire it;

(II) acquired under circumstances giving rise to a duty to maintain its secrecy or limit its use; or

(III) derived from or through a person who owed a duty to the person seeking relief to maintain its secrecy or limit its use; or

(C) before a material change of his [or her] position, knew or had reason to know that it was a trade secret and that knowledge of it had been acquired by accident or mistake.

(3) "Person" means a natural person, corporation, business trust, estate, trust, partnership, association, joint venture, government, governmental subdivision or agency, or any other legal or commercial entity.

(4) "Trade secret" means information, including a formula, pattern, compilation, program, device, method, technique, or process, that:

(i) derives independent economic value, actual or potential, from not being generally known to, and not being readily ascertainable by proper means by, other persons who can obtain economic value from its disclosure or use, and

(ii) is the subject of efforts that are reasonable under the circumstances to maintain its secrecy.

COMMENT

One of the broadly stated policies behind trade secret law is "the maintenance of standards of commercial ethics." *Kewanee Oil Co. v. Bicron Corp.,* 416 U.S. 470 (1974). The Restatement of Torts, Section 757, Comment (f), notes: "A complete catalogue of improper means is not possible," but Section 1(1) includes a partial listing.

Proper means include:

1.   Discovery by independent invention;

2.   Discovery by "reverse engineering", that is, by starting with the known product and working backward to find the method by which it was developed. The acquisition of the known product must, of course, also be by a fair and honest means, such as purchase of the item on the open market for reverse engineering to be lawful;

3.   Discovery under a license from the owner of the trade secret;

4.   Observation of the item in public use or on public display;

5.   Obtaining the trade secret from published literature.

Improper means could include otherwise lawful conduct which is improper under the circumstances; *e.g.,* an airplane overflight used as aerial reconnaissance to determine the competitor's plant layout during construction of the plant. *E. I. du Pont de Nemours & Co., Inc. v. Christopher,* 431 F.2d 1012 (CA5, 1970), cert. den. 400 U.S. 1024 (1970). Because the trade secret can be destroyed through public knowledge, the unauthorized disclosure of a trade secret is also a misappropriation.

The type of accident or mistake that can result in a misappropriation under Section 1(2)(ii)(C) involves conduct by a person seeking relief that does not constitute a failure of efforts that are reasonable under the circumstances to maintain its secrecy under Section 1(4)(ii).

The definition of "trade secret" contains a reasonable departure from the Restatement of Torts (First) definition which required that a trade secret be "continuously used in one's business." The broader definition in the proposed Act extends protection to a plaintiff who has not yet had an opportunity or acquired the means to put a trade secret to use. The definition includes information that has commercial value from a negative viewpoint, for example the results of lengthy and expensive research which proves that a certain process will *not* work could be of great value to a competitor.

Cf. Telex Corp. v. IBM Corp., 510 F.2d 894 (CA10, 1975) per curiam, cert. dismissed 423 U.S. 802 (1975) (liability imposed for developmental cost savings with respect to product not marketed). Because a trade secret need not be exclusive to confer a competitive advantage, different independent developers can acquire rights in the same trade secret.

The words "method, technique" are intended to include the concept of "know-how."

The language "not being generally known to and not being readily ascertainable by proper means by other persons" does not require that information be generally known to the public for trade secret rights to be lost. If the principal person persons who can obtain economic benefit from information is are aware of it, there is no trade secret. A method of casting metal, for example, may be unknown to the general public but readily known within the foundry industry.

Information is readily ascertainable if it is available in trade journals, reference books, or published materials. Often, the nature of a product lends itself to being readily copied as soon as it is available on the market. On the other hand, if reverse engineering is lengthy and expensive, a person who discovers the trade secret through reverse engineering can have a trade secret in the information obtained from reverse engineering.

Finally, reasonable efforts to maintain secrecy have been held to include advising employees of the existence of a trade secret, limiting access to a trade secret on "need to know basis", and controlling plant access. On the other hand, public disclosure of information through display, trade journal publications, advertising, or other carelessness can preclude protection.

The efforts required to maintain secrecy are those "reasonable under the circumstances." The courts do not require that extreme and unduly expensive procedures be taken to protect trade secrets against flagrant industrial espionage. See *E. I. du Pont de Nemours & Co., Inc. v. Christopher, supra.* It follows that reasonable use of a trade secret including controlled disclosure to employees and licensees is consistent with the requirement of relative secrecy.

SECTION 2. INJUNCTIVE RELIEF.

(a) Actual or threatened misappropriation may be enjoined. Upon application to the court, an injunction shall be terminated when the trade secret has ceased to exist, but the injunction may be continued for an additional reasonable period of time in order to eliminate commercial advantage that otherwise would be derived from the misappropriation.

(b) In exceptional circumstances, an injunction may condition future use upon payment of a reasonable royalty for no longer than the period of time for which use could have been prohibited. Exceptional circumstances include, but are not limited to, a material and prejudicial change of position prior to acquiring knowledge or reason to know of misappropriation that renders a prohibitive injunction inequitable.

(c) In appropriate circumstances, affirmative acts to protect a trade secret may be compelled by court order.

COMMENT

Injunctions restraining future use and disclosure of misappropriated trade secrets frequently are sought. Although punitive perpetual injunctions have been granted, *e.g., Elcor Chemical Corp. v. Agri–Sul, Inc.,* 494 S.W.2d 204 (Tex.Civ.App.1973), Section 2(a) of this Act adopts the position of the trend of authority limiting the duration of injunctive relief to the extent of the temporal advantage over good faith competitors gained by a misappropriator. See, *e.g., K–2 Ski Co. v. Head Ski Co., Inc.,* 506 F.2d 471 (CA9, 1974) (maximum appropriate duration of both temporary and permanent injunctive relief is period of time it would have taken defendant to discover trade secrets lawfully through either independent development or reverse engineering of plaintiff's products).

The general principle of Section 2(a) and (b) is that an injunction should last for as long as is necessary, but no longer than is necessary, to eliminate the commercial advantage or "lead time" with respect to good faith competitors that a person has obtained through misappropriation. Subject to any additional period of restraint necessary to negate lead time, an injunction accordingly should terminate when a former trade secret becomes either generally known to good faith competitors or generally knowable to them because of the lawful availability of products that can be reverse engineered to reveal a trade secret.

For example, assume that A has a valuable trade secret of which B and C, the other industry members, are originally unaware. If B subsequently misappropriates the trade secret and is enjoined from use, but C later lawfully reverse engineers the trade secret, the injunction restraining B is subject to termination as soon as B's lead time has been dissipated. All of the persons who could derive economic value from use of the information are now aware of it, and there is no longer a trade secret under Section 1(4). It would be anti-competitive to continue to restrain B after any lead time that B had derived from misappropriation had been removed.

If a misappropriator either has not taken advantage of lead time or good faith competitors already have caught up with a misappropriator at the time that a case is decided, future disclosure and use of a former trade secret by a misappropriator will not damage a trade secret owner and no injunctive restraint of future disclosure and use is appropriate. See, *e.g., Northern Petrochemical Co. v. Tomlinson*, 484 F.2d 1057 (CA7, 1973) (affirming trial court's denial of preliminary injunction in part because an explosion at its plant prevented an alleged misappropriator from taking advantage of lead time); *Kubik, Inc. v. Hull*, 185 USPQ 391 (Mich.App.1974) (discoverability of trade secret by lawful reverse engineering made by injunctive relief punitive rather than compensatory).

Section 2(b) deals with the special situation in which future use by a misappropriator will damage a trade secret owner but an injunction against future use nevertheless is inappropriate due to exceptional circumstances. Exceptional circumstances include the existence of an overriding public interest which requires the denial of a prohibitory injunction against future damaging use and a person's reasonable reliance upon acquisition of a misappropriated trade secret in good faith and without reason to know of its prior misappropriation that would be prejudiced by a prohibitory injunction against future damaging use. *Republic Aviation Corp. v. Schenk*, 152 USPQ 830 (N.Y.Sup.Ct.1967) illustrates the public interest justification for withholding prohibitory injunctive relief. The court considered that enjoining a misappropriator from supplying the U.S. with an aircraft weapons control system would have endangered military personnel in Viet Nam. The prejudice to a good faith third party justification for withholding prohibitory injunctive relief can arise upon a trade secret owner's notification to a good faith third party that the third party has knowledge of a trade secret as a result of misappropriation by another. This notice suffices to make the third party a misappropriator thereafter under Section 1(2)(ii)(B)(I). In weighing an aggrieved person's interests and the interests of a third party who has relied in good faith upon his or her ability to utilize information, a court may conclude that restraining future use of the information by the third party is unwarranted. With respect to innocent acquirers of misappropriated trade secrets, Section 2(b) is consistent with the principle of 4 Restatement Torts (First) § 758(b) (1939), but rejects the Restatement's literal conferral of absolute immunity upon all third parties who have paid value in good faith for a trade secret misappropriated by another. The position taken by the

Uniform Act is supported by *Forest Laboratories, Inc. v. Pillsbury Co.,* 452 F.2d 621 (CA7, 1971) in which a defendant's purchase of assets of a corporation to which a trade secret had been disclosed in confidence was not considered to confer immunity upon the defendant.

When Section 2(b) applies, a court is given has discretion to substitute an injunction conditioning future use upon payment of a reasonable royalty for an injunction prohibiting future use. Like all injunctive relief for misappropriation, a royalty order injunction is appropriate only if a misappropriator has obtained a competitive advantage through misappropriation and only for the duration of that competitive advantage. In some situations, typically those involving good faith acquirers of trade secrets misappropriated by others, a court may conclude that the same considerations that render a prohibitory injunction against future use inappropriate also render a royalty order injunction inappropriate. See, generally, *Prince Manufacturing, Inc. v. Automatic Partner, Inc.,* 198 USPQ 618 (N.J.Super.Ct.1976) (purchaser of misappropriator's assets from receiver after trade secret disclosed to public through sale of product not subject to liability for misappropriation).

A royalty order injunction under Section 2(b) should be distinguished from a reasonable royalty alternative measure of damages under Section 3(a). See the Comment to Section 3 for discussion of the differences in the remedies.

Section 2(c) authorizes mandatory injunctions requiring that a misappropriator return the fruits of misappropriation to an aggrieved person, *e.g.,* the return of stolen blueprints or the surrender of surreptitious photographs or recordings.

Where more than one person is entitled to trade secret protection with respect to the same information, only that one from whom misappropriation occurred is entitled to a remedy.

SECTION 3. DAMAGES.

(a) Except to the extent that a material and prejudicial change of position prior to acquiring knowledge or reason to know of misappropriation renders a monetary recovery inequitable, a complainant is entitled to recover damages for by misappropriation. Damages can include both the actual loss caused by misappropriation and the unjust enrichment caused by misappropriation that is not taken into account in computing actual loss. In lieu of damages measured by any other methods, the damages caused by misappropriation may be measured by imposition of liability for a reasonable royalty for a misappropriator's unauthorized disclosure or use of a trade secret.

(b) If willful and malicious misappropriation exists, the court may award exemplary damages in an amount not exceeding twice any award made under subsection (a).

COMMENT

Like injunctive relief, a monetary recovery for trade secret misappropriation is appropriate only for the period in which information is entitled to protection as a trade secret, plus the additional period, if any, in which a misappropriator retains an advantage over good faith competitors because of misappropriation. Actual damage to a complainant and unjust benefit to a misappropriator are caused by misappropriation during this time alone. See *Conmar Products Corp. v. Universal Slide Fastener Co.*, 172 F.2d 150 (CA2, 1949) (no remedy for period subsequent to disclosure of trade secret by issued patent); *Carboline Co. v. Jarboe*, 454 S.W.2d 540 (Mo.1970) (recoverable monetary relief limited to period that it would have taken misappropriator to discover trade secret without misappropriation). A claim for actual damages and net profits can be combined with a claim for injunctive relief, but, if both claims are granted, the injunctive relief ordinarily will preclude a monetary award for a period in which the injunction is effective.

As long as there is no double counting, Section 3(a) adopts the principle of the recent cases allowing recovery of both a complainant's actual losses and a misappropriator's unjust benefit that are caused by misappropriation. *E.g., Tri–Tron International v. Velto*, 525 F.2d 432 (CA9, 1975) (complainant's loss and misappropriator's benefit can be combined). Because certain cases may have sanctioned double counting in a combined award of losses and unjust benefit, *e.g., Telex Corp. v. IBM Corp.*, 510 F.2d 894 (CA10, 1975) (per curiam), cert. dismissed, 423 U.S. 802 (1975) (IBM recovered rentals lost due to displacement by misappropriator's products without deduction for expenses saved by displacement; as a result of rough approximations adopted by the trial judge, IBM also may have recovered developmental costs saved by misappropriator through misappropriation with respect to the same customers), the Act adopts an express prohibition upon the counting of the same item as both a loss to a complainant and an unjust benefit to a misappropriator.

As an alternative to all other methods of measuring damages caused by a misappropriator's past conduct, a complainant can request that damages be based upon a demonstrably reasonable royalty for a misappropriator's unauthorized disclosure or use of a trade secret. In order to justify this alternative measure of damages, there must be competent evidence of the amount of a reasonable royalty.

The reasonable royalty alternative measure of damages for a misappropriator's past conduct under Section 3(a) is readily distinguishable from a Section 2(b) royalty order injunction, which conditions a misappropriator's future ability to use a trade secret upon payment of a reasonable royalty. A Section 2(b) royalty order injunction is appropriate only in exceptional circumstances; whereas a reasonable royalty measure of damages is a general option. Because Section 3(a) damages are awarded for a misappropriator's past conduct and a Section 2(b) royalty order injunction regulates a misappropriator's future conduct, both remedies cannot be awarded for the same conduct. If a royalty order injunction is appropriate because of a person's material and prejudicial change of position prior to having reason to know that a trade secret has been acquired from a misappropriator, damages, moreover, should not be awarded for past conduct that occurred prior to notice that a misappropriated trade secret has been acquired.

Monetary relief can be appropriate whether or not injunctive relief is granted under Section 2. If a person charged with misappropriation has acquired materially and prejudicially changed position in reliance upon knowledge of a trade secret acquired in good faith and without reason to know of its misappropriation by another, however, the same considerations that can justify denial of all injunctive relief also can justify denial of all monetary relief. See *Conmar Products Corp. v. Universal Slide Fastener Co.*, 172 F.2d 1950 (CA2, 1949) (no relief against new employer of employee subject to contractual obligation not to disclose former employer's trade secrets where new employer innocently had committed $40,000 to develop the trade secrets prior to notice of misappropriation).

If willful and malicious misappropriation is found to exist, Section 3(b) authorizes the court to award a complainant exemplary damages in addition to the actual recovery under Section 3(a) an amount not exceeding twice that recovery. This provision follows federal patent law in leaving discretionary trebling to the judge even though there may be a jury, *compare* 35 U.S.C. Section 284 (1976).

Whenever more than one person is entitled to trade secret protection with respect to the same information, only that one from whom misappropriation occurred is entitled to a remedy.

SECTION 4.   ATTORNEY'S FEES.

If (i) a claim of misappropriation is made in bad faith, (ii) a motion to terminate an injunction is made or resisted in bad faith, or (iii) willful and malicious misappropriation exists, the court may award reasonable attorney's fees to the prevailing party.

COMMENT

Section 4 allows a court to award reasonable attorney fees to a prevailing party in specified circumstances as a deterrent to specious claims of misappropriation, to specious efforts by a misappropriator to terminate injunctive relief, and to willful and malicious misappropriation. In the latter situation, the court should take into consideration the extent to which a complainant will recover exemplary damages in determining whether additional attorney's fees should be awarded. Again, patent law is followed in allowing the judge to determine whether attorney's fees should be awarded even if there is a jury, *compare* 35 U.S.C. Section 285 (1976).

SECTION 5.   PRESERVATION OF SECRECY.

In an action under this [Act], a court shall preserve the secrecy of an alleged trade secret by reasonable means, which may include granting protective orders in connection with discovery proceedings, holding in-camera hearings, sealing the records of the action, and ordering any person involved in the litigation not to disclose an alleged trade secret without prior court approval.

COMMENT

If reasonable assurances of maintenance of secrecy could not be given, meritorious trade secret litigation would be chilled. In fashioning safeguards of confidentiality, a court must ensure that a respondent is provided sufficient information to present a defense and a trier of fact sufficient information to resolve the merits. In addition to the illustrative techniques specified in the statute, courts have protected secrecy in these cases by restricting disclosures to a party's counsel and his or her assistants and by appointing a disinterested expert as a special master to hear secret information and report conclusions to the court.

SECTION 6.   STATUTE OF LIMITATIONS.

An action for misappropriation must be brought within 3 years after the misappropriation is discovered or by the exercise of reasonable diligence should have been discovered.

For the purposes of this section, a continuing misappropriation constitutes a single claim.

COMMENT

There presently is a conflict of authority as to whether trade secret misappropriation is a continuing wrong. *Compare Monolith Portland Midwest Co. v. Kaiser Aluminum & Chemical Corp.,* 407 F.2d 288 (CA9, 1969) (no not a continuing wrong under California law—limitation period upon all recovery begins upon initial misappropriation) with *Underwater Storage, Inc. v. U. S. Rubber Co.,* 371 F.2d 950 (CADC, 1966), cert. den., 386 U.S. 911 (1967) (continuing wrong under general principles—limitation period with respect to a specific act of misappropriation begins at the time that the act of misappropriation occurs).

This Act rejects a continuing wrong approach to the statute of limitations but delays the commencement of the limitation period until an aggrieved person discovers or reasonably should have discovered the existence of misappropriation. If objectively reasonable notice of misappropriation exists, three years is sufficient time to vindicate one's legal rights.

SECTION 7.   EFFECT ON OTHER LAW.

(a) Except as provided in subsection (b), this [Act] displaces conflicting tort, restitutionary, and other law of this State providing civil remedies for misappropriation of a trade secret.

(b) This [Act] does not affect:

(1) contractual remedies, whether or not based upon misappropriation of a trade secret;

(2) other civil remedies that are not based upon misappropriation of a trade secret; or

(3) criminal remedies, whether or not based upon misappropriation of a trade secret.

COMMENT

This Act does not deal with criminal remedies for trade secret misappropriation and is not a comprehensive statement of civil remedies. It applies to a duty to protect competitively significant secret information that is imposed by law. It does not apply to a duty voluntarily assumed through an express or an implied-in-fact contract. The enforceability of covenants not to disclose trade secrets and covenants not to compete that are intended to protect trade secrets, for example, are is governed by other law. The Act also does not apply to a duty imposed by law that is not dependent upon the existence of competitively significant secret information, like an agent's duty of loyalty to his or her principal.

SECTION 8.   UNIFORMITY OF APPLICATION AND CONSTRUCTION.

This [Act] shall be applied and construed to effectuate its general purpose to make uniform the law with respect to the subject of this [Act] among states enacting it.

SECTION 9.   SHORT TITLE.

This [Act] may be cited as the Uniform Trade Secrets Act.

SECTION 10.   SEVERABILITY.

If any provision of this [Act] or its application to any person or circumstances is held invalid, the invalidity does not affect other provisions or applications of the [Act] which can be given effect without the invalid provision or application, and to this end the provisions of this [Act] are severable.

SECTION 11.   TIME OF TAKING EFFECT.

This [Act] takes effect on _____, and does not apply to misappropriation occurring prior to the effective date. With respect to a continuing misappropriation that began prior to the effective date, the [Act] also does not apply to the continuing misappropriation that occurs after the effective date.

COMMENT

The Act applies exclusively to misappropriation that begins after its effective date. Neither misappropriation that began and ended before the effective date nor misappropriation that began before the effective date and continued thereafter is subject to the Act.

SECTION 12.   REPEAL.

The following Acts and parts of Acts are repealed:

(1)

(2)

(3)

X. Restatement (First) of Torts

(Selected Sections & Comments)

■ ■ ■

Table of Sections

Division Nine. Interference with Business Relations
Part 1. By Trade Practices
Chapter 36. Miscellaneous Trade Practices

§ 757 Liability for Disclosure or Use of Another's Trade Secret—General Principle

One who discloses or uses another's trade secret, without a privilege to do so, is liable to the other if

(a) he discovered the secret by improper means, or

(b) his disclosure or use constitutes a breach of confidence reposed in him by the other in disclosing the secret to him, or

(c) he learned the secret from a third person with notice of the facts that it was a secret and that the third person discovered it by improper means or that the third person's disclosure of it was otherwise a breach of his duty to the other, or

(d) he learned the secret with notice of the facts that it was a secret and that its disclosure was made to him by mistake.

Comment:

b. Definition of trade secret. A trade secret may consist of any formula, pattern, device or compilation of information which is used in one's business, and which gives him an opportunity to obtain an advantage over competitors who do not know or use it. It may be a formula for a chemical compound, a process of manufacturing, treating or preserving materials, a pattern for a machine or other device, or a list of customers. It differs from other secret information in a business (see § 759) in that it is not simply information as to single or ephemeral events in the conduct of the business, as, for example, the amount or other terms of a secret bid for a contract or the salary of certain employees, or the security investments made or contemplated, or the date fixed for the announcement of a new policy or for bringing out a new model or the like. A trade secret is a process or device for continuous use in the operation of the business. Generally it relates to the production of goods, as, for example, a machine or formula for the production of an article. It may, however, relate to the sale of goods or to other operations in the business, such as a code for determining discounts, rebates or other concessions in a price list or catalogue, or a list of specialized customers, or a method of bookkeeping or other office management.

Secrecy. The subject matter of a trade secret must be secret. Matters of public knowledge or of general knowledge in an industry cannot be appropriated by one as his secret. Matters which are completely disclosed by the goods which one markets cannot be his secret. Substantially, a trade secret is known only in the particular business in which it is used. It is not requisite that only the proprietor of the business know it. He may, without losing his protection, communicate it to employees involved in its use. He may likewise communicate it to others pledged to secrecy. Others may also know of it independently, as, for example, when they have discovered the process or formula by independent invention and are keeping it secret. Nevertheless, a substantial element of secrecy must exist, so that, except by the use of improper means, there would be difficulty in acquiring the information. An exact definition of a trade secret is not possible. Some factors to be considered in determining whether given information is one's trade secret are: (1) the extent to which the information is known outside of his business; (2) the extent to which it is known by employees and others involved in his business; (3) the extent of measures taken by him to guard the secrecy of the information; (4) the value of the information to him and to his competitors; (5) the amount of effort or money expended by him in developing the information; (6) the ease or difficulty with which the information could be properly acquired or duplicated by others.

Novelty and prior art. A trade secret may be a device or process which is patentable; but it need not be that. It may be a device or process which is clearly anticipated in the prior art or one which is merely a mechanical improvement that a good mechanic can make. Novelty and invention are not requisite for a trade secret as they are for patentability. These requirements are essential to patentability because a patent protects against unlicensed use of the patented device or process even by one who discovers it properly through independent research. The patent monopoly is a reward to the inventor. But such is not the case with a trade secret. Its protection is not based on a policy of rewarding or otherwise encouraging the development of secret processes or devices. The protection is merely against breach of faith and reprehensible means of learning another's secret. For this limited protection it is not appropriate to require also the kind of novelty and invention which is a requisite of patentability. The nature of the secret is, however, an important factor in determining the kind of relief that is appropriate against one who is subject to liability under the rule stated in this Section. Thus, if the secret consists of a device or process which is a novel invention, one who acquires the secret wrongfully is ordinarily enjoined from further use of it and is required to account for the profits derived from his past use. If, on the other hand, the secret consists of mechanical improvements that a good mechanic can make without resort to the secret, the wrongdoer's liability may be limited to damages, and an injunction against future use of the improvements made with the aid of the secret may be inappropriate.

Information not a trade secret. Although given information is not a trade secret, one who receives the information in a confidential relation or discovers it by improper means may be under some duty not to disclose or use that information. Because of the confidential relation or the impropriety of the means of discovery, he may be compelled to go to other sources for the information. As stated in Comment *a,* even the rule stated in this Section rests not upon a view of trade secrets as physical objects of property but rather upon abuse of confidence or impropriety in learning the secret. Such abuse or impropriety may exist also where the information is not a trade secret and may be equally a basis for liability. The rules relating to the liability for duties arising from confidential relationships generally are not within the scope of the Restatement of this Subject. As to the use of improper means to acquire information, see § 759.

f. Improper means of discovery. The discovery of another's trade secret by improper means subjects the actor to liability independently of the harm to the interest in the secret. Thus, if one uses physical force to take a secret formula from another's pocket, or breaks into another's office to steal the formula, his conduct is wrongful and subjects him to liability apart from the rule stated in this Section. Such conduct is also an improper means of procuring the secret under this rule. But means may be improper under this rule even though they do not cause any other harm than that to the interest in the trade secret. Examples of such means are fraudulent misrepresentations to induce disclosure, tapping of telephone wires, eavesdropping or other espionage. A complete catalogue of improper means is not possible. In general they are means which fall below the generally accepted standards of commercial morality and reasonable conduct. See also, § 759, Comment *c.*

§ 759   Procuring Information by Improper Means

One who, for the purpose of advancing a rival business interest, procures by improper means information about another's business is liable to the other for the harm caused by his possession, disclosure or use of the information.

Comment:

b.   Kind of information. The rule stated in this Section applies to information about one's business whether or not it constitutes a trade secret (see § 757, Comment *b,* where trade secret is defined). The Section states the rule of liability applicable only when the information is procured by improper means. Sections 757 and 758 deal specially with the liability for the disclosure and use of trade secrets, whether they are discovered by improper means or otherwise. Examples of information, other than trade secrets, included in this Section are: the state of one's accounts, the amount of his bid for a contract, his sources of supply, his plans for expansion or retrenchment, and the like. There are no limitations as to the type of information included except that it relate to matters in his business. Generally, however, if the improper discovery of the information is to cause harm, the information must be of a secret or confidential character. Thus, if one freely gives full information about the state of his accounts to trade associations, credit agencies or others who request it, the possession, disclosure or use of the same information by one who procured it through improper means can hardly cause him harm. On the other hand, if one has a closely guarded trade secret, another's discovery of it may reduce its sale value even before any other disclosure or use is made of the secret.

XI. RESTATEMENT (SECOND) OF AGENCY

(Selected Sections & Comments)

■ ■ ■

Table of Sections

Chapter 1. Introductory Matters
Topic 1. Definitions

Chapter 1. Introductory Matters
Topic 1. Definitions

§ 2   Master; Servant; Independent Contractor

(1) A master is a principal who employs an agent to perform service in his affairs and who controls or has the right to control the physical conduct of the other in the performance of the service.

(2) A servant is an agent employed by a master to perform service in his affairs whose physical conduct in the performance of the service is controlled or is subject to the right to control by the master.

(3) An independent contractor is a person who contracts with another to do something for him but who is not controlled by the other nor subject to the other's right to control with respect to his physical conduct in the performance of the undertaking. He may or may not be an agent.

Chapter 7. Liability of Principal to Third Person; Torts
Topic 2. Liability for Authorized Conduct or Conduct Incidental Thereto
Title B. Torts of Servants

§ 220 Definition of Servant

(1) A servant is a person employed to perform services in the affairs of another and who with respect to the physical conduct in the performance of the services is subject to the other's control or right to control.

(2) In determining whether one acting for another is a servant or an independent contractor, the following matters of fact, among others, are considered:

(a) the extent of control which, by the agreement, the master may exercise over the details of the work;

(b) whether or not the one employed is engaged in a distinct occupation or business;

(c) the kind of occupation, with reference to whether, in the locality, the work is usually done under the direction of the employer or by a specialist without supervision;

(d) the skill required in the particular occupation;

(e) whether the employer or the workman supplies the instrumentalities, tools, and the place of work for the person doing the work;

(f) the length of time for which the person is employed;

(g) the method of payment, whether by the time or by the job;

(h) whether or not the work is a part of the regular business of the employer;

(i) whether or not the parties believe they are creating the relation of master and servant; and

(j) whether the principal is or is not in business.

Chapter 13. Duties and Liabilities of Agent to Principal
Topic 1. Duties
Title C. Duties of Loyalty

§ 387 General Principle

Unless otherwise agreed, an agent is subject to a duty to his principal to act solely for the benefit of the principal in all matters connected with his agency.

§ 388 Duty to Account for Profits Arising out of Employment

Unless otherwise agreed, an agent who makes a profit in connection with transactions conducted by him on behalf of the principal is under a duty to give such profit to the principal.

§ 389 Acting as Adverse Party without Principal's Consent

Unless otherwise agreed, an agent is subject to a duty not to deal with his principal as an adverse party in a transaction connected with his agency without the principal's knowledge.

§ 390 Acting as Adverse Party with Principal's Consent

An agent who, to the knowledge of the principal, acts on his own account in a transaction in which he is employed has a duty to deal fairly with the principal and to disclose to him all facts which the agent knows or should know would reasonably affect the principal's judgment, unless the principal has manifested that he knows such facts or that he does not care to know them.

§ 391 Acting for Adverse Party without Principal's Consent

Unless otherwise agreed, an agent is subject to a duty to his principal not to act on behalf of an adverse party in a transaction connected with his agency without the principal's knowledge.

§ 392 Acting for Adverse Party with Principal's Consent

An agent who, to the knowledge of two principals, acts for both of them in a transaction between them, has a duty to act with fairness to each and to disclose to each all facts which he knows or should know would reasonably affect the judgment of each in permitting such dual agency, except as to a principal who has manifested that he knows such facts or does not care to know them.

§ 393 Competition as to Subject Matter of Agency

Unless otherwise agreed, an agent is subject to a duty not to compete with the principal concerning the subject matter of his agency.

§ 394 Acting for One with Conflicting Interests

Unless otherwise agreed, an agent is subject to a duty not to act or to agree to act during the period of his agency for persons whose interests conflict with those of the principal in matters in which the agent is employed.

§ 395 Using or Disclosing Confidential Information

Unless otherwise agreed, an agent is subject to a duty to the principal not to use or to communicate information confidentially given him by the principal or acquired by him during the course of or on account of his agency or in violation of his duties as agent, in competition with or to the injury of the principal, on his own account or on behalf of another, although such information does not relate to the transaction in which he is then employed, unless the information is a matter of general knowledge.

§ 396 Using Confidential Information after Termination of Agency

Unless otherwise agreed, after the termination of the agency, the agent:

(a) has no duty not to compete with the principal;

(b) has a duty to the principal not to use or to disclose to third persons, on his own account or on account of others, in competition with the principal or to his injury, trade secrets, written lists of names, or other similar confidential matters given to him only for the principal's use or acquired by the agent in violation of duty. The agent is entitled to use general information concerning the method of business of the principal and the names of the customers retained in his memory, if not acquired in violation of his duty as agent;

(c) has a duty to account for profits made by the sale or use of trade secrets and other confidential information, whether or not in competition with the principal;

(d) has a duty to the principal not to take advantage of a still subsisting confidential relation created during the prior agency relation.

§ 397 When Agent Has Right to Patents

Unless otherwise agreed, a person employed by another to do noninventive work is entitled to patents which are the result of his invention although the invention is due to the work for which he is employed.

Comment:

a. A person who has discovered a principle or device for which a patent is issued is entitled to the ownership of the patent unless, at the time of the employment or subsequently, he agrees to convey it to another. Such an agreement may be found in specific terms in a contract of employment or from the circumstances surrounding the employment, the nature of the work done, and the relations of the parties during the employment. For the employer to be entitled to a patent it is not necessary that the contract should specifically so provide. Whether or not the inventions of the employee are to belong to the employer is a question to be decided upon all the facts of the individual case. There is no inference from the mere fact of employment that an employee agrees that his employer is to own patentable ideas which are discovered in the course of or as a consequence of the work which the employee is employed to do. This is true although the employee uses the tools and facilities of the employer in developing the idea. If, however, one is employed to do experimental work for inventive purposes, it is inferred ordinarily, although not so specifically agreed, that patentable ideas arrived at through the experimentation are to be owned by the employer. This is even more clear where one is employed to achieve a particular result which the invention accomplishes. On the other hand, if one is employed merely to do work in a particular line in which he is an expert, there is no inference that inventions which he makes while so working belong to the employer.

b. *License to use patent.* Although the facts do not show an agreement that the employer is to own a patent which is the result of the employee's invention, if the invention is made by an employee using the employer's facilities for the purpose of experimentation and invention in connection with the work for which he is employed, it is the reasonable inference that the employer is to have, without charge, a nonexclusive license to manufacture and use the patented device or process in the regular course of the business in which the employee is employed at the time of the invention.

c. *Use of employer's time or facilities.* The fact that an employee uses time which he should have devoted to his employer's affairs in perfecting a patent does not entitle the employer to the patent. This is true even though, in addition, the employee has used improperly the employer's tools. However, if the employer's time or facilities are used without his permission, and the employee invents a device which can be used in the regular business of the employer, the latter is given a nonexclusive license to manufacture and use it.

Illustrations:

1. A, employed as a shop foreman by P, improperly uses his own time and the tools of his employer in perfecting a device not used in the employer's business, and obtains a patent. P is not entitled to an assignment of the patent or to manufacture or use the device. He is entitled to compensation for the use of the tools.

2.   Same facts as in Illustration 1, except that the device is an improvement on a machine manufactured by the employer. The employer is entitled to manufacture and use the device.

§ 398   Confusing or Appearing to Own Principal's Things

Unless otherwise agreed, an agent receiving or holding things on behalf of the principal is subject to a duty to the principal not to receive or deal with them so that they will appear to be his own, and not so to mingle them with his own things as to destroy their identity.

XII. RESTATEMENT (THIRD) OF AGENCY

(Selected Sections & Comments)

■ ■ ■

Table of Sections

Chapter 8. Duties of Agent and Principal to Each Other
Topic 1. Agent's Duties to Principal
Title A. General Fiduciary Principle

§ 8.01 General Fiduciary Principle

An agent has a fiduciary duty to act loyally for the principal's benefit in all matters connected with the agency relationship.

Title B. Duties of Loyalty

§ 8.05 Use of Principal's Property; Use of Confidential Information

An agent has a duty

(1) not to use property of the principal for the agent's own purposes or those of a third party; and

(2) not to use or communicate confidential information of the principal for the agent's own purposes or those of a third party.

Comment:

c. Confidential information. Many employees and other agents are given access by the principal to information that the principal would not wish to be revealed or used, except as the principal directs. Such information may pertain to the principal's business plans, personnel, nonpublic financial results, and operational practices, among a range of possibilities. The value of some types of confidential information is recognized by trade-secret law, which protects "any information that can be used in the operation of a business or other enterprise and that is sufficiently valuable and secret to afford an actual or potential economic advantage over others." Restatement Third, Unfair Competition § 39.

An agent may, additionally, acquire confidential information about a principal or otherwise in the course of an agency relationship that does not have competitive or other economic value. For example, in the context of a lawyer-client relationship, confidential client information encompasses all information, not generally known, that relates to representation of the client. See Restatement Third, The Law Governing Lawyers § 59. An agent's relationship with a principal may result in the agent learning information about the principal's health, life history, and personal preferences that the agent should reasonably understand the principal expects the agent to keep confidential. An agent's duty of confidentiality extends to all such information concerning a principal even when it is not otherwise connected with the subject matter of the agency relationship.

An agent's duty of confidentiality is not absolute. An agent may reveal otherwise privileged information to protect a superior interest of the agent or a third party. Thus, an agent may reveal to law-enforcement authorities that the principal is committing or is about to commit a crime. An agent's privilege to reveal such information also protects the agent's revelation to a private party who is being or will be harmed by the principal's illegal conduct. Many statutes provide protection against termination to employees who engage in "whistleblowing."

An agent's duties concerning confidential information do not end when the agency relationship terminates. An agent is not free to use or disclose a principal's trade secrets or other confidential information whether the agent retains a physical record of them or retains them in the agent's memory. If information is otherwise a trade secret or confidential, the means by which an agent appropriates it for later use or disclosure should be irrelevant. Feats of human memory, however commendable and intriguing in many respects, should not be privileged as instruments of disloyal conduct.

Illustrations:

6.   P, who owns a commercial cleaning service, maintains a list of customers and prospective customers, noting particulars about each. P's list would be of competitive use to others. P maintains the list on a computer in P's office and restricts access to high-level employees within P's organization. A, P's general manager, who wishes to establish a competing cleaning service, retains a hard copy of the list that P gave to A to use in A's work. A resigns, taking the list and planning to use it to solicit business for A's new competing firm. A has breached A's duty to P.

7.   Same facts as Illustration 6, except that A commits the list to memory, memorizing a portion each day and then typing that portion into A's home computer each evening. Same result.

An agent's use of the principal's confidential information for the agent's own purposes breaches the agent's duty as stated in subsection (2) although the agent's use of the information does not necessitate revealing it. Thus, it is a breach of an agent's duty to use confidential information of the principal for the purpose of effecting trades in securities although the agent does not reveal the information in the course of trading.

XIII. COMPUTER FRAUD AND ABUSE ACT
(18 U.S.C. § 1030)

■ ■ ■

Table of Sections

Section

1030.   Fraud and related activity in connection with computers

---

§ 1030.   Fraud and related activity in connection with computers

(a) Whoever—

(1) having knowingly accessed a computer without authorization or exceeding authorized access, and by means of such conduct having obtained information that has been determined by the United States Government pursuant to an Executive order or statute to require protection against unauthorized disclosure for reasons of national defense or foreign relations, or any restricted data, as defined in paragraph y. of section 11 of the Atomic Energy Act of 1954, with reason to believe that such information so obtained could be used to the injury of the United States, or to the advantage of any foreign nation willfully communicates, delivers, transmits, or causes to be communicated, delivered, or transmitted, or attempts to communicate, deliver, transmit or cause to be communicated, delivered, or transmitted the same to any person not entitled to receive it, or willfully retains the same and fails to deliver it to the officer or employee of the United States entitled to receive it;

(2) intentionally accesses a computer without authorization or exceeds authorized access, and thereby obtains—

(A) information contained in a financial record of a financial institution, or of a card issuer as defined in section 1602(n) of title 15, or contained in a file of a consumer reporting agency on a consumer, as such terms are defined in the Fair Credit Reporting Act (15 U.S.C. 1681 et seq.);

(B) information from any department or agency of the United States; or

(C) information from any protected computer;

431

(3) intentionally, without authorization to access any nonpublic computer of a department or agency of the United States, accesses such a computer of that department or agency that is exclusively for the use of the Government of the United States or, in the case of a computer not exclusively for such use, is used by or for the Government of the United States and such conduct affects that use by or for the Government of the United States;

(4) knowingly and with intent to defraud, accesses a protected computer without authorization, or exceeds authorized access, and by means of such conduct furthers the intended fraud and obtains anything of value, unless the object of the fraud and the thing obtained consists only of the use of the computer and the value of such use is not more than $5,000 in any 1–year period;

(5)(A) knowingly causes the transmission of a program, information, code, or command, and as a result of such conduct, intentionally causes damage without authorization, to a protected computer;

(B) intentionally accesses a protected computer without authorization, and as a result of such conduct, recklessly causes damage; or

(C) intentionally accesses a protected computer without authorization, and as a result of such conduct, causes damage and loss.

(6) knowingly and with intent to defraud traffics (as defined in section 1029) in any password or similar information through which a computer may be accessed without authorization, if—

> **(A)** such trafficking affects interstate or foreign commerce; or

> **(B)** such computer is used by or for the Government of the United States;

(7) with intent to extort from any person any money or other thing of value, transmits in interstate or foreign commerce any communication containing any—

> **(A)** threat to cause damage to a protected computer;

> **(B)** threat to obtain information from a protected computer without authorization or in excess of authorization or to impair the confidentiality of information obtained from a protected computer without authorization or by exceeding authorized access; or

> **(C)** demand or request for money or other thing of value in relation to damage to a protected computer, where such damage was caused to facilitate the extortion;

shall be punished as provided in subsection (c) of this section.

(b) Whoever conspires to commit or attempts to commit an offense under subsection (a) of this section shall be punished as provided in subsection (c) of this section.

(c) The punishment for an offense under subsection (a) or (b) of this section is—

(1)(A) a fine under this title or imprisonment for not more than ten years, or both, in the case of an offense under subsection (a)(1) of this section which does not occur after a conviction for another offense under this section, or an attempt to commit an offense punishable under this subparagraph; and

(B) a fine under this title or imprisonment for not more than twenty years, or both, in the case of an offense under subsection (a)(1) of this section which occurs after a conviction for another offense under this section, or an attempt to commit an offense punishable under this subparagraph;

(2)(A) except as provided in subparagraph (B), a fine under this title or imprisonment for not more than one year, or both, in the case of an offense under subsection (a)(2), (a)(3), or (a)(6) of this section which does not occur after a conviction for another offense under this section, or an attempt to commit an offense punishable under this subparagraph;

(B) a fine under this title or imprisonment for not more than 5 years, or both, in the case of an offense under subsection (a)(2), or an attempt to commit an offense punishable under this subparagraph, if—

(i) the offense was committed for purposes of commercial advantage or private financial gain;

(ii) the offense was committed in furtherance of any criminal or tortious act in violation of the Constitution or laws of the United States or of any State; or

(iii) the value of the information obtained exceeds $5,000; and

(C) a fine under this title or imprisonment for not more than ten years, or both, in the case of an offense under subsection (a)(2), (a)(3) or (a)(6) of this section which occurs after a conviction for another offense under this section, or an attempt to commit an offense punishable under this subparagraph;

(3)(A) a fine under this title or imprisonment for not more than five years, or both, in the case of an offense under subsection (a)(4) or (a)(7) of this section which does not occur after a conviction for another offense under this section, or an attempt to commit an offense punishable under this subparagraph; and

(B) a fine under this title or imprisonment for not more than ten years, or both, in the case of an offense under subsection (a)(4), or (a)(7) of this section which occurs after a conviction for another offense under this section, or an attempt to commit an offense punishable under this subparagraph;

(4)(A) except as provided in subparagraphs (E) and (F), a fine under this title, imprisonment for not more than 5 years, or both, in the case of—

    (i) an offense under subsection (a)(5)(B), which does not occur after a conviction for another offense under this section, if the offense caused (or, in the case of an attempted offense, would, if completed, have caused)—

        (I) loss to 1 or more persons during any 1–year period (and, for purposes of an investigation, prosecution, or other proceeding brought by the United States only, loss resulting from a related course of conduct affecting 1 or more other protected computers) aggregating at least $5,000 in value;

        (II) the modification or impairment, or potential modification or impairment, of the medical examination, diagnosis, treatment, or care of 1 or more individuals;

        (III) physical injury to any person;

        (IV) a threat to public health or safety;

        (V) damage affecting a computer used by or for an entity of the United States Government in furtherance of the administration of justice, national defense, or national security; or

        (VI) damage affecting 10 or more protected computers during any 1–year period; or

    (ii) an attempt to commit an offense punishable under this subparagraph;

(B) except as provided in subparagraphs (E) and (F), a fine under this title, imprisonment for not more than 10 years, or both, in the case of—

    (i) an offense under subsection (a)(5)(A), which does not occur after a conviction for another offense under this section, if the offense caused (or, in the case of an attempted offense, would, if completed, have caused) a harm provided in subclauses (I) through (VI) of subparagraph (A)(i); or

(ii) an attempt to commit an offense punishable under this subparagraph;

(C) except as provided in subparagraphs (E) and (F), a fine under this title, imprisonment for not more than 20 years, or both, in the case of—

(i) an offense or an attempt to commit an offense under subparagraphs (A) or (B) of subsection (a)(5) that occurs after a conviction for another offense under this section; or

(ii) an attempt to commit an offense punishable under this subparagraph;

(D) a fine under this title, imprisonment for not more than 10 years, or both, in the case of—

(i) an offense or an attempt to commit an offense under subsection (a) (5)(C) that occurs after a conviction for another offense under this section; or

(ii) an attempt to commit an offense punishable under this subparagraph;

(E) if the offender attempts to cause or knowingly or recklessly causes serious bodily injury from conduct in violation of subsection (a)(5)(A), a fine under this title, imprisonment for not more than 20 years, or both;

(F) if the offender attempts to cause or knowingly or recklessly causes death from conduct in violation of subsection (a)(5)(A), a fine under this title, imprisonment for any term of years or for life, or both; or

(G) a fine under this title, imprisonment for not more than 1 year, or both, for—

(i) any other offense under subsection (a)(5); or

(ii) an attempt to commit an offense punishable under this subparagraph.

[**(5)** Repealed. Pub.L. 110–326, Title II, § 204(a)(2)(D), Sept. 26, 2008, 122 Stat. 3562]

(d)(1) The United States Secret Service shall, in addition to any other agency having such authority, have the authority to investigate offenses under this section.

(2) The Federal Bureau of Investigation shall have primary authority to investigate offenses under subsection (a)(1) for any cases involving espionage, foreign counterintelligence, information protected against unauthorized disclosure for reasons of national defense or foreign relations, or Restricted Data (as that term is defined in section 11y of the Atomic Energy Act of 1954 (42 U.S.C. 2014(y)), except for offenses affecting the duties of the United States Secret Service pursuant to section 3056(a) of this title.

(3) Such authority shall be exercised in accordance with an agreement which shall be entered into by the Secretary of the Treasury and the Attorney General.

(e) As used in this section—

(1) the term "computer" means an electronic, magnetic, optical, electrochemical, or other high speed data processing device performing logical, arithmetic, or storage functions, and includes any data storage facility or communications facility directly related to or operating in conjunction with such device, but such term does not include an automated typewriter or typesetter, a portable hand held calculator, or other similar device;

(2) the term "protected computer" means a computer—

(A) exclusively for the use of a financial institution or the United States Government, or, in the case of a computer not exclusively for such use, used by or for a financial institution or the United States Government and the conduct constituting the offense affects that use by or for the financial institution or the Government; or

(B) which is used in or affecting interstate or foreign commerce or communication, including a computer located outside the United States that is used in a manner that affects interstate or foreign commerce or communication of the United States;

(3) the term "State" includes the District of Columbia, the Commonwealth of Puerto Rico, and any other commonwealth, possession or territory of the United States;

(4) the term "financial institution" means—

(A) an institution, with deposits insured by the Federal Deposit Insurance Corporation;

(B) the Federal Reserve or a member of the Federal Reserve including any Federal Reserve Bank;

(C) a credit union with accounts insured by the National Credit Union Administration;

(D) a member of the Federal home loan bank system and any home loan bank;

(E) any institution of the Farm Credit System under the Farm Credit Act of 1971;

(F) a broker-dealer registered with the Securities and Exchange Commission pursuant to section 15 of the Securities Exchange Act of 1934;

(G) the Securities Investor Protection Corporation;

(H) a branch or agency of a foreign bank (as such terms are defined in paragraphs (1) and (3) of section 1(b) of the International Banking Act of 1978); and

(I) an organization operating under section 25 or section 25(a) of the Federal Reserve Act;

(5) the term "financial record" means information derived from any record held by a financial institution pertaining to a customer's relationship with the financial institution;

(6) the term "exceeds authorized access" means to access a computer with authorization and to use such access to obtain or alter information in the computer that the accesser is not entitled so to obtain or alter;

(7) the term "department of the United States" means the legislative or judicial branch of the Government or one of the executive departments enumerated in section 101 of title 5;

(8) the term "damage" means any impairment to the integrity or availability of data, a program, a system, or information;

(9) the term "government entity" includes the Government of the United States, any State or political subdivision of the United States, any foreign country, and any state, province, municipality, or other political subdivision of a foreign country;

(10) the term "conviction" shall include a conviction under the law of any State for a crime punishable by imprisonment for more than 1 year, an element of which is unauthorized access, or exceeding authorized access, to a computer;

(11) the term "loss" means any reasonable cost to any victim, including the cost of responding to an offense, conducting a damage assessment, and restoring the data, program, system, or information to its condition prior to the offense, and any revenue lost, cost incurred, or other consequential damages incurred because of interruption of service; and

(12) the term "person" means any individual, firm, corporation, educational institution, financial institution, governmental entity, or legal or other entity.

(f) This section does not prohibit any lawfully authorized investigative, protective, or intelligence activity of a law enforcement agency of the

United States, a State, or a political subdivision of a State, or of an intelligence agency of the United States.

(g) Any person who suffers damage or loss by reason of a violation of this section may maintain a civil action against the violator to obtain compensatory damages and injunctive relief or other equitable relief. A civil action for a violation of this section may be brought only if the conduct involves 1 of the factors set forth in subclauses (I), (II), (III), (IV), or (V) of subsection (c)(4)(A)(i). Damages for a violation involving only conduct described in subsection (c)(4)(A)(i)(I) are limited to economic damages. No action may be brought under this subsection unless such action is begun within 2 years of the date of the act complained of or the date of the discovery of the damage. No action may be brought under this subsection for the negligent design or manufacture of computer hardware, computer software, or firmware.

(h) The Attorney General and the Secretary of the Treasury shall report to the Congress annually, during the first 3 years following the date of the enactment of this subsection, concerning investigations and prosecutions under subsection (a)(5).

(i)(1) The court, in imposing sentence on any person convicted of a violation of this section, or convicted of conspiracy to violate this section, shall order, in addition to any other sentence imposed and irrespective of any provision of State law, that such person forfeit to the United States—

> **(A)** such person's interest in any personal property that was used or intended to be used to commit or to facilitate the commission of such violation; and

> **(B)** any property, real or personal, constituting or derived from, any proceeds that such person obtained, directly or indirectly, as a result of such violation.

(2) The criminal forfeiture of property under this subsection, any seizure and disposition thereof, and any judicial proceeding in relation thereto, shall be governed by the provisions of section 413 of the Comprehensive Drug Abuse Prevention and Control Act of 1970 (21 U.S.C. 853), except subsection (d) of that section.

(j) For purposes of subsection (i), the following shall be subject to forfeiture to the United States and no property right shall exist in them:

> **(1)** Any personal property used or intended to be used to commit or to facilitate the commission of any violation of this section, or a conspiracy to violate this section.

> **(2)** Any property, real or personal, which constitutes or is derived from proceeds traceable to any violation of this section, or a conspiracy to violate this section.

XIV. Economic Espionage Act of 1996
(18 U.S.C. §§ 1831–1832)

■ ■ ■

Table of Sections

Section

§ 1831.   Economic espionage

(a) In general.—Whoever, intending or knowing that the offense will benefit any foreign government, foreign instrumentality, or foreign agent, knowingly—

(1) steals, or without authorization appropriates, takes, carries away, or conceals, or by fraud, artifice, or deception obtains a trade secret;

(2) without authorization copies, duplicates, sketches, draws, photographs, downloads, uploads, alters, destroys, photocopies, replicates, transmits, delivers, sends, mails, communicates, or conveys a trade secret;

(3) receives, buys, or possesses a trade secret, knowing the same to have been stolen or appropriated, obtained, or converted without authorization;

(4) attempts to commit any offense described in any of paragraphs (1) through (3); or

(5) conspires with one or more other persons to commit any offense described in any of paragraphs (1) through (3), and one or more of such persons do any act to effect the object of the conspiracy,

shall, except as provided in subsection (b), be fined not more than $5,000,000 or imprisoned not more than 15 years, or both.

(b) Organizations.—Any organization that commits any offense described in subsection (a) shall be fined not more than the greater of $10,000,000 or 3 times the value of the stolen trade secret to the organization, including expenses for research and design and other costs of reproducing the trade secret that the organization has thereby avoided.

439

§ 1832. Theft of trade secrets

(a) Whoever, with intent to convert a trade secret, that is related to a product or service used in or intended for use in interstate or foreign commerce, to the economic benefit of anyone other than the owner thereof, and intending or knowing that the offense will, injure any owner of that trade secret, knowingly—

(1) steals, or without authorization appropriates, takes, carries away, or conceals, or by fraud, artifice, or deception obtains such information;

(2) without authorization copies, duplicates, sketches, draws, photographs, downloads, uploads, alters, destroys, photocopies, replicates, transmits, delivers, sends, mails, communicates, or conveys such information;

(3) receives, buys, or possesses such information, knowing the same to have been stolen or appropriated, obtained, or converted without authorization;

(4) attempts to commit any offense described in paragraphs (1) through (3); or

(5) conspires with one or more other persons to commit any offense described in paragraphs (1) through (3), and one or more of such persons do any act to effect the object of the conspiracy,

shall, except as provided in subsection (b), be fined under this title or imprisoned not more than 10 years, or both.

(b) Any organization that commits any offense described in subsection (a) shall be fined not more than $5,000,000.

XV. ILLINOIS TRADE SECRETS ACT
(765 ILCS §§ 1065/1 TO 1065/9)

■ ■ ■

Table of Sections

1065/1.   Short title

§ 1. This Act shall be known as and may be cited as the "Illinois Trade Secrets Act".

1065/2.   Definitions

§ 2. As used in this Act, unless the context requires otherwise:

(a) "Improper means" includes theft, bribery, misrepresentation, breach or inducement of a breach of a confidential relationship or other duty to maintain secrecy or limit use, or espionage through electronic or other means. Reverse engineering or independent development shall not be considered improper means.

(b) "Misappropriation" means:

(1) acquisition of a trade secret of a person by another person who knows or has reason to know that the trade secret was acquired by improper means; or

(2) disclosure or use of a trade secret of a person without express or implied consent by another person who:

(A) used improper means to acquire knowledge of the trade secret; or

441

(B) at the time of disclosure or use, knew or had reason to know that knowledge of the trade secret was:

> **(I)** derived from or through a person who utilized improper means to acquire it;

> **(II)** acquired under circumstances giving rise to a duty to maintain its secrecy or limit its use; or

> **(III)** derived from or through a person who owed a duty to the person seeking relief to maintain its secrecy or limit its use; or

(C) before a material change of position, knew or had reason to know that it was a trade secret and that knowledge of it had been acquired by accident or mistake.

(c) "Person" means a natural person, corporation, business trust, estate, trust, partnership, association, joint venture, government, governmental subdivision or agency, or any other for-profit or not-for-profit legal entity.

(d) "Trade secret" means information, including but not limited to, technical or non-technical data, a formula, pattern, compilation, program, device, method, technique, drawing, process, financial data, or list of actual or potential customers or suppliers, that:

> **(1)** is sufficiently secret to derive economic value, actual or potential, from not being generally known to other persons who can obtain economic value from its disclosure or use; and

> **(2)** is the subject of efforts that are reasonable under the circumstances to maintain its secrecy or confidentiality.

1065/3. Injunctions

§ 3. (a) Actual or threatened misappropriation may be enjoined. Upon application to the court, an injunction may be terminated when the trade secret has ceased to exist, provided that the injunction may be continued for an additional reasonable period of time in appropriate circumstances for reasons including, but not limited to an elimination of the commercial advantage that otherwise would be derived from the misappropriation, deterrence of willful and malicious misappropriation, or where the trade secret ceases to exist due to the fault of the enjoined party or others by improper means.

(b) If the court determines that it would be unreasonable to prohibit future use due to an overriding public interest, an injunction may condition future use upon payment of a reasonable royalty for no longer than the period of time the use could have been prohibited.

(c) In appropriate circumstances, affirmative acts to protect a trade secret may be compelled by a court order.

1065/4.   Damages

§ 4. (a) In addition to the relief provided for by Section 3, a person is entitled to recover damages for misappropriation. Damages can include both the actual loss caused by misappropriation and the unjust enrichment caused by misappropriation that is not taken into account in computing actual loss. If neither damages nor unjust enrichment caused by the misappropriation are proved by a preponderance of the evidence, the court may award damages caused by misappropriation measured in terms of a reasonable royalty for a misappropriator's unauthorized disclosure or use of a trade secret.

(b) If willful and malicious misappropriation exists, the court may award exemplary damages in an amount not exceeding twice any award made under subsection (a).

1065/5.   Attorney's fees

§ 5. If (i) a claim of misappropriation is made in bad faith, (ii) a motion to terminate an injunction is made or resisted in bad faith, or (iii) willful and malicious misappropriation exists, the court may award reasonable attorney's fees to the prevailing party.

1065/6.   Protection of secrecy

§ 6. In an action under this Act, a court shall preserve the secrecy of an alleged trade secret by reasonable means, which may include granting protective orders in connection with discovery proceedings, holding in-camera hearings, sealing the records of the action, and ordering any person involved in the litigation not to disclose an alleged trade secret without prior court approval.

1065/7.   Limitations

§ 7. An action for misappropriation must be brought within 5 years after the misappropriation is discovered or by the exercise of reasonable diligence should have been discovered. For the purposes of this Act, a continuing misappropriation constitutes a single claim.

1065/8.   Legislative intent; exceptions

§ 8. (a) Except as provided in subsection (b), this Act is intended to displace conflicting tort, restitutionary, unfair competition, and other laws of this State providing civil remedies for misappropriation of a trade secret.

(b) This Act does not affect:

   (1) contractual   remedies,   whether   or   not   based   upon misappropriation of a trade secret, provided however, that a contractual or other duty to maintain secrecy or limit use of a trade secret shall not be deemed to be void or unenforceable solely for lack of durational or geographical limitation on the duty;

(2) other civil remedies that are not based upon misappropriation of a trade secret;

(3) criminal remedies, whether or not based upon misappropriation of a trade secret; or

(4) the definition of a trade secret contained in any other Act of this State.

1065/9.   Effective date and application

§ 9. This Act takes effect on January 1, 1988, and does not apply to misappropriation occurring prior to its effective date.

XVI. MAINE REVISED STATUTES
(10 M.R.S. §§ 1541–1548)

■ ■ ■

Table of Sections

---

§ 1541.   Short title

This Act shall be known and may be cited as the "Uniform Trade Secrets Act."

§ 1542.   Definitions

As used in this Act, unless the context otherwise indicates, the following terms have the following meanings.

1. Improper means. "Improper means" means theft, bribery, misrepresentation, breach or inducement of a breach of duty to maintain secrecy or espionage through electronic or other means.

2. Misappropriation. "Misappropriation" means:

A.   Acquisition of a trade secret of another by a person who knows or has reason to know that the trade secret was acquired by improper means; or

B.   Disclosure or use of a trade secret of another without express or implied consent by a person who:

(1) Used improper means to acquire knowledge of the trade secret;

(2) At the time of disclosure or use, knew or had reason to know that his knowledge of the trade secret was:

445

(i) Derived from or through a person who had utilized improper means to acquire it;

(ii) Acquired under circumstances giving rise to a duty to maintain its secrecy or limit its use; or

(iii) Derived from or through a person who owed a duty to the person seeking relief to maintain its secrecy or limit its use; or

(3) Before a material change of his position, knew or had reason to know that it was a trade secret and that knowledge of it had been acquired by accident or mistake.

3. **Person.** "Person" means a natural person, corporation, business trust, estate, trust, partnership, association, joint venture, government, governmental subdivision or agency or any other legal or commercial entity.

4. **Trade secret.** "Trade secret" means information, including, but not limited to, a formula, pattern, compilation, program, device, method, technique or process, that:

A. Derives independent economic value, actual or potential, from not being generally known to and not being readily ascertainable by proper means by other persons who can obtain economic value from its disclosure or use; and

B. Is the subject of efforts that are reasonable under the circumstances to maintain its secrecy.

§ 1543. Injunctive relief

1. **Misappropriation restrained or enjoined.** Actual or threatened misappropriation may be restrained or enjoined. Upon application to the court, an injunction shall be terminated when the trade secret has ceased to exist, but the injunction may be continued for an additional reasonable period of time in order to eliminate commercial advantage that otherwise would be derived from the misappropriation.

2. **Exceptional circumstances.** In exceptional circumstances, an injunction may condition future use upon payment of a reasonable royalty for no longer than the period of time for which use could have been prohibited.

A. Exceptional circumstances include, but are not limited to, a material and prejudicial change of position prior to acquiring knowledge or reason to know of misappropriation that renders a prohibitive injunction inequitable.

3. Protection of trade secret compelled. In appropriate circumstances, affirmative acts to protect a trade secret may be compelled by court order.

4. Application. This section applies to all forms of injunctive relief, including temporary restraining orders, preliminary injunctions and permanent injunctions.

§ 1544. Damages

Except to the extent that a material and prejudicial change of position prior to acquiring knowledge or reason to know of misappropriation renders a monetary recovery inequitable, a complainant is entitled to recover damages for misappropriation.

1. Measurement of damages. Damages may include both the actual loss caused by misappropriation and the unjust enrichment caused by misappropriation that is not taken into account in computing actual loss. In lieu of damages measured by any other methods, the damages caused by misappropriation may be measured by imposition of liability for a reasonable royalty for a misappropriator's unauthorized disclosure or use of a trade secret.

2. Willful, malicious misappropriation. If willful and malicious misappropriation exists, the court may award exemplary damages in an amount not to exceed twice any award made under subsection 1.

§ 1545. Attorneys fees

If a claim of misappropriation is made in bad faith, a motion to terminate an injunction is made or resisted in bad faith or willful and malicious misappropriation exists, the court may award reasonable attorneys fees to the prevailing party.

§ 1546. Preservation of secrecy

In an action under this Act, a court shall preserve the secrecy of an alleged trade secret by reasonable means, which may include granting protective orders in connection with discovery proceedings, holding in camera hearings, sealing the records of the action and ordering any person involved in the litigation not to disclose an alleged trade secret without prior court approval.

§ 1547. Statute of limitations

An action for misappropriation must be brought within 4 years after the misappropriation is discovered or, by the exercise of reasonable diligence, should have been discovered. For the purposes of this section, a continuing misappropriation constitutes a single claim.

§ 1548.   Effect on other laws

1.   No effect. Except as provided in this section, this Act displaces conflicting tort, restitutionary and other laws of this State providing civil remedies for misappropriation of a trade secret. This Act does not affect:

A.   Contractual remedies, whether or not based upon misappropriation of a trade secret;

B.   Other civil remedies that are not based upon misappropriation of a trade secret;

C.   Criminal remedies, whether or not based upon misappropriation of a trade secret;

D.   The duty of any person to disclose information where expressly required by law; or

E.   The provisions of the Maine Tort Claims Act, Title 14, chapter 741.

XVII. RACKETEER INFLUENCED AND CORRUPT ORGANIZATIONS ACT
(18 U.S.C. §§ 224, 1341, 1343, 1961–1964, 2319A; 19 U.S.C. § 1981)

■ ■ ■

Table of Sections

---

§ 224.   Bribery in sporting contests

(a) Whoever carries into effect, attempts to carry into effect, or conspires with any other person to carry into effect any scheme in commerce to influence, in any way, by bribery any sporting contest, with knowledge that the purpose of such scheme is to influence by bribery that contest, shall be fined under this title, or imprisoned not more than 5 years, or both.

(b) This section shall not be construed as indicating an intent on the part of Congress to occupy the field in which this section operates to the exclusion of a law of any State, territory, Commonwealth, or possession of the United States, and no law of any State, territory, Commonwealth, or possession of the United States, which would be valid in the absence of the section shall be declared invalid, and no local authorities shall be deprived of any jurisdiction over any offense over which they would have jurisdiction in the absence of this section.

(c) As used in this section—

(1) The term "scheme in commerce" means any scheme effectuated in whole or in part through the use in interstate or foreign commerce of any facility for transportation or communication;

(2) The term "sporting contest" means any contest in any sport, between individual contestants or teams of contestants (without regard to the amateur or professional status of the contestants therein), the occurrence of which is publicly announced before its occurrence;

(3) The term "person" means any individual and any partnership, corporation, association, or other entity.

§ 1341.   Frauds and swindles

Whoever, having devised or intending to devise any scheme or artifice to defraud, or for obtaining money or property by means of false or fraudulent pretenses, representations, or promises, or to sell, dispose of, loan, exchange, alter, give away, distribute, supply, or furnish or procure for unlawful use any counterfeit or spurious coin, obligation, security, or other article, or anything represented to be or intimated or held out to be such counterfeit or spurious article, for the purpose of executing such scheme or artifice or attempting so to do, places in any post office or authorized depository for mail matter, any matter or thing whatever to be sent or delivered by the Postal Service, or deposits or causes to be deposited any matter or thing whatever to be sent or delivered by any private or commercial interstate carrier, or takes or receives therefrom, any such matter or thing, or knowingly causes to be delivered by mail or such carrier according to the direction thereon, or at the place at which it is directed to be delivered by the person to whom it is addressed, any such matter or thing, shall be fined under this title or imprisoned not more than 20 years, or both. If the violation occurs in relation to, or involving any benefit authorized, transported, transmitted, transferred, disbursed, or paid in connection with, a presidentially declared major disaster or emergency (as those terms are defined in section 102 of the Robert T. Stafford Disaster Relief and Emergency Assistance Act (42 U.S.C. 5122)), or affects a financial institution, such person shall be fined not more than $1,000,000 or imprisoned not more than 30 years, or both.

§ 1343.   Fraud by wire, radio, or television

Whoever, having devised or intending to devise any scheme or artifice to defraud, or for obtaining money or property by means of false or fraudulent pretenses, representations, or promises, transmits or causes to be transmitted by means of wire, radio, or television communication in interstate or foreign commerce, any writings, signs, signals, pictures, or sounds for the purpose of executing such scheme or artifice, shall be fined under this title or imprisoned not more than 20 years, or both. If the violation occurs in relation to, or involving any benefit authorized, transported, transmitted, transferred, disbursed, or paid in connection with, a presidentially declared major disaster or emergency (as those terms are defined in section 102 of the Robert T. Stafford Disaster Relief and Emergency Assistance Act (42 U.S.C. 5122)), or affects a financial institution, such person shall be fined not more than $1,000,000 or imprisoned not more than 30 years, or both.

§ 1961.   Definitions

As used in this chapter—

(1) "racketeering activity" means (A) any act or threat involving murder, kidnapping, gambling, arson, robbery, bribery, extortion, dealing in obscene matter, or dealing in a controlled substance or listed chemical (as defined in section 102 of the Controlled Substances Act), which is chargeable under State law and punishable by imprisonment for more than one year; (B) any act which is indictable under any of the following provisions of title 18, United States Code: Section 201 (relating to bribery), section 224 (relating to sports bribery), sections 471, 472, and 473 (relating to counterfeiting), section 659 (relating to theft from interstate shipment) if the act indictable under section 659 is felonious, section 664 (relating to embezzlement from pension and welfare funds), sections 891–894 (relating to extortionate credit transactions), section 1028 (relating to fraud and related activity in connection with identification documents), section 1029 (relating to fraud and related activity in connection with access devices), section 1084 (relating to the transmission of gambling information), section 1341 (relating to mail fraud), section 1343 (relating to wire fraud), section 1344 (relating to financial institution fraud), section 1351 (relating to fraud in foreign labor contracting), section 1425 (relating to the procurement of citizenship or nationalization unlawfully), section 1426 (relating to the reproduction of naturalization or citizenship papers), section 1427 (relating to the sale of naturalization or citizenship papers), sections 1461–1465 (relating to obscene matter), section 1503 (relating to obstruction of justice), section 1510 (relating to obstruction of criminal investigations), section 1511 (relating to the obstruction of State or local law enforcement), section 1512 (relating to tampering with a witness, victim, or an informant), section 1513 (relating to retaliating against a witness, victim, or an informant), section 1542 (relating to false statement in application and use of passport), section 1543 (relating to forgery or false use of passport), section 1544 (relating to misuse of passport), section 1546

(relating to fraud and misuse of visas, permits, and other documents), sections 1581–1592 (relating to peonage, slavery, and trafficking in persons)., section 1951 (relating to interference with commerce, robbery, or extortion), section 1952 (relating to racketeering), section 1953 (relating to interstate transportation of wagering paraphernalia), section 1954 (relating to unlawful welfare fund payments), section 1955 (relating to the prohibition of illegal gambling businesses), section 1956 (relating to the laundering of monetary instruments), section 1957 (relating to engaging in monetary transactions in property derived from specified unlawful activity), section 1958 (relating to use of interstate commerce facilities in the commission of murder-for-hire), section 1960 (relating to illegal money transmitters), sections 2251, 2251A, 2252, and 2260 (relating to sexual exploitation of children), sections 2312 and 2313 (relating to interstate transportation of stolen motor vehicles), sections 2314 and 2315 (relating to interstate transportation of stolen property), section 2318 (relating to trafficking in counterfeit labels for phonorecords, computer programs or computer program documentation or packaging and copies of motion pictures or other audiovisual works), section 2319 (relating to criminal infringement of a copyright), section 2319A (relating to unauthorized fixation of and trafficking in sound recordings and music videos of live musical performances), section 2320 (relating to trafficking in goods or services bearing counterfeit marks), section 2321 (relating to trafficking in certain motor vehicles or motor vehicle parts), sections 2341–2346 (relating to trafficking in contraband cigarettes), sections 2421–24 (relating to white slave traffic), sections 175–178 (relating to biological weapons), sections 229–229F (relating to chemical weapons), section 831 (relating to nuclear materials), (C) any act which is indictable under title 29, United States Code, section 186 (dealing with restrictions on payments and loans to labor organizations) or section 501(c) (relating to embezzlement from union funds), (D) any offense involving fraud connected with a case under title 11 (except a case under section 157 of this title), fraud in the sale of securities, or the felonious manufacture, importation, receiving, concealment, buying, selling, or otherwise dealing in a controlled substance or listed chemical (as defined in section 102 of the Controlled Substances Act), punishable under any law of the United States, (E) any act which is indictable under the Currency and Foreign Transactions Reporting Act, (F) any act which is indictable under the Immigration and Nationality Act, section 274 (relating to bringing in and harboring certain aliens), section 277 (relating to aiding or assisting certain aliens to enter the United States), or section 278 (relating to importation of alien for immoral purpose) if the act indictable under such section of such Act was committed for the purpose of financial gain, or (G) any act that is indictable under any provision listed in section 2332b(g)(5)(B);

(2) "State" means any State of the United States, the District of Columbia, the Commonwealth of Puerto Rico, any territory or possession of the United States, any political subdivision, or any department, agency, or instrumentality thereof;

(3) "person" includes any individual or entity capable of holding a legal or beneficial interest in property;

(4) "enterprise" includes any individual, partnership, corporation, association, or other legal entity, and any union or group of individuals associated in fact although not a legal entity;

(5) "pattern of racketeering activity" requires at least two acts of racketeering activity, one of which occurred after the effective date of this chapter and the last of which occurred within ten years (excluding any period of imprisonment) after the commission of a prior act of racketeering activity;

(6) "unlawful debt" means a debt (A) incurred or contracted in gambling activity which was in violation of the law of the United States, a State or political subdivision thereof, or which is unenforceable under State or Federal law in whole or in part as to principal or interest because of the laws relating to usury, and (B) which was incurred in connection with the business of gambling in violation of the law of the United States, a State or political subdivision thereof, or the business of lending money or a thing of value at a rate usurious under State or Federal law, where the usurious rate is at least twice the enforceable rate;

(7) "racketeering investigator" means any attorney or investigator so designated by the Attorney General and charged with the duty of enforcing or carrying into effect this chapter;

(8) "racketeering investigation" means any inquiry conducted by any racketeering investigator for the purpose of ascertaining whether any person has been involved in any violation of this chapter or of any final order, judgment, or decree of any court of the United States, duly entered in any case or proceeding arising under this chapter;

(9) "documentary material" includes any book, paper, document, record, recording, or other material; and

(10) "Attorney General" includes the Attorney General of the United States, the Deputy Attorney General of the United States, the Associate Attorney General of the United States, any Assistant Attorney General of the United States, or any employee of the Department of Justice or any employee of any department or agency of the United States so designated by the Attorney General to carry out the powers conferred on the Attorney General by this chapter. Any department or agency so designated may use in investigations authorized by this chapter either the investigative provisions of this chapter or the investigative power of such department or agency otherwise conferred by law.

§ 1962. Prohibited activities

(a) It shall be unlawful for any person who has received any income derived, directly or indirectly, from a pattern of racketeering activity or through collection of an unlawful debt in which such person has participated as a principal within the meaning of section 2, title 18, United States Code, to use or invest, directly or indirectly, any part of such income, or the proceeds of such income, in acquisition of any interest in, or the establishment or operation of, any enterprise which is engaged in, or the activities of which affect, interstate or foreign commerce. A purchase of securities on the open market for purposes of investment, and without the intention of controlling or participating in the control of the issuer, or of assisting another to do so, shall not be unlawful under this subsection if the securities of the issuer held by the purchaser, the members of his immediate family, and his or their accomplices in any pattern or racketeering activity or the collection of an unlawful debt after such purchase do not amount in the aggregate to one percent of the outstanding securities of any one class, and do not confer, either in law or in fact, the power to elect one or more directors of the issuer.

(b) It shall be unlawful for any person through a pattern of racketeering activity or through collection of an unlawful debt to acquire or maintain, directly or indirectly, any interest in or control of any enterprise which is engaged in, or the activities of which affect, interstate or foreign commerce.

(c) It shall be unlawful for any person employed by or associated with any enterprise engaged in, or the activities of which affect, interstate or foreign commerce, to conduct or participate, directly or indirectly, in the conduct of such enterprise's affairs through a pattern of racketeering activity or collection of unlawful debt.

(d) It shall be unlawful for any person to conspire to violate any of the provisions of subsection (a), (b), or (c) of this section.

§ 1963. Criminal penalties

(a) Whoever violates any provision of section 1962 of this chapter shall be fined under this title or imprisoned not more than 20 years (or for life if the violation is based on a racketeering activity for which the maximum penalty includes life imprisonment), or both, and shall forfeit to the United States, irrespective of any provision of State law—

(1) any interest the person has acquired or maintained in violation of section 1962;

(2) any—

(A) interest in;

(B) security of;

(C) claim against; or

(D) property or contractual right of any kind affording a source of influence over;

any enterprise which the person has established, operated, controlled, conducted, or participated in the conduct of, in violation of section 1962; and

(3) any property constituting, or derived from, any proceeds which the person obtained, directly or indirectly, from racketeering activity or unlawful debt collection in violation of section 1962.

The court, in imposing sentence on such person shall order, in addition to any other sentence imposed pursuant to this section, that the person forfeit to the United States all property described in this subsection. In lieu of a fine otherwise authorized by this section, a defendant who derives profits or other proceeds from an offense may be fined not more than twice the gross profits or other proceeds.

(b) Property subject to criminal forfeiture under this section includes—

(1) real property, including things growing on, affixed to, and found in land; and

(2) tangible and intangible personal property, including rights, privileges, interests, claims, and securities.

(c) All right, title, and interest in property described in subsection (a) vests in the United States upon the commission of the act giving rise to forfeiture under this section. Any such property that is subsequently transferred to a person other than the defendant may be the subject of a special verdict of forfeiture and thereafter shall be ordered forfeited to the United States, unless the transferee establishes in a hearing pursuant to subsection (l) that he is a bona fide purchaser for value of such property who at the time of purchase was reasonably without cause to believe that the property was subject to forfeiture under this section.

(d)(1) Upon application of the United States, the court may enter a restraining order or injunction, require the execution of a satisfactory performance bond, or take any other action to preserve the availability of property described in subsection (a) for forfeiture under this section—

(A) upon the filing of an indictment or information charging a violation of section 1962 of this chapter and alleging that the property with respect to which the order is sought would, in the event of conviction, be subject to forfeiture under this section; or

(B) prior to the filing of such an indictment or information, if, after notice to persons appearing to have an interest in the property and opportunity for a hearing, the court determines that—

(i) there is a substantial probability that the United States will prevail on the issue of forfeiture and that failure to enter the order will result in the property being destroyed, removed from the jurisdiction of the court, or otherwise made unavailable for forfeiture; and

(ii) the need to preserve the availability of the property through the entry of the requested order outweighs the hardship on any party against whom the order is to be entered:

Provided, however, That an order entered pursuant to subparagraph (B) shall be effective for not more than ninety days, unless extended by the court for good cause shown or unless an indictment or information described in subparagraph (A) has been filed.

(2) A temporary restraining order under this subsection may be entered upon application of the United States without notice or opportunity for a hearing when an information or indictment has not yet been filed with respect to the property, if the United States demonstrates that there is probable cause to believe that the property with respect to which the order is sought would, in the event of conviction, be subject to forfeiture under this section and that provision of notice will jeopardize the availability of the property for forfeiture. Such a temporary order shall expire not more than fourteen days after the date on which it is entered, unless extended for good cause shown or unless the party against whom it is entered consents to an extension for a longer period. A hearing requested concerning an order entered under this paragraph shall be held at the earliest possible time, and prior to the expiration of the temporary order.

(3) The court may receive and consider, at a hearing held pursuant to this subsection, evidence and information that would be inadmissible under the Federal Rules of Evidence.

(e) Upon conviction of a person under this section, the court shall enter a judgment of forfeiture of the property to the United States and shall also authorize the Attorney General to seize all property ordered forfeited upon such terms and conditions as the court shall deem proper. Following the entry of an order declaring the property forfeited, the court may, upon application of the United States, enter such appropriate restraining orders or injunctions, require the execution of satisfactory performance bonds, appoint receivers, conservators, appraisers, accountants, or trustees, or take any other action to protect the interest of the United States in the property ordered forfeited. Any income accruing to, or derived from, an enterprise or an interest in an enterprise which has been ordered forfeited under this section may be used to offset ordinary and necessary expenses to the enterprise which are required by law, or which are necessary to protect the interests of the United States or third parties.

(f) Following the seizure of property ordered forfeited under this section, the Attorney General shall direct the disposition of the property by sale or any other commercially feasible means, making due provision for the rights of any innocent persons. Any property right or interest not exercisable by, or transferable for value to, the United States shall expire and shall not revert to the defendant, nor shall the defendant or any person acting in concert with or on behalf of the defendant be eligible to purchase forfeited property at any sale held by the United States. Upon application of a person, other than the defendant or a person acting in concert with or on behalf of the defendant, the court may restrain or stay the sale or disposition of the property pending the conclusion of any appeal of the criminal case giving rise to the forfeiture, if the applicant demonstrates that proceeding with the sale or disposition of the property will result in irreparable injury, harm or loss to him. Notwithstanding 31 U.S.C. 3302(b), the proceeds of any sale or other disposition of property forfeited under this section and any moneys forfeited shall be used to pay all proper expenses for the forfeiture and the sale, including expenses of seizure, maintenance and custody of the property pending its disposition, advertising and court costs. The Attorney General shall deposit in the Treasury any amounts of such proceeds or moneys remaining after the payment of such expenses.

(g) With respect to property ordered forfeited under this section, the Attorney General is authorized to—

(1) grant petitions for mitigation or remission of forfeiture, restore forfeited property to victims of a violation of this chapter, or take any other action to protect the rights of innocent persons which is in the interest of justice and which is not inconsistent with the provisions of this chapter;

(2) compromise claims arising under this section;

(3) award compensation to persons providing information resulting in a forfeiture under this section;

(4) direct the disposition by the United States of all property ordered forfeited under this section by public sale or any other commercially feasible means, making due provision for the rights of innocent persons; and

(5) take appropriate measures necessary to safeguard and maintain property ordered forfeited under this section pending its disposition.

(h) The Attorney General may promulgate regulations with respect to—

(1) making reasonable efforts to provide notice to persons who may have an interest in property ordered forfeited under this section;

(2) granting petitions for remission or mitigation of forfeiture;

(3) the restitution of property to victims of an offense petitioning for remission or mitigation of forfeiture under this chapter;

(4) the disposition by the United States of forfeited property by public sale or other commercially feasible means;

(5) the maintenance and safekeeping of any property forfeited under this section pending its disposition; and

(6) the compromise of claims arising under this chapter.

Pending the promulgation of such regulations, all provisions of law relating to the disposition of property, or the proceeds from the sale thereof, or the remission or mitigation of forfeitures for violation of the customs laws, and the compromise of claims and the award of compensation to informers in respect of such forfeitures shall apply to forfeitures incurred, or alleged to have been incurred, under the provisions of this section, insofar as applicable and not inconsistent with the provisions hereof. Such duties as are imposed upon the Customs Service or any person with respect to the disposition of property under the customs law shall be performed under this chapter by the Attorney General.

(i) Except as provided in subsection (l), no party claiming an interest in property subject to forfeiture under this section may—

(1) intervene in a trial or appeal of a criminal case involving the forfeiture of such property under this section; or

(2) commence an action at law or equity against the United States concerning the validity of his alleged interest in the property subsequent to the filing of an indictment or information alleging that the property is subject to forfeiture under this section.

(j) The district courts of the United States shall have jurisdiction to enter orders as provided in this section without regard to the location of any property which may be subject to forfeiture under this section or which has been ordered forfeited under this section.

(k) In order to facilitate the identification or location of property declared forfeited and to facilitate the disposition of petitions for remission or mitigation of forfeiture, after the entry of an order declaring property forfeited to the United States the court may, upon application of the United States, order that the testimony of any witness relating to the property forfeited be taken by deposition and that any designated book, paper, document, record, recording, or other material not privileged be produced at the same time and place, in the same manner as provided for the taking of depositions under Rule 15 of the Federal Rules of Criminal Procedure.

(*l*)(1) Following the entry of an order of forfeiture under this section, the United States shall publish notice of the order and of its intent to dispose of the property in such manner as the Attorney General may direct. The Government may also, to the extent practicable, provide direct written notice to any person known to have alleged an interest in the property that is the subject of the order of forfeiture as a substitute for published notice as to those persons so notified.

(2) Any person, other than the defendant, asserting a legal interest in property which has been ordered forfeited to the United States pursuant to this section may, within thirty days of the final publication of notice or his receipt of notice under paragraph (1), whichever is earlier, petition the court for a hearing to adjudicate the validity of his alleged interest in the property. The hearing shall be held before the court alone, without a jury.

(3) The petition shall be signed by the petitioner under penalty of perjury and shall set forth the nature and extent of the petitioner's right, title, or interest in the property, the time and circumstances of the petitioner's acquisition of the right, title, or interest in the property, any additional facts supporting the petitioner's claim, and the relief sought.

(4) The hearing on the petition shall, to the extent practicable and consistent with the interests of justice, be held within thirty days of the filing of the petition. The court may consolidate the hearing on the petition with a hearing on any other petition filed by a person other than the defendant under this subsection.

(5) At the hearing, the petitioner may testify and present evidence and witnesses on his own behalf, and cross-examine witnesses who appear at the hearing. The United States may present evidence and witnesses in rebuttal and in defense of its claim to the property and cross-examine witnesses who appear at the hearing. In addition to testimony and evidence presented at the hearing, the court shall consider the relevant portions of the record of the criminal case which resulted in the order of forfeiture.

(6) If, after the hearing, the court determines that the petitioner has established by a preponderance of the evidence that—

(A) the petitioner has a legal right, title, or interest in the property, and such right, title, or interest renders the order of forfeiture invalid in whole or in part because the right, title, or interest was vested in the petitioner rather than the defendant or was superior to any right, title, or interest of the defendant at the time of the commission of the acts which gave rise to the forfeiture of the property under this section; or

(B) the petitioner is a bona fide purchaser for value of the right, title, or interest in the property and was at the time of purchase reasonably without cause to believe that the property was subject to forfeiture under this section;

the court shall amend the order of forfeiture in accordance with its determination.

(7) Following the court's disposition of all petitions filed under this subsection, or if no such petitions are filed following the expiration of the period provided in paragraph (2) for the filing of such petitions, the United States shall have clear title to property that is the subject of the order of forfeiture and may warrant good title to any subsequent purchaser or transferee.

(m) If any of the property described in subsection (a), as a result of any act or omission of the defendant—

(1) cannot be located upon the exercise of due diligence;

(2) has been transferred or sold to, or deposited with, a third party;

(3) has been placed beyond the jurisdiction of the court;

(4) has been substantially diminished in value; or

(5) has been commingled with other property which cannot be divided without difficulty;

the court shall order the forfeiture of any other property of the defendant up to the value of any property described in paragraphs (1) through (5).

§ 1964.   Civil remedies

(a) The district courts of the United States shall have jurisdiction to prevent and restrain violations of section 1962 of this chapter by issuing appropriate orders, including, but not limited to: ordering any person to divest himself of any interest, direct or indirect, in any enterprise; imposing reasonable restrictions on the future activities or investments of any person, including, but not limited to, prohibiting any person from engaging in the same type of endeavor as the enterprise engaged in, the activities of which affect interstate or foreign commerce; or ordering dissolution or reorganization of any enterprise, making due provision for the rights of innocent persons.

(b) The Attorney General may institute proceedings under this section. Pending final determination thereof, the court may at any time enter such restraining orders or prohibitions, or take such other actions, including the acceptance of satisfactory performance bonds, as it shall deem proper.

(c) Any person injured in his business or property by reason of a violation of section 1962 of this chapter may sue therefor in any appropriate United States district court and shall recover threefold the damages he sustains and the cost of the suit, including a reasonable attorney's fee, except that no person may rely upon any conduct that would have been actionable as fraud in the purchase or sale of securities to establish a violation of section 1962. The exception contained in the preceding sentence does not apply to an action against any person that is criminally convicted in connection with the fraud, in which case the statute of limitations shall start to run on the date on which the conviction becomes final.

(d) A final judgment or decree rendered in favor of the United States in any criminal proceeding brought by the United States under this chapter shall estop the defendant from denying the essential allegations of the criminal offense in any subsequent civil proceeding brought by the United States.

§ 2319A. Unauthorized fixation of and trafficking in sound recordings and music videos of live musical performances

(a) Offense.—Whoever, without the consent of the performer or performers involved, knowingly and for purposes of commercial advantage or private financial gain—

    (1) fixes the sounds or sounds and images of a live musical performance in a copy or phonorecord, or reproduces copies or phonorecords of such a performance from an unauthorized fixation;

    (2) transmits or otherwise communicates to the public the sounds or sounds and images of a live musical performance; or

    (3) distributes or offers to distribute, sells or offers to sell, rents or offers to rent, or traffics in any copy or phonorecord fixed as described in paragraph (1), regardless of whether the fixations occurred in the United States;

shall be imprisoned for not more than 5 years or fined in the amount set forth in this title, or both, or if the offense is a second or subsequent offense, shall be imprisoned for not more than 10 years or fined in the amount set forth in this title, or both.

(b) Forfeiture   and   destruction   of   property;   restitution.— Forfeiture, destruction, and restitution relating to this section shall be subject to section 2323, to the extent provided in that section, in addition to any other similar remedies provided by law.

(c) Seizure and forfeiture.—If copies or phonorecords of sounds or sounds and images of a live musical performance are fixed outside of the United States without the consent of the performer or performers involved, such copies or phonorecords are subject to seizure and forfeiture in the United States in the same manner as property imported in violation of the customs laws. The Secretary of Homeland Security shall issue regulations by which any performer may, upon payment of a specified fee, be entitled to notification by United States Customs and Border Protection of the importation of copies or phonorecords that appear to consist of unauthorized fixations of the sounds or sounds and images of a live musical performance.

(d) Victim impact statement.—**(1)** During preparation of the presentence report pursuant to Rule 32(c) of the Federal Rules of Criminal Procedure, victims of the offense shall be permitted to submit, and the probation officer shall receive, a victim impact statement that identifies the victim of the offense and the extent and scope of the injury and loss suffered by the victim, including the estimated economic impact of the offense on that victim.

(2) Persons permitted to submit victim impact statements shall include—

    (A) producers and sellers of legitimate works affected by conduct involved in the offense;

    (B) holders of intellectual property rights in such works; and

    (C) the legal representatives of such producers, sellers, and holders.

(e) Definitions.—As used in this section—

    (1) the terms "copy", "fixed", "musical work", "phonorecord", "reproduce", "sound recordings", and "transmit" mean those terms within the meaning of title 17; and

    (2) the term "traffic" has the same meaning as in section 2320(e) of this title.

(f) Applicability.—This section shall apply to any Act or Acts that occur on or after the date of the enactment of the Uruguay Round Agreements Act.

§ 1981. General authority

(a) Proclamation of increase in, or imposition of, any duty or other import restrictions; report to Congress; adoption of resolution of approval; request for additional information

(1) After receiving an affirmative finding of the United States International Trade Commission under section 1901(b) of this title with respect to an industry, the President may proclaim such increase in, or imposition of, any duty or other import restriction on the article causing or threatening to cause serious injury to such industry as he determines to be necessary to prevent or remedy serious injury to such industry.

(2) If the President does not, within 60 days after the date on which he receives such affirmative finding, proclaim the increase in, or imposition of, any duty or other import restriction on such article found and reported by the United States International Trade Commission pursuant to section 1901(e) of this title—

    (A) he shall immediately submit a report to the House of Representatives and to the Senate stating why he has not proclaimed such increase or imposition, and

    (B) such increase or imposition shall take effect (as provided in paragraph (3)) upon the adoption by both Houses of the Congress (within the 60–day period following the date on which the report referred to in subparagraph (A) is submitted to the House of Representatives and the Senate), by the yeas and nays by the affirmative vote of a majority of the authorized membership of each House, of a concurrent resolution stating in effect that the Senate and House of Representatives approve the increase in, or imposition of, any duty or other import restriction on the article found and reported by the United States International Trade Commission.

For purposes of subparagraph (B), in the computation of the 60–day period there shall be excluded the days on which either House is not in session because of adjournment of more than 3 days to a day certain or an adjournment of the Congress sine die. The report referred to in subparagraph (A) shall be delivered to both Houses of the Congress on the same day and shall be delivered to the Clerk of the House of Representatives if the House of Representatives is not in session and to the Secretary of the Senate if the Senate is not in session.

(3) In any case in which the contingency set forth in paragraph (2)(B) occurs, the President shall (within 15 days after the adoption of such resolution) proclaim the increase in, or imposition of, any duty or other import restriction on the article which was found and reported by the United States International Trade Commission pursuant to section 1901(e) of this title.

(4) The President may, within 60 days after the date on which he receives an affirmative finding of the United States International

Trade Commission under section 1901(b) of this title with respect to an industry, request additional information from the United States International Trade Commission. The United States International Trade Commission shall, as soon as practicable but in no event more than 120 days after the date on which it receives the President's request, furnish additional information with respect to such industry in a supplemental report. For purposes of paragraph (2), the date on which the President receives such supplemental report shall be treated as the date on which the President received the affirmative finding of the United States International Trade Commission with respect to such industry.

(b) Maximum rate of increase

No proclamation pursuant to subsection (a) of this section shall be made—

(1) increasing any rate of duty to a rate more than 50 percent above the rate existing on July 1, 1934, or, if the article is dutiable but no rate existed on July 1, 1934, the rate existing at the time of the proclamation,

(2) in the case of an article not subject to duty, imposing a duty in excess of 50 percent ad valorem.

For purposes of paragraph (1), the term "existing on July 1, 1934" has the meaning assigned to such term by paragraph (5) of section 1886 of this title.

(c) Reduction, termination, or extension of increase in, or imposition of, any duty or other import restriction

(1) Any increase in, or imposition of, any duty or other import restriction proclaimed pursuant to this section or section 7 of the Trade Agreements Extension Act of 1951—

(A) may be reduced or terminated by the President when he determines, after taking into account the advice received from the United States International Trade Commission under subsection (d)(2) of this section and after seeking advice of the Secretary of Commerce and the Secretary of Labor, that such reduction or termination is in the national interest, and

(B) unless extended under section 2253 of this title, shall terminate not later than the close of the date which is 4 years (or, in the case of any such increase or imposition proclaimed pursuant to such section 7, 5 years) after the effective date of the initial proclamation or October 11, 1962, whichever date is the later.

(2) Repealed. Pub.L. 93–618, Title VI, § 602(d), Jan. 3, 1975, 88 Stat. 2072.

(d) Review of developments with respect to industries concerned; annual report to President; advice of probable economic effect; considerations; investigations; hearings

(1) So long as any increase in, or imposition of, any duty or other import restriction pursuant to this section or pursuant to section 7 of the Trade Agreements Extension Act of 1951 remains in effect, the United States International Trade Commission shall keep under review developments with respect to the industry concerned, and shall make annual reports to the President concerning such developments.

(2) Upon request of the President or upon its own motion, the United States International Trade Commission shall advise the President of its judgment as to the probable economic effect on the industry concerned of the reduction or termination of the increase in, or imposition of, any duty or other import restriction pursuant to this section or section 7 of the Trade Agreements Extension Act of 1951.

(3) Repealed. Pub.L. 93–618, Title VI, § 602(d), Jan. 3, 1975, 88 Stat. 2072.

(4) In advising the President under this subsection as to the probable economic effect on the industry concerned, the United States International Trade Commission shall take into account all economic factors which it considers relevant, including idling of productive facilities, inability to operate at a level of reasonable profit, and unemployment or underemployment.

(5) Advice by the United States International Trade Commission under this subsection shall be given on the basis of an investigation during the course of which the United States International Trade Commission shall hold a hearing at which interested persons shall be given a reasonable opportunity to be present, to produce evidence, and to be heard.

(e) Conformity of trade agreements with this section

The President, as soon as practicable, shall take such action as he determines to be necessary to bring trade agreements entered into under section 1351 of this title into conformity with the provisions of this section. No trade agreement shall be entered into under section 1821(a) of this title unless such agreement permits action in conformity with the provisions of this section.

XVIII. Sherman Act
(15 U.S.C. §§ 1–2)

■ ■ ■

Table of Sections

---

§ 1.   Trusts, etc., in restraint of trade illegal; penalty

Every contract, combination in the form of trust or otherwise, or conspiracy, in restraint of trade or commerce among the several States, or with foreign nations, is declared to be illegal. Every person who shall make any contract or engage in any combination or conspiracy hereby declared to be illegal shall be deemed guilty of a felony, and, on conviction thereof, shall be punished by fine not exceeding $100,000,000 if a corporation, or, if any other person, $1,000,000, or by imprisonment not exceeding 10 years, or by both said punishments, in the discretion of the court.

§ 2.   Monopolizing trade a felony; penalty

Every person who shall monopolize, or attempt to monopolize, or combine or conspire with any other person or persons, to monopolize any part of the trade or commerce among the several States, or with foreign nations, shall be deemed guilty of a felony, and, on conviction thereof, shall be punished by fine not exceeding $100,000,000 if a corporation, or, if any other person, $1,000,000, or by imprisonment not exceeding 10 years, or by both said punishments, in the discretion of the court.

XIX. 15 U.S.C. § 4

■ ■ ■

§ 4. Jurisdiction of courts; duty of United States attorneys; procedure

The several district courts of the United States are invested with jurisdiction to prevent and restrain violations of sections 1 to 7 of this title; and it shall be the duty of the several United States attorneys, in their respective districts, under the direction of the Attorney General, to institute proceedings in equity to prevent and restrain such violations. Such proceedings may be by way of petition setting forth the case and praying that such violation shall be enjoined or otherwise prohibited. When the parties complained of shall have been duly notified of such petition the court shall proceed, as soon as may be, to the hearing and determination of the case; and pending such petition and before final decree, the court may at any time make such temporary restraining order or prohibition as shall be deemed just in the premises.

XX. Clayton Act
(15 U.S.C. §§ 15, 15a, 18, 26)

■ ■ ■

Table of Sections

Section

---

§ 15.   Suits by persons injured
(Clayton Act § 4)

(a) Amount of recovery; prejudgment interest

Except as provided in subsection (b) of this section, any person who shall be injured in his business or property by reason of anything forbidden in the antitrust laws may sue therefor in any district court of the United States in the district in which the defendant resides or is found or has an agent, without respect to the amount in controversy, and shall recover threefold the damages by him sustained, and the cost of suit, including a reasonable attorney's fee. The court may award under this section, pursuant to a motion by such person promptly made, simple interest on actual damages for the period beginning on the date of service of such person's pleading setting forth a claim under the antitrust laws and ending on the date of judgment, or for any shorter period therein, if the court finds that the award of such interest for such period is just in the circumstances. In determining whether an award of interest under this section for any period is just in the circumstances, the court shall consider only—

> **(1)** whether such person or the opposing party, or either party's representative, made motions or asserted claims or defenses so lacking in merit as to show that such party or representative acted intentionally for delay, or otherwise acted in bad faith;

> **(2)** whether, in the course of the action involved, such person or the opposing party, or either party's representative, violated any applicable rule, statute, or court order providing for sanctions for

471

dilatory behavior or otherwise providing for expeditious proceedings; and

(3) whether such person or the opposing party, or either party's representative, engaged in conduct primarily for the purpose of delaying the litigation or increasing the cost thereof.

(b) Amount of damages payable to foreign states and instrumentalities of foreign states

(1) Except as provided in paragraph (2), any person who is a foreign state may not recover under subsection (a) of this section an amount in excess of the actual damages sustained by it and the cost of suit, including a reasonable attorney's fee.

(2) Paragraph (1) shall not apply to a foreign state if—

(A) such foreign state would be denied, under section 1605(a)(2) of Title 28, immunity in a case in which the action is based upon a commercial activity, or an act, that is the subject matter of its claim under this section;

(B) such foreign state waives all defenses based upon or arising out of its status as a foreign state, to any claims brought against it in the same action;

(C) such foreign state engages primarily in commercial activities; and

(D) such foreign state does not function, with respect to the commercial activity, or the act, that is the subject matter of its claim under this section as a procurement entity for itself or for another foreign state.

(c) Definitions

For purposes of this section—

(1) the term "commercial activity" shall have the meaning given it in section 1603(d) of Title 28, and

(2) the term "foreign state" shall have the meaning given it in section 1603(a) of Title 28.

§ 15a. Suits by United States; amount of recovery; prejudgment interest (Clayton Act § 4A)

Whenever the United States is hereafter injured in its business or property by reason of anything forbidden in the antitrust laws it may sue therefor in the United States district court for the district in which the defendant resides or is found or has an agent, without respect to the amount in controversy, and shall recover threefold the damages by it sustained and the cost of suit. The court may award under this section, pursuant to a motion by the United States promptly made, simple interest on actual damages for the period beginning on the date of service of the pleading of the United States setting forth a claim under the antitrust laws and ending on the date of judgment, or for any shorter period therein, if the court finds that the award of such interest for such period is just in the circumstances. In determining whether an award of interest under this section for any period is just in the circumstances, the court shall consider only—

(1) whether the United States or the opposing party, or either party's representative, made motions or asserted claims or defenses so lacking in merit as to show that such party or representative acted intentionally for delay or otherwise acted in bad faith;

(2) whether, in the course of the action involved, the United States or the opposing party, or either party's representative, violated any applicable rule, statute, or court order providing for sanctions for dilatory behavior or otherwise providing for expeditious proceedings;

(3) whether the United States or the opposing party, or either party's representative, engaged in conduct primarily for the purpose of delaying the litigation or increasing the cost thereof; and

(4) whether the award of such interest is necessary to compensate the United States adequately for the injury sustained by the United States.

§ 18. Acquisition by one corporation of stock of another (Clayton Act § 7)

No person engaged in commerce or in any activity affecting commerce shall acquire, directly or indirectly, the whole or any part of the stock or other share capital and no person subject to the jurisdiction of the Federal Trade Commission shall acquire the whole or any part of the assets of another person engaged also in commerce or in any activity affecting commerce, where in any line of commerce or in any activity affecting commerce in any section of the country, the effect of such acquisition may be substantially to lessen competition, or to tend to create a monopoly.

No person shall acquire, directly or indirectly, the whole or any part of the stock or other share capital and no person subject to the jurisdiction of the Federal Trade Commission shall acquire the whole or any part of the assets of one or more persons engaged in commerce or in any activity affecting commerce, where in any line of commerce or in any activity affecting commerce in any section of the country, the effect of such acquisition, of such stocks or assets, or of the use of such stock by the voting or granting of proxies or otherwise, may be substantially to lessen competition, or to tend to create a monopoly.

This section shall not apply to persons purchasing such stock solely for investment and not using the same by voting or otherwise to bring about, or in attempting to bring about, the substantial lessening of competition. Nor shall anything contained in this section prevent a corporation engaged in commerce or in any activity affecting commerce from causing the formation of subsidiary corporations for the actual carrying on of their immediate lawful business, or the natural and legitimate branches or extensions thereof, or from owning and holding all or a part of the stock of such subsidiary corporations, when the effect of such formation is not to substantially lessen competition.

Nor shall anything herein contained be construed to prohibit any common carrier subject to the laws to regulate commerce from aiding in the construction of branches or short lines so located as to become feeders to the main line of the company so aiding in such construction or from acquiring or owning all or any part of the stock of such branch lines, nor to prevent any such common carrier from acquiring and owning all or any part of the stock of a branch or short line constructed by an independent company where there is no substantial competition between the company owning the branch line so constructed and the company owning the main line acquiring the property or an interest therein, nor to prevent such common carrier from extending any of its lines through the medium of the acquisition of stock or otherwise of any other common carrier where there is no substantial competition between the company extending its lines and the company whose stock, property, or an interest therein is so acquired.

Nothing contained in this section shall be held to affect or impair any right heretofore legally acquired: *Provided*, That nothing in this section shall be held or construed to authorize or make lawful anything heretofore prohibited or made illegal by the antitrust laws, nor to exempt any person from the penal provisions thereof or the civil remedies therein provided.

Nothing contained in this section shall apply to transactions duly consummated pursuant to authority given by the Secretary of Transportation, Federal Power Commission, Surface Transportation Board, the Securities and Exchange Commission in the exercise of its jurisdiction under section 79j of this title, the United States Maritime Commission, or the Secretary of Agriculture under any statutory provision vesting such power in such Commission, Board, or Secretary.

§ 26.   Injunctive relief for private parties; exception; costs (Clayton Act § 16)

Any person, firm, corporation, or association shall be entitled to sue for and have injunctive relief, in any court of the United States having jurisdiction over the parties, against threatened loss or damage by a violation of the antitrust laws, including sections 13, 14, 18, and 19 of this title, when and under the same conditions and principles as injunctive relief against threatened conduct that will cause loss or damage is granted by courts of equity, under the rules governing such proceedings, and upon the execution of proper bond against damages for an injunction improvidently granted and a showing that the danger of irreparable loss or damage is immediate, a preliminary injunction may issue: *Provided,* That nothing herein contained shall be construed to entitle any person, firm, corporation, or association, except the United States, to bring suit for injunctive relief against any common carrier subject to the jurisdiction of the Surface Transportation Board under subtitle IV of Title 49. In any action under this section in which the plaintiff substantially prevails, the court shall award the cost of suit, including a reasonable attorney's fee, to such plaintiff.

XXI. Robinson–Patman Act
(15 U.S.C. §§ 13, 13a, 13b, 21a)

■ ■ ■

Table of Sections

---

§ 13. Discrimination in price, services, or facilities

(a) Price; selection of customers

It shall be unlawful for any person engaged in commerce, in the course of such commerce, either directly or indirectly, to discriminate in price between different purchasers of commodities of like grade and quality, where either or any of the purchases involved in such discrimination are in commerce, where such commodities are sold for use, consumption, or resale within the United States or any Territory thereof or the District of Columbia or any insular possession or other place under the jurisdiction of the United States, and where the effect of such discrimination may be substantially to lessen competition or tend to create a monopoly in any line of commerce, or to injure, destroy, or prevent competition with any person who either grants or knowingly receives the benefit of such discrimination, or with customers of either of them: *Provided*, That nothing herein contained shall prevent differentials which make only due allowance for differences in the cost of manufacture, sale, or delivery resulting from the differing methods or quantities in which such commodities are to such purchasers sold or delivered: *Provided, however*, That the Federal Trade Commission may, after due investigation and hearing to all interested parties, fix and establish quantity limits, and revise the same as it finds necessary, as to particular commodities or classes of commodities, where it finds that available purchasers in greater quantities are so few as to render differentials on account thereof unjustly discriminatory or promotive of monopoly in any line of commerce; and the foregoing shall then not be construed to permit differentials based on

477

differences in quantities greater than those so fixed and established: *And provided further*, That nothing herein contained shall prevent persons engaged in selling goods, wares, or merchandise in commerce from selecting their own customers in bona fide transactions and not in restraint of trade: *And provided further*, That nothing herein contained shall prevent price changes from time to time where in response to changing conditions affecting the market for or the marketability of the goods concerned, such as but not limited to actual or imminent deterioration of perishable goods, obsolescence of seasonal goods, distress sales under court process, or sales in good faith in discontinuance of business in the goods concerned.

(b) Burden of rebutting prima-facie case of discrimination

Upon proof being made, at any hearing on a complaint under this section, that there has been discrimination in price or services or facilities furnished, the burden of rebutting the prima-facie case thus made by showing justification shall be upon the person charged with a violation of this section, and unless justification shall be affirmatively shown, the Commission is authorized to issue an order terminating the discrimination: *Provided, however*, That nothing herein contained shall prevent a seller rebutting the prima-facie case thus made by showing that his lower price or the furnishing of services or facilities to any purchaser or purchasers was made in good faith to meet an equally low price of a competitor, or the services or facilities furnished by a competitor.

(c) Payment or acceptance of commission, brokerage, or other compensation

It shall be unlawful for any person engaged in commerce, in the course of such commerce, to pay or grant, or to receive or accept, anything of value as a commission, brokerage, or other compensation, or any allowance or discount in lieu thereof, except for services rendered in connection with the sale or purchase of goods, wares, or merchandise, either to the other party to such transaction or to an agent, representative, or other intermediary therein where such intermediary is acting in fact for or in behalf, or is subject to the direct or indirect control, of any party to such transaction other than the person by whom such compensation is so granted or paid.

(d) Payment for services or facilities for processing or sale

It shall be unlawful for any person engaged in commerce to pay or contract for the payment of anything of value to or for the benefit of a customer of such person in the course of such commerce as compensation or in consideration for any services or facilities furnished by or through such customer in connection with the processing, handling, sale, or offering for sale of any products or commodities manufactured, sold, or offered for sale by such person, unless such payment or consideration is available on proportionally equal terms to all other customers competing in the distribution of such products or commodities.

(e) Furnishing services or facilities for processing, handling, etc.

It shall be unlawful for any person to discriminate in favor of one purchaser against another purchaser or purchasers of a commodity bought for resale, with or without processing, by contracting to furnish or furnishing, or by contributing to the furnishing of, any services or facilities connected with the processing, handling, sale, or offering for sale of such commodity so purchased upon terms not accorded to all purchasers on proportionally equal terms.

(f) Knowingly inducing or receiving discriminatory price

It shall be unlawful for any person engaged in commerce, in the course of such commerce, knowingly to induce or receive a discrimination in price which is prohibited by this section.

§13a. Discrimination in rebates, discounts, or advertising service charges; underselling in particular localities; penalties

It shall be unlawful for any person engaged in commerce, in the course of such commerce, to be a party to, or assist in, any transaction of sale, or contract to sell, which discriminates to his knowledge against competitors of the purchaser, in that, any discount, rebate, allowance, or advertising service charge is granted to the purchaser over and above any discount, rebate, allowance, or advertising service charge available at the time of such transaction to said competitors in respect of a sale of goods of like grade, quality, and quantity; to sell, or contract to sell, goods in any part of the United States at prices lower than those exacted by said person elsewhere in the United States for the purpose of destroying competition, or eliminating a competitor in such part of the United States; or, to sell, or contract to sell, goods at unreasonably low prices for the purpose of destroying competition or eliminating a competitor.

Any person violating any of the provisions of this section shall, upon conviction thereof, be fined not more than $5,000 or imprisoned not more than one year, or both.

§13b. Cooperative association; return of net earnings or surplus

Nothing in this Act shall prevent a cooperative association from returning to its members, producers, or consumers the whole, or any part of, the net earnings or surplus resulting from its trading operations, in proportion to their purchases or sales from, to, or through the association.

§ 21a.   Actions and proceedings pending prior to June 19, 1936; additional and continuing violations

Nothing herein contained shall affect rights of action arising, or litigation pending, or orders of the Federal Trade Commission issued and in effect or pending on review, based on section 13 of this title, prior to June 19, 1936: *Provided*, That where, prior to June 19, 1936, the Federal Trade Commission has issued an order requiring any person to cease and desist from a violation of section 13 of this title, and such order is pending on review or is in effect, either as issued or as affirmed or modified by a court of competent jurisdiction, and the Commission shall have reason to believe that such person has committed, used or carried on, since June 19, 1936, or is committing, using or carrying on, any act, practice or method in violation of any of the provisions of said section 13 of this title, it may reopen such original proceedings and may issue and serve upon such person its complaint, supplementary to the original complaint, stating its charges in that respect. Thereupon the same proceedings shall be had upon such supplementary complaint as provided in section 21 of this title. If upon such hearing the Commission shall be of the opinion that any act, practice, or method charged in said supplementary complaint has been committed, used, or carried on since June 19, 1936, or is being committed, used or carried on, in violation of said section 13 of this title, it shall make a report in writing in which it shall state its findings as to the facts and shall issue and serve upon such person its order modifying or amending its original order to include any additional violations of law so found. Thereafter the provisions of section 21 of this title, as to review and enforcement of orders of the Commission shall in all things apply to such modified or amended order. If upon review as provided in said section 21 of this title the court shall set aside such modified or amended order, the original order shall not be affected thereby, but it shall be and remain in force and effect as fully and to the same extent as if such supplementary proceedings had not been taken.